THE LAST CHARGE
The 21st Lancers
and the Battle of Omdurman
2 September 1898

First published in 1998 by
The Crowood Press Ltd
Ramsbury, Marlborough
Wiltshire SN8 2HR

© Terry Brighton
Colour plates © The Crowood Press Ltd
Edited by Martin Windrow

Design by Tony Stocks/Compendium

All rights reserved. No part of this publication
may be reproduced or transmitted in any form or
by any means, electronic or mechanical, including
photocopy, recording, or in any information
storage and retrieval system, without permission in writing
from the publishers.

British Library Cataloguing-in-Publication Data
A CIP catalogue record for this book
is available from the British Library

Standard edition
ISBN 1 86126 189 6

De luxe edition
ISBN 1 86126 193 4

Printed and bound in Great Britain by
Biddles Ltd, Guildford & King's Lynn

THE LAST CHARGE

The 21st Lancers
and the Battle of Omdurman
2 September 1898

Terry Brighton

Colour plates by
Douglas N. Anderson

The Crowood Press

Dedication
To Janet in our 25th year
for her love and support

Acknowledgements
The author acknowledges the assistance of those individuals and institutions who have helped in the preparation of this book, particularly RHQ The Queen's Royal Lancers, The National Army Museum and The Imperial War Museum; and those descendants of men who charged at Omdurman who have deposited letters and diaries in the regimental archives or otherwise made them available for use. The extract from *My Early Life* is used by permission of Curtis Brown Ltd, London, on behalf of the Estate of Sir Winston S.Churchill.

Special thanks are due to Captain J.M. Holtby, who researched the uniforms worn by the regiment in Egypt and the Sudan, and to Mr Douglas Anderson, who translated that research into the highly evocative colour plates reproduced here.

Finally the author wishes to pay tribute to Lieutenant-Colonel R.L.C.Tamplin, the first and foremost historian of the 21st Lancers.

CONTENTS

FOREWORD
by the Marquis of Granby 7
PROLOGUE 8

CHAPTER ONE   9

English Origins

The birth of light cavalry in England; the Marquis of Granby and Lord Robert Manners. Granby's Regiment: the 21st Light Dragoons, 1760-1763. Douglas's Regiment: the 21st Light Dragoons, 1779-1783. Beaumont's Regiment: the 21st Light Dragoons, 1794-1820; service during the war with France in San Domingo and South Africa; guarding Napoleon on Saint Helena; fighting the Marathas in Bengal.

CHAPTER TWO   17

Indian Origins

The Great Mutiny, 1857; the East India Company forms European light cavalry, distinguished by French grey uniforms. Company armies taken over by the Crown, 1861; 3rd Bengal European Light Cavalry becomes the 21st Light Dragoons, later Hussars. "The French Greys". Improved firearms threaten the role of l'arme blanche. A soldier's life in India.

CHAPTER THREE   25

Into the Sudan

Popular uprisings in Egypt and the Sudan; General Gordon besieged in Khartoum. The Gordon Relief Expedition; 21st Hussars included in Camel Corps, 1884; arrives too late. Bangalore: the regiment to India, 1887; Major Pigott commands Yonni expedition - first use of Maxim gun in action. India as a social station. Secunderabad: the 21st trains alongside artillery; fears for the future of the cavalry charge. Temperance versus the canteen; the horse racing mania; the frustration of peacetime soldiering. Anglo-Egyptian force formed in 1896 to reconquer the Sudan; the 21st Hussars shipped to Cairo.

CHAPTER FOUR   37

Towards Omdurman

Kitchener's army moves into the Sudan; the 21st trains for a desert campaign; khaki service dress. April 1897, the 21st Lancers: the restyled regiment adopts the lance. June 1898, the 21st included in Kitchener's army; attachment of Lieutenant Churchill. The desert advance: journey by train, steamer and desert march to Wadi Hamed. 27 August, the final advance begins; 30 August, first skirmish with Dervishes; 31 August, 21st Lancers patrol locates Dervish camp in Kerreri Hills.

CHAPTER FIVE   52

The First Dervish Attack

1 September: the 21st reconnoitre ahead of Kitchener's army; first sight of Omdurman and the Dervish army; gunboats shell the city. The Dervish advance; construction of the zariba; the 21st recalled at dusk. 2 September, 4.30a.m.: the regiment out before dawn; exchange of fire. 6.15a.m.: the regiment recalled as infantry and artillery open fire; the first Dervish attack repelled.

CHAPTER SIX — 74
The Charge at Omdurman
7.30 a.m.: the 21st sent out to clear the route to Omdurman; ordered to intercept Dervishes returning to the city. 8.30 a.m.: patrol encounters 800 Dervishes blocking Omdurman road; Dervishes reinforced by 2,000 men hidden in the dry Khor Abu Sunt. 9.30a.m.: the 21st reaches the Dervish position; 200 enemy open fire at 300 yards. The charge: the dash under fire; the 2,600 enemy in the khor sighted at a hundred yards' range; the Lancers leap into them. The mêlée: horror and gallantry. The survivors regroup; enemy advance driven off by carbine fire; the dead and wounded.

CHAPTER SEVEN — 90
Survivors' Accounts
Captain Eadon's letter: "I said, 'Now, men, get your lances down'". Lieutenant de Montmorency's letter: "I was in the khor and among them. They were as thick as bees...". Lieutenant Pirie's diary: "Every man down was cut to pieces". Lieutenant Smyth's letter: "Blood, blood, blood everywhere, horses and men smothered". Lieutenant Churchill's account: "Stabbed and hacked at by spear and sword." Private Rix's account: "It was parry and thrust as I spurred my horse on through the mêlée."

CHAPTER EIGHT — 99
The Second Dervish Attack
The infantry follow the 21st towards Omdurman; MacDonald's brigade isolated and attacked; enemy repelled by infantry and artillery fire; MacDonald attacked by a third force. The 21st Lancers' wounded operated upon in the midst of battle; MacDonald reinforced by the Lincolnshire Regiment; the battle won. Into Omdurman; the 21st Lancers patrol outside, turning back groups of unbeaten enemy.

CHAPTER NINE — 105
Aftermath, Reactions and Rewards
3-5 September: the regiment continues its patrols; Gordon's memorial service amid the ruins; officers and men explore Omdurman. 6 September: the return march to Cairo begins; first press reports of the charge. Pour la gloire? - the merits of the charge debated. Queen Victoria's Lancers - the Queen grants the 21st the title Empress of India's Lancers. The three VCs honoured at Osborne House.

CHAPTER TEN — 112
Riding in the Twilight
Detachments of the 21st in South Africa; a new kind of war. The North-West Frontier, 1912: the charge at Shabkadar, 5 September 1915. The Great War: the 21st in France; the lance and the machine gun; the expectation of the charge and the reality of the trenches. 1922: the 17th and 21st Lancers are amalgamated.

EPILOGUE 121
APPENDIX: The Omdurman Roll 122
COLOUR PLATES & COMMENTARIES 64-73
MAPS 43, 58, 60, 76, 79, 102
BIBLIOGRAPHY 124
NOTES 125
INDEX 127

FOREWORD

When Mr Brighton asked me to write the foreword to this book I was only too pleased to agree; my ancestor, the first Marquis of Granby, raised the 21st in 1760 and appointed his brother Lord Robert Manners its commanding officer. My wider family and I are justly proud of these our forbears, and of the history of what became the 21st Lancers.

The fact that many public houses around the country are named The *Marquis of Granby* stems from the first Marquis' fame as one of the first British generals to look after his men in the long term. As his troopers left the army he bought cottages for them, many of which were later converted into pubs named after him in gratitude. The first Marquis also set up homes for disabled troopers from the two regiments with which he was directly involved, the 21st (Granby's) Light Dragoons and the Blues. As a result of his generosity – unparalleled in the more brutal world of 18th century soldiering – he was deeply in debt by the end of the war with France.

This book tells the story of the regiment from its earliest days, and – for the first time – gives a full account of its part in the Battle of Omdurman in 1898. It is wonderfully researched, with clear maps and fine illustrations. Whether you are an historian or a layman you will find this a fascinating insight into our military history at the time of the Empire. I commend this volume to you all.

Granby

Belvoir Castle, stately home of the Manners family from 1487 to the present day. From a watercolour by Turner painted in 1816. (His Grace The Duke of Rutland)

PROLOGUE

"The bloody cavalry charge to end them all.... It was a bloody flourish at the height of British imperialism, as the British Army mounted what is generally considered to be its last cavalry charge." So wrote *The Times* of 26 March 1997, reporting the auction of a survivor's diary.

Lieutenant Winston Churchill, who rode with the 21st Lancers at Omdurman on 2 September 1898, estimated that the charge lasted two minutes. Yet a hundred years later it can still excite our fascination with the mad dash of the cavalry and the clash with the enemy.

In 1898 the British press presented the charge as avenging the death of General Gordon at Khartoum in 1885, the kind of "great deed nobly done" — as Lieutenant Robert Smyth described it in his diary — that made the Empire newsworthy. However, the realities of the battlefield were not for the public at large. "Blood, blood, blood everywhere", Smyth wrote, describing a scene of carnage which even today probably could not be transmitted in convincing detail by the BBC on grounds of taste.

When she heard of the charge Queen Victoria awarded the 21st Lancers the title "Empress of India's"; she later authorised the use of her Imperial cypher on the uniform, a unique distinction marking out the 21st as Queen Victoria's Lancers.

Yet unlike the great charge at Balaklava, which has to be understood in terms of what was happening above the level of the regiments concerned, the charge of the 21st Lancers at Omdurman can only be understood in terms of what was happening within the regiment. Pressures which had built up over almost 140 years led directly to the regiment's behaviour in this action.

The frustrations vented at Omdurman began when the regiment was raised as the 21st Light Dragoons in 1760 by the Marquis of Granby, to fight with him against the French in central Europe - but was kept at home. This frustration increased through service in the West Indies, South America, South Africa, and India. Despite playing its part in defeating Napoleon and establishing the British Empire, the 21st was denied the ultimate act for which cavalry had been created: a full charge against a standing enemy.

Later, restyled the 21st Hussars, the regiment was kept almost permanently in India, a "social station" in the time of the Raj. The only enemies able to kill — chiefly cholera and syphilis — were hardly susceptible to a cavalry charge; and frustration was released in measured quantities on the polo field, in hunting big game, and in riding to hounds (with the jackal standing in for the fox). Yet there remained the feeling that a regiment first mounted on horses of the Belvoir Hunt had yet to be truly blooded in battle.

In 1884 a detachment of the 21st joined the force sent to the Sudan to rescue General Gordon, besieged in Khartoum by an army of Dervishes. Hopes of a glorious charge were dashed when the Hussars found themselves escorting the baggage rather than leading the advance. Worse still, the expedition arrived too late, finding Khartoum in ruins and Gordon dead.

The 21st became Lancers in 1897, and the following year the regiment was included in Kitchener's army sent to retake the Sudan. Taunted by fellow cavalrymen that the motto of the 21st should be "Thou shalt not kill", the regiment journeyed towards the new capital, Omdurman, with one intent: that there would be a charge.

Kitchener's army advanced on Omdurman on 2 September 1898. The 21st Lancers was sent ahead to reconnoitre the Kerreri plain, where the Dervishes believed the bones of their enemies would one day whiten the desert. Discovering the route to Omdurman blocked by some 200 warriors, the regiment took this opportunity to charge — discovering much too late that a dry watercourse concealed a further 2,600 Dervishes.

While it had little effect on the outcome of the battle — Kitchener's victory was assured by the Maxim gun and the Lyddite high explosive shell — in England the charge caught the public imagination. The press dismissed the wider battle as an unequal contest between modern weapons and spearmen, focusing instead on the gallantry of 440 Lancers fighting for their lives in the midst of 2,800 Dervish warriors intent on hacking every one of them to pieces. *The Times* missed a sensational scoop when its correspondent Hubert Howard, who rode with the regiment and survived the charge, was killed before he could file his story. This left Lieutenant Churchill, who was writing for the *Morning Post*, to provide a first-hand account, shaming those correspondents who reported blindly from afar.

Yet while Churchill could tell the story of the charge from the inside, as an attached officer (from the 4th Hussars) he could not tell the inside story of the 21st Lancers, which is crucial to a full understanding. In any case, one man's experience can hardly convey the whole gamut of horror through which the 440 Lancers charged, and their numerous acts of valour.

Wherever possible, then, I have allowed the officers and men of the 21st to tell their own story; and they tell it well. The charge at Omdurman is particularly well documented by survivors, and five of their graphic accounts are published here, alongside Churchill's own. In these we come as close as we ever can to experiencing the mad dash of the charge, the reality of the clash with the enemy, and the carnage that followed.

Terry Brighton
The Regimental Museum
Belvoir Castle

CHAPTER ONE

English Origins

Before the birth of light cavalry in England, King George II issued this descriptive command: "His Royal Highness cannot approve of the large footed, hairy leg'd Cart Horse that are too commonly bought for the Dragoons; Dragoon Horses should be nimble and active movers"[1].

Commanding officers, who had to purchase the mounts at their own expense, were reluctant to pay seven guineas or more for a hunter when a cob could be had for half as much. In any case, dragoons were mounted infantry, moving into position on horseback but dismounting to fight. Their horses had to carry a large amount of baggage and were chosen for strength, not speed.

When the Scots invaded England in 1745 these dragoons were poorly matched against lightly armed and fast-moving clansmen. The Duke of Kingston quickly raised a regiment in Nottinghamshire, copying the light cavalry (or hussars) he had seen in Europe. "Kingston's Light Horse" was mounted on hunters and lightly equipped, to maximise both speed and manoeuvrability, and the men were trained to fight from the saddle.

The regiment was made up of six troops of about 60 men each. Lord Robert Manners Sutton was one of its troop captains. He had been born Lord Robert Manners at Belvoir Castle in 1722, second son of the Duke of Rutland and younger brother of the Marquis of Granby. His mother was heiress of Robert Sutton, whose estates lay by Sherwood Forest; because the Marquis of Granby was to inherit the Rutland estates the Sutton estates passed to Lord Robert, who took that surname and settled in Nottinghamshire. He found the 60 men for his troop of the Light Horse from among those who worked on Sutton land.

The Scots reached Derby but were turned back by a large English force. They retreated northwards, and Kingston's Light Horse joined the advance in a pursuit that culminated in the savage battle on Culloden Moor in April 1746, where a general pursuit of the defeated Scots left the battlefield strewn with dead. Its task completed, the regiment was returned to Nottingham and disbanded. However, the Duke of Cumberland had been so impressed by this first use of light cavalry in England that he persuaded the King to allow him to raise a similar regiment, to be known as "Light Dragoons" and to serve in the war against France.

Most of the officers and men who had served in Kingston's Light Horse were re-engaged into this new regiment, and Cumberland appointed Lord Robert Manners Sutton, who had distinguished himself as a troop captain, to command it. Cumberland's Light Dragoons went to Flanders in 1747 and quickly proved itself. Its speed and manoeuvrability allowed an effective charge against the French at Lauffeld on 2 July when the heavy cavalry could only sit and watch. During this action Lord Robert was badly wounded, became separated from the regiment and was taken prisoner.

The War of the Austrian Succession ended with the peace treaty of Aix-la-Chappelle in October 1748. Although this second experiment with light cavalry had been as successful as the first, the British army remained too short-sighted to see any long term role for regiments of light dragoons. Despite Cumberland's argument in favour of its retention, his regiment was disbanded. As a compromise, a troop of 65 light dragoons was added to each of the existing regiments of dragoons.

Lord Robert was released and returned to Nottinghamshire. Many of those who had fought in both Kingston's Light Horse and Cumberland's Light Dragoons continued to work on his estates; and it was there that the memory of the charge at Lauffeld, and the knowledge of what a full regiment of light dragoons could do on the battlefield, lived on.

Granby's Regiment

In 1756 a new war against the French began – this would come to be known as the Seven Years' War, and would have incalculable results for Britain's future. Lord John Manners, Marquis of Granby, commanded a cavalry brigade against the French in Germany. He led several charges to good effect; but this was heavy cavalry, and a prolonged trot before coming into action seriously reduced the pace of the horses and thus their shock effect. Granby was aware of the need for light dragoons in the British force, cavalry able to manoeuvre at speed and charge without loss of pace. His voice – with others – convinced George II to allow two regiments to be raised. As there were 14 regiments of dragoons, the new regiments were numbered 15th and 16th. A few months later five more regiments of light dragoons were authorised, numbered 17th to 21st.

It was the practice for regiments to be raised by individual gentlemen after receiving the king's permission, and the Marquis of Granby hoped to raise one of these five. Early in 1760 he put this proposition before the king: "The Marquis of Granby ventures to flatter himself that many tenants and people of the counties where the family estates lay would eagerly enlist in a Light Dragoon Regiment of 6 Troops … Lord Granby and the Troop Captains to find the men and horses without expense to the Public within two months"[2].

On 28 March the King approved Granby's request, the new regiment to rank as the 21st Light Dragoons. Because of its origin in the area of Sherwood Forest the title "The Royal Foresters" was authorised. But among the people a regiment still took the name of the man who raised it, and the 21st became popularly known as "Granby's Regiment". Commanded by his brother, Lord Robert Manners Sutton, it consisted of 30 officers, 18 sergeants, 12 drummers and 345 troopers. The officers were Nottinghamshire gentlemen and friends of the Manners family. The men were found easily enough, for many who had served with Lord Robert in Kingston's Light Horse and Cumberland's Light Dragoons still lived and worked on the Sutton estates. Lord Robert boasted that they would be mounted on horses selected from among the finest hunters in the land, most likely a reference to the mounts of the Belvoir Hunt. On its formation the 21st was presented with three swallow-tailed flags known as guidons. The first ("the King's") was embroidered with the royal crest, the second and third with the regimental motto *Hic et ubique*, indicating the ability to move quickly about a battlefield, appearing to be *here, there and everywhere*.

The uniform worn in 1760 included a painted brass helmet, knee-length red coat, white waistcoat and shirt worn with a red stock, tight fitting buff leather breeches and soft black leather jackboots. Each man was armed with a straight 36-inch sword, a pair of flintlock saddle pistols with 9-inch barrels, and a carbine with a 30-inch barrel and a 12-inch bayonet. Pistols and carbine took the same size lead ball, although neither were particularly accurate. The carbine was attached to a crossbelt by a swivelling spring clip and hung muzzle-down when not in use; it could be brought up and fired from the saddle while still attached to the belt.

Hair was worn long, usually gathered into a pigtail at the back, and cutting it was strictly forbidden except for medical reasons, when a wig had to be worn. The Marquis of Granby, although bald from the age of 24, excused himself from this requirement, arguing that a wig was an encumbrance on the battlefield and that a hat sufficed. In July 1760 he led three heavy cavalry charges which broke the French line at Warburg; in one of these his hat blew off and he finished the charge with his shining pate exposed. In England this action was widely reported, and gave rise to the popular expression for recklessly dashing behaviour - "going for it bald-headed". Granby's fame grew with each further report home; as a result his new 21st Light Dragoons was able to attract more recruits than it needed while other regiments struggled to reach full strength.

The Marquis hoped that after a period of training in England the 21st would join him in Europe. However, on 25 October 1760 George II died and the following day George III became King. A French invasion was still feared by much of the population and, eager for the good opinion of his new subjects, the 22-year-old King announced his intention to take to the field in person to repel it. The 21st Light Dragoons, as one of the regiments detailed to fight under his command, was retained in England to await the invasion.

The French had committed troops along a wide front, and both Parliament and the British army considered an invasion unlikely. It is surprising, then, that such a high profile regiment should be committed to the home defence force. Possibly Granby's fame, and the ease with which his regiment attracted recruits, persuaded the authorities to keep it in England and draw from its ranks the men needed to reinforce those cavalry regiments fighting abroad which could not recruit for themselves.

The 21st spent the winter of 1760 escorting French prisoners of war, who arrived by sea at Scarborough, to

Lord John Manners, Marquis of Granby, eldest son of the 3rd Duke of Rutland. This portrait by Sir Joshua Reynolds hangs in the State Dining Room at Belvoir Castle. (His Grace The Duke of Rutland)

compounds in Hull and elsewhere. But if the French were the enemy abroad, new grievances among the poor made an enemy of them at home, and in an age before the creation of a regular constabulary the army was responsible for maintaining order. In February and March of 1761 the regiment was to be found "aiding the Civil Powers at Durham, where certain miners and other disorderly persons were committing breaches of the peace"[3]. Later it was moved south to Hertford and put down something of a riot on 8 August:

"A dispute having happened between the farmers of Kings Langley and the Irish reapers about wages, the Royal Foresters was sent for and a great skirmish ensued in which several were wounded. Six were taken and committed to St.Alban's jail and the rest dispersed"[4].

Disquiet grew within the 21st too, because it had been held in England on what were seen as lesser duties. It was said that the primary aim of a cavalry officer was to charge the enemy and die sword in hand. This overstated the case, for most had country estates which they hoped to enjoy when the war was won; but there was much frustration that they had not yet been allowed to join the Marquis of Granby in his famous exploits against the French. On 22 September the regiment was present in London for ceremonial duty at the Coronation of their Majesties King George III and Queen Charlotte. This was followed in November by the death of the commanding officer, Lord Robert Manners Sutton; given the increasing likelihood of peace being achieved in Europe without them, the men ended the year in low spirits.

The Marquis of Granby leading his regiment, The Blues, in the charge by two brigades of British heavy cavalry against the French at the battle of Warburg on 31 July 1760, his bald head shining "conspicuous in the sun". The French lost some 8,000 dead, wounded and captured, and twelve guns. (Royal Horse Guards)

Early in 1763 the war with France came to an end and the 21st was ordered back to Nottingham to be disbanded. Frustration that a regiment mounted on hunters from the Belvoir had not been "blooded" in battle now boiled over: the men refused to leave their barracks or surrender their weapons. This refusal was no mere token, for the 3rd Hussars had to be sent from Romford to assist in disbanding them: "The Royal Foresters was publicly disbanded in the Market Place by order of the Crown. Their arms were given up to be forwarded to the Tower; and their horses were sold in the neighbourhood, and realised about £7 each. This was one of the finest regiments in the service, broken up and dispersed"[5].

The regiment was gone, but the frustration remained. Captain Robert Hinde of the 21st was the model for Uncle Toby in Laurence Sterne's *Tristram Shandy*, published in several volumes during the 1760s. Uncle Toby is portrayed as a retired soldier fighting imaginary campaigns against the French, acted out on the local bowling green. The caricature was somewhat unfair to Hinde, a most accomplished cavalry officer who himself later wrote a book, *The Discipline of the Light Horse*, published in 1778. This manual covered every aspect of training and correct practice, and set the standards for light cavalry regiments in the British army for decades to come.

The Marquis of Granby died in 1770 without succeeding to the dukedom. All that remains of his regiment are the three guidons presented on its formation. These now hang near the entrance to the regimental museum, which has returned to Belvoir Castle, to this day the home of the Manners family.

Douglas's Regiment

In 1778 France declared its support for the American colonists who had rebelled against British rule, and with a large part of the British army abroad the threat of a French invasion reappeared. Three new regiments of light dragoons were authorised and one of these, raised at Stamford in Lincolnshire on 25 April 1779 by Colonel John Douglas, took rank as the 21st. In order to bring these regiments quickly to full strength the light dragoon troops attached to dragoon regiments were abolished and transferred to them.

The colonel had to provide horses, saddles, swords and uniforms at his own expense, and prices were rising: the cost of a hunter had more than doubled since 1760 to 15 guineas. However, a regiment became the property of the man who raised it and was considered a sound investment. The sons of gentlemen would pay in excess of £500 for a commission; in addition, the colonel drew the pay of those on the muster roll who had died, deserted, or never existed. Douglas could expect a return of about £3,000 a year, an enormous sum then. The men enlisting in the 21st were not so well rewarded. Each was paid eight pence a day (up from five pence in 1760), plus one penny a day grass money (up from three farthings).

The uniform of Douglas's Regiment was red with white facings, and silver lace and buttons. A significant change in the formation of the regiment since the days of Granby's 21st was brought about by the King's decision to replace drummers with trumpeters, one to each troop. Orders previously issued by drum beat were now to be sounded by trumpet call.

The first call of the day was Reveille at 5.30a.m., and the last Tattoo (or *tap-to*, meaning no more liquor was to be drawn) at 9.00p.m. Drill and musket practice, and the cleaning of arms and horse furniture, filled most of the day, with little opportunity for or recourse to entertainment. Standing Orders required all men to remain in their quarters whenever any bull-baiting or football match took place. No gambling of any kind was allowed. All that remained was women and drink, and it must be supposed that the men partook of both in considerable quantities.

Although marriage was discouraged, a small number of men were allowed to marry and have their wives live in the barrack room, and in such circumstances a married man could screen off his bed from the rest. The women were expected to wash, cook and mend for all the men in their barrack room. Standing Orders required: "Great care to be taken that those Women who wash, do not make use of the Men's Cloaks to Iron upon as is the usual custom"[6].

The colonel proprietor was not required actually to reside with his regiment or lead it in battle; he could appoint a lieutenant-colonel to do that on his behalf. Douglas appointed Lieutenant-Colonel Phillip de la Motte to command the 21st, and Major John Floyd to train the recruits. Floyd was well qualified for the task. Years earlier, aged only 12, he had taken part in the charge of the 15th Light Dragoons against the French at Emsdorff. Now an experienced veteran of 31, he also had Captain Hinde's *Discipline of the Light Horse* to advise him. Published just six months before Douglas raised the 21st, the book covered every aspect of preparing a regiment for service: "To form a light troop, your movements at first must be slow, and quickened by degrees, as the men grow ready; when they are got to be pretty quick and accustomed to charge without halting ... the men should be taught to fire with ball, and to point their swords well on horseback"[7].

Major Floyd trained his men in the area around Stamford and Peterborough through the harsh winter of 1779. Hinde had insisted that work on horseback be confined to the summer months, and that only dismounted exercises take place in the winter, but Floyd was having none of that. In a letter dated 15 December he wrote: "They ride ill, but do their Business in the Field very well for all that. We had much Frost and Rain lately, so that our poor Horses began to suffer ... Numbers of the men are ill and I have buried two; however the Sick List decreases. I make them live on horseback and it answers very well"[8]. Sooner than

Mounted private of the 21st Light Dragoons in 1762. This painting by David Morier hangs in the Royal Collection in Windsor Castle, and gives an accurate representation of the first uniform. (Royal Collection © Her Majesty The Queen)

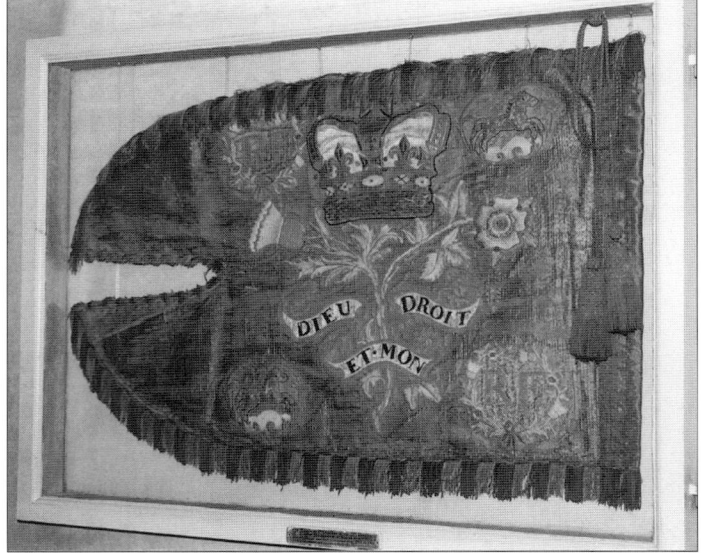

One of the three guidons presented to the 21st Light Dragoons on its formation in 1760. This, the first or King's guidon, bears the royal crest and 'RF' for 'Royal Foresters'. (The Queen's Royal Lancers)

expected, the regiment was ready for service.

While the population feared a French invasion another enemy had long since reached the eastern and southern coasts of England: smugglers. Rum was brought in by the barrel, but this was not the only contraband. Tea from China and India was becoming established as the national drink, and because of its bitter taste the demand for sugar from the West Indies was growing too. As import duties kept the price of both tea and sugar artificially high, smugglers could make huge profits ferrying contraband from Holland and France. There were few good roads along the coasts of England and the task of patrolling, moving rapidly from cove to cove, was best performed by light dragoons.

The 21st was first posted to Whitby for revenue duty along the Yorkshire coast. Apart from a period in Manchester, where poverty and unemployment led to unrest and required a constant military presence in aid of the civil powers, Douglas's Regiment was committed exclusively to the battle against smugglers. It patrolled the Sussex coast through the winter of 1781, then moved to Canterbury to perform the same duties along the Kent coast.

The war with America ended in November 1782 and peace was made with France two months later. Regiments serving abroad returned home, so that those raised to take their place were no longer required. The 21st Light Dragoons was disbanded in March 1783. Once again, having served only in England and being denied any sight of that enemy for which a light dragoon regiment was designed, it was with a sense of purpose unfulfilled that the officers and men returned to their homes.

Yet just as Granby's Regiment bequeathed to the British cavalry the experience of Captain Hinde, so Douglas's gave the experience of Major Floyd. He was appointed colonel of the 19th Light Dragoons, a regiment specially raised to assist the private army of the English East India Company. The Company ruled most of Bengal and Madras and, desiring a trading monopoly, engaged in military operations against both the native population and the French East India

Lord Robert Manners Sutton, younger brother of the Marquis of Granby. As commanding officer of the 21st (Granby's) Light Dragoons, he required that all recruits be "light and straight and by no means gummy". (National Portrait Gallery)

Company. Floyd distinguished himself in leading charges against the Marathas, inland tribes armed by the French. He later raised several regiments of native cavalry, local horsemen prepared to fight in the pay of the Company. Trained by Floyd and led by officers of the 19th, these were the origin of that native cavalry without which the British could not have extended their power across the whole subcontinent.

Beaumont's Regiment

Following the Revolution of 1789 the French offered to assist other peoples who wished to abolish their monarchies. Britain, Holland and Spain saw this as deliberately provocative and united in opposition to the Republic. In February 1793 France declared war on all three countries. Britain increased its army by 30,000 men, including 14 regiments of light dragoons. This took some time and it was not until 24 February 1794 that the 21st Light Dragoons was re-embodied at Doncaster by Colonel T.R.Beaumont, one of the largest landowners in the north of England. His regiment forsook the scarlet uniform of its forbears for the less conspicuous blue now adopted by the whole corps of light dragoons.

After only three months' training at Doncaster, Gainsborough and Retford, Beaumont's Regiment was moved to Manchester. There were only so many recruits to be found and, like many of the newly created regiments, the 21st was still not up to strength. For the poor and unemployed of the new industrial cities the offer of food, shelter and a regular wage was often sufficient temptation to enlist.

However, there was a second, more pressing reason for this early move. The ideas of liberty and equality that inspired the French had crossed the channel and found a voice in Thomas Paine's *The Rights of Man*, published in 1791. Manchester was the only centre of organised protest in England. It was there that the Abolitionists — demanding an end to Britain's part in the slave trade — had most support, and it was thought such a dissident movement might form the basis of an English Revolution. In 1792, 20,000 people had signed a petition calling for an end to the slave trade, out of a total city population of 75,000. The trade was crucial to the British economy. British ships transported African slaves to work on plantations in the West Indies, particularly the islands of San Domingo (Hispaniola, later Haiti) and Jamaica, returning with cheap cotton, coffee, sugar, rum and tobacco. The shipowners, some of them leading politicians of the day, were making huge profits. Furthermore, it was this source of cheap cotton that fuelled the industrial revolution and allowed British trade to dominate the world. The Abolitionists were unlikely revolutionaries, but their increasing popular support threatened both the slave trade and the empire growing with it.

The mere presence of cavalry was sufficient to ensure order and no record exists of any encounter between the Manchester Abolitionists and the 21st. Had it been necessary, force would undoubtedly have been used, although mounted troops were expected to break up a crowd without resort to the sword. (The later massacre of the Manchester Reformers resulted from indiscipline in the regiment then concerned.) Ironically, the only open fighting occurred within the ranks of the 21st when it was brought up to full strength by drafting in men of the 23rd (Ulster) Light Dragoons. The Irishmen were not well received, and the 4th Light Dragoons had to be called in to restore order and supervise the incorporation.

By 1795 the ideas of the Revolution had spread to the French colony of San Domingo in the West Indies. Several of the French regiments garrisoned there declared themselves for the Republic and sided with the plantation slaves, who took this opportunity to rebel. The plantation owners called on Britain for support. Because the island was crucial to its economy, both as a market for slaves and a source of cheap cotton, Britain was quick to respond.

The 21st Light Dragoons (dismounted) was included in a force of infantry and cavalry which reached San Domingo in June 1796. Along with the 14th and 18th Light Dragoons and the Prince of Wales' Hussars, the regiment was quartered at Port au Prince and remounted on horses from America. Although the British garrison was pitted against the French Republicans and the plantation slaves, who to some extent united against them, the first enemy to strike was yellow fever. A muster roll dated December 1796 records that during the first six months on the island 85 men of the 21st died of fever, and the other cavalry regiments were just as badly hit. Thus weakened, the British force could do little more than defend itself, and only one notable action occurred.

The French troops occupying the town and fort of Mirebalais had declared for the Republic. Detachments of all four Light Dragoon regiments were included in a party sent over the mountains to take the town by surprise. A gripping account of their passage over terrain most unsuit-

An engraving from The Discipline of The Light Horse *published in 1778, by Captain Robert Hinde. Although equipped with both sword and carbine the former was the dragoon's primary weapon. (The Queen's Royal Lancers)*

able for cavalry was recorded in the narrative of Sergeant Landsheit:

"There was no riding up the face of that rock, which here and there opened up into terrible fissures, of which no bottom could be discerned. On we went, each man leading his horse, which gathered up its feet like a cat at the edge of the gulf, and sprang over. Yet all passed not thus. From time to time a cry from the lookers-on told of man and horse having missed their spring; and a crash amongst the branches was all that proclaimed their progress to annihilation"[9].

When this force reached Mirebalais the town was taken by the infantry and set alight. At this, French soldiers manning the fort attempted to escape. The dragoons pursued them, killing many with the sword and driving the rest into the river Artibonite, where they either swam and drowned or returned to the bank and were cut down.

Despite this success, the British garrison at Port au Prince was too small to take control of the island, and developments elsewhere soon made that unnecessary. The availability of cheap cotton from slave plantations along the American coast, together with the establishment of sugar cane and coffee plantations in Brázil, meant that the islands of the West Indies were no longer crucial to Britain. The British force was evacuated in April 1798. The plantation slaves declared both themselves and San Domingo free, and gave their island the new name of Haiti. Nine years later Britain abolished the slave trade — not quite the concession to the Abolitionists that it seemed, for the market was nearing saturation and the trade no longer so profitable.

★ ★ ★

Immediately it arrived back in England the regiment was ordered to Bridgenorth in Shropshire, and brought back to near full strength by a draft of 150 men from the 13th Light Dragoons. Bridgenorth lay at the centre of the Industrial Revolution now gathering pace. Coal and steam, factories and iron foundries were changing the landscape and the working conditions of the people. The government feared that rising discontent among poorly paid workers and the unemployed would lead to violence against merchants and machines, and stationed mounted regiments in likely trouble spots to discourage rashness.

After two years in Shropshire the regiment was moved to Ireland. The great Irish rebellion of 1798 had been put down, but unrest naturally persisted; the eight troops of the 21st (comprising 80 men per troop) were posted to separate locations around the countryside to discourage any further rising. This was the least desirable station available to the British army, and when the celebrated Lieutenant-General Sir Banastre Tarleton was appointed colonel of the regiment both officers and men hoped for something better. Tarleton had earned a reputation for energetic, even ruthless leadership during the American War of Independence. He was known for the green uniform he and his men wore in America in preference to the official scarlet, and it can be assumed that the men of the 21st shared many a joke about the likely effect of a change to Tarleton's green in the countryside of Ireland.

Spain had allied itself with France in the continuing battle for colonies and markets; and in 1806 two troops were detached from the regiment to join a force sent to reinforce the British garrison holding Buenos Aires, capital of Spanish South America. They arrived to find the Spanish had retaken Buenos Aires two months earlier. In preparation for a counter-attack this force advanced on the town of Maldonado, defended by a small party of Spanish troops protected by sandhills. A charge was ordered, swords were drawn, and the men of the 21st spurred their horses forward; but the Spanish fled before the horsemen could reach the gallop.

The remains of the British garrison expelled from Buenos Aires joined with these reinforcements in an attack on Montevideo. Several cavalry skirmishes occurred as Spanish patrols were pressed back, until the town could be taken by the infantry. The British force then advanced toward Buenos Aires, leaving the 21st to garrison Montevideo. This attempt on the capital failed, the British surrendered, and the two troops of the 21st Light Dragoons sailed for Cape Town where the main body of the regiment had recently been stationed.

★ ★ ★

The Cape of Good Hope, the Dutch colony at the tip of South Africa, was of no mercantile value to the British; but its strategic harbour facilities were of the highest importance to the security of the shipping routes to India and China, which by now made an enormous contribution to national wealth. The 21st Light Dragoons, under the command of Lieutenant-Colonel Pigot, arrived at Cape Town in August 1806.

Most of the native population had fled across the Great

Fish River, although some remained to work on the farms. There were 30,000 Dutch settlers who seemed unlikely to cause the British trouble. The infantry was kept on the coast, ready to repel any French attack. The cavalry patrolled inland, and each man was billeted on a farmer who was required to feed both dragoon and horse: "Each Dragoon to be supplied daily with 1¼ lbs. Bread, 1 lb. Meat, 9 lbs. Barley, and 7 lbs. Chaff"[10]. This imposition caused much ill-feeling among the Dutch.

The Great Fish River was recognised by the British and Dutch as the northern frontier of the colony, but not by the Pondo and Xhosa tribes, who periodically crossed and attempted to reclaim the Zuurveld, a fertile plain south of the river where they had lived before the Dutch came. By 1811 some areas had been reoccupied by about 4,000 members of the two tribes, and the Governor issued a stern proclamation: "Whereas the Kaffir chiefs wandering in the Zuurveld continue to annoy the inhabitants and to plunder the farmers ... Now to put a stop to these calamities I have authorised a military force for the purpose of driving these marauders over the Great Fish River, the acknowledged boundary of His Majesty's settlement"[11]. "Kaffir" was not then the term of abuse it later became, but the Dutch collective name for the Pondo and Xhosa tribes; the British borrowed the word, and the area around the Great Fish River (and often the whole colony) became known as Kaffirland or Kaffraria.

A large British force commanded by Colonel Graham, including a detachment of the 21st Light Dragoons, advanced through the Zuurveld, burning rebuilt villages and driving the Pondo and Xhosa tribes back across the river. Observation posts were then built along the frontier and men of the 21st detailed to patrol between them. One post was named Trumpeter's Drift after a trumpeter of the regiment swimming in the river there was carried away by the current. In addition to patrolling the frontier, light dragoons were the only letter carriers in the colony and these riders became known as "dragoon-expresses".

Increasing tension between the British and the Dutch led to the regiment's involvement in a most serious affair. The Governor, while striking firmly against the native population when conceived as the enemy (as in the Zuurveld), could not condone the ill-treatment of native workers employed on Dutch farms. In 1815 a farmer named Bedizenhout, who had been charged with ill-treating a worker, was shot by British soldiers while resisting arrest. Several days later 400 settlers, some armed with hunting rifles, attacked a British post. A troop of the 21st Light Dragoons was present and immediately advanced with drawn swords; the farmers fled and the troop gave chase, capturing 90. The six leaders were tried and sentenced to death, and hanged in public at Schlacters Nek. When the scaffold broke under their combined weight, spectators joined the convicted men in crying for mercy, but the sentence was carried out. The incident became a focus for hatred of the British and was the root of much subsequent trouble.

During this period the finer details of the uniform changed almost annually, if all reports can be believed, though there was many a slip between the issue of regulation patterns and the dress actually worn, particularly by regiments serving far from home. Prior to 1812 the uniform of the 21st was shown in the Army List as blue with yellow facings and silver lace. The Royal Military Panorama of 1814 gave it as blue with pink facings and silver lace. The Army List for 1815 described it as blue with black facings and silver lace. In later Army Lists it appeared as blue with black velvet facings and gold lace.

★ ★ ★

After the final defeat of Napoleon Bonaparte at Waterloo in 1815 the Emperor was sent into exile on the remote South Atlantic island of Saint Helena. The British garrison on the island was strengthened by a detachment of 21st Light Dragoons from the Cape: Lieutenant McConchey and 20 men. As Napoleon was not restricted to his official residence, Longwood House, during the early years of captivity he took long daily rides across the island, escorted everywhere and on every occasion by men of the 21st. To prevent a rescue attempt being mounted from Tristan da Cunha to the south this island was occupied by a further 12 men of the regiment under Captain Cloeté, and a detachment of artillery.

The garrison commander, the notoriously disagreeable General Sir Hudson Lowe, seems to have taken a dislike to the light dragoons under his command. He replaced Lieutenant McConchey with Cornet Hoath, also of the 21st, but later fell out with him too - and ordered Hoath to

Thomas, 3rd Earl of Effingham in the uniform of an officer of the 21st (Douglas's) Light Dragoons at the time of the American War of Independence. He wears a scarlet coat, a white waistcoat and white breeches. (Courtesy G. Gibbs)

An officer of the 21st (Beaumont's) Light Dragoons in 1795. He wears a blue jacket with yellow facings and silver lace. The GR cypher on the silver plate of the crossbelt has '21' and 'LD' to either side. (Courtesy G. Gibbs)

Martin French of the 21st (Beaumont's) Light Dragoons, showing the hussar-style uniform worn from about 1805. The blue jacket has yellow facings and silver lace. (Courtesy G. Gibbs)

hand over command to an infantry officer! Hoath took this as an insult to both himself and the cavalry, and left the island with his mess bills unpaid.

Leaving these detachments on Saint Helena and Tristan da Cunha, the remainder of the regiment was ordered to India. The only opposition to British control of the subcontinent came from the Marathas, native cavalrymen who occupied large areas of the interior. After years of operating independently, attacking colonists for plunder, Maratha bands were uniting under Baji Rao with the intention of expelling the British from India. Additional troops were needed urgently in Bengal.

The 21st Light Dragoons arrived in India in September 1817 and occupied areas already taken by the main British force, while a detachment under Captain O'Reilly joined Bengal native troops in action on the frontier. There were no set-piece battles, the Marathas preferring to fight a war of skirmishes rather than engage the British directly; certainly the 21st suffered more casualties from cholera and heatstroke than from clashes with the enemy. By 1819 the territory under British control had been extended sufficiently that the Marathas no longer posed a threat, and the 21st once again provided dragoon-expresses to maintain communication between the seat of government and forces inland.

That same year a financial crisis in the British army led to a reduction in the number of regiments, and the 21st Light Dragoons was one of those chosen for disbandment. The regiment was returned to England and disbanded in April 1820, although the detachment guarding Napoleon on Saint Helena was allowed to continue after this date. Napoleon was by then seriously ill and remained inside Longwood House. Frederick Allison of the 21st was employed to carry messages for the British orderly officer based there, and awarded himself the title of "Napoleon's Orderly". When Napoleon died in May 1821 the last men of the 21st Light Dragoons attended his funeral.

A number of officers had remained in Bengal, choosing to join the private army of the East India Company rather than return to England. Their regiments were composed of native troops under British officers, and ironically it would be the eventual mutiny of these troops which would cause the restructuring of Company forces and the reappearance of the 21st in India.

★   ★   ★

In the year that Beaumont's Regiment was disbanded Muhammad ʿAli, Viceroy of Egypt – nominal representative of the Turkish Ottoman empire, and actual ruler – sent an army to conquer the Sudan. Lying south of Egypt and bisected by the Nile, the Sudan's one million square miles of desert and scrub made it the largest country in Africa. By 1821 Muhammad ʿAli controlled the area north of the Sudanese capital, Khartoum, and proceeded to strip the country of its wealth — mostly gold, livestock and slaves.

An attempted rebellion against Egyptian rule was brutally suppressed. Left with little more than their Islamic faith, the Sudanese could do no more than worship Allah, honour his Prophet and dream of the day they would rise again. Nationalism and religion fused in a potent yearning for independence from Egypt. A sense of messianic expectation persisted among the devout, who believed that a second great Prophet — known as *al-Mahdi* — would be sent to expel the foreigners and establish the rule of Islam on earth.

CHAPTER TWO

Indian Origins

The 18-year-old Princess Victoria became Queen of England in 1837. The early years of her reign were marked by unrest at home, with riots and strikes among the poor in England and famine and armed insurrection in Ireland. Meanwhile the Empire grew steadily wider and stronger; and once it was believed that Russian expansion had been halted in the Crimea in 1855 Britain's world power seemed unchallenged.

In 1851 the Great Exhibition at the Crystal Palace in Hyde Park displayed Britain's unrivalled technological achievements. "The workshop of the world" sent out not only its goods but its warships and soldiers. The British Empire was now so large that it was possible to sail around the world and at all points come under the protection of British ships from nearby naval bases, and in all countries where trade was conducted to travel under the protection of Her Majesty's Forces.

The one exception was India, where "Queen's regiments" were few and far between, and such protection was largely provided by the private armies of the three regional Residencies of the East India Company, the largest being in Bengal. The Bengal Light Cavalry had seen much fighting as the Company took control of most of the subcontinent; its native troopers and NCOs were led by Indian warrant ranks but commanded by British officers. The 11 regiments were distinguished by the colour of their uniform jackets — "French grey", a cool grey-blue. These close-fitting garments could not have been more unlike the loose native dress: "A cavalryman can neither mount nor dismount without the danger of bursting both his jacket and trousers"[1]. It might be said that the native troops felt their religious beliefs and practices to be similarly constrained by their European masters; and in the 1850s a number of different grievances festered into an explosive mood of sullen discontent.

It has passed into legend that the final spark which detonated the Great Mutiny of 1857 was the use of beef and pork fat in the grease used to lubricate cartridges for the newly issued Enfield rifles and carbines: biting off the end of the paper cartridge to load was thus offensive to both Hindus (to whom the cow was sacred) and Muslims (to whom the pig was unclean). The truth was that the Company insisted that its officers respect the religious beliefs of their native troops. Immediately the concerns of the men became known, officers of the 3rd Bengal Light Cavalry based at Meerut - a major station for both Bengal and British troops, about 30 miles from Delhi - had the cartridge lubricant made up by the men themselves using beeswax and clarified butter, both bought locally. On 24 April 1857 the regiment's 90 skirmishers were paraded and told that the cartridge could be torn with the fingers instead of the teeth. Only five men accepted the cartridge; the 85 who refused were tried (by a court of Indian officers), and sentenced to ten years' hard labour.

The sentence was announced on 9 May; and on the following evening a British officer of the 3rd was one of the first to learn of the high price to be paid for complacency. He was riding towards the barracks to investigate a report of unrest, certain that it would amount to nothing of consequence:

"As I looked down the road to the lines, it was full of Cavalry Troopers galloping towards me ... before I knew what was happening, I found myself warding off as well as I could a fierce onslaught from many blades". The native troops were not only rebelling against their white officers, but attacking all Europeans, shouting that the Company's Raj was over for ever. "I was horror-struck to see a carriage being dragged along by its driverless horse, while beside it rode a Trooper of the 3rd Cavalry plunging his sword repeatedly through its open window into the body of an unfortunate European woman"[2].

The mutineers moved on Delhi and took the city; within days they controlled all the main centres of population. Because British regiments were spread widely over the great expanse of India a response to the Mutiny took time to organise, and it was September before Delhi was retaken. Men who had lost wives and children in the massacres, and their countrymen, took terrible revenge on their captives. Surrendered rebel leaders were shot without trial and their bodies thrown down in the bazaars. The conflict degenerated into a cycle of massacre and counter-terror of which neither side can be proud. At Cawnpore 500 British men, women and children were slaughtered by the rebels. At Lucknow 2,000 mutineers were massacred with rifle and bayonet; native leaders were tied to the muzzles of cannon

The British Residency at Lucknow after attack by Indian artillery during the Great Mutiny of 1857. (The Queen's Royal Lancers)

British troops putting down the Mutiny. Artistic licence allows the cavalry charge to rout a massed enemy. (The Queen's Royal Lancers)

and literally blown to pieces.

The senior officers of Her Majesty's Forces in England and around the world came almost exclusively from the land-owning nobility and gentry; certainly the system of purchasing commissions ensured that only the wealthy could attain such rank. In contrast, British officers of native regiments in the employ of the East India Company — which gave commissions freely to men of ability — were predominantly middle-class. Although they were paid almost twice as much as their British army equivalents this was still too little to cover the cost of uniforms, equipment, and maintaining themselves in the necessary style of life. Lacking the private incomes upon which Queen's officers depended, many of them remained in debt throughout their period of service.

This debt, together with the fact that a commission freely obtained could not be sold on leaving Company service, meant that regimental officers soldiered on long after officers in the service of the Crown had given up their posts to younger men — 30 years was not uncommon. Ironically, then, the Company's system of commissions awarded on ability produced elderly and lethargic officers, while the much-criticised system of purchasing commissions ensured a continual intake of young officers for Her Majesty's forces.

The native troops of the Bengal Light Cavalry had no particular allegiance to Queen or country. Their allegiance was to their regimental officers, and when these no longer commanded respect regimental discipline broke apart as inevitably as the close-fitting uniform split on the stoop. The causes of the Mutiny were many and complex, but this shallowness of allegiance must rank significantly among them.

Once the Mutiny had been suppressed the Company reorganised its private army so that it no longer had to depend on the loyalty of native troops. Its British officers were given command of five new regiments of light cavalry made up wholly of recruits from England. Those who had served in the 4th and 6th Bengal Light Cavalry now officered the newly created 3rd Bengal European Light Cavalry stationed at Lucknow. Continuity with the old regiments was maintained by the colour of the uniform jacket — French grey.

Given the need to attract recruits for service in a theatre whose recent reputation was uninviting, the height requirement set by the Company was lower than that set for the Queen's service, so that the average height of men arriving to join the Bengal European Light Cavalry was two to three inches shorter than in Her Majesty's regiments. An average height below 5 feet 4 inches and a chest measurement of less than 33 inches gave rise to the unfortunate nickname "Dumpies", understandably never heard within the Company's regiments themselves except in rare instances of self-mockery.

By Act of Parliament in 1858 the territories administered by the East India Company, together with its several armies, were taken over by the Crown. The French-grey regiments could not be fully absorbed into Crown service, their men having enlisted only for service in India. "Her Majesty's Forces in India" thus remained administratively separate from "Her Majesty's General Forces". Two years later the decision of Prime Minister Lord Palmerston that this Indian army should be absorbed into the British army proper and should be available for service elsewhere almost led to a "white mutiny". The young recruits still considered themselves employed by the East India Company, some proposing "three cheers for the Company and three groans for the Queen"[3]. The officers were uneasy too; fiercely proud of their Bengal Cavalry origins, these middle-class Englishmen feared for their future if absorbed into Queen's cavalry regiments long officered by the English aristocracy.

The 21st Hussars

In May 1861 "Her Majesty's Forces in India" were transferred to "Her Majesty's General Forces". Three regiments

Sketch of the Mess Room of the 3rd Bengal European Light Cavalry by Lieutenant H.C.Kemble, who served from 1858. It shows officers at dinner, sharing four bottles of port and served by five waiters. (The Queen's Royal Lancers)

Below: *An officer of the 21st Hussars wearing the earliest uniform adopted in 1863, with a dark blue tunic and a scarlet sabretache. His busby has a white plume and a French grey bag. (Courtesy G.Gibbs)*

of light dragoons were formed from the Bengal cavalry, the 3rd Bengal European Light Cavalry being redesignated the 21st Light Dragoons. That July, only two months after its re-embodiment, a change in the classification of cavalry regiments meant that the 21st was restyled "Hussars". The change was largely administrative and little changed except the uniform, and since that did not arrive from England until August 1863 the officers and men of the 21st Hussars spent their first two years dressed as light dragoons.

Men who did not wish to transfer from the Bengal Cavalry to the 21st were given free passage home, and many of the older officers also took this opportunity to retire. The regiment was brought back to full strength by officers and men from 16 Crown regiments. While this transfer of younger officers and men brought much-needed new blood to the 21st, some of those forcibly transferred from long-established Crown regiments resented the move. Deprived of the higher status that went with ancient pedigree and battle honours, they looked down on a regiment that had until a moment ago been part of Her Majesty's Indian Forces. There was considerable tension between those who transferred from the Company's service and those from regiments which had always been in Crown service, this divide sometimes being made physically apparent by the height difference.

The 21st was allowed to retain French grey as the colour of the facings of the uniform jacket, indicating the regiment's Indian origins and a victory for the Company transfers (the nickname "Dumpies" was a less welcome inheritance).

When Colonel Pigot, the last commanding officer of the 21st (Beaumont's) Light Dragoons disbanded in 1820, wrote to the re-embodied regiment conveying his best wishes, this reminder of a second lineage of inheritance was of special interest to the Crown transfers. An application was immediately made for the battle honours of Beaumont's Regiment to be transferred to the Bengal regiment: 'Saint Domingo', 'Monte Video' and 'Kaffraria'. The refusal of this request caused much resentment, particularly as the 5th

The dry Indian plains around Lucknow, where the 21st trained in the unrelenting heat. (The Queen's Royal Lancers)

Lancers (raised in 1858) had been allowed to assume the battle honours of the 5th Royal Irish Dragoons (disbanded in disgrace in 1799). It seemed to the officers of the 21st (though quite without substantive evidence) that their regiment's Indian origins had counted against its assuming the battle honours of its English origins. To some extent this had a beneficial effect, uniting Company and Crown transfers in resentment against their London masters and in determination to prove their regiment as good as any in the Queen's service.

Nevertheless, there remained a considerable and long-lasting tension between the two groups; and when ten years later a correspondent referred in the *Regimental Gazetteer* to the 21st as being "formed in 1861" he was heavily rebuked in the next issue: "The word should have been *reformed*, for everyone knows that the 21st Light Dragoons had existed long before 1861"[4]. Lest anyone had forgotten, a brief history of the three previous regiments designated 21st Light Dragoons then followed.

Tension between the two constituent parts of the regiment was compounded by the unrelenting heat. British cavalry regiments in India were garrisoned on the hot plains close to large cities, and the men were continually exposed to epidemics — the most deadly being cholera, typhoid and enteric fever. In 1862 cholera broke out among the men of the 21st Hussars and the regiment was sent to the cool hill station of Abbotabad while the epidemic ran its course. Experiencing more than 50 deaths in that isolated place, the 21st returned to the Bengal plains with the old animosity tempered as if in battle against a deadly common foe.

Disease continued to be the chief enemy; during a ten-year period the regiment lost 116 men, none of them in combat. Surgeon Fairland of the 21st was so concerned that he wrote a paper arguing, at some risk to his own military career, that posting only the sick to a hill station achieved nothing: "The real value of these mountain regions is in preserving health before it is broken down, their curative powers being comparatively small"[5]. He proposed "prevention not cure", moving whole regiments permanently from the plains to the hills.

The political and military powers in London were not impressed by Fairland's argument. India generated enormous revenue for Britain — half of China's total imports consisted of opium supplied from the subcontinent. India itself was a vital market for British cotton exports, taking one third of the total output, the East India Company having destroyed the local textile industry as a competitor with Lancashire. This in effect funded Britain's balance of payments surplus, and foreign policy towards India was based on a no-risk premise. Therefore cavalry regiments were left to suffer the hot, cholera-haunted barracks on the plains, deliberately located close to the cities and able to react immediately to any threat of further rebellion.

In fact no rebellion was forthcoming, and with no real fighting to be done, combat readiness had to be maintained by war games. In a typical exercise, the 21st Hussars marched out from Lucknow with orders to take a position held by two "enemy" infantry regiments in the river fort of Jellalabad. As the position could not be taken by a cavalry charge, the regiment dismounted and opened fire with carbines: "A smart fusilade was kept up for about three hours, when the sun was discovered to be unpleasantly hot and the forces returned to quarters, convinced that nothing is so unlike real war as sham war"[6].

This experience, together with the army's approval of its first universal pattern breech-loading carbine (the Westley Richards "Monkey-tail" in 1861), sparked a heated debate in the 21st. Although light cavalry were armed with both sword and carbine, the first was their primary and offensive weapon — they were taught to charge "down the blade" of a drawn sword. Indeed, the whole ethos of the cavalry was *l'arme blanche* ("white weapons", i.e. blades). The carbine was purely defensive. Although even the old muzzle-loading carbines had been possible to fire and reload while mounted, this was a slow and clumsy process. The issue of rifled breech-loaders made it quicker and more practical under battlefield conditions, but most practice was still conducted dismounted (the combination of a short barrel and an unsteady seat made firing from the saddle inherently inaccurate). It was assumed that carbines would be used only by dismounted troops defending a fixed position, a role which would not normally fall to the cavalry.

However, powerful voices in the British army proposed that the rifle should replace the sword as the cavalryman's primary offensive weapon; and even that he should be retrained to fire with precision at the gallop (though how whole regiments of circus trick-shooters were to be created does not seem to have been addressed). It was further and more realistically suggested that regiments of light cavalry should be transformed into "Mounted Rifles", the men equally able to deploy mounted or on foot. It was this latter prospect which caused most consternation among both officers and men of the 21st Hussars. All were darkly convinced - totally without evidence, and based solely on the regimental sense of inferiority - that the cavalry regiments chosen for this indignity would be those whose heritage lay in Her Majesty's Indian Forces and not their more blue-blooded comrades.

Major Schmid ridiculed these proposals in the *Gazetteer* with the (at that time) satirical suggestion that infantry regiments mounted on bicycles might better meet the army's need: "If Mounted Rifles are thought necessary, why not take advantage of a modern Invention and train men to ride on By-cycles? With practice men so mounted could make faster or longer marches than even Cavalry. On arrival at the position to be held, the By-cycles could be thrown down and left on the ground under a slight guard, and in view of the possibility of their being captured by the enemy, the linch-pin should be removed on dismounting"[7].

While failing to act - yet - on Major Schmid's suggestion, the army decided not to create regiments of Mounted Rifles. It was not the protests of the 21st Hussars that won the day, but the lobbying of more socially confident regiments of lancers, concerned that such a change, once introduced, might spread throughout the cavalry. Major-General Tombs wrote scathingly: "If you accustom Cavalry Soldiers to trust more to their firearms than their spurs, swords and lances, you destroy their dash, their élan, the speciality of this arm of the services"[8].

There was real fear that the hell-for-leather spirit of the cavalry would be lost in an age of the rifled breech-loader. As a result these regiments continued to use the sword and lance as offensive weapons long after they were effectively obsolete. Incredibly, as a compromise, the army considered mounting an infantryman behind each cavalryman, two men to each horse. Rough Rider Matthew Muttonfist of the 21st commented of such an unwelcome passenger that "he would not be likely to sit there long"[9].

The "French Greys"

On its arrival from England the new dark blue hussar uniform was found to be tight and unsuitable for the Indian climate: "Most of the men have found the Stable Jacket most uncomfortable, and the shoulder strap causes great pain across the chest ... and the unpleasant feeling that something is bound to go, either the braces, brace buttons, or overall tabs"[10]. Despite this it was generally well received. The regiment's Indian inheritance was retained in the French grey of the busby bag — part of the high fur cap (colpack) which had evolved in Western Europe from the native headgear of the original Hungarian hussars of an earlier century. At the same time, the tunic was identical to that worn by regiments with distinguished records of Crown service. Both Company and Crown transfers could wear it with pride.

United by continuing fatalities from disease, the threat from modern firearms which struck at the very idea of *l'arme blanche*, and the new uniform, the 21st Hussars now made a conscious effort to establish an alternative nickname to the hated "Dumpies". A regimental musical troupe adopted the name "French Grey Minstrels"; and before long the regiment was known, at least to its own officers and men, as the "French Greys".

Nevertheless, the regimental sense of inferiority persisted. Throughout India the unofficial league of top British cavalry regiments was determined on the polo ground. This sport required considerable investment and was dominated by regiments officered by men with large private incomes who could purchase the necessary strings of ponies specially bred for the game. The members of the 21st's mess possessed none of the required ponies and had never won a polo tournament.

This sense of inferiority within the cavalry establishment existed alongside the sense of superiority over the Indian people which pervaded the Raj. India introduced the officers of the 21st to a way of life which they could never have expected at home even in that Victorian heyday. Native servants cooked and served their food, groomed and saddled their horses, and saw to their every need. A married officer, occupying a bungalow in its own grounds within walking distance of the mess, would typically have two personal servants and a groom for his horse. For the rank and file, too, life in India was easier than life at home. Although horses had to be exercised morning and evening, apart from the routine of drills, parades and weapon training there was nothing to be done between 10.00a.m. and 5.00p.m. each day.

In such a situation sport was crucial, not only to maintain personal fitness but simply to fill the hours of leisure time. Football and cricket were popular among the men, while officers preferred big-game hunting — tiger, bear, panther and elephant; and if these proved elusive, snipe and parrot could be had in abundance. Mounted sports were most appropriate for the cavalry, and although polo matches were played with some success against the less accomplished native teams, hunting proved more popular. Although local jackals were slower than English foxes, the regimental officers had a pack of hounds shipped out from England to

A typical Indian hill station, where the sick were sent to recover in the cooler air. Surgeon Fairland of the 21st thought that it was pointless to send only convalescent cases to such stations as Abbotabad - prevention would have made more sense than attempted cure. (The Queen's Royal Lancers)

Lucknow for their own use.

The popularity of the Lucknow Hounds was exceeded only by that of pig-sticking, which was considered more testing for both pony and rider. Spears up to 12 feet long were used in the manner of lances. As wild boar were ferocious and fast-moving, able to manoeuvre swiftly and turn unexpectedly to charge, there was an element of real danger; the chase honed all the skills of quick thinking and precise horsemanship that a cavalryman needed.

In the lethal heat of the plains only so many leisure hours each day could be filled with physical activity, and time had to be occupied in other ways. The Regimental Library was particularly well stocked, its 1,402 volumes covering every subject — perhaps surprisingly, hypnotism and theology were well represented — and including a broad selection of fiction, from the great French novels to "shilling shockers". These were augmented by the regular arrival of English newspapers and periodicals. While one end of the library was reserved for quiet reading the other had tables equipped with chess, backgammon, dominoes and playing cards.

However, those readers who know their Kipling will appreciate that most of the men inevitably found less constructive pastimes, illustrated by the inquest held into the death by drowning of Private Mills. The day following his disappearance his helmet had been found by the river, and three days later fishermen brought up his body in their nets. "One of his comrades who had been with him, had seen him standing in the river up to his knees, he being partly intoxicated at the time, and failing to persuade him to return to Barracks, had left him, and he was never afterwards seen alive"[11].

The *arrack* (local spirit) sold in the bazaars was strong and cheap enough that a man could get drunk for a halfpenny. The 21st introduced a system of fines for drunkenness; in the three years to May 1872, 283 fines were imposed amounting to £114. One man had been fined 20 times. In a further attempt to save the men from themselves the purchase of arrack in the bazaars was banned and a limited supply made available in the regimental canteen. The canteen opened for one hour each evening, and to discourage the consumption of spirits English beer was

Above: *Lance-Corporal Grigsby of the 21st Hussars photographed at Lucknow in 1870. His single-breasted tunic is laced across the front, and Austrian knots decorate the cuffs; his white foreign service helmet has a brass spike, and he has a riding whip tucked under his right arm. (The Queen's Royal Lancers)*

Below: *Non-commissioned officers of the 21st Hussars photographed at Lucknow in the late 1860s; some sport the full beards fashionable at that date. (The Queen's Royal Lancers)*

Above: The earliest known photograph of the 21st Hussars on parade, taken at Lucknow in 1871. *(The Queen's Royal Lancers)*

Left: Pig-sticking was a more popular sport than polo among officers of the 21st in India. Wild boar were fierce and fast, which added a welcome element of risk. *(The Queen's Royal Lancers)*

available at a subsidised price. This hardly helped. During the canteen hour between 300 and 400 men crowded into the large, hot and humid room, each with the sole intent of downing as much as he could within the time allowed.

The heat and the drink could hardly be blamed (though both were) for a high rate of venereal disease. A Royal Commission reported that British soldiers in India were "gregarious in their amours"[12]. Less than ten per cent of the men had wives living with them, and this phrase was a euphemistic allusion to the fact that the rest made overmuch use of prostitutes. Sexually transmitted diseases were rife, particularly syphilis, and the Bengal regiments fared worst of all with a staggering one-third of the men infected. Because it was common for individual prostitutes to be shared by ten or more men at a time, one infected woman could quickly spread the disease through a barrack room. It was reckoned that every soldier who did not marry would become infected before the age of 30.

There was of course a severe shortage of single European women of the soldiers' social class, and the death of a married man would be quickly followed by his widow's remarriage, although stories of proposals made and accepted on the day of the funeral are probably apocryphal. The death of Sergeant Rothwell in Lucknow on 15 June 1871 was followed a little over a year later by this announcement in the Marriages column of the *Gazetteer*: "At Lucknow, on the 25th June 1872, Sergt William Griffiths to Jane, widow of the late Sergeant S. Rothwell"[13]. The dates are perhaps significant; wives received a small allowance which continued to be paid for exactly one year after a husband's death.

The library and the canteen represented extremes, between which was lived a hectic sporting and social life. Regimental events for Christmas week 1872 were: cricket match; polo match; meeting of Masonic Lodge "Morning Star"; picnic in the Padshah Bagh; dance at the Chutter Munzil; theatrical performances of *The Castle Spectre*; croquet tournament; meet of the Lucknow Hounds; privates' dance ("the Regimental Recreation room was crowded with a merry party of the fair sex"); sergeants' dance ("dancing in the Mess was kept up with great spirit till ½ past 4a.m."); officers' ball[14].

Men continued to arrive from the regiment's Home Depot near Canterbury, Kent, where new recruits were received and trained before joining the regiment in India. On Christmas Day Cornet Martin arrived with a draft of 38 men. By now the Dumpies were history, the average height having risen to 5 feet 6 inches, reflecting the fact that the number of officers and men from previous Crown service had become greater than the number still continuing from Company service. Significantly, this did not lead to a denial

Indian Origins

The bazaars of Lucknow town offered British soldiers a number of temptations which threatened their health, among them local alcohol stronger and cheaper than any European spirit - a lethal indulgence in the blazing climate of the plains. (The Queen's Royal Lancers)

or belittling of the regiment's Indian in favour of its English origins; by now all were proud to be known as French Greys. Furthermore the purchase system had been abolished in the British army and all regiments placed on the same footing for promotion; so when the 21st Hussars prepared to sail for England in 1873 it was with new confidence in their equality with those cavalry regiments of long standing with which the British public were more familiar.

By chance an event in England brought the regiment to the notice of that public. The Home Depot was located within sight of Canterbury Cathedral, and Captain Spottisford, exercising his troop, noticed flames coming from the ancient building. He and his men immediately rode down and organised the crowd which had gathered, and Spottisford later reported that his troop had been instrumental in extinguishing the fire. The papers of the day questioned this version of events, the *Daily Telegraph* going so far as to assert that the men of the 21st had been of no use. All the feelings of inferiority resurfaced with heartfelt indignation, and Spottisford appealed to the archdeacon to put the record straight. In a subsequent letter in the *Telegraph* Canon Thomas confirmed that had it not been for the troops the Cathedral would have been demolished.

* * *

In November 1873, after 12 years in Bengal, the 21st Hussars embarked on Her Majesty's Troop Ship *Serapis* for the five-week passage to Portsmouth via the Suez Canal. As the ship passed through the Red Sea it followed the eastern coast of the Sudan north towards Egypt.

Trade between Europe and North Africa had increased rapidly over the preceding years. The Viceroy Isma'il was determined to transform Egypt and the Sudan into a modern, Western-style state. To finance his reforms and his own extravagant Westernised lifestyle he accepted high-interest loans from British and French investors, promising in return to end the slave trade. In northern areas of the Sudan where Egyptian control was absolute he had some success. But large areas south and west of Khartoum were controlled by powerful slave merchants, their fortified stations garrisoned by tribesmen. In these remote deserts of the Sudan Isma'il found it more advantageous to appease the merchants than his distant investors, and went so far as to appoint the most powerful of the slave traders, az Zubayr, as governor of the south-west province.

In his drive to modernise the Sudan Isma'il posted many Western administrators to Khartoum. This increasing Christian presence caused much resentment among the devout Moslem population, who acknowledged the power of the slave traders as the only alternative to the infidel. Thus to the existing combination of nationalism and Islam was added the private armies of the traders. Only one element was lacking before the Sudanese would rise to evict their Egyptian and Western masters — a charismatic leader.

In 1873, as the *Serapis* followed the eastern coast of the Sudan north towards the canal, Mohammed Ahmed ibn 'Abd Allah was studying the Koran on a secluded island of the White Nile. Born in 1848, the son of a boat-builder who claimed descent from the Prophet Mohammed, he had travelled to Khartoum at the age of 14 to train as a Muslim priest. Now 25, he lived in seclusion on Abba Island 150 miles up river from the capital. He knew that the devout expected a second great Prophet to appear soon, in what were now believed to be the "last days". *Al-Mahdi* ("He who is guided by God") would establish the rule of Islam in the Sudan and throughout the world. Mohammed Ahmed was at this time struggling with the enormous idea taking form in his mind - that he himself might be the expected Mahdi.

As the *Serapis* left the coast of the Sudan behind the officers and men of the 21st Hussars looked forward to a respite from the sea at Suez, where fresh supplies would be taken on. None could have guessed that they would next see foreign service in the impoverished and powerless land to the south.

The Chutter Munzil Officers' Club, Lucknow, where the most elaborate balls were held. (The Queen's Royal Lancers)

CHAPTER THREE

Into the Sudan

Arriving in Portsmouth during the week before Christmas 1873, the 21st Hussars marched to Aldershot. The regiment moved to Hounslow the following year, with a detachment at Kensington Palace. The 21st quickly discovered that the gap dividing them from crack cavalry regiments officered by sons of the aristocracy had not been closed by the abolition of purchase. A private income — an allowance of more than £500 a year in addition to pay — was necessary to sustain a fitting position in society. This was many times the amount required in India, and acted as a social filter which still disqualified the 21st from aspiring to the cavalry élite.

For the Other Ranks the return to England proved equally deflating. Having swapped the heat of India for the cold and damp of an English winter, they found it impossible to dry the clothes they washed in the wooden tubs provided, for no more than six items at a time could be hung about the barrack room fire. The fire itself was inadequate to warm the room and men were not allowed to wear their cloaks when off duty; cold and dispirited, they sought relief in the regimental canteen, where beer was sold at 3d (three old pence) a quart.

However, it must be remembered that the soldier's lot compared favourably with that of a worker in the new industrial cities. His pay was 1s 2d a day (14 old pennies - about 6 new pence - or more than eight pints of beer, to use another medium of conversion…); accommodation, regimental clothing, and bread and meat were provided free, and other foodstuffs cost 3d a day. There was money left for saving, although more often it was spent in the canteen or the town — drunkenness remained a problem, and the number of men treated each year for venereal disease was never less than ten per cent.

Queen Victoria assumed the title "Empress of India" in 1877. Tea and other goods from the subcontinent had reached a peak of popularity, and among the public (to whom the social distinction between exclusive cavalry regiments and the rest meant little) the 21st Hussars found its Indian origins a cause for celebration. When the regiment marched through Tuxford its welcome was reported in the local newspaper: "As a troop of the 21st Hussars was seen rising the hill, Mr Bridges, a farmer, suggested that they should be treated to a drink. As soon as Captain Fisher arrived at the Newcastle Arms Hotel, he was asked would he allow his men to each have a glass of ale. He said he would be pleased to do so, but one glass only. 'Then', said the landlord, 'they shall have the very best', and soon glasses were filled with Warwicks Sparkling"[1].

In rural areas such a welcome was not unusual. But there was a growing gulf between rich and poor, and in urban areas where unemployment was rife and cavalry regiments were posted to keep order, soldiers in public houses were more likely to be beaten up. The regiment was moved to Leeds as the General Election of 1880 approached, in aid of the civil authorities. Irish Home Rule was the most hotly debated issue of the campaign, and differences boiled over onto the streets. According to regimental records, on 8 April 1880 "D Troop under Captain Hayes marched to

Lieutenant P.M.King in mounted full dress in 1879, with leopardskin saddle cloth, valise marked '21H', and the French grey sabretache adopted in 1876. (The Queen's Royal Lancers)

Mapplewell, where rioting on account of the General Election was expected". The presence of hussars prevented trouble, but on the following day "F Troop under Captain Taylor was sent by rail to Marsborough and at 9.00p.m. was called upon to assist police in quelling a riot. The Troop cleared the streets without difficulty"[2].

Although the Tory government was ousted by Gladstone's Liberals the new prime minister was frustrated in his attempts to resolve the Irish problem, and that country continued to be heavily garrisoned by British troops. The 21st Hussars was ordered to Dublin in August 1881.

★ ★ ★

Britain had abolished the slave trade over 60 years earlier, and the very different public values of the high Victorian age required that the might of the Empire be used to wipe out the evil of slavery wherever it continued. In 1877 the Viceroy of Egypt (given the new title *Khedive*) had promised his Western investors that traffic in slaves would be eradicated by 1880, and appointed General Charles Gordon as Governor-General of the Sudan to ensure that this was done. The charismatic and independently minded Gordon - who had operated energetically against the slave traders further south in Central Africa in 1874-76 - took up resi-

This portrait photograph of Lieutenant King provides an excellent view of the uniform jacket worn in 1879, with six acorn-loop fastenings, gold plaited braid cord and Austrian knots to the cuffs. The busby of black sable fur has a white plume and a French grey bag. (The Queen's Royal Lancers)

Men of the Mounted Infantry Camel Regiment, part of the Camel Corps which joined the Gordon Relief Expedition. Major Berkeley Pigott, 21st Hussars, was attached to the Mounted Infantry. (The Queen's Royal Lancers)

dence in Khartoum, bringing in more Christian administrators and officers to go about the country breaking up markets and imprisoning traders.

Disraeli's Conservative government had been convinced that adequate reforms were being made in the Sudan, and to ensure the free movement of British shipping £4 million worth of shares in the Suez Canal (representing a controlling interest) were purchased from the Khedive Isma'il. Gladstone had warned against greater British involvement in North Africa, but the Empire was at its height of power and neither Egypt nor the Sudan seemed likely to prove troublesome. Despite this huge payment, by 1880 Isma'il was unable to pay the interest on his ever-increasing debts to European investors, and declared Egypt bankrupt. An Anglo-French commission was appointed to oversee Egyptian finances and in effect to administer the country. In January 1880 Gordon was recalled from Khartoum by the new Khedive, Isma'il's son Tewfik, with his task only partly completed. As the Sudan was administered by Egypt, Britain and France were now the *de facto* overseers of a country in which the slave trade continued.

In August 1881, the same month that the 21st Hussars was ordered to Dublin, Mohammed Ahmed publicly proclaimed himself to be the Mahdi. He had gathered a band of followers during a tour of the country west of Khartoum, and seen that the discontent of the people required only leadership to break out in open rebellion. In an impover-

Above: The 21st Hussars on mounted parade at Bangalore in 1888. The foremost officer is Lieutenant-Colonel Thomas Hickman, who took command of the regiment the previous year. (The Queen's Royal Lancers)

Right: Major Charles Berkeley Pigott of the 21st, detached in 1888 to lead the Yonni expedition in West Africa, during which he ordered the first use of the Maxim gun in action. (The Queen's Royal Lancers)

ished and occupied land where nationalism and religious fervour were inextricably linked, he found both the poor and the pious ready to commit themselves to a holy war, to free the Sudan and to conquer the world for Islam. He was supported by those slave merchants who had avoided Gordon's crusade, and most crucially by the Baggara tribes of Kordofan and Dofur, who resented the taxes imposed from Khartoum. The vast number of these warriors, together with the sizeable private armies of the slavers, seemed likely to compensate for their primitive weapons.

Hoping to pre-empt a country-wide rebellion, the Egyptians sent a force to arrest the Mahdi. He escaped and retreated into the desert, leaving Khartoum to the Egyptians but claiming for himself the deserts of Kordofan to the south and west of the capital. At first there seemed no need for British involvement. Events in the Sudan were considered of no consequence, despite the continuing public distaste for slavery. In opposition, Gladstone had been against British involvement in North Africa; now in government, he sought to reduce that involvement and was happy to leave matters to the Khedive.

Rebellion, however, teaches its own lessons; and in December 1881 Colonel Ahmet Arabi Pasha led the Egyptian army in a nationalist revolt against the nominal authority of the Turkish sultan and the actual control of the European powers, with the none too original slogan "Egypt for the Egyptians". The deposed Khedive fled to the safety of the British fleet harboured at Alexandria. When Arabi added extra guns to the harbour forts, a clear threat to the fleet, the British shelled the city. This bombardment of July 1882 was counter-productive, extending Arabi's support from the army into the civilian population.

Gladstone had reluctantly approved an Egyptian Expeditionary Force, not so much to reinstate the Khedive as to protect British investments in Egypt and the Suez Canal, this latter being vital for an Empire founded on ocean-going naval power and financed by global trade. For more than a year the Sudan was ignored by both Britain and Egypt as they confronted one another. The Mahdi, now able to consolidate and extend his power unopposed, told his followers that God had set these foreign powers at each others' throats for the sake of Islam.

The British force led by Sir Garnet Wolseley landed at Alexandria and took control of the Canal and the railway before moving on Cairo. At Magfar, although the Egyptians advancing to meet them were turned back, the British heavy cavalry was unable to give chase, its horses exhausted by the long desert march. A body of 30 mounted infantry had been formed in Alexandria and its small Egyptian ponies, supplied by the Khedive's own stables, were still fresh (although such a small force could hardly pursue an army). The lesson was not lost on Lieutenant Charles Berkeley Pigott of the 60th Rifles, serving with the mounted infantry; he resolved that at the earliest opportunity he would join a regiment of light cavalry.

The Egyptians attacked again and were repulsed at Kassassin. Pigott was wounded twice, and for him the war was over. A night attack on Arabi's 38,000-strong army at Tel-el-Kebir on 13 September 1882 brought about a decisive victory. The British occupied Cairo and established a sizeable garrison there in support of the reinstated Khedive and to secure the Canal. The French, who protested that Egypt was not a British colony and that the troops should be withdrawn, were duly ignored: this was a period of naked colonial competition in North Africa.

Lieutenant Pigott, once recovered, returned to England. Although the Rifles had a considerable cachet his infantry background and his financial status were not to the liking of the smart cavalry regiments he might have preferred, and in

January 1883 he joined the 21st Hussars in Dublin. Although such a station was hardly desirable, worse was to follow. In October the regiment was spread thinly across rural areas, operating as eight independent troops. Deprived of the social life of the city, Pigott was eager to return to a theatre of war, and had not long to wait.

The Gordon Relief Expedition

The Mahdi was by now the acknowledged leader of the desert tribes of the Sudan, his followers known as Mahdists or *ansar*. Informed by the press, the British came to know them (less accurately, though more popularly) as Dervishes. Only Khartoum - held by 8,000 Egyptian troops - and a number of smaller garrisons remained outside the Mahdi's control.

The defeated Egyptian army was quickly reorganised and British officers took command. In October 1883 Colonel William Hicks led 11,000 of the best Egyptian troops south into Dervish-controlled territory, anticipating an easy victory over undisciplined spearmen. The Dervishes retreated, destroying the wells as they went until Hick's army was exhausted; then, on 3 November at Kashgil (el Obeid) they attacked in force. The Egyptian troops were virtually wiped out, less than 1,000 escaping alive. The Dervishes took their Remington breech-loader rifles and ammunition, and although the Baggara never accepted the superiority of firearms over spears and swords, other tribes took to them with great alacrity (if not always great accuracy).

To the Mahdi's followers this overwhelming victory proved that he was indeed the Expected One, guided by God. To Gladstone it confirmed only that British involvement in North Africa was a costly mistake, and that the remaining Egyptian troops in the Sudan should be evacuated. As the garrison at Khartoum was now surrounded by the Mahdi's army, General Gordon was sent to negotiate the withdrawal of its 8,000 troops, women and children. While his previous experience as Governor-General of the Sudan seemed to qualify him for the task, he was in fact the one man to whom the Mahdi could not make concessions without losing the support of the slave traders.

At the same time, Anglo-Egyptian troops attempted to relieve the small garrison at Suakin and destroy the army of the most able Dervish commander in the field, the former slaver Osman Digna. Several officers and men of the 21st Hussars had by now managed to escape the drudgery of service in Ireland by getting themselves attached to the Egyptian cavalry, and the *Standard* war correspondent reporting from Suakin described the first encounter between a member of the regiment and the Dervishes: "Lieutenant Beech (21st Hussars) came across two Dervishes at a moment when he was separated by a considerable distance from the Egyptian Cavalry. Not expecting any resistance, he offered the men quarter, but they suddenly attacked him. In the struggle which followed he killed one with his sword and wounded the other with his revolver"[3].

Although the beleaguered garrison at Suakin was

A programme, expensively printed in several colours and cut in the shape of the sabretache, produced for a 21st Hussars ball held at Bangalore in December 1890. The reverse lists the dances, and the ladies to whom this officer was engaged for each. (The Queen's Royal Lancers)

The Trimulgherry Barracks at Secunderabad. (The Queen's Royal Lancers)

relieved, Osman Digna's army stood its ground and many lives were lost on both sides. This hardly assisted Gordon's attempt to negotiate at Khartoum; the Mahdi refused even to meet him. By May 1884 the Dervishes had stopped all traffic on the Nile and cut all telegraph wires into the city. Gordon was besieged in Khartoum.

While Gladstone hesitated, the newspapers of the day had a keen eye for a popular cause and ensured that Gordon's fate became the nation's primary concern. In August 1884 the prime minister agreed to send a Gordon Relief Expedition under Wolseley to rescue him and complete the evacuation of the Sudan. For this purpose a Camel Corps was hastily formed, consisting of four regiments: the Heavy Camel, Light Camel, Guards Camel, and Mounted Infantry Camel Regiments. Each of these *ad hoc* units was formed by detachments of men from all regiments then serving in England or Ireland. On 19 September a detachment of the 21st Hussars — Major Crole Wyndham, Lieutenants Fowle and Higgs, and 43 men — proceeded to Aldershot to join the Light Camel Regiment. Pigott (now promoted captain) was attached to the Mounted Infantry Camel Regiment, where his previous experience would be of most use.

The Light Camel Regiment arrived at Cairo in October 1884 and sailed up the Nile to Korti, north of Khartoum, where the full expeditionary force was assembling. From there the infantry would continue by boat. Operating independently of this River Column, a Desert Column of cavalry would make a 200-mile overland dash to take the Mahdist army by surprise and hold the city until the infantry arrived. Sufficient camels should have been available at Korti to mount the whole Corps, but local sources could not provide the number required. During the two weeks' wait while scouts went out to purchase more, one camel was provided to each three men for practice. Most of the 21st Hussars had served in India, where camel racing had been a popular pastime, and took to these new mounts without the extreme difficulty experienced by some.

On 30 December the Camel Corps of 2,000 men began the march to Khartoum; the continuing shortage of beasts meant that much of the stores had to be left at Korti. At Gakdul, the half-way point, the Corps halted while the Light Camel Regiment was sent back with most of the camels to bring up extra stores. The men of the 21st, escorting camels and stores from oasis to oasis, were closely watched by local Arabs, and guessed (rightly) that news of the Desert Column's overland "dash" would reach Khartoum long before the first British soldier.

Leaving the Light Camel Regiment to guard the stores at Gakdul the rest of the Corps advanced to the wells at Abu Klea, arriving to find the area occupied by a large Dervish force. On 17 January 1885 the column formed a single large square and advanced in this formation, with Captain Pigott's Mounted Infantry at the front left corner. A hollow in the ground ran parallel to the route this square had to take to the wells, and from that cover the enemy opened fire, killing and wounding many. Pigott returned fire with a shotgun charged with buckshot, previously a favourite weapon among officers but by now condemned as barbaric in the English press. The nickname "Bloody-minded Pigott" had not been earned by appeasing the confused sentiments of armchair critics; he fired at any Dervish head appearing above the hollow, "riddling it like the rose of a watering can"[4].

After advancing slowly in this fashion for two miles, the square was rushed by 600 Dervishes who rose suddenly from the hollow and made for the left leading corner. An artillery piece was quickly moved to that point and fired. Smoke from this shot hid the rapidly advancing enemy from the defenders, and Captain Pigott was the first to realise that if another shot were fired the smoke would conceal the Dervishes until they were right into the square. The gun was being prepared for firing, and in the noise and confusion his shouted order went unheard. He rushed to the gun and stood in front of the muzzle with both hands raised. The smoke of the first shot cleared; the defending infantry could see to fire into an enemy now only yards away, and the square held. Pigott, who had offered his back to the Dervish spears, remained unhurt.

Once the wells had been won Captain Pigott was selected for the dangerous task of riding back across the desert to Korti with despatches. The Arab guide who accompanied him lost the path between distant wells, and for two days the pair wandered the desert. When their water ran out the guide told Pigott they would "die together like brave men". "Not together", Pigott replied; "You will die first. I shall drink your blood and that may give me strength to find the path"[5]. No doubt encouraged, the guide discovered the path a few hours later.

The Light Camel Regiment now escorted the stores and baggage on to Abu Klea, remaining there as rearguard while the main force advanced to Metemmeh and again met strong resistance. A convoy of wounded returning to Abu Klea came under attack and the Light Camel Regiment went to the rescue; the Dervishes withdrew, but returned later and had to be repulsed by carbine fire.

News of the defeat at Abu Klea quickly reached the Mahdi, who concluded that the British force must soon reach Khartoum. Before light on 26 January 1885 he sent his army into the city, giving strict orders that Gordon was to be taken alive. Egyptian troops manning the walls, in no condition to put up much of a fight, were easily overrun. Before the palace could be taken the general appeared at the top of its stone steps, making a last desperate appeal to be taken to the Mahdi. At the sight of this most hated infidel fanaticism overcame discipline; a Dervish mob rushed him, stabbing until he fell dead, and then cut off his head.

Decapitation was not quite the pointless barbarity it seemed to the Christian West, for Moslem warriors believed it despatched an enemy to eternal exile from heaven. According to one report the head was carried to the Mahdi, but in view of his express order that Gordon was not to be killed this seems unlikely. Certainly the guilty men were severely punished. There is no record of what became of the body.

Gordon's death ended any hope that the Egyptian troops might escape with their lives, for all knew that their surrender would not be accepted. In the mania of religious frenzy the Mahdi's followers massacred the men and raped the women before killing these too. The Westerners of Gordon's party were butchered with particular venom.

Advance troops of the expeditionary force reached Khartoum two days later to find the palace and the city in ruins, and the dead everywhere. They returned to Metemmeh, from where a general withdrawal north to Dongola began. The 21st Hussars, with the Light Camel Regiment and the baggage, had advanced no further than Abu Klea. No officer or man of the 21st had been killed or wounded in action, although during the retreat across the desert three men died of enteric fever and one of dysentery. The sense of failure after coming so far must have been profound. One member of the expedition, Major Herbert Kitchener of the Royal Engineers, took it particularly badly. Holding the Dervishes collectively responsible for Gordon's murder and decapitation, he became obsessed with the need to avenge this atrocity.

Although Khartoum could have been rebuilt from the ruins, the marshy land between the White and Blue Niles was not to the Mahdi's liking and would prevent the city expanding. Instead he ordered the construction of a new capital on the west bank where the fort and village of Omdurman stood. In June 1885, with this new city hardly begun and a planned advance to drive Egyptian troops back across the border yet to be put into execution, the Mahdi died of typhus. He was succeeded by Abdullah el Taaisha, the *Khalifa* ("Deputy"), who loyally ordered the planned attack. In December 1885 this was repulsed at Ginnis, though instead of following up the success the Egyptian force withdrew further north to Wadi Halfa.

That same month the Tories returned to power in Britain. Having blamed Gladstone's anti-imperialist sentiments for the failure of the Gordon Relief Expedition the new prime minister, the Marquis of Salisbury, now followed Gladstone's policy of non-interference in the Sudan. The Khalifa's intentions were uncertain and Salisbury decided to watch and wait. It was hoped that the defeat at Ginnis, together with the withdrawal of Egyptian troops to within a few miles of the border, would convince this new Mahdist ruler to settle for the territory that was now his.

Bangalore

India was by now the main overseas station for British cavalry regiments; and in 1887 the 21st Hussars was ordered from Ireland to Aldershot en route to Bangalore. Before proceeding to Portsmouth the regiment took part in both the Queen's Birthday Parade and the Grand Review in the presence of Her Majesty the Queen Empress in commemoration of the Jubilee of her accession.

Lieutenant-Colonel Thomas Hickman, an austere man and a total abstainer, now took command of the 21st and dedicated himself to making the regiment the equal of any serving in India. An accomplished horseman and polo enthusiast, he knew any such ambition required a competitive polo team able to draw on a stable of ponies bred for the game. He was determined that the money for this would be found (although exactly how remained unclear) and that success and the esteem of the cavalry establishment would follow.

At the same time that Hickman took command, Lieutenant the Honourable René de Montmorency transferred into the 21st from the Lincolnshire Regiment. Taller than average — throughout his time of service he was the tallest officer in the 21st — this former infantry officer had

Inside a barrack room at Trimulgherry.
(The Queen's Royal Lancers)

A mounted private of the 21st Hussars in Secunderabad wearing "half-khaki" dress - a khaki "frock" with dark blue pantaloons striped yellow. Khaki was authorised for wear in India from 1885. (The Queen's Royal Lancers)

ridden to hounds from an early age, preferred horse racing and hunting to polo, and rode as often as possible with the Belvoir Hunt. He was the cousin of Violet Manners (whose husband Henry was the son of John Manners, heir-presumptive to the sixth Duke of Rutland). The regiment took some satisfaction from this connection by marriage with the family of its founder, as if de Montmorency in French grey finally reconciled its English and Indian origins. This satisfaction was increased when the sixth duke died childless, John Manners became the seventh Duke of Rutland, and Henry as his eldest son became Marquis of Granby (he would become the eighth duke on the death of his father in 1906). De Montmorency wrote regularly to his aunt, now Lady Granby, and must have kept her informed of events within the regiment.

The 21st Hussars embarked from Portsmouth on Her Majesty's Indian Troop Ship *Crocodile*, disembarking in Bombay one month later and arriving in Bangalore in January 1888. Service dress — a khaki jacket and brown belt — was now authorised for use in India, and while preferring it for everyday wear to their "ornamental uniform" few of the men gave it an unqualified welcome. The free clothing provided under their terms of service was designated to be the traditional hussar dress, and the khaki had to be paid for by the men themselves.

Colonel Hickman's disappointment on arriving at the new garrison was profoundly felt: "The chief defect of Bangalore as a cavalry station is its very bad polo ground"(6). The ground was virtually unplayable, rough and lumpy and covered with red dust which rose in clouds when disturbed. There was, Lieutenant de Montmorency quickly noted, a decent racecourse. The colonel intended to establish a stable of polo ponies; either by ignorance (which is unlikely) or the sly intent of those entrusted with the task, 30 racing ponies were purchased, probably from regimental funds. De Montmorency, his riding skills honed by the Belvoir, excelled equally at the race and the steeplechase, and spent his considerable winnings on entertaining fellow officers and others in Bangalore society. In this way, if not by success on the polo field, the 21st Hussars acquired a higher social standing among British cavalry regiments in India than might otherwise have been expected.

Although there was little chance of the regiment seeing active service — Bangalore was in the south, while continuing troubles with the Mohmand tribes occurred on the distant North-West Frontier — in October 1888 Pigott (now a major) was detached for special service with the Gold Coast Constabulary in West Africa. The Yonnis were a loose confederation of inland tribes in the area of Sierra Leone, some 4,000 warriors armed with machetes. Discovering that the river tribes by the Rokel were trading with the British, the Yonnis made regular raids to loot and take slaves. As the tribes attacked were under British protection, an expedition was sent to their assistance: Major Pigott and 300 troops, most from the 1st West India Regiment, supported by a seven-pounder mountain gun, a rocket tube, and the first Maxim machine gun to be issued for active service.

The Maxim, capable of firing 650 rounds per minute, was fed by cartridges lined up in a looped canvas belt, its recoil forces being harnessed to reload, fire and eject continuously for as long as the trigger was held back; it was cooled by a water-jacket around the barrel. While the declared purpose of the expedition was to discourage the Yonni warriors it undoubtedly offered the required conditions in which to test the Maxim gun in action — that is, this new-fangled gun's potential failure in the face of tribesmen armed only with machetres was unlikely to place British troops at mortal risk. The reverse was equally true – that the Maxim had to be tested against moving flesh even if the use of such a brutal tool proved unnecessary - and "Bloody-minded Pigott" was clearly the man to command.

The Yonni town of Robari, protected by a 12-foot mud wall and a gate of logs, was reached on 20 November. Pigott had the mountain gun, rocket tube and Maxim gun set up outside the gate. After four shells from the gun and four rockets the Yonnis fled through a rear exit, offering no opportunity for the Maxim to be brought into operation.

Above: Officers and senior NCO of the 21st Hussars photographed at the Beder Camp of Exercise in 1893. Khaki and the foreign service helmet had by now become commonplace in the regiment. Lieutenant de Montmorency sits on a chair at far left, and Lieutenant-Colonel Martin at centre right. Martin and the officer seated far right can be seen to wear black mourning bands for Martin's predecessor Lieutenant-Colonel Hickman. (The Queen's Royal Lancers)

Right: Lieutenant-Colonel Rowland Martin photographed at Secunderabad on becoming Commanding Officer of the 21st Hussars in 1892. Note the lavish additional embellishment to the collar and sleeves of the uniform, indicating an officer of field rank. (The Queen's Royal Lancers)

The remaining towns were taken without resistance, except at Romielto. Shells and rockets were fired, and "the Maxim gun did great execution on the Yonnis who fled in all directions"[7]. At each town Pigott had the fetish tree — worshipped in the belief that a powerful spirit inhabited it — blown up. He let it be known that the seven-pounder, the rocket tube and the Maxim gun were the white man's fetishes, containing spirits of much greater power.

The contents of Pigott's official report confirm the point of the expedition: "4 carriers were required for the Maxim gun and 1 for each box of ammunition. The gun could be brought into action in 12 seconds and worked smoothly without jamming. At 100 yards the bullets penetrated 2 inches of hard stockade plank. At Romielto the gun was placed 70 yards from the gate and every Yonni who attempted to escape was killed"[8]. The Maxim had proven itself and, mounted on a carriage rather than manhandled, would be used to great effect by Kitchener's army at Omdurman.

In India the 21st Hussars continued with outdated carbines — incredibly, the regiment had not yet been issued with the Martini-Henry introduced 17 years earlier in 1871. Some officers wanted their men re-equipped with modern firearms; one, inspired by Major Pigott's experience, suggested that each troop be given a Maxim gun mounted on a "galloper" carriage. Others urged caution, out of the continuing fear that the cavalry, once granted such firepower, might become Mounted Infantry by default.

Young officers of the regiment, denied an opportunity to apply the rider spirit of the cavalry on the battlefield, continued to prove their excellence and dash on the Bangalore racecourse. In January 1889 they were joined by Lieutenant Paul Kenna, a friend of de Montmorency's from their time together at the Royal Military College, Sandhurst. On his arrival at Bangalore his fellow officers were not at first impressed — average height had risen above 5 feet 7 inches, yet Kenna was only 5 feet 5½ inches, a fact made inescapably conspicuous by his renewed friendship with the tallest officer in the regiment. Kenna transferred from the 2nd West India Regiment; the 1st had been included in the Yonni expedition the previous year, much to his frustration. Officers of the West India Regiments were viewed with contempt by the cavalry élite, but Kenna was readily accepted by the 21st Hussars, the one regiment in which he could be certain not to attract the nickname Dumpy. While at Sandhurst he had ridden to hounds, accompanying de Montmorency to the Belvoir, and he now quickly supplanted his friend as the best rider in the regiment.

Lieutenant Pirie joined the 21st straight from Sandhurst, one month after Kenna; yet another racing enthusiast, he immediately befriended de Montmorency and Kenna. The 21st Hussars polo team, formed under the personal supervision of Colonel Hickman, had yet to excel; meanwhile de Montmorency and Kenna, and to a lesser extent Pirie, dominated the Bangalore racecourse, their winnings and their generosity funding for the regiment the high life expected of officers of the Raj.

Bangalore was high and cool, and essentially a society station: "We were young and giddy and were continually organising fun of some sort or other"[9]. In July 1890 the officers gave a Grand Ball for 300 guests, including the Maharajah of Mysore and the élite of Bangalore society. The dance card listed 21 dances, though there were always "extras". The *Madras Mail* reported: "Dancing began at 10.00p.m. and the 'Queen' was not played till 3.30a.m.; indeed the livelier spirits remained on till the first streak of dawn"[10]. Such balls were not isolated events, though the 21st excelled itself in August 1891 when the regimental calendar included nine.

Because of the heat it was desirable for those attending a ball to take the air at intervals, and gentlemen "signed up" for each alternate dance; the fainthearted who feared even such a duty retreated to the smoking tent, strictly out of bounds to ladies. As there were in general two men to each lady, the ladies were required to take every dance; they did, however, retire at the official end of the proceedings, usually between 3.30 and 4.00 in the morning. Not so the gentlemen.... War games were now organised, several men lining up as infantry while others, playing the dashing cavalry, formed pairs to charge piggy-back style. "Many gallant actions were performed and the shouts of the hard-pressed and wounded were carried afar on the morning air ... All was over by 6.30a.m. A gallop to the racecourse was then considered best to prepare ourselves for the day"[11].

Secunderabad

The 21st Hussars left Bangalore in November 1891, travelling by rail to Trimulgherry barracks at Secunderabad. Colonel Hickman, conscious that polo had been neglected at Bangalore, was encouraged to discover a far better ground

D Squadron football team, which won the 21st Hussars regimental cup in Secunderabad in 1894. A full sporting calendar was one of the ways regiments tried to keep their men fit and occupied during boring, unhealthy garrison duty in India. (The Queen's Royal Lancers)

Left: *For the officers there was polo, although the regiment's less than glittering performance always grated on Colonel Hickman, who did not live to see this team win the Hyderabad Trophy in 1894. From left to right: Lieutenant Pirie, Captain Bowley, Lieutenant de Montmorency, Lieutenant Kenna. (The Queen's Royal Lancers)*

Right: *The first photograph of a member of the regiment in full khaki dress, taken at Secunderabad in 1896. That same year, as the regiment prepared to sail for Cairo, the khaki service dress was authorised for use outside India. (The Queen's Royal Lancers)*

at the new station. His officers noted less happily that the barracks were 12 miles from the racecourse.

Early in 1892 a squadron system was introduced into the British army. A regiment, previously divided into eight troops, was now to consist of four squadrons designated A to D, each of two troops. Of greater concern to the 21st, exercises were to be conducted alongside infantry *and* artillery. While previously the cavalry had been allowed an offensive role, it was now restricted to advance-guard work: reconnoitring enemy positions and reporting back, then keeping watch until the infantry and artillery came up for the attack.

Given the cavalry's underlying paranoia it was predictable that this should spark a major debate within the regiment, concerned that the days of the cavalry were past and that in future battles only the infantry and artillery would engage the main enemy force. Sergeant-Major Laughton feared that the cavalry must "become an arm of secondary importance — the long range of modern weapons render the occasions on which cavalry can charge with sword and lance more and more rare"[12]. The possibility that no further cavalry charges would be made by the British army was particularly horrendous for a regiment which had yet to charge.

Sir Frederick Roberts, Commander-in-Chief in Madras, must have been aware of this fear when he addressed the 21st Hussars: "During the confusion of battle, opportunities will offer for a timely charge of cavalry. Depend upon it, gentlemen. Prepare yourselves and your men; opportunities are fleeting, and unless seized instantaneously, are lost for ever"[13]. Among those listening and taking his words to heart sat Major Martin, who would command the regiment at Omdurman where he would, in his estimation, be offered just such a fleeting opportunity.

While such considerations weighed heavily upon the officers, of greater interest to the men were changes to the canteen. Already open longer hours, it now boasted Private Lane on the piano, and a system for keeping beer cool — wet sods of grass packed on and around the barrels. Whether Private Lane or cool beer was the greater attraction, the canteen manager was soon able to report that "...during the hours at which it is open, the place is thronged with Hussars and their friends ... a constant flow of songs helps to shorten the long tropical evenings"[14].

The Regimental Temperance Society was quick to respond. Colonel Hickman, as a total abstainer himself, had provided a meeting room and attendance was increasing. It was particularly well supported by young ladies, and not all of the men who joined them were convinced abstainers. The August 1892 meeting was followed by a magic lantern show, *All Around The World In A Camera*, accompanied by the regimental string band. This novelty attracted almost a quarter of the regiment's full strength and was loudly applauded, although the finale — a step-dance by Privates Flusty and Reid — probably added little.

When Colonel Hickman died in October after a three-day illness, Major Martin was promoted lieutenant-colonel to command the regiment. A most able commander, Martin was free of his predecessor's single-minded self-assurance, and sought the esteem of his senior regimental officers over that of the cavalry establishment at large. Hickman's plans for a competitive polo team were dropped. The social activities of the regiment, still supported for the most part by the winnings of de Montmorency and Kenna at the racecourse, could (after a decent period of mourning) now flourish unrestrained.

In May 1894 Captain Doyne gave a dinner-party in his bungalow at which the male guests were invited to "attire themselves as ladies". The party, including Lieutenant de Montmorency in "becoming golden locks" and Lieutenant Smyth "gowned in green and pink and wigged in yellow"[15], dined to the accompaniment of the string band. The following month a Fancy Dress Ball was held and all commanded to dress as officers or ladies of the 1760s, when the regiment was first raised and gentlemen of the 21st wore their hair long or sported wigs (with the honourable exception of the Marquis of Granby). Not enough wigs could be found in Bangalore and telegrams were sent to Bombay,

Calcutta and Madras for further supplies. Wigs came in from all parts of the country, but the following notice posted in the Mess disappointed many: "It is a fact that no more white silk-stockings (men's size) can be obtained throughout India"[16].

Success at the racecourse continued. The slightly-built Kenna made a natural jockey; during the three years 1893-95 he rode more winners annually than any other rider, topped the list of Gentlemen Riders in India (followed by de Montmorency), and was recognised as one of the finest horsemen anywhere in the British army. Such recognition was most welcome to the regiment, and the *Madras Mail* extolled him as "the curled darling of the 21st Hussars"[17].

The sports editor of the London *Globe* was not so complimentary, writing in October 1894 that "...the riding of matches on Sunday is practised by the 21st Hussars ... this would not be done here and, as a matter of good taste, not to mention religion, it should not be allowed away from home"[18]. The reply from the 21st — that the racecourse was visited on Sundays not for racing but for taking the air on horseback, this made necessary by the climate, and that some rivalry at the gallop then ensued — was far from convincing. Mrs Martin had been ill since the move from Bangalore and Colonel Martin spent several months with her at the hill station of Rajpuntama. His absence may perhaps have contributed to the problem, although there is no evidence that he disapproved of the social and sporting activities of his officers.

The *Globe* report prompted the editor of the regimental magazine, renamed the *Vedette*, to suggest that if time spent on racing had been devoted to polo, the 21st would not now face the prospect of leaving India without winning a tournament. This failing was "mainly due to the racing mania which took possession of the regiment and held it fast ... With the material we possessed, had we not wasted energy on racing which would have been devoted to polo, we ought to have carried off the big trophy"[19]. Colonel Martin, back with the regiment and finding a general acknowledgement that polo had been neglected, authorised the purchase of nine pairs of tournament-ponies bred for the game. With Kenna and de Montmorency as the backbone of the team, and the addition of Pirie and Bowley, the 21st Hussars beat several native teams and the 4th Lancers to win the Hyderabad Polo Tournament. This was not the "big trophy", however, and they had left it too late to challenge giants of the game such as the 17th Lancers.

The social calendar of Secunderabad — a continuous round of parties, dinners and dances — meant that the dashing young officers of the 21st were much in demand, and especially the darlings of the racecourse, Kenna and de Montmorency. At one such event de Montmorency met Pamela Plowden, daughter of a senior diplomat, and a romance ensued. At this same time he introduced Kenna to Lady Cecil Bertie, daughter of the Earl of Abingdon and a family acquaintance, and thus began a second courtship. The two couples were invited to all the smart occasions and missed none. In July 1895 Kenna married Lady Cecil at Saint Mary's Catholic Church in the hill station of Ootacamund (known as "Snooty Ooty" because it was inhabited largely by wealthy plantation owners). The Kennas remained there for their honeymoon.

The regiment was in high spirits when the couple returned, and unprepared for what quickly followed. In

August the colonel's lady died after a long and painful illness, and was buried at Trimulgherry. She had been popular with the regiment and her loss was deeply felt. But worse was soon to follow; in October Lady Cecil Kenna died of typhoid fever, aged 22, after only three months of marriage. Kenna fell into a deep depression, and told de Montmorency that he now wished only for an opportunity to meet an honourable death in battle.

Kenna's wish for an enemy to ride at was shared by many in the regiment, though without his tragic reason and in the hope of avoiding his longed-for consequence. Bangalore and Secunderabad were both in the south of India; the only opportunities for active service occurred on the faraway North-West Frontier; and even there the terrain and the tactical realities put Queen's cavalry low on the list of priorities when task forces were assembled. There was increasing frustration at the lack of opportunity to fulfill the purpose for which light cavalry had been invented. Repressed by the energy with which officers threw themselves into the social whirl of Secunderabad, this frustration surfaced in self-parody in the hours after dark when the ladies had left the ball and piggy-back charges ran the length of the mess.

It was not only within the regiment that this lack of engagement with an enemy was noted. Fellow cavalry regiments were by now suggesting that the motto of the 21st should be *Thou Shalt Not Kill*. This cut more deeply than any officer or man of the 21st would admit.

★ ★ ★

After three years in opposition the Marquis of Salisbury's Conservatives were returned to power in 1895. Salisbury may not have been the arch-imperialist portrayed by Gladstone, but he now came to office with the will to reconquer the Sudan if a politically acceptable opportunity arose; and there was not long to wait.

Ethiopia, where the Italians were belatedly seeking a major colonial possession, lay on the south-east border of the Sudan; and in March the following year an Ethiopian army partly supplied with French weapons sensationally defeated a large Italian force at Adowa. An alliance between Ethiopia and the Sudan then seemed likely to some, giving the Khalifa in Omdurman access to French arms and a wider power base from which to attack Egypt. In fact the Khalifa rejected an alliance with the Christian Emperor Menelek, but this could hardly have been predicted from London. In any case, it was not the Dervish threat to Egypt that concerned Salisbury most. French assistance to Ethiopia was part of a wider scheme to build a corridor of client states from west to east which would divide British power on the continent, located mainly in the north and south. Bluntly stated, Britain had to take the Sudan before the French could do so.

When Salisbury announced in March 1896 that an Anglo-Egyptian force — primarily Egyptian troops led by British officers — was to invade the Sudan, he knew that popular newspapers would lead national opinion in supporting the expedition under the banner of "avenging Gordon". The phrase was virtually the personal motto of General Herbert Kitchener, now *Sirdar* (Commander-in-Chief) of the Egyptian army. But while a campaign was planned that could take Omdurman and Khartoum, at this time Salisbury authorised only the first stage: an advance to Dongola 200 miles south of the Egyptian border.

General Herbert Kitchener, Sirdar (Commander-in-Chief) of the Egyptian Army, who led the Anglo-Egyptian army sent to reconquer the Sudan. (The Queen's Royal Lancers)

Egyptian troops were transported south by rail and by the river steamers of Thomas Cook & Sons. Both forms of transport were to prove crucial for the rapid movement of troops, for all major towns and cities in the Sudan lay on the Nile. The Dervish outpost at Akasha was abandoned as the enemy, vastly outnumbered, concentrated resistance at Firket. On 7 June Kitchener's army of 9,000 Egyptian troops attacked the 3,000 Dervishes defending Firket, while gunboats fired on the town from the river. Over 1,000 were killed or wounded before the rest retreated south to Dongola. Although the Khalifa considered this a strategic withdrawal, it seriously dented the morale of warriors whose religious fervour had convinced them of invincibility. Kitchener waited for additional troops to be brought up; then, in September 1896, he advanced on Dongola with 13,000 men and four gunboats. After an artillery bombardment the 5,000 Dervishes, again outnumbered and outgunned, withdrew further south to Metemmeh, and Dongola was taken without major engagement. The first stage had been completed, and in October Kitchener travelled to London to argue the case for continuing.

That same month the 21st Hussars left Secunderabad and embarked on the Hired Transport *Britannia* for two years' service in Egypt. En route to Cairo, the regiment had high hopes of being included in any further expedition against the Khalifa. News of Kitchener's effective use of gunboats and artillery had reached them; and many believed that the advance on Omdurman and Khartoum might be the final opportunity for a cavalry charge which would ever be open to the British army.

CHAPTER FOUR

Towards Omdurman

While Kitchener was in London presenting the case for pressing on from Dongola deeper into the Sudan, the 21st Hussars arrived at its new barracks at Abbassia three miles from Cairo. The regiment was disappointed to discover that polo and horse racing were impossible at Abbassia — sand stirred up by the horses choked and blinded both participants and spectators — but relieved to find adequate facilities six miles away at Ghezireh. An island in the Nile and the only green spot in the vicinity, Ghezireh was known as "the Officers' playground", boasting two polo grounds, a golf course, a racecourse and a steeplechase course.

A greater grievance was provoked by the barracks themselves: "Each officer has but one room and his horses are kept in the regimental lines, instead of having a whole bungalow, stabling and coach houses to himself as in India. The married officers are expected to live in the same passages as the others"[1]. In fact few married officers put up with the indignity, most choosing to live in hotels in Cairo. Even single officers dined more often at the hotels than in the mess, and remained for the evening entertainment. The larger hotels each had a ballroom and dancing took place two or three times a week, often to a military band. The prospect of meeting European tourists, particularly the young ladies among them, was bait enough.

Abbassia was connected with Cairo by an electric tramway, much used by the men, who found every imaginable diversion in the city. Officers preferred to ride in on horseback, but complained, "The tram cars at night, ablaze with electric light and making a hideous noise with their electric bells, frighten our horses"[2]. Bicycles were sometimes pressed into service, not always without incident, as Lieutenant de Montmorency recorded in his diary: "Had bad fall off Wyndham's bike — running full tilt into donkey en route to dinner"[3].

Three miles from Abbassia in the opposite direction lay the ancient town of Heliopolis. This much quieter road was used to exercise the horses each morning and evening. Heliopolis had been the scene of one of the largest ever cavalry charges when, in 1800, a reputed 20,000 Arab cavalrymen charged 10,000 French troops formed in squares. Officers of the 21st regularly visited the site and must have pondered the charge at Heliopolis with envy.

Faced with all these novel diversions the regimental officers tended to divide their time between Ghezireh and Cairo and were little in evidence at Abbassia. Indeed, in December 1896, after less than three months in Egypt, Kenna was named as the top Gentleman Rider in the country. Yet two events that same month radically changed the outlook of the 21st. Kitchener returned from London with permission for the next stage of the Sudan campaign, an advance to Berber (not yet Omdurman and Khartoum, although there was a general assumption that the advance would proceed to the capital). Every British regiment stationed in Egypt had a good chance of a place in the expedition. The second event, with a more direct bearing on the 21st Hussars, was a dinner held by the regimental officers at the Continental Hotel in Cairo, at which their principal guest was Slatin Pasha.

This Austrian officer was a protégé of Gordon who had previously been appointed by the Khedive as governor of Dofur in western Sudan, where Mahdist support was strongest. During his campaign against the slavers he had converted to Islam, which probably saved his life when taken prisoner before the fall of Khartoum. While held in captivity he had been consulted by the Mahdi and later by the Khalifa on British intentions in the Sudan. In 1895 he escaped after ten years' captivity and joined the Sirdar's intelligence service, where his knowledge of the Mahdist leadership was highly valued. At the time of his visit to the 21st Slatin had recently completed a book about his years of imprisonment (*Fire and Sword in the Sudan* would be published the following year).

Addressing the regiment, he described Mahdism as an evil power and accused the Khalifa of mass political murder. Certainly there were massacres, and whole villages had been wiped out merely because the men denied the Mahdist cause (though in the context of a life of marginal subsistence the general population suffered more from plagues and famine than from the exemplary cruelties of an insecure ruler). Slatin was an impassioned speaker, and it was through his eyes that officers of the 21st now viewed their potential adversary. From this date their diaries and letters elevate the conflict to the quasi-religious level always latent in Victorian attitudes to non-Christian peoples, as the great battle of civilisation against barbarism. De Montmorency believed that at Omdurman the Khalifa would "make his last stand … to save his own life and stem the advance of civilisation"[4].

Whether the greater influence was Kitchener's news or Slatin's passion, the 21st Hussars began 1897 with a new sense of purpose. In January, while the racecourse and the ballroom were far from neglected, Colonel Martin initiated a programme of training for both men and horses intended to prepare the regiment for a desert campaign. In March Martin himself led a 205-mile desert march completed in five days, with 32 Australian horses, 32 Hungarians and 32 Arabs, each horse heavily laden to replicate campaign conditions. The aim was to test the stamina of the horses; the Arabs and Australians stood the march equally well, while the Hungarians went to pieces. Further desert route marches were planned to test the men to the same degree, and local Arabs became familiar with columns of "khaki hussars" crossing the open desert. The field service dress worn by the 21st was the same khaki cotton tunic worn by the infantry, but with fawn Bedford breeches reinforced on

Band of the 21st Hussars outside a Cairo hotel early in 1897. The band played in the ballrooms of all the city's major hotels. (The Queen's Royal Lancers)

the inside leg with soft leather; puttees (long bands of cloth) were wrapped round the leg from ankle to knee. The cork foreign service helmet had a khaki cotton cover and a wide, floppy sun-shade of quilted cotton taped in place around its whole circumference — known by the men as the "lamp-shade", this was unique to the 21st, as the neck curtains worn by the infantry hung from the sides and rear of the helmet only. A brown leather bandolier was worn over the left shoulder, holding 50 rounds of .303-inch ammunition for the new Lee-Enfield magazine carbine with which the regiment had been equipped on arrival in Cairo, and which was carried in a brown leather "boot" or scabbard attached to the saddle behind the rider's right leg. Even the sword scabbard was covered in brown leather (for officers) or khaki cloth (for the men) to prevent reflections from its bright steel betraying a man's position to the enemy.

The 21st Lancers

Army Orders of 1 April 1897 informed Colonel Martin: "Her Majesty The Queen has been generously pleased to approve, with effect from the 31st March 1897, of the following changes: the 21st Hussars will be designated the 21st Lancers and armed, clothed, equipped and recruited as Lancers of the Line"[5].

This change was wholly unexpected and was made solely for administrative reasons. The army had decided to "twin" existing lancer regiments — while one was posted abroad, its twin would serve at home — and as there was an odd number of such regiments it became necessary to create another. Thus the 21st Hussars became the 21st Lancers.

The news was unwelcome, not least because while French grey had previously distinguished the regiment's "ornamental uniform", the full dress lancer tunic was to have scarlet facings and would be worn with a lance cap with a red top and a white plume, depriving the 21st of the link with its Indian origins. This was not an immediate concern, as subsequent War Office orders indicated that the change of uniform would not take place until the regiment returned to England. The 21st Lancers continued to parade as hussars, and in any case, since the adoption of field service khaki dress the ornamental uniform was less in evidence.

More significantly, of course, the men (not the officers) would be equipped with a nine-foot lance, a weapon with which they had no experience. Unlike the uniform, this change was to be immediate. One of the most influential cavalry manuals of the time and required reading for officers, Denison's *Modern Cavalry* (published in 1868), insisted that while the lance was an effective weapon in the hands of trained men it was worthless when used by the inexperienced. Lance drill was particularly difficult for both men and horses, and it was unlikely that the regiment could become proficient in the use of the weapon before the advance on Omdurman began. This fact alone, it seemed, might deny the 21st active service in the Sirdar's army.

Despite this worrying turn of events Colonel Martin maintained the momentum of regimental training. Lance drill began immediately, with hog spears standing in for lances until a full complement was acquired. Officers who had experience with the hog spear — pig-sticking required manoeuvres similar to lance drill — quickly began to instruct their men in these skills. Their practice was not, however, refined, and these lancers remained hussars at heart. (After the charge at Omdurman, when it seemed that the regiment might make a second charge, several men asked permission to throw down their lances and use the sword instead.)

Although the early cavalry lance had a wooden shaft (usually ash), the standard pattern introduced in India in 1868 had a bamboo shaft with a triangular-section steel spearhead and a steel butt ferrule. Because male bamboo of a suitable diameter was comparatively rare, and female bamboo snapped too easily, an ash lance was reintroduced in 1885; lancer regiments were unhappy with this, and in 1890 a bamboo lance was reintroduced. It was with this that the 21st Lancers was eventually equipped. Each lance weighed about five pounds, with a hand sling tied to the shaft at armpit height (which could be individually adjusted to suit each man). When carried mounted, the butt sat firmly in a leather lance-bucket fixed to the stirrup iron. The red-over-white swallowtail pennon attached beneath the spearhead was kept tightly furled when on active service.

Desert training continued, and during the latter part of 1897 the 21st Lancers undertook a series of exacting route marches, each squadron spending three weeks in the desert carrying full campaign kit. Colonel Martin insisted that his officers and men spend more time in the saddle than in the ballroom or the canteen, and hoped that word of his preparations would reach Kitchener.

★   ★   ★

In the Sudan, Kitchener's advance to Berber was outstanding as a logistical rather than a military victory. The Dervishes holding the town could be outnumbered and outgunned only if the Anglo-Egyptian army's vast numbers of troops and enormous quantities of supplies could be transported across hundreds of miles of open desert. As an engineer, Kitchener felt this would best be achieved by building a railway from Wadi Halfa (near the Egyptian border) to within striking distance of Berber - a distance of 400 miles, more than half of it across the heart of the Nubian Desert. Experts dismissed it as impossible; Kitchener had it built anyway. To be certain of success, he also required additional gunboats to destroy the wooden Dervish forts protecting river towns. The boats were built in England, shipped out in pieces and reassembled beside the Nile.

When the small Dervish garrison at Abu Hamed, through which the railway had to pass, refused to surrender or withdraw, its defenders were overrun by an advance force of the Egyptian army that went ahead of the track-laying gangs. This force included Sudanese troops — after each earlier battle captives had joined the Egyptian army rather than suffer imprisonment or worse; nevertheless, at Abu Hamed the Mahdists were slaughtered. The gunboat flotilla then moved up to the town to secure this stretch of the river while the railway advanced across the desert towards it.

The fate of the defenders of Abu Hamed led to the evacuation of Berber and the concentration of Mahdist forces further south at Metemmeh. Kitchener occupied Berber at the end of August 1897 without resistance. The Sudan Military Railway, completed two months later, spanned two-thirds of the 600 miles between the Egyptian border and Omdurman, cutting out the great "Dongola loop" of the Nile which extended the river journey to almost 900 miles. A fortified camp was established south of Berber at the confluence of the Nile and the Atbara. The Egyptian brigades and General Gatacre's British brigade were then brought up, along with the gunboats, so that by January 1898 a large Anglo-Egyptian army was concentrated at Fort Atbara.

Kitchener now waited at Berber for further troops and supplies to be brought up in preparation for the final stage of the campaign. There was still no indication that the 21st Lancers or indeed any British cavalry regiment would be included in further action, but Captain Fair of the 21st was detached to act as staff officer to General Gatacre. Fair was accompanied by his servant Private Denton.

Dervish spies kept the Khalifa informed of these activities, and in mid-February he decided to take the initiative. The commander at Metemmeh, Sharif Mahmoud Ahmad, was ordered to advance and retake Berber, his 11,000 men

A squadron of the regiment encamped near the Pyramids during a desert exercise. Colonel Martin pursued a rigorous programme of desert training for men and horses alike. (The Queen's Royal Lancers)

Colonel Martin and officers of the 21st Lancers - still in hussar uniform, worn here with the pillbox cap - photographed at the Abbassia barracks in Cairo in 1897. (The Queen's Royal Lancers)

reinforced by Osman Digna's 5,000. However, the Khalifa was not alone in having spies in the field. Kitchener had appointed Colonel Reginald Wingate as Director of Intelligence. An academic with a superb command of Arab dialects, Wingate had translated Slatin Pasha's book into English, and with his assistance had organised a network of Arab spies which extended into Omdurman itself. These agents tracked Mahmoud across the desert, sending regular messengers to Wingate with the latest enemy position and direction of advance.

Rivalry between the two Dervish commanders led to their disagreement over tactics. Mahmoud wished to continue along the Nile and confront Kitchener's army at the Atbara, while Osman Digna preferred a desert route, avoiding Kitchener by crossing the Atbara (little more than a dry watercourse) well south of his fortified camp and taking Berber unawares. They could not agree; orders had to be sent from Omdurman, the Khalifa backing the desert route.

When it became clear from Wingate's intelligence reports that this Dervish force did not intend to engage the Anglo-Egyptian army in its fortified position, Kitchener sent out the Egyptian cavalry to confirm their numbers and disposition. This force was strongly attacked and avoided something of a massacre only by bringing four Maxim guns to bear on its assailants. Three days later Kitchener led his infantry brigades (11,000 men) out to confront Mahmoud at Nakheila on the Atbara. From first light on 8 April a one-hour artillery bombardment reduced the number and morale of the enemy. The only counter-attack, a charge by Dervish cavalrymen, was stopped most abruptly by Maxim guns. Then Kitchener ordered in the infantry. Although outnumbered, they advanced with regular volleys of rifle fire against Dervishes armed mainly with spears and swords. It was all over in 40 minutes.

While many prisoners were taken, the most prized was Mahmoud himself, one of the Khalifa's most senior lieutenants. Osman Digna and most of his men, who had deployed to one side and escaped the brunt of the attack, withdrew south towards Omdurman. Wingate interviewed Mahmoud, although at this point the man had little to say beyond assuring his captors that they would pay dearly for this at Omdurman. The Anglo-Egyptian dead totalled 83; the number of Dervishes killed was variously reported, from an unlikely low of 1,000 up to 3,000. Arab historians put the true number at 7,000, and suggest that this was concealed from the English press because Kitchener thought the battle at the Atbara would seem unequal and unnecessarily brutal, and his political masters might not then authorise the final stage of the campaign.

In fact, by this time the British government viewed the occupation of Omdurman and Khartoum as politically essential. A French expedition had already entered the south-west province of the Sudan, heading for Fashoda on the upper Nile. Ironically, British pressure on the Dervish army from the north had assisted French progress in the south. Until Kitchener had taken the capital the upper Nile remained inaccessible to British gunboats and no claim could be made for British rule.

Despite this urgency the advance had to wait until the rising waters of the Nile made it navigable as far as Khartoum. Kitchener returned to Cairo to plan the taking of the Sudan's old and new capitals. While there, in an interview with Hubert Howard of *The Times*, he was uncharacteristically revealing: " ... after the fall of Khartoum, the end of Mahdism leaves the way open for

France … occupation will be a great factor"[6]. The British occupation of Omdurman and Khartoum would open up the river and allow gunboats to proceed south to Fashoda, raising the possibility of an actual armed confrontation between Britain and France in this remote land.

★ ★ ★

The 21st Lancers was at this time returning from a Camp of Exercise at Mena, where much of the regiment's training in desert warfare had been put to the test as they manoeuvred alongside infantry and artillery in mock battlefield conditions. On arriving back at the Abbassia barracks and learning of Kitchener's victory at the Atbara, every man knew the way was now clear for the final advance. There was of course still no reason to suppose that the 21st would be involved, and it was with mixed emotions that the lancers visited the 32nd Field Battery on 11 April to watch a rehearsal for the taking of Omdurman. An exact replica of the six-foot-thick wall protecting the inner city had been built in the desert, and gunners expressed their concern in crude terms when the shells damaged but failed to demolish it.

In May 1898, with the final advance of the Anglo-Egyptian army planned to begin in three months time, Colonel Martin optimistically stepped up the programme of training for his regiment. This included manoeuvring squadrons at speed, the training of over 300 Arab mounts, and turning out "on alarm" with campaign equipment and desert rations in less than one hour. The 21st was ready to join the advance; it only waited to be asked.

On 14 June the regiment was inspected by General Kitchener himself. On the following evening the officers gave a lavish dinner with Kitchener as their principal guest, and he received a thunderous ovation. While this lengthy standing applause was most likely for his victory at the Atbara, it is possible that the regiment's own spy in Kitchener's ranks — General Gatacre's staff officer Captain Fair — had already intimated the content of an order that would be received one week later: that the 21st was to join the Sirdar's army. Kitchener had asked the War Office for additional artillery, a second British infantry brigade, and a cavalry regiment which he himself specified should be the 21st Lancers.

Initially six additional officers were to be attached to the regiment for the Sudan campaign, but two deaths early in July (from diphtheria and enteric fever) increased this number to eight. This circumstance enabled Lieutenant Winston Churchill of the 4th Hussars to pull strings in London and scrape in, despite the fact that Kitchener disliked him and had previously denied him a place. The officers of the 21st similarly viewed Churchill's attachment with alarm. No one doubted the man's abilities as a soldier; all feared his abilities as a newspaper correspondent. Despite promising Kitchener that he would not write about the campaign, Churchill got round this in a rather underhand way by writing highly descriptive (and highly impersonal) letters supposedly to his mother, which the ever-supportive and well-connected Lady Randolph kindly made available to the *Morning Post*.

By this time most officers of the 21st had employed Egyptian servants — Lieutenant Pirie had Mahomed and Major Fowle had Abdul — and these were to accompany them on the campaign. Lieutenant de Montmorency did

The first photograph of the regiment mounted and carrying lances, on parade in Cairo in 1897. Under magnification this seems to show half-khaki hussar uniform - khaki frocks and dark blue pantaloons, with the white foreign service helmet. (The Queen's Royal Lancers)

Kitchener's Sudan Military Railway advances south, sleepers and rails being brought up to the railhead by train. (Churchill Archives Centre)

Egyptian troops check some of the several thousand Dervish dead after the battle of the Atbara on 8 April, and (far right) gather up discarded spears. His heavy losses in this action convinced the Khalifa to concentrate his forces much further south at Omdurman. (The Queen's Royal Lancers)

better still, employing a Sudanese servant of the Jaalin tribe, and bragging at irritating length about this coup; the man's name, his brother officers were forced to conclude, could only be "my-Jaalin". The Jaalin tribe inhabited northern areas of the Sudan and, when they refused to follow the Khalifa, had seen their villages burned and many young men slaughtered. Those who fled into Egypt had good reason to support the Anglo-Egyptian campaign.

The Desert Advance

B Squadron, 21st Lancers left Cairo on 31 July 1898. The first stage of the journey was by rail and the rest of the regiment saw the men off from the station with much singing and mutual encouragement. Hubert Howard, correspondent for *The Times*, noted their enthusiasm. He struck up a friendship with officers of the remaining squadrons, and determined to ride with the regiment during the campaign.

Churchill arrived in Cairo on 2 August, in time to leave with A Squadron on the following day. C Squadron followed on 6 August (a regiment on active service normally travelled with three service squadrons of about 130 men each). The 22-hour rail journey to Khizam was particularly unpleasant, the movement of the train lifting the sand and forming a gritty cloud that enveloped its entire length and at first filled the carriages, so that windows had to be closed despite the fierce heat. The horses, too closely packed, also suffered badly.

As each squadron arrived at Khizam the horses and baggage were transferred to barges, and the men boarded Thomas Cook's large tourist steamers *Cleopatra* and *Princess* for the second stage of the journey up the Nile to Aswan and Shellah. In addition to the official rations of preserved mutton and biscuits the regiment took a number of live sheep to be killed at intervals to provide fresh meat. At

Shellah they transferred to two smaller steamers, *Alexandria* and *Amara*, each with two barges attached (one on either side) for the horses and baggage, for the third stage across the Egyptian border to Wadi Halfa.

Here they transferred back from steamers to trains — on Kitchener's Sudan Military Railway — for the fourth stage of the journey, crossing the great Nubian Desert to Fort Atbara from where the march south was planned to begin. By now the horses were suffering badly, and much time was wasted in getting them onto the train; de Montmorency received a kick in the back, and Kenna a kick on the leg. Two squadrons were behind schedule and Colonel Martin, unusually, lost his temper with his senior officers. Pirie (now Adjutant) wrote: "The old man is getting very fidgety … I wish he'd try to keep calm, things go so much better when he does"[7]. Both officers and men were accommodated in open-sided goods vans covered by awnings to give some protection from the sun and sand. Rest periods were important for the men but crucial for the horses, which had to be watered and exercised, and perhaps unwisely Martin ordered these periods to be cut short. The result was that all three squadrons reached Atbara on schedule.

Both Generals Kitchener and Gatacre visited the Lancers

Sharif Mahmoud Amad, one of the most senior Dervish leaders, guarded by men of the 10th Sudanese Battalion after his capture at the Atbara. Note the fine quality of his decorative jibbah, and the bloodstains on his left thigh. (National Army Museum)

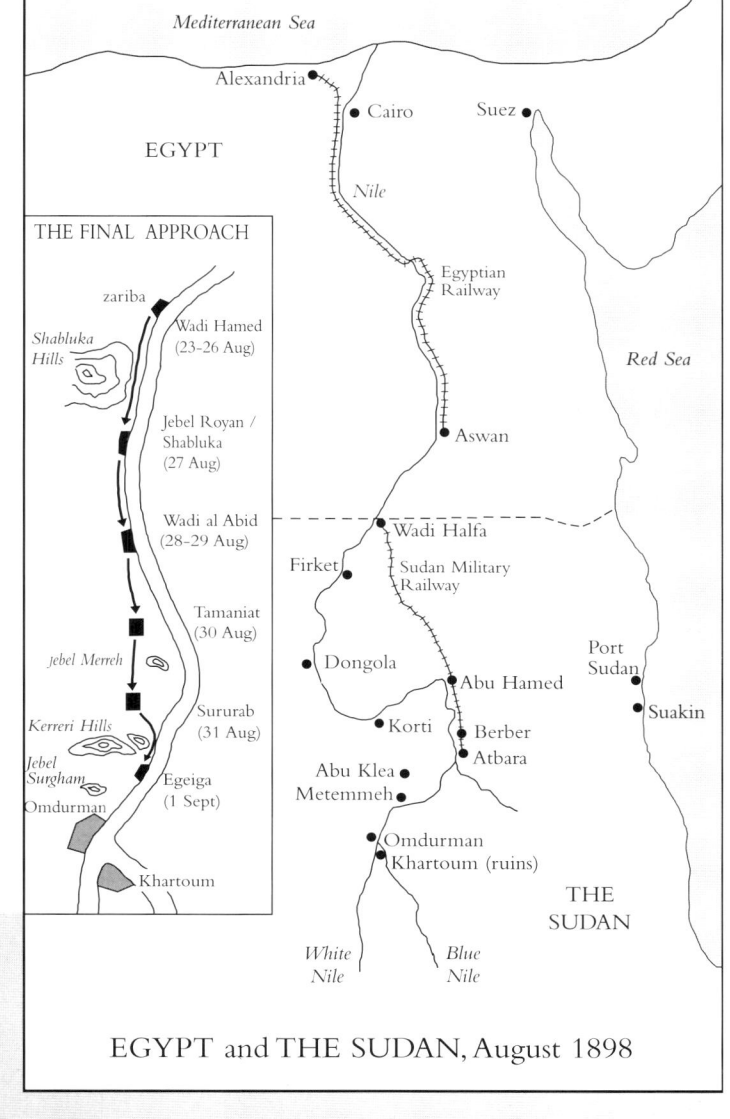

soon after their arrival, and Captain Fair rejoined his regiment. He had met the captured Dervish leader Mahmoud, who was now boasting that 175,000 Dervishes awaited them at Omdurman. As Wingate's spies put the number at approximately 50,000 this was taken to prove only the Mahdist mastery of hyperbole.

It was at Atbara that the 21st had its first bad experience with the press. Hubert Howard had become a friend and had nothing but praise for the regiment; but G.W.Steevens, correspondent for the *Daily Mail*, was less than complimentary: "It was their first appearance in war ... they were the only regiment in the British army which had never been on active service ... at this first glimpse of British cavalry in the field, they looked less like horsemen than Christmas

Left: Lieutenants Molyneux, Royal Horse Guards, and Churchill, 4th Hussars, on a steamer en route to join the 21st Lancers in Cairo in preparation for the Sudan campaign. Both men arrived only 24 hours before the regiment left to join the Anglo-Egyptian army. (National Army Museum)

Below: Officers and attached officers, 21st Lancers, photographed in 1898 at the Abbassia barracks. Under magnification, students of uniform details will see that some variation was tolerated in service dress. Some officers (e.g. O. W. Brinton, second row, far right) favoured jackets with doubled breast pockets, a straight flap showing above the three-point flap; Finn (front row, third from right) has cartridge loops above his pockets; Dunlop-Smith (second row, third from right) has his collar pressed open over the white hunting stock; Wormald and Vaughan (third row, left, and second row, second left) wear their Sam Brownes with cartridge loops on a single brace. (The Queen's Royal Lancers)

tree "⁽⁸⁾. There was some truth in it: from man and horse there dangled haversack, cloak, sword and carbine, corn feed, canvas bucket, waterproof and water bottles. The men, yet to experience the full treachery of the correspondents' art, took it in good part and henceforth referred to themselves as being in "Christmas Tree Order".

A and B Squadrons prepared to march the fifth and final stage of the journey to Wadi Hamed, where the whole army was concentrating; C Squadron was to continue by steamer. But now came further orders: the two marching squadrons were to escort over 2,000 mules, donkeys and camels, keeping to a schedule devised by Kitchener himself. Furthermore, although the main Dervish force was located much further south, enemy parties up to 350 strong were known to be shadowing the Anglo-Egyptian troops. The squadrons' firepower was therefore enhanced by two Maxim guns.

It rained heavily on the night of 15 August, so that when the lancers set off on the following morning with their column of baggage animals the rising Nile had overflowed. The *khors* — dry watercourses running down to the river — appeared to be tributaries of the Nile, but when the river was in flood water ran up the khors into the desert. Now filled, some were so deep that it was necessary for the three-mile-long animal train to make a wide detour into the desert, where the thick mimosa (large thorn bushes) made progress difficult, adding considerably to the distance to be travelled and the time taken. Colonel Martin found it impossible to keep to Kitchener's schedule and became most agitated; Pirie wrote, " he does not manage well, I'm afraid"⁽⁹⁾.

On 17 August the regiment rose at 3.00a.m. to water, feed and saddle the horses, all accomplished in the dark; they commenced the day's march — measured by Kitchener as 20 miles — at first light, about 4.30. Stores had been dropped by boat at set intervals along the river bank, so the schedule of march had to be kept to. Hubert Howard noted in the pocket diary from which he compiled his reports: "21st march till 1, some 28 miles, and cannot get to stores for the flood of the river, which has run up a long hollow between us"⁽¹⁰⁾. A further detour was required, making a total of 32 miles actually marched to complete Kitchener's theoretical twenty.

The regiment marched an average of 30 miles a day for nine days, the necessity of reaching the next cache of stores forcing them to continue through the scorching midday heat - there was insufficient moonlight to allow night marches. Almost 50 horses had to be destroyed, most suffering from laminitis caused by the hot sand. One man (Private Bishop) died of sunstroke and exhaustion; several others, unable to continue, were put on a passing steamer. Others were sent into the desert after straying animals and became lost; unable to find their regiment, they found the Nile and a steamer instead. Infantrymen proceeding south by steamer claimed to have seen a dozen lancers standing by the river thumbing a lift, and correspondents who should have known better duly relayed this "news" home. Bennet Burleigh of the *Daily Telegraph*, ignorant of the regiment's preparation and misled by Kitchener's measurements, used

The sergeants of the 21st Lancers at Abbassia, with Major Crole-Wyndham and Colonel Martin. (Queen's Royal Lancers)

Lieutenant de Montmorency with NCOs and men of his troop photographed in Cairo in 1898 before leaving for the Sudan. The foreign service helmet now has a khaki cover, but the distinctive sunshade has yet to be added. (The Queen's Royal Lancers)

these circumstances to suggest that the 21st was ill-prepared for the march.

As the regiment's press coverage grew worse their relationship with Lieutenant Churchill became strained. The feeling was mutual. Given the task of leading two donkeys and a mule, he had already complained to his mother of having "a fearful lot of work of a petty and tedious kind"[11]. Now he wrote: "The 21st Lancers are not on the whole a good business and I would much rather have been attached to the Egyptian cavalry staff. They hate all the attached officers and some of them take little pains to conceal their dislike"[12]. Although the senior officers of the 21st were undeniably a close-knit bunch there is no evidence for a general dislike of the attached officers, and only Churchill seems to have been treated as an outsider.

The Final Approach

The great camp at Wadi Hamed where Kitchener's army was concentrating extended for two miles along the bank of the Nile, protected on the desert side by a *zariba*, a defensive hedge formed of thorn bushes cut down and pressed together. A and B Squadrons of the 21st Lancers arrived on 23 August, and C Squadron arrived by steamer three days later. There was now time for men and horses to recover from the march from the Atbara and to prepare for the final advance on Omdurman and Khartoum.

The first night it rained heavily, and although tents had been provided for officers the men had to sleep on the sand beneath their waterproofs — lances and waterproofs were sometimes strung together to form an improvised shelter. All were aware that Mahdist forces might attempt a pre-emptive attack under cover of darkness, although General Gatacre's advice that men on guard duty stay alert lest Dervishes surprise them and leap into the zariba using their spears as vaulting poles caused only amusement.

While at Wadi Hamed the regiment had to form a fourth squadron. The system of having three field squadrons of 130 men each was considered by many to be unwieldy, and four squadrons of 100 men were preferred. Kitchener had said that he wanted a regiment of four squadrons, and Churchill rightly suspected that rather than be left behind the 21st Lancers would have formed 40 if required. The fourth squadron was formed by first taking one troop from each squadron to make four squadrons of three troops each, and then taking a number of men from each troop to form a fourth troop for each squadron.

Kitchener had now gathered his army for the final advance. The force concentrated at Wadi Hamed comprised two British and four Egyptian brigades — a total of 8,200 British and 17,600 Egyptian and Sudanese troops, with 44 artillery pieces and 20 Maxims, and an additional 36 guns and 24 Maxims on ten armour-plated gunboats.

While the 21st Lancers was the only British cavalry regiment included, the Egyptian cavalry (nine squadrons commanded by Lieutenant-Colonel Robert Broadwood) had fought under Kitchener throughout the Sudan campaign and considered the 21st to be untried in battle. This undoubted fact lay behind Churchill's wish to transfer: "The whole matter is reaching its climax and I think a great battle is imminent. I am trying to get to Egyptian cavalry as ... it is a much better business"[13]. Eager to see action, he reasoned that when a task arose for the cavalry that might bring it into contact with the enemy Kitchener was more likely to entrust this to the Egyptians than to the 21st. A similar thought had occurred to the lancers, who feared that they might be held back in a secondary role.

The latest intelligence from Omdurman indicated that the Khalifa intended to meet this Anglo-Egyptian army on the Kerreri plain outside the city. Wingate's spies were reporting a Dervish army increased by the forced enlistment of every able-bodied man in the city to 55,000, and he let this be known among the troops to counter rumours running through the camp which had by now inflated Mahmoud's 175,000 to an incredible 250,000.

At first light on 27 August the cavalry was sent forward to reconnoitre the Shabluka hill where the Dervishes were known to have an outpost, and to check the wooden forts nearby on the banks of the Nile. Broadwood's Egyptian cavalry went first, with the 21st Lancers in support, which seemed to confirm the regiment's worst fears. The lancers rode in close formation and Pirie complained privately: "Dust awful — Martin never seems to think of the Sqdns in rear & had them all close up, quite unnecessary & very hard for men & horses"[14]. They found both the outpost and the forts abandoned (Osman Digna had wanted to make a stand here, but the Khalifa ordered him to withdraw his men to Omdurman).

A new camp was established at Royan Island and the main army came up, now only 40 miles from Khartoum. The 21st found itself encamped with the Egyptian cavalry, one officer remarking that "All our river front is occupied by black troops washing etc, most unpleasant"[15].

The following day was a Sunday and the Anglican chaplain, likening the British troops to the Crusaders, called down the blessing of God on their rifles and swords. After church parade General Gatacre addressed them, and — none too helpfully — he took the opportunity to accuse everyone of gross inefficiency so far. Colonel Martin took this personally and was in a furious rage, which he took out on his officers. The army then moved six miles further south to Wadi el Abid, the 21st Lancers providing the Sirdar's escort. On arrival at the new camp they led their horses down to the river, where the bank was extremely steep; after one horse fell in and was drowned they were forced to water the rest from nose-bags and canvas buckets.

Monday 29 August was a rest day. The Sirdar sent out the Egyptian cavalry to reconnoitre for a camp for the following day, and to feel for Dervish activity nearby. The 21st felt aggrieved that the regiment had not been allowed to

Above: A lancer encouraging his horse to board the train after an exercise break. Cramped conditions required regular stops for both horses and men. (National Army Museum)

Below: Officers of the regiment in a sleeping car on the Egyptian railway during the first stage of their journey to the Sudan. The accomodation and comforts may look basic, but they would find conditions on the Sudan Military Railway even less luxurious. (National Army Museum)

Men of the 21st on board one of the two steamers which conveyed the regiment between Aswan and Wadi Halfa en route to the Sudan. Horses can be seen on the lower deck. (National Army Museum)

perform this duty, and that the Egyptians seemed always to be given the lead role in cavalry work. Pirie spoke to Colonel Martin about it, urging him to see Kitchener. After lunch Martin went to the Sirdar and, choosing his words carefully (for Kitchener would not countenance any form of protest), expressed concern that his men might reach the coming battle without some lesser work to prepare them for the greater. Kitchener assured Martin that this would not be the case.

The Egyptian cavalry reported no Dervish activity, although Arab historians insist that the Khalifa's intelligence officer, Abd al Baqi, was tracking the army's movement south with a force of 300 men. This group kept to the desert side, and sent three reports daily back to Omdurman. Abd al Baqi claimed that some of his men actually walked in amongst the Egyptian and Sudanese troops and gathered further intelligence.

On Tuesday 30 August the great army started southwards at 5.30a.m. in heavy rain. One hour earlier the Egyptian cavalry and the 21st Lancers had been sent out as an advance screen, reconnoitring ten miles ahead, keeping pace with the gunboats on the river and a party of Jaalin on the east bank. The Egyptian cavalry was to the right, protecting the desert flank, and the 21st Lancers to the left, beside the Nile.

The ground was mostly flat, with an occasional khor running up from the river, and a thick covering of thorn bushes which ran from the river bank several hundred yards into the desert. This mimosa made it difficult to search thoroughly. Every lancer had been told how effectively dismounted Dervish patrols could use such camouflage, for three of those now riding towards Omdurman were veterans of the 1884 Gordon Relief Expedition — Major Crole-Wyndham, Major Fowle and Sergeant-Major Wood had served with the Light Camel Regiment, and knew how Dervishes could appear suddenly from khors and bushes to slash at the horses' hocks and spear fallen riders. In places the mimosa was so thick that troopers were ordered to dismount and search on foot, carbines at the ready.

Each squadron put out forward patrols, and Major Finn (commanding A Squadron) sent out Lieutenant Churchill with five men. At about 8.00a.m. this party was stunned to see a Dervish suddenly appear from the mimosa and walk calmly towards them. Churchill rode quickly at the man, who readily surrendered and gave up his spears. Colonel Martin ordered the prisoner to be taken immediately to Kitchener. The lancers (and Churchill most vocally of all) made much of the incident, boasting of the ease with which they took their first Dervish. Much to their embarrassment and the amusement of the Egyptian cavalry, the man was found to be one of Colonel Wingate's spies returning with an urgent report on the situation in Omdurman.

The 21st pressed on towards Jebel Merreh ("the hill of Merreh"), 25 miles from Khartoum; Kitchener had ordered them to occupy the hill and report any Dervish position on the plain ahead. It was reached by 1.00p.m.; from its summit the desert stretched southwards towards Omdurman and Khartoum, revealing not a single Dervish. This news was heliographed back to the Sirdar, who had stopped the main force at Tamaniat four miles north of the hill and ordered the construction of a zariba for the night's bivouac. At 2.30p.m., with the 21st still reporting no sign of the enemy, Kitchener signalled the regiment to come in but to leave one squadron to keep watch until sunset.

Finn's A Squadron was left on the hill, and he put out two patrols (led by Lieutenants Smyth and Conolly) a further two miles south. Almost immediately Smyth's patrol made contact with about 70 mounted Dervishes who had inexplicably not been seen from the summit. In turning aside, the enemy rode across the path of Conolly's patrol. He ordered his men to dismount and open fire with their carbines at 750 yards, although no Dervish was hit at this great range. This was thought to be part of Abd al Baqi's force, which had seen the 21st withdraw from the hill and failed to realise that one squadron remained.

There were no further sightings, and A Squadron abandoned Jebel Merreh at 5.00p.m. in time to reach the zariba by sunset. No lights were allowed and many guards posted, lest the Khalifa bring his troops out of Omdurman and attempt a night attack. However, the main talking point among the troops was a snippet of the news brought back by Colonel Wingate's spy, which had somehow leaked to

Left: The gunboat Fateh *at Fort Atbara, preparing for the final advance. (Churchill Archives Centre)*

Below: A trooper of the 21st Lancers (left) reporting sick to be returned to Cairo by steamer. This clearly contrasts the quilted helmet sunshade unique to the regiment with the infantry neck protector worn by the Grenadier Guardsman (centre). (National Army Museum)

the men. The Khalifa had announced that an ancient prophecy — that the bones of the Sudan's enemies would one day whiten the Kerreri desert (north of Omdurman, and through which Kitchener's army must pass) — was about to be fulfilled. The officers and men of the 21st knew that as the army advanced in reconnoitring formation the cavalry would lead the way across the Kerreri plain.

Wednesday 31 August

The cavalry went out at 5.30a.m. in advance of the main army to reconnoitre the route to Sururab, eight miles further south. Captain Douglas Haig, commanding a squadron of the Egyptian cavalry, must by now have heard of Colonel Martin's intercession with the Sirdar, for he wrote sourly: "21st Lancers anxious to do some scouting, so they precede, and the Egyptian Cavalry are ordered to support them"[16].

By 6.00a.m. the lancers had reached higher ground from which the Kerreri hills could be seen 12 miles further south. Inspecting the area below the hills by telescope the officers spotted the tents and flags of a Dervish camp. It was a clear morning and the light was sufficient for Lieutenant Clerk (commanding the 21st Lancers Signals Party) to heliograph this information back to the Sirdar. More immediately pressing, Dervish cavalry was seen about three miles south of the lancers' position. As the 21st continued south Colonel Martin sent Major Fowle's B Squadron ahead as advance squadron. The Dervish cavalry retired, maintaining a distance of about two miles.

Watching from the higher ground recently vacated by the regiment, Haig noted "The 21st patrols going on in a somewhat careless way … cantering recklessly through the scrub"[17]. Frank Rhodes, chief correspondent for *The Times* and watching from the same position, saw it differently: "In front of the Lancers' scouts we could see bodies of Dervish horsemen falling back …"[18]. These Dervishes, part of Abd al Baqi's shadowing force of 300, were under orders not to engage the enemy. De Montmorency's troop, sent ahead of B Squadron, followed them to within a mile of the Kerreri hills, but at this point Colonel Martin (perhaps fearing his men were being led into an ambush) sent Pirie forward to bring back the advance squadron.

Pirie delivered the order to Fowle; then went after de Montmorency and his troop, still in pursuit of the Dervish horsemen, and reached them just as they lost sight of the enemy. A large number of flags could be seen above the thick bush, suggesting a large Dervish camp. Deciding that the situation superseded their colonel's order, these two officers left the troop behind and went closer, taking de Montmorency's Jaalin servant to hold the horses when they dismounted. At 250 yards from the flags they discovered about 20 Dervishes, who spotted them at the same time. Pirie wrote: "One of them was out on a flank. de M went up & fired at him, two of them fired at us from about 100 yards & I'm glad to say missed us though one bullet went close to de M's head"[19]. As the Dervishes moved casually away Pirie and de Montmorency retired too.

The sound of gunfire had caused some consternation in the squadron waiting at a distance, as Steevens of the *Daily Mail* reported: "'Where's Montmorency?' 'Gone into the bush, sir.' Pop! Very faint and muffled, but all hearts leaped; it was the first shot of the campaign. 'Where's Montmorency?'"[20].

The troop rejoined B Squadron, and Fowle withdrew to

Right & far right: Men of the 21st during halts on the southward march to Omdurman. The welcome shade of palm trees became less frequent as the regiment moved up the Nile. (Churchill Archives Centre)

the regiment. Pirie expected an immediate advance on the Dervish position to be ordered, but the Egyptian cavalry had been left behind and Colonel Martin felt the regiment was too exposed. The location of the Dervish camp was heliographed back to Kitchener, who sent a gunboat up to shell it.

The chief significance of the incident was not the apparent recklessness of the two officers, but Colonel Martin's caution. After Omdurman it was suggested that the regiment's commanding officer, overly eager for the charge, would have taken any chance, at any risk to his men. If this had been the case it is likely he would have advanced on the Dervish camp at Kerreri as Pirie expected, heedless of a concealed enemy whose strength was unknown. Ironically, Kitchener himself thought that the 21st should have done more. Pirie wrote: "We got back to camp about 2.00p.m. De Montmorency sent in a report to Sirdar & I went round after lunch. He seemed rather annoyed that we hadn't turned them out of Kerreri, but will do it tomorrow"[21]. Martin might reasonably have taken this as a measure of the man, and determined not to annoy him again with such a show of caution.

It began to rain heavily at 9.00p.m. and continued throughout the night, though the lancers' sleep was disturbed more by their own sense of anticipation: on the following day, they would have the chance to put matters right with the Dervishes encamped below the Kerreri hills and "turn them out". Pirie feared that the 30 shells fired at this position by the gunboat might already have done so. He realised sooner than most that the formidable firepower of the boats would prove more useful to the Sirdar than any number of lancers: "I'm afraid they may spoil our show a bit, blow them"[22].

Below: *The regiment formed a fourth squadron at the Atbara; and this photograph (although taken in Cairo) clearly shows the formation in which the 21st went into battle: Colonel Martin in the foreground, with (left to right) Major Finn's A Squadron, Major Fowle's B Squadron, Captain Doyne's C Squadron and Captain Eadon's D Squadron. (The Queen's Royal Lancers)*

CHAPTER FIVE

The First Dervish Attack

Thursday 1 September

It rained hard throughout the night and the camp became a sandy swamp. The thunderstorms and the continual downpour proved too much for the improvised lance-and-waterproof shelters of the 21st Lancers, and at Reveille all were very wet. Nevertheless it was the first day of September, the opening of the partridge shooting season, and while making ready their horses officers joked about the bag they expected. Hubert Howard of *The Times* was to ride with them and joined in the banter: Captain Eadon was "rather excited at the prospect of first meeting the enemy"[1].

At 5.30a.m. the Anglo-Egyptian army advanced towards Omdurman, 18 miles to the south. Kitchener sent the cavalry out ahead of the infantry, to reconnoitre the Kerreri hills and ascertain whether the Dervish camp there was still occupied after the gunboat shelling of the previous day. While any position not occupied in strength was to be captured, the primary objective was to close on Omdurman and locate the Khalifa's army.

The cavalry moved south in parallel columns, the 21st Lancers on the left beside the Nile, Colonel Broadwood's Egyptians on the right. This advance group moved several miles ahead of the main army, keeping pace with the gunboats on the river to their left and the Jaalin "friendlies" on the far bank. Colonel Martin sent an officer's patrol (Lieutenant Smyth and six men) ahead of the regiment to give advance warning of enemy activity. Although the ground was flat, deep khors and a thick covering of thorn scrub offered ample cover for dismounted Dervishes waiting in ambush.

The Egyptian cavalry, now moving off at an angle to guard the desert flank as they approached the hills, expected the 21st to reduce its pace in order to keep the two in line. However, the eager lancers edged ahead; to the jaundiced eye of Captain Haig with the Egyptian cavalry it seemed that "the 21st kept near the river, working independently of us, and (I thought) somewhat recklessly"[2].

As the rain stopped and the sky brightened about a hundred vultures appeared from the desert and accompanied the lancers, flying or watching from the ground and – both officers and men were convinced – always looking at *them*. This dampened the excitement more effectively than the rain, the consensus being that from their high vantage point these carrion birds saw two armies converging and knew a considerable feast must follow. The conflict would not, however, be immediate — Smyth's patrol reported back with news that the Dervish camp on the Kerreri hills was deserted. Just before 7.30 the regiment halted on the lower slopes of Kerreri only eight miles from Omdurman. The Egyptian cavalry was approaching the western end of the hills, more than a mile to their right, and Kitchener's army were coming up six miles behind.

A party of the 21st was sent to the summit to see what

Left: *Major Crole-Wyndham, the regimental second-in-command, mounted and in field service kit. Although he wears the regulation holstered Webley revolver on his right hip, he also has a privately purchased 1896 "broom-handle" Mauser pistol strapped to the saddle wallet in its wooden holster-stock. This, the very latest handgun available, was the world's first practical, mass-produced semi-automatic. At 7.63mm its calibre was smaller than that of the Webley, but the round had a higher muzzle velocity and considerable stopping power, and the magazine held ten rounds. Compare the size of his charger with the smaller Arab ridden by Sergeant–Major Hutton opposite. (The Queen's Royal Lancers)*

Right: *Sergeant-Major Rough Rider Hutton in field service kit at Abbassia barracks, his foreign service helmet as yet without a cover. His Sam Browne is worn with both braces, over the strap of the haversack on his left hip; the waterbottle is not visible here, but it would have been slung on top of the haversack in the field. Some men claimed to find the 1890 pattern cavalry sabre a little too heavy to wield easily from the saddle, but Mr Hutton does not look like that kind of soldier.... His rank and appointment are marked by a gold crown and chevrons separated by a spur, all on red backing on his right sleeve. Since this rank carried neither lance nor carbine Hutton has room for a corn-sack and his messtin attached to the saddle behind his right leg; a picket pin is just visible on top of the rolled and strapped cloak behind the saddle. Note the cord fly screen on the horse's bridle. Hutton rode with C Squadron at Omdurman. (The Queen's Royal Lancers)*

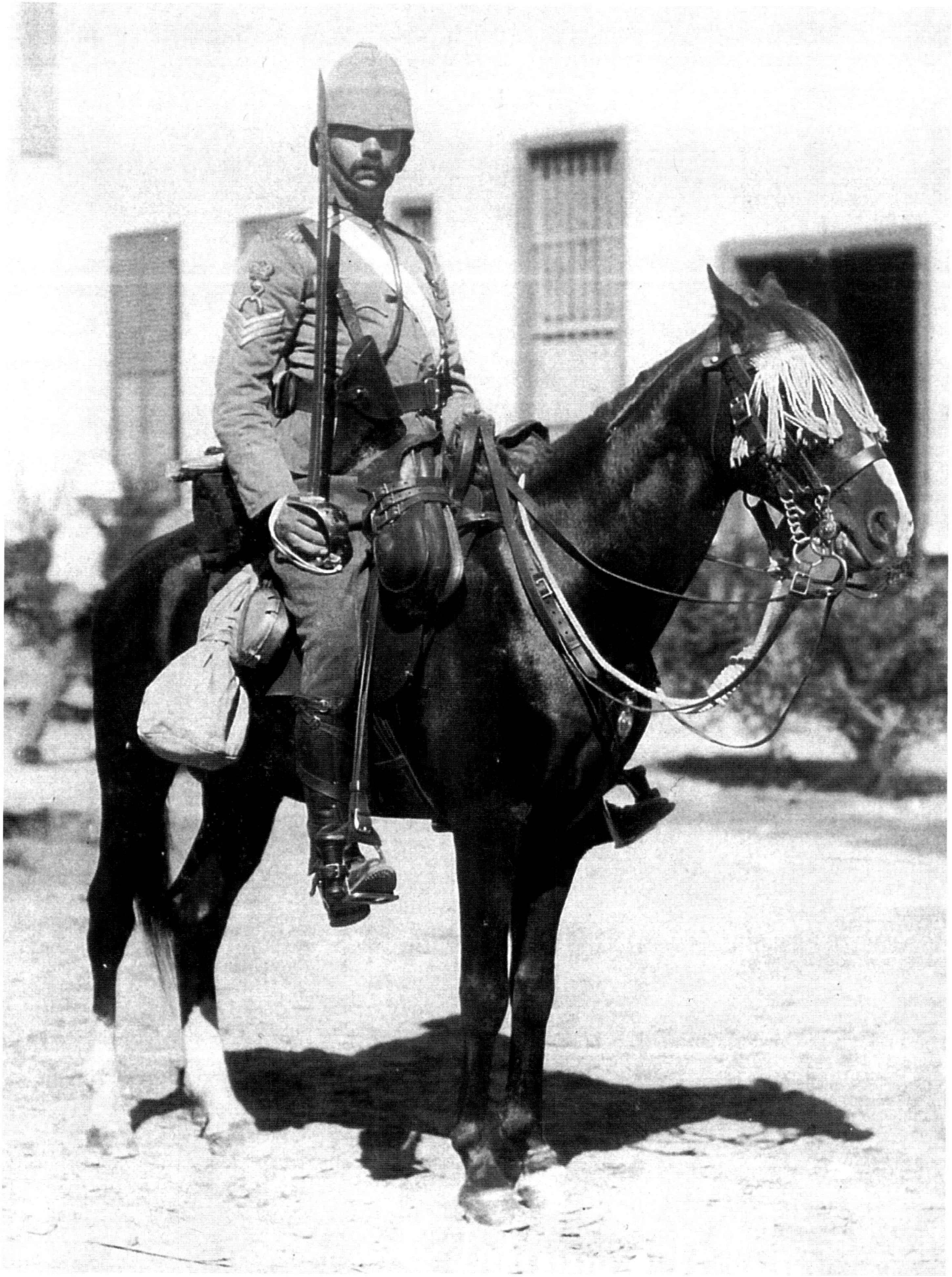

Sketch made by an unidentified officer of the 21st as the regiment gained its first view of Omdurman; the drawing is said to have been damaged by a gust of wind that blew it from his hand as he worked. (The Queen's Royal Lancers)

lay ahead. Lieutenant Clerk, the Signals Officer, was the first to reach the top and the first man in the British force to see Omdurman. He had an open view southwards across the Kerreri plain, an apparently flat expanse of sand between the distant hills to his right and the Nile, almost a mile wide, to his left. Straight ahead lay the Khalifa's capital — hundreds of flat-roofed mud houses stretching for more than three miles along the river, and rising above them the enormous pale yellow dome of the Mahdi's Tomb. Immediately south of the city the river divided into the White and Blue Niles. Between these two, thick clumps of palm trees on Tuti Island masked the ruins of Khartoum, untouched since the Dervishes stormed its walls 14 years earlier.

A single hill, Jebel Surgham, stood halfway between Kerreri and Omdurman. Although at first the Kerreri plain appeared otherwise flat, Lieutenant Clerk now saw that a sand ridge ran from the Surgham across the desert, high enough to conceal an enemy force encamped below the line of sight. He informed Colonel Martin that only from this ridge could they make a full inspection of the plain. To their right the Egyptian cavalry continued in a wide arc, rounding the western end of the hills and making for the same ridge.

As the four squadrons of the 21st left the Kerreri hills behind and headed due south across the plain, Major Finn cannot have been alone in feeling how small and vulnerable the regiment was in a landscape of such proportions. Although the ground underfoot was now sand patched with coarse grass, giving no cover for dismounted Dervish patrols, every man knew they were in an exposed position and closing fast on the Khalifa's army. All had heard of the ancient prophecy which the Khalifa believed was about to be fulfilled, that the bones of the Sudan's enemies would whiten the sands of Kerreri.

The lancers reached the sand ridge at a position just below Jebel Surgham and gained an uninterrupted view of Omdurman now only five miles away, the mud huts along the river and the thick stone walls of the inner city dwarfed by the dome of the Mahdi's tomb. A long black line ran from the city out across the desert, and this at first seemed to be some kind of fortification. Several of the men, thinking it a barrier of thorn bushes, offered ribald comments on the fate of kilted Scottish regiments when these had to cross it. Lieutenant Pirie was first to realise that it was a line of Dervishes:" ... only about 800 or 900, but they were coming out of Omdurman fast"[3]. Lieutenant Churchill, coming up with Major Finn's A Squadron at the rear of the regiment, first saw the line some 15 minutes after Pirie, and in that short interval the enemy force had grown: "A long black line with white spots ... it seemed to us, as we looked, that there might be 3,000 men"[4].

At 9.45 the signal party began the ascent of Jebel Surgham to establish a heliograph post. The Egyptian cavalry had now reached the sand ridge further to the west and had seen the enemy. Kitchener's army was approaching the Kerreri hills only four miles behind. On the Nile the gunboats were nearing Omdurman. The thunderstorms had cleared and there was no cloud cover. As Lieutenant Clerk climbed Jebel Surgham he knew there would be no difficulty in flashing the news back to Kitchener, providing the main army had rounded the Kerreri hills by the time the signal party reached the summit.

Colonel Martin, seeing the Egyptian cavalry to his right continuing over the ridge, and eager for the 21st to remain at the forefront of the advance, left the signal party on Surgham and led the regiment a further two miles across the plain, closing warily on the enemy. At the hollow of Khor Shambat, left swampy by the rain, hooves sank several inches into the sand, yet insufficient water lay on the surface to refresh the horses. After crossing the khor the regiment halted two miles from the long line of Dervishes. The Egyptian cavalry crossed the khor at a point further west and halted at about the same distance from the enemy.

Now for the first time the lancers had a clear view of the Dervish force and could distinguish individual horsemen riding about in front of the line. A few of these advanced to inspect the British and Egyptian cavalry. One squadron of lancers dismounted and opened fire at 800 yards. Two horsemen fell to the ground, one wounded, one dead; others recovered the wounded man and made away at a steady pace.

A small village and a wooden fort lay on the river bank a little further south to their left. When de Montmorency was sent forward with his troop to inspect these, Hubert Howard (perhaps with the incident at the Kerreri hills in mind) borrowed a Lee-Enfield carbine and went with them. The village seemed deserted, but as de Montmorency rode forward alone to check the fort a small party of Dervishes appeared and fired at him. Although not hit, he was forced

Lieutenant Clerk (front centre) was photographed in Cairo with his signals party before marching. The equipment includes lamps, flags, heliograph mirrors and telescopes; most signals at Omdurman were sent by heliograph. The sergeant wears his crossed flags badge above his chevrons of rank on the right sleeve, the junior ranks on the left forearm. (The Queen's Royal Lancers)

to dismount and take cover and was in danger of being cut off from his troop. Howard and two men ran at the Dervishes, firing as they went, and drove them away. The troop returned to the regiment. Howard, already the only correspondent to find favour with the 21st, had in all probability saved the life of one of its most popular officers, and was now held in great esteem.

★   ★   ★

The 21st Lancers and the Egyptian cavalry held their positions two miles from the Dervish line as Kitchener's army rounded the Kerreri hills. Officers and men watched as the enemy force continued to grow; Pirie noted, "They were increasing in numbers very quickly & suddenly were forming up ... they appeared to be about 15,000 formed in 3 lines"[5].

At 10.50a.m. the regiment's attention was distracted to the river as the gunboats, having reached the northern outskirts of Omdurman, opened fire on the wooden forts and gun batteries protecting the city. The lancers watched the river as a cloud of black smoke followed by a loud report signalled each shot, at which they turned towards the city for the result. The aim of the gunboats was accurate and several forts were quickly demolished in clouds of debris, to much cheering from the 21st. Between each shell and the next the Maxim guns could be heard firing at Dervish infantry in the trenches alongside the river.

The merriment halted abruptly as every second or third lancer drew the next man's attention back to the three long lines of Dervishes, which had begun to move forward. As they did so a fourth line, just as long, appeared behind them. When this line had come fully into view a fifth line appeared, soon followed by a sixth – and thus the great Dervish army seemed to grow out of the very sand. Only now did those watching realise that the original line of Dervishes stood at the top of a sand ridge — the Omdurman ridge — with the Khalifa's entire army forming up below the line of sight.

As the Dervish troops advanced the hundreds of banners waving above their heads and the sun glinting on their spearpoints made a formidable sight. Hubert Howard, jotting down his first impression for *The Times*, saw "a great black line covering a front of two miles or more, advancing over the plain ... with many flags and horsemen galloping across their front"[6]. The enemy advance was slow, and for some time the four squadrons of lancers sat and watched in awe as Pirie's 15,000 doubled and tripled before their eyes. Captain Eadon saw "over 20,000 men"[7]; Lieutenant Smyth reported "their army about 30,000 strong drawn up in battle array"[8]; Major Finn wrote that "the whole hillside seemed to move ... we estimated their numbers at not less than 40,000"[9]; Lieutenant Churchill, not to be outdone, made it 56,000. All agreed, however, that this movement marked the beginning of the Dervish attack.

The signal station on Jebel Surgham was now operational and Colonel Martin sent an urgent heliograph message to Kitchener: "To Sirdar. Dervish army coming out of Omdurman in battle array, estimated 35,000 advancing NORTH. Col Martin"[10].

Taken literally, this would suggest that the Dervish army was coming out of the city itself to form up on the plain. On such evidence, later commentators argued that the Khalifa planned to keep his army inside the city walls and fight Kitchener's army in its streets, and that only the shelling by the gunboats forced him out. In fact the 21st Lancers had observed the first line of Dervishes on the plain and the movement out from Omdurman before the shelling began. In any case, at this point the gunboats were firing only on defensive positions along the river bank.

As the greater part of the Khalifa's army had encamped immediately outside the city, the first movement witnessed by the 21st was of men leaving camp to form up on the plain, while most remained out of sight below the sand ridge. This army then advanced up over the Omdurman ridge, so that at each moment more were visible to the Lancers than a moment before. Colonel Martin used "out of Omdurman" in this sense, for no army of such a size could leave the city confines "in battle array".

One might think that for the 21st Lancers the appearance of the Dervish mass from below a ridge apparently occupied by less than 1,000 men would have been a sobering lesson in the enemy's use of dead ground in apparently featureless terrain; the events of the next day suggest that it was a lesson ignored. The Khalifa had similarly failed to learn the lessons of the campaign so far. That the Dervish army was still coming out of camp and forming up while advance troops of the Anglo-Egyptian force were already on the Kerreri plain confirms Wingate's intelligence that the Khalifa intended to meet them at Kerreri but underestimated Kitchener's rate of advance. However, the Dervish army had been mobilised rapidly; and it now seemed to the 21st Lancers that if the enemy continued at its present rate of advance north, and the Sirdar continued south, the two must clash before nightfall.

The response to Colonel Martin's signal soon reached Lieutenant Clerk: "To Signal Station. I am falling troops in position and wish to be informed of every movement of enemy without delay. Sirdar"[11]. Kitchener's brigades took up a defensive position at the riverside village of Egeiga north of Jebel Surgham, forming a semicircle with their backs to the Nile, and the troops began the construction of a thorn-bush zariba.

Martin, deciding that Kitchener should receive an eye-witness account, sent for an officer whose horse was still fresh, and Major Finn selected Lieutenant Churchill. Martin told him to report to the Sirdar exactly what he had seen. As Churchill rode away the Dervish army moved steadily forward. The 21st, along with the Egyptian cavalry to the west, began to fall back, maintaining a distance of about one and a half miles from the enemy. The Dervish ranks were now variously estimated at between two and four miles from end to end, so that it seemed as if the whole near horizon was advancing menacingly on the four squadrons of lancers. The continuous shouting of religious exhortations, unintelligible to the British cavalry, sounded like one long war cry.

Seeing the lancers retreating, the Dervishes put out advance parties of five or six men each which came within a few hundred yards of the regiment. Dervish cavalrymen carried captured Remington rifles and presented a considerable threat if allowed to come within range. Colonel Martin put out patrols to the rear and both flanks to keep them at bay. Every so often a Dervish party ventured too close and a lancer patrol dismounted and opened fire, taking advantage of the relatively longer range of the Lee-Enfield carbine to kill or wound about six of the enemy in all.

While work on the zariba continued Kitchener rode up the eastern slopes of Jebel Surgham to see the enemy for himself, now only three miles away and still advancing. In his official despatch he claimed to have seen the Khalifa's black flag at the centre of the mass, and estimated the number of men at 35,000. This was in fact Colonel Martin's figure, and even as Kitchener returned to the zariba Lieutenant Churchill arrived with a verbal report and a much higher estimate.

Jaalin tribesmen ("friendlies") prepare for battle. The 21st witnessed this same excitement among the Dervish warriors coming out of Omdurman to form up on the plain. (National Army Museum)

The gunboat Melik, *which played a major role in the bombardment of Omdurman. (National Army Museum)*

Once the gunboats had destroyed the forts protecting Omdurman a battery of 5.5-inch howitzers was landed on the bank across from the city. These were equipped to fire Lyddite, a new high explosive adopted for the bursting charge of their 50-pound shells. Kitchener wanted them brought into action as soon as possible. Four days earlier he had sent a letter by messenger to the Khalifa warning him to remove all women and children from Omdurman, as he intended to bombard the city. Taking the Mahdi's Tomb as a range mark the howitzers now began to shell the walled city of Omdurman.

As the 21st Lancers fell steadily back in front of the advancing Dervish army they watched this spectacular demonstration of firepower beside the river. It was the first time any of those watching had seen Lyddite high explosive in use — the shells had never before been used in battle — and the sight was enough to distract their attention from the enemy. The almost pointed dome of the Tomb rising above Omdurman, a place holy to the Mahdists, made an irresistible target; its destruction in the sight of the enemy might fatally injure Dervish morale. A shell burst directly above the dome with a great flash and a white ball of smoke, then the dull thud of a distant explosion. Several more followed, some leaving holes in the dome, until the Tomb disappeared in a cloud of red dust. When this cleared the peak of the dome was gone, and a great cheer went up from the men of the 21st.

This scene may be argued to mark a turning point in the history of warfare: a regiment of lancers whose history ran back to the beginnings of light cavalry in England, watching the first high-explosive bombardment of a city. Yet while they marvelled at the firepower and accuracy of the howitzers, none doubted the crucial role yet to be played by the mounted soldier and the lance.

Watching from the plain, they were unable to see the casualties inflicted in the city. The Khalifa had failed to evacuate the whole population, either because he underestimated Kitchener's rate of advance or because he never intended doing so. The women and children were in the vast suburbs of mud huts outside the city walls, most at a safe distance except from stray shells. Those left inside were mainly older men unfit to join the fighting troops, and survivors of the 4,000 Dervishes who had manned the defensive forts, batteries and trenches. These suffered badly as the Lyddite shells rained down - shells that could blast a hole more than a foot deep in solid stone. Major Elmslie commanding 37th Field Battery saw one man running "as a shell happened to burst close to him, and he disappeared altogether; there was no body that I could see"[12].

Kitchener, aware that the Dervish army had formed up on the plain and was moving away from Omdurman, nevertheless allowed the bombardment to continue. For the sake of his fighting men he had to ensure that the Khalifa could not return to the city and fortify the Dervish army within its stone buildings; storming and street-fighting is a notoriously bloody affair. For his own sake, he had to avenge the death of Gordon and the humiliation of the British 14 years earlier. The Khalifa had left Khartoum in ruins and Gordon dead: Kitchener was determined to do as much to Omdurman and the Khalifa.

★   ★   ★

Again the lancers had their attention drawn abruptly to the enemy army, which halted at the long hollow of Khor Shambat in about the position the regiment had previously occupied. Dervish riflemen now fired into the air and a long cloud of white smoke rose above them. Many of the lancers supposed that this heralded the imminent outbreak of battle.

The regiment continued to fall back until it reached the ridge running out from Jebel Surgham, where two squadrons dismounted and fired on pursuing Dervish patrols. Lieutenant Clerk, still at his heliograph position on the summit and under orders to report all developments without delay, sent an urgent signal: "To Sirdar. Dervish army halted three miles S.W. and are firing in the air. Two Sqdns Lancers holding ridge 300 yards S.W. with dismounted fire and have shot several advanced scouts. Lieutenant Clerk (Signal Station)". The reply came quickly: "To Col. Martin. Please let the Sirdar know

MOVEMENTS of 1 SEPTEMBER 1898

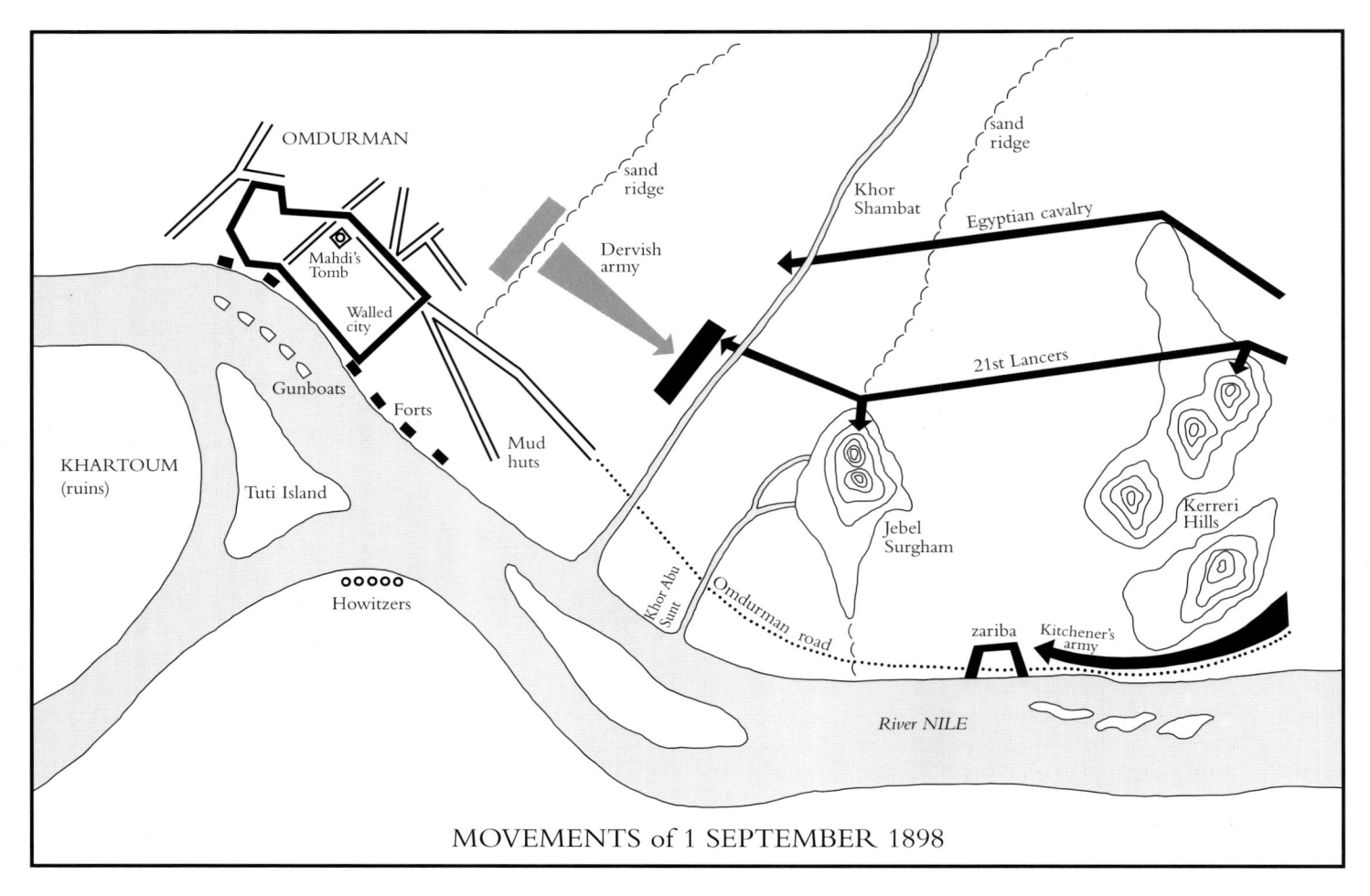

immediately they move"[13].

In fact the Dervishes began to make camp and lit many fires. Lieutenant Churchill returned from the zariba to find that the decisive battle was now unlikely to take place that day. Reaction among the lancers was divided between relief and disappointment. Lieutenant Pirie was happy to hold his position on the ridge: "We kept a dismounted party on the ridge on the hill as they were busy sending out small parties to stalk us but we managed to keep them well out & shot several of them"[14]. Captain Eadon seemed eager for a different outcome: "We made two demonstrations to try and make them advance but they did not"[15].

There was no cloud cover, the heat was by now intense, and the horses were beginning to suffer. One squadron at a time retired to the zariba to water the horses in the Nile; despite this, several died of dehydration during the afternoon. Skirmishes continued between patrols; three Dervishes were killed and eight or nine wounded, while Corporal Harris was wounded in the left knee and his horse killed. Throughout the long, hot afternoon lancers not engaged in skirmishes watched the enemy from the Surgham ridge in fascination. Begging the loan of field glasses and telescopes, they passed these from man to man.

The Mahdi had ordered his earliest followers to wear the *jibbah* (a loose white cotton tunic worn by the poor) to symbolise their commitment to a life of austerity and devotion. By 1898 this had become a stylised uniform, with coloured patches — mostly red, blue, black or tan — stitched on in imitation of the patches used to repair poor men's clothing, but now forming formalised patterns. The precise dress differed from tribe to tribe. Some wore the jibbah with white cotton trousers, others wore the trousers only; some wore turbans, others shaved their heads and wore skull caps. The tribes of eastern Sudan, particularly the Hadendoa, grew their hair long, and these caught the attention of watching lancers. The term "Fuzzy Wuzzies" (which the British applied indiscriminately to all Dervishes) derived from their frizzed and stiffened hair which stood out up to eight inches from the head.

The spearmen who formed the majority of the Khalifa's

The Mahdi's Tomb after the shelling of 1 September. The damage could be seen by the 21st Lancers watching from the Kerreri plain. (The National Army Museum)

warriors were armed with throwing spears, broad-bladed stabbing spears, double-edged slashing swords and knives. Some carried shields made from rhinoceros hide (which was said to stop a bullet more certainly than metal). Riflemen, and the cavalrymen with whom the lancers skirmished throughout the afternoon, were mostly armed with Remington "rolling-block" .44 cal. rifles captured from the Egyptian army; these were reliable single-shot breech-loaders.

By this time the gunboats on the river had moved to the southern end of Omdurman and joined the howitzers in shelling the city. The lancers, looking over the encamped Dervish army, could no longer see the centre of Omdurman because of the low cloud of red dust which had drifted up from the shell-torn buildings and now hung over the whole area. It was hoped that the sight would have a suitably depressing effect on the enemy.

Before the light failed Kitchener called the regiment in. Lieutenant Clerk, seeing an enemy patrol slip round the lancers' flank, flashed a final signal to the main army: "To Sirdar. Patrol of ten men from enemy's extreme right advancing straight on you. Lt Clerk (Signal Station)"[16]. At 5.30p.m. both the 21st Lancers and the Egyptian cavalry returned to the zariba by the river at Egeiga. The gunboats steamed northward away from Omdurman. The Dervish army of up to 55,000 men was encamped only four miles from the Anglo-Egyptian force of 25,800. Although the enemy had apparently bivouacked for the night the continuing activity of forward patrols suggested the possibility of a night attack.

The 21st Lancers had been in the saddle for 12 hours. As they rode through the British force concentrated in the zariba officers and men called out, asking whether the enemy was coming. When they dismounted men gathered round to hear what had been seen. A naval officer on one of the gunboats threw a bottle of champagne to the regiment; it dropped short and Lieutenant Churchill was first in the water to the rescue. This prize had to be consumed later by moonlight, as no lamps were allowed.

The gunboats were moored in line along the west bank, making their firepower available in the event of an attack. As it became fully dark the boats played their powerful searchlights over the plain, and this continued throughout the night. The men slept in their clothes and equipment and with their weapons by their side. Immediately outside the wall of thorn bushes double sentries were posted every 35 yards; further out, patrols moved continuously about the zariba. Kitchener had good reason to fear a night attack. If the enemy penetrated the zariba under cover of darkness and close-quarter fighting ensued, the firepower of his Maxim guns and artillery would become useless and the Khalifa's warriors — outnumbering the Anglo-Egyptian troops two to one — might prove unbeatable.

The few elderly villagers left in Egeiga, finding their mud huts engulfed by a foreign army, were understandably eager to co-operate. Several were sent out towards the Dervish camp to gather intelligence, having been given the impression that Kitchener himself intended a night attack. It was presumed that these men, once within the safety of the Dervish force, would swap allegiance and tell all they knew to the Khalifa, who would then hold his position. Lest this ruse failed reliable Sudanese scouts were sent out to give advance warning of an enemy advance. So that these men could be distinguished from Dervishes on their return it was agreed that they would come in only in pairs; after dark any man approaching alone, or any group of three or more, would be shot without challenge.

The 21st Lancers were bivouacked at the southern tip of the zariba between the river and the British infantry. While most of the men placed little trust in the Egyptian brigades and felt it to be the safest place, the three veterans of the 1884 expedition believed that if the Khalifa did attack during the night then this was the point at which he would break in. The wall of thorn bushes built by the British infantry offered defenders no protection against bullets and forced them to stand while firing. The Egyptian and Sudanese troops in the centre and northern sectors had dug a shallow trench behind a low ridge of sand, which gave protection against bullets and enabled them to fire kneeling or lying.

Kitchener views the Dervish army from the summit of Jebel Surgham. The signallers standing centre and right seem, from their helmet sunshades, to be men of the 21st Lancers signals party. (The Queen's Royal Lancers)

2 SEPTEMBER: FIRST DERVISH ATTACK

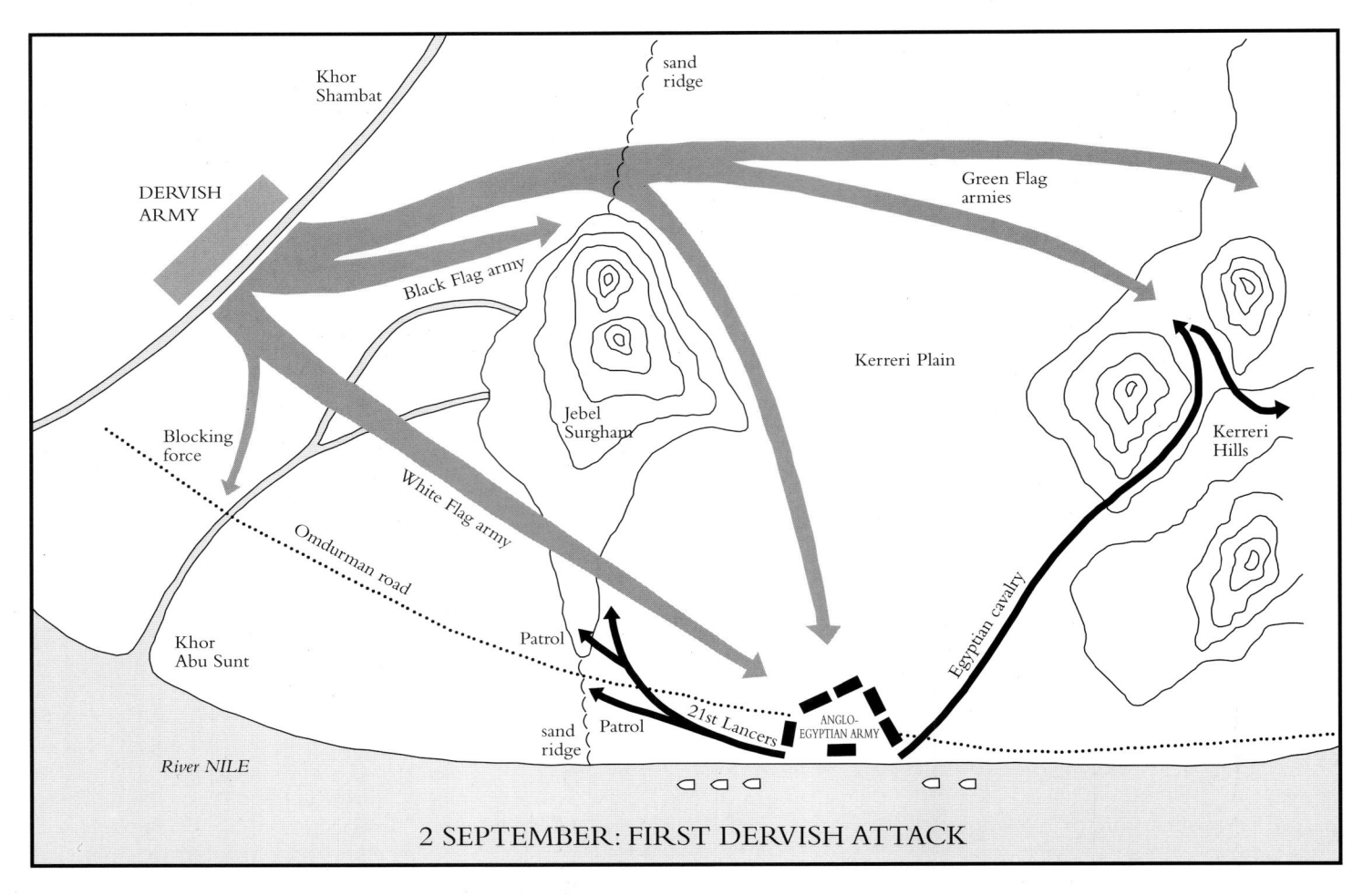

Orders were issued to the 21st that in the event of a Dervish attack breaking into the zariba every man was to lead his horse down to the river, then one man hold four horses while the rest of the regiment formed round them, the men armed only with lances, the officers with swords. Firearms were not to be used in close-quarter combat.

The alarm was sounded at 11.00p.m. when several shots were fired. The men turned out quickly and the gunboats' searchlights probed the darkness for the Dervish army, but there was nothing. Four of Kitchener's Sudanese scouts, surprised by an enemy patrol on the slopes of Jebel Surgham, had withdrawn in such haste that they approached the zariba together and were shot at, though they managed to make themselves known before being hit.

Some of the men took this as evidence that the enemy was preparing to attack, and refused to sleep. Others slept soundly, perhaps convinced by rumours that the Khalifa believed the British to be cowards and would not attack until daylight, when his warriors could see better to kill men running away than they could in the dark. The men of the 21st were weary and most slept well, despite having seen the enemy in full strength and knowing that a mighty battle was imminent.

Friday 2 September

It was still dark when trumpeters sounded stand-to-arms at 4.30a.m. Kitchener now thought that the Khalifa might attack at daybreak, and ordered the infantry and artillery to stand to. If the enemy did not come within sight by first light the cavalry was to go out and establish the position of Dervish forces. The 21st Lancers worked by the light of lanterns, checking horses and weapons. Those who could stomach it ate a breakfast of porridge, biscuits and bully beef. Corporal Wade Rix summed up the mens' feelings: " We stood by our horses, each man with his private thoughts, knowing that out there in the desert thousands of Dervishes fired with religious fervour were about to descend on us, their determined aim being literally to cut us to pieces"[17].

By 5.00a.m. the 21st and the Egyptian cavalry were mounted and waiting outside the zariba. At 5.20 it was light enough to move out, and they were ordered to reconnoitre the Kerreri plain to establish the Khalifa's position and assess his intentions. They made for the Surgham ridge from where the plain could be surveyed, the lancers heading

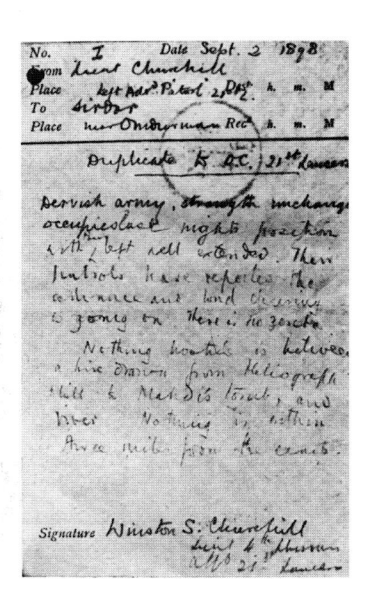

Message sent by Lieutenant Churchill to Kitchener on 2 September, with a copy to Colonel Martin: "Dervish army, strength unchanged, occupies last night's position with their left well extended. Their patrols have reported the advance and loud cheering is going on. There is no action. Nothing hostile is between a line drawn from heliograph hill to Mahdi's tomb and river. Nothing is within three miles from the camp." (Estate of Winston S. Churchill)

east of the hill, the Egyptians heading west. Colonel Martin sent Major Finn's A Squadron forward to scale the ridge between the hill and the river; meanwhile the rest of the regiment moved cautiously below the hill. It was believed from intelligence brought in by Sudanese scouts that the Dervishes had occupied the summit during the night; if so, the lancers would make easy targets as the light strengthened.

Finn approached the Surgham ridge with caution, lest his squadron come suddenly upon a Dervish army lying in wait below the level of sight. He sent out two patrols led by Lieutenants Smyth and Churchill; both officers left their patrols just below the top of the ridge and approached dismounted, each with one man to lead two horses in readiness for a rapid retreat. Topping the ridge, Churchill immediately saw the great Dervish army on the plain below, exactly where the regiment had left it on the previous day, one and a half miles to the south-west. He sent a rider back to Colonel Martin with the news. Smyth sent an almost identical message from his position further up the ridge, although he made the distance only 1,000 yards.

Minutes later, at 5.45a.m., these two officers reported the Dervish army to be moving directly towards their positions, although Arab sources insist that the advance began at 5.20 (just as the lancers left the zariba). Perhaps it was only as the light increased that Churchill and Smyth realised the Dervishes were not stationary, though Smyth's 1,000-yard estimate suggests as much. This news was relayed to Colonel Martin, who dictated an urgent signal for the Sirdar informing him that the enemy were on the move. The light was still inadequate for the heliograph and Major Crole-Wyndham was sent to report personally. (The sky remained overcast throughout the day; although some heliograph signals were successful, many reports and orders had to be sent by hand of messenger). The Egyptian cavalry to the west had also seen this advance and informed Kitchener. Rivalry between the 21st and the Egyptians was such that both later made passionate claims to have been the first to locate the enemy.

Churchill watched almost spellbound as the Dervish troops came on: "They are advancing fast, cheering for God, his Prophet and his Holy Khalifa ... they think they are going to win"[18]. Their religious invocations, shouted out en masse, sounded like one long war cry to the regiment hidden below Jebel Surgham, who had yet to catch a glimpse of the enemy. Dervish commanders put out advance cavalry patrols and some of these came within range of Smyth and Churchill, concealed below the ridge. A correspondent approaching Smyth's position remained mounted and was spotted by an enemy patrol. Smyth noted: "Bullets whistling & splashing on rocks very close. Col hearing this sends for me to retire at once ... much excited & annoyed & saying I was unnecessarily exposing myself. It was the correspondent's fault ..."[19].

As the Dervish force drew closer it could be seen to comprise three main armies or divisions — the latter term is used here for clarity, though not in its formal European sense — each subdivided into tribal groups. At its centre was the black flag of the Khalifa, with his brother Yaqub and a force of about 13,000 men. To the desert side the green flags of Sheikh el Din, the Khalifa's son, and Abi Wad Helu fluttered above the largest division with 22,000 men. To the river side white flags identified Osman Digna and Osman Azrak with 6,000 men. The whole army was thus 41,000 strong. The numbers have always been disputed; those given here are from the Arab historian Zulfo. Wingate's spies variously reported an army of 40,000 to 55,000. Perhaps understandably, estimates made by British spectators were generally higher, with totals of between 52,000 and 66,000. To the lancers watching from little more than half a mile away the precise figures were at this point academic.

The Khalifa rode on a donkey at the centre of his army. He had inspected them before first light and had told his commanders that both Mohammed and the Mahdi had appeared to him in a vision during the night, to foretell a great victory and promise immediate entry into paradise for all who died in battle with the infidel. Now advancing across the Kerreri plain, the victorious battlefield promised in legend, he must have felt certain of victory. He knew something of the superior firepower of Kitchener's army, but counted that as nothing against faith, vision and prophecy.

Major Crole-Wyndham returned from delivering his report to the Sirdar. Colonel Martin, aware that the Jebel Surgham would soon be taken by the advancing Dervish army, now sent him to recall Major Finn's A Squadron before the 21st retired to the protection of the zariba. Finn reported that Lieutenant Churchill's patrol had failed to

The view from inside the zariba, where the infantry - here, from their hackle-shaped helmet flashes, the 1st Grenadier Guards - peer out over the thorn bushes for a first sight of the advancing Dervish army. (National Army Museum)

return and its exact location was unknown. Martin was furious to learn that Churchill was still on the Surgham ridge, as the Dervishes were coming on fast and the regiment's retreat could be delayed no longer. He sent Corporal Rix out to locate him with this message: "With the Colonel's compliments, you are to return to the zariba immediately"[20].

Churchill had moved his position as the Dervish army came on, in order to see while not being seen. He watched as the mass of men neared the hill, dividing as it marched — the black flag division headed straight for Jebel Surgham as if to pass right over the summit, the green flags moved to the west to round the hill on the desert side, the white flags to the east. This third division was likely to pass within yards of Churchill's position, but still he remained.

By now Dervish advance patrols had reached the slopes of Surgham and spotted the lancers. The regiment continued to retire at a steady pace under sporadic fire (though from too great a range to trouble them unduly). Hubert Howard was still with them, and the final entry in his diary — he would be killed a few hours later in Omdurman — records their retreat: "21st behave steadily under fire, retiring slowly in squadrons. Under fire no uneasiness apparent"[21].

As the regiment neared the zariba the following Dervish patrols fell back towards their infantry, and the regiment galloped in through the gap left for their return. The Egyptian cavalry had returned a little earlier and had been sent to occupy the Kerreri hills to the north. It was just before 6.30a.m. and the Dervish infantry was only 3,000 yards behind the lancers; the attack was imminent.

Back on the Surgham ridge, Corporal Rix found Churchill still entranced by the spectacle of the mass of Dervishes, and repeated Colonel Martin's message. Churchill dictated his reply without turning his eyes from the enemy now only a few hundred yards away and coming on fast: "My compliments to the Colonel, tell him that I am watching the enemy's front and will return to the zariba shortly". Rix turned his horse and sped away at the gallop: "On returning to the regiment I delivered Mr Churchill's reply, the Colonel gave a brief nod of the head and paced up and down giving sharp flicks with his stick at the ground as though warding off a pack of dogs. There was no doubt that he was extremely angry"[22].

★   ★   ★

The green flag division was already rounding Jebel Surgham to the west and turning to make a frontal attack. The white flag force was swarming over the lower slopes to the east to attack the zariba's left flank. At 6.40a.m. the shouts of the advancing Dervishes could be heard by the waiting Anglo-Egyptian troops, and a few minutes later their flags appeared over the Surgham.

The Dervishes could now see Kitchener's army and riflemen fired into the air while all chanted invocations to God and his Prophet. They in turn could be seen by the 32nd Field Battery, which opened fire at 6.45 at a range of 2,800 yards. Within minutes the whole artillery and several

An English infantry battalion prepare to meet the Dervishes with volley fire and fixed bayonets. The absence of taped-on neck protectors is unusual among photographs of Omdurman. Rectangular helmet flashes were worn by the 1st Royal Warwicks (red) and 2nd Lancashire Fusiliers (yellow). (The Queen's Royal Lancers)

of the gunboats were in action. The first shells went high and warriors yelled in derision, but the gunners soon got the range and shells rained down on the Dervish army. Shrapnel cut many men to pieces; others disappeared altogether in the bursts of Lyddite.

Churchill, mounted and ready to retire if spotted, still watched from the Surgham ridge, and although he does not say so he was a little too close to the falling shells for his own good: "Some burst in the air, others in their faces, others in the sand and dashed clouds of red dust and splinters amid their ranks. The white flags toppled over ... yet they rose up again, as other men pressed forward to die for Allah's sacred cause ... It was a terrible sight, for as yet they had not hurt us at all, and it seemed an unfair advantage"[23].

His line of retreat would soon be cut, and a second message was sent ordering him back into the zariba at once as the infantry were about to open fire. He rejoined the regiment only minutes before the first volley was fired on the Dervishes swarming over the eastern slopes of Surgham. Their ceaseless chant as they came on — *La llaha illa wa Mohammed rasul ullah!* ("There is but one God and Mohammed is the Messenger of God") — was soon lost in the rapid rattle of the Royal Irish Fusiliers' Maxim guns.

The 21st Lancers waited at the southern tip of the zariba, and from there Captain Eadon watched the attack: "I can only say the attack of the Dervish army was too magnificent for words — reckless in its bravery and devoid of all tactics. To hear the hum and cries and beating of drums of 30,000 men, who could be seen slowly advancing, was as magnificent a spectacle as could be imagined ... I could see the shells dropping into their dense masses and killing heaps at a shot, but they still advanced, till they came under the infantry and Maxim fire, which stopped them"[24]. Eadon overestimated the number — the first attack involved about 15,000 men, although there undoubtedly seemed twice as many to those in their path.

The first volleys were fired by the British regiments, armed with the longer-ranged .303-inch Lee-Metford magazine rifle; Kitchener personally ordered Private Parragreen of the 1st Bn., Grenadier Guards to fire a ranging shot at 2,000 yards, and then the regular section volleys began. It was no longer necessary to wait until "the whites of their eyes" could be seen; "the whites of their jibbahs" would do. Egyptian troops equipped with the older Martini-Henry joined in as the range decreased, until a total of 10,000 rifles were firing.

The British infantry stood in two ranks behind the zariba, firing and reloading as quickly as possible. Normal practice was to fire and reload the bolt-action rifles with single cartridges, leaving the eight or ten rounds in the magazine for short-range emergencies, closed off with a swivelling cover. Even so, old sweats like the Grenadiers, the Royal Warwicks, the Northumberland Fusiliers or the Cameron Highlanders - to say nothing of the proud specialists of the Rifle Brigade - could fire 12 rounds a minute. Some rifles became too hot to hold and had to be exchanged for others from the reserve. Apart from one Egyptian brigade on the far right, the whole army was now hotly engaged. Lieutenant Pirie was astounded that the Dervishes continued to move forward: "They made most beautiful practice but came on with wonderful pluck, they came right up within 800 yards & caused some loss to the infantry"[25].

They came on still, running and leaping over the bodies of the dead and wounded, never allowing a flag to lie on the ground longer than it took the next man to raise it, impelled by the belief that they were racing into paradise. Those advancing on the Lee-Metfords were stopped at between 600 and 800 yards; those running towards the Martini-Henrys got as close as 300 yards; few men got nearer, except the occasional mounted, mail-clad emir, his men lost, making a courageous but hopeless last charge. Not a single Dervish penetrated the zariba.

Despite this easy victory there was some confusion about the Khalifa's intentions. The white flag division and a part of the green flag force had turned to attack and had been stopped, but the remainder of the green flag warriors – almost as many again as the total involved in this first attack – had continued straight on towards the Kerreri hills. This led some to conclude that the Khalifa was unsure where the Sirdar's army was and, seeing infantry within the zariba and the Egyptian cavalry on the hills, had divided his army to attack each with equal strength.

However, it is unlikely that Dervish scouts would have lost a stationary army of 26,000 men within six miles of Omdurman. Crucially, the Khalifa's black flag division held its position below Jebel Surgham, hidden from the Sirdar. The disposition and line of advance of the green and white flag forces suggest that he anticipated that the first attack would be turned back with heavy loss — sacrificed for the greater victory — and expected that the whole Anglo-Egyptian army would then come out onto the plain in pursuit. Once in the open, the infidels would be attacked by the green flags on their right flank, coming down from the Kerreri hills, and by the black flags on their left flank, appearing from behind Jebel Surgham. There on the Kerreri plain, as the prophecy foretold, victory would be his.

By 7.15 the attack had come to a standstill and the Dervish spearmen began falling back. Riflemen armed with Remingtons took cover behind sand mounds and opened fire on the zariba, and although most were firing from too great a range some found their mark. The artillery and Maxim guns were brought to bear on their various positions, and it took another 30 minutes to clear the enemy from the field.

The first Dervish attack had been repulsed with less than 60 British and Egyptian casualties. Immediate Dervish losses were estimated at 2,000 dead and 4,000 wounded; few of the seriously wounded would survive. Yet while the troops inside the zariba congratulated each other on the victory, Kitchener knew better. At most, only half of the Khalifa's total force had been committed to this first attack, and all but 6,000 of these had retired and might regroup. The battle was far from won, and the retreating Dervishes sorely tempted Kitchener to move his army out onto the Kerreri plain in pursuit.

COLOUR PLATES A – D

A1: Dervish warrior of Hadendoa tribe
The 800 Dervishes blocking the road to Omdurman, first spotted by a patrol of the 21st Lancers, were of the Hadendoa tribe. The Hadendoa wore their hair long, frizzed and stiffened to stand out up to eight inches from the head - the style which gave rise to the British soldier's entirely respectful nickname "Fuzzy-Wuzzies". Unlike most tribesmen the Hadendoa did not wear the jibbah, preferring a white cotton cloth wound around the waist and slung over the left shoulder, then tied above waist level; however, coloured patches were often sewn onto these, jibbah-style. The waist cloth was worn alone, or with a sleeveless vest of white or striped cotton. While the Hadendoa were equipped with the traditional weapons of broadsword, spears and knives, a number were armed with Remington rolling-block rifles - single-shot breech-loaders captured from the Egyptians - and these men wore leather bandoliers around the waist above the cloth.

A2: Dervish warrior of Baggara tribe
Before the regiment arrived at the Omdurman road and the charge was ordered the 800 Hadendoa had been reinforced by some 2,000 warriors of the Baggara tribe. These wore the traditional jibbah, a loose-fitting tunic of off-white cotton, originally worn by the poor but adopted by the Mahdists to symbolise their commitment to a life of austerity. By 1898 the jibbah had become a stylised uniform with aesthetic patterns of coloured patches - mostly red, blue, black and tan - stitched on to simulate those originally added to repair wear and damage. Beneath the jibbah many warriors wore loose cotton trousers falling to just above the ankles. The white turban was wrapped so that its folds formed an inverted V to the front, with one end hanging loose. The Baggara spurned rifles in favour of traditional weapons, which included a straight double-edged sword carried in a red leather scabbard slung over the shoulder, a broad-bladed stabbing spear, throwing spears, and short curved knives. A few carried shields, mostly of rhinoceros hide but occasionally of metal.

B1: Officer in Hussar full dress
The 21st Hussars became the 21st Lancers in 1896 while in Egypt, but continued to dress as hussars until after the Sudan campaign in 1898. As can be seen from this figure, representing Lieutenant-Colonel Martin, the dark blue hussar tunic had remained essentially unchanged since the British cavalry copied the Austro-Hungarian hussar style during the Napoleonic Wars, even down to detailed embellishments such as the Austrian knot of plaited gold cord on the cuffs. The hussar fur cap (black sable for officers) was known as a "Busby" after the London hatter who originally supplied them. It was open at both ends, a cloth bag being attached to the inside and drawn up through the top to cover the head and fall at one side. Originally the colour of the busby plume denoted the regiment, but by 1898 this was indicated by the colour of the busby bag — French grey for the 21st.

The mount's throat ornament of horsehair was of regimental colour for all hussar regiments except the 14th and 21st, for whom it was white. The shabraque, leather-lined and completely covering the saddle, was of leopardskin for senior officers.

B2: Lieutenant in Hussar undress
This figure, representing Lieutenant de Montmorency, wears the pillbox hat with a wide lace band for officers, and epaulettes of ringmail ("shoulder chains") adopted from the Indian cavalry and bearing rank insignia. When mounted and wearing the busby his gold cap lines would be attached to the rear of the cap so that it could not be lost while on the move. The shoulderbelt, of gold lace with a central French grey stripe, supported a silver pouch at his back, originally for ammunition but now largely decorative, although often used for carrying letters. The sabretache, suspended by slings from the sword waistbelt, was also a stylised evolution of what was once a practical pouch; by the late 19th century it had become flat and stiffened, laced all round and embellished with regimental devices. Previously of scarlet, the 21st sabretache was by now French grey.

C1: Corporal Farrier in Hussar undress
NCOs and men wore the undress order depicted here during the 1890s in India, and this continued after the move to Egypt and into 1898, although some wore the same jacket with dark blue overalls and a white foreign service helmet. The jacket was blue serge with a five-button fastening, two unpleated breast pockets and shoulder chains. The yellow cap lines are plaited and looped up to the right shoulder, the free end fastened to the second tunic button. The white drill overalls were fastened by a strap and buckle under the instep of the boot. The pillbox hat had yellow worsted bands. The corporal's rank insignia to the right arm has an inverted horseshoe above denoting a farrier. The black half-Wellington boots have fixed swan-neck steel spurs.

C2: Private in Hussar full dress
Based on a photograph of the regiment's first parade as lancers in Cairo, this figure shows the uniform worn by NCOs and men in 1897/98. The jacket is of blue serge, with six acorn-and-loop fastenings, plaited yellow shoulder cords and the Austrian knot to the cuffs. Additional yellow cord decorates the front and rear, and the collar and skirt of the jacket. The pantaloons are of blue serge with a double yellow stripe. The busby has been replaced by a white foreign service helmet as first worn in India, with pugaree (bands of cloth, originally a turban wrapped round to reduce the heat of the sun), a brass chin chain, and a removable brass spike. Despite the hussar style of the uniform the lance was now issued. It was nine feet long, of male bamboo, with a red-over-white pennon (the colours of the Polish flag; both France and Britain copied the original Polish lancers).

D1: Officer in service dress
The Sudan campaign of 1898 was the first "all-khaki" campaign outside India; khaki drill had been worn in India since 1885 but was not approved for service elsewhere until 1896. This officer, representing Captain Kenna, wears a Wolseley helmet (without the sunshade adopted for the men) and a khaki frock with five-button fastening, four pockets, a white hunting stock beneath the collar, and shoulder chains with rank insignia. The cord breeches were reinforced on the inside leg with soft leather. Laced brown leather boots were worn with Stohwasser gaiters and detachable steel spurs. Officers wore the Sam Browne belt with a leather holster and ammunition pouch for the regulation issue Webley revolver. The officer's 1887 pattern heavy cavalry sabre, with a leather-covered scabbard and metal shoe, was attached to the near side of the saddle by a frog sewn onto the horseshoe case. Officers did not carry the lance — except for Captain Kenna, possibly the only cavalry officer to have charged with this weapon. Photographs of several officers show what seems to be some kind of water bag slung behind the right leg.

D2: Corporal Trumpeter in service dress
NCOs and men wore the same khaki drill frock with two breast pockets as the infantry, but with the addition of shoulder chains. Bedford cord breeches were worn with boots and khaki puttees, with detachable steel spurs. The cork foreign service helmet was now given a khaki cover, but unlike the infantry, who wore a neck protector hung from the rear of the helmet, the 21st Lancers wore a wide, quilted sunshade fitted around its whole perimeter - a device unique to the regiment. The trumpeter shown here is distinguished by gold chevrons of rank on a red backing with crossed trumpets above. The trumpet was used for dismounted calls; when mounted a bugle was used. He is armed with the Webley revolver.

PLATE A

A1: Hadendoa rifleman

A2: Baggara warrior

PLATE B

B1: Lieutenant-Colonel, Hussar full dress

B2: Lieutenant, Hussar undress

PLATE C

C1: Corporal Farrier, Hussar undress

C2: Private, Hussar full dress

PLATE D

D1: Captain, service dress

D2: Corporal Trumpeter, service dress

68

PLATE E

E1: Lieutenant, service dress

E2: Signaller, service dress

69

PLATE F

F1: Private, service dress

F2: Squadron Sergeant Major (Rough Rider), service dress

PLATE G

G1: Officer, Lancer full dress

G2: Private, Lancer full dress

71

PLATE H

H1: Sergeant Rough Rider, Lancer undress

H2: Lieutenant-Colonel, Lancer undress

72

COLOUR PLATES E – H

E1: Lieutenant in service dress
This figure represents Lieutenant Winston Churchill, attached to A Squadron of the 21st from the 4th Hussars. While most officers wore a Sam Browne belt with double braces, Churchill and some others preferred a single brace over the right shoulder. Several officers also replaced the regulation Webley revolver with the latest Mauser semi-automatic pistol, and Churchill purchased his in London before leaving to join the regiment in Cairo. This 7.63mm Mauser C96 took ten cartridges, and was carried in a wooden holster-stock which could be slotted on to the grip of the pistol so that it could be fired from the shoulder like a carbine. During the charge officers such as Churchill and Crole-Wyndham used it conventionally, however; its "broomhandle" butt gave an awkward grip, but the ability to fire ten rounds rapid was invaluable in hand-to-hand fighting. The saddle is the universal pattern steel arch type, with regulation bridle, and strands of plaited string sewn to the brow strap to keep flies away from the horse's eyes. A pair of leather wallets and a binocular case are suspended from the saddle. The mounts of the 21st Lancers in the Sudan were mostly Syrian Arab ponies. These appeared small and frail in comparison with the larger Indian troop horses, but were in fact extremely tough, and could survive up to 24 hours in the desert without water.

E2: Private Signaller in service dress
While all Other Ranks were armed with the 1896 Lee-Enfield bolt-action magazine carbine, this was of most importance to the signaller. Working at a distance from the regiment, dismounted and often exposed on high ground, he was vulnerable to attack by enemy patrols; the long-range carbine and his command of the ground were his only defence. The Lee-Enfield was 40 inches long and weighed 7^1/2 lbs; it fired the standard .303 round — with a considerable kick — and magazine capacity was six rounds. The signaller shown here wears the 50-round leather bandolier which replaced the hussar pouch belt. Signallers were equipped with square flags (used for Morse code and Semaphore), and a telescope on double tripods for reading distant signals. The most effective means of transmitting signals over a long distance, however, was by heliograph, its variable-angle mirror reflecting flashes of sunlight. The 21st Lancers signals party proved particularly proficient, having trained in the Indian hills, and so impressed Kitchener that on one occasion he spent some time speaking with them and asking questions about the equipment. Most signals in the Sudan were sent by heliograph.

F1: Private in service dress
This figure represents Private Byrne in khaki dress, mounted with full campaign kit. Two red inverted chevrons to the lower left arm of the khaki frock are good conduct stripes. Twin leather wallets hang over the pommel, one to each side, with spare boots strapped over the wallets. A feed bag and canvas water bucket hang from the saddle on the near side (left), and a haynet from each side of the girth. He carries the 1890 pattern sabre with steel scabbard covered with khaki cloth, attached to the near side of the saddle by a frog sewn onto the horseshoe case. The nine-foot bamboo lance, with a steel spear point and shoe, is carried (on active service) with the pennon furled, although some photographs of the 21st at this time show them with no pennon attached. The shoe or ferrule of the lance sat in a leather lance bucket — one attached to each stirrup leather and iron, so that the lance could be carried on either side. The carbine was carried in a leather boot on the offside (right) of the saddle, with a picketing post and rope attached to the boot.

F2: Squadron Sergeant-Major (Rough Rider) in service dress
This sergeant-major wears the khaki drill frock with badges of rank to the right arm: sergeant's chevrons of gold lace on a red backing, with a crown to denote sergeant-major and a spur to denote Rough Rider. He carries the 1890 pattern cavalry sabre. Previous cavalry swords had been found to bend and break, and this pattern was made stronger (and therefore heavier); some of the men, many of whom were of small stature, complained that it was too heavy to wield with comfort, but on 2 September 1898 it still broke under blows from Dervish broadswords or against ringmail armour. Sergeants were armed with the Webley revolver and therefore wore a Sam Browne belt; the pattern shown here, with double braces, differs only slightly from the one-armed General Browne's original design of 1860. A haversack and water bottle were worn over the right shoulder; the men (but not sergeants) wore the carbine bandolier over the left shoulder.

G1: Officer in Lancer full dress
Although the 21st became Lancers in 1896, the lancer uniform was not adopted until after the charge at Omdurman in 1898. The dark blue tunic was originally intended to have a scarlet plastron front, but by then Victoria had authorised French grey facings, thus preserving the link with the regiment's Indian origins. The officer shown here has a French grey plastron front, collar and cuffs, the latter embellished with gold lace, with French grey piping from below the plastron, running down the front edge and around the skirt of the tunic. The shoulder cords of twisted gold bear his rank insignia. Gold plaited cap lines were worn across the right shoulder, the double acorn ends secured above the left breast, the loop end secured to the cap. The pouch belt was of gold lace with a French grey centre stripe. The czapska (lance cap — the word is Polish for 'hat') is of black leather with a French grey top and a plume of white swan feathers, decoration in gold cord and lace, and a silver cap plate. The sabretache of black leather bears a gilt regimental device of the VRI monogram and crossed lances. Officers now adopted a black sheepskin saddle cloth edged in French grey.

G2: Private in Lancer full dress
NCOs and men wore the same style of blue jacket as officers, with French grey plastron front and piping, but without the gold lace embellishments. The standard cavalry girdle was of yellow and crimson. Dark blue overalls with a double yellow stripe were worn when dismounted, fastening beneath the boot with a leather strap and buckle; when mounted, pantaloons were worn. The black Wellington boots had fixed steel swan-neck spurs. The czapska was as worn by officers, but with yellow cord decoration and a plume of white horse hair. A white leather pouch belt was worn with a black leather pouch to the back. It appears odd that a black pouch was used with a white belt — the original cartouche box had been black so as not to show greasy finger marks from the lubricant on paper cartridges, and this custom was continued. He carries the 1890 pattern cavalry sword.

H1: Sergeant Rough Rider in Lancer undress
The blue serge frock with V-shaped breast pockets flaps is worn here with chevrons of rank, and the spur badge denoting Rough Rider, to the right sleeve; and the two Omdurman campaign medal ribbons (Queen's Sudan Medal and Khedive's Sudan Medal) to the left breast. He wears a field service cap of regimental pattern; dark blue strapped overalls with double yellow stripes, and Wellington boots with fixed spurs. He carries his riding crop under one arm.

H2: Officer in Lancer undress
This figure represents Lieutenant-Colonel Crole-Wyndham, who took command of the regiment on its return from the Sudan. He wears a dark blue patrol frock with five rows of wide mohair braid across the chest with pointed ends and olivettes, sewn to allow the free ends to fall either side of the concealed hook-and-eye fastening. The collar and cuffs are embellished with mohair braid, which also runs along the jacket edges and trims the two side pockets. With the frock he wears the pillbox hat with officer's ornament to the top, overalls fastened beneath the instep of the boot, and half-Wellington boots with fixed swan-neck spurs. White gloves were often worn with this order of dress. In place of a swagger stick Crole-Wyndham favoured a walking cane.

CHAPTER SIX

The Charge at Omdurman

Once the first Dervish attack had been repulsed, Kitchener had two options — to hold his army inside the zariba and await a second attack from those forces not yet engaged, or to take the offensive and move south across the Kerreri plain to occupy Omdurman. It seemed unlikely that the Khalifa would send a second army to perish in front of the zariba; more likely, he would now regroup his scattered forces and retire to make a stand in the shell-battered capital, where street fighting might still inflict heavy casualties on the Anglo-Egyptian force. Kitchener was determined to occupy Omdurman before the Khalifa could do so, but before ordering the infantry out of the zariba he needed to be certain the enemy had not already blocked his route of march to the city. Therefore at 7.30a.m. he sent out the 21st Lancers on a second reconnaissance.

Immediately General Gatacre was seen galloping along the line to Colonel Martin, waiting by the river with the 21st at the southern tip of the zariba, a buzz of excitement passed through the regiment. Such was this anticipation that even as the two men spoke officers were already ordering their men to mount and make ready. The Sirdar's orders were delivered verbally by Gatacre: the regiment was to return to the Surgham ridge on the river side of the hill (the position lately vacated by Lieutenant Churchill), to observe Dervish dispositions on the plain and the direction of retreat of those turned back from the zariba. If the lancers reported a clear route of march from the zariba to the city, the infantry would follow. At this point the regiment received no order to proceed further south than Jebel Surgham; Kitchener's instructions specified reconnaissance, not engagement.

As the artillery had yet to clear the final Dervish riflemen sniping from within range of the zariba, Colonel Martin led the regiment south along the bank of the Nile before turning west towards the sand ridge and the lower slopes of Jebel Surgham. It was, nevertheless, a most dangerous route. The killing ground was littered with the dead and dying, both men and horses, and every sand mound might conceal one or more of the less badly wounded, poised to strike a final, desperate blow. Several lay as if dead until the lancers passed by, then rose to hurl spears at their backs; no injury to men of the 21st was recorded, though several Dervishes had to be shot.

As they mounted the Surgham ridge the plain opened up before them and they saw a long column of wounded Dervishes heading back towards the city. While these presented no threat to Kitchener's advance, among them were parties of armed men who seemed not yet to have been involved in the battle. "Thousands were retreating in confusion towards Omdurman. Stragglers opened fire, and one gentleman dropped a bullet at the feet of the B Squadron commander [Major Fowle]"[1]. The 21st was in an exposed position on the ridge; perhaps alerted by these first shots, Dervish snipers lodged high on Jebel Surgham now opened fired too. Although both groups were at too

The view south towards the Jebel Surgham as the 21st Lancers left the zariba at 7.30a.m. on 2 September. Dead Dervishes littered the plain, and some of the walking wounded were still determined enough to present a threat. (National Army Museum)

Thought to be the only photograph of the 21st Lancers to have been taken on 2 September, showing one squadron dismounted below the southern slopes of Jebel Surgham. If so, it must have been taken at approximately 8.20a.m. while the regiment awaited further orders from the Sirdar. (National Army Museum)

great a range for serious effect, Colonel Martin led the regiment within the shelter of the hill and dismounted the men. The bodies of fresh troops among the wounded presented a clear threat to the Anglo-Egyptian advance, and he dictated an urgent message informing Kitchener. The signals officer, Lieutenant Clerk, took a considerable risk to climb higher up the Surgham towards enemy positions to send a heliograph signal.

In the zariba, Captain Egerton received the message from a signaller and carried it immediately to Kitchener. The Sirdar was at that moment studying the Kerreri hills, where Broadwood with the Egyptian cavalry, the Camel Corps and the horse artillery had moved out of sight to the north pursued by a Dervish division apparently as large as that which attacked the zariba. The gunboat *Melik* had been sent downstream to give assistance, but if the Dervishes trapped the cavalry in the hills a major upset seemed likely.

Kitchener stood for some time before replying to Martin's signal. The battlefield situation was far from clear. At first it had been thought that the Khalifa had divided his great army into two, sending one against the zariba and another after Broadwood's cavalry (supposing this to be the tail end of a much greater force). Taking the lowest estimate of the Khalifa's total force to be 40,000 men, this meant that each of his two divisions had to comprise at least 20,000 and probably many more — yet these were now put at about 15,000 each. The figures did not add up, and raised the possibility of a third division yet to be engaged. As the two forces already encountered had advanced from the eastern and western sides of Jebel Surgham respectively, it was likely any such third force would be held in reserve behind the hill. The Khalifa and his black flag, clearly visible at the centre of the army on the previous day, had yet to be spotted, and might well be with this hidden reserve.

While tempted to move his brigades out in pursuit of the defeated first army, Kitchener realised that once on the Kerreri plain they would be exposed to attack by any third force. Now Colonel Martin's signal, reporting *fresh* Dervish troops retiring towards Omdurman, suggested that this hidden reserve too was withdrawing south to occupy the city. It seemed to Kitchener that if he did not move south to the capital the Khalifa might beat him to it.

★   ★   ★

Kitchener moved his army out of the zariba to march on Omdurman. The 21st Lancers was ordered to proceed further south and if possible to clear the enemy from the route of march: "All attacks on our position having failed, and the enemy having retired out of range, I sent out the 21st Lancers to clear the ground on our left front and head off any retreating Dervishes from the direction of Omdurman"[2].

The order, timed at precisely 8.30a.m., reached the 21st on the Surgham ridge just minutes later: "To Colonel Martin. Annoy them as far as possible on their flank and head them off if possible from Omdurman. Sirdar"[3]. Martin correctly understood this to mean that he was to ignore the great number of wounded flowing towards the city but to head off any parties of unbeaten troops likely to interfere with the infantry advance. The order clearly changed the regiment's primary task from reconnaissance to engagement.

While leading the regiment south at a walk towards the enemy, Martin sent out two advance patrols under Lieutenants Pirie and Grenfell. Grenfell's patrol followed the foot of the Jebel Surgham along the south-west slopes of the hill, and soon came under heavy fire from the summit. Lieutenant de Montmorency (but no other officer) wrote

2 SEPTEMBER: approx. 9.40am

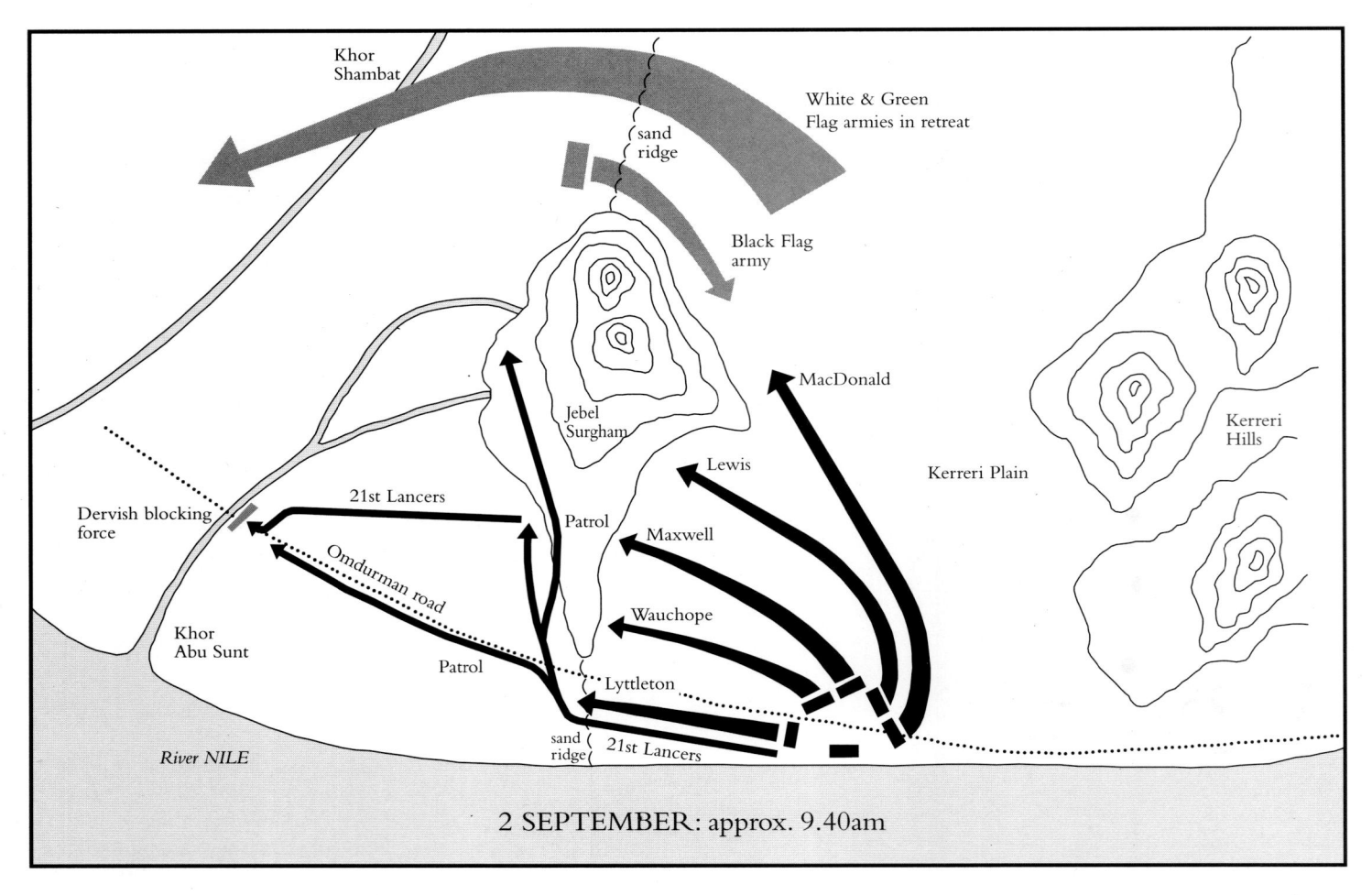

that the Sirdar's original 7.30a.m. order, delivered verbally by Gatacre, required a reconnaissance south-west of the hill to ascertain whether the Khalifa's reserve force was located there; if so, then Martin sent Grenfell's patrol in that direction with this aim. Certainly Grenfell was rounding the slopes that would eventually present a view of the hidden third division, and perhaps for this reason the fire from above became so intense that he was forced to turn back before seeing it.

Pirie's patrol headed south towards the Omdurman road, the route most of the wounded were taking and where parties of unbeaten troops had been spotted, to test the strength of opposition. Moving alongside and parallel with the wounded at a distance of only 100 yards, the patrol were occasionally fired on, though without effect. After almost a mile Pirie became aware of a line of Dervishes (he estimated 1,000) apparently holding their position on open ground and prepared to block the patrol's advance. Trumpeter Steele — at 17 the youngest member of the patrol, and of the regiment — thought there were 700. These were fresh troops; Pirie, guessing that they had been left there to secure the Omdurman road, turned back to report to the regiment. He had every expectation that his colonel, abandoning the caution which had irritated Kitchener two days earlier, would bring the 21st into action against them.

Arab historians confirm that these men of the Hadendoa tribe, in fact numbering 800, had been stationed there to protect the Khalifa's line of retreat back into Omdurman. They had 40 horses and 31 rifles; the rest were spearmen and swordsmen on foot. They held the Omdurman road at a point where it crossed the Khor Abu Sunt; this dry watercourse lay below a slight sand ridge, so that although Pirie

The original order sent by Kitchener which led to the charge at Omdurman: "Annoy them as far as possible on their flank & head them off if possible from Omdurman". It was sent by heliograph, received by Lieutenant Clerk on the summit of Jebel Surgham, and forwarded by messenger to Colonel Martin waiting out of sight below the hill. (The Queen's Royal Lancers)

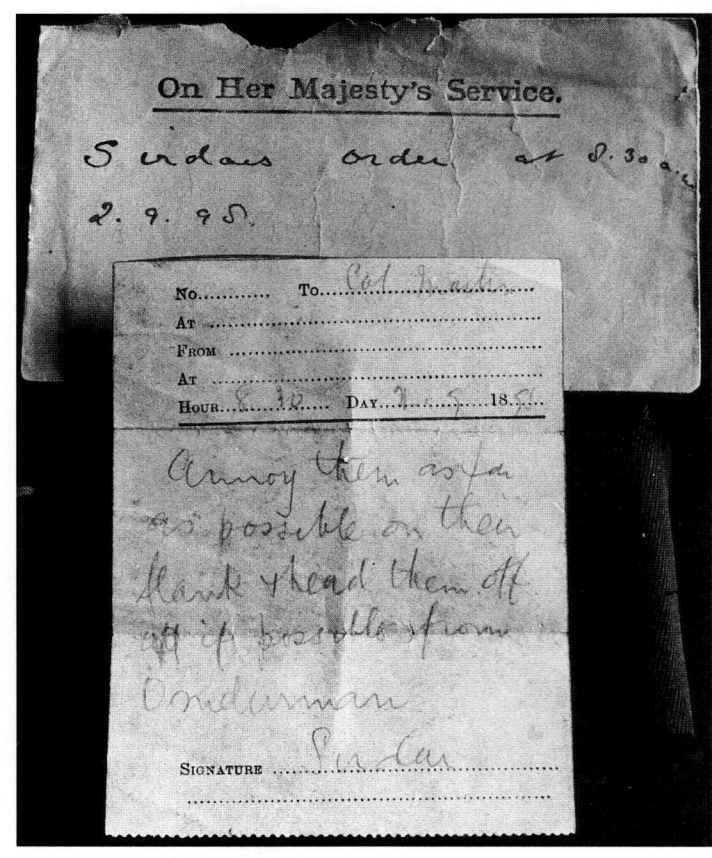

Warriors of the Hadendoa tribe; note the teased-out hairstyle, and the large double-edged Sudanese broadswords with cruciform hilts. The Hadendoa charged by the 21st Lancers were similarly dressed and armed, although about 30 also carried Remington rifles captured from defeated Egyptian forces at Kashgil in 1883 and Suakin in 1884 - see Plate A. (The National Army Museum)

The Khor Abu Sunt ran up from the river and swung round behind the hill, so that reinforcements could be moved from the Khalifa's hidden reserve to the Omdurman road without being seen. These remained hidden in the khor — which varied in width from ten to 20 feet, and was at this point deep enough for men to stand upright and remain unseen — expecting that a smaller number visible on the sand ridge might tempt the lancers into a trap. It was supposed that once the horsemen were among them the Baggara would prove invincible in close quarter combat. This was a standard Dervish tactic, and the Khalifa believed that the enemy cavalry would be cut to pieces — a small but significant revenge for the slaughter outside the zariba.

Some Arab accounts claim that the Khalifa left his position behind Jebel Surgham to watch the trap being sprung. This seems unlikely, unless he expected the infantry to quickly follow the cavalry, allowing a much greater trap to be sprung using the whole of his reserve. After the charge several lancers did report seeing the Khalifa mounted and urging his men back into the fray, although this was almost certainly a subordinate emir.

By 9.00a.m., as Pirie's patrol encountered the Hadendoas and turned back to report to the regiment, five brigades of the Anglo-Egyptian army had formed up on the Kerreri plain; these now began their march south towards Omdurman. It was imperative that the 21st clear the route of march with all haste.

ventured close enough to see the line of men manning the ridge he cannot have been aware of the khor immediately behind.

Arab accounts reveal that Dervish scouts watching from the top of Jebel Surgham had reported to the Khalifa immediately they saw the 21st Lancers leave the zariba and head southwards. The Khalifa then ordered the Hadendoa force to be reinforced with a further 2,000 men. These were Baggara spearmen, who preferred their traditional weapons to captured Remingtons and were well used to dealing with cavalry at close quarters. The choice of reinforcements indicated the nature of the encounter planned.

The Charge

Pirie reported a force of 1,000 men on open ground, apparently holding the Omdurman road and intent on blocking the advance. Colonel Martin could hardly ignore such a number of unbeaten troops. The lancers had been moving south at a walk; Martin now increased the pace to a trot and headed for the enemy.

If, as seems likely, he relished the opportunity to blood a

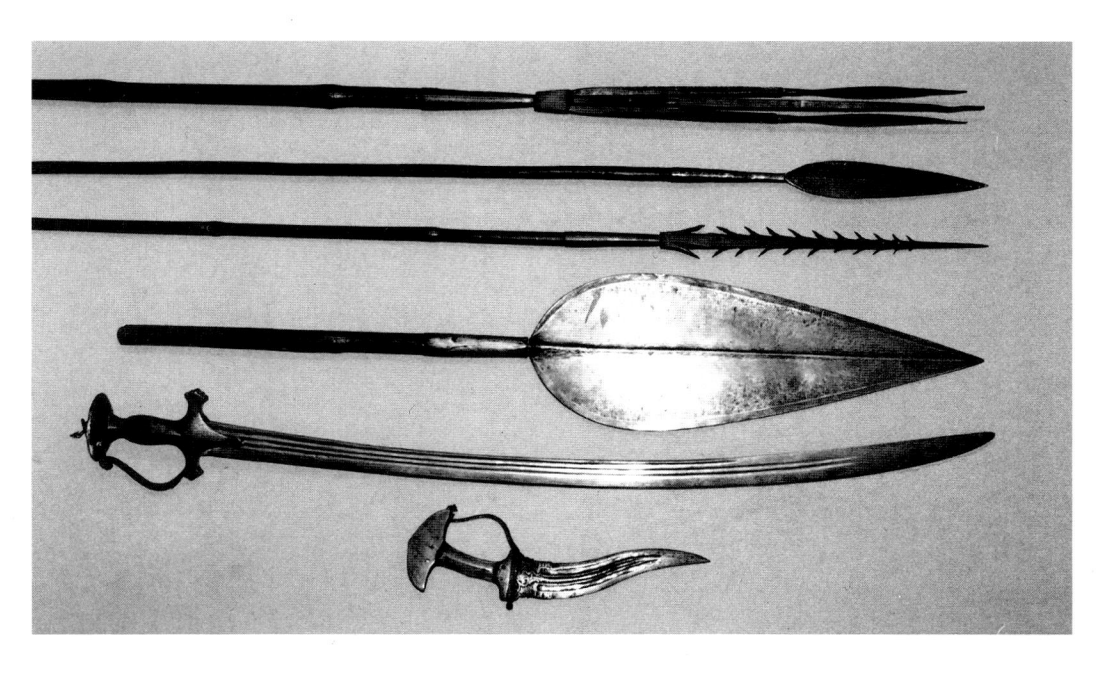

Dervish weapons collected by the regiment following the charge included these throwing spears (note the unpleasant double-barbed head - some wounded lancers reached the aid post by the river with such weapons still lodged in their bodies), a very broad-headed stabbing spear, a knife typical of the kind carried by warriors of all tribes, and a single-edged sword. Sudanese swords were invariably straight and double-edged with straight crossguards; although several of the type illustrated, which immediately recalls an Indian style, were used against the 21st, it is not known how they came to be in Dervish hands in 1898. (The Queen's Royal Lancers)

regiment that until now had played no major role in this or any previous action of the campaign, it cannot be inferred that he rushed the 21st into an unwise and unauthorised engagement with superior forces (as some commentators have persistently claimed). His orders were clear: *head them off if possible from Omdurman*. His assessment of the situation, based on Pirie's report, was that which any cavalry commander would have made: that 440 lancers could be expected to clear 1,000 infantry from open ground without difficulty or serious loss. Perhaps later critics were influenced by press reports — written by correspondents who were not present — that Martin rushed the regiment into action without putting out forward patrols. Lieutenant de Montmorency wrote that as the 21st neared the Hadendoa position, "our combat patrols were suddenly driven rapidly back on us"[4].

By 9.20 the leading brigades of the Sirdar's infantry had reached the Surgham ridge and halted, to allow the rear brigades to close up before venturing further. Unknown to Kitchener the Khalifa's reserve force, still 15,000 strong after detaching 2,000 to reinforce the Omdurman road, waited on the far side of the hill. Concerned that he had received no further reports on Dervish dispositions from Colonel Martin, Kitchener sent his ADC, Captain the Marquis of Tullihardine (Royal Horse Guards) to locate the 21st Lancers and assess the situation. The regiment was at this time approaching the Hadendoa position. Tullihardine arrived and, sensing that the cavalry was likely to come into action, rather than reporting back to Kitchener he remained with the 21st.

As the regiment came within sight of the Dervish line Major Finn saw "a couple of hundred Dervishes on a slight eminence"[5], and Lieutenant Smyth confirmed this figure. Clearly there were far less than the 1,000 reported by Pirie. It was later suggested that Colonel Martin dismissed Pirie's figure as an overestimate and took what he now saw as their true total strength. While he could not see the khor from his present position, it was evident that the Dervish party stood atop a slight ridge which might easily conceal the remainder of the original 1,000 men, and it is likely that in all that followed Martin assumed an enemy strength of 1,000. He could not know that the Hadendoa had been reinforced by Baggara warriors to make a total of 2,800 men, of whom 2,600 were concealed in the khor of which the ridge was the near edge.

A fine example of the Dervish jibbah, worn by an emir and thus far more elaborately decorated than that worn by the mass of warriors. (The Queen's Royal Lancers).

An officer's pattern cavalry sword carried by Lieutenant de Montmorency, and the .303 Lee-Enfield magazine carbine borrowed and carried in the charge by Times *correspondent Hubert Howard. (The Queen's Royal Lancers)*

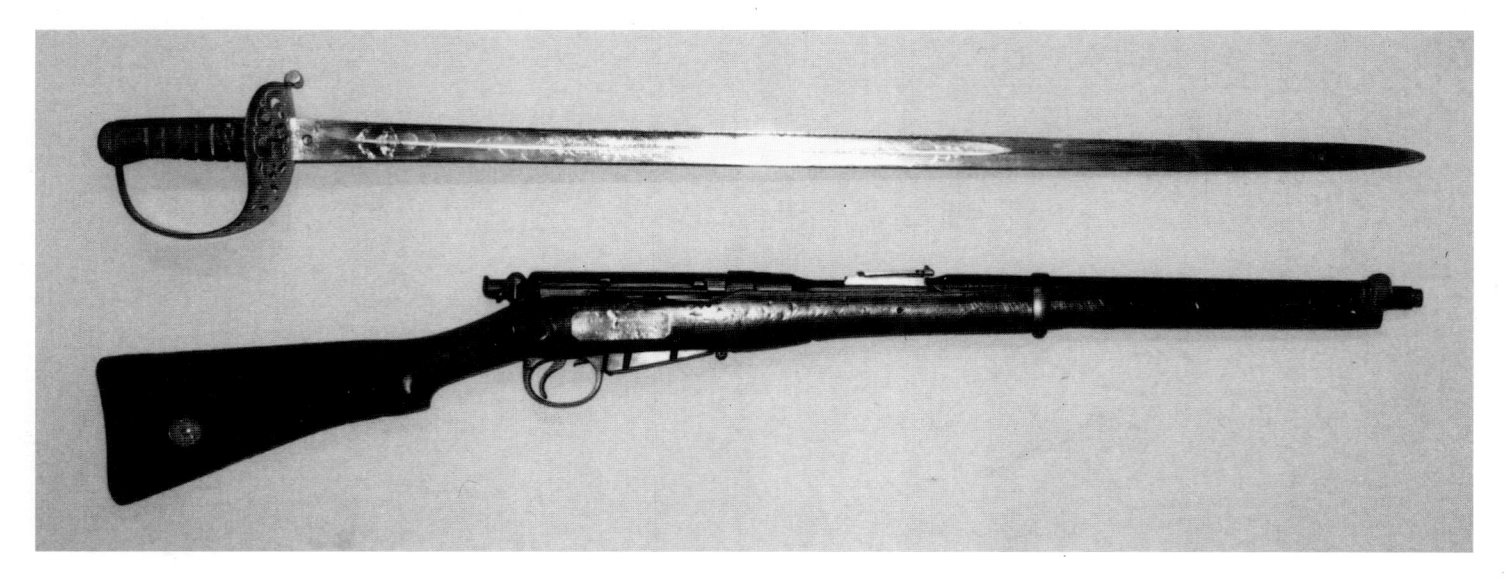

Photographed in Cairo, Captain Kenna of B Squadron — the only officer to carry a lance in the charge. (The Queen's Royal Lancers)

The 21st approached the enemy from the north. Rather than advance straight on them, Martin decided to take a look at them from the south. He wheeled the regiment to the left into column of troops (each troop followed by the next) and trotted across the Dervish front at about 300 yards. This would enable him to position the 21st between the enemy and Omdurman, from where he could reassess their strength and, dismounting, drive them away from the city with carbine fire, thus fulfilling Kitchener's order.

This was undoubtedly the correct manoeuvre, and only one aspect of Martin's decision can be faulted — that in moving in column of troops across the Dervish front at only 300 yards he placed his men within range of the 31 Hadendoa riflemen and made casualties likely. Although most of the men still thought of the Dervishes solely as spearmen, Martin should hardly have assumed this. There is some uncertainty about whether Pirie's patrol, which first located the Hadendoa, had come under fire — Finn wrote that it had, but Pirie made no mention of this in his report to Martin, and it is likely that the riflemen held their fire the better to spring the trap. Now again, with disciplined patience, they held their fire until the lancers were spread across their whole front.

The Hadendoa were not particularly experienced with their captured Remingtons, but mounted cavalrymen offering their right flank at the trot made easy targets. When these riflemen dropped to their knees and opened fire their habit of aiming high undoubtedly reduced the number of casualties, but a number of men and horses were hit. Seconds later de Montmorency, forgetting himself, shouted out, "Why the blazes don't we charge those ...... before they shoot us down?"[6]. The words were meant for Colonel Martin, and it is likely that every man who dared would have said as much.

Some commentators make Martin a blundering fool who rushed his regiment blindly into the charge without a second thought. In fact, as de Montmorency's exasperated

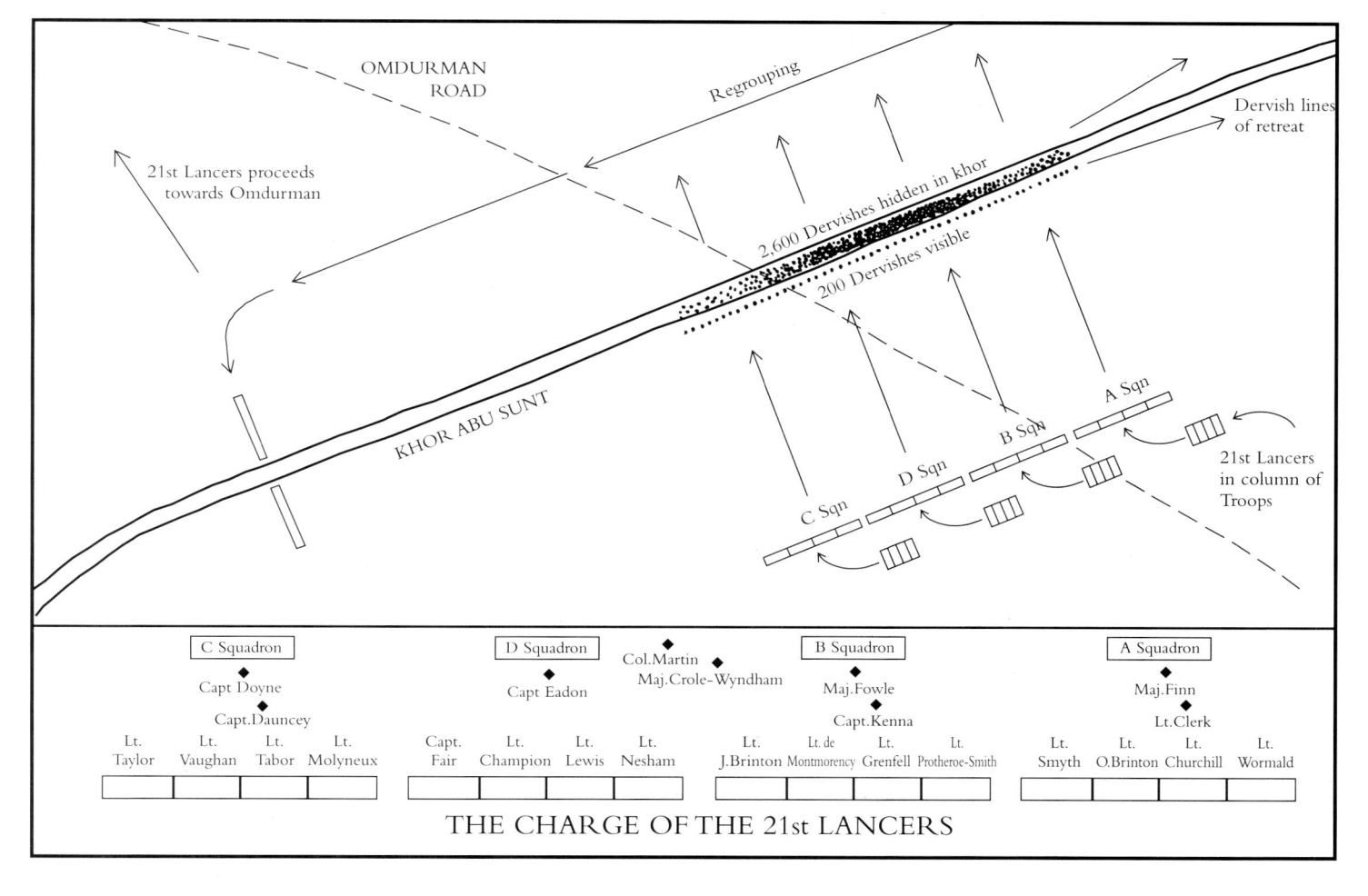

THE CHARGE OF THE 21st LANCERS

Painting by J.Mathews giving an enemy's eye view of Colonel Martin leading the charge, with the squadron leaders immediately behind him, followed by the troop leaders and their men. (The Queen's Royal Lancers)

cry indicates, he hesitated, caught between two options. He could wheel his regiment to the right and charge the enemy's front under constant fire; or he could wheel left, move out of range, then proceed south to outflank the riflemen in safety, dismount his men and clear them from the ridge with his regiment's longer-range carbine fire. While turning away and engaging the Dervishes with carbines was tactically the better option, it required the 21st Lancers to behave more like mounted infantry than cavalry. Turning towards them offered what was likely to be the regiment's only opportunity for true cavalry action against a standing enemy — and for the first charge in its history

We can hardly know what went through Martin's mind during these crucial seconds, but the sentiments recorded by his officers indicate the human pressures he had to balance against tactical discretion. De Montmorency believed that "there was only one way out of a disaster and that was to charge home"[7]. Finn wrote bluntly: "Only one course was possible"[8]. Churchill summed it up: "Everyone expected that we were going to make a charge. That was the one idea that had been in all our minds since we started from Cairo. Of course there would be a charge …"[9].

None of this makes Martin's decision to charge reckless or tactically wrong. He was aware of a potential enemy strength of 1,000, of whom 200 were visible and less than one quarter of these equipped with rifles. A charge from 300 yards was unlikely to sustain high casualties (and did not), and the shock effect of 440 lancers on the enemy might result in their immediate withdrawal, while carbine fire from a safe distance might take some time to produce the same effect, delaying the regiment from continuing south towards Omdurman.

Martin called *Right Wheel into Line*, and Sergeant Trumpeter Knight sounded the order. (Trumpeters carried both trumpet and bugle, but when mounted all orders were sounded on the bugle — it must have been mere careless habit which led several survivors to refer to the trumpet sounding the call). Immediately all 16 troops swung round into one long line of men, and as the regiment completed this movement Sergeant Knight sounded *Trot*. In fact the squadron leaders and the men behind them immediately spurred their horses on to greater speed; Knight later confirmed that the further orders which would normally have followed to increase the pace by degrees — *Canter, Gallop and Charge* — were never sounded. Once these cavalrymen were facing the enemy at less than 300 yards further orders became as superfluous as at the opening of stalls on the racecourse.

The Hadendoa were spread thinly along the ridge, offering a front of about 400 yards. Once turned towards them the 21st Lancers, over 440 strong, had a longer frontage. Colonel Martin, riding 30 yards ahead of the regiment, made for the centre of the enemy line. Behind him were C Squadron (commanded by Captain Doyne) on the left, then D (Captain Eadon), B (Major Fowle), and A (Major Finn) on the right. The outermost troops of C Squadron to the left and A Squadron to the right seemed likely to overlap the enemy.

The charge took 30 seconds, and Martin spent most of this time looking back over his shoulder, urging his men on. He knew that if (as seemed likely) additional men rose from behind the ridge at the last moment and strengthened the enemy line to 1,000 then only the greatest possible pace could carry the regiment through them. Churchill, too, rode the first 100 yards looking back at the men of his troop to see what effect the Dervish fire was having, but thought it small; the Dervishes still persisted in firing high. Captain Kenna and Major Fowle rode head down for the illusion of protection their flimsy helmets offered against the bullets.

Most officers now held their swords pointing forward at the enemy, "riding down the blade" in true cavalry fashion. There were four exceptions. Colonel Martin was so preoccupied with the pace of the regiment that he drew neither sword nor revolver. Fowle and Churchill had each armed themselves with the latest Mauser semi-automatic pistol (purchased in preference to the standard issue Webley revolver), and charged with this in hand. Captain Kenna inexplicably carried a lance; it seems unlikely that he would choose this cumbersome weapon in preference to the sword, but the evidence is convincing. A photograph taken in Cairo shows Kenna mounted and holding a lance, and no less an authority than Colonel Martin himself confirmed that this officer carried it in the charge. Perhaps the lance's unpopularity among the men of his troop, most of whom would gladly have swapped it for the sword, prompted Kenna to lead by example.

After the first 100 yards confidence remained high. Private Hewitt, riding a grey Arab pony in B Squadron, later recalled: "During the charge I sat firm and tight in the saddle, with lance in hand ... we were in a fine line and worked up to a good speed before the shock, fit to take anything in front, so it would have taken something rather solid to stop us"[10]. On the right of the regiment Major Finn now saw that his outermost two troops would overlap the enemy front, and gave the order *Right Shoulders*, turning A Squadron to attack in a crescent shape. On the left of the regiment no such order was given and C Squadron continued in line; the outermost troop would overlap the enemy and charge into thin air.

At 150 yards — the halfway point — a number of horsemen could be seen riding behind the Dervish line, and several brightly coloured flags appeared bearing texts in Arabic. Suddenly a mass of spears and swords and faces were visible on the sand, seeming to indicate that the remainder of the original 1,000 Dervishes were, as suspected, hidden behind a low sand ridge ready to spring up from a prone position. The khor itself was still hidden, and every man remained confident that the shock effect of 440 lancers would destroy the enemy line.

At between 100 and 50 yards the khor became visible. The faces that had appeared just above ground level, taken to be those of men lying on the sand, were now seen to be Baggara spearmen already standing upright: "A long, dense white mass became visible ... they were about 12 deep"[11]. This was at the right of the line; at the centre where the khor was wider they were reckoned to be 20 deep. At once every officer and man realised that a trap had been sprung.

The charge reaches the lip of the khor — a drawing by René Bull, correspondent for Black and White, *a weekly illustrated paper published in London. (The Queen's Royal Lancers)*

Another impression, by John Charlton, of the moment of impact. (The Queen's Royal Lancers)

This enemy could not be galloped through, nor the khor jumped. Already at the gallop and within seconds of engagement, the 21st was committed to the charge, and could do no other than leap down into the packed mass of the enemy. Men frantically spurred their horses on to gain the greatest possible momentum, which alone might carry them through and out the other side. All now saw that the struggle would be equal, and that the 21st might suffer as heavily as the enemy.

When under 50 yards from the khor they were staring into the faces of the 200 Dervishes topping the ridge. While the 31 kneeling riflemen fired and reloaded as quickly as possible the rest sat calmly on the sand, a sight which perplexed some of the troopers bearing down on them. In fact these men sat ready to fall back as the cavalrymen reached them, hamstringing the horses with knife slashes — a tactic they had perfected against mounted swordsmen, for in falling back they fell below the arc of the rider's blade. As they were about to discover, lances had a much longer reach. Several officers realised what the sitting Dervishes intended and called out to their men, telling them to lower their lances — these were already in the *Engage infantry* position, but if they were not to pass over warriors who fell back onto the sand it was essential to drop the point to near ground level.

As the 21st Lancers reached the khor and made for the leap they let out a great cheer, answered immediately by a cry of *Allah il Allah!* from the Dervishes. So eager were some of the enemy that they sprang from the khor and rushed forward to meet the regiment, although most held their position. The charge could not be seen by the Anglo-Egyptian infantry halted behind the Surgham ridge; but Lieutenant McNeill of the Seaforths, out on a mission for General Gatacre, noticed "a great commotion going on

First into the khor: Lieutenant Colonel Martin (left) and his second-in-command, Major Crole-Wyndham. The latter was unhorsed, but incredibly managed to fight his way clear on foot with sword and Mauser pistol. (The Queen's Royal Lancers)

about a mile away to the south of Surgham. Crackling rifle fire, unmistakable British cheers and high clouds of dust"[12].

At the moment when they reached the khor the lancers were riding at about 20 miles per hour; with an average man-and-horse weight of up to half a ton the shock effect on the line of 200 Dervishes was tremendous, and the majority of the enemy killed in the action must have been among these men. Almost all were thrown into the air or sent crashing back into the khor. In a letter to a friend Churchill wrote that "they all fell knocked A.O.T. [arse over tip]"[13]. Several were transfixed by the nine-foot lances and carried into the khor. Such was its depth that several lancers instinctively checked their horses as they reached the edge, losing the momentum that alone could force a way through the dense mass: "The men jumped actually on to the spears of the enemy, whose heads were scarcely level with the horses' knees"[14].

As the 21st closed on the enemy Private Byrne was hit by a bullet which passed through his right arm and inflicted a severe wound. His lance fell from his hand and, pulling up his horse, he managed with great difficulty to draw his sword. The momentum of his charge lost, his sword arm all but disabled, Byrne was the last man to enter the khor.

Colonel Martin in the midst of the enemy — a romanticised but probably fairly realistic impression by John Charlton; Martin rode through the enemy unarmed. (The Queen's Royal Lancers)

B Squadron (left to right): Major Fowle, Captain Kenna, and Lieutenant de Montmorency. (The Queen's Royal Lancers)

B Squadron: Private Brown (left) was awarded the DCM for saving the lives of both Privates Varley and Rowlett (centre & right) although he himself was already wounded. Rowlett, dragged clear after being unhorsed and wounded in both arms, was probably the last man to leave the khor alive. (The Queen's Royal Lancers)

The Mêlée

At the moment of initial impact the advantage was undoubtedly with the lancers; but immediately their mounts began the leap into the khor the situation was abruptly reversed. While horses were in mid-air knifes and swords were swung in well-practised hamstringing cuts, and broad-bladed stabbing spears were thrust straight up into their unprotected bellies. Where the Dervishes were most thickly packed the horses came down directly onto a bed of blades turned upward to receive them. As disabled horses threw their riders four or more warriors fell upon each dismounted trooper, hacking frantically at the head and neck (as the helmets of the dead testified) and stabbing at the chest.

Many horses, though not wounded, stumbled as they hit the rocky floor of the khor, and some "grassed" their riders. Colonel Martin was first in, having drawn neither sword nor pistol. His charger landed badly, went forward on its head, and almost unhorsed him. Dervishes rushed at him with raised swords as the horse recovered; he spurred it forward, struggling through the packed mass, remarkably still unarmed.

Just behind Martin came Major Crole-Wyndham, second-in-command. His horse Mafeesh landed on its feet, but as it did so a Dervish pressed the muzzle of a rifle into its hide and fired. Despite being hideously wounded the horse continued for several yards through the enemy mass before falling, giving Crole-Wyndham time to draw his Mauser pistol. As the horse collapsed beneath him he landed on his feet, sword in one hand, pistol in the other, slashing and firing as Dervishes pressed at him from all directions, knowing he had little chance of escape without help.

Behind these two came the squadron leaders, followed by the troop leaders, and finally the full force of 440 lancers. Most of those who died fell at this point. The Dervishes were so thickly packed that horses which recovered from the leap were quickly brought to a halt by the dense mass of the enemy. It took up to a minute (to them, an endless minute) for the lancers to fight their way through the mêlée, spurring on their terrified horses, fighting off multiple assailants aiming sword blows at their heads and shoulders and thrusting spears at their chests, while others cut at their bridle reins and stirrup leathers. Few who sustained a serious wound or became unhorsed were able to escape by their own efforts.

The lances that had proved so effective against the line of men on the lip of the khor now proved to be an encumbrance. Several of those who had skewered an enemy found it impossible to disengage the lance and had to abandon it; in other cases the lance snapped on impact. Once the lance had been lost the men found it difficult to draw their swords – from scabbards attached to the saddle behind their left leg – and at the same time control a terrified horse while yelling enemies pressed in from every side.

Those who still had their lances found them impossible to wield effectively in close-quarter combat, where the enemy was not nine feet away but inside their reach. As a regiment new to the weapon the 21st was perhaps not as practised with the lance as it might have been; but in such close fighting years of additional lance drill would hardly have helped — this was the classic deathtrap for the spear-armed horseman since the dawn of cavalry soldiering. Had the men charged as hussars, sword in hand, they might well have cut a faster path through the enemy. It is a tribute to their discipline that no man is known to have abandoned a serviceable lance and resorted to the sword. Private Hewitt remembered "getting a pierce in when and where I could"[15]. Captain Eadon considered that his squadron "could not advance in any formation nor [at] sufficient pace to get our lances well home"[16].

Those who did use the 1887 officer's and 1890 cavalry swords found them too light for this sort of fighting. Many Dervishes swung heavy double-edged blades which were virtually medieval broadswords; they cut right through the lancers' slimmer blades as they parried, and went on to bite deep into man or horse. Even if such a cut were successfully blocked its weight was enough to unseat the lancer — this almost put an end to de Montmorency, though he just managed to stay in the saddle. The most appropriate weapon in the mêlée was the revolver or self-loading pistol, carried only by officers and sergeants. Fowle used his Mauser pistol to shoot a man blocking his path as he reached the rim, fired at another as he landed but missed, then killed another with his third shot.

D and B Squadrons, at the centre of the line, entered the khor at its widest point and where it was most densely packed; the far bank was at its steepest opposite where B entered, and that squadron had the most difficult passage of all. C Squadron to the left and A to the right entered where the khor was neither so wide nor deep and the enemy not so closely packed; the outermost troop of C Squadron overlapped the enemy flank altogether and galloped through the khor unhindered. Thus there was no real mêlée at the two

C Squadron: Captain Doyne (left) and Lieutenant Taylor. Riding through the enemy where they were less densely packed, Taylor quickly got his troop dismounted and began delivering the carbine fire which drove them back. (The Queen's Royal Lancers)

extreme ends of the line, where the momentum of the charge carried the lancers through and any man who remained in the saddle came out relatively unscathed.

★ ★ ★

Major Fowle's B Squadron entered the khor where the enemy were so closely packed that the ground was literally invisible. Fowle's charger, though leaping from the gallop, was brought to an abrupt standstill. He attempted to clear a path with his Mauser pistol and was most disconcerted to see the dead remain upright, held in place by the crush around them.

Captain Kenna, his second-in-command, was riding a grey charger named Rainbow. He landed well, and immediately came across the unhorsed Major Crole-Wyndham, fighting for his life. (None of those who witnessed Kenna's actions in the khor mention a lance, and it must be supposed that he jettisoned it — or left it in the body of a Dervish — as he leapt down.) Kenna reached out and pulled Crole-Wyndham up behind him, but this pause allowed the enemy to close around them, and for one desperate moment the two men sat pinned there, firing their pistols into the heaving mass of enemies around them. When this gave a little, Kenna spurred the horse forward; but Rainbow found the load and the crowd too much and threw the two of them, though both men landed on their feet. Two critical yards had been gained, and Crole-Wyndham attempted to fight his way towards the far side of the khor; Kenna managed to remount, but by then the Dervish mass had closed between them and he could see no sight of Crole-Wyndham, and thought him lost.

Only yards away, although unseen through the enemy crowd, Lieutenant Grenfell and his troop had entered the khor where it was most thickly packed. The horses came down onto the spears and many were fatally wounded before hitting the ground. Their riders, once unhorsed, had little chance of escape. Grenfell was pitched from his horse as it landed. Its wounds were not fatal and he attempted to remount; as he did so he was struck by a sword across his back, and almost simultaneously by another across one wrist. Severely wounded, he was pounced upon by several warriors and literally hacked to death, suffering multiple sword and spear wounds to his chest, neck and head, his helmet alone taking 11 cuts.

Those men of B Squadron who remained in the saddle were immediately surrounded and set upon by the enemy; spears were thrust at the horses, swords swung at the riders. This squadron was the only one in which an officer was killed, and Grenfell's troop suffered the heaviest casualties of all, with ten killed and 11 wounded. Lieutenant de Montmorency, commanding the troop immediately to Grenfell's left, had a narrow escape when a sword blow came down heavily on his arm but with the flat forward. Private Brown, already wounded, performed a remarkable double rescue. Seeing Private Varley unhorsed and surrounded by Dervishes, he turned his mount into them and literally dragged Varley out of the khor. He then returned to the rim where Private Rowlett, unhorsed and wounded in both arms, was unable to climb out and shouting for help; Brown pulled him clear of the enemy.

Private Byrne, riding with B Squadron but wounded before entering the khor, saw the impossibility of getting through this most densely packed spot with his sword arm all but disabled, and pulled sharply to the left, crossing behind D Squadron and entering the khor at the rear of C

Below & right: Private Byrne of B Squadron, posing here in field marching order in Cairo, was awarded the VC for rescuing Lieutenant Molyneux when that officer was dismounted, wounded and surrounded by the enemy; Byrne was himself wounded twice. Note the near and off side stowage of equipment: carbine boot behind right leg with picket post attached; a forage net hanging from the girth, and a corn sack from the near side cantle; boots strapped to wallets; waterbottle and haversack slung high under the left arm, and sword slings hooked up to the belt; sabre behind the left leg, with what appear to be a feeding bag and picket rope attached. Note the lance pennon furled and covered with black fabric. (The Queen's Royal Lancers)

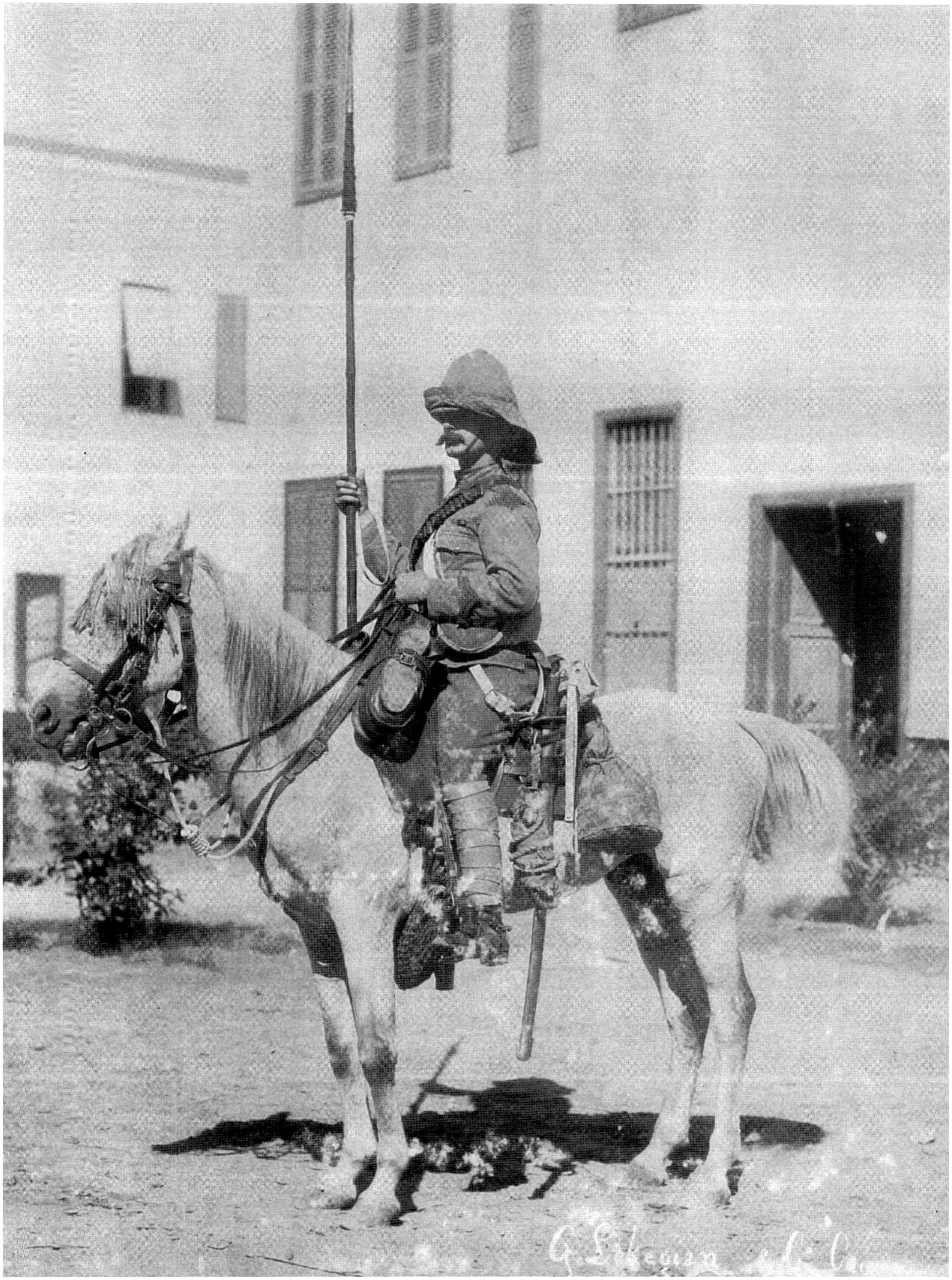

Squadron on the far left. He swung his sword at the enemy, compounding his injury until he could barely keep a grasp on the hilt. His course through the Dervishes continued to take him to the left, until he spotted a clear route of escape and spurred his horse on.

★ ★ ★

Captain Doyne's C Squadron entered the khor where the Dervishes were spread most thinly, and all who remained mounted got through, although several suffered spear wounds. However, any man who was unhorsed had little chance of escape. Private Ayton, without pulling up his own mount, rescued an unhorsed man by grasping and dragging him through the enemy and out of the khor.

Lieutenant Molyneux had his horse killed beneath him and continued on foot, racing for the far side of the khor. Dervishes closed across his path and the first sword blow left a deep cut across his right hand; his pistol fell to the ground, and a second blow was likely to prove fatal. Looking round frantically for help, Molyneux found that the easy passage offered his troop meant that he stood alone. He dodged several sword blows from the four Dervishes surrounding him, buying precious seconds but finding no escape. At this moment a private rode in from the right, his lance gone, his sword arm badly wounded, heading for the far bank of the khor. Molyneux called out for help; without hesitation Private Byrne replied, "All right, Sir, I won't leave you!", and turned his horse back. He rode straight at the four Dervishes, battering them with his horse, but at the first blow of his sword it fell from his hand; at the same time a spear was thrust into his chest, though not deeply enough to embed itself. While the enemy paid attention to Byrne, Molyneux reached the far side of the khor unhindered and scrambled out. Seeing this, Byrne turned his horse and quickly followed, now twice wounded and reeling in the saddle from loss of blood.

Byrne rejoined B Squadron and went about seeking the men of his troop — only Lieutenant de Montmorency and six men had come out of the khor. De Montmorency rode back in search of the missing, and at this moment Major Crole-Wyndham appeared from the khor, incredibly having fought his way though on foot. He had yet to reach safety, as a Dervish horseman gave chase with a spear — de Montmorency rode at the horseman and, when he turned away, shot him in the back.

The bottom of the khor was covered with the dead and wounded, both lancers and Dervishes, and de Montmorency came across Grenfell's body, badly mutilated by multiple wounds. Seeing Captain Kenna and Corporal Swarbrick nearby he called them both to the body. While these two men remained mounted to ward off the enemy, de Montmorency lifted the blood-soaked corpse onto his horse, which (perhaps startled by the gruesome load) bolted, Grenfell falling to the ground. Kenna and Swarbrick rode after the terrified animal while de Montmorency, armed only with a revolver, stood guard over the body. The horse was returned, but now a large number of Dervishes were closing on them from both sides and within seconds there would be no possibility of escape. With the greatest regret de Montmorency mounted and all three men withdrew. The Dervishes who gave chase were turned back by carbine

Captain Eadon, commanding D Squadron, got through with only a dent to his helmet from a sword cut; but his squadron suffered 11 dead and 13 wounded. (The Queens Royal Lancers)

Left: *An oil painting by G.D.Rowlandson, illustrating the moment when the regiment broke through the enemy ranks into the open desert. (The Queen's Royal Lancers)*

Right: *D Squadron: Lieutenant Nesham (left), the youngest officer in the regiment, was badly wounded, and only escaped because his spurs raked his horse when two Dervishes tried to drag him from the saddle by his legs. Sergeant Freeman (right), who had most of his face hideously cut off by a Dervish swordsman, finished rallying his troop before reporting to Captain Eadon at attention and asking permission to fall out "to have his nose put on". (The Queen's Royal Lancers)*

fire from a troop which had by now regrouped on the far side of the khor.

★   ★   ★

Captain Eadon's D Squadron entered the khor to the left of B and where the Dervishes were packed just as thickly. He crashed through with only a blow to the head which dented his helmet. Behind him Captain Fair clashed swords with a Dervish, saving himself but seeing his sword snap off at the hilt. He flung this at his opponent, and before the man could get in a second blow Fair's mount had carried him a crucial few feet further on, out of reach.

These two officers had a remarkably easy passage compared to most of D Squadron, which suffered the highest number of deaths with 11 killed and 13 wounded (although B Squadron had the most casualties with nine killed and 25 wounded, one of whom later died). D Squadron's survivors also suffered the most gruesome injuries. Sergeant Freeman was struck by a blow to the face that sliced through his nose, one cheek, and his lips, leaving these hanging from his face on bloody strings and blood covering his chin, neck and shoulders.

Lieutenant Nesham, the youngest officer in the regiment, had the most unlikely escape when death seemed certain. Both man and horse made their way through the mêlée and scaled the steep far side of the khor unscathed; the horse paused briefly to recover from the jump — Nesham thinking himself safely out of it — when a Dervish sprang up after him and took hold of the bridle. As Nesham brought his sword down on the man an enemy swordsman struck his bridle hand, almost severing it. Within seconds he had suffered a further deep sword cut to his leg, and a third to his right shoulder, deep enough to paralyse the arm. Nesham was defenceless, his left hand almost severed and his right arm useless. Reaching up from the khor one Dervish took hold of his right leg, another his left, and together they tried to pull him back down to his death. This very action pressed his spurs into the horse's flanks; the charger sprang forward and carried Nesham away, seriously wounded and bleeding profusely, but hardly believing himself free of the hands that within seconds would have hacked him to pieces.

★   ★   ★

Major Finn's A Squadron, at the right of the regiment, entered the khor where the Dervishes were less thickly packed and the gully in places only eight feet wide. Finn charged through without pause, firing at six Dervishes and killing four of these. Behind him Lieutenant Clerk (the Signals Officer) landed badly; his horse stumbled and almost threw him, but recovered. Lieutenant O. W. Brinton ducked to dodge the slash of a sword from the right, only to be cut across the shoulder by a blow from the left; still in the saddle, he managed to escape.

Lieutenant Smyth was attacked by two swordsmen, shot at by a rifleman, and had a spear thrown at him from close range — incredibly, parrying the sword blows and ducking in the saddle, he rode through unscathed, although his horse received wounds to the neck and shoulder. Lieutenant Wormald came under attack from a mounted emir dressed in ringmail. Wormald slashed heavily at the man with his sword, which bent almost double on impact, then hit out desperately with the buckled blade as the emir moved in for the kill. Luckily a private coming up behind aimed his lance well, and with the momentum of the charge maintained on this less densely packed flank its point went through both mail and emir. Surgeon-Major Pinches, riding with A Squadron, had his horse shot under him. Private Pedder, his own mount badly wounded and unable to leap from the khor, managed to capture two stray horses while fighting off the Dervishes who closed around him, bringing one to the stranded officer and enabling both men to escape.

Regrouping

The time elapsed between the first man entering the khor (Colonel Martin) and the last man leaving it (probably Private Rowlett) was variously estimated at between two and four minutes, although time in its common sense can hardly be used to measure the lancers' passage through that living hell.

Once out it, they came to a halt about 150 yards away and regrouped as best they could by troop and squadron. Although few had come through without a scratch, every possible assistance was given to the seriously wounded. Lieutenant Brinton came across Lieutenant Nesham, bleeding profusely from his all but severed left hand. Himself wounded and unable to help, Brinton explained to a private how to put on a tourniquet; despite this he thought it likely that Nesham would bleed to death. The total number of officers and men wounded to the extent that they were unable to continue in action was 71, and more than 100 horses. Few escaped without a cut of some kind; most made little of their injury and — like Sergeant Diggs, who had two fingers sliced off by a Dervish sword — refused to fall out for medical attention until the seriously wounded had been seen to.

Many men stood around in a stupor. Some later reported experiencing a sense of unreality while in the khor, which continued for some time after their escape. For one corporal the whole charge was a blank, and it was with great alarm that he discovered his sword arm red to the shoulder. He searched for the wound beneath the khaki, but found himself unhurt — the blood was that of Dervishes he must have killed. A private said that he heard nothing at all while in the khor, fighting his way through an eerie silence. Churchill reported much the same: "The whole scene flickered exactly like a cinematograph picture … I remember no sound; the whole event seemed to pass in absolute silence. The yells of the enemy, the shouts of the soldiers, the firing of many shots, the clashing of sword and spear, were unnoticed by the senses, unregistered by the brain"[17].

Yet during these first moments of regrouping some officers and men (particularly those who had come through relatively unscathed) were eager to be allowed a second charge. Most can be forgiven such absurd bravado by their ignorance, as yet, of the heavy losses incurred by the regiment. Few joined Lieutenant Churchill in knowingly seeking further losses; he was "quite clear that we should have charged back at once ... another 50 or 60 casualties would have made the performance historic"[18]. During this period when a second charge seemed likely many of the men asked permission to abandon their lances and draw their swords.

While Major Finn's A Squadron had a comparatively easy passage, the sight of the casualties suffered further along the line soon discouraged any thought of "having another go": "The men were anxious to cut their way back through their enemies. But some realisation of the cost of that wild ride began to come to all of us"[19]. They watched as riderless horses struggled from the khor, some galloping away across the plain, others staying on their feet with difficulty as the blood flowed from wide, deep wounds. Then came wounded men, clinging precariously to their mounts, some lurching in the saddle and about to fall, most covered with blood from multiple wounds. With this sight came an awareness that others were missing, and that any man left among the Dervishes was most certainly dead.

By 9.50a.m. the 21st had regrouped. Colonel Martin considered a second charge to bring out the missing, but decided that no lancer still in the khor could be alive, and that to charge a reformed Dervish line was likely to double or triple the regiment's losses. Instead he now led his men south and turned to face the khor at right angles to the line of charge, dismounting two squadrons and opening fire with carbines. Churchill's quip that the Colonel "remembered for the first time that we had carbines"[20] was hardly fair comment when he himself had preferred to lead his men back into the Dervish mass.

Within minutes of the charge one of the horses that had continued in terror over the Surgham ridge reached the waiting Anglo-Egyptian army, its empty saddle red with blood. Kitchener, angry that he had still received no signal from Colonel Martin and that the Marquis of Tullibardine had not returned with news, sent a scout over the ridge to see what had happened; on this man's return the infantry called out to him, asking what he had seen. He shouted back, "The 21st Lancers have caught it hot"[21].

The regiment still had work to do. The Dervish force had recovered as emirs ordered their men out to form a line

A Squadron: Major Finn (left) shot his way through, killing four of the enemy. The regimental Signals Officer, Lieutenant Clerk (centre), got through unscathed; Lieutenant O. W. Brinton (right) was wounded by a sword cut to the shoulder. (The Queen's Royal Lancers)

A Squadron: Lieutenant Smyth (left) escaped attacks by two swordsmen, a rifleman and a spearman. Lieutenant Wormald (centre) broke his sword on a mounted emir's ring-mail armour. Surgeon Major Pinches (right) was saved from death when Private Pedder caught two loose horses for them. (The Queen's Royal Lancers)

at right angles to the khor, facing the lancers, and began to advance. Despite the dead and wounded they still numbered well over 2,000 fighting men, and had yet to be pressed from the field. But before long the carbine fire told and they fell back, though slowly and in good order, taking their wounded with them — not at all the beaten rabble some correspondents were later to describe for readers at home. That they retired without further fighting was, however, much to do with the charge: "There can be little doubt that the moral effect of the charge had been very great, and that these brave enemy were no longer unshaken"[22].

Once out of range the Dervishes turned north-west, making for the Khalifa's third division hidden behind Jebel Surgham, from which they had been detached. Before they could reach the protection of the hill they passed within range of 32nd Artillery Brigade, which opened fire at 2,000 yards. Though the 21st must take credit for pressing the enemy back from Omdurman — for 440 lancers to drive 2,800 infantry from an entrenched position was no small accomplishment — it was undoubtedly the artillery which applied the coup de grâce.

The success of the regiment's carbine fire in forcing the enemy from the field without further loss was much quoted later in evidence that the charge was pointless and that Martin should have turned away at the outset, outflanked the enemy, and used carbine fire to clear the area. That might not have been accomplished so easily before the Dervish force had been demoralised by the charge. The Baggara spearmen had confidently expected to destroy the British cavalry as a fighting unit, and their failure to do so delivered a serious blow to morale; while they could comprehend defeat by Maxim gun or high explosive shell, defeat by an outnumbered force of enemy "spearmen" had been unthinkable.

In any case, the pressures which had built up within the regiment over many years made it unlikely that Martin could have declined any reasonable opportunity to charge. Nor would any man of his regiment, living or dead, have wished him to do so. Having invented light cavalry and encouraged its essential animating spirit it would have been unreasonable to expect it to do other than its nature dictated, which had more to do with dash and valour than a cold calculation of tactical effectiveness. That is far from saying that the charge could not have proved effective. A charge by 440 lancers against a standing enemy of 1,000 on open ground could reasonably have been expected to show the effectiveness of light cavalry at its best, and to clear the ground most rapidly; the khor and the hidden reinforcements might have been anticipated, but in the passion of the hour, fuelled by Kitchener's order to head them off from Omdurman, they were not.

The 21st was now left in command of the Omdurman road and the khor, though at a heavy cost. Troop leaders were ordered to each select a party of men and collect the dead. Private Hewitt recalled that "Captain Kenna asked for volunteers to pick out our dead and wounded from the battlefield. Some of our poor chaps were cut about terribly, some with arms or legs off, others with heads split open"[23]. The scene was gruesome, and gallows humour passed between men who knew that the day's bloody proceedings had far to run. A private whose thumb had been sliced off during the fight and who seemed to be making too much of it was told by another man, "That's nothing to make a fuss about. Here's poor Sam with his head cut off, and he's not saying a word"[24].

The 21 bodies — Lieutenant Grenfell and 20 men — were recovered and laid in a row. All had suffered horrific, multiple wounds inflicted by several assailants at once, which gave rise to tales of ritual mutilation (but there had been no time for this). Grenfell's body was carried back with the wounded, who were now sent under escort towards the medical post still located within the zariba. The 20 fallen men were buried together — not in the khor, but in the ground over which they had charged. Captain Cordeaux was left in charge of the burial party while the regiment made ready to proceed south. When the burial was complete Cordeaux broke a lance, tied it in the shape of a cross, and stuck it in the sand so that its red and white pennon fluttered over the grave.

The number of Dervish dead has never been confirmed. Churchill made it 30 to 40; Finn thought 60; de Montmorency counted 72 — 52 killed in the charge and 20 by carbine fire — which seems credibly precise. But a Seaforths officer who visited the scene about two hours later counted only 21. Haig claimed that the total was not more than 15, though the source of this information is unclear, and it possibly reflects regimental rivalry more than an accurate count.

Back below the Surgham ridge, Tullihardine reported the charge to Kitchener (although there is conflicting evidence, it seems likely that Tullihardine charged with the regiment). Kitchener was extremely angry that Colonel Martin had allowed the 21st to become engaged in a major action. He now knew that a third Dervish division had indeed been hidden behind Jebel Surgham, and thought the 21st might have discovered and reported this earlier. This sentiment was much quoted by later commentators who accused Martin of exceeding the order to "annoy them" and "head them off". Yet these are terms of engagement, not reconnaissance, and Kitchener himself wrote that "I sent out the 21st Lancers to clear the ground"[25].

Only 30 minutes after the regiment had wheeled right into line to charge it had regrouped, taken possession of the khor, and was once more moving south towards Omdurman in compliance with the Sirdar's order. Finn records this at 9.30, but de Montmorency has 10.00 and this is most likely correct. A regimental tradition dating back to the day of the charge relates that Lieutenant Grenfell's pocket watch was struck and broken by a spear during his last forlorn struggle, poignantly recording the time of his death as 9.40. In fact the watch suffered no damage other than a slight dent to its outer case and remained in working order. However, the general acceptance of the anecdote by the men of the 21st suggests that the time quoted was correct, and therefore that the mêlée still raged at 9.40a.m.

Drawing by the war artist W. T. Maud, showing Lieutenant de Montmorency and his troop regrouping after the charge. De Montmorency is supposedly restraining a man eager to charge back into the enemy; some may well have been ready to do so, but none were eager. (The Queen's Royal Lancers)

CHAPTER SEVEN

Survivors' Accounts

Captain F.H. Eadon
Frank Eadon commanded D Squadron, which entered the khor at its widest point and where the Dervishes were most densely packed. In a letter to his father written on 22 September during the return journey to Cairo he gives an account of the charge, in which his squadron suffered the highest number of deaths[1].

"It seems months instead of only a few days since our charge, which I still can hardly realise. How we four squadron leaders got through, and the CO, will always seem to me an extraordinary feat of good luck, or I should say, a kind of providence ...

"We had gone out on the left near the river, and had several small encounters with their infantry. We were keen to make some mark in history in this our first campaign, and when we got the, to us, memorable message — 'Annoy them and if possible cut off their retreat from Omdurman. SIRDAR' — off we went in the direction of what we thought were a few of their infantry.

"We wheeled into line to the right and galloped, when I at once saw lumps of them concealed in a nullah [the Indian term for a watercourse] within 100 yards of us, and by that time bullets flew by in hundreds. I turned round to my squadron and said, 'Now, men, get your lances down', and off I galloped as hard as I could split, and strange to say I got through them with nothing worse than a blow on the head, which only crushed my helmet, and a sword cut, slight, on my horse's quarters.

"Not so my poor squadron, which suffered more than any of the others. I had 11 killed and 13 wounded out of the total casualties. When I got through I saw Nesham being run away with, and smothered in blood, and so weak he could hardly sit on his horse. I gave my sword to my trumpeter and went after him, but he fell off from exhaustion and loss of blood before I could catch him, his left hand nearly severed and a bad gash on his leg. I sent him to the rear as soon as I could, and then rushed back to my squadron. I then met a man whom I could not recognise, as his nose was cut off and his face covered with blood. He was one of my sergeants, and having rallied his troop as far as he was able, rode up to me sitting at attention and asked if he might fall out and get his nose put on. After the rally we again attacked the enemy with dismounted fire, and finally drove them on to their own main body, where they were nicely caught by our infantry advancing.

"We then collected all the dead and laid them in a row, and proceeding in the direction of Omdurman, kept heading off the retreating army from the river and Omdurman. So we carried out to the letter the Sirdar's orders."

Lieutenant R.H. de Montmorency
René de Montmorency led a troop in B Squadron, to the right of Eadon and where the Dervishes were just as thickly packed. His letter to a friend written on 28 September gives a graphic account of the charge and the action for which he would be awarded the Victoria Cross[2].

"I have just remembered that I have not fulfilled my promise to send you in writing my first impression of a battle — so I will now attempt to do so ...

"At 7.30a.m. we received orders to move south along the river bank and report if the enemy had any large reserves behind Jebel Surgham hill and ridges. When we reached the rising ground 3,000 yards south of the zariba, we were fired at from the top of Jebel Surgham and also by small bodies of wounded and unwounded enemy retiring from the battlefield.

Captain Eadon in the hussar "ornamental uniform" worn before the charge. (The Queen's Royal Lancers)

Survivors' Accounts

Colonel Martin in the lancer uniform adopted after the charge. He wears his two Omdurman medals and a black armband in mourning for the dead. (The Queen's Royal Lancers)

"About 2,400 yards from the zariba the enemy were lying dead and wounded in heaps of six or seven and a lot of wounded horses and donkeys were here and there. We dismounted under a hill 500 yards east of Jebel Surgham and opened fire on the enemy while two officer's patrols under Lieutenants Pirie and Grenfell were sent to report on the enemy S.W of Jebel Surgham. Both these patrols were fired at heavily by the enemy at a range of under 200 yards but had no casualties. They reported that several bodies of the enemy were moving about S and S West of Jebel Surgham, most of them apparently unbroken, and that there was one formed body of about 1,000 strong one mile S of hill.

"At 8.45a.m. we received orders from the Sirdar to annoy enemy's right flank and if possible head them off from Omdurman. We immediately moved SW towards the retiring enemy's right flank and our combat patrols immediately reported enemy in front of us — about 600 they thought they had seen, but they could not get close enough to the enemy to report exact numbers. We continued to push on at a walk for another ten minutes when our combat patrols were suddenly driven rapidly back on us and we came under heavy fire from a body of the enemy 600 yards to our front.

"Our CO immediately moved us to the left in column of troops so as to take the enemy in flank, when we suddenly again came under fire of a large body of the enemy hidden in a khor 300 yards on our right flank. Men and horses began to go down under the hail of bullets and there was only one way out of a disaster and that was to charge home — which we accordingly did.

"I will now endeavour to record what I actually saw myself during this part of the fight. Before we wheeled into line to charge I could see over my right shoulder about 300 yards away a dense mass of Dervish footmen pouring a hail of bullets into us — luckily as usual most of them were too high. But it was not comfortable work riding along slowly in column of troops with the enemy blazing into our right flank, and I found myself calling out, 'Why the blazes don't we charge those — before they shoot us down?'; but directly we were wheeled into line and charged a wild feeling of satisfaction and a wish to put sword into an enemy came over me and as our pace quickened into a fast gallop, a wild cheer of excitement and deep satisfaction burst from us for at last for the first time in the history of the regiment, the 21st Lancers were charging in earnest and the prayer of generation upon generation of 21st Lancers was being granted — and nothing could have stopped us but absolute and complete annihilation.

"The Dervishes answered us with fierce hoarse yells of 'Allah il Allah, Khalifa Rasoul Allah' which completely drowned our cheers and some of them actually bounded joyfully forward to meet us as if victory was already theirs — for they had yet to learn what British Cavalry was. As we closed on them I noticed that my Squadron Leader and Squadron 2nd in command were riding with heads down as if riding against a hail storm and I found myself doing the same — and it was very much like riding against a hail storm as the bullets seemed to hail among us and there was a continuous 'whizz' 'whizz' 'whizz' and an occasional clink as a bullet hit a sword or lance point.

"Just before we hit them I saw straight in front of me a khor with rocks on either side filled with a dense mass of Dervishes packed round three flags, yelling defiance at us waving their spears and swords and firing their Remingtons, and amidst the smoke and waving arms I could see their upturned faces grinning hate, defiance and satisfaction at us.

Below left: *Lieutenant de Montmorency in khaki service dress. He was awarded the VC for his attempt to bring away the body of Lieutenant Grenfell. (The Queen's Royal Lancers)*

Above: *Lieutenant de Montmorency's troop sergeant — "I especially missed Sergeant Carter ... a magnificent soldier and a very skilful man-at-arms, and I knew he would have been with me unless something had happened to him." Carter had been killed in the Khor. (The Queen's Royal Lancers)*

Captain Kenna was awarded the VC (worn here on his later lancer full dress uniform) for going to the assistance of Major Crole-Wyndham, and later assisting de Montmorency's efforts to bring out Grenfell's body. (The Queen's Royal Lancers)

My charger attempted to incline to his left, but I managed to keep him straight and the next moment he jumped the rocks and I was in the khor and among them. They were as thick as bees and hundreds must have been knocked over by our horses. My charger — a polo pony — behaved magnificently, literally trampling straight through them. He only received a slight spear wound and I got through scot free except for a blow from some blunt weapon across my left arm and the left flap pocket of my coat cut through, which let out all my food (biscuits) for the day! Also my sword scabbard, sword frog, and one rein were cut.

"The two Dervishes that gave me most trouble as I pressed through the khor were — a fine clean-shaved light skinned, well bred looking swordsman who cut at me with a huge sword, right hand on hilt, left hand on right wrist. I can remember him well and also the hissing yell of 'Allah' and the look of ferocious hate with which he struck. I parried the blow but the strength of his cut knocked me half off my horse and as I recovered my seat a coal-black fiend put his rifle straight at my chest but before he fired I threw myself onto the other side of my horse's neck and he missed me.

"At this moment my horse and Pte.Miller's cannoned at the bottom of the khor and we passed out of the khor side by side — each of us having thus only one side to defend. Directly we got through the khor and had gone some 100 yards, we halted and faced about and we then saw the enemy had begun to retire westward all the time keeping up a heavy fire on us and we could see their Emirs rushing forward and trying to induce them to attack us while we were rallying but their followers weren't for it — they had already had enough of British Cavalry!

"At this moment I noticed that Pte.Byrne of my troop was as pale as death and reeling in his saddle from loss of blood so I told him he might fall out, but he answered, 'No, no Sir, I'm all right, fall in No. 2 Troop — where are the Devils?' I now began to get very annoyed with my troop for not rallying sooner for I could only find six men, but I soon learnt the reason for one of them called out to me, 'This is all that remains of No. 2 Troop', so I told them to rally with the rest of the Squadron while I went to see if I could find any of my troop still alive in the khor. I especially missed Sergeant Carter — my troop sergeant, a magnificent soldier and a very skilful man-at-arms, and I knew he would have been with me unless something had happened to him.

"En route to the khor I met Major Wyndham on foot running in magnificent style considering the length of his legs and holding his revolver up in the air in his right hand. This little scene was very amusing as I could see he was in no immediate danger there being no Dervishes near him except one horseman 40 yards behind him galloping after him with a spear, and directly I rode at this horseman he turned and attempted to make off and I consequently had to shoot him in the back.

"Near and in the khor I passed over the bodies of several of our men — terribly mutilated — also a number of bodies of the enemy and some wounded and also unwounded Dervishes who had stayed behind to loot or to mutilate — probably both. The sight of our mutilated dead made me 'see Red' and use very bad language and go for every Dervish I met like a Fury. It had the same effect afterwards on our men. I could not find Carter's body but suddenly I came upon the body of an officer lying face downwards. At first I thought it was Smyth's. At this moment I saw Kenna and Cpl.Swarbrick riding about near me so I called them both to the body and dismounting found it to be Grenfell's — terribly mutilated.

"As the regiment was now 400 yards away and the enemy, who had begun to advance again firing heavily, were only 200 yards off, we determined to bring Grenfell's body away before it was more mutilated and after a great effort — for a dead man is a terrible burden to lift — I managed to get him on to my horse, who took fright at the unusual burden and suddenly plunged forward, broke away from us and galloped off, Grenfell's body falling off him. Kenna and Cpl.Swarbrick immediately went in pursuit of my horse and most gallantly brought it back to me. I then made one more effort to get the body on my horse but I found it impossible to lift him quickly and as we were only three and in a few more moments several hundred Dervishes would be round us there was nothing for us to do but to retire. So I mounted my horse and we rode off together amidst a hail of bullets. There is no doubt that the Dervishes are the worst shots in the world and that not one of them in a hundred could hit a haystack at 50 yards!

"As we retired Taylor, who had rallied his troop, first opened fire on the advancing Dervishes — and he was soon reinforced by several other dismounted troops. This fire soon checked the enemy and drove them back again and they retreated westward in confusion. The Regiment mounted and advanced slowly after them, and we recovered

Corporal Swarbrick received the Distinguished Conduct Medal — and his third stripe — for his part in helping de Montmorency and Kenna. (The Queen's Royal Lancers)

all our dead, also three of their standards and some 72 of their dead were left in our hands. As they retired they crossed the front of the 2nd British Brigade who we could see just coming over the ridges W of Jebel Surgham Hill — and almost at the same moment the 32nd FBRA opened fire at about 2,000 yards range on the confused mass of the enemy and we could see the shrapnel bursting right over them — much to our joy for we didn't bear any feeling of kindness for that black mass who had just mutilated so many of our gallant comrades. They now retired westward into the great mass of broken enemy who were slowly and sullenly strolling from the battlefield towards the SW corner of Omdurman.

"We were masters of the khor, they having lost 52 killed in the charge and 20 by our carbine fire and no doubt they had a great number of wounded. Our loss was 1 officer and 20 men killed and 4 officers and 45 men wounded and 118 horses killed and wounded — a heavy price to pay for victory, but though perhaps it may have had no immediate effect on the result of the battle, it had a far-reaching result for it proved that the British Cavalry of today is imbued with the same spirit as the British Cavalry of the past, and that the boasted Dervish is absolutely no match in a hand to hand fight for the British trooper ... we knew that in our first battle the Regiment had behaved in a manner worthy of the traditions of the British Cavalry."

Lieutenant A.M.Pirie

Arthur Pirie, the Adjutant, received a spear wound in the shoulder during the mêlée. In his diary entry for 2 September, which was probably written the following morning, he fails to mention that his patrol first located the Hadendoa force blocking the Omdurman road[3].

"...When the Dervish attack had been beaten off on the left we were sent out on to the ridge again to see if they were retiring behind it & keep them off the river. We halted at the ridge and reconnoitred round. Grenfell & I went on & could see them all retiring.

"About ¼ of an hour after we returned, the Sirdar sent us orders to go out & head them all back from Omdurman. After going about a mile Picquet's [his horse's] bandage came untied & I had to wait & have it tied on again. Just as I got up to the regiment again I found them wheeling into line to charge about 200 dervishes who were firing at us from about 400 yards.

"I just had time to get into line & we were in it. They gave us a very hot time, luckily firing high as we had few men hit but it was an awful row, they kept up firing till we were among them, & then we came upon 2,000 of them who had been hiding in a nullah just behind. They came at us perfectly straight but the men came on beautifully & we got through them, how we did I don't know, as they were about 10 deep on bad ground. A lot of horses fell owing to the nullah & every man down was of course cut to pieces. We rallied on the far side & found them retiring so we dismounted 2 squadrons & gave them a very hot time. They retired right in towards our infantry which was what our object had been to make them do.

The account of the charge left by the Adjutant, Lieutenant Pirie, has a matter-of-fact style and comes quickly to the point...(The Queen's Royal Lancers)

"The regiment all went perfectly straight & one may well feel proud of the men. We lost very heavily with poor Grenfell killed. Nesham, Molyneux, Brinton, severely wounded, self slightly wounded. 20 NCOs & men killed & 45 wounded & 90 horses killed & wounded. De Montmorency & Kenna did a most plucky thing going back & getting poor Grenfell's body out. All the killed were awfully cut about. Luckily they didn't have time to mutilate them. I got a slight spear stab in the shoulder but had a very narrow escape. Picquet came right down on his head & didn't recover himself, for about ¼ of a minute I had both feet on the ground & six of them were round close to me, luckily they paused for me to roll over & he recovered himself & I got through.

"After we collected the dead & sent on the wounded, we went on on the right flank of the infantry …"

Lieutenant R.N.Smyth

Robert Smyth commanded the troop on the far left of A Squadron, where the enemy were still thickly packed. In a letter to his sister Alice written on 4 September from Omdurman, in which he refers to the battleground as the Range, his almost breathless prose beats with the adrenaline rush of the charge(4).

"Herewith a full account of my experience. You will have read the whole account by now in the papers so I shall confine myself to what I saw and did …

"Artillery duel goes on, having good view of it. Frightful slaughter of enemy, not much damage to zariba. We are ordered to high ground right of the Range to await orders to pursue. Good view of battlefield, horrible sight of dead & dying, wounded horses & men trying to get away, men on all fours creeping, finally giving up & lying down to die, horses neighing & galloping about aimlessly, a regular inferno.

"Retreating enemy cross the Range, & no longer under fire begin to try & reform. We are ordered to stop them, & clear plain Omdurman side of Range of any formed or forming bodies. We mount & go down at a sharp trot to plain in line of Squadron Columns.

"The aforesaid body about 200, 600 yards from left front. 'Troops left wheel.' Immediately met by volleys fairly accurately aimed, my right-hand man drops, his horse shot under him. Bullets seem whistling splashing all round. 'Right wheel into line.' 'Charge.' We are right Squadron & get orders 'Right Shoulders'. Manoeuvre well carried out. I am left Troop leader. Look round, see khor (ditch) 8 feet wide & 4 feet deep in front, other side a compact mass of white robed men apparently soundless, still firing, waving swords.

"Find myself at khor, man bolts out leaving 2 donkeys in my way, catch hold of horse hard by head, knowing to fall would be fatal. He blunders against donkey, recovers & scrambles out. Am met by swordsman on foot, cuts at my right front, I guard it with sword. Next man, fat face, all in white, having fired & missed me, throws up both hands, I cut him across the face, he drops. Large bearded man in blue with 2 edged sword in both hands cuts at me, think this time I must be done but pace tells & my guard carries it off. Duck my head to spear thrown, just misses me. Another cut at my horse, miss guard but luckily cut is too far away & only cuts through my breast plate [part of harness] & gives my horse a small flesh wound in neck & shoulder.

"Then I remember no more till I find myself outside with 4 or 5 of my troop. See Major Wyndham running, gallop to help him. Am just too late, Kenna has seized him & he takes him out not me. Rally my troop as well as I can. Horrible sights, everyone seems to be bleeding including my own horse. I don't know then if he badly hurt or not. It seems to be blood, blood, blood everywhere, horses & men smothered, either their own or other people's. Wounded men being carried off by others, as one sees in

… While that of Lieutenant Smyth spills out with hardly the time to form sentences, as if he were truly reliving the fight. (The Queen's Royal Lancers)

Lieutenant Winston Churchill photographed wearing khaki service dress in 1898 while attached to the 21st Lancers. Note that he wears a jacket with double breast pocket flaps and the ribbon of the 1895-1902 India General Service Medal — just a year before the charge he had narrowly escaped death in a fierce infantry mêlée in the Mamund Valley on the North-West Frontier. In this photo he has his Mauser pistol in its wooden holster-stock attached but forwards to the right side of his Sam Browne. (The Queen's Royal Lancers)

pictures, horses dropping down & being carried away. See Nesham led away with left hand hanging down. Words are passed on, 'Poor Grenfell killed', '2,000 men', 'Brinton shot' & 'Poor little Smyth killed' etc. (The Colonel, de Montmorency & Dauncey at first mistook Grenfell for me, he was so horribly mutilated).

"We reform. Take up their position & use dismounted fire. Men fire steadily. The break up is complete, the once formed band is dispersed, our charge has been successful. We are left in possession of the ground & the whole plain is ours. Some say we did right, others wrong, but the fact remains that we achieved our object & did what we were told to do. 300 cavalrymen had dispersed 1,500 to 2,000 riflemen who stood their ground. They may say that the charge was 'pour la gloire' but it was not only a brave feat but a successful one. The casualties were big for these times, 1 officer killed, 4 wounded, 20 men killed & 40 to 50 wounded, not counting the horses.

"After we saw the complete success of work we revisited the scene of the charge. I was told off to get six men of my troop to collect our dead. The less said or written about that the better. It was a ghastly sight. The tears streamed down my cheeks & I was physically sick. It was terrible. At this present moment I don't wish the morn' repeated, it cost too dear. I have always wanted to be in a charge & have got my desire & am satisfied.

"We appear to be the only lot who had real hard fighting & suffered to any extent ... It was an experience, & what struck me most was that you always hear that there are cases in every action where some men want dash & courage, in this instance I can't quote *one*. I would if I could because I value the statistics.

"As far as cavalry goes it is the biggest thing since Balaklava & I am proud of belonging to the 21st Lancers. Wise or unwise, it was a brave deed nobly done, & as Colonel Martin said, he was so proud & pleased that it had happened, as it proved that cavalry still existed & that we did not come here to play at mounted infantry."

Lieutenant W.S.Churchill

Winston Churchill, attached to the 21st Lancers from the 4th Hussars, commanded a troop on the right of A Squadron. He wrote immediate reports for the Morning Post, and a full account in The River War (1899). This more personal account was first published in My Early Life in 1930 (5).

"Immediately after the first attack had been repulsed we were ordered to leave the zariba, ascertain what enemy forces, if any, stood between Kitchener and the city, and if possible drive these forces back and clear the way for the advancing army ...

"Presently I noticed, 300 yards away on our flank and parallel to the line on which we were advancing, a long row of blue-black objects, two or three yards apart. I thought there were about 150. Then I became sure that these were men — enemy men — squatting on the ground. Almost at the same moment the trumpet sounded 'Trot', and the whole long column of cavalry began to jingle and clatter across the front of these crouching figures. Forthwith from every blue-black blob came a white puff of smoke, and a loud volley of musketry. Such a target at such a distance could scarcely be missed, and all along the column here and there horses bounded and a few men fell. ... The trumpet sounded 'Right wheel into line', and all the 16 troops swung round towards the blue-black riflemen. Almost immediately the regiment broke into a gallop, and the 21st Lancers were committed to their first charge in war!

"The troop I commanded was, when we wheeled into line, the second from the right of the regiment. I was riding a handy, sure-footed, grey Arab polo pony. Before we wheeled and began to gallop, the officers had been marching with drawn swords. On account of my shoulder I had always decided that if I were involved in hand-to-hand fighting, I must use a pistol and not a sword. I had purchased in London a Mauser automatic pistol, then the newest and the latest design. I had practised carefully with this during our march and journey up the river. This then was the weapon with which I determined to fight. I had first of all to return my sword into its scabbard, which is not the easiest thing to do at a gallop. I had then to draw my pistol from its wooden holster and bring it to full cock.

The available records are contradictory as to the precise date of Wade Rix's promotion to corporal – whether before or after the charge. This portrait was taken during his Great War service with the Mounted Military Police. (Courtesy R.W.Rix)

This duel operation took an appreciable time, and until it was finished, apart from a few glances to my left to see what effect the fire was producing, I did not look up at the general scene.

"Then I saw immediately before me, and now only half the length of a polo ground away, the row of crouching blue figures firing frantically, wreathed in white smoke. On my right and left my neighbouring troop leaders made a good line. Immediately behind was a long dancing row of lances couched for the charge. We were going at a fast but steady gallop. There was too much trampling and rifle fire to hear any bullets. After this glance to the right and left and at my troop, I looked again towards the enemy. The scene appeared to be suddenly transformed. The blue-black men were still firing, but behind them there now came into view a depression like a shallow sunken road. This was crowded and crammed with men rising from the ground where they had hidden. Bright flags appeared as if by magic, and I saw arriving from nowhere Emirs on horseback among and around the mass of the enemy. The Dervishes appeared to be ten or twelve deep at the thickest, a great grey mass gleaming with steel, filling the dry watercourse. In the same twinkling of an eye I saw also that our right overlapped their left, that my troop would just strike the edge of their array, and that the troop on my right would charge into air. My subaltern comrade on the right, Wormald of the 7th Hussars, could see the situation too; and we both increased our speed to the very fastest gallop and curved inwards like the horns of the moon ...

"The collision was now very near. I saw immediately before me, not ten yards away, the two blue men who lay in my path. They were perhaps a couple of yards apart. I rode at the interval between them. They both fired. I passed through the smoke conscious that I was unhurt. The trooper immediately behind me was killed at this place and at this moment, whether by these shots or not I do not know. I checked my pony as the ground began to fall away beneath his feet. The clever animal dropped like a cat four or five feet down on to the sandy bed of the watercourse, and in this sandy bed I found myself surrounded by what seemed to be dozens of men. They were not thickly packed enough at this point for me to experience any actual collision with them. Whereas Grenfell's troop next but one on my left was brought to a complete standstill and suffered very heavy losses, we seemed to push our way through as one has sometimes seen mounted policemen break up a crowd. In less time than it takes to relate, my pony had

Corporal Payne of C Squadron and the horse he rode in the charge; the original photograph is entitled "Omdurman Heroes". (The Queen's Royal Lancers)

The stone obelisk erected in 1899 on the site of the charge, on the plain between Jebel Surgham and Omdurman. (The Queen's Royal Lancers)

scrambled up the other side of the ditch. I looked round.

"Once again I was on the hard, crisp desert, my horse at a trot. I had the impression of scattered Dervishes running to and fro in all directions. Straight before me a man threw himself on the ground ... I saw the gleam of his curved sword as he drew it back for a ham-stringing cut. I had room and time enough to turn my pony out of his reach, and leaning over on the offside I fired two shots into him at about three yards. As I straightened myself in the saddle, I saw before me another figure with uplifted sword. I raised my pistol and fired. So close were we that the pistol actually struck him. Man and sword disappeared below and behind me. On my left, ten yards away, was an Arab horseman in a bright-coloured tunic and steel helmet, with chain-mail hangings. I fired at him. He turned aside. I pulled my horse into a walk and looked around again.

"... I saw two or three riflemen crouching and aiming their rifles at me from the fringe of it. I crouched over the saddle, spurred my horse into a gallop and drew clear of the melee. Two or three hundred yards away I found my troop already faced about and partly formed.

"I was still prepossessed with the idea that we had inflicted great slaughter on the enemy and had scarcely suffered at all ourselves. Three or four men were missing from my troop. Six men and nine or ten horses were bleeding from spear-thrusts or sword cuts. We all expected to be ordered immediately to charge back again. The men were ready, though they all looked serious. Several asked to be allowed to throw away their lances and draw their swords. I asked my second sergeant if he had enjoyed himself. His answer was: 'Well, I don't exactly say I enjoyed it, Sir; but I think I'll get more used to it next time.' At this the whole troop laughed.

"But now from the direction of the enemy there came a succession of grisly apparitions; horses spouting blood, struggling on three legs, men staggering on foot, men bleeding from terrible wounds, fish-hook spears stuck right through them, arms and faces cut to pieces, bowels protruding, men gasping, crying, collapsing, expiring. Our first task was to succour these; and meanwhile the blood of our leaders cooled. They remembered for the first time that we had carbines. Everything was still in great confusion. But trumpets were sounded and orders shouted, and we all moved off at a trot towards the flank of the enemy. Arrived at a position from which we could enfilade and rake the watercourse, two squadrons were dismounted and in a few minutes with their fire at 300 yards compelled the Dervishes to retreat. We therefore remained in possession of the field. Within 20 minutes of the time when we had first wheeled into line and begun our charge, we were halted and breakfasting in the very watercourse that had so very nearly proved our undoing. There one could see the futility of the much vaunted *Arme Blanche*. The Dervishes had carried off their wounded, and the corpses of 30 or 40 enemy were all that could be counted on the ground. Among these lay the bodies of over 20 Lancers, so hacked and mutilated as to be mostly unrecognisable."

Private W. Rix

Wade Rix was, like Churchill, his troop commander in A Squadron, only 23 at the time of the charge, in which his lance shattered on impact with the first Dervish. His recollections, written down years later, have a sense of immediacy that never left those who took part(6).

"The regimental lines were based at the southern end of the zariba near to the river Nile. We had taken no active part in the battle and so far had no idea if we would or no. The combined sound of rifle fire from our infantry, the shelling of the field guns and the rat, tat, tat of the Maxims had been intense though very reassuring. At about 8.30a.m. there was a lull in the battle. Then we noticed that there was some activity amongst our Officers and we soon learned that General Kitchener had given orders that we were to move out and make for Omdurman to prevent the retreating Dervishes from occupying the town. We tightened the girth on the horses, looked to our arms, mounted and were away within minutes.

"Two patrols scouted ahead to make sure that our path, which passed between the hill Jebel Surgham and the river, was clear of the enemy. We had barely covered a couple of miles when the patrols came galloping back to report, enemy ahead. The regiment continued at a walk when suddenly we came under sporadic fire. It came from a line of kneeling Dervishes, I should say they numbered around 100, then the bullets began to fly and several men and horses were hit. The Colonel had to make a quick decision, ignore this enemy group and push on to Omdurman or dispose of this group first. He took the latter course and the trumpet call 'right wheel into line' gave the answer.

"As we completed the movement the trumpet sounded 'trot'. Now here are 400 cavalry men, facing an enemy shooting to kill, there is nothing that will stop them from digging their spurs in and urging the horses into a gallop. The die is cast and down go the lances into the 'engage infantry' position. The galloping horses, beating hooves and the flying bullets produced an increased awareness of the action, a mixture of excitement and fear as we raced on towards the enemy. But what is this, 100 yards to go and before us an alarming sight presents itself. A dry stream bed is crammed with hundreds of dervishes who were hidden and waiting for the kill. Too late, it's a trap, nothing for it now, must go on, and on we go.

"As my horse leapt into the deep depression my lance entered the left eye of a white robed figure who had raised his double-edged sword to strike. The enormous impact and the weight of the man's body shattered the lance and I cast the broken pieces from me. I quickly drew my sword just in time as another man pointed his flintlock, I struck him down and blood splattered his white robe. Then it was parry and thrust as I spurred my horse on through the melee. Luck was with us, the horse bravely scrambled up the opposite bank of the stream bed and we were through without a scratch.

"Once out of the shambles of the stream bed the scene was one of confusion. Many horses were dead, others were trotting around riderless, some were in a distressing state standing with their heads down, most of them streaming with blood from the many gashes received from the fearsome double-edged swords wielded by the Dervishes. Mr. Churchill wanted the men to charge the enemy again but the Colonel wisely forbade it, instead we formed line, wheeled round to face the enemy's flank, dismounted and opened up a sustained rifle fire. This was more than they could stand and they finally retreated.

"I managed to get a chance to speak to my friend the Trumpet Major and he confirmed that the 'charge' was never sounded. Having sorted ourselves out we continued our delayed ride to Omdurman heading off the remnants of the enemy. It was a day that I shall never forget."

A later photograph taken after the memorial obelisk was protected by railings, showing men of the regiment revisiting the site. Interestingly, this shows part of the khor itself — and it is just as hard to distinguish the lip from the dead ground as it was on 2 September 1898. The ground falls away, obscured by vegetation, just above the tourist's scrawled note and the two rocks in the foreground. (The Queen's Royal Lancers)

98

CHAPTER EIGHT

The Second Dervish Attack

As five brigades of the Anglo-Egyptian army moved south in echelon towards Omdurman, the heights of Jebel Surgham stood in their path. General Lyttleton (commanding the 2nd British Brigade) was on the far left by the river; then General Wauchope (1st British Brigade), and Colonel Maxwell (2nd Egyptian Brigade), with Colonel Lewis (3rd Egyptian Brigade) passing over the eastern slopes of Surgham. This left Colonel MacDonald (1st Egyptian Brigade) on the far right, heading away from the rest to round the western slopes of the hill, from where he could turn south and rejoin the main army. Major Collinson with the 4th Egyptian Brigade remained in the rear to escort the baggage.

Those brigades heading almost due south, thinking the battle over and the final victorious march into Omdurman begun, pulled ahead at a faster pace than Kitchener would have wished, each eager to be first into the city. This had the effect of increasing the gap between MacDonald's brigade and the rest of the army. At 9.30a.m. a halt was ordered at the Surgham ridge to enable the rear brigades to catch up.

While the leading brigades waited, Lewis moved over the eastern slopes of Surgham, MacDonald headed towards the western slopes, and the hill came between the two like a wedge, pressing each further from the other as they advanced. This continued until MacDonald's 3,000 men were in effect isolated from the rest of the army — a fact quickly reported to the Khalifa by Dervish scouts. The lone brigade seemed easy prey to his black flag divison waiting in hiding behind the hill. Although the 15,000 warriors were almost all spearmen, the disparity in numbers and the advantage of surprise seemed to the Khalifa an assurance of victory, and he ordered an attack. Yaqub (his half-brother, given command of the black flag force) was not so confident. Informed that the second division in the Kerreri hills had already turned back, he delayed his attack in the hope of adding the riflemen of the green flag force to his own.

The Khalifa believed that Kitchener had made a serious mistake in allowing one brigade to become isolated from the rest. Captain Haig thought so too: "Having six brigades, is it tactics to fight a very superior enemy with one of them and to keep the others beyond supporting distance?"[1]. Haig was, of course, writing with hindsight. Kitchener certainly suspected that while the first Dervish division attacked the zariba and a second headed north after the Egyptian cavalry a third force remained in reserve, but at this time its strength and location were unknown. Some later accused him of deliberately allowing MacDonald to become isolated on the plain to tempt the Khalifa into revealing this force.

It is far more likely that Kitchener believed, on the basis of intelligence received from the 21st Lancers (to the effect that groups of fresh troops were heading south into Omdurman), that the Khalifa was withdrawing his third division with the intention of occupying the city. It then appeared crucial to Kitchener that he do so first, given his priority of avoiding costly street fighting. The possibility that this force might in fact have remained behind Jebel Surgham ready to launch a second attack seems to have been overlooked in his eagerness to take Omdurman.

At about 9.40a.m. — while two miles to the south the 21st Lancers struggled with the enemy in the khor — Hector MacDonald became aware of scattered parties of Dervishes on the slopes of the hill to his left flank. Although not yet a large enough number to indicate the presence of Yaqub's army (still hidden from view), MacDonald was concerned by his brigade's isolation, and sent Lieutenant Pritchard back to Kitchener to ask for support. Still thinking it a race between himself and the Khalifa to reach Omdurman first, Kitchener refused.

At 9.45 — as the 21st Lancers scrambled from the khor — Yaqub decided that he could wait no longer for the green flag riflemen to return from the north. MacDonald's brigade was closing fast and would soon be within sight. Yaqub told his men that God had delivered the enemy into their hands, and ordered the advance.

When MacDonald saw Yaqub's force round the Surgham, he realised that his brigade was now confronted by as great a number of the enemy as had earlier attacked all six brigades, and this time without the protection of a zariba. Nevertheless, he calmed his Egyptian and Sudanese troops, and when in their nervousness the latter opened fire at an impossible range he rode along the front line knocking up their rifles and ordering them to cease fire. The 15,000 Dervish spearmen walked steadily forward, and MacDonald allowed them to come on unhindered.

At 400 yards the enemy broke into a charge and immediately the first volley was fired into their front line; as each man fell another filled the gap, and on they came. The constant fire from MacDonald's riflemen was so intense that within each six- or seven-second period the whole Dervish front line dropped down dead or wounded. Those behind leapt over the bodies and came on regardless, steadily narrowing the distance until they were within 100 yards. Yaqub's spearmen had to come within ten yards before they could strike, and the absence of green flag riflemen meant that no covering fire was available; nevertheless, with 15,000 men he could bear heavy losses in closing with the enemy, certain that once within striking distance his superior numbers would quickly tell.

This second Dervish attack might well have gone as Yaqub planned had it not been for MacDonald's Maxim guns. Their massive rate of fire increased Dervish casualties to the point at which the advance faltered. Watching from the rear, Babikr Bedri had little idea exactly what a Maxim gun was, but he knew what it sounded like and what it did

In this naif but lively impression by A.Sutherland dated 1898, artistic licence fills the Kerreri plain in front of the main Anglo-Egyptian position with the opposing armies, and has the 21st Lancers — seen at top left behind Jebel Surgham, in two ranks — charging many times the number they actually faced. However, despite the false curvature the relative position of the opposing forces is more accurately conveyed than in some sketch maps of the battle. (The Queen's Royal Lancers)

to his comrades: "We saw them advance ... and the enemy fired on them with a sound like 'Runnnn'. They did not return"[2].

Meanwhile Kichener, hearing the sounds of battle, moved quickly to correct his earlier error. He ordered Maxwell to turn his brigade, cross directly over Jebel Surgham and advance down the hill to attack the enemy's right flank. Lyttleton was to move round the hill and come at the enemy from behind; Lewis was to turn back and reinforce MacDonald (as previously requested). Captain Sparkes, with Lewis's brigade, wrote: "We received orders to go to his help and you may guess we didn't waste time, but still only got into about the last quarter of an hour of the fight. We fired however 37,000 rounds of ammunition in the time and did considerable damage"[3]. Under heavy fire from these reinforcements, and forced to turn a large part of his force to meet the attack on his right flank, Yaqub could no longer keep up the pressure on MacDonald, and soon the Dervishes fell back under the immense firepower now turned against them.

At about this time an artillery shell landed at Yaqub's feet, instantly killing him and all the men of his bodyguard. Arab accounts state that the Khalifa, seeing that the attack had failed and hearing of his brother's death, fell to his knees in prayer and seemed deaf to those imploring him to flee the battlefield. He may have realised that the firepower of the Anglo-Egyptian army was unassailable, and that his mistake was failing to do what Kitchener assumed he would — retreat to Omdurman and force the enemy to come after him. Both men allowed their personal convictions to lead them into error, Kitchener believing that it was a race to the capital, the Khalifa certain that the bones of his enemies would whiten the Kerreri plain. In the event the overwhelming firepower of the Anglo-Egyptian army, thrown into the balance, alleviated Kitchener's mistake and compounded the Khalifa's.

*   *   *

The balance swung suddenly back in the Khalifa's favour with the reappearance of the green flag division from the Kerreri hills. At the outset of the first Dervish attack this force had moved north after the Egyptian cavalry, the Camel Corps and the horse artillery, the Khalifa taking these to be the rear of a much larger force. Broadwood deliberately led the enemy away from the zariba to divide the Dervish force, and both Kitchener (after despatching a gunboat) and the Khalifa then became embroiled in the battle and "forgot" their forces to the north. During the chase the Camel Corps and horse artillery found the rocky ground in the hills hard going, and only fire from the gunboat *Melik* prevented the Dervishes overwhelming them. In turning back to the zariba the Camel Corps now led the enemy back too.

MacDonald's brigade was facing west, firing on the last of the Khalifa's black flag division, when Uthman al Din (the Khalifa's son) came down unexpectedly from the Kerreri hills with his green flags — 10,000 men reinforced by Ali Wad Ulla's 5,000. MacDonald swung his brigade from west to north, completing the manoeuvre just as the enemy came within 200 yards. Much of the support ordered forward by Kitchener was still moving into position, and MacDonald felt that his brigade alone was taking on the full might of the Dervish army.

Wauchope rushed his brigade forward, sending the 1st Battalion, The Lincolnshire Regiment to reinforce MacDonald's right, yet still out of range. The Dervishes were within 100 yards of MacDonald's front and coming on quickly. Once again artillery and Maxim fire was put to good effect; but the Dervish infantry swept on over the dead and wounded careless of loss, and it seemed that nothing could stop them.

The medical station had remained in the zariba, its staff tending the wounded as best they could, although the three barges equipped to act as floating hospitals had earlier been towed to the far bank so as not to obstruct the gunboats and no boats were now available to return them. At this point, when it seemed possible that the Dervish attack from the north might slip round MacDonald's right flank, overrun the medical post and slaughter all within it, the 49 wounded officers and men of the 21st Lancers arrived. The most seriously injured were immediately loaded onto an ammunition barge, but still no boat was available to tow this across to the operating equipment waiting on the hospital barges. The infantry dead (and Grenfell, whose body the Lancers had brought in with them from the khor) were hastily buried beside the Nile for fear they might fall into the hands of the enemy.

Medical staff were shocked by the severity of the lancers' wounds. Until this point the only casualties had been infantrymen suffering clean bullet wounds, for nowhere had the Dervish spearmen yet come within striking distance of the front line. These cavalrymen had deep, gaping wounds. Some arrived still impaled by spears, the barbs below the spearhead — pointing in both directions along the shaft — making it impossible to either pull out or push through without a great wad of flesh being torn away with it. Several men had to be operated upon immediately, despite the lack of sterile conditions, with empty ammunition boxes serving as an operating table.

The Dervishes were now within 40 yards of MacDonald's brigade and his Sudanese troops were down to their last few rounds of ammunition; within seconds they would be forced to resort to the bayonet in hand-to-hand combat as the enemy reached their front line. The foremost warriors came within ten yards and the first spears were hurled. At this last possible moment, A Company of the Lincolns came up on the right and within firing range. The Lincolns claimed to fire volleys faster and more accurately than any other British battalion, and MacDonald's fate depended on the truth of this boast. The first volley was insufficient to stop the Dervish advance but gained precious seconds. As further companies of the Lincolns came up, and volley after volley struck the enemy ranks, the advance faltered to a halt just yards from MacDonald's bayonets.

The remainder of Wauchope's brigade arrived at the left of the line and added their firepower, and soon the Dervishes were falling back. The second Dervish attack, quickly and rightly named "MacDonald's Battle" by the men, was over. MacDonald could claim to have borne the brunt of the fighting, though both Lewis and Wauchope (and particularly the 1st Lincolns) had played an essential part. Perhaps it was regimental rivalry or an imperfect view of the battlefield that led Captain Sparkes (with Lewis) to write that "Wauchope's brigade got up too late and never fired a shot"[4].

As the Dervish infantry retreated, among the dead and wounded littering the battlefield there remained a considerable party of Baggara cavalry (100 according to Haig, although Sparkes thought them 200, and Churchill, who was two miles away with the 21st Lancers and cannot have seen them, wrote of 400 — later commentators added even to that). The number was irrelevant, for the act was magnificent. Sparkes watched as they chose to die rather than retire from the field: "One of the finest things I've ever seen was during this attack, some 200 Baggara cavalry made a desperate charge against MacDonald's line. They hadn't a chance against the terrific fire he poured on them, but not one man faltered, each rode to his death without flinching, a few got so close that officers drew their revolvers but none got up to the line"[5].

This last charge of the Dervish cavalry was tactically pointless, the battle already lost, and yet left many of the Anglo-Egyptian troops feeling that they had witnessed the greatest act of valour on the field that day. It was a fitting parallel to the earlier charge of the 21st Lancers, the last full regimental charge against a standing enemy made by the British cavalry. This too was dismissed as tactically pointless, the battle being won elsewhere, yet caught the imagination of those at home as an act of dash and valour unmatched by infantry regiments partly dependent on field guns and Maxims to keep the enemy at bay.

The battle was effectively over and Kitchener, still concerned that he might be beaten to the capital, sent the Egyptian cavalry to harass the retreating warriors. Haig wrote that "little groups of men dropped on their knees in submission, though some firmly resisted until killed by our lances"[6]. Dervish riflemen, retreating but unbeaten, opened fire and made it impossible for the cavalry to proceed. Brought to a stop in the midst of the enemy, the Egyptians were in danger of being surrounded and overwhelmed and had to withdraw at the gallop.

At 11.30a.m. Kitchener claimed the victory that was rightly MacDonald's, and immediately began the delayed march south to the capital with Lyttleton's and Maxwell's

Kitchener (second from left) leads his army into Omdurman. In the right background can be seen the defeated Khalifa's black flag. (The Queen's Royal Lancers)

2 SEPTEMBER: FINAL DERVISH ATTACK

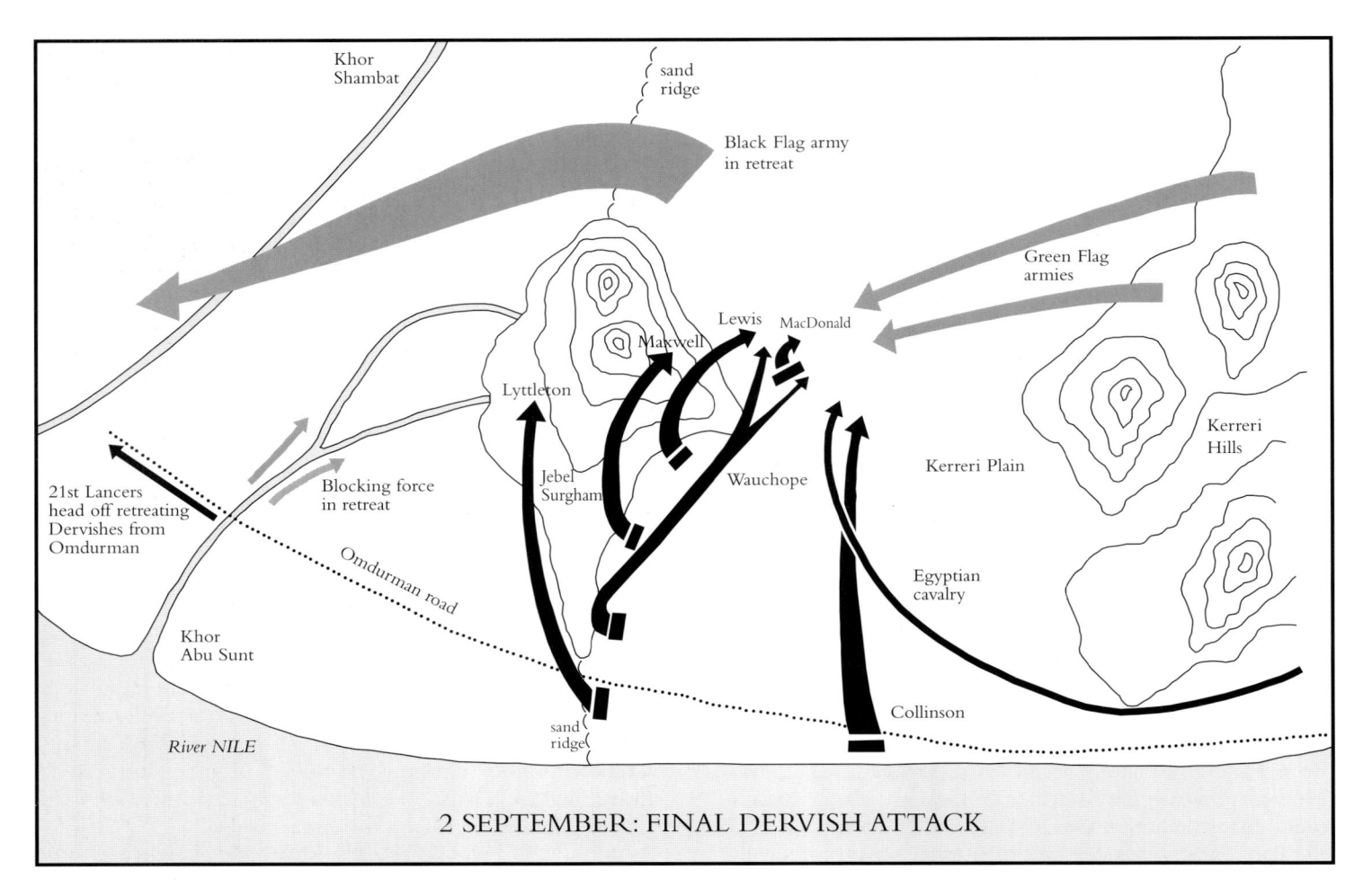

brigades, leaving the rest to regroup and follow on as soon as possible.

Into Omdurman

Further south the 21st Lancers continued to head off retreating Dervishes in accord with the Sirdar's order. W.T.Maud, a great artist if not so distinguished a correspondent, claimed that "the Lancers were practically useless after their magnificent charge"[7]. In fact the regiment had returned immediately to the task Kitchener had set, in effect closing the Omdurman road to the enemy. After MacDonald had repulsed the black flag and green flag divisions the numbers retreating southwards became huge and the lancers' task impossible. They could see many Dervishes making a wide arc, moving out into the desert to avoid them, then turning back into Omdurman. The need to patrol the direct route the infantry would take prevented the 21st from intercepting those who took a desert route.

As a further handicap, many of the walking wounded came forward to surrender, throwing down their weapons and holding up their hands, saying *"Amaan, amaan"*. At first they were ignored, but some then retrieved their spears and hurled them after the lancers. Major Finn was concerned that some of his men, having seen the hacked bodies of their comrades in the khor, and infuriated by this ruse, might disgrace the regiment; but "not a single wounded Dervish was killed except by order of an officer, which was rarely given, and only when necessary to save a man from treachery"[8]. Once it was seen that surrender was accepted large numbers of the enemy came in, and an increasing number of lancers had to be detailed to disarm and escort a growing column of prisoners.

Thousands more kept their distance. The 21st could certainly no longer "head them off" but could, however, "annoy them": "Those still intent on flight made a wide detour to avoid the cavalry, and streamed past our front at a mile's distance in uninterrupted succession ... thousands of Dervishes escaped into Omdurman. To harry and annoy the fugitives a few troops were dismounted with carbines and a constant fire was made on such as did not attempt to come in and surrender"[9].

Among those who reached Omdurman was the Khalifa himself. Because the 21st Lancers patrolled the area between the battlefield and the city he and his bodyguard had taken the wide detour. He may have returned to the capital in the hope of gathering men for further resistance; the numbers prepared to rally proved inadequate, and in any case the howitzer and gunboat bombardment had breached the city walls and left most of the fortified buildings in ruins. Acknowledging that his army was defeated and his city lost, the Khalifa collected his family and valuables and made good his escape.

Kitchener, unaware of this but informed of unbeaten troops retiring towards Omdurman, was concerned that a large force might build up in the city and offer considerable resistance. His brigades were exhausted, and when at 12.30p.m. they reached the waters of Khor Shambat he ordered a halt to rest and water, so that they would be prepared for renewed battle when they reached Omdurman. The 21st continued to patrol between the Shambat and the outermost mud houses of the city suburbs. These stretched for almost two miles along the Nile, to the walled enclosure within which the main buildings lay, and where any last stand would be mounted.

At about 1.30p.m., 30 minutes before leaving the Khor Shambat, Kitchener sent a message to Colonel Martin ordering him to inspect the camp just outside Omdurman (where the Dervish army had been located the previous day before leaving to form up on the plain), to ascertain whether it had been reoccupied. Martin sent a patrol — Lieutenant Smyth and four men — towards the camp; Smyth found it to be deserted, but his patrol was fired on from a building within the city: "As I could get no cover I had to retire about 100 yards as they were firing straight at us ... think I am entitled to say I was first in Omdurman, as the camp was part of it"[10]. Possibly because of this intelligence, Kitchener ordered the area of the Mahdi's tomb (likely to be the focus of any last stand) to be shelled. He then left the Khor Shambat and approached with Maxwell's brigade and the 32nd Field Battery.

Passing untroubled through the suburbs of Omdurman where only women and children peered in fear from mud huts, the Sirdar reached the walled city. Stationing two guns and three battalions at the main approach, he sent four guns and one battalion along the river bank to enter the city through breaches in the wall made by the howitzers. This force met only token resistance and quickly located a straight road leading to the Mahdi's Tomb and the Khalifa's residence. When it was clear that no organised resistance lay in wait Kitchener led the remainder of his troops in to occupy the city. The 21st Lancers' favourite correspondent, Hubert Howard, had by now detached himself from the regiment and entered Omdurman with the Sirdar.

Perhaps in his eagerness to see final victory, Kitchener led his men straight towards the Tomb, forgetting that his order to shell the area had not been rescinded. Four shells were fired just in advance of his approach and he quickly retreated, sending immediate orders for the shelling to cease. Sadly this was too late to stop a fifth shell, and Hubert Howard, who had gone ahead of the troops, was at the entry to the Khalifa's residence when this exploded nearby, killing him instantly. The 21st Lancers heard the shelling from the plain but had no reason to fear that they had lost a friend.

By 3.00p.m. Wauchope, MacDonald and Lewis arrived with their brigades at the Khor Shambat and halted. Soon afterwards Collinson arrived escorting the baggage. It is unclear exactly when the 21st Lancers was called in to rest and water. According to Churchill this was at 2.00,

An accurate reconstruction of the Khalifa's residence in Omdurman built on its original site. (Khalifa's House Museum, Omdurman)

The gateway to the Khalifa's residence in Omdurman, shelled as Kitchener approached. Times correspondent Hubert Howard and several Sudanese civilians were killed at this point, and bodies can be distinguished beneath the debris. (National Army Museum)

although Pirie records it as 3.00 and de Montmorency has 4.00p.m. It is unlikely that Kitchener would bring the regiment in from the approaches to Omdurman before he had reached the city, given his fear of resistance in strength, but by 3.00 the city had been secured and the lancers could be safely retired. Pirie says that the regiment rested from 3.00 to 5.00 and this is most likely correct, for they found the regiment's mess camels at the Shambat with the baggage, which arrived a little after 3.00.

The water of Khor Shambat was badly polluted. De Montmorency described it as "thick and muddy and strongly flavoured with dead camel, dead donkey and dead Dervish", though the lancers "drank quarts of it all the same and found it most refreshing"[11]. They then settled down to a feast of bully-beef and biscuits from the mess camels.

At 5.00 those brigades still at the Shambat were ordered to join the Sirdar in Omdurman. The 21st Lancers and the Egyptian cavalry were to continue patrolling north and west of the city, turning away any groups of unbeaten warriors attempting to enter. Finn complained that they were "everywhere obstructed and delayed by the surrender of hundreds of prisoners"[12]. This was particularly frustrating, because among the vast numbers of women and children leaving the town far away to the south they could see armed horsemen. The 21st became convinced that the Khalifa escaped with these, and they may have been right. Kitchener believed that the Khalifa left Omdurman shortly before the first Anglo-Egyptian troops entered the city, but Arab accounts indicate that he departed some time after the occupation and barely avoided capture.

At about 7.00p.m. fresh orders were received. Broadwood was to take the Egyptian cavalry and the Camel Corps south in pursuit of the Khalifa; Colonel Martin was to continue patrolling the outskirts of the city, lest Dervish troops regroup in the desert and return under cover of darkness. It had been a long day, the men and horses were exhausted, and neither commanding officer relished the task allotted him. Martin felt that the 21st Lancers should have been called in — it was at this time that the infantry brigades bivouacked around the town. Broadwood felt that the Khalifa could have been captured much earlier and his present task avoided. De Montmorency agreed: "The mounted troops could easily have gone round to the SW of Omdurman and cut off the Khalifa's line of retreat, but ... they were simply wasted"[13].

De Montmorency later wrote of his own part in the chase after the Khalifa; possibly, then, Colonel Martin allowed this officer a temporary attachment to the Egyptian cavalry. As the main route south followed the Nile a gunboat went with them, carrying the forage and rations. The increasingly marshy ground by the river forced the cavalry into the desert and contact with the gunboat was lost. Without essential supplies, Broadwood abandoned the chase after 30 miles.

Outside Omdurman, when by 8.00p.m. Colonel Martin had still not been called in, he became most concerned. His men and horses had been in action from first light, all were exhausted, and yet they were left out patrolling in total darkness — a hazardous task of doubtful value. By 9.00 he was forced to conclude (probably rightly) that Kitchener had simply forgotten the 21st Lancers. No order to come in and bivouac was received, and at 9.15 Martin made the decision himself.

The regiment moved at a walk between the rows of mud huts lit only by an occasional fire, wary of half-seen figures watching from the gloom. At about 10.00 the 21st bivouacked next to the infantry beside the city wall. As they unsaddled and picketed the horses, Captain Eadon noticed "a small bundle" close to his horse's leg: "Found it was small Dervish baby not long born, and quite lively"[14]. When it began to cry Lieutenant Wormald picked it up and pressed it into the arms of a wounded Dervish.

Only now did they hear of Hubert Howard's death. Howard had ridden with them in the charge and afterwards had been first to ride up and congratulate Martin; his loss was as keenly felt as if he had been a member of the regiment. In the days that followed, as inaccurate reports of the charge appeared in the press, the 21st deeply regretted the loss of the one correspondent who had grown close enough to the regiment to write a fair and accurate account.

Several officers, eager for a glimpse of the city, ventured inside that night — one indignantly reported seeing the Sirdar (who had forgotten his cavalry) sleeping soundly. They came back with a supper of sausages and tea, these luxuries begged from British cooks encamped with the baggage by the ruins of the Mahdi's Tomb. There turned out to be few with whom they could share these spoils; most were by now asleep.

De Montmorency, who had gone after the Khalifa with the Egyptian cavalry and bivouacked with them in the desert, slept soundly too: "I lay down — helmet and all on — and tied my horse to my wrist, and though he walked about during the night and pulled me after him, I slept like a top"[15].

Kitchener had issued a General Order to all troops that evening, congratulating them on their excellent behaviour and announcing that their total defeat of the Khalifa's forces had avenged Gordon at last. The forgotten 21st Lancers had come in too late to hear it.

CHAPTER NINE

Aftermath, Reactions and Rewards

Before first light on 3 September the 21st Lancers received orders to move to a point by the river five miles south of Omdurman, to patrol the southern approach to the city and report immediately any sighting of formed groups of Dervishes returning from the desert. Although the Khalifa had fled it was conceivable that he might regroup some part of his scattered army and turn back in a desperate counter-attack.

The regiment reached its allotted point by the Nile at 8.00a.m. Patrols went out continuously several miles west, crossing the plain south of Omdurman and returning to the river. Each returned with several times its own number of Dervishes, who had abandoned their weapons and surrendered. Many of these were walking wounded seeking medical attention. Others were deserters from the Khalifa's retreating army, trusting the mercy of the victor over the pitiless rigours of the desert. All had to be escorted into the city, where the wounded received rudimentary treatment and the deserters were (by all accounts, without undue pressure) enrolled in the Sirdar's army — a normal procedure in that part of the world. The first task given these recruits was clearing the streets of Omdurman of corpses and rubble from the howitzer and gunboat bombardment.

Between patrols the lancers watered the horses, washed in the river, and cooked. Many Dervishes had fled taking their livestock with them, and on their surrender these animals were taken into custody too. Captain Eadon noted that the lancers "captured many sheep and goats which men soon made into good dinners"[1]. Shortly after 3.00p.m. the regiment was ordered to return north, pass by Omdurman and bivouac at the Khor Shambat. There was some disgruntlement that the 21st had not yet been given an opportunity to explore the capital, particularly as the infantry had already enjoyed a 24-hour head start in looting everything of interest — the victors' traditional reward.

Early on the morning of 4 September Colonel Martin visited the wounded, now on one of the hospital barges moored by the city wall. Pirie went too and was relieved to discover that Lieutenant Nesham would not after all lose his hand, although it would never again be of much use to him. Later that day the wounded officers — Captains Fair and King, and Lieutenants Brinton and Nesham — were due to leave by steamer.

At 9.00a.m. detachments of men from each regiment were ferried across the Nile by the gunboats and steamers to the ruins of Khartoum, to attend a memorial service for General Gordon and all those killed during this present campaign. The 21st Lancers was represented by 12 officers and 24 men — all wanted to attend, and these numbers were selected by drawing lots. Several walls of Government House (better known among the men as "Gordon's Palace") still stood, but the inside of the building had been gutted. At the top of one partly demolished wall two flag staffs were erected, and the representatives of the several regiments lined up in front of these, with the Sirdar to the front. At precisely 10.00a.m. the gunboat *Melik* fired a single shell; the band played the British national anthem while the Union Jack was raised, followed by the Egyptian national anthem while the Khedive's Crescent was raised. After scripture readings and prayers, and "Abide With Me" (Gordon's favourite hymn), the *Melik* fired a 21-gun salute; no blanks were available and live shells were aimed south of Omdurman.

After the service most of those present visited the steps on which Gordon was killed. Some wanted to have the single word "Avenged" chiselled into the stone, and Major Finn thought the same should be done to Gordon's statue in Trafalgar Square. Pirie found that many officers of other

Dervish prisoners being escorted into Omdurman by infantry; every patrol sent out by the 21st returned with several times its own number of surrendered Mahdists. (National Army Museum)

105

Raising the flags over the ruins of Government House during the Gordon Memorial Service held in Khartoum on 4 September. (National Army Museum)

regiments wanted to hear more about the 21st Lancers' charge, and recorded with obvious satisfaction that it had made a great impression on everyone.

Captains Eadon and Cordeaux, not among those chosen to attend the memorial service, revisited the grave of the lancers north of Omdurman and went on to inspect the site of the infantry battle. By now they had heard of the "last charge" of the Baggara cavalry, and sought out the spot where these men fell: "The sights and smells were very disgusting, but it was a sight to see especially where their cavalry had bravely charged down on our square. In one place they left one straight line of dead horses which had evidently been swept away by the Maxims"[(2)].

Over the whole extent of the battlefield the dead lay on average three yards apart, but so thickly in some places that no part of the ground beneath them was visible. Two days beneath the desert sun had left these corpses in a hideous state, hugely swollen and hardly recognisable as human beings. Yet more horrific was the sight of badly wounded men among the dead, still lying where they fell 48 hours earlier. (Estimates of Dervish casualties vary wildly. It is likely that at least 5,000 were killed on the day of the battle, and that as many again, seriously wounded, lay where they fell. Although the walking wounded who surrendered received some attention, the seriously wounded were taken water by a convoy of 150 mules but otherwise left to die.)

Both Eadon and Cordeaux were disappointed to find few weapons left on the ground, but collected several spears. The infantry had taken many as souvenirs for themselves before quitting the battlefield, and Kitchener had most of the remainder collected and burned.

Pirie (as Adjutant) spent the early hours of 5 September determining which of the wounded men were incapable of making the return march to Cairo and would need to follow the officers by boat, and selecting wounded horses to be left behind. The rest of the day was free, the first chance he and many of the lancers had to explore Omdurman. Pirie and Kenna toured the city in search of souvenirs, but there was little to be found; the infantry had taken everything that was not under guard. The more enterprising among these men now auctioned their booty, and the lancers, coming late onto the scene, found that they had to purchase their souvenirs dearly. Nevertheless Pirie was pleased with the loot he bought, and Kenna was delighted with a copy of the Koran.

Eadon and Finn made straight for the arsenal, its rooms packed with Remington rifles and ammunition, all of which the Khalifa had left unissued while most of his warriors attacked the zariba armed only with spears. The lancers were most interested in several suits of ringmail armour; traditionally such items were always said to have been "taken centuries earlier from the Crusaders", although they were far more likely to be of more recent Persian make. By now, however, the arsenal had been placed under guard and nothing could be removed.

After the arsenal, everyone made a point of visiting the Mahdi's Tomb. Rubble from the huge holes blown in its roof covered the stone tomb and the floor, and by now the brass railings surrounding the tomb had been stripped of their hangings. (These four black panels bearing a text from the Koran in yellow lettering were later acquired by an officer of the 21st). The building was unsafe and soon had to be demolished, although Kitchener would no doubt have had it pulled down in any case.

At this stage the stone tomb itself had not been defiled. Kitchener, believing that because it contained the embalmed body of the Mahdi it might become the focal point of any future Dervish uprising, had the body removed and decapitated. This was arguably a more barbaric act than that committed by the Dervishes on the body of Gordon, which had at least been motivated by the belief that it would have an effect on the victim in the afterlife. The body was thrown into the Nile and the head retained. While the Egyptian and Sudanese troops approved, most of the British officers thought this wrong, among them Captain Sparkes: "The bones of the Mahdi have been

Bodies of Dervishes on the Kerreri plain two days after the battle. The seriously wounded had been given water but were otherwise left to die where they lay. (National Army Museum)

General Gordon's telescope recovered in Omdurman, held here by a slightly built trooper of the 21st and a Guardsman of the Grenadiers. (National Army Museum)

chucked into the river, which I think rather bad form"(3). Worse still, Kitchener planned to have the head mounted in silver to serve as an inkwell. Word of this reached Queen Victoria, who ensured that her general heard of her disgust. He decided to have the skull buried, as the Queen desired.

★   ★   ★

Before beginning the return march to Cairo on 6 September the 21st Lancers were entertained to a farewell lunch by the Egyptian cavalry. The Sirdar then came to see them off at 3.00p.m., and the regiment formed up to receive him. His farewell speech was short and to the point:

"Colonel Martin, officers and men of the 21st Lancers, I am proud to have had you under my command: the fine charge you made the other day will long go down to history in the annals of your regiment and be looked upon with pride by the whole of the British cavalry. I will not keep you any longer, but I hope you will have a pleasant march down to the Atbara"(4). The regiment gave three cheers for the Sirdar before moving off north towards Kerreri, where the first night's bivouac was planned.

En route, Colonel Martin paused at the scene of the charge. The dead had been buried in the ground over which they had charged rather than in the bottom of the khor where they fell. Now the survivors formed a square with the grave at its centre. Martin spoke briefly — his words were nowhere recorded, but Finn wrote that he "paid a well earned tribute to those around whose simple grave we were standing"(5). While some men held the horses the remainder collected large stones from the surrounding area, each man adding his stone to the grave as he passed by. The broken lance tied to make a cross and erected at the time of the burial was now fixed between the stones at the summit of this rough cairn. Martin had already spoken with his officers and decided that a stone obelisk should later be erected on this spot, inscribed with the names of the dead. In total silence the regiment proceeded two miles further north to the grave of Lieutenant Grenfell by the river, placing a second broken lance at its head.

From Grenfell's grave the lancers rode north, passing over the battlefield, its sights more horrific still and its sweetish stink so appalling that not until they bivouacked beneath the Kerreri Hills could they breath free of the smell and (it seemed to some) the acid taste of death. Here and elsewhere they were afflicted by scorpions which appeared from the cracked earth as they slept and "particularly liked a bit of good Captain ... whiskey, inwardly and outwardly applied, was the usual remedy"(6). Lieutenant Churchill now detached himself from the 21st to join a passing steamer and return by river with the Guards.

During the days that followed the regiment proceeded north, marching from 5.30a.m. to 1.00p.m. each day, by which time all were exhausted. Many found the return march worse than the advance; the sun seemed stronger, and one man (Private Case) died of heat exhaustion. Because of the rising Nile, khors that had been dry on the march south were now full and required lengthy detours. There were extra swampy areas, making it difficult to reach the bank and pick up supplies from the boats carrying rations and barley, though the regiment never went hungry — when flocks of sand grouse flew over the officers bagged several apiece, and no herd of gazelle was allowed to pass without contributing to the regimental pot.

On their passing through one small village an elderly woman brought them water, and explained that all the men of the village had been killed by the Khalifa. When De Montmorency (via his Jaalin servant) told of the battle and the Dervish losses, she raised her eyes and hands to heaven and gave thanks to Allah.

On arriving at the Atbara on 19 September Colonel Martin found 100 waiting telegrams congratulating the regiment on its charge, among them: "Congratulations and sympathy" (5th Lancers); "Many congratulations, brilliant performance" (7th Hussars); "Congratulations on your brilliant victory" (12th Lancers).

At the same time the regiment saw the first newspaper reports, and these were not so wholehearted in their praise. *The Times* was fair enough: "This maiden charge of the 21st

A morbid cairn erected on the site of the Dervish attack by Anglo-Egyptian troops. The regiment built a simple rock cairn over the grave of its dead. (The Queen's Royal

Wounded officers in the British Military Hospital at Abadia, including Lieutenants J. C. Brinton (third from left) and Nesham (far right). (The Queen's Royal Lancers)

Lancers is regarded as an extremely brilliant affair"[7]. But the *Daily Mail* was blunt: "... a gross blunder"[8]. Bennet Burleigh, who wrote for the *Daily Telegraph*, summed up the approach most correspondents took: "One cannot refuse to admire the gallant deed ... but the obvious comment will be that made about the Balaklava charge — *C'est magnifique, mais ce n'est pas la guerre*"[9]. *The Globe* suggested that the charge was made *pour la gloire*: "... not to win the battle, for that was virtually over, but merely to seize the opportunity to prove of what stuff the 21st Lancers and the British cavalry are made"[10]. The report in *The Graphic* was so inaccurate that many of the men were merely amused, but de Montmorency admitted to being disappointed. Eadon told his father that "there are some curious accounts in the papers of our charge. Poor Howard was killed ... he was quite one of us and was the only correspondent who had a complete idea of our charge"[11].

From the Atbara the Lancers travelled north by train on Kitchener's Sudan Military Railway to Wadi Halfa. Once across the Egyptian border they continued by steamer to Khiva, and transferred to rail for the final part of the journey, arriving back at Abbassia on 26 September — to be welcomed by a band on the platform playing "Soldiers of the Queen".

On 2 October, just one week after returning from the Sudan, Colonel Martin handed over command of the regiment to Major Crole-Wyndham and left for England. At an emotional farewell dinner given by the officers Crole-Wyndham spoke warmly of their colonel — "We have never been more of a happy family than during the last six years ..." — and echoed an anti-establishment sentiment that had become almost a tradition of the 21st: "Colonel, I would point out that this is no ceremonious dinner; we have asked no Big Wigs of the civil service, no bloated aristocrats of the staff ..."[12].

The Big Wigs and bloated aristocrats of the staff were, it was thought, behind Martin's indecently hasty departure. Colonel Martin was too much an officer and a gentlemen to question the decision of the War Office, where it seemed to be believed (though no one said as much) that he had rushed his regiment blindly into an unnecessary charge.

Others had made the accusation publicly, and this allowed Martin to put the record straight in a newspaper interview given in Portsmouth immediately upon his arrival home:

"I have seen the way the German Military Attaché criticised the charge, but I did not pay much attention to his remarks, as he has formed them on quite erroneous grounds. In the first place, he was not there, and has no knowledge of the actual situation ... He says that we had no patrols out. That is wrong. In fact, he is quite inaccurate throughout his criticism. We were sent to head the enemy off from Omdurman, and we did it"[13].

Pour La Gloire?

What stung the lancers was not the unspoken reproach of "aristocrats of the staff", or the criticism — half-informed at best — of newspaper correspondents, but the remarks passed privately between fellow officers, many of which nevertheless came to their attention. Only those written down have been preserved, but they typify the rest.

Captain Sparkes considered that the 21st made "a fine but useless charge ... a very gallant but foolish action"[14]. If such a comment could be dismissed as the view of the infantry and of no account, accusations made by British officers of the Egyptian cavalry could not. Captain Haig wrote to Sir Evelyn Wood: "You will hear a lot of the charge made by the 21st Lancers. The regiment seems to have advanced without any patrols in front ... the loss inflicted on the enemy was trifling, 14 or 15 at most ... for the cavalry really jumped over the Dervishes in most cases. We onlookers [sic] in the Egyptian Cavalry have feared this all along, for the regiment was keen to do something and meant to charge something before the show was over. They got their charge ... The Promotion Board puts duffers in command of regiments"[15].

The same points appeared in reports filed by a number of correspondents who, in common with Haig, did not witness the charge. Crucially, the lancers were kept out of Omdurman on patrol throughout the day following the battle. A story had to be filed, and as officers of the 21st were not available to present the facts it seems that a version of events was cobbled together from the half-truths and

Aftermath, Reactions and Rewards

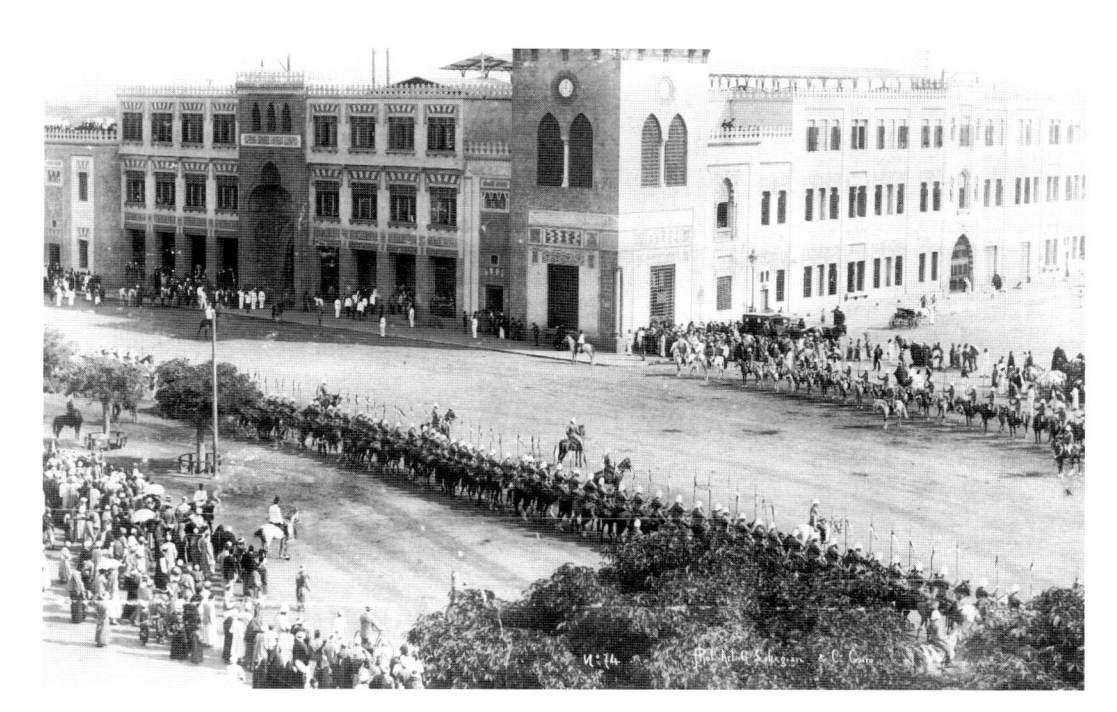

The 21st Lancers line the streets of Cairo on Kitchener's return from the Sudan. (The Queen's Royal Lancers)

rumours passing between the regiments inside the city.

The assertion that the 21st had no forward patrols out as it advanced towards the enemy was clearly false, as the accounts of several officers (and Colonel Martin himself) later confirmed. Haig's figure of 14 or 15 Dervish dead was lower than that reported by anyone who actually saw the bodies, and was in any case irrelevant, for success in clearing the enemy was not determined by the number killed — 2,800 fresh infantrymen had been driven from the field. Haig's dismissal of the mêlée on the basis that the lancers jumped right over the Dervishes is hardly credible — there is no account of any officer or man achieving this (and if he did then his mount was a most remarkable animal, the khor being up to 20 feet wide where B and D Squadrons entered and filled from side to side with Dervishes thrusting their spears upwards). Perhaps Haig unwittingly reveals himself in the phrase "we onlookers in the Egyptian Cavalry"; for within hours of the charge, despite the much greater battle of which it was but an episode and in which Haig had played his part, the charge of the 21st Lancers was being talked about by everyone.

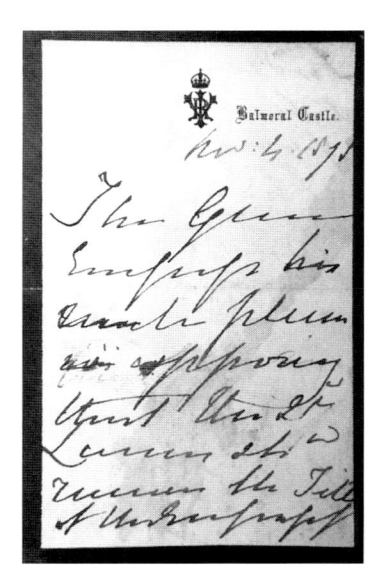

Letter written in Victoria's own hand at Balmoral on 4 November 1898, granting the 21st Lancers the title "Empress of India's" regiment and approving French grey facings for the new lancer uniform — see body text for transcription. (The Queen's Royal Lancers)

It is Haig's final criticism — that the lancers went out looking for a charge and "they got their charge" — that has enough truth in it to stick. The crucial question is not whether the regiment hoped for a reasonable opportunity to charge — that is what the cavalry was for. Its twin roles of reconnaissance and engagement were both required by Kitchener on 2 September; engagement was specified in his 8.30a.m. order; and the most effective form of engagement at the disposal of light cavalry facing enemy infantry on open ground was the charge. The question is whether in the particular circumstances facing Colonel Martin at the khor he was right to order the charge, rather than withdrawing and pressing the enemy back with carbine fire.

Clearly this question cannot be asked at the point when the khor packed with additional Dervishes first became visible, for the regiment was at the gallop and the die cast. It can be asked only at a distance of 300 yards, when the regiment first came under fire and before it wheeled right into line, when neither the khor nor the reinforcements were apparent.

At 300 yards Martin was free to withdraw his regiment to a safe distance and engage the enemy with carbine fire, and to that extent the charge was avoidable. However, the Sirdar's order specified that he "head them off if possible from Omdurman", and time was of the essence, for the 21st was to clear a route for the infantry to follow. It seems reasonable for Martin to have supposed that the shock effect of 440 lancers would clear the enemy from the field more quickly than dismounted carbine fire, and that this was required by Kitchener's order.

Major Finn certainly felt that "there was no choice but to charge or gallop away — the definite order excluded the latter"[16]. Lieutenant Smyth agreed — "Some say we did right, others wrong, but the fact remains that we did what we were told to do …" — although he acknowledged that "we did not come here to play at mounted infantry"[17]. Martin was under considerable pressure from his officers (whose approval he sought rather than ignored) to deliver an engagement with the enemy, and few would have been satisfied with anything less than a full-blooded charge. However, it cannot be concluded from this that he led the

109

Trophies of Omdurman line the walls of the Officers' Mess. (The Queen's Royal Lancers)

21st into a charge when withdrawal was the only correct tactical decision.

Correspondents who were not present, but who immediately declared Martin a duffer and the charge an error of command to rival that at Balaklava, did so on the assumption that dismounted carbine fire *instead* of the charge could have cleared the field as quickly as it did *following* the charge — not at all the same thing. It is not surprising that when Major Finn compiled an official report of the charge published early in 1899, he began: "What really happened was ..."[18].

By then, of course, it was too late to correct the version of events established by the popular press, which was keen to present the charge at Omdurman as a second Balaklava — nothing sold newspapers so well as copy that ridiculed a senior cavalry officer as incompetent at the same time as extolling the valour of men thrown needlessly into a veritable valley of death. As Bennet Burleigh expected, few correspondents denied the magnificence of the charge, but most doubted its efficacy on the battlefield. Churchill, unrepentant, wrote to a friend that "there is no merit in making one charge. Three touches on the splendid"[19]. Yet this particular magnificence or splendour only attaches itself to the unavoidable. If Martin had chosen to charge a second time such a number of the enemy in such a position there would have been neither magnificence nor splendour, but only the pointless sacrifice of brave men's lives.

The charge at Omdurman was ordered when neither the strength of the enemy nor their advantageous position was known to Martin, these becoming apparent only after the regiment was committed and unable to turn back; only therein lies the magnificence and the tragedy. The ancient Greeks understood it — the magnificence of men rushing headlong at the unavoidable, not the chosen. Had the 21st found a poet of the stature of Tennyson, Omdurman might have outdone Balaklava in the public consciousness of this tragic splendour. As it was, the feat was recorded by lesser poets, though the first into print (published on 6 September) incorporated a subtle dig at the 17th Lancers' famous motto that the men of the 21st greatly savoured:

Over the sand, bronzed and tanned,
Clank of sword and jingle of spur,
Pennons that droop in the sultry air,
Ready to fight, morn and night,
Death or Glory! What do we care?
Lance in hand, over the sand,
Ride! For death and the foe are there[20].

In England, Colonel Martin made no particular effort to exonerate himself beyond the interview given on arriving home. He did, however, attempt to gain proper recognition for his former regiment. With no friend in Kitchener and no one in the War Office ready to speak for him, Martin wrote directly to Queen Victoria, suggesting how she might honour the 21st Lancers. He had little hope that his letter would be well received.

At least (and at last) a most prized battle honour had been won. Finn in his report concluded: "It was the Regiment's baptism of fire and steel. The 21st had no long list of battles on its appointments and on its crest. It had no proud traditions handed down from wars in France and the Low Countries. But we will now with contented pride inscribe the word 'Khartoum' as the first honour on our arms and an inheritance to our successors; an inheritance which had been denied us"[21]. An idea of the frustrations loosed in the charge can be gained from this revealing statement made by one of the regiment's most senior officers, its genuine passion reaching a climax in the final phrase.

Colonel Martin rightly has the last word on the matter. Speaking after his return to England in October 1898 he said: "We were sent to head the enemy off from Omdurman, and we did it. If cavalry are going to wait first to calculate the strength of the foe, and are only to attack if they find him weak enough, what is the use of them on the field of battle? The 21st Lancers was a fine body of men. Nearly all had over six years' service, they were splendidly mounted, and in my opinion, we could have gone through twice as many of the enemy as we did"[22].

Queen Victoria's Lancers

On 17 November 1898 Lieutenant-Colonel Crole-Wyndham received a letter from Lord Lansdowne, Secretary of State for War, enclosing a letter written in Queen Victoria's own hand: "Balmoral Castle, 4th November 1898: The Queen Empress has much pleasure in approving that the 21st Lancers should assume the title of 'Empress of India's Regiment' and have French Grey facings, their bravery deserves recognition. Victoria, RI"[23].

Officers and men of A Troop in Cairo, wearing the new lancer uniform with French grey facings. The use of the Royal cypher on the uniform was not authorised until January 1899. (The Queen's Royal Lancers)

The regimental drum horse early in 1899; the Royal cypher — inset — and the new battle honour for Khartoum are prominent on the drum banner. (The Queen's Royal Lancers)

This response to Colonel Martin's special pleading exceeded every expectation, conferring a double honour. While the right to wear French grey facings instead of scarlet on the lancer tunic (yet to be adopted) restored a treasured link with the regiment's Indian origins, the title 'Empress of India's' distinguished the 21st as Queen Victoria's Lancers. There was much satisfaction among both officers and men that a regiment which once felt itself snubbed by the cavalry establishment should now bear this most sought-after title.

Greater distinction soon followed. The *London Gazette* announced that the Victoria Cross was to be awarded to Captain Kenna, Lieutenant de Montmorency and Private Byrne for their valour at Omdurman, and all three men sailed for England to receive the award. On 6 January 1899 they were received by Queen Victoria at Osborne House. The two officers were transported from Cowes in the royal carriage and dined with Her Majesty; Byrne had to be content with a hackney carriage and dinner with the servants. The Queen was determined that the 21st should be clearly marked as the Empress of India's, and after awarding each man the Victoria Cross she granted the regiment the right to wear her Imperial Cypher, a unique distinction otherwise reserved for aides-de-camp to the Sovereign.

Further awards followed. At a parade at Abbassia on 7 March the Duke of Connaught presented the Distinguished Conduct Medal to seven of the men, telling them that it was second only to the VC (most of them had been recommended for the supreme award). The recipients included Sergeant Swarbrick, who had helped de Montmorency and Kenna in their attempt to bring Grenfell's body out of the khor; Private Brown, who returned twice to the khor to rescue disabled comrades; and Private Pedder, who brought a stray horse to Surgeon-Major Pinches and enabled him to escape. The parade was significant for another reason too, as Swarbrick described in a letter home: "We were in full dress, mounted and, being the first time that the Lancer tunic had been seen on a mounted parade, attracted much attention"[24].

While survivors of the charge at Omdurman were honoured for their valour, the regiment did not forget the dead. On 25 April a memorial stone was despatched to Khartoum to be erected near the spot where they fell. Inscribed on it were 22 names — the 20 men buried on the site of the charge, Lieutenant Grenfell who was buried by the Nile, and Private Hadley, who had died in October 1898 at Abbassia from spear wounds received in the khor.

The regiment remained in Egypt for twelve months after returning from the Sudan. During that period it is likely that some men experienced the symptoms of a stress which they could not have acknowledged to their comrades, but which might have included recurrent nightmares in which the horror of the mêlée was replayed. This may have led to an otherwise inexplicable tragedy that occurred as the first anniversary of the charge approached. Sergeant Swarbrick came off guard duty in the early hours of the morning and returned to the sergeants' room: "I found that Sergeant Dyer had taken a revolver and shot himself shortly after midnight. There were two other Sergeants in the room at the time, and they were awfully shocked when the report of the pistol woke them up and they saw what had occurred. We are all very sorry, as no reason whatever can be assigned for this rash act." Despite that, the anniversary on 2 September 1899 was properly celebrated: "All the regiment had a beanfeast on that night … there was any amount of beer and singing"[25].

CHAPTER TEN

Riding in the Twilight

Having completed its time in Egypt, the 21st (Empress of India's) Lancers returned to England for a period of home service. The 50 recruits who had arrived only months before to bring the regiment up to full strength were transferred to the 16th Lancers in India. The rest, all veterans of the Sudan campaign, left Cairo in November and arrived at Southampton — only to discover that they were to proceed immediately to Ireland. The Falls Road barracks in Dublin, although counted as home service, had not been what the lancers had had in mind during their voyage home.

In South Africa the Dutch settlers had long sought independence from Britain, and by November an uprising had begun, although no one expected these Boers — farmers with little or no military training — to unduly trouble the British garrison there. There seemed no chance that the 21st would see service in the Boer War; having just returned from Egypt it was last on the roll for foreign service. However, a number of officers and men contrived to have themselves transferred to this latest arena of action. All three of the VC recipients embarked for South Africa, Captain Kenna to serve on the Staff of Cavalry Division, Captain de Montmorency to raise and command De Montmorency's Scouts in the Stormberg District of Cape Colony, and Private Byrne as de Montmorency's servant. Captain Smyth was granted leave to proceed to South Africa on special service attached to the 13th Hussars, and others soon followed.

The Boers were to trouble the British army more than anyone yet imagined, and already in the early months of 1900 casualties were mounting. On 23 February Captain de Montmorency was killed by a Boer rifleman at Shoeman's Farm. Private Byrne was with him when he was killed. On informing the regiment, Colonel Crole-Wyndham spoke of the loss of an Omdurman hero and a friend: "His death on active service, facing the foe at the head of the Corps of Scouts he himself raised and trained, is the death he would have himself chosen"[1].

In March 1900 Queen Victoria visited Ireland and inspected the 21st Lancers in a grand review in Phoenix Park, Dublin. It was to be the only occasion on which the Empress of India was present with her regiment. By now the War Office realised that the Boer War was not to be a colonial skirmish, and that faced with a well-armed European enemy adopting guerrilla tactics British troops might be found wanting. Reinforcements were urgently needed, and immediately after Queen Victoria had inspected her regiment in Dublin a detachment of 70 men from the 21st sailed for South Africa to serve with the 16th Lancers; a further detachment of 60 followed in September 1900.

The death of Queen Victoria in January 1901 plunged the nation and her regiment into mourning, officers wearing black crêpe on the left arm of the uniform. Three officers and 100 men of the 21st Lancers journeyed to London to join the funeral procession on 1 February, but the country remained at war and immediately afterwards this party embarked for South Africa. At the coronation of King Edward VII the 21st was represented by Colonel Crole-Wyndham, seven officers and 38 men, together with the 36 men of the regimental band — a smaller party than might have been expected, for by now a majority of all officers and men of the regiment had been detached for active service.

This was a new kind of war, particularly for the cavalry. The Boers would not stand and wait to be charged; they attacked in small commando groups and disappeared before they could be engaged. There was little use for the sword or lance; only the rifle and the machine gun could engage an enemy who refused to close. Yet when the war was over a Royal Commission set up to examine the state of the army in the light of its failings in South Africa still did not declare the lance obsolete.

At the end of 1903 the 21st Lancers left Ireland, being ordered to Hounslow with a detachment at Hampton Court. During the next seven years it provided escorts for visiting sovereigns and heads of state and took part in ceremonial parades for the opening of Parliament, while the names of successive commanding officers amounted almost to a roll call of those at Omdurman — Cordeaux, Fowle, Kenna, Smyth.

In September 1910, two weeks after Colonel Kenna handed over command to Smyth, the 21st Lancers embarked for Egypt and their old barracks at Abbassia. Colonel Smyth wrote (via the War Office) inviting Queen Mary to become Colonel-in-Chief of the regiment, but the reply was not what he hoped for: "Her Majesty regrets that She is unable to see Her Way to comply with the request. The Regiment was entitled 'Empress of India's' — that is 'Queen Empress Victoria's' — inasmuch as Queen Victoria was actually the Reigning Sovereign. Queen Mary has the title as wife of the King Emperor, which is rather different"[2].

A heated debate now broke out within the regiment on the value of the lance, which many felt had proven itself obsolete in the Boer War. A letter in the *Vedette* put it bluntly: "The weapon is of no use whatever ... a small boy with a pea-shooter would be just as dangerous. It may be pleasant to read about pennons fluttering in the breeze, but only practical weapons are required in war"[3]. In the magazine's next issue others rushed to the defence: "Does not the fame of the charge at Omdurman rest on the lance points of the regiment?"; "I certainly would not mind meeting your correspondent in mounted combat and having the

Officers and men of the 21st Lancers detached for service in the Boer War. Increasing numbers were sent out to bolster the strength of other regiments serving in South Africa. (The Queen's Royal Lancers)

choice of a lance against his pee-shooter". The original writer replied to the challenge: "He ought to know that the pea-shooter is a dismounted weapon and to challenge me to mounted combat with one is ridiculous"[4]. This seemed to many within the 21st, and indeed the cavalry as a whole, to be precisely the point — those who argued against the lance argued against the cavalry, for without the lance it must become mounted infantry.

The Charge at Shabkadar

In 1912 the regiment, commanded by Lieutenant-Colonel Scriven, was posted to Risalpur in the north-west corner of India. Mohmand tribesmen mounted regular night-time raids across the border to loot and burn villages, and an increased British presence in the area was required to guard against more serious incursions.

At the outbreak of the Great War in 1914 the 21st Lancers was the only British cavalry regiment retained in India. Unrest on the North-West Frontier had increased, and intelligence reports indicated that the Mohmands were being armed by German agents and encouraged to invade the Punjab through the Khyber Pass. By the end of August 1915 several thousand tribesmen had gathered north of the administrative frontier between tribal and British territory.

On 28 August, Colonel Scriven with B and C Squadrons of the 21st marched from the barracks at Risalpur to Shabkadar, an old fort in the Himalayan foothills three miles north of the Kabul River and about 15 miles north of the main British base at Peshawar; close by was the village of Shankargarh, which had been burned down during the last major Mohmand incursion in 1897. These squadrons patrolled the foothills while the infantry was brought up. On 4 September Mohmands were seen in the hills overlooking the town; throughout the day their number increased to an estimated 2,500, and many advanced to within a few hundred yards. General Campbell, in command of the British force, decided to take the initiative rather than wait to be attacked.

At 6.00a.m. on 5 September the infantry formed up along a four-mile front between Shabkadar and the enemy. This line would prevent any Mohmand advance while the artillery shelled their positions in the hills.

To the left of the line a sand ridge ran from the foothills as far as the Michni irrigation canal and village, offering cover for the enemy to advance on this left flank. At 8.30 Campbell sent the 21st Lancers through the line to reconnoitre the area. The two squadrons immediately came under fire from the hills to their front and the sand ridge to their left, indicating that the enemy had already reached the canal in an attempt to get behind the infantry. Two troops of B squadron went forward while the rest dismounted and

113

Panoramic photograph of the camp at Adazai during the regiment's Mohmand operations on the North-West Frontier in 1915, giving a useful reminder of the amount of organisation and impedimenta involved in taking a horsed cavalry regiment to war. (The Queen's Royal Lancers)

gave covering fire, but enemy fire became so heavy that Scriven was forced to withdraw his men.

By 10.15a.m. the artillery bombardment had forced the enemy back from their advance position in the foothills and the guns had moved forward; but the Mohmands still holding the sand ridge on the left flank now threatened to cross the canal, occupy the village and get behind the guns. The situation was critical and Campbell ordered the 21st Lancers to attack and clear them from the ridge. Colonel Scriven led C Squadron along the north bank of the canal, from where he could charge across open ground towards the ridge. He sent B Squadron across the canal towards the village.

Seeing the cavalry advance, the Mohmands immediately crossed the canal and occupied the village, so that as Colonel Scriven led his men towards the sand ridge he came under heavy fire from the canal bank and the houses to his left. He immediately swung C Squadron round and charged towards the canal and the enemy firing from the far bank. Meanwhile B Squadron found that fields to the south of the canal had recently been flooded; the horses sank in up to their hocks, and taking the village was impossible.

C Squadron reached the canal under heavy fire: "We came into line facing the enemy, and went for them, neck-or-nothing; and then misfortune befell us. At the moment of impact we came to a dyke fourteen feet wide and six feet deep. We were no longer in any formation. Those whose horses did not fall at the jump went straight on. Many were shot as they were trying to get out of the water"[5].

Colonel Scriven was the first man across — his charger cleared the canal in a single leap — followed by Captain Anderson and Lieutenant Thompson. The men who followed, riding horses of lesser quality, went in and out of the water (three to four feet deep), some being dismounted in the process and becoming easy targets for Mohmand riflemen. Scriven rode through the enemy on the bank, killing two with his sword before his horse was shot and fell, pinning him to the ground. Corporals Ballard and Lucas, coming up behind, rescued their colonel; Scriven refused to mount Ballard's horse when this was offered — he and Lucas each held one of Ballard's stirrups, and together they moved forward.

Behind them, many of the men dismounted in the canal were shot dead as they left the water, or found themselves in hand-to-hand combat with Mohmand swordsmen. Most had dropped their lances and drawn their swords as they struggled from the canal, and were now engaged in a desperate struggle, outnumbered by the enemy. Those still mounted fared little better. Captain Anderson, Lieutenant Thompson and Sergeant Simpson were shot from their saddles before reaching the village, then attacked by swordsmen. "Tommy [Lieutenant Thompson] was seen fighting against the odds. The squadrons were all split up into groups. Tommy protested with the men who took him out of it and told them to leave him and look out for themselves"[6]. Captain Learoyd's horse was shot and he found himself on foot surrounded by the enemy — Private Hull turned his horse at the Mohmands, forcing a path through to the officer and bringing the enemy's attention upon himself. Incredibly he avoided the swords swung at him, took Learoyd up behind and galloped to safety.

Many others, still mounted and lance in hand, ran at the enemy but were turned from their task by the need to rescue dismounted comrades: "We used our lances with terrible effect. I stopped once to pick up a sergeant who had lost his horse. Together we went into them. He held on to my stirrup and used his sword with his left hand. Men were falling in all directions. How we came through that fierce affray alive, God alone knows"[7].

Colonel Scriven was shot through the heart (though one account has it through the head) and killed. At the same time Corporal Ballard's horse was badly wounded and he was forced to dismount. Ballard and Lucas dragged the colonel's body into the cover of a field of eight-foot high maize, then lay firing over it to keep the enemy at bay. Men who had reached cover in the village or the maize fields opened fire on the Mohmands and eventually drove them away.

B Squadron, unable to reach the village from the south, had turned back and followed the route taken by C Squadron, and arrived at this point. Two troops deployed to give covering fire while the remaining two crossed the canal to help evacuate the dead and wounded. They found Lieutenant Thompson and Sergeant Simpson lying side by side beneath a tree, both seriously wounded. Doctor Cathcart, the Medical Officer with the 21st, was called to Thompson: "Tommy was perfectly conscious when I got up to him. His wounds were bullet wounds through spleen, groin, and neck, one finger blown off; sword cuts over head and face (one of which had divided his frontal bone"[8].

The survivors of C Squadron helped carry out the dead and wounded: "Here I have to relate the most terrible sight of all. We found some of our men mutilated beyond description with knives, and still alive at that. Others had heads missing, and limbs and bodies cut in the most atrocious manner. The sights were maddening"[9].

By 11.00a.m. the dead and wounded had been brought out and the 21st was withdrawn behind the infantry lines. Five hours of shelling had forced the Mohmands out of the hills above Shabkadar, the enemy's only initiative — an attempt to get round the infantry's left flank — having been turned back by the lancers. The 21st lost three officers and five men killed during the charge; Lieutenant Thompson died later that same day of his wounds, and 16 others suffered serious wounds. Private Hull was awarded the Victoria Cross for saving Captain Learoyd, and the regiment had won a second battle honour — "North-West Frontier, India'.

There were obvious parallels with Omdurman, and the press made much of them. According to the *Daily Express* correspondent, writing beneath the headline "Lancers' Splendid Charge: … The action of the two squadrons is spoken of in the highest terms and their charge saved the day. It is worthy of note that only two days separated the anniversary of this regiment's charge at Omdurman in 1898, from this new achievement"[10].

With the death of Colonel Scriven, Major Brinton took command of the regiment and the remaining two squadrons were brought up to Shabkadar. In action again on 8 October, facing a similar situation to that in which a charge had been ordered on 5 September, the regiment was employed dismounted, repelling the enemy with rifle and machine gun fire.

The Great War

As the situation in Europe worsened many officers and men of the 21st in India were granted leave to serve with regiments fighting in France. After the first few months of mobile warfare congealed in late 1914 into a solid double line of trenches from the sea to Switzerland, it was generally expected that the cavalry would be held behind the front line until the infantry broke through; then the cavalry would be released to exploit the breech and fan out across

A striking image from the days of horsed cavalry on the Frontier: a troop of the 21st Lancers returning from watering the horses. (The Queen's Royal Lancers)

The Michni canal near Shabkhadar. On 5 September 1915, C Squadron charged Mohmand tribesmen across the canal (from right to left in this view) under heavy fire; many men were unhorsed, and then killed as they left the water. (The Queen's Royal Lancers)

the enemy's rear areas, the pursuit of retreating German troops across open ground giving every opportunity for the charge and the use of sword and lance. A member of the 21st, having arrived in France, wrote back to the regiment in Risalpur to correct this picture: "My horse was killed in a charge on a wood full of machine guns ... lucky at least I did not break my neck as we were going some when he came down with 3 hits"[11].

Worse news soon followed. From Mons: "One does not have a chance at all, nothing but shells and shrapnel all day long, they leave nothing standing, we have to leave our horses 3 to 4 miles away and foot it which is bad as it is mud everywhere. Most of the towns and villages are in ruins"[12]. From Ypres: "It's like hell, 2-hundredweight shells, Bang! Half a trench blown up and all in it. Nearly all day we have to lay in the bottom of the trench as we are between our own artillery and the enemy, then at night it's fix bayonets and blaze away until daylight. Three or four days in the trenches, then a day out to dress the wounds of the horses"[13].

Worst of all was the news from Gallipoli, where Kenna was commanding the 3rd Mounted Brigade (although they had no horses with them). A man of the 21st serving under him wrote: "I cannot say that trench warfare appeals to me much, I should prefer my own trade. We landed in Gallipoli and ... our Brigade took over a section of trenches and started an advance trench 100 yards ahead. Whilst inspecting this, the second night of digging, Colonel Kenna got a bullet which hit him in the left elbow, and turning over entered his side. I am sorry to say he died two hours later"[14]. It was not how a hero of Omdurman would have wished to die. Colonel Brinton, writing from Shabkadar, noted that it "must have occurred on the same day as the fight here. How he would have gloried to have been here and died mounted, sword in hand"[15].

Through the early months of 1916 the officers and men of the 21st Lancers became increasingly frustrated at being retained in India when their services were clearly required elsewhere. Brinton persuaded the BEF to authorise the formation of a Service Squadron to fight in France. This squadron, 250 strong, was raised in June 1916 and served as part of 14th Corps Cavalry. Despite letters from those already engaged in the conflict these men expected to be used as cavalry. In fact they were sent immediately to dig trenches, and were quickly initiated into the new way of war: "Enemy aircraft dropped bombs, which wounded nine horses, five of which had to be destroyed. Splinters of bombs passed through the officers' mess tent and the men's bivouac"[16].

In Flanders from June to September 1916, the lancers were put to work (dismounted) laying communication cables, often taking these up to front line trenches under bombardment. As the winter approached it became impossible for wheeled vehicles to reach the worst areas, and they were used mounted to carry orders to the front; this work continued until March 1917.

On the 17th of that month the squadron was ordered forward for mounted duty. On 24 February British patrols had first detected the enemy withdrawal from the great Arras-Peronne-Soissons salient left at the close of the Somme fighting the previous November, back towards their newly prepared Hindenburg Line. Cavalry were required to act as "feelers", probing in advance of the infantry who were unable to keep in touch with the rapidly retreating enemy. Perhaps a knowledge of the regimental history influenced the wording of an order received by Captain Wheeler, who was told to "follow and watch the Germans and not to charge"[17]. The first advance patrols went out east of Combles, in the southern sector of the 4th Army front, on the following day. They had to dismount and lead their horses through terrain south of Saillisel torn up by months of artillery bombardments; even so several horses missed their footing and tumbled into shellholes full of water. Once through this, mounted and making faster

Private Charles Hull, awarded the VC for rescuing Captain Learoyd, dismounted and in extreme danger in the midst of the enemy at Shabkadar. (The Queen's Royal Lancers)

progress through the villages of Hermies and Etricourt, these men of the 21st were the first British troops to enter villages evacuated by the enemy only hours earlier.

Day after day the squadron moved ahead of the infantry, often engaged by the enemy rearguard and losing a number of men. Night patrols were particularly hazardous in shell-holed areas and the men walked on foot, each guiding himself by holding the tail of the horse in front. On 6 April three patrols were sent to reconnoitre Havrincourt Wood, still occupied by the enemy. They came under heavy fire and only one patrol was able to approach the objective. Two sergeants and a private were severely wounded and, despite every effort to bring them out — Corporal Dinsdale remaining with them until the last possible moment — the fire became so intense that these men had to be left.

In September 1917, when infantry losses became so great as to require all available men in the trenches, the Service Squadron was disbanded. Its last duty was to form a Royal Escort for King George V when he visited 14th Corps. In all the squadron had lost 12 officers and 93 men. The lancers handed in their cavalry equipment, were issued infantry kit, and received just five days of infantry training before being distributed among a number of front line regiments.

★ ★ ★

After the Great War the 21st Lancers remained in India. Peace was inevitably followed by a reduction in the size of the army, and in 1921 it was decided that four cavalry regiments were to be disbanded — the 19th and 20th Hussars and the 5th and 21st Lancers. Protests failed to reverse the decision; on the contrary, it was announced that a further four regiments might have to go — the 14th and 15th Hussars and the 16th and 17th Lancers. The howl of pain at the loss of so many famous cavalry regiments now reached the highest echelons of the War Office, where Sir Charles Harris suggested amalgamation as an alternative to disbandment. Thus were created the 14th/20th and 15th/19th Hussars, and the 16th/5th and 17th/21st Lancers.

The 21st was returned to England, reduced to one squadron and amalgamated with two squadrons of the 17th Lancers. The squadrons at first retained the name of their original regiment, so that in the new 17th/21st Lancers, C Squadron was styled "C (21st Lancer) Squadron" and wore the 21st Lancer badge — Queen Victoria's Imperial cypher. The battle honours "Khartoum" and "North-West Frontier" were among those inherited by the new regiment, but the title "Empress of India's" was lost. In 1927 the lance was abolished as a weapon, the cavalry retaining it for ceremonial use only.

In 1929 the colonels of amalgamated regiments were required to decide on a single badge to be worn by all their squadrons, and the 17th/21st chose the famous "motto" (as it is always styled) of the 17th — a skull and crossed thigh bones, with the words "Or Glory" below. It was with great sadness that those who had served in the 21st Lancers gave up the cap badge of their old regiment, the last overt sign of Queen Victoria's Lancers.

Lieutenant N.R. Thompson was unhorsed and surrounded by the enemy at Shabkadar; he died later the same day of multiple wounds. This photograph was taken in 1912. (Courtesy F.K. Mitchell)

A cartoon of the Great War contrasting the cavalry's expectation of the charge with the reality of the trenches. (The Queen's Royal Lancers)

Lancers, incredibly still burdened with the lance in the age of the machine gun and heavy artillery, pass through a shattered town in France during the Great War. (Imperial War Museum)

The cavalry, now without lances, cross a trench line on reconnaissance duties in France, 1917. (Imperial War Museum)

Right: *The Kerreri plain and Jebel Surgham today, with telegraph poles and vehicle tracks crossing the site of the charge, and the stone obelisk erected by the 21st Lancers in memory of those who died. (The Queen's Royal Lancers)*

EPILOGUE

In 1964, at the invitation of His Grace the Duke of Rutland whose ancestor raised the 21st Light Dragoons in 1760, the regimental museum of the 17th/21st Lancers was established in Belvoir Castle.

In 1993 the 17th/21st Lancers was amalgamated with the 16th/5th Lancers, bringing together four old and famous cavalry regiments in a new regiment styled The Queen's Royal Lancers with Her Majesty the Queen as its Colonel-in-Chief. Among the battle honours on the new guidon presented by Her Majesty, "Khartoum" commemorates the last full regimental charge made by the British cavalry against a standing enemy.

In the Republic of Sudan the Mahdi's Tomb was reconstructed on its original site in Omdurman. A Russian-built radar station now stands on the summit of the Jebel Surgham, a legacy of the Cold War. A military airfield marks the spot by the Nile where Kitchener's zariba was constructed, and anti-aircraft installations are dotted about the Kerreri plain. The only reminder of the charge of the 21st Lancers is the stone obelisk erected by the regiment in memory of those killed.

★   ★   ★

The charge at Omdurman brought the 21st its first battle honour and three Victoria Crosses, and caught the imagination of late Victorian Britain. Infantry regiments protested sourly that it was they who had defeated the Dervish army; that was, of course, to miss the point.

When 100 Baggara horsemen of the Dervish cavalry rode to certain death against the massive firepower of MacDonald's brigade after all hope of victory had gone, Captain Eadon called the act "too magnificent for words". Eadon was measuring not by arms or tactics, and clearly not by outcome, but by boldness and valour. So did the British public of 1898 measure the charge of the 21st. What is more, the British cavalry considered the magnificence of the charge (as displayed at Balaklava and Omdurman) to have a real effect on the outcome of the battle, almost in reverse proportion to the apparent pointlessness of the act, by mortally wounding the morale of the enemy.

It could hardly last. Just sixteen years after the charge at Omdurman - the same period which separates the Falklands War of 1982 from the publication of this book - an entirely new kind of war handed dominance of the battlefield to machine guns and heavy artillery, and very soon to poison gas, armoured tanks, and ground-attack aircraft. The ages-old martial magnificence of the horseman, lance or sword in hand, found no place on this new battlefield. During at least the first half of that war there were cavalry officers who argued that when the anticipated breakthrough was finally achieved by the other arms the charge would once more have a tactical contribution to make; but in their hearts they clung to the forlorn hope that its role might yet be judged more by style than by outcome.

The 21st Lancers typified this stubborn belief that the rider-spirit of the cavalry and the esprit de corps of regiments committed to *l'arme blanche* — bonded by courage, style and dash — could weigh heavier in the balance than numbers killed and ground occupied. It was magnificent, but it was not true.

APPENDIX

The Omdurman Roll

Roll of officers and men of the 21st Lancers who charged at Omdurman on 2 September 1898. This excludes 39 men who left Cairo with the regiment but did not charge (36 were returned sick, and three died during the advance south). The total who charged were 447 (34 officers, 412 men and one civilian). Casualties are marked **[K]** for killed and **[W]** for wounded. The roll is copied directly from a document dated January 1899; some abbreviations indicating regimental NCOs' and warrant officers' appointments rather than ranks remain obscure.

Headquarters
Martin, R.H., Lieutenant-Colonel Commanding
Crole-Wyndham, W.G., Major, Second in Command
Pirie, A.M., Lieutenant, Adjutant **[W]**
Cordeaux, W.W., Captain, Transport Officer
King, W.H., Captain, Riding Master **[W]**
Graham, G.L., Captain, Quartermaster

Others
Surgeon Major Pinches, Royal Army Medical Corps
Captain the Marquis of Tullihardine (Royal Horse Guards), ADC to Kitchener
Captain Drage, Army Veterinary Department
Lieutenant Smith, Army Veterinary Department
Private J.Cope (7th Hussars) Lieutenant Wormald's servant
Hubert Howard, correspondent of *The Times*

A Squadron
Finn, H., Major Commanding
Clerk, C.J., Lieutenant, Second in Command
Smyth, R.N., Lieutenant
Brinton, O.W., Lieutenant **[W]**
Wormald, F.W., Lieutenant (7th Hussars)
Conolly, T., Lieutenant (Scots Greys)
Churchill, W. L. S., Lieutenant (4th Hussars)

Acres, G., Private
Albury, J., Lance-Corporal
Allchin, P., Pte
Baddeley, H., Pte
Bateman, J., Pte
Baker, G., Pte **[W]**
Behan, T., Pte
Benz, A., L/Cpl
Blythe, G., Pte
Bonnett, F., Lance-Sergeant
Brading, A., Pte
Burnell, G., Pte
Buxton, G., Pte
Byrne, S., Pte
Chalmers, W., L/Sgt
Chambers, T., Pte
Chapman, R., Pte
Clayton, J., Pte
Clements, C., Cpl
Coats, S.M., Pte
Colbourne, G., Pte
Coleman, J., Pte
Dale, A., L/Cpl
Dobbing, C., L/Sgt
Easton, A., Pte
Edwards, A., Pte
English, A., SSM (Sqn Sgt-Maj) **[W]**
Ewart, J., Pte
Farndell, G., SS Cpl (Sqn Signals Cpl?)
Fisher, T., SS (Sqn Signaller?)
Fowler, E., Pte
Gammon, H., Pte
Gerrard, J., Pte
Gordon, R., Pte
Gordon, G., Pte
Gore, W., Pte
Hagger, T., L/Sgt
Ham, J., Pte
Harris, R., Sgt
Harrison, P., Pte
Hawken, H., Sgt **[W]**
Hill, W., Pte
Hilton, G., Pte
Hiscock, T., Pte
Keane, A., Pte
Kelly, W., Pte
Knowles, F., L/Cpl
Legerton, J., Pte
Locke, G., SQMS (Sqn Quartermaster Sgt)
Lynch, W., Sgt
Marsh, W., Pte
Mean, W., Pte
Morgan, P., Pte
Morhall, F., Pte **[K]**
Mulligan, H., Pte
Newman, R., L/Cpl
Norris, M., Trumpeter
Pearson, W., Pte
Pedder, F., Pte
Pendred, E., L/Cpl
Penn, H., L/Cpl
Pinkney, M., Pte
Pink, E., Pte
Pollard, W., Pte
Pollock, G., FQMS (Farrier QMS?)
Pothecary, F., Pte
Robinson G., Tptr **[W]**
Rix, W., Pte
Roddis, C., Pte
Robinson, F., Pte
Sands, C., Pte
Scabrooke, A., L/Sgt
Scotchman, C., Pte
Shrubb, J., Pte
Shillcock, R., Pte
Short, E., Pte
Signal, W., Pte
Smith, A., Pte
Smith, J., Pte
South, J., Pte
Stace, B., Pte
Staples, W., Pte
Stander, F., Cpl
Stevens, T., Pte **[W]**
Steward, J., Pte
Swan, G., Pte
Sykes, J., L/Cpl
Tapsell, A., Pte
Tempest, J., Pte
Titmus, W., Pte
Titley, J., Pte
Thompson, G., Pte
Tomsett, A., Pte
Turner, T., Pte
Thwaites, H., Pte
Voisey, W., Pte
Watkins, W., Pte
Wilde, E., L/Cpl
Williams, J., Pte
Wise, F., Pte
Wood, E., L/Cpl
Wood, J., Pte **[W]**
Wright, G., Pte

B Squadron
Fowle, J., Major Commanding
Kenna, P.A., Captain, Second in Command
de Montmorency, R.H., Lieutenant the Hon.
Protheroe-Smith, H.B., Lieutenant
Brinton, J.C., Lieutenant (2nd Life Guards) **[W]**
Grenfell, R.S., Lieutenant (12th Lancers) **[K]**
Allen, R., Sgt **[K]**
Baker, H., Pte
Binns, Pte
Birch, T., Pte
Bradshaw, H., Pte **[K]**
Brown, W., Pte
Bushell, E., Pte **[W]**
Bushell, W., Pte
Byrne, T., Pte **[W]**
Carter, E., L/Sgt **[K]**
Case, H., Pte
Cooke, C., Pte **[W]**
Dyer, H., Cpl
Edmunds, H., Pte **[W]**
Etherington, W., Pte **[K]**
Everest, E., Pte
Farndell, E., Pte **[W]**
Farrington, W., Pte
Gadenne, W., Pte
Gainey, J., Pte
Goacher, W., Pte
Goodenough, A., Pte
Green, F., Pte
Grocock, C., Pte
Hadley, W., Pte **[K]**
Hannah, T., Pte **[K]**
Harpley, E., Pte **[W]**
Harris, W., SS Cpl
Hatter, E., Pte **[K]**
Head, T., SS **[W]**
Heslop, A., Pte
Hewitt, A., Pte
Higgs, A., Sgt **[W]**
Hills, J., Pte
Holland, W., Pte
Hotchkiss, T., Sgt **[W]**
Hunter, W., Pte
James, G., Pte
Jones, H., Pte
Jones, R., Pte
Kelly, J., L/Cpl
King, T., Cpl **[W]**
Knight, F, Sgt Tptr
Leonard, W., Pte
Lovett, H., L/Cpl
Lowe, J., L/Cpl
McWean, W., Pte
March, F., Pte
Mangan, T., Pte
Marsden, A., Pte

McLennan, A., SQMS
Meek, R., Pte
Miller, C., Sgt
Miller, S., Pte
Mooney, W., Pte
Morgan, J., Pte
Mulholland, W., Pte
Norman, F., ORSM
   (Regt Ordnance S-M?)
Old, W., Pte
Penfold, C., Pte
Perkins, G., Pte
Plowman, G., Pte
Plumb, J., Pte
Porch, F., Pte [W]
Potter, G., Pte
Poules, T. Pte [W]
Quigley, J., Pte [W]
Range, J., Cpl [W]
Reynolds, M., Pte [W]
Rice, T., Pte [W]
Robinson, H., Pte
Rowlett, A., Pte [W]
Randall, C., Pte
Scattergood, J., Cpl [K]
Scholes, F., SSF
   (Sqn Sgt Farrier?) [W]
Searle, H., Pte
Sherring, G., Pte
Skelton, W., Pte
Smith, C., Pte
Smythe, C., Pte
Stanton, F., L/Cpl
Steele, W., Tptr
Swarbrick, F., Cpl
Thompson, C., Pte [W]
Thompson, R., Pte
Varley, J., Pte
Vessey, G., SSM [W]
Walker, W., L/Cpl
Walton, A., Pte
Warburton, W., Pte
Watson, J., Pte
Watson, W., Pte
Western, G., Pte [W]
Williams, G., Pte
Wilson, R., Tptr
Wilson, W., L/Cpl [W]
Wood, F., RSM
   (Regt Sgt-Maj)
Woodside, F., Pte [W]
Wright, C., L/Cpl [K]
Young, H., Sgt

C Squadron

Doyne, W.M., Captain
   Commanding
Dauncey, T.H.E., Captain,
   Second in Command
Taylor, A.H., Lieutenant
Vaughan, J., Lieutenant (7th
   Hussars)
Tabor, A.M., Lieutenant (3rd
   Hussars)
Molyneux, R., Lieutenant the
   Hon. (Royal Horse Guards)

Abbott, T., Pte
Akester, W., Pte
Atkins, I., Sgt
Ayton, B., Pte
Badger, R., Pte
Barrett, W., Pte
Barrow, J., Pte

Beattie, G., Pte
Blower, B., Pte
Brennan, J., SSM
Brooker, J., Pte
Brown, A., Pte
Bullock, T., Pte
Bushell, A., Pte
Butchers, C., Pte
Butler, E., Pte
Carey, P., Pte
Carr, R., Pte
Carter, J., Pte
Chattaway, D., Pte
Clarke, W., Pte
Coates, G., Pte
Cofax, T., Pte
Cole, A., Pte
Copley, A., Pte
Corthine, J., Sgt
Daly, W., Pte
Deamer, E., Pte
Denton, E., Pte
Donegan, W., Pte
Dovey, J., Pte
Drew, W., Cpl
Eadie, A., Sgt
Ellins, C., Pte
Farr, T., Pte
Fennell, N., Pte
Fox, G., Pte
Fry, H., Pte
Gallagher, P., Tptr
Graham, R., L/Cpl
Gregory, R., Pte
Haines, J., SSF
Hallam, W., Pte
Hammond, L., Pte
Hankinson, A., Pte
Hutton, F., RRSSM
   (Rough Rider SSM)
Jackson, A., SSF
Jackson, H., Sgt
Jewkes, J., Pte
Johnson, W., Pte
Jones, H., Pte
Kelly, M., Pte
Kemble, C., Pte
Knight, J., Pte
Laughton, A., RQMS
Lelliott, G., Sgt
Linton, C., Pte
Lodge, C., Pte [W]
Long, W., Pte
Lowery, R., Pte
Lynch, D., Pte
Mann, A., Pte
Mansfield, A., L/Cpl
Martin, A., Pte
Mitchell, F., Pte
Mitchell, W., Pte
Morris, W., Pte
Nazer, G., Pte
Owens, T., Pte
Overton, H., S/Cpl
Park, G., Pte
Paul, A., Pte
Payne, W., L/Cpl
Pawson, D., Pte
Peacock, J., Pte
Price, H., Pte
Puttick, A., L/Sgt
Roff, W., Pte
Rose, C., Pte
Scanlon, C., Pte
Shepherd, J., Pte 2301

Shepherd, J., Pte 3724
Sparshott, F., Pte
Stauton, A., SQMS
Thomas, A., Pte
Thomas, G., Pte
Tickner, H., Pte
Tillman, A., Pte
Trimmer, S., L/Cpl
Trodd, D., Cpl/F
   (Cpl Farrier)
Walton, G., Pte
Ward, J., Pte
Ward, R., Pte
Wardrop, D., Pte
Warrington, G., SSM
Waters, M., Pte
Watson, H., Tptr
Watts, W., Pte
Wells, S., Pte
Westwood, A., Pte
Westwood, R., Pte
Whitebread, H., Pte
Wiggins, C., Pte
Williams, A., Pte
Wilson, A., Pte
Winton, H., SS
Woolley, E., Pte

D Squadron

Eadon, F.H., Captain
   Commanding
Fair, J.G., Captain, Second
   in Command
Champion, A.D., Lieutenant
Lewis, E.H., Lieutenant
Nesham, C.S., Lieutenant [W]

Ash, J., Pte
Atherton, P., Pte
Baninster, S., Pte
Barnes, H., Pte
Berville, J., Pte
Bohan, J., Pte
Borthwick, G., Cpl [K]
Brettle, G., Pte
Brown, W., Pte
Carswell, G., Pte
Clarke, J., Pte
Coppins, G., L/Cpl
Corry, J., Pte
Cowley, W., Pte
Craythorne, W., Sgt
Curran, M., Pte [W]
Dale, W., Tptr
Darling, W., L/Cpl
Davis, F., Cpl
Elliott, F., L/Cpl [K]
Elliott, J., Pte
Emby, F., SI of S&G
   (Sgt Instructor of ?)
Fitch, H., L/Cpl
Foote, G., Sgt
Foreman, F., Pte
Fowler, F., Pte
Fowler, W., Pte
Foy, J., Pte
Freeman, G., Sgt [W]
Freeman, J., Pte
Fuller, A., Pte
Gardner, C., Pte [W]
Godfrey, W., Pte
Grantham, A., L/Sgt [K]
Green, R., Pte
Hand, B., Pte

Harper, W., Pte
Haycocks, R., SSF
Hiatt, W., Pte
Hill, C., SF
Hope, J., Pte [W]
Honeysett, J., Pte [W]
Hunt, H., Pte [K]
Ives, G., Pte
Ing, J., Pte
Johnson, A., Pte
Jones, H., L/Cpl
Jones, T., Pte
Kelly, F., Pte [K]
Kevins, T., Pte
Lawrence, T., Sgt [W]
Lewis, J., Pte
Lloyd, H., Pte
Long, T., Pte
Lonie, Pte
Lovatt, J., Pte
McGinn, B., Pte
Morton, H., Pte
Mackereth, J., Pte
McKenna, J., Pte
Morris, W., Pte
Miles, T., Pte [K]
Oldbury, J., Pte [K]
Osgood, A., L/Sgt
Payne, J., Pte
Pepper, E., Pte
Pocock, H., Pte
Poole, W., Pte
Pothecary, F., Cpl [W]
Rawle, F., Pte [K]
Raynor, E., L/Cpl [W]
Readymartcher, W., Pte
Redfearn, J., Pte [W]
Roberts, A., Pte [K]
Roberts, W., Pte
Robins, W., Pte
Saddler, A., L/Cpl [W]
Sargent, W., L/Cpl
Sawkins, F., L/Cpl
Saxby, C., Pte
Scott, J., Pte
Scrivener, J., L/Cpl
Seston, W., Pte
Simons, J., L/Sgt
Skelton, P., SS [W]
Smith, F., L/Sgt
Smith, M., Pte
South, R., Pte
Sparey, H., Pte
Thompson, J., L/Cpl
Thorp, F., L/Cpl
Turner, S., L/Sgt
Warner, W., Pte
Weller, W., L/Cpl [K]
Whittaker, E., Pte
Wilkinson, F., Pte
Williams, B., Pte
Wood, F., Tptr
Wood, I., L/Cpl [K]
Wood, J., Pte

BIBLIOGRAPHY

While the published works listed below have been consulted and may be of interest to the general reader, this present account draws most heavily on original material in the regimental archives. As will be seen from the source notes, most quotations are taken directly from letters, diaries and other writings of officers and men of the 21st. My intent has been to tell the history of the regiment and the story of the charge at Omdurman in words as closely akin as possible to the experience of those who lived it. Where their account differs from that published elsewhere, unless it is clearly mistaken, I have preferred the cavalry perspective over all else.

Published works:

Alford, H.S. & Sword, W.D., *The Egyptian Sudan. Its Loss and Recovery* (1898)
Anglesey, Marquis of, *History of the British Cavalry*, Vols. 2 (1975) & 3 (1982)
Bennett, E.N., *The Downfall of the Dervishes* (1898)
Burleigh, Bennett, *The Khartoum Campaign* (1899)
Churchill, Randolph S., *Winston S. Churchill, Companion Vol.1* (1967)
Churchill, Winston S., *My Early Life* (1930, paperback 1959)
Churchill, Winston S., *The River War* (1899)
Hinde, Capt.Robert, *The Discipline of the Light Horse* (1778).
Howard, Hubert, *Extracts from the Diaries and Letters of Hubert Howard* (1899)
Steevens, G.W., *With Kitchener to Khartoum* (1898)
Tamplin, Lt.Col.R.L.C., *A Short History of the 17th/21st Lancers* (1959)

United Services Magazine, 'Notes on the History and Services of the Twenty First Regiment of Dragoons', (July 1876)
Ziegler, Philip, *Omdurman* (1973)
Zulfo, Ismat, *Karari: the Sudanese Account of the Battle of Omdurman* (trans. 1980)

Archival works *(held by The Queen's Royal Lancers Regimental Museum and Archive):*

Brinton, Maj.O.W., letter, 12 September 1915
Cox, Capt.G., record of heliograph signals sent and received on 1 & 2 September 1898
Eadon, Capt.F.H., diary, 1898
Eadon, Capt.F.H., letter, 22 September 1898
Finn, Maj.H., 'Our Baptism', report of the Sudan campaign published in the *Vedette*, January 1899
Gazetteer, 21st Hussars regimental magazine, from 1872
Hewitt, Pte., memoir of 2 September 1898
McCombie, F., unpublished biography of Capt.Kenna
Montmorency, Lieut.R.H. de, diary, 1898
Montmorency, Lieut.R.H. de, letter, 28 September 1898
Pirie, Lieut.A., diary, 1898
Regimental History Book, 21st Hussars, hand-written in 1862 by the Adjutant
Rix, Cpl.W., memoirs recorded by his son Reginald Rix
Service Squadron Diary, 21st Lancers, 1916-1917
Smyth, Lieut.R.N., letter, 4 September 1898
Sparkes, Capt.N.S., transcript letter, 13 September 1898
Swarbrick, Cpl.F., letters, 1899
Vedette, 21st Hussars/Lancers regimental magazine, from 1887

NOTES

For full details of published and archival works, see Bibliography under author.

Chapter One: English Origins
(1) 'Standing Orders to be observed by the whole Corps of Dragoons, by His Royal Highness' Order' (circa 1755) among the Cumberland Papers in the Royal Library, Windsor Castle
(2) Tamplin, p.21
(3) United Services Magazine, p.338
(4) Annual Register, note for 8 August 1761
(5) Nottingham Date-Book (1763)
(6) as note 1
(7) Hinde, p.112
(8) Tamplin, p.23
(9) Gleig, Revd.G.R., 'The Hussar' (1837)
(10) United Services Magazine, p.350
(11) ibid., p.351

Chapter Two: Indian Origins
(1) Carman, W.Y., 'The Bengal Light cavalry' in The Journal of the Society for Army Historical Research, 1980, p.132
(2) Mackenzie, Col.A.R.D., in 'The Pioneer', 9 December 1890
(3) Anglesey, Vol.2, p.234
(4) Gazetteer, July 1872
(5) ibid., September 1872
(6) ibid., April 1783
(7) ibid., October 1782
(8) ibid.
(9) ibid., June 1873
(10) ibid., May 1872
(11) ibid., June 1873
(12) Royal Sanitary Commission, 1858
(13) Gazetteer, June 1872
(14) ibid., January 1873

Chapter Three: Into The Sudan
(1) Retford Times, 1879, reproduced 11 December 1959
(2) Vedette, August 1911
(3) QRL Archive
(4) Anglesey, Vol.3, p.337
(5) Obituary by "an old comrade", QRL Archive
(6) Vedette, 31 March [1897?]
(7) Vedette, 1 December 1888
(8) ibid.
(9) ibid., 31 March 1898
(10) Madras Mail, July 1890
(11) Vedette, September 1891
(12) ibid.
(13) ibid., June 1890
(14) ibid., July 1894
(15) ibid., August 1894
(16) ibid., September 1894
(17) Madras Mail, quoted Vedette, October 1894
(18) The Globe, 24 October 1894
(19) Vedette, November 1894

Chapter Four: Towards Omdurman
(1) Vedette, March 1897
(2) ibid
(3) Montmorency, diary
(4) Montmorency, letter
(5) AO 4.1.c, quoted Vedette, September 1911
(6) Howard, p.222
(7) Pirie
(8) Steevens, p.219
(9) Pirie
(10) Howard, p.250
(11) Churchill, 'Companion', letter of 16 August 1898
(12) ibid., letter of 24 August
(13) ibid., letter of 26 August
(14) Pirie, 27 August
(15) ibid.
(16) McCombie, p.110
(17) Anglesey, Vol.3, p.372
(18) The Times, 5 September 1898
(19) Pirie, 31 August
(20) Steevens, p.253
(21) Pirie, 31 August
(22) ibid.

Chapter Five: The First Dervish Attack
(1) Eadon, 1 September
(2) Anglesey, Vol.3, p.373
(3) Pirie, 1 September
(4) Churchill, 'The River War', p.258
(5) Pirie, 1 September
(6) Howard, p.292
(7) Eadon, diary
(8) Smyth
(9) Vedette, January 1899
(10) Cox
(11) ibid.
(12) Ziegler, p.94
(13) Cox
(14) Pirie, 1 September
(15) Eadon, diary, 1 September
(16) Cox
(17) Rix
(18) Churchill, 'My Early Life', p.189
(19) Smyth
(20) Rix

(21) Howard, p.293
(22) Rix
(23) Churchill, 'The River War', p.273
(24) Eadon, letter
(25) Pirie, 2 September

Chapter Six: The Charge At Omdurman
(1) Vedette, January 1899
(2) Kitchener's official despatch
(3) QRL Museum
(4) Montmorency, letter
(5) Vedette, January 1899
(6) Montmorency, letter
(7) ibid.
(8) Vedette, January 1899
(9) Churchill, 'My Early Life', p.195
(10) Hewitt
(11) Vedette, January 1899
(12) Ziegler, p.156
(13) Churchill, 'Companion', letter of 16 September
(14) Vedette, January 1899
(15) Hewitt
(16) Eadon, diary, 2 September
(17) Churchill, 'Companion', letter of 14 September
(18) ibid.
(19) Vedette, January 1899
(20) Churchill, 'My Early Life', p.200
(21) Ziegler, p.158
(22) Vedette, January 1899
(23) Hewitt
(24) Vedette, January 1899
(25) Kitchener's official despatch

Chapter 7: Survivors' Accounts
(1) Eadon, letter
(2) Montmorency, letter
(3) Pirie
(4) Smyth
(5) Churchill, 'My Early Life', Chapter 15 (abridged)
(6) Rix

Chapter Eight: The Second Dervish Attack
(1) Zeigler, p.163
(2) ibid., p.167
(3) Sparkes
(4) ibid.
(5) ibid.
(6) Anglesey, p.386
(7) The Graphic, 22 October 1898
(8) Vedette, January 1899
(9) ibid.
(10) Smyth
(11) Montmorency, letter
(12) Vedette, January 1899
(13) Montmorency, letter
(14) Eadon, diary, 2 September (also noted in letter)
(15) Montmorency, letter

Chapter Nine: Aftermath, Reactions and Rewards
(1) Eadon, diary, 3 September
(2) ibid., 4 September
(3) Sparkes
(4) Vedette, January 1899
(5) ibid.
(6) Vedette, January 1899
(7) The Times, 6 September 1898 (report by Frank Rhodes)
(8) QRL Archive
(9) Burleigh, p.178
(10) The Globe, 10 September 1898
(11) Eadon, letter
(12) Vedette, January 1899
(13) QRL Archive
(14) Sparkes
(15) McCombie, p.181
(16) Vedette, January 1899
(17) Smyth
(18) Vedette, January 1899
(19) Churchill, 'Companion', letter of 17 September
(20) QRL Archive
(21) Vedette, January 1899
(22) QRL Archive
(23) QRL Museum
(24) Swarbrick
(25) ibid.

Chapter Ten: Riding in the Twilight
(1) Vedette, April 1900
(2) QRL Archive
(3) Vedette, February 1911
(4) Vedette, March 1911
(5) QRL Archive
(6) Cathcart, G.G., letter, 3 December 1915, QRL Archive
(7) QRL Archive
(8) as note 6
(9) QRL Archive
(10) Daily Express, report dated 9 September 1915
(11) Vedette, March 1915
(12) ibid.
(13) ibid.
(14) Vedette, December 1915
(15) Brinton
(16) Service Squadron Diary

INDEX

Page numbers in Roman type refer to text entries; in *italic* type, to illustrations

Abbassia barracks, Cairo, 37, 41, 108, 111-112
Abd al Baqi, Dervish commander, 48-49
Abi Wad Helu, 61
Abolitionists, 13-14
Abu Hamed, 39
Abu Klea, 29-30
Adazai camp, N.W. Frontier, *114*
Ali, Muhammad, Viceroy of Egypt, 16
Ali Wad Ulla, Dervish commander, 100
Allison, Pte., 21st LD, 16
Anderson, Capt., 21st L, 114-115
Anglo-Egyptian Army (1896-1898), 39, 46, 59, 63, 74-75
Arabi, Col, Egyptian rebel leader, 27
artillery, 41, 57, 62-63, 88, 100
Atbara, action at, 40, *42, 43*
Atbara, river/Fort, 39, 40, 46, 107
Ayton, Pte., 21st L, 86

Babikr, Bedri, Dervish Army, 99
Baggara tribe 27-28, 64, 77-78, 81, 88, 101, 106, 121
Ballard, Corp., 21st L, 114-115
Bangalore, 30-33
Beaumont, Col., 21st LD, 13
Beech, Lt., 21st H, 28
Belvoir Castle, 7, 9, 11, 121
Belvoir Hunt, 10, 31, 33
Berber, 37, 39
Bishop, Pte., 21st L, 45
Bowley, Capt., 21st H, 34-35
Brinton, Lt. JC, 2nd LG att. 21st L, 105, *108*
Brinton, Lt. OW, 21st L, 87, *88*, 116-117
Broadwood. Lt. Col., EC, 46, 52, 75, 100, 103-104
Brown, Pte., 21st L, *83*, 111
Buenos Aries, 14
Burleigh, Bennet., correspondent, 45, 108, 110
Byrne VC, Pte., 21st L, 73, 82-86, *84, 85*, 92, 111-112

Cairo, 27, 37, 42, 109
Campbell, Gen., 113-114
Canterbury home depot, 21st H, 23-24
Carter, Sgt., 21st L, *91*, 92
Case, Pte., 21st L, 107
casualties, 21st L, 87-89, 93-95, 100-101, 115-116; Dervish, 40, 63, 74, 89-90, 93
Cathcart, Dr., 115
Charlotte, Queen, 11
Churchill, Lt. Winston, 4th H att. 21st L, 8, 41, 42, *44*, 46, 48, 54-56, 58-62, 73-74, 80-82, 87-89, 95-98, *95*, 101, 103, 107, 110
Clerk, Lt., 21st L, 49, 54, *55*, 56-57, 59, 75, *88*

Cloeté, Capt., 21st LD, 15-16
Collinson, Maj., 4th E.B., 99, 103
Connaught, Duke of, 111
Conolly, Lt., 21st L, 48
Cordeaux, Capt., 21st L, 89, 106, 112
Crole-Wyndham, Maj., 21st L, 29, *45*, 48, *52*, 61, 73, *82*, 83-84, 86, 92, 108, 110, 112
Culloden Moor, battle of, 9
Cumberland, Duke of, 9

Denton, Pte., 21st L, 39
Dervishes, (see also under tribes: Baggara, Hadendoa), 28-30, 36-37, 39-40, 46, 48-49, 54-63, 99-104
Dinsdale, Corp., 21st L, 118
Disraeli, Prime Minister, 26
Dongola, 36
Douglas, Col., 21st LD, 11-12
Doyne, Capt., 21st L, 34, 80, *84*, 86
Dyer, Sgt., 21st L, 111

Eadon, Capt., 21st L, 52, 55, 58, 63, 80, 83, *86*, 87, 90, *90*, 104-106, 108, 121
East India Company, English, 13, 16-18, 20
East India Company, French, 13
Edward VII, King, 112
Effingham, Thomas, 3rd Earl of, 21st LD, 15
Egeiga village, 56, 59-60
Egerton, Capt., staff, 75
Egypt, 16, 24, 26-27, 36-41, 108, 111-112
Egyptian Cavalry, 40, 46-47, 49, 52, 54-55, 59-61, 63, 75, 99-100, 103-104, 107-109
Elizabeth II, Queen, 121
Elmslie, Maj., 37th F.B., 57
Emsdorff, charge at, 12

Fair, Capt., 21st L, 39, 41, 44, 87, 105
Fairland, Surgeon, 21st H, 20
Fashoda, 40-41
Finn, Maj., 21st L, 48, 54-56, 60-61, 78-81, 87-89, *88*, 102-103, 105-107, 109-110
Firket, 36
Fisher, Capt., 21st H, 25
Floyd, Maj., 21st L, 12,13
Flusty, Pte., 21st H, 34
Fowle, Maj., 21st L, 41, 48-49, 74, 80-81, 83, *83*, 112
Freeman, Sgt., 21st L, 87, *87*
French, Pte., 21st LD, 16

Gatacre, Gen., 39, 43, 46-47, 74, 76
George II, King, 9-10
George III, King, 10-11
George V, King, 118
Gladstone, Prime Minister, 26-29
Gordon, Gen. Charles, 26-30, 36, 105
Gordon Relief Expedition, 28-30, 48

Granby, Marquis of, 7, 9-11, *10, 13*, 31
Great War, 113-118
Grenfell, Lt., 12th L att. 21st L, 75-76, 86, 89, 92, 101, 107, 111
Griffiths, Sgt., 21st H, 23
Grigsby, Corp., 21st H, *22*
Gunboats, 50-52, 56, 59, 102
Fateh, *49*
Melik, *57*, 75, 100, 105

Hadendoa tribe, 64, 76-80, 77
Hadley, Pte., 21st L, 111
Haig, Capt., EC, 49, 52, 99, 101, 108-109
Harris, Corp., 21st L, 58
Harris, Sir Charles, 118
Hayes, Capt., 21st H, 25
Hewitt, Pte., 21st L, 81, 83, 89
Hickman, Lt. Col., 21st H, 30, 33
Hicks, Col., 28, 34
Higgs, Lt., 21st H, 29
Higgs, Sgt., 21st L, 87
Hinde, Capt., 21st LD, 11-13
Hoath, Cornet, 21st LD, 16
horses, 9, 30, 37, 41, *47, 48*, 82
Howard, Hubert, correspondent, 8, 40, 42, 44-45, 52, 54-55, 62, 103-104, 108
Hull VC, Pte., 21st L, 115-116, *118*
Hutton, Sgt. Maj., 21st L, *53*

India, 13, 16-24, 30-31, 33-36, 113-116
Ireland, 14, 26, 28, 112
Isma'il, Viceroy of Egypt, 24

Jaalin tribe, 42, 48, 52, 56
Jebel Merreh, 48
Jebel Surgham, 54-58, 60, 62-63, *74, 75*, 76-77, 88-89, 99-100, 121

Kashgil, 28
Kassassin, 27
Kemble, Lt., 3rd BELC, 19
Kenna VC, Capt., 21st L, 33-35, *34*, 37, 43, 64, *79*, 80-81, *83*, 86, 89, 92, 106, 111-112, 117
Kenna, Lady Cecil, 35-36
Kerreri hills, 49-52, 54-55, 62-63, 75, 99-100, 107
Kerreri plain, 46, 49, 54, 56, 61, 74, 77, 99-100, 107, *121*
Khalifa, (Abdullah el Taaisha), 30, 37, 48-49, 54, 56-57, 59, 61, 63, 74-78, 99-100, 102-107
Khartoum, 16, 24-26, 30, 36, 40-41, 54, 105, 111
Khedive, Isma'il, 24, 26; Tewfik, 26, 27
Khor Abu Sunt, 76-78, 81
Khor Shambat, 54, 57, 102-103, 105
King, Capt., 21st L, 105
King, Lt., 21st H, *25, 26*
Kingston, Duke of, 9

127

Kitchener, Gen., 30, 36-37, *36*, 40-41, 43, 46, 48, 50, 52, 55-57, *59*, 61, 74-75, 78, 89, 99-104, *101*, 106-107
Knight, Sgt. Tpt., 21st L, 80

lance, 38-39, 81-83, 112-113, 115
Landsdown, Lord, 110
Lane, Pte., 21st L, 34
Lauffeld, charge at, 9
Laughton, Sgt. Maj., 21st H, 34
Learoyd, Capt., 21st L, 115-116
Lee Enfield carbine, 38, 54, 56, 78, *78*
Lewis, Col., 3rd E.B., 99-101, 103
Lowe, Gen. Sir Hudson, 16
Lucas, Corp., 21st L, 114-115
Lucknow, 18-24, *24*
Lyttleton, Gen., 2nd B.B., 99, 101

MacDonald, Col., 1st E. B., 99-103
Magfar, 27
Mahdi, (Mohammed Ahmed ibn 'Abd Allah), 16, 24, 26-30, 37, 61, 106
Mahdi's Tomb, 54, 57, *58*, 103-104, 106
Mahmoud, Sharif, Dervish commander, 39-40, *43*, 44
Maldonado, charge at, 14
Manners, Lord John, see under Granby, Marquis of
Manners, Violet, 31
Manners Sutton, Lord Robert, 7, 9-11, *11*
Marathas, Indian tribesmen, 13, 16
Martin, Lt.Col., 21st L, 23, *32*, 34-35, 37-39, 41, 43, 45, *45*, 47-50, 52, 54-57, 60-62, 64, 74-81, *82*, 83, 87-89, *91*, 102-111
Mary, Queen, 112
Maud, W.T., correspondent, 102
Maxim gun, 31-33, 40, 45-46, 55, 59, 63, 99-101, 106
Maxwell, Col., 2nd E. B., 99-101, 103
McConchey, Lt., 21st LD, 15-16
McNeil, Lt., Seaforths, 82
Metemmeh, 29-30, 36, 39
Miller, Pte., 21st L, 92
Mills, Pte., 21st H, 22
Mirebalais, 14
Mohmand tribesmen, 31, 113-116
Molyneux, Lt., RHG att. 21st L, *44*, 86
Montmorency VC, Lt. de, 21st L, 30-31, *32*, 34, *34*, 35, 37, 41-43, *46*, 49, 64, 75, 78-80, 83, *83*, 86, 89-93, *91*,103-104, 107-108, 111-112
Motte, Lt. Col. de la, 21st LD, 12
Mutiny, Indian, 17-18, *18*
Muttonfist, Rough Rider, 21st H, 21
Mysore, Maharajah of, 33

Nakheila, 40
Napoleon, Bonaparte, 15, 16
Nesham, Lt., 21st L, 87, *87*, 105, *108*
North-West Frontier, India, 31, 113-116

Omdurman, 30, 36, 40, 44, 46-48, 54-57, 59, 74, 102-104, 106, 121
Omdurman, charge at, 8, 34, 77-98, 108-110
O'Reilly, Capt., 21st LD, 16
Osman Asrak, Dervish commander, 61
Osman Digna, Dervish commander, 28-29, 40, 47, 61

Paine, Thomas, 13
Parragreen, Pte., 1st Batt. G.G., 63
Payne, Corp., 21st L, 96

Pedder, Pte., 21st L, 87, 111
Pigot, Lt.Col., 21st LD, 15, 19
Pigott, Maj., 21st H, 27, *27*, 29, 31-32
Pinches, Surgeon Maj., 87, *88*, 111
Pirie, Lt., 21st L, 33, *34*, 35, 41, 43, 45, 48-50, 54-55, 58, 63, 75-79, 93-94, *94*, 103, 105-106
Plowden, Pamela. 35
Pritchard, Lt., 1st E.B., 99

Randolph, Lady, 41
Rao, Baji, Indian leader, 16

REGIMENTS (see also Anglo-Egyptian Army, Egyptian Cavalry)
Cavalry:
Bengal Light Cavalry, 3rd, 17-18; 4th, 18; 6th, 18
Camel Corps (1884)
  Light camel regiment, 29-30, 48;
  Mounted Infantry Camel Regiment, *26*, 29
Camel Corps (1898), 75, 100, 103
Cumberland's Light Dragoons, 9
Hussars: 3rd, 11; 7th, 107; 13th, 112; 14th, 118; 15th, 118; 19th, 118; 20th, 118; Prince of Wales, 13
Kingston's Light Horse, 9
Lancers: 4th, 35; 5th, 19-20, 107, 118; 12th, 107; 16th Lancers, 112, 118; 17th Lancers, 110, 118; 16th/5th Lancers, 118, 121; 17th/21st Lancers, 118, 121; Queen's Royal Lancers, 121
Light Dragoons: 4th, 13; 13th, 14; 14th, 13; 15th, 12; 18th, 13; 19th, 13; 23rd (Ulster), 13

3rd Bengal European Light Cavalry, 18, 19, *19*
21st Hussars, 18-25, 30-31, 33-38
21st Lancers, 38-39, 41-63, 74-98, 102-118
21st Light Dragoons:
  Granby's Regiment, 7-11
  Douglas's Regiment, 11-13
  Beaumont's Regiment, 13-16

Infantry:
Lincolnshire Regiment, 30, 100-101
West India Regiments, 1st, 31; 2nd, 33

Batteries:
32nd Field Battery, 41, 62, 88, 93, 103
37th Field Battery, 57

Reid, Pte., 21st H, 34
Rhodes, Frank, correspondent, 49
Rix, Corp., 21st L, 60-62, 97-98, *97*
Roberts, Sir Frederick, 34
Royal Military College Sandhurst, 33
Rothwell, Sgt.,21st H, 23
Rowlett, Pte., 21st L, *83*, 87
Rutland, Duke of, 9, 31, 121

Saint Helena, 15-16
Salisbury, Marquis of, 30, 36
San Domingo (Haiti), 13-14
Schmid, Maj., 21st H, 21
Scriven, Lt. Col., 21st L, 113-116
Secunderabad, 33-36
Service Squadron, 21st L., 117-118
Shabkadar, N.W. Frontier, charge at, 113-116
Shabluka hill, 46
Sheik el Din, Dervish commander, 61

Simpson, Sgt., 21st L, 115
Slatin Pasha, 37, 40
Smyth, Lt., 21st L, 8, 34, 48, 52, 55, 61, 78, 87, *88*, 94-95, *94*, 109, 112
South Africa, 14-15, 112
South America, 14
Sparkes, Capt., 3rd EB, 100-101, 106
Spottisford, Capt., 21st H, 24
Steele, Tpt., 21st L, 76
Steevens, G.W., correspondent, 44, 49
Sterne, Laurence, 11
Sudan, 8, 16, 24, 26-30, 36, 39-40, 43-63, 74-89, 99-106
Sudan Military Railway, 39, *42*, 43, 108
Suez Canal, 24, 26-27
Sururab camp, 49
Sutton, Robert, 9
Swarbrick, Corp., 21st L, 86, 92, *93*, 111

Tamaniat camp, 48
Tarleton, Lt. Gen. Sir Banastre, 21st LD, 14
Taylor, Capt., 21st H, 26
Taylor, Lt., 21st L, *84*
Tel-el-Kebir, 27
Thompson, Lt., 21st L, 114-116, *118*
Tombs, Maj.Gen., 21
Trimulgherry barracks, Secunderabad, *29*, 33, 36
Tristan da Cunha, 15-16
Tullihardine, Marquis of, R.H.G., 78, 88-89

uniform, 21st LD, 10-11, 13-15; 21st H, *19*, 21, *22*, *25*, *26*, 31-32, 37-38; 21st L, 38, *40*, *44*, 45, 49, *110*; Dervish, 58, 63, *78*
Uthman al Din, Dervish commander, 100

Varley, Pte., 21st L, *83*
Victoria Cross, 111
Victoria, Queen, 17, 25, 30, 38, 107, 110-112

Wadi el Abid, 47
Wadi Halfa, 30, 36, 39, 108
Wadi Hamed, 45-46
Warburg, charges at, 10, 13
Wauchope, Gen., 1st B.B., 99, 101, 103
weapons, British (see also artillery, lance, Lee Enfield carbine, Maxim gun), 20-21, 33, 63, 81-83, 112; Dervish, 28, 56, 58-59, 63, 77, 79, 81, 83, 106
West Indies, 13-14
Wheeler, Capt., 21st L, 117
Wingate, Col., 40, 46, 48, 56, 61
Wolseley, Sir Garnet, 27, 29
Wood, Sgt, Maj., 21st L, 48
Wood, Sir Evelyn, 108
Wormald, Lt., 7th H att. 21st L, 87, *88*, 104

Yaqub, Dervish commander, 61, 99-100
Yonni Expedition, 31-32

zariba, 46, 48, 56, 58-60, 62-63, 75

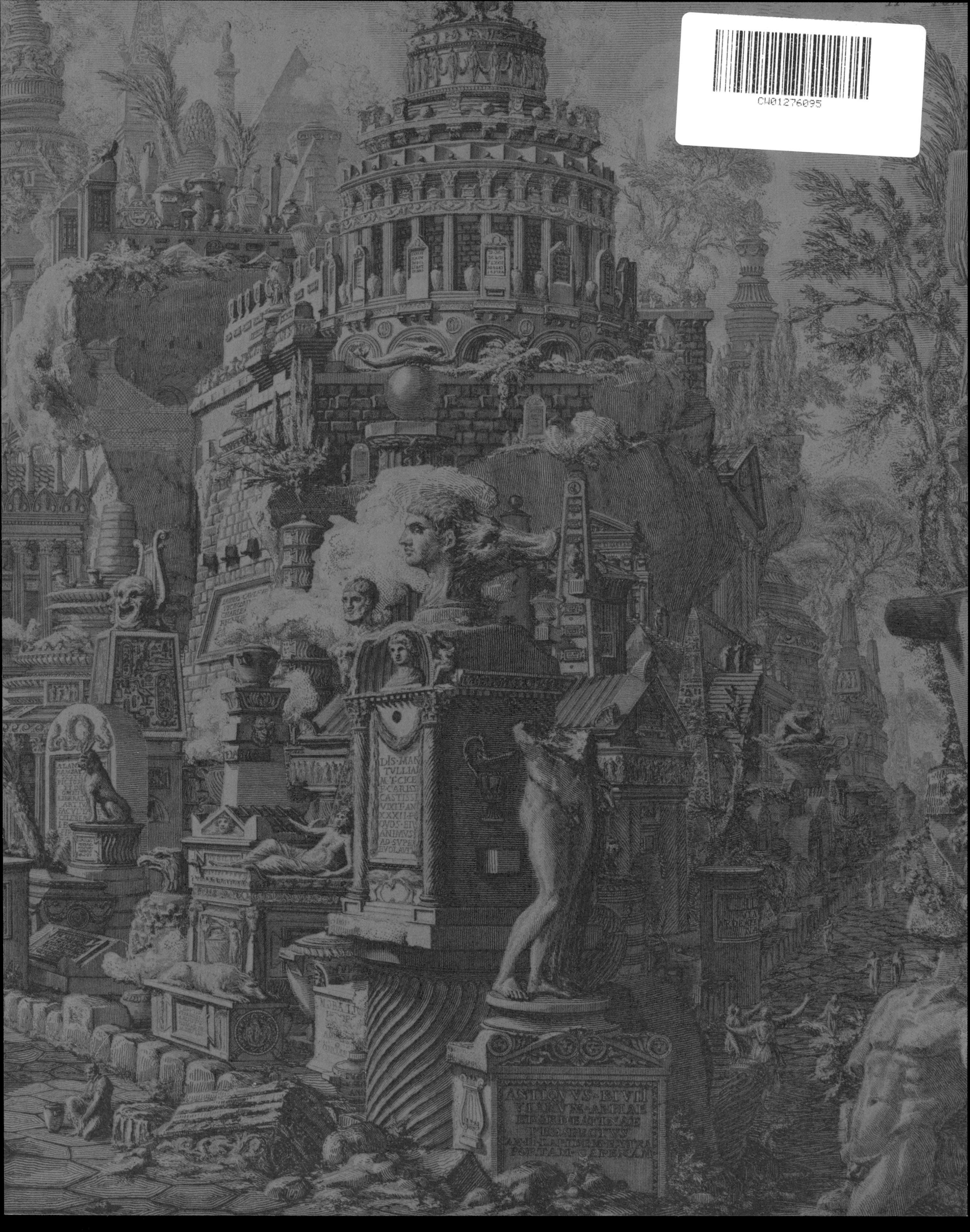

THE ETERNAL LETTER

QVAM VER
PERIER
VS POSSIT
DATVS E C
I NVMEN
VENIT H

THE ETERNAL LETTER

TWO MILLENNIA OF THE CLASSICAL ROMAN CAPITAL

EDITED BY PAUL SHAW

THE MIT PRESS | CAMBRIDGE, MASSACHUSETTS AND LONDON, ENGLAND

Copyright © 2015 Massachusetts Institute of Technology.
Individual articles are the copyright property of their authors.

All rights reserved. No part of this book may be reproduced in any form by any electronic or mechanical means (including photocopying, recording, or information storage and retrieval) without permission in writing from the publisher.

MIT Press books may be purchased at special quantity discounts for business or sales promotional use. For information, please email: special_sales@mitpress.mit.edu.

Library of Congress Cataloging-in-Publication Data
The eternal letter : two millennia of the classical roman capital / edited by
    Paul Shaw. pages cm. — (A codex book)
Includes bibliographical references and index.
ISBN 978-0-262-02901-8 (hardcover : alk. paper)
1. Roman capitals (Lettering) I. Shaw, Paul, editor. II. Shaw, Paul. Eternal letter.
NK3625.R66E84   2015
745.6'1978—dc23
2014039749

Printed and bound in China by Everbest.
10 9 8 7 6 5 4 3 2

Frontispiece: Detail of the inscription on the tomb of the children of Sextus Pompeius Justus on the Via Appia, Rome, 2nd century AD. (CIL VI 24520)

Endleaves: Front, Giovanni Battista Piranesi, *Via Appia Imaginaria*, 1756 (detail). Back, View of the Las Vegas Strip, altered photograph by James Brandon.

Facing page: Brush kinetics exercise by Father Edward Catich from *The Origin of the Serif* (1968), p. 165.

This publication is made possible, in part, by the generosity of Adobe Typekit, Monotype Imaging, Mark Simonson Studios, and Courier Corporation.

The Eternal Letter is set in Carat, a contemporary face in the Venetian Renaissance vein by Dieter Hofrichter (Hoftype, 2012). The jacket and binding are set in a combination of Stevens Titling by John Stevens (Linotype, 2012) and Magma by Sumner Stone (Stone Type Foundry, 2004). Robert Slimbach's Trajan Sans Pro (Adobe, 2012) and Magma appear on the title page.
   The first section divider has quotations by Jan Tschichold, Wolfgang Weingart, and Jeremy Tankard set, respectively, in Sistina (Hermann Zapf, D. Stempel, 1951), ITC Golden Cockerel (Dave Farey and Richard Dawson, 1996 after Eric Gill, 1929) and Forum Titling (Frederic W. Goudy, 1911). The latter is also used for the title of "Goudy's Inscriptional Letters." The title of "Eric Gill's Capital Letter" is set in a wood type version of Perpetua Titling by Gill (1928). The second section divider has quotations by Jim Parkinson, Eric Gill and Peter Bil'ak set, respectively, in Mantinia (Matthew Carter, Carter & Cone, 1993), Penumbra Sans (Lance Hidy, Adobe, 1994) and Senatus (Werner Schneider, H. Berthold, 2003). The title of "Penumbra: The Offspring of Trajan and Futura" is set in Penumbra Flare Light, while the titles of "The Origins of Senatus," "Mantinia," and "Requiem," are set in those faces. The title of "Waters Titling" is set in Waters Titling Condensed (Julian Waters, Adobe, 1996).

CODEX STUDIES IN LETTERFORMS

EDITOR IN CHIEF
Paul Shaw

DESIGNER
Linda Florio

PRODUCER AND EDITOR
Scott-Martin Kosofsky

CODEX EDITORIAL BOARD
John Boardley, *founder*
  Ho Chi Minh City, Vietnam
Patricia Belen
  New York, New York, USA
Peter Bil'ak
  The Hague, The Netherlands
James Clough
  Milan, Italy
Catherine Dixon
  London, England
Greg D'Onofrio
  New York, New York, USA
Jost Hochuli
  St. Gallen, Switzerland
Alastair Johnston
  Berkeley, California, USA
Scott-Martin Kosofsky
  Lexington, Massachusetts, USA
Indra Kupferschmid
  Saarbrücken, Germany
Mathieu Lommen
  Amsterdam, The Netherlands
Sébastien Morlighem
  Amiens, France
James Mosley
  London, England
Claudio Rocha
  São Paulo, Brazil
Helmut Schmid
  Osaka, Japan

A B C D
E F G H I
K L M N
O P Q R

Introduction: The Classical Roman Capital
PAUL SHAW, EDITOR

The Eternal Letter: The Classical Roman Capital is the first of what is intended to be a series of thematic books, Codex Studies in Letterforms. The history of the classical Roman capital (*capitalis monumentalis* to epigraphers) over the course of two millennia is a fascinating subject, though one far too vast to be properly encompassed in a single book. Instead, *The Eternal Letter* is a collection of articles, primarily biographies and case studies, focused on two moments when the classical Roman capital was ascendent: the Renaissance and, more importantly, the 20th century.

Thus, despite their strong presence throughout its pages, the book is not about inscriptions from the Roman Empire. They are merely the starting point for an investigation into how and why the Classical Roman capital has been revived, altered, and adapted not only as a letter carved into stone, but as one cut into wood, written with ink and paint, cast into lead, and converted into pixels.

The Eternal Letter opens with my overview of the roller-coaster reputation of the classical Roman capital during its two-thousand-year history, accompanied by a timeline. These are supplemented by a short, visual definition of classical Roman capitals—in a broad sense rather than a narrow, antiquarian one—and their antagonists: "industrial" Roman capitals. Together, these three items provide a contextual framework for the articles and a guide to many of the subtle aesthetic discussions that appear within them.

The specific incarnation of the classical Roman capital that dominates the book is the inscription on the base of Trajan's Column, in Rome. It is the lodestar and lightning rod for nearly all of the individuals—both authors and subjects—in *The Eternal Letter*. It is either an exemplary model to be extolled, worshipped, and replicated or it is an overhyped specimen to be adamantly avoided. The principal individual in the first camp is Father Edward M. Catich, a Chicago signwriter turned Iowa priest, while those in the second camp include designer and educator Walter Kaech, and the stonecarvers Eric Gill, Michael Harvey, and the three generations of the Benson family of Rhode Island: John Howard, John E., and Nicholas.

Catich played a seminal role in creating our current understanding of the forces shaping the Imperial Roman capital, especially as found in the Trajan inscription. He is the author of one essay and the subject of two others in *The Eternal Letter*, one by me and one by Gregory MacNaughton, but his spirit hovers over the entire book, extending beyond stonecarving to calligraphy and type design.

Centuries before Father Catich discovered the charms of the Trajan inscription, it was an object of obsession to Renaissance and Baroque artists and scholars, among them antiquarian Felice Feliciano (1433–1479), sculptor Andrea Bregno (1418–1506), and writing master Giovanni Francesco Cresci (c.1534/5–early 17th century). Their attempts to solve the mystery of the beauty of the Imperial capitals and to apply them to tombs and monuments are taken up in two articles by James Mosley and one by Garrett Boge and me. The latter includes a reduced scale facsimile of a rubbing of an entire quattrocento inscription.

From Feliciano (1460) to Johannes Muess (1989), many have tried but failed to recreate the Trajan letters using compass and set-square. In "The Trajan Secrets," contemporary British lettercarver Tom Perkins approaches the idea from a novel perspective that promises more success.

The Benson family, proprietors of The John Stevens Shop since 1929, have forged their own contemporary take on the classical Roman capital—including sans serif variants—in the inscriptions they have carved for tombs, monuments, and buildings throughout the United States. British lettercarver Richard Kindersley, himself part of the Gill legacy and the inheritor of a family tradition, interviews John E. and Nicholas Benson for *The Eternal Letter*.

The migration of the classical Roman capital from stone to lead in the 1470s is a key moment in the history of printing and, by extension, graphic design. Frank Blokland has

Roman majuscules from *Lo presente libro...* by Giovanntonio Tagliente (Venice, 1524). Cut in wood by Eustachio Celebrino. From the 1525 edition.

supplied an article that sheds some much-needed light on the details of that transition, a subject often shrouded in ignorance.

Eric Gill is arguably as important a figure as Catich in any discussion of the classical Roman capital in the 20th century. He was a type designer as well as a stonecarver—and much else besides. The full range of his lettermaking activities, along with his legacy in English lettercarving, is the subject of two articles by Ewan Clayton. I profile Michael Harvey, one of those heavily influenced by Gill, who represents another link between lettercarving and type design.

William Morris and the Arts & Crafts Movement spawned not only Gill, but also Frederic W. Goudy, Jan van Krimpen, and Hermann Zapf, four type designers from four different cultures who each breathed new life into the classical Roman capital in the 20th century. Their work in this area is surveyed respectively by Steve Matteson, Martin Majoor, and me.

The allure of the Trajan letter has not been confined to Western Europe and the United States, as Maxim Zhukov reminds us in his survey of attempts by Soviet designers, especially Vadim Lazurski, to create a Cyrillic interpretation.

The spark that flamed up to become *The Eternal Letter* is "Trajan Revived Redux," my overview of a surprising concatenation of digital typefaces inspired by the classical Roman capital that all appeared in 2011. Zhukov and Gerry Leonidas weigh in with their opinions on the Cyrillic and Greek extensions of Adobe Trajan.

Scott-Martin Kosofsky narrates the story of Adobe Trajan, the typeface designed by Carol Twombly, but rooted in Catich's researches, that has become as widely recognized as Helvetica. Similar backstories of digital typefaces by Lance Hidy (Penumbra), Werner Schneider (Senatus), Matthew Carter (Mantinia), Jonathan Hoefler (Requiem), Garrett Boge (The Baroque Set), and Julian Waters (Waters Titling) provide a reminder that there is far more to the classical Roman capital than Adobe Trajan.

Calligraphic interpretations of the classical Roman capital are an undercurrent in *The Eternal Letter*. They burst forth in the work of John Stevens, the preeminent calligrapher in the world today, whose book *Scribe: Artist of the Word* is reviewed here.

Rounding out *The Eternal Letter* are appendices intended to provide additional resources for those who, we hope, have become entranced, or at least intrigued, by the classical Roman capital in the course of reading these essays.

The Decline of the West by Oswald Spengler (New York: Alfred A. Knopf, 1962). Book jacket design by George Salter.

OSWALD SPENGLER

An abridged edition of **THE DECLINE OF THE WEST**

Alfred A. Knopf: PUBLISHER, New York

salter

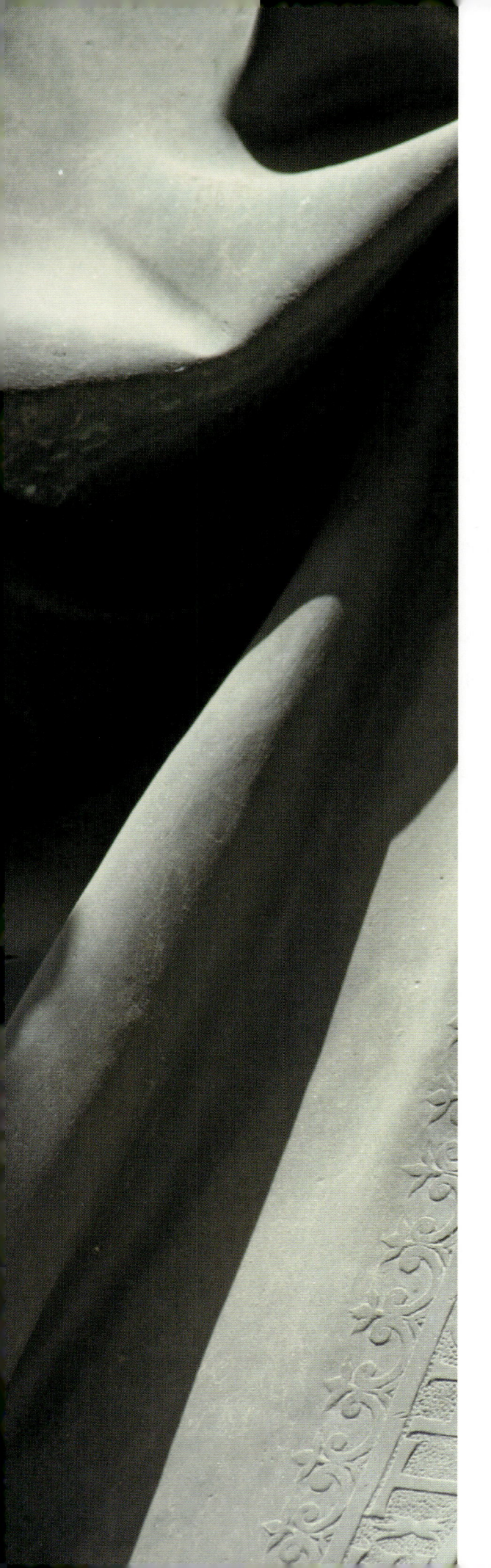

CONTENTS

1   The Eternal Letter: The Fluctuating Fortunes of the Classical Roman Capital
PAUL SHAW

23   Defining The Classical Roman Capital
PAUL SHAW

25   Father Edward M. Catich and the Trajan Inscription
PAUL SHAW

32   The Genetrix
FATHER EDWARD M. CATICH

34   The Trajan Secrets
TOM PERKINS

37   Walter Kaech, Craftsman
JOST HOCHULI

40   On the Origin of Capital Proportions in Roman Type
FRANK E. BLOKLAND

49   Felice Feliciano and the Inscriptions on the Macello of Verona
JAMES MOSLEY

52   The Tomb of Niccolò Forteguerri
PAUL SHAW AND GARRETT BOGE

59   The Baroque Inscriptional Letter in Rome
JAMES MOSLEY

64   The Baroque Set
GARRETT BOGE

69   Goudy's Inscriptional Letters
STEVE MATTESON

85   Eric Gill's Capital Letter
EWAN CLAYTON

105   Jan van Krimpen and Roman Capitals
MARTIN MAJOOR

111   Hermann Zapf's Roman Capitals: An Appreciation
PAUL SHAW

127   The Trajan Letter in Russia
MAXIM ZHUKOV

133   Gill's Legacy
EWAN CLAYTON

138	Straight, No Chaser: The Work of Michael Harvey	
	PAUL SHAW	
143	The John Stevens Shop: Three Generations of Lettercarvers	
	RICHARD KINDERSLEY	
165	Penumbra: The Offspring of Trajan and Futura	
	LANCE HIDY	
175	Father Catich at Reed College	
	GREGORY MACNAUGHTON	
181	Democratizing the Empire: The Birth of Adobe Trajan	
	SCOTT-MARTIN KOSOFSKY	
185	Trajan Revived Redux	
	PAUL SHAW / MAXIM ZHUKOV / GERRY LEONIDAS	
202	Artist of the Written Word	
	PAUL SHAW	
209	The Origins of Senatus	
	WERNER SCHNEIDER WITH DAN REYNOLDS	
213	Mantinia	
	MATTHEW CARTER	
221	Requiem: A True Renaissance Letter	
	JONATHAN HOEFLER	
225	Waters Titling	
	JULIAN WATERS	
232	Typefaces with Classical Roman Influences: 1900 – 2012	
235	Trajan at the Movies	
	YVES PETERS	
236	Learning from Chairs	
	CYRUS HIGHSMITH	
238	Census of Trajan Inscription Reproductions	
242	Selected Collections of Roman Inscriptions	
245	Further Reading on Roman Capitals	
251	Recording Inscriptions: Methods and Tips	
256	Acknowledgments	Credits	Contributors	

Details from bronze statue of St. John the Baptist by Lorenzo Ghiberti (1412–1416) located in one of the niches of Orsanmichele, Florence. The letters are one of the earliest examples of Renaissance artists reviving classical Roman capitals, though they are apparently derived from manuscript sources and not from ancient Roman inscriptions.

A·MARCEI·VERGILEI·EVRYSACIS·PISTORIS·REDEMPTORIS·APPARE

THE ETERNAL LETTER: THE FLUCTUATING FORTUNES OF THE CLASSICAL ROMAN CAPITAL

PAUL SHAW

THE YEARS IMMEDIATELY preceding and following the fiftieth anniversary of Helvetica (née Neue Haas Grotesk, in 1957), the most famous of all sans serif typefaces, were marked by a frenzy previously unknown in the staid world of typography. It began with *Helvetica: Homage to a Typeface* (2002), compiled by Lars Müller, reached an apotheosis with the release of Gary Hustwit's *Helvetica* (2007), the first movie ever made about a typeface, and culminated in the publication of *Helvetica Forever: Story of a Typeface*, edited by Müller and Victor Malsy, first in German (2008) and soon after in English (2009). The excitement over Helvetica is part of a long-running narrative in which the graphic design elite have, since the 1920s, continually declared sans serif to be the typeface of modernity, first of the machine age and now of the computer age.

The sans serif has been constantly lauded as the perfect embodiment of a rational, functional letterform, one that has been stripped to its essentials and, thus, in harmony with machines and the simplicity of digital data. But if the sans serif, especially as epitomized by Helvetica, has triumphed in the 21st century, how does one explain the fact that serif typefaces, most notably Times New Roman, still dominate the great bulk of all printed matter and retain a strong presence in screen-based communication? The truth is that seriffed romans have not gone away, they simply have made room for sans serifs. And the strongest proof of their resilience is the astonishing popularity—despite the mockery—of Adobe Trajan, the digital incarnation of the most famous example of the most tradition-bound of all seriffed romans: the classical Roman capital. Helvetica's fiftieth birthday, in 2007, may have seemed like quite an achievement, but it pales in comparison to the nineteen hundredth birthday, in 2014, of Trajan's Column and its renowned inscription. The pervasiveness and persistence of classical Roman capitals today obscures the fact that they have not been held continuously in high favor over the past two millennia. Furthermore, they did not emerge miraculously, Athena-like, fully formed.

The earliest extant example of classical Roman capitals—often referred to as *capitalis monumentalis* or Imperial Roman capitals—dates to 43 BC, a year after the assassination of Julius Caesar and the beginning of the transformation of Rome from a republic into an empire.[1] The letters differ from their predecessors, the Republican Roman capitals, in three key aspects: there is variation in the thickness of the strokes, a greater variety of widths, and the serifs are longer and more fully bracketed. [1, 2] Several of these features are traceable to the use of a flexible, broad-edged brush to lay out inscriptions as a guide to carving. (An instance of brush-written letters, albeit as graffiti, is still to be found at Pompeii.) [3] However, the Imperial Roman capitals do not fully come to the fore until the early 1st century AD, reaching their apogee in the 2nd century. Since the publication of Edward Johnston's *Writing & Illuminating, & Lettering*, in 1906, the general—though not universal—consensus has been that the best example of the Imperial Roman capitals is the inscription at the base of Trajan's Column.[2] [4] (See p. 24 for Father Edward M. Catich's summation of this position.)

Although much of the adulation of the Trajan inscription has taken on the nature of rote, there are several good reasons why it deserves its preeminence. As part of the column commissioned by Emperor Trajan to commemorate the successful Roman campaign against the Dacians, it is of great historical importance. It remains in its original location and, with the exception of a triangular chunk missing at the bottom edge (containing six letters) and

[1] The tomb of Marcus Vergilius Eurysaces (The Baker's Tomb), Rome, c. 50–20 BC. The letters are Republican capitals.

2   The tomb of Publius Cacurius Philocles (CIL VI 10020), along the Via Appia, Rome, 1st c. BC. The letters are Republican capitals.

a ding caused by a cannonball near the top edge, it is essentially intact. [5] The text contains every letter of the Roman alphabet then in use, save *H*. Finally, the layout is well done with generally excellent letter- and wordspacing; the margins are generous and, through the use of a subtle adjustment of scale from line to line, justification has been accomplished without ligatures and with a minimum of abbreviations. [6] There are Roman inscriptions that have letters that are equal or even better in quality, but none of them meet all of these criteria. (See frontispiece, tomb of the children of Sextus Pompeius Justus on the Via Appia, Rome, 2nd c. AD.)

The Imperial Roman capital spread along with the Roman Empire itself. Versions of varying degrees of quality can be found throughout Italy, as well as in France, Germany, Great Britain, Turkey, Syria, and other areas of Europe and the Middle East that came under Roman domination. The style lasted into the 5th century, dissipating only when the western half of the Empire collapsed with the deposition of Romulus Augustulus by the Germanic leader Odoacer, in 476. [7]

A century earlier, the primacy of the Imperial Roman capital had been challenged by the so-called Damasian letter, created by Filocalus to record the names of Christian martyrs. [8]

The first revival of the classical Roman capital occurred in the late 8th century, as part of Charlemagne's program to recreate the culture of the Roman Empire. The most important Carolingian inscription in this respect is that of Pope Hadrian I, commissioned by Charlemagne in 795 and now preserved in the portico of St. Peter's.[3] [10] Interpreted by the Church as evidence of imperial loyalty to the papacy, it was one of the few monuments from Old St. Peter's to be transplanted into the new building. It is overshadowed, however, by the numerous examples of pen-made copies of Imperial Roman capitals in Carolingian manuscripts, such as the Moutier-Grandval Bible (834–843) and the Second Bible of Charles the Bald (871–877). [11]

Imperial Roman capitals—called *capitalis quadrata* in their pen-made form—were at the top of Alcuin of York's hierarchy of scripts, followed, in descending and chronological order, by rustics, uncials, and the newly minted Carolingian minuscules. [9, 12] However, they were not faithful copies. The scale of a manuscript is markedly smaller than that of an inscription, and the quill a less flexible tool than the soft, broad-edged brush used to lay out the *capitalis monumentalis* prior to carving. Despite this, the Carolingian capitals had the same unmistakable air of authority as their Roman forebears.

Charlemagne's heirs lacked both his political skill and his passion for the ancient world. The supple Carolingian minuscule declined, metamorphosing during the Middle Ages into the rotunda and the rigid textura. In medieval texts, the resurrected capitals of antiquity were blended with drawn uncials to serve as initial letters, often called versals. In that capacity, their widths were further distorted and homogenized in order to fit the uniform spaces set aside by scribes for rubrication.[4] [14]

The classical Roman capitals were revived a second time in the 15th century, as part of the Italian Renaissance and its passionate interest in the art and culture of Greek and Roman antiquity. However, the earliest examples of "ancient" Roman

3 Graffiti, Pompeii, 79 AD. Political notices painted on the house of Aulus Trebius Valens, Via dell'Abbondanza. Photograph from 1916. Of the large letters, all but the two on the right were destroyed by a bomb on 19 September 1943.

capitals by the Florentine sculptors Lorenzo Ghiberti, Donatello, Michelozzo, and Luca della Robbia were actually Romanesque in origin. [13] They had strokes of varying thickness, but instead of serifs they had wedge-shaped or flared terminals. Nicolete Gray dubbed these capitals, which emerged around 1410, "Florentine Sans Serifs."[5] [15] They were ascendant until the middle of the century and, despite Gray's appellation, can be found in Rome, Siena, Perugia, Milan, Venice, and other northern Italian cities. Instances in S. Croce, in Florence, became the models for Hermann Zapf's Optima typeface.[6] (See p. 118.)

Exactly when a more accurate *capitalis monumentalis* emerged in the quattrocento has been a matter of much debate among art historians, paleographers, and epigraphers. Among those put forth as the originators have been Donatello (his signature on the base of the statue of the *condottiero* Erasmo da Narni, Gattamelata in Padua, completed in 1450); Andrea Mantegna (the trompe l'oeil inscription in the background of the Martyrdom of St. James fresco, c.1448–1454 in the Cappella Ovetari, Chiesa di Eremitani, Padua); Andrea Bregno (the inscription on the tomb of Ludovico d'Albret [d. 1465] in S. Maria in Aracoeli, Rome—see p. 57, figs. 4 and 5), and Leon Battista Alberti (the inscription on the Cappella Rucellai [1467] in S. Pancrazio, Florence).[7] [17, 18] The dispute devolves upon the features required to define letters as sufficiently classical: thick/thin stroke contrast, variable widths, presence of bracketed serifs, and specific forms of key letters such as *E*, *M*, *P*, and *R*. Star Meyer and I argued for Bregno in our contribution to *Andrea Bregno: il senso della forma nella cultura artistica del Rinascimento* (2008), but more recently I have come to believe that Poggio Bracciolini and the unidentified carver of his epitaph (1438), in S. Maria Bambina, in Terranuova Bracciolini, deserve first place of honor.[8] [16]

Regardless of who deserves credit, it is clear that letters with the basic properties of the Imperial Roman capitals had emerged before 1465, when the first printers in Italy, Conrad Sweynheym and Arnold Pannartz, arrived in Subiaco. The Paduan calligraphers Biagio di Saraceno and Bartolomeo Sanvito had already been employing pen-made versions of the Imperial Roman capitals in their manuscripts since the early 1450s. [19] They not only used them in multicolored rubrications, but as the majuscule companion to the humanist book hand, successor to the Carolingian minuscule, a combination that became enshrined in the early roman types of Wendelin da Spira and Nicolas Jenson at the beginning of the 1470s, though the exigencies of typecasting (the need to limit the number of widths) may have influenced the lateral proportions of the capitals so that they never wholly emulated their lapidary models.[9] (See article by Frank E. Blokland, p. 40.)

Beginning with Felice Feliciano's *Alphabetum Romanum* of 1460, a succession of treatises began to appear over the course of the next seventy years—and continued sporadically into the 20th century—that tried to discover the secrets of the Imperial Roman capitals through their reconstructions via geometrical means. [20] The most famous of these constructed alphabets by Feliciano, Damiano da Moylle, Luca Pacioli, Albrecht Dürer, and Geoffroy Tory have fascinated art historians, typographers, and others out of all proportion to their actual impact on contemporary practice.[10] No matter how complex or convoluted the constructions,

THE ETERNAL LETTER 3

4 The Forum of Trajan with Trajan's Column, c.1860–1870.

none of these attempts—or modern ones by David Lance Goines and Johannes Muess—succeed in matching letters such as those of the Trajan Inscription.[11] [21]

Successful or not, the string of treatises attempting to construct classical Roman capitals is testament to the importance in which these letters were held in the quattrocento, a value that continued through the Renaissance and into the Baroque period. Classical Roman capitals became a part of the manuals produced by the new profession of writing master that sprung up in the wake of the Gutenbergian printing revolution. Among the most celebrated of these alphabets are those by Arrighi (see p. 223), Tagliente (see p. vi), and, especially, Giovan Francesco Cresci (see p. 58). A measure of how deeply absorbed the classical Roman capitals had become by the middle of the 16th century is their presence as the underlying structure of a fantastical and bizarre alphabet in the *Opera* of Frate Vespasiano Amphiareo (1548), built out of tree trunks and branches.[12] [24]

It was Cresci, who, in his *Essemplare di piu sorti lettere* (1560) and *Il perfetto scrittore* (1571), achieved a nearly perfect imitation of the Trajanic capital by breaking free of the mania for geometrical construction. [22] His models, created freehand, were copied by other Italian writing masters well into the second half of the 17th century. In the hands of his pupil Luca Horfei, they adorn the obelisks and aqueducts erected between 1585 and 1590 as part of Sixtus V's restoration of Rome. [23] Thus, Cresci's capitals became the basis of the Baroque version of the Imperial Roman capitals.[13]

The eclipse of the Baroque Roman capital began with the creation of the Romain du Roi typeface, in the 1690s. [25] The decision of the commission headed by Abbé Bignon, to design the letters on a grid of 2304 squares, using arcs of circles, returned geometry to a position of prominence.[14] The prestige of the resulting typeface, cut by Philippe Grandjean and first used in 1702, influenced the typefounders Pierre Simon Fournier le jeune, Louis Luce, and ultimately Firmin Didot and Giambattista Bodoni. Out of the Romain du Roi was born the neoclassical capital with features that were in direct opposition to those of classical Roman capitals. [26] The lateral proportions were regularized, the contrast between thick and thin strokes was exaggerated, and bracketing of serifs was either reduced or dispensed with altogether.

The neoclassical letterforms that emerged in the 1780s dominated the world of typography through the end of the 19th century. They also became the armature for

5 Inscription at the base of Trajan's Column.

SENATVS·POPVLVSQVE·ROMANVS
IMP·CAESARI·DIVI·NERVAE·F·NERVAE
TRAIANO·AVG·GERM·DACICO·PONTIF
MAXIMO·TRIB·POT·XVII·IMP·VI·COS·VI·P·P
AD·DECLARANDVM·QVANTAE·ALTITVDINIS
MONS·ET·LOCVS·TANTIS·OPERIBVS·SIT·EGESTVS

6 Recreation of the text of the Trajan nscription using Adobe Trajan. The letters in gray are those that are missing today from the inscription.

THE ETERNAL LETTER 5

7 The Arch of Constantine (north side), Rome, 315 AD. The main inscription was originally filled with bronze letters.

the new advertising type styles developed in England between 1803 and 1834. The Fat Faces, Egyptians, and Grotesques that that Thomas Hansard, in his *Typographia* (1825), assailed as "typographic monstrosities" were the vanguard of the shift from types designed for books to types designed for commerce. There was no place in the world of Victorian publicity for the elegance and nuance of the classical Roman capital, nor for its cultural associations. The brash but functional industrial letter was now in demand. [27, 28]

Traditional accounts of printing history describe the 19th century as an aesthetic nadir, attributable to the absence of classical discipline coupled with a decline in the quality of craftsmanship that accompanied the rapid mechanization of the industry. Although typefounding and composition were not mechanized until late in the century, with the twin inventions of the Linotype and Monotype in the mid-1880s, typography had already suffered a loss of quality, with the introduction of stereotyping and electrotyping decades earlier. The rejuvenation of both printing and typography started in 1891 with the founding of the Kelmscott Press by William Morris. Its books immediately spawned a wave of private presses in England and America that subsequently spread to Germany and Holland, almost all of which, following Morris's lead, looked to the work of Nicolaus Jenson as the model of the ideal Roman letter. At nearly the same time, and no doubt not coincidentally, there began a tentative rebirth of interest in the classical Roman capital. Edward F. Strange's *Alphabets* (1898) reproduced Tagliente's capitals, an inscription by Horfei, and an alphabet by Antonio Sacchi in the Crescian vein, but, curiously, no examples of ancient Roman inscriptions. Dürer's complete alphabet of constructed Roman capitals is included as an exemplar for making Roman capitals.

Edward Johnston, widely recognized as the father of modern calligraphy, who at first looked to Strange for paleographic knowledge, is responsible for initiating the modern fascination with the Trajan inscription. A reproduction of it, based on the cast in the Victoria & Albert Museum, is included as plates I and II in his seminal *Writing & Illuminating, & Lettering* (1906) and in the portfolio *Manuscript & Inscription Letters* (1909).[15] In the wake of Johnston's works, every new lettering book felt obliged to include its own reproduction of the Trajan inscription (always taken from the same V&A cast), thus establishing its letters as the *sine qua non* of Imperial Roman capitals. One of these books was *Roman Lettering* by L. C. Evetts (1938), which reintroduced the notion of constructing the "Trajan letters" with compass and straightedge, albeit with some adjustments. The culmination of this trend in England was the establishment, in 1949, of a guide for signwriters by the Ministry of Public Building and Works, based on Evetts' model alphabet.[16]

Both of Johnston's works included plates on lettercarving by his pupil Eric Gill. Gill's letters deviated from the Trajan ideal, influenced in part by Florentine sans serif inscriptions and in part by William Caslon's typefaces. [29] Gill quickly gained a reputation for his lettercarving work, which, along with his charismatic personality, touched off a renaissance of manual lettercarving in England that is still vibrant today and which still feels Gill's influence. The classical influence of Johnston and Gill even extended to the world of type, beginning with Johnston's 1916 design of a sans serif for use in the London Underground [30] and, a dozen years later, Gill's design of Gill Sans for Monotype Corporation. Both typefaces clearly show their classical origins, though deviate in several respects from the Trajanic ideal, most noticeably in the form of *M*.[17]

A revival of interest in classical Roman capitals was occurring in the United States at the same time as in England, but it emerged from a source other than the British Arts & Crafts movement. It can be traced back to the early 1890s and the interest of Charles Follen McKim (founder of the famed architectural firm McKim, Mead and White) in the Italian Renaissance and its classical antecedents. This interest was first made visible in his design of the Boston Public Library (1895), whose facade is festooned with the names of cultural immortals carved in the classical style.[18] Soon afterwards, Boston architect Frank Chouteau Brown wrote *Letters and Lettering* (1902), which contained nearly forty plates of classical Roman capitals—photographs, rubbings, and drawings—from antiquity and the Renaissance, though not of the Trajan inscription. Although Brown promoted an interpretation of Sebastiano Serlio's 16th-century capitals drawn by Albert R. Ross as a model, he also showed letters from the Arch of Constantine and other ancient sources. [31] Brown's book went through five editions by 1906 and was instrumental in spreading the classical Roman capital among architects and designers in the United States in the ensuing twenty-five years. [32, 33] The classicizing trend that remained strong through the 1920s was eventually overtaken by Art Deco and Bauhaus modernism in the 1930s and never quite recovered.

The third individual who deserves credit for reviving interest in the classical Roman capital in the United States is Frederic W. Goudy, whose typefaces Kennerley, Forum, Hadriano, and Goudy Oldstyle—designed between 1910 and 1914—became instantly popular, not only for books but for advertising. Goudy Oldstyle, in particular, was so successful that Morris Fuller Benton of American Type Founders extended it into a family, showcased in a special supplement to the famed 1923 ATF catalogue.[19] (See p. 73, fig. 9.) In his writings, Goudy added an American voice to the English chorus championing the Trajan inscription. His books *The Alphabet* (1918) and *Elements of Lettering* (1922) spread the gospel of clas-

8 (*left*). Detail of inscription in S. Sebastiano fuori le Mura, Rome, 4th c. The distinctive Damasian capital letter, used for tablets memorializing Christian martyrs, was designed by Furius Dionysius Filocalus, secretary to Pope Damasus I (reigned 366–384).

9 (*right*). Detail of Virgil, *Veterum Fragmentorum Manuscriptis Codicibus detractorum collectio* Tom. I., late 4th c. (Cod. Sang. 1394, p. 15.) Written in square capitals (*capitalis quadrata*).

10 Rubbing of detail of the Epitaph of Pope Hadrian I (reigned 772–795), portico of St. Peter's, Rome, 795 AD.

sicism throughout the American printing, design, and advertising communities—just at the moment when modernist designers in Europe were beginning to promote the grotesque sans serif as the type for the machine age.

Despite the persistence of blackletter, there was a significant classical strain in the typography and graphic design of pre-Nazi Germany, part of what Rudolf Koch saw as the country's unique dual tradition of *antiqua* and *fraktur*. Yet despite their reverence for the Imperial Roman capitals, Koch and other German type designers never attempted to recreate them faithfully, instead giving the types their own distinctive spin on form and proportion. This is evident in such typefaces as Koch Antiqua, Weiss Antiqua, and, after World War II, in Palatino and Trump Mediaeval. (See p. 111.) Some of these designs may be viewed as stretching the definition of classical to its outer limits, but they succeeded in revitalizing the classical tradition in an age often hostile to it—and in a country caught in an ideological tug-of-war between modernists advocating sans serif and *volkisch* fascists advocating blackletter.[20] Even more importantly, Koch and Paul Renner infused the geometric sans serif genre with the spirit of classicism. Both Kabel and Futura, two of the three most influential sans serifs of the interwar era (the other being Gill Sans) have capitals that are, at their core, indebted to Imperial Roman capitals. In the case of Futura, the "*Schrift unserer Zeit*," this seems like a delicious irony.

Not surprisingly, the Italian Fascists latched onto the classical Roman capital as part of the visual aspect of Mussolini's Terza Roma, though many of the architects of the regime were more interested in geometrical sans serifs in the Futura vein. [34]

After World War II, the ascendancy of the neo-grotesques (especially Akzidenz Grotesk and the newer Univers and Helvetica) put an end to the resurgence of the classical Roman capital. For the remainder of the 20th century, the industrial sans serif dominated graphic design. However, two typefaces—Optima by Hermann Zapf (1958) and Syntax by Hans Ed. Meier (1969)—attempted to find a meeting ground between the classical and the modern. These "humanist" sans serifs, an oddity in their time, have, since the advent of the Macintosh, sparked one of the fastest growing categories of type.[21]

In the 1960s, an Iowa priest with experience as a signwriter, shook up the staid world of calligraphy with two books that presented radically new ways of looking at Imperial Roman capitals and, in particular, the Trajan inscription. Father Edward M. Catich's theories, expressed in *Letters Redrawn from the Trajan Inscription in Rome* (1961) and *Origins of the Serif* (1968), upended the widely held views on the methods used to construct these hallowed

11 (*above*). *Evangelium secundum quatuor Evangelistas* (BM Abbeville, Ms 4, fol. 154), end of the 8th c.

12 (*right*). The Evangelary of Wolfcoz (Cod. Sang. 367, p. 53), c.835–840. An excellent example of the Carolingian hierarchy of scripts: square capitals, rustics, uncials, and Carolingian minuscule.

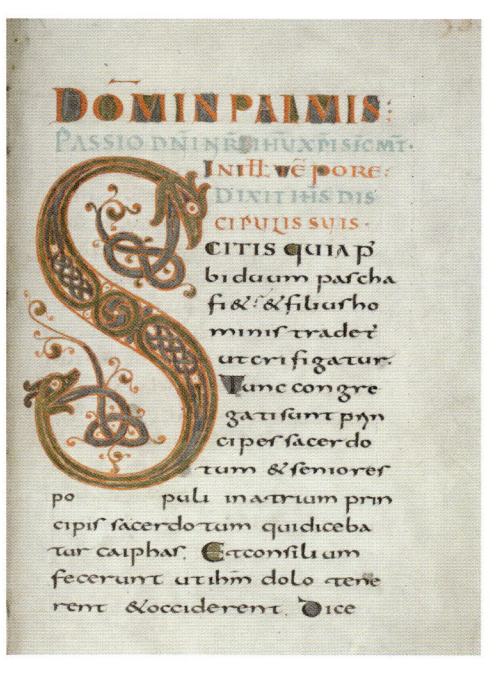

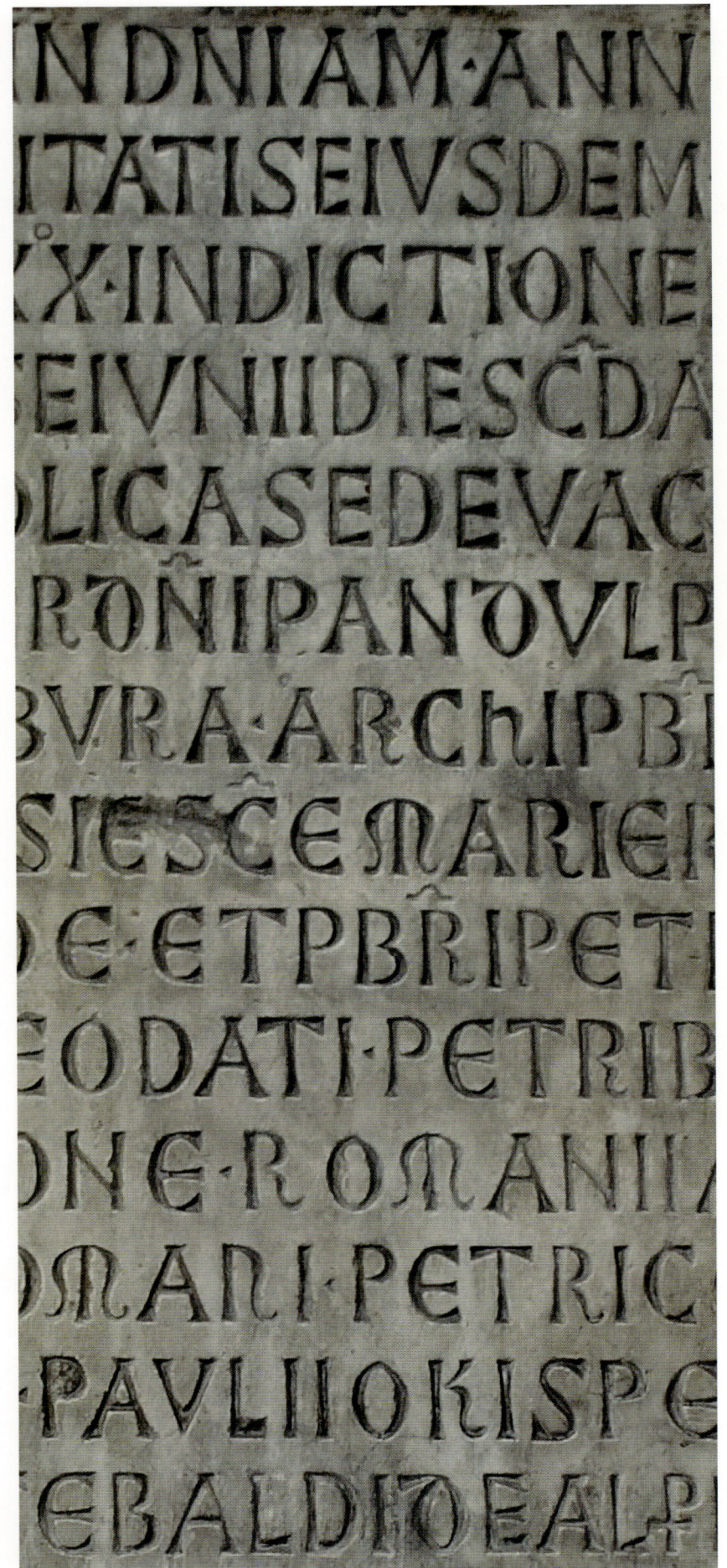

13 (*left*). Detail of Romanesque inscription recording the addition of a campanile to the Pantheon, Rome, 1270. Note the alternate uncial forms of *D*, *E*, *H*, *M* and *N*.

14 (*above*). Page of medieval versals from a scribal pattern book by Gregorius Bock, c. 1510–1517. (Beinecke MS 439, f.33v). Note the open-minded medieval attitude toward form, including a willingness to violate classical convention and place the tail of the leftmost *Q* on the left where it has room to flourish.

letters. His emphasis on the brush as the determinative tool, rather than the chisel or the pen, caused an uproar at the time, but have since become received wisdom. Although Catich's work occurred far from the realms of type design and graphic design, they have since had an impact on both. His research and arguments led Sumner Stone, the typographic director at Adobe, to commission Carol Twombly to design a typeface based on the Trajan inscription. The result, Adobe Trajan (1989), has turned out to be one of the most visible typefaces of the past quarter century and it was its redesign that sparked the idea for *The Eternal Letter*.[21]

Over the course of two millennia, the classical Roman capital has been on a roller coaster ride with peaks of intense interest alternating with valleys of neglect and hostility. It is doubtful that it will ever recapture the imagination of the culturally literate quite the way it did in the Renaissance and Baroque eras, but neither will it go away entirely. [35, 36] It has survived the attacks of the grid-besotted modernists and the indifference of the vernacular-soaked populists. It is an inescapable part of the DNA of Western culture.

15 (*above*). Epitaph of Filippo Brunelleschi, Duomo, Florence, 1446. The letters are a superb example of the Florentine sans serif that flourished between 1410 and the early 1450s.

16 (*left*). Detail of lines 14–17 of the Epitaph of Poggio Bracciolini, S. Maria, Terranuova Bracciolini, 1437. The inscription evolves erratically, line by line, from Florentine sans serif capitals (e.g. *M*) to Imperial Roman capitals (e.g. *E, N, Q, R*).

17 (*below*). Detail of the inscription on the tomb of Martin V (reigned 1417–1431), S. Giovanni in Laterano, Rome, c.1445. The design of the tomb and its inscription has been attributed variously to Donatello, an unknown follower of his, Michelozzo, Simone Ghini, or some combination of these.

18 (*bottom*). Detail of the large inscription that wraps around the upper portion of the Sepolcro Rucellai in S. Pancrazio, Florence, 1467. Leon Battista Alberti designed the geometrically constructed marble inlaid letters.

THE ETERNAL LETTER 11

19 (*above*). Rubricated capitals by Bartolomeo Sanvito (1435–1511). Detail from *Epigrammata* by Martial, c.1477–1483 (Biblioteca Raccolta Durazzo, Ms. A III 3, f.1). The miniature in the *all'antica* style, including the Colosseum, is by Gaspare da Padova.

20 (*right*). *M* and *N* from *Alphabetum Romanum* by Felice Feliciano (Vat. Lat. 6852), c.1460.

THE ROOTS OF THE CLASSICAL ROMAN CAPITALS

~770 BC	First evidence of Greek writing in Italy.
750 BC	First Etruscan inscriptions.
740 BC	The Dipylon inscription (Athens) and the Nestor Cup (Pithekoussai); earliest known Greek inscriptions in Greece.
753 BC	**Legendary founding of Rome by Romulus; though ancient sources give dates ranging from 814 BC to 729 BC.**
~625–600 BC	Tita inscription (Gabii) and Vendia inscription (Rome?); pottery with the first examples of epigraphic Latin letters.
~580–570 BC	Duenos vase inscription (Rome); yet to be deciphered.
~575–550 BC	Forum Cippus, Roman Forum; oldest extant Latin inscription in stone; written in *boustrephedon* (bidirectional) style.
~550–525 BC	Castor and Pollux dedicatory inscription (Lavinium) in Latinized Greek.
~550–500 BC	Lapis Niger inscription (Rome); written in *boustrephedon* style.
~525–500 BC	Tufa inscription (Tivoli); written in serpentine style of the Sabines.
510 BC	**Beginning of Roman Republic and of Roman expansion in Italy.**
~500 BC	Lapis Satricanus inscription (Satricum) in Archaic Latin; important for comparative Indo-European grammar.
Before c. 500 BC	Latin inscriptions show considerable diversity of letterforms and direction of writing. Most writing is left to right in the late 7th c. BC but right to left in the 6th c. BC.
5th c. BC	Modular Greek inscriptions (*stoichedon*) using chisel width as stroke length.
312 BC	**Construction of the Appian Way.**
334 BC	Dedication of the Temple of Athena Polias (Priene) by Alexander the Great; first Greek inscription with serifs.
Late 4th c. BC	Late 4th c. BC Ardea Krater (now in Museo Nazionale Romano, Terme di Diocleziano) with overpainted inscription of uncertain interpretation.
264 BC	**First Punic War between Rome and Carthage begins.**
After 259 BC	Epitaph (in Musei Vaticani) of Lucius Cornelius Scipio (consul of Rome and grandfather of Scipio Africanus) in sans serif capitals.
~250 BC	According to Plutarch, letter *G* created by Spurius Carvilius Ruga, founder of the first private elementary school in Rome; Roman alphabet fixed at 21 letters.
221 BC	**Hannibal begins conquest of Hispania (Spain).**
218–203 BC	**Second Punic War. Scipio Africanus defeats Hannibal at Zama (now Sers, Tunisia).**
167 BC	Early Latin inscription with serifs (Delphi; now in Musei Vaticani).
1st c. BC	Temple of Vesta (Tivoli) inscription.
73–71 BC	**Slave revolt led by Spartacus.**
~50 BC	Tomb of Publius Gessius family inscription (Viterbo; now in Museum of Fine Arts, Boston). Arco dei Gavi (Verona) built by architect Vitruvius.
~50 BC	
~50–20 BC	Tomb of Marcus Vergilius Eurysaces (the Baker's Tomb) (Rome).
44 BC	**Julius Caesar assassinated.**
44–30 BC	**Roman civil wars.**
43 BC	First extant Roman inscription in "Imperial" style
32–30 BC	**Final War of the Roman Republic; Octavian defeats Antony and Cleopatra.**
~28 BC	Tomb of Caecelia Metella (via Appia, Rome).
27 BC	**Octavian becomes Caesar Augustus, first Roman Emperor.**
17 BC	Theatre of Marcellus (Rome).
27 BC–14 AD	**Reign of Augustus.**
14	**Augustus dies.**
25	Pantheon built by Agrippa.
41–54	**Reign of Claudius. Rome invades Britain.** Claudius introduces three new letters to the alphabet, but they do not survive his reign.
51	Arch of Claudius dedicated.
69–79	**Reign of Vespasiano.**
79–81	**Reign of Titus.** Pompeii and Herculanum destroyed by eruption of Mt. Vesuvius.
79	Arch of Titus dedicated; Colosseum completed.
98–117	**Reign of Trajan.**
106	**Trajan defeats Dacians.**
112	Trajan Forum dedicated.
113	Trajan column dedicated along with inscription.
117–138	**Reign of Hadrian.**
122	**Hadrian's Wall built across northern Britain.**
130	Wroxeter inscription (Forum Viroconium, Britannia—England).
161–180	**Reign of Marcus Aurelius**.
2nd c.	Tomb of family of Sextus Pomponius (via Appia, Rome).
193–211	**Reign of Septimius Severus; Roman Empire a military dictatorship.**
203	Arch of Septimius Severus dedicated.
311–337	**Reign of Constantine I**.
313	**Edict of Milan ends persecution of Christians.**
315	Arch of Constantine dedicated.
359	**Constantinople becomes the capital of the Roman Empire.**
366–384	Papacy of Damasus; commissioned inscriptions, carved by Furius Dionysius Philocalus, honoring Christian martyrs.
395	**Roman Empire divided by Theodosius into Eastern and Western Empires.**
4th c.	Vatican Virgil (Vat. lat. 3225); written in *capitalis rustica* (rustics).
4th c.	Codex Augusteus (Georgics of Virgil) (Vat. lat. 3256); written in *capitalis quadrata* (square capitals).
476	**Fall of Roman Empire in the West; Romulus Augustulus deposed by Odoacer.**
5th c.	Codex Sangallensis (works of Virgil) (St. Gall, Stiftsbibliothek 1394); written in *capitalis quadrata* (square capitals).

THE REJUVENATION OF THE CLASSICAL ROMAN CAPITAL

795	Epitaph of Pope Hadrian I commissioned by Charlemagne.
800	**Charlemagne crowned Holy Roman Emperor by Pope Leo III.**
~830–834	Latin Vulgate Bible (Abbey of St. Martin, Tours; now Munich, Bayerische Staatsbibliothek CLM 12741); Carolingian versals.
834–843	Moutier-Grandval Bible (Tours, now British Library, Add. MS. 10456); written in Carolingian minuscules.
871–877	Second Bible of Charles the Bald (Paris, Bibliothèque Nationale, Ms. Lat. 2); Carolingian versals with classical Roman proportions.
963–984	Benedictional of Aethelwold; its versals are the basis for Adobe Charlemagne typeface.
Early 11th c.	The Trinity Gospels (Trinity College, Cambridge, Ms. B.10.4 (215).

THE REDISCOVERY OF THE CLASSICAL ROMAN CAPITAL

1403	Poggio sent classical inscriptions from Rome to Coluccio Salutati in Florence.
1409	Sylloge Signorilliana; first collection of classical Roman inscriptions.
1412–1416	Statue of John the Baptist (Orsanmichele, Florence) by Ghiberti; inscription with humanist majuscules.
1417–1431	**Revival of Rome under papacy of Martin V.**
1424	First visit of Ciriaco di Ancona to Rome to study inscriptions.
1425	Tomb of anti-Pope John XXIII (Battistero, Florence) by Donatello and Michelozzo.
1431–1437	Cantoria (Florence) by Luca della Robbia; inscription is basis for Donatello typeface.
1432–1433	Second visit of Ciriaco di Ancona to Rome to study inscriptions.
1439–1440	Shrine of St. Zenobius (S. Lorenzo, Florence) by Ghiberti; inscription in *lettere antiche*.
1440	Giovanni Marcanova begins collecting epigraphs.
1447–1452	Tempio Malatestiano (Rimini) by Alberti with monumental inscription on façade (1453).
1447–1455	**Continued revival of Rome under papacy of Nicholas V.**
1449–1452	Funerary monument to Leonardo Bruni (S. Croce, Florence) by Bernardo Rossellino.
1450	*Chronicle* of Eusebius (Biblioteca Marciana, Lat. IX.1 = 3496) by Biagio di Saraceno; first manuscript with epigraphic capitals.
1453	**Fresco of St. James (Ovetari Chapel, Padua) with inscriptions in epigraphic capitals.**
1453	Constantinople sacked by Ottoman Turks; end of Byzantine Empire (eastern portion of Roman Empire).
1455	Tomb of Pope Nicholas V (Grotte Vaticane).
1455	42-line Bible completed by Johannes Gutenberg.
~1453	First manuscript by Paduan scribe Bartolomeo Sanvito.
1459	Strabo *Geographia* (Bibliothèque Municipale, Albi, MS 77) with epigraphic initials.
1460	*Alphabetum Romanum* (Vat. lat. 6852) by Felice Feliciano; first constructed alphabet.
1460	Livy (Biblioteca Nazionale e Universitaria di Torino, J.II.5) by Sanvito; one of first manuscripts with a monumental frontispiece.
1464	Felice Feliciano, Mantegna, Samuele da Tradate and Giovanni Antenori search for Roman inscriptions near Lake Garda.
1465	Second Marcanova recension of collection of epigraphs completed.
1465	Tomb of Cardinal Ludovico d'Albret (S. Maria in Aracoeli, Rome) by Andrea Bregno.
1467	Cappella Rucellai (Florence) by Alberti.
1468	Pescheria (Verona) inscription attributed to Feliciano.
1468–1476	House of Lorenzo Manilio (Rome) with façade incorporating mix of antique and imitation antique inscriptions.
1470	Façade inscription on S. Maria Novella (Florence) by Alberti.
1470	Roman typeface by Nicholas Jenson.
1471–1484	**Papacy of Sixtus IV led urban revival of Rome; associated with revival of Roman capitals.**
1471	**Capitoline Museum established by Pope Sixtus IV.**
1473	Tomb of Cardinal Niccolò Forteguerri (S. Cecilia in Trastevere, Rome) by Andrea Bregno and Mino da Fiesole.
1475	Ponte Sisto inscriptions attributed to Sanvito.
1470s	Pomponio Leto began collecting epigraphs.
1475–1477	**Latin and Greek libraries created at Vatican.**
1478	1478 First redaction of Fra Gioconda *silloge*.
1479–1483	*Libellus Inscriptionum* printed by Jacopo Zaccaria.
~1480	Constructed alphabet by Chicago Anonymous.
1480	Codice Barberiniano (Barb. Lat. 4424) by Giuliano Sangallo; contains drawings of Roman inscriptions and monuments.
1482	Inscription in courtyard of Palazzo Ducale, Urbino.
1483	Constructed alphabet by Damiano Da Moylle.
1484–1499	**Construction of the Cancelleria (Rome).**
~1490–1516	Taccuino Senese di Giuliano Sangallo (Biblioteca Comunale degli Intronati, S.IV.8); includes complete alphabet of Roman capitals.
1491–1509	Codex Escurialensis (Codex 28.11.12) by Domenico Ghirlandaio; includes drawings of Tomb of Cecelia Metella, Trajan's Column and alphabet of Roman capitals.
1495	Roman typeface by Francesco Griffo da Bologna.

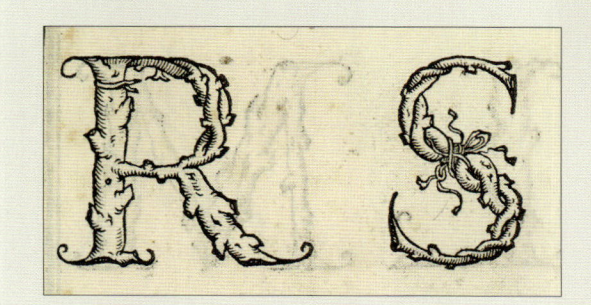

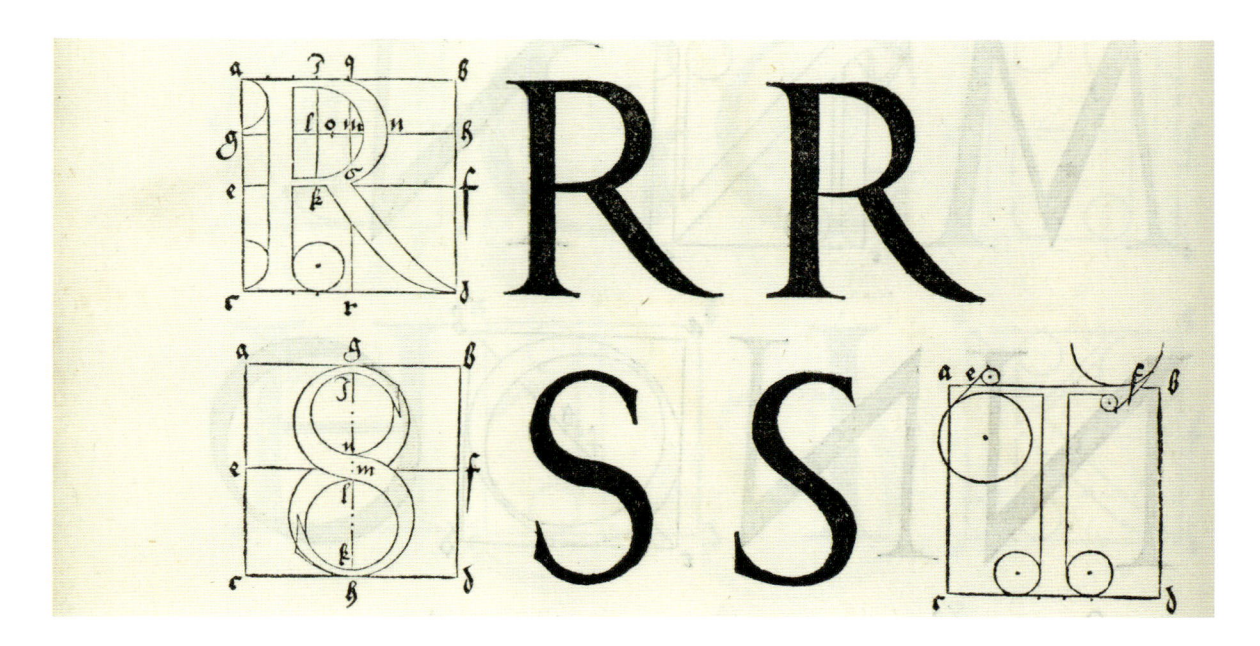

21 (*above*). Constructed capitals from *Vnderweysung der Messung* (1525) by Albrecht Dürer. Note the inconsistency between the diagrams and the solid letters.

22 (*right*). Detail of Roman capitals from *Il perfetto scrittore* (1570) by Giovantonio Francesco Cresci. Cut in wood by Francesco Aureri da Crema.

23 (*right, below*). Plate 38 from *Varie inscrittioni del santiss. S. N. Sixto V Pont. Max.* (1589) by Luca Horfei (Newberry Library, Wing ZW 14 .067). The text was inscribed on the four sides of the platform added to Trajan's Column during the pontificate of Sixtus V.

24 (*opposite*). Woodcut letters from *Opera di Frate Vespasiano Amphiareo* (1554).

THE ETERNAL LETTER 15

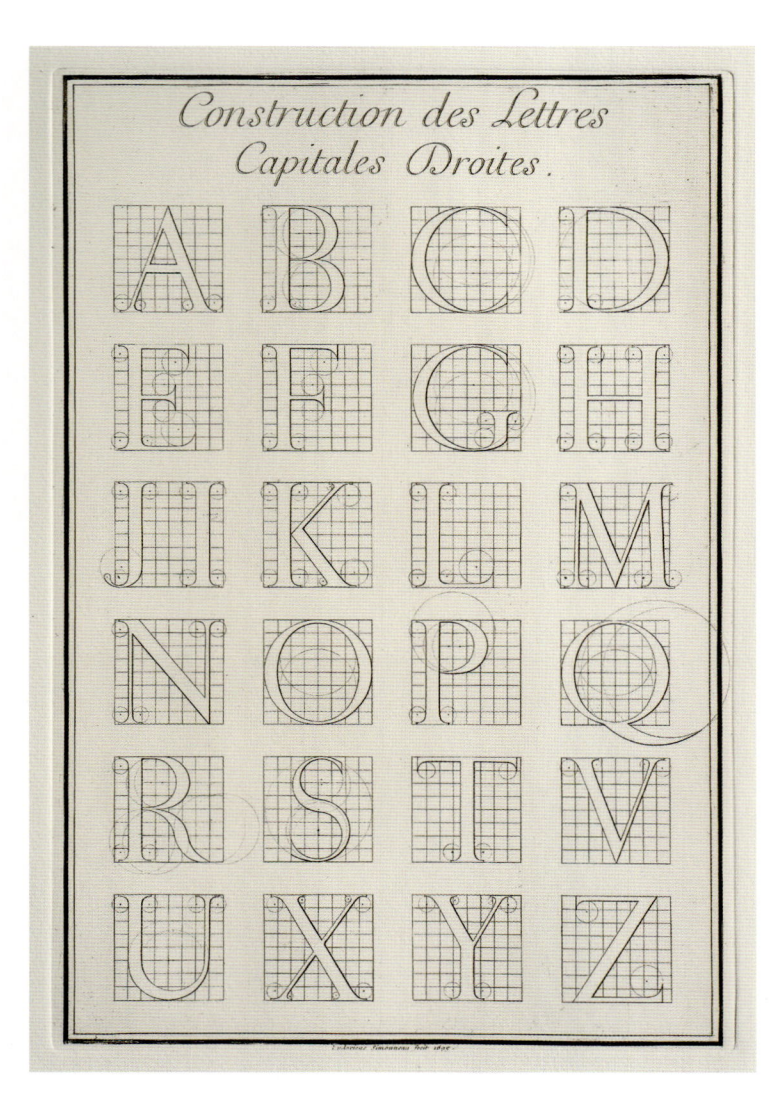

25 (*above left*). "Lettres Capitales Droites" engraved by Louis Simonneau, 1695. This is one of nine plates engraved by Simonneau that punchcutter Philippe Grandjean used as a model for the first series of the Romain du Roi types.

26 (*above right*). "Numero I" Roman capitals from *Serie di maiuscole e caratteri cancellareschi* (1788) by Giambattista Bodoni. Margins cropped.

27 (*right*). Fat face type (Fourteen Line Pica Roman) from *Specimen of Plain and Ornamental Wood Type, Cut by Machinery* by Wells & Webb (1840).

28 (*right, lower*). Sans serif type (Twelve Line Pica Gothic Condensed) from *Specimen of Plain and Ornamental Wood Type, Cut by Machinery* by Wells & Webb (1840).

THE REJUVENATION OF THE CLASSICAL ROMAN CAPITAL

- 1509 *Divina Proportione* by Luca Pacioli published in Venice; contains alphabet of constructed Roman capitals.
- 1517 *Opera del mondo de fare le littere maiuscole antique* by Francesco Torniello.
- 1523 *Il Modo Temperare de le Penne* by Ludovico degli Arrighi da Vicenza.
- 1524 *Lo presente libro Insegna La Vera arte* by Giovannantonio Tagliente.
- 1525 *Vnderweysung der Messung* [Of the Just Shaping of Letters] by Albrecht Dürer.
- ~1527 *Luminario* by Giovambaptista Verini; alphabet of constructed Roman capitals.
- 1529 *Champ Fleury* by Geoffroy Tory; contains alphabet of constructed Roman capitals.
- ~1530 First roman typeface by Claude Garamont.
- 1540 *Libro nuovo d'imparare a scrivere* by Giovambattista Palatino.
- 1540 *On Antiquities* by Sebastiano Serlio, second of his "Seven Books."
- 1548 *Un novo modo d'insegnare a scrivere* by Vespasiano Amphiareo.
- 1554 *Sette Alphabeti di varie lettere* by Ferdinando Ruano.
- 1560 *Essemplare di piu sorti lettere* by Giovanni Francesco Cresci.
- 1570 *Il Perfetto Scrittore* by Giovanni Francesco Cresci.
- **1585–1589 Papacy of Sixtus V; responsible for the systematization of Rome with the creation of new arteries and plazas marked by the erection of obelisks on Roman bases; and the restoration of the Acqua Alessandrina (renamed Acqua Felice, 1586).**
- 1587 *Alphabeto Delle Maiuscole Antiche Romane* by Luca Horfei da Fano.
- 1589 *Varie iscrittioni del santiss....* by Luca Horfei da Fano; designs for program of graphic exposition to accompany urban restoration under Sixtus V.
- 1638 *De Caratteri* by Leopardo Antonozzi.

THE DECLINE OF THE CLASSICAL ROMAN CAPITAL

- 1692–1745 Romain du Roi; first "designed" typeface; first printed appearance 1702.
- 1725 First typeface by William Caslon.
- **1738 Excavations of Herculanum begun.**
- **1748 Excavations of Pompeii begun.**
- 1754 John Baskerville type specimen.
- **~1760–1840 Industrial Revolution.**
- 1766 "Fry's Baskerville" cut by Isaac Moore.
- 1784 First type by Firmin Didot.
- 1788 *Serie di maiuscole* by Giambattista Bodoni.
- **1789 French Revolution.**
- **1804–1815 Napoleon Emperor of the French.**
- 1818 *Manuale Tipografico* by Giambattista Bodoni; printed posthumously.
- 1846 Lyons Titling (Caractères Augustaux) by Louis Perrin; revived "antique" Roman capitals.
- 1872 Cast of base of Trajan's Column made for Victoria & Albert Museum.
- 1894 The American School of Architecture in Rome (the American Academy in Rome, after 1897) opened; championed by architect Charles Follen McKim.
- 1895 Boston Public Library (McKim, Mead and White) completed.

THE RESURRECTION OF THE CLASSICAL ROMAN CAPITAL

- 1906 *Writing & Illuminating, & Lettering* by Edward Johnston published.
- 1906 Eric Gill visits Rome for first time.
- 1911 Forum Title by Frederic W. Goudy.
- 1914 Centaur by Bruce Rogers. (Released by Monotype, 1929.)
- **1914–1918 World War I.**
- 1916 Goudy Old Style (American Type Founders) by Frederic W. Goudy.
- 1918 Hadriano Title by Frederic W. Goudy.
- **1919 Bauhaus (Weimar) opened.**
- **1922 Fascist March on Rome; Mussolini become prime minister of Italy.**
- 1927 Futura (Bauer) by Paul Renner.
- 1927 Kabel (Klingspor) by Rudolf Koch; promotional material included constructed capital diagrams.
- 1927 John Stevens Shop (est. 1705) purchased by John Howard Benson.
- 1927 Open Capitals (Enschedé) by Jan van Krimpen.
- 1928 *Die neue Typographie* [The New Typography] by Jan Tschichold published.
- 1925–1930 Perpetua (Monotype) by Eric Gill.
- 1930 Trajan Title by Frederic W. Goudy.
- 1931 *Four Gospels* printed by Golden Cockerel Press; with type, illustrations, lettering, and ornaments by Eric Gill.
- **1933 Bauhaus (Weimar) closed by the Nazis.**
- 1934 Felix Titling (Monotype) based on constructed capitals of Felice Feliciano.
- 1935–1939 First trip to Rome by Father Edward M. Catich.
- 1936 David Kindersley sets up as independent lettercarver.
- 1937 Schneidler Initials [Bauer Text] (Bauer) by F. H. E. Schneidler.
- 1938 *Roman Lettering* by L.C. Evetts published.
- 1938–1940 *Res Gestae Divi Augusti* inscribed on wall of the building housing the Ara Pacis (Rome) as part of Fascist celebration of Augustan Bimillenary; letters based on Trajan capitals.
- 1939 Palazzo degli Uffici dell'Ente Autonomo (EUR, Rome) completed; façade bears inscription announcing "Terza Roma"; bas relief depicts Mussolini as direct descendent of Roman consuls and emperors.
- **1939–1945 World War II.**
- 1943 Palazzo della Civiltà Italiana ("the Square Colosseum") (EUR, Rome) completed.

THE RESURRECTION OF THE CLASSICAL ROMAN CAPITAL

1946 Jan van Krimpen designed numeral stamps for the Dutch post office.
1950 Michelangelo (Stempel) by Hermann Zapf. Sistina (Stempel) by Hermann Zapf.
1951 Augustea (Nebiolo) by Alessandro Butti and Aldo Novarese.
1951 Columna (Bauer) by Max Caflisch.
1955 *Rhythm and Proportion in Lettering* by Walter Kaech published.
1956 National Monument on the Dam square (Amsterdam) with inscription designed by Jan van Krimpen.
1957 Castellar (Monotype) by John Peters.
1957 Univers (Deberny & Peignot) by Adrian Frutiger.
1957 Neue Haas Grotesk (Haas) [later Helvetica (Stempel)] by Max Miedinger and Eduard Hoffmann.
1958 Optima (Stempel) by Hermann Zapf.
1960s David Kindersley designs alphabet for Cambridge, England street signs; modeled on classical Roman capitals.
1961 John E. Benson takes over the John Stevens Shop.
1961 *Letters Redrawn from the Trajan Column in Rome* by Father Edward M. Catich published.
1964 John F. Kennedy Memorial, Arlington Cemetery carved by John E. Benson and John Hegnauer.
1964 Father Edward M. Catich makes polyester cast of Trajan inscription.
1967 *Printing and the Mind of Man* catalogue (based on London exhibition, 1963) with title page engraved by Reynolds Stone.
1968 *The Origins of the Serif* by Father Edward M. Catich published.
1976 Lida Lopes Cardozo begins collaboration with David Kindersley; eventually becomes partner in Cardozo Kindersley Workshop.
1982 *A Constructed Roman Alphabet* by David Lance Goines published.
1989 Lithos, Trajan, and Charlemagne (Adobe) by Carol Twombly.
1991 Arrus (Bitstream) by Richard Lipton.
1993 Mantinia (Carter & Cone) by Matthew Carter; based on the engraved lettering of Mantegna.
1993 Nicholas Benson takes over ownership of the John Stevens Shop.
1994 Penumbra (Adobe) by Lance Hidy.
1996 Cresci, Pontif, and Pietra (LetterPerfect) by Garrett Boge.
1997 Franklin Delano Roosevelt Memorial, National Mall, carved by John E. Benson.
1998 Waters Titling (Adobe) by Julian Waters.
1999 Capitolium by Gerard Unger; inspired by capitals by Cresci. Requiem (Hoefler & Frere-Jones) by Jonathan Hoefler, based on capitals by Arrighi.
2003 Senatus (Berthold) by Werner Schneider.
2004 National World War II Memorial, National Mall, carved by Nicholas Benson.
2011 Stevens Titling (Linotype) by John Stevens and Ryuichi Tateno.
2012 Trajan Pro 3 and Trajan Sans (Adobe) by Robert Slimbach.

29 Inscription on Hopton Wood stone by Eric Gill, 1926. The text, "Ex divina pulchritudine esse omnia derivatur" (From divine beauty comes all that is) is by Thomas Aquinas.

30 (*top*). Revision of Railway Sans capitals (4–12 March 1916) by Edward Johnston for the London Underground. First drawn February 1916.

31 (*middle*). Plate 22 ("Classic Roman Inscription in Stone") from *Letters & Lettering* by Frank Chouteau Brown (1902). Redrawn from a rubbing by F.C.B.

32 (*bottom*). Working drawing of Centaur capitals by Bruce Rogers for Monotype version of typeface, 1929.

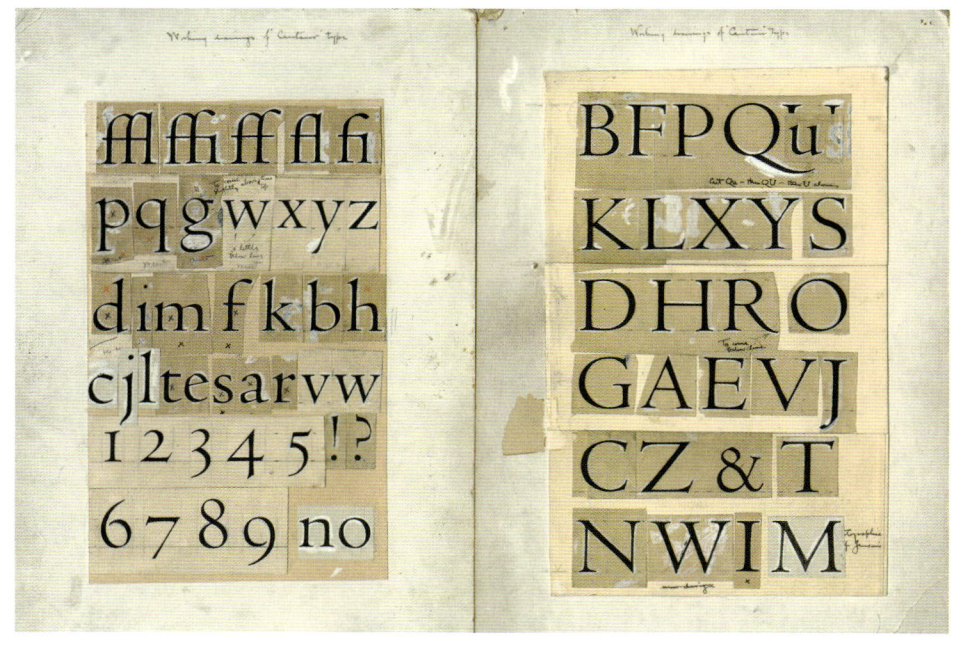

33 (*above*). New York City subway station name in mosaic tile. Rector Street, 1918.

34 (*right*). Monument to the Bersaglieri, Piazzale di Porta Pia, Rome, 1932. Design by Italo Mancini and sculpture by Publio Morbiducci.

35 *S/Z: An Essay* by Roland Barthes (Hill & Wang, 1975). Jacket design by Charles Skaggs. The title and author's name are hand lettered.

36 *Eros* magazine (Summer 1962). Cover design by Herb Lubalin. Masthead lettering by John Pistilli.

1. The earliest surviving example of a Roman inscription in the Imperial style is CIL VI 37077 from 43 BC. See Arthur Gordon and Joyce Gordon, *An Album of Dated Latin Inscriptions*. (Berkeley and Los Angeles: University of California Press, 1958), Plates 5a and 5b, which are reproduced as figs. 8 and 9 on p. 254 of this book.
2. "Trajan Revived" by James Mosley, in *Alphabet 1964: International Annual of Letterforms*, vol. 1 (London: James Moran Ltd. for The Kynoch Press, 1964), pp. 17–48, is the best survey of how the Trajan letter became the singular model of what Roman capitals should look like.
3. See Joanna Story, "Charlemagne's Black Marble: The Origin of the Epitaph of Pope Hadrian I," in *Papers of the British School at Rome*, vol. 73 [2005], pp. 157–190.
4. A notable exception to this trend are the versals of the Benedictional of St. Aethelwold, written by the scribe Godeman for St Æthelwold, Bishop of Winchester from 963-984. They provided the inspiration for Carol Twombly's Charlemagne typeface (1989).
5. Although some of its dating has since been challenged, the basic source for the Florentine sans serif is Nicolete Gray, "Sans Serif and Other Experimental Inscribed Lettering of the Early Renaissance," in *Motif* (1960), pp. 67–76. A reprint with corrections and additional commentary, edited by Paul Shaw, was published by LetterPerfect in 1997.
6. For more on Optima, see p. 118.
7. Though now out of date, the standard overview of the revival of classical Roman capitals in the Quattrocento is Millard Meiss, "Toward a More Comprehensive Renaissance Paleography" in *The Art Bulletin* XLII, 1960, pp. 97–112.
    The key texts for the competing claims of primacy are these. For Donatello: Stanley Morison, *Politics and Script: Aspects of Authority and Freedom in the Development of Graeco-Latin Script from the Sixth Century B.C. to the Twentieth Century A.D.* The Lyell Lectures 1957. ed. Nicolas Barker. (Oxford: Clarendon Press, 1972). For Andrea Mantegna: Meiss, Millard. *Andrea Mantegna as Illuminator: An Episode in Renaissance Art, Humanism and Diplomacy*. (New York: Columbia University Press, 1957). Also see "Mantinia." p. 213. For Felice Feliciano: Giovanni Mardersteig, ed. *Alphabetum Romanum. Felice Feliciano Veronese*. (Verona: Officina Bodoni, 1960). For Leon Battista Alberti: Giovanni Mardersteig, "Leon Battista Alberti e la Rinascita del Carattere Lapidario Romano nel Quattrocento" in *Italia medioevale e umanistica* 2 (1959), pp. 285–307; translated into English by James Mosley as "Leon Battista Alberti and the revival of the roman inscriptional letter in the fifteenth century" in *Typography Papers* 6 (2005), pp. 49–65. For Andrea Bregno: Starleen Meyer and Paul Shaw, "Towards a New Understanding of the Revival of Roman Capitals and the Achievement of Andrea Bregno" in *Andrea Bregno: il senso della forma nella cultura artistica del Rinascimento*. Edited by Claudio Crescentini and Claudio Strinati, eds. (Rome: Artout—Maschietto Editore, 2008), pp. 276–331. Also see "The Tomb of Niccolò Forteguerri," p. 52.
8. See Paul Shaw, "Poggio's Epitaph" in *Alphabet: Journal of the Friends of Calligraphy*, vol. 33, no. 3 Summer 2008.
9. Most notably in the legs of *M*, the tail of *Q* and the leg of *R*. Also see "On the Origin of Capital Proportions in Roman type," p. 40.
10. See "Towards a New Understanding of the Revival of Roman Capitals and the Achievement of Andrea Bregno." I also delivered a talk on this subject, "The Myth of the Renaissance Constructed Roman Capital," at TypeCon 2008 in Buffalo, New York.
11. See "Further Reading," p. 245 for a list of some of the most important titles dealing with the geometric construction of capitals.
12. See A.S. Osley, *Luminario: An Introduction to the Italian Writing-Books of the Sixteenth and Seventeenth Centuries* (Nieuwkoop: Miland Publishers, 1972) for more information on Italian writing books and the evolution of lettering styles from Arrighi to Cresci and beyond. Also see the capitals by Arrighi in "Requiem: A True Renaissance Letter," p. 221 and the capitals by Tagliente in "Eric Gill's Capital Letter," p. 85.
13. See "Trajan Revived" and "The Baroque Inscriptional Letter in Rome," p. 59. Crescian letters appear often in Baroque engraved title pages and they were also the model for the large woodcut letters used on the title page of the Sistine Vulgate (1590).
14. For more on the Romain du Roi, see James Mosley, *Le Romain du roi: la typographie au service de l'État, 1702–2002* (Lyon: Musée de l'Imprimerie, 2002), André Jammes, *La naissance d'un caractère: le Grandjean—la réforme de la typographie royale sous Louis XIV* (Paris: Librairie Paul Jammes, 1961); and Jacques André and Denis Girous, "Father Truchet, the typographic poit, the Romain du roi, and tilings" at https://www.tug.org/TUGboat/tb20-1/tb62andr.pdf.
15. Johnston's reproduction of the Trajan inscription came not from the Trajan Column in Rome, but from a cast of it in the Victoria & Albert Museum in London. For the history of this cast, see "Census of Trajan Inscription Reproductions," p. 238. The cast, as Father Catich pointed out, has a flaw in the inscription (most obvious in the letter *M*) which has adversely affected alphabets based on it.
16. See "Trajan Revived" and John Nash, "In Defence of the Roman Letter" at http://www.ejf.org.uk/Resources/JRNarticle.pdf. Also, it should be noted that *An Alphabet of Roman Capitals* by George Woolliscroft Rhead (London: B.H. Batsford, 1903) has a plate of Trajan capitals.
17. See "Eric Gill's Capital Letter," p. 85.
18. For the lettering on the Boston Public Library, see "Mantinia," p. 214.
19. See "Goudy's Inscriptional Letters," p. 69.
20. See "Hermann Zapf's Roman Capitals: An Appreciation," p. 111.
21. For Optima, see "Hermann Zapf's Roman Capitals: An Appreciation," p. 111. Also see "Penumbra: The Offspring of Trajan and Futura," p. 165.
22. See "Democratizing the Empire: The Birth of Adobe Trajan," p. 181; "Trajan at the Movies," p. 235; and "Trajan Revived Redux, p. 185.

THE ETERNAL LETTER 21

IETOM
IETOM

1 Comparison of classical and industrial roman capital proportions: Trajan (top) vs. Modern no. 20 (bottom).

EEEEEEE

2 Comparison of the stroke width/letter height ratio of classically influenced digital typefaces. From left to right: Schneidler Text, Senatus, Trajan, Requiem, Arrus, Waters Titling, and Mantinia.

3 Key Trajanic capitals.

MN
CQ
BR

4 Comparison of key letters from Roman capitals and oldstyle typefaces: Trajan (left) vs. Minion (right).

Ee
Mm
Rr

5 Comparison of key classical and industrial roman capital letters: Trajan (left) vs. Craw Clarendon (right).

KK
QQ
MM
RR

6 Comparison of classical and industrial sans serif capital letters: Syntax (left) vs. Helvetica (right).

EE
GG
MM
RR

DEFINING THE CLASSICAL ROMAN CAPITAL

IT SEEMS ESSENTIAL AT THE OUTSET to explain what we mean in *The Eternal Letter* by the adjective *classical*. And to describe what its alternative is. Collectively, classical Roman capitals are characterized by variable widths. Individually, they are letters with optically balanced proportions, a modest thick-thin stroke contrast, and bracketed serifs. Their ancestry can be traced to the Imperial Roman capitals that arose in the mid-1st century AD with the inscription at the base of Trajan's Column commonly considered to be the embodiment of the form at its peak.

In his article "The Trajan Secrets," Tom Perkins has matched the varying widths of the Trajan letter to a series of shapes that form a geometric system of proportions: root-five rectangle (*B*, *E*, *F*, *P*), half square rectangle (*L*, *S*, *X*), double golden rectangle (*A*, *H*, *R*, *T*), double root-five rectangle (*C*, *D*, *G*, *N*, *V*), and square (*M*, *O*, *Q*). *J*, *K*, *U*, *W*, *Y*, and *Z* are missing because they were not part of the Latin alphabet used by the Romans; *I* is left out because its width is defined by the tool used to make its stem. (See "The Trajan Secret," p. 34.) [1]

Classical Roman capitals have a "Goldilocks" weight: not too heavy, not too light, but just right. Their weight is determined by the ratio of stroke thickness to letter height. Exactly what that ratio is has been the subject of vigorous debate since the Renaissance, with various commentators arguing for proportions ranging from 1:8 to 1:12, though 1:9 and 1:10 are the most favored. (See "Typefaces with Classical Roman Influences: 1900 to 2012," p. 232.) [2]

The Trajan letters have several key features that have become closely identified with classical Roman capitals: *A*, *M*, and *N* lack serifs at their apexes; *M* has slightly splayed legs; and *R* has a diagonal leg that juts out beyond the bowl. [3] The first of these is not essential; the latter two are crucial yet problematic. All have been challenged over the past two thousand years as lettermakers—whether wielding pen, brush, or graver—have found them obstacles to achieving greater functionality when employed in lengthy texts at small sizes. The subtle yet strong bracketing of the serifs has been a target of adjustment for similar reasons. [4]

Despite such tinkering there remains a core identity of the classical Roman capital within oldstyle typefaces and their contemporary offspring, from the 1470 roman of Nicolas Jenson to Arno Pro by Robert Slimbach (2007). This influence has even infiltrated sans serif letters, beginning with Futura, continuing with Optima and Syntax, and most recently, underpinning Peter Bil'ak's History. [6]

In opposition to classical Roman capitals are so-called industrial Roman capitals, born in the late 18th century but at their zenith in the 19th century. These letters are nearly uniform in width—the exceptions being *I*, *J*, *M*, and *W*—having been squeezed and stretched, like the victims of Procrustes, to fit a rigid module. The legs of the *M* are vertical, the leg of the *R* is pulled in and often curved, and the *O* has become oval. [5] What industrial Roman capitals lack in beauty and harmony they make up for in efficiency and utility, as they are easier to design and easier to assemble (to space). They are also more malleable, effortlessly lending themselves to changes in weight and width, which is why they dominate the category of sans serifs.

The fact that classical Roman capitals require more discipline and skill to make than industrial Roman capitals is surely part of their allure. They are a challenge to everyone who takes the making of letters seriously. They do not have to be embraced or even accepted, but they do have to be confronted. —*P.S.*

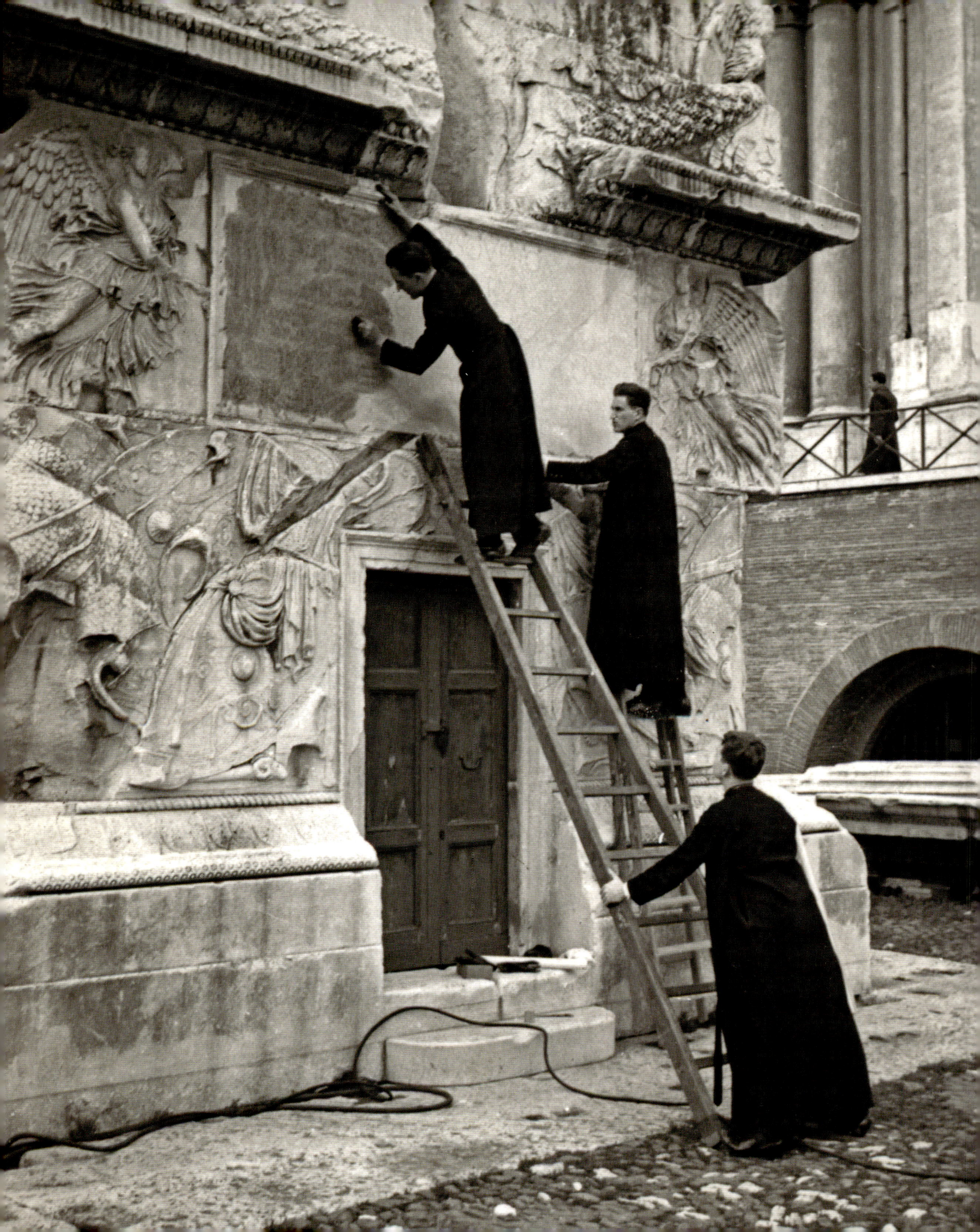

FATHER EDWARD M. CATICH AND THE TRAJAN INSCRIPTION

PAUL SHAW

SINCE ITS REDISCOVERY, first in the middle of the 15th century and again early in the 20th, the inscription at the base of Trajan's Column, in Rome, has come to represent the classical Roman capital at its apex, and its letters have served as a benchmark for judging the excellence of all other capitals. Their exalted status has been the result of the continual fascination they have exerted on artists, architects, and scholars, all of whom have sought to unlock the secret to their perfection. From Felice Feliciano (1460) to Johannes Muess (1989), many have assumed the key lay in geometry and have constructed ever more elaborate edifices to replicate the carved letters, yet have failed each time to match their subtle grace.[1] One stumbling block has been the thick/thin stroke contrast of the letters. Another has been their bracketed serifs, often thought to be the inevitable result of carving letters into stone with a chisel.

The various theories about the making of the Trajan inscription letters that originated in the Renaissance and those that surfaced in the wake of the British Arts & Crafts movement—which brought a renewed interest in classical letters in reaction to the eclecticism of the Victorian era—were all upended in the 1960s when Father Edward M. Catich, a Catholic priest in Iowa, self-published two books: *Letters Redrawn from the Trajan Inscription in Rome* (1961) and *The Origin of the Serif* (1968).[2] In them he argued that the form of the Imperial Roman capitals, including their serifs, was determined by a flat, flexible brush and not by geometric tools, the chisel, or the broad-edged pen.[3] [6] His arguments were supported by brush-written and carved letters in the Trajanic mode that he made himself.

Even before the publication of the first of these books, Catich had begun to illustrate his theory by carving brush-written alphabets and stroke kinetics—a seminal idea that he credited to conversations with W. A. Dwiggins in the late 1940s—in small slate stones for individuals and institutions.[4] [2] (Two of the earliest of these stones were acquired in 1961 by the Portland Art Museum at the urging of Lloyd J. Reynolds, professor of art at Reed College, who, from the mid-1950s on, was one of Catich's staunchest supporters.[5]) In the decade that followed the publication of *Origin of the Serif*, Catich popularized his theories in a series of talks under the title, "The Origin of Letter Forms: Praenotanda," given throughout the United States.[6] They were usually accompanied by bravura demonstrations of his ability to quickly render the Trajanic capitals with a broad brush. In these talks, he summarized his arguments:

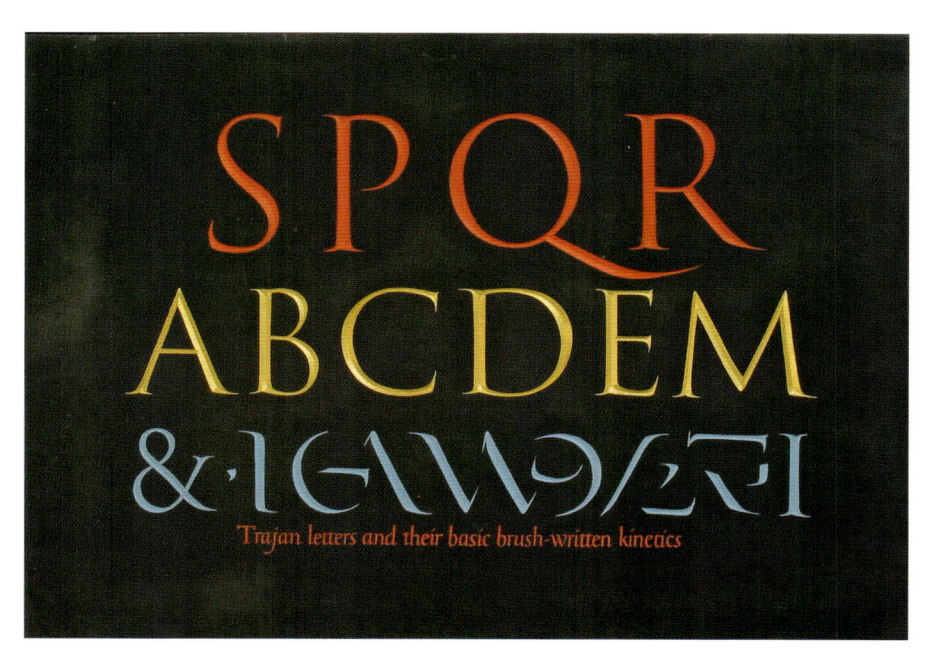

---

1 Father Catich making a rubbing of the Trajan inscription, assisted by two unidentified seminary students, c. 1950.

2 Inscription (C.33) carved and painted by Father Catich, date unknown. The bottom line shows all of the basic brush strokes used to write the Imperial capitals.

3 Detail of rubbing of the Trajan inscription made by Father Catich, 1966.

1. The Imperial stone letterer was the craft brother of today's signwriter;
2. The instrumental cause of the Roman stonecut letters was the flat, square-edged brush;
3. A master signwriter manipulating such a brush wrote the inscription directly on stone then chiseled what he had written;
4. A "double line" layout, as some contend, was not used, that is, letters were not outlined then filled in;
5. Serifs and stroke endings are not the product of chisel-handling and glyptic influences, rather they were the result of the skillful but natural behavior of the brush;
6. The chisel added nothing to the outlines and shapes of the letters;
7. The chisel cut only what was written;
8. It is no more difficult to chisel curved than straight letter parts;
9. The chisel can cut any shape written by the brush;
10. The written inscription was the important element and not the cutting;
11. Cast shadows of chiseled V-cuts did not [as some insist] influence and alter the basic letter shapes made by the brush.
12. The chisel, by sinking the writing below the surface, served only to guard the writing from effacement by weathering;
13. After chiseling, the letters were repainted with minium ("red lead") to restore the original writing.

It was not until the 1990s, spurred by the popularity of the Trajan typeface issued by Adobe in 1989, that Father Catich's theories became the orthodoxy they are today. The typeface was derived directly from his publications as well as from rubbings and a plaster cast he made of the inscription.[7] [3] The latter currently resides, in a polyester version, in the corporate headquarters of the giant printing company R. R. Donnelley & Sons, in Chicago.[8] (See p. 239.)

Edward M. Catich was born in Montana, in 1906.[9] At the age of twelve, following the death of his parents, he moved to an orphanage outside of Chicago. There he learned signwriting as a teenage apprentice to Walter Heberling. In the 1920s he became a union signwriter in Chicago, making showcards, rag signs, banners, and theatrical posters. [4] A slowdown in the sign trade in the middle of the decade led Catich to enroll in the Art Institute of Chicago to study anatomy, painting, art history, and design, and to enhance his lettering skills.

It was at the Art Institute that he came under the influence of calligrapher Ernst F. Detterer, a student of Edward Johnston, who introduced him to letterers in Chicago.[10] One of them was Ray DaBoll, who for awhile worked for the type designer Oswald Cooper. Catich visited DaBoll in the late 1920s to show him his portfolio and seek advice. DaBoll told him how to improve his broad-edged pen writing and urged him to undertake a comprehensive study of the history of the alphabet, lending him Frederic Goudy's books *The Alphabet* (1918) and *The Elements of Lettering* (1922). Plate I in the latter, entitled "Forum Title," shows "stone-cut capitals" from Trajan's Column as rendered by Goudy. It was probably not the first time that Catich encountered the Trajan inscription, as Detterer had made a rubbing of it in 1922 that was shown to his students at the Art

4 Chicago poster lettercase letters written out by Father Catich with a flexible, broad-edged brush. The bottom line shows how the capital letters are built up with compound strokes. From *Reed, Pen & Brush Alphabets for Writing and Lettering* (plate 230).

CATICH AND THE TRAJAN INSCRIPTION 27

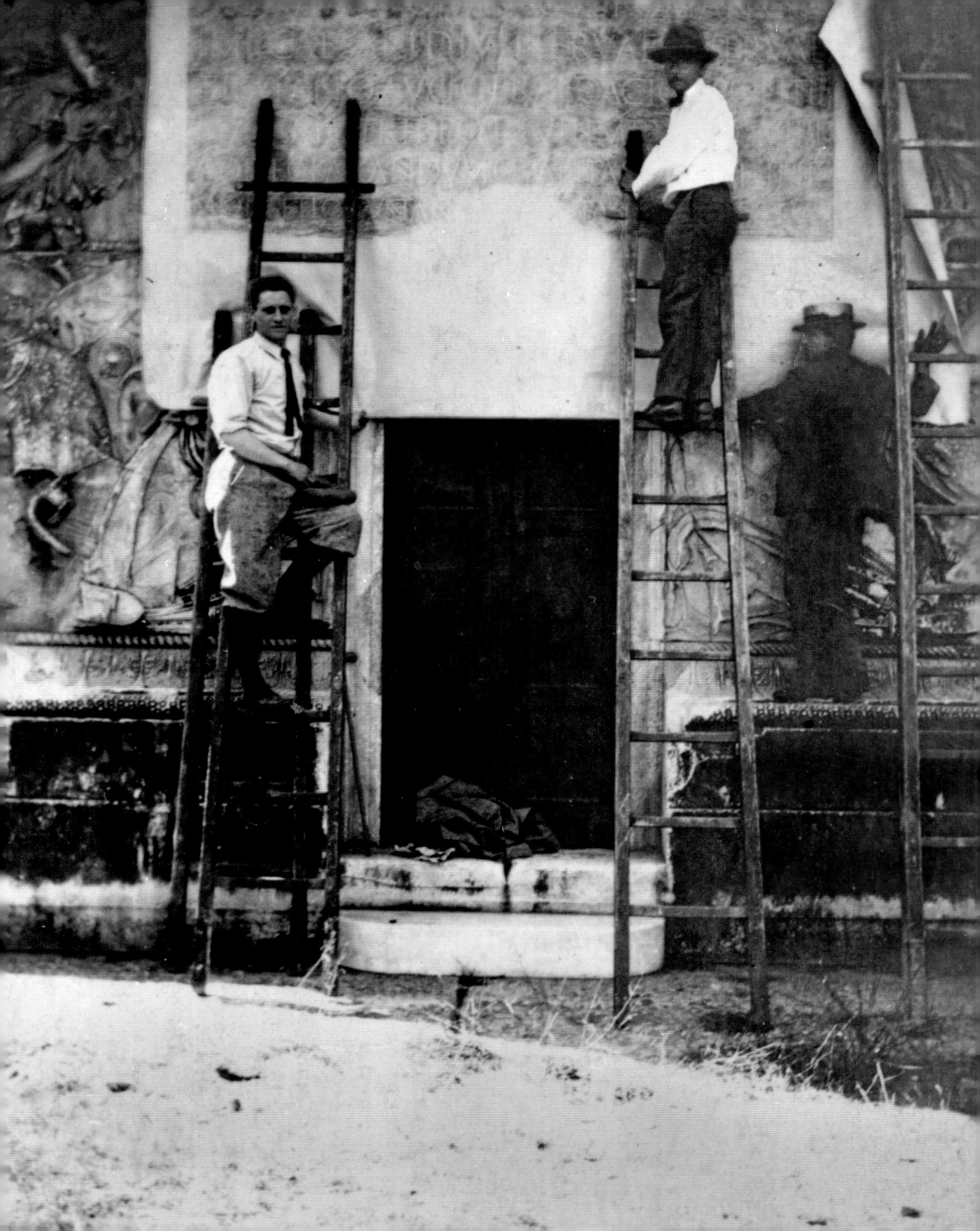

Institute. [5] But it was Goudy's views on the Trajan inscription in these books and in *The Capitals from the Trajan Column at Rome* (1936) that came to play a key role later in Catich's life.[11]

The onset of the Great Depression pushed Catich out of the signwriting trade. From 1931 to 1934 he attended St. Ambrose College (now University) in Davenport, Iowa, and graduated with a degree in art. In 1935, he was awarded a scholarship to study for the priesthood at the Pontifical Gregorian University in Rome. It was there that he first viewed Imperial inscriptions of the 1st century BC and the 1st and 2nd centuries AD. He later wrote, "fortified by my Chicago sign-writing experience, I sensed immediately that the square-edged brush was the formative tool behind Imperial, chiseled inscriptions. I could see not only the shaping of the curves, tails, swells; horizontal, vertical, and oblique widths & proportions, but even terminal finials—fillets, serifs, and tails—as having been produced by a brush similar to the tool we showcard & sign-writers used in Chicago."[12] [6]

During his four years in Rome, Catich conducted intensive paleographic and epigraphic studies, even going so far as to make rubbings of the Trajan inscription in 1936. [1] "I used Goudy's book on Trajan letters [*The Capitals from the Trajan Column at Rome*, 1936] as a note book in which I put down all my jottings and research pertinent to the letters and to the Imperial alphabet in general," Catich later told Donald Anderson.[13] [7, 8] His studies ended with his return to the United States, where he became a teacher of art, music, mathematics, and engineering at St. Ambrose.

From 1947 to 1952, Catich traveled each summer to Hingham, Massachusetts, to spend several weeks studying calligraphy and type design with W. A. Dwiggins. During this period he revived his explorations into the Trajan inscription. The two men shared a fascination with the kinesthetics of writing, which led Dwiggins to suggest Catich make the alphabet kinetics stone that catalyzed his theories about the making of the Imperial Roman capitals. By 1952 he had nearly finished the text that was eventually published, with a preface by Dwiggins, as *Letters Redrawn from the Trajan Inscription in Rome* (1961).[14]

Catich returned to Rome many times between 1950 and 1970 to further his study of Roman epigraphic capitals, each time making new rubbings and squeezes of the Trajan inscription.[15] His easy access was facilitated by his friendship with Prof. Guglielmo Gatti of Reparto X (Belle Arti) of the Comune di Roma, who directed the excavation of Trajan's Forum from 1935 through the 1970s.[16] In the 1960s, Catich began selling his rubbings of the Trajan inscription to finance his trips. (See p. 239.) He also began carving inscriptions for the Los Angeles County Museum of Art, which are now destroyed, as well as for Reed College in Portland, Oregon,[17] the Cathedral of Learning at the University of Pittsburgh, and Rensselaer Polytechnic Institute in Troy, New York. (See "Father Catich At Reed College, p. 175.") He also carved alphabet stones for individuals and institutions. [10] Catich died in 1979, too soon to see his theories about the making of Imperial Roman capitals be widely adopted. Yet his legacy lives on in typefaces such as Adobe Trajan, Arrus, and Stevens Titling, all of which owe a tremendous debt to his research. (See pp. 181–199).[18]

5 (*opposite*) Ernst Detterer making a rubbing of the Trajan inscription with the assistance of two unidentified men, 1922.

6 Father Catich's basic brush strokes used in making Imperial capitals. Figs. 222 and 223 from *The Origin of the Serif* (1968).

Some Rs seem to have a forward slant. Check this. Evidently the good calligrapher's unconscious effort to balance the tail.

"BUILT-UP LETTERS" → this form shows that the author built the letter from without rather from within. i.e. understanding the primal character of the letter such mistakes as the lobe would not be.

serifs a little too big.

Check Rs for slant of stem.

the tail is too long & the lobe & its counter too small.

the lobe doesn't seem to be spontaneously functional *

mid-bar too high.

this is a type face not an inscription shape.

Somehow I feel that the joint with lobe & stem should be more sympathetically related to lobe & stem * i.e. the stroke should not be rigidly perpendicular with stem; more of an upward-ever so slight slant. The juncture is harsh.

tail too big inner serif too big.

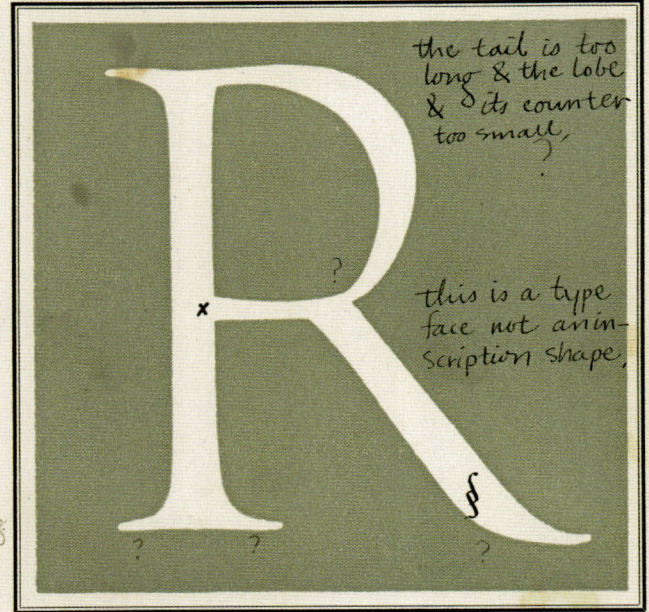

R Interests me most of all the letters in the Trajan alphabet, probably because so few letter artists seem able to draw an R of distinction; the tail often is wrongly attached, or the angle is wrong, or the whole effect is weak. In this R the form of the upper bowl follows more nearly that of the B, except that it is slightly larger, the curve ending at about the middle of the letter where the tail begins. It is interesting to note how the tail joins the bowl; in many instances the tail, instead of ending practically on the base line, is projected slightly below and under the following letter in the attempt to diminish the gap of white between them. This is especially desirable when R is followed by A.

astonishing! Actually the letter above reproduced is deadly an ugly form

§ In Trajan ltrs. the R's tail is thickest here & thinnest at lobe-juncture.

* the functional form would probably be R, but because the 3 strokes coming together would make an undue black, the tail was moved out. and to add clear distinction (in Gk ltrs from which Roman ltrs were derived) between the open Greek Pi ΠΠΠ and the closed Greek Rho Ρ Ρ Ρ. See my paper, "The P & R."

[sic;] R R

Most stems in R are definitely above the baseline.

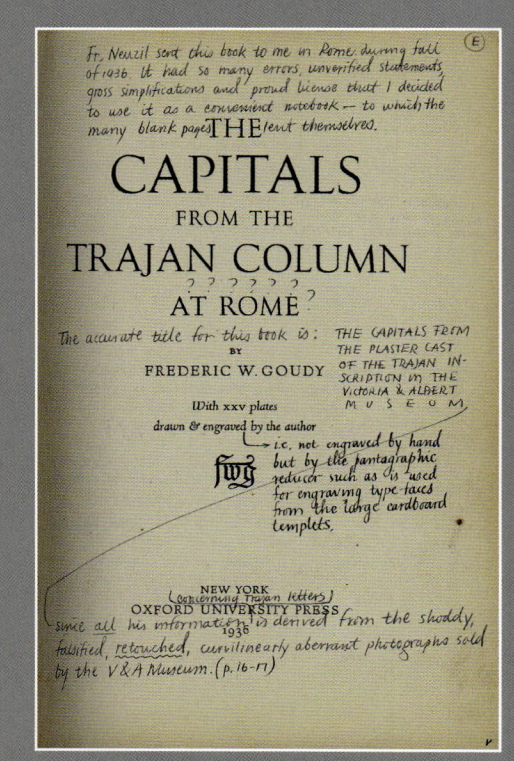

over

57

F. Neuzil sent this book to me in Rome during fall of 1936. It had so many errors, unverified statements, gross simplifications and proud bisnes that I decided to use it as a convenient notebook — to which the many blank pages **THE** lent themselves.

CAPITALS
FROM THE
TRAJAN COLUMN
AT ROME

The accurate title for this book is: THE CAPITALS FROM THE PLASTER CAST OF THE TRAJAN INSCRIPTION IN THE VICTORIA & ALBERT MUSEUM

BY
FREDERIC W. GOUDY

With xxv plates
drawn & engraved by the author

i.e. not engraved by hand but by the pantographic reducer such as is used for engraving type faces from the large cardboard templets.

fwg

(NEW YORK reproducing Trajan letters)
OXFORD UNIVERSITY PRESS
1936

since all his information is derived from the shoddy, faulted, retouched, curvilinearly aberrant photographs sold by the V&A Museum. (p. 16-17)

1 The first constructed alphabet was by Felice Feliciano (1460). It was followed by Damiano da Moylle (1483), Luca de Pacioli (1509), Sigismond Fanti (1514), Francesco Torniello da Novara (1517), Albrecht Dürer (1525), Giambattista Verini (c. 1526), and Geoffroy Tory (1529). In the 20th century, L. C. Evetts (1938), David Lance Goines (1982), and Johannes Muess (1989) have been among those to offer constructed interpretations of the Trajan capitals. Tom Perkins ("Trajan Secrets" in *The Edge* [January 1997]) and Richard Grasby (*The Making of Roman Inscriptions*, Studies 7–11 [2009]) have both suggested new geometric theories of Roman inscription-making that try to accommodate Catich's brush conclusions.

2 In *The Origin of the Serif: Brush Writing and Roman Letters* (Davenport, Iowa: Catfish Press, 1968), Catich gleefully attacks Frederic Goudy, Warren Chappell, Oscar Ogg, Clarence P. Hornung, Eric Gill, L. C. Evetts, Walter Kaech, and Albert Kapr, among others, for their beliefs that the Trajan capitals were constructed geometrically or had to be drawn rather than written ("[Trajan] letters of the same size are so stereotyped and alike in effect that this could only be obtained by drawing-like copying." Walter Kaech, *Rhythm and Proportion in Lettering*, p. 37), that serifs are the product of the chisel ("The manipulation of the chisel in stone caused the element known as the *serif* to come to be." Oscar Ogg, *An Alphabet Source Book*, p. 35), that it was difficult for lettercutters to carve curves ("V in Latin inscriptions stood normally for *U* as well as *V*, and is easier to cut in stone." Frederic W. Goudy, *The Capitals from the Trajan Column in Rome*, p. 35), that brush letters are inferior to pen-made ones ("Their [brushes'] popularity comes more from the needs of the show-card writer than the refined requirements of the letter designer. Acceptable brush lettering depends more on dexterity than on a knowledge of form." Warren Chappell, *The Anatomy of Lettering*, p. 4). (For more on Walter Kaech, see p. 37; and for more on Frederic W. Goudy, see p. 69.)

3 In *Origin of the Serif*, pp. 182–83, Catich summarizes fifteen differences between reed (pen) writing and brush writing. The key ones are that the brush can make strokes in any direction, that the change in strokes from thick to thin is slow and gradual, that brushstrokes vary in width with writing speed and pressure, and that it is easier to make frequent changes of cant (pen angle). William Lethaby, in his preface to Edward Johnston's *Writing & Illuminating, & Lettering* (1906), pp. ix–x, anticipated Catich's argument: "The Roman characters, which are our letters to-day, although their earlier forms have only come down to us cut in stone, must have been formed by incessant practice with a flat, stiff brush or some such tool. The disposition of the thicks and thins, and the exact shape of the curves, must have been settled by an instrument used rapidly; I suppose, indeed, that most of the great monumental inscriptions were designed *in situ* by a master writer, and only cut in by the mason, the cutting being merely a fixing, as it were, of the writing, and the cut inscriptions must always have been intended to be completed by painting." The key difference is his suggestion that the tool used was a stiff brush as opposed to a flexible one.

4 Father E. M. Catich to Lloyd J. Reynolds, 31 August 1958. Reed College, Lloyd J. Reynolds Archives, Box 1, Folder 1 (hereafter cited as LJR Archives).

5 The stones were exhibited at the Portland Art Museum in 1958, but not purchased until 1961, made possible by the help of the Portland Craftsman Club. Lloyd J. Reynolds to Father E. M. Catich, 27 January 1961, LJR Archives; *Portland Craftsman* 38, nos. 3 and 4 (November 1960 and December 1960).

6 "The Origin of Letter Forms: Praenotanda," published from a lecture Catich gave 4 May 1972 to the Washington, DC, chapter of the AIGA.

7 See Scott-Martin Kosofsky's article on the development of Adobe Trajan, p. 181.

8 For the story of the Donnelley cast, see Edward M. Catich, *The Trajan Inscription in Chicago* (Chicago: Lakeside Press, R. R. Donnelley & Sons Co., c. 1964). Also Catich to Lloyd J. Reynolds, 30 August 1966, LJR Archives.

9 Most of the biographical information about Father Catich in this essay is taken, with permission, from Paul Herrera's overview of his life on the Art Legacy League website, artlegacyleague.org/

10 In *Calligraphy Broadside* 24 (March 1969), in The Catich Collection, St. Ambrose University, Catich made a distinction between signwriters and signpainters: "The ancient, Roman inscription maker was, in reality, what we today in Chicago call a sign writer; mind, not a sign painter but a sign writer. The distinction is a simple one. The sign writer works in the same shop and belongs to the same union as the painter and both make signs. Their working methods differ. The sign writer does just that; he writes out his signs directly without retouching or retracing his brush strokes, i.e., he makes his letters directly and completely just as one does who writes a letter to friend.... The sign painter however outlines, fills-in, & builds-up his letters. Such lettering may be seen on highway bulletins, gold-leaf window signs, etc." The information on Catich's career in the 1920s comes from an undated typescript by Edward M. Catich in Special Collections, St. Ambrose University; the information about his 1936 rubbing of the Trajan inscription is from the flyleaf of Iowa State University's copy of Catich's *The Trajan Inscription: An Essay* (Boston: Society of Printers, 1973).

11 There are two known rubbings by Detterer from 1922 in existence: one at the Newberry Library, the other at the King Library Press, University of Kentucky. See also Edward M. Catich to Lloyd J. Reynolds, 29 January 1961, LJR Archives.

12 *Calligraphy Broadside* 03 (n.d., but post-1968), The Catich Collection, St. Ambrose University.

13 Father E. M. Catich to Donald Anderson, 31 December 1970. Donald M. Anderson Papers, Newberry Library.

14 Father E. M. Catich to Robert Hunter Middleton, 19 February 1952. Robert Hunter Middleton Papers, Newberry Library.

15 Catich is known to have made trips to Rome in 1950, 1952, 1956, 1966, and 1970. The census of Trajan inscription rubbings on p. 238 has details of the whereabouts of his rubbings today. There are some fanciful rumors of how he managed to obtain access to Trajan's Column. Ryan Roth to James Mosley, private email, 20 December 2007: "The story I gather is that Catich had apparently financed his trips to Rome by offering to bring back rubbings, charging at least in one instance $100 (this I've gathered from Bob Williams in Chicago, who at the time couldn't afford it). Susie Taylor at SF [San Francisco] public library remembers Catich report[ed] that he had bribed persons with nylons and cigarettes apparently to make (at least some of the rubbings) though this may be untrue."

16 Father E. M. Catich to Donald Anderson, 31 December 1970. Donald M. Anderson Papers, Newberry Library. There is very little information online about Professor Gatti's activities beyond his biography of Gabriele d'Annunzio and his masterwork, *Topografia ed edilizia di Roma antica, Studi e materiali del Museo della civiltà*, 13 (Rome: "L'Erma" di Bretschneider, c. 1989), covering his researches from 1934 to 1979.

17 For details of Father Catich's inscriptions at Reed College, see the article by Gregory MacNaughton on p. 175.

18 Both Richard Lipton and John Stevens, the designers of Arrus and Stevens Titling, respectively, learned how to make Imperial roman capitals from reading Father Catich's books.

7 (*left*). Annotated page from Father Catich's copy of *The Capitals from the Trajan Column at Rome* by Frederic W. Goudy (1936). On the title page (right) Catich wrote, "Fr. Neuzil sent this book to me in Rome during fall of 1936. It had so many errors, unverified statements, gross simplifications and proud biases that I decided to use it as a convenient notebook—to which the many blank pages lent themselves.'

8 (*right*). Annotated title page of Father Catich's copy of The Capitals from the Trajan Column at Rome: "The accurate title for this book is THE CAPITALS FROM THE PLASTER CAST OF THE TRAJAN INSCRIPTION IN THE VICTORIA & ALBERT MUSEUM since his information is derived from the shoddy, falsified, retouched, curvilinearly aberrant photographs sold by the V&A Museum (p. 16–17) [sic]."

THE GENETRIX

THE TRAJAN INSCRIPTION: AN ESSAY
FATHER EDWARD M. CATICH
BOSTON: SOCIETY OF PRINTERS, 1973
excerpt, pp. 12–13

ROMAN, SHADED WRITING IS THE GENETRIX of our present roman alphabet. The principal tool for writing it was the square-edged reed. Shaded writing reached its peak and transformation in the larger, architectonic, scriptura monumentalis of the Imperial age. The tool used here was the soft, chisel-edged brush.

Since the tool helps determine writing size, the smallest writing is done with stylus tools such as pen and pencil; larger writing, with square pen and reed; and the largest writing, with the chisel-edged sign-writer's brush.

It is cramping to brush-write majuscules less than one inch tall. A comfortable size for brush-writing Imperial majuscules, scriptura monumentalis, having swells, serifs, bows, cant-twirled arms, etc., is about four to five inches tall.

The specifics for beautiful letters are not easy to fix. The consensus of practicing calligraphers is that roman capitals eight and one-half to nine stem-widths tall are best, that letters *B, E, F, L, P,* and *S* should be about one-half as wide as tall, that round letters *C, D, G, O,* and *Q* should be geometrically narrower, but appear to be equal in height and width, that letter *N* should be broad, that no letter should descend below the baseline (*Q*'s tail excepted); further, that some kind of serif should terminate letter parts, that counters should be spacious enough to balance and buttress visible letter parts, that there should be an absolute economy of parts, and that each should perform its function to an exact degree for the letter's overall unity; and finally, that each part should be clearly stated without prejudice to other parts or letters. Trajan letters score perfectly in all these specifics.

Good writing or lettering always indicates in some fashion its kinesthetic structure, that is, its tool origins and manipulation. Inasmuch as Trajan letters openly show their basic brush kinetics, and since brush-writing is easily manipulated in Trajan-letter size, and since that size is well accommodated to human vision, I trust we can agree that the Trajan alphabet is the best roman letter designed in the Western world, and the one which most nearly approaches an alphabetic ideal.

The Trajan alphabet remains the noblest of all letter forms, despite centuries of efforts at letter improvement, invention, and innovation. When one considers all the formative factors that preceded its invention, and its perfectly poised optical adjustments, one cannot avoid praising it as a staggering monument of super-calligraphy. It is simply phenomenal.

During the past two thousand years, many changes in letter shapes have occurred. However, Trajan letters remain constant in their classic proportions after every twist in calligraphic taste. They are the immutable lodestar for all Western writing and lettering. Bold and clear, logical and impersonal, they gleam for us as a fulfilled expression of the classical spirit begun in Greece in the 5th century BC.

It is hazardous to use superlatives in praise of any artistic production, because the taste of one age may well be the bane of another. Yet no improvement has been made on the Imperial majuscules written and cut eighteen to twenty centuries ago, and among those majuscules, the place of honor goes to the Trajan inscription.

Admiration for these letters is not a recent phenomenon. Trajan letters were admired and copied centuries ago. It is quite certain that they were researched and reproduced by writing masters in the early Renaissance and later. The very precision of the Trajan letters may well have convinced Renaissance calligrapher-authors that the only way such perfection could have been achieved would have been by a compass-and-square, geometric procedure. This influenced these Renaissance calligraphers to develop their own compass-and-square methods for letter shaping. By doing so they unwittingly testified to Trajan superiority.

There is no better evidence of their beauty and legibility than the fact that they have served as models and a source of inspiration for those seeking perfection in what we call capital letters for almost two thousand years. No matter how doggedly calligraphers try, no lettering has been created to challenge the supremacy of the Trajan inscription.

1 Trajanic *E* written with a flexible, broad-edged brush (unretouched) by Father Catich. From *The Origin of the Serif* (p. 236).

2 Trajanic *R* written with a flexible, broad-edged brush (retouched) by Father Catich. From *The Origin of the Serif* (p. 257).

3 Detail of the Trajan inscription. Photograph by Father Catich, n.d. (probably early 1950s).

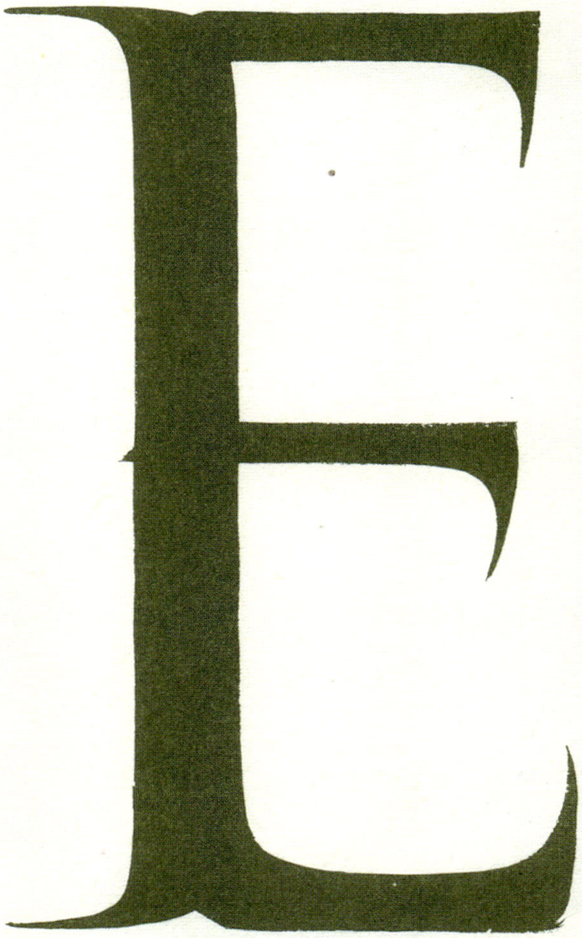

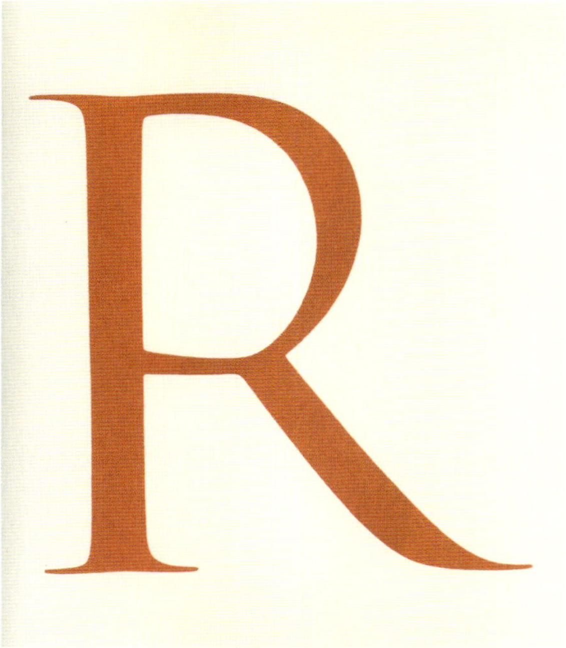

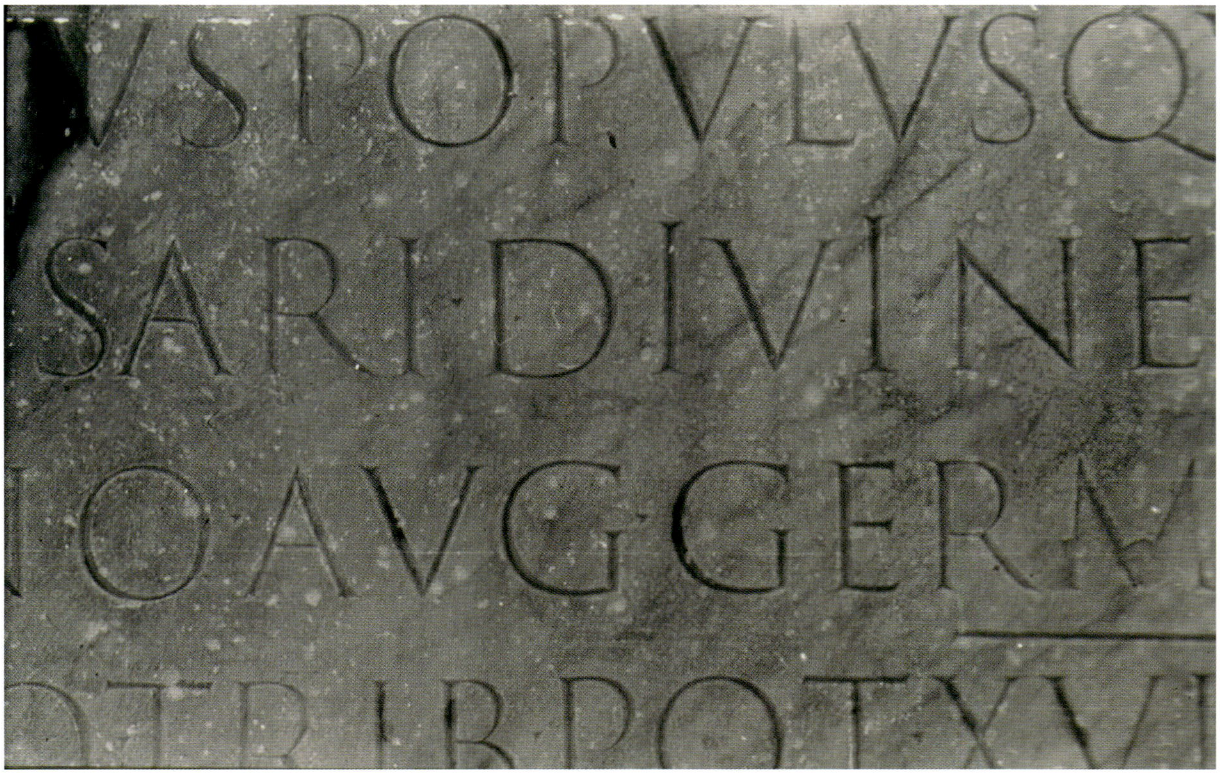
VSPOPVLVSQ
SARIDIVINE
OAVGGER
TRIBPOTXV

THE TRAJAN SECRETS

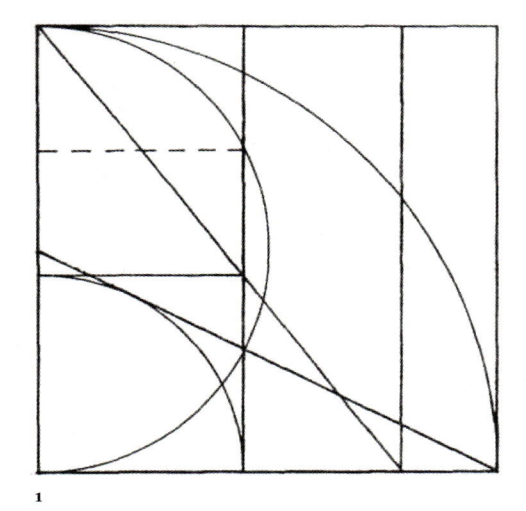

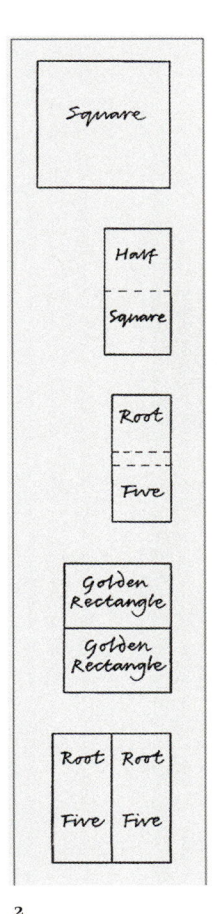

TOM PERKINS

FOR SEVERAL YEARS I have been carrying out research concerning a geometric system for proportioning the letters on the base of Trajan's Column, in Rome (114 AD). Using Father Edward M. Catich's outline drawings, traced directly from the rubbings he made of the Trajan inscription and published as a boxed set in 1961, I was able to analyze the letters very closely using a system of geometric proportions described by Jay Hambidge (1867–1924) in *The Elements of Dynamic Symmetry*.[1] [1]

I analyzed the letter proportions using the square, half square, and, importantly, the root-five rectangle and golden rectangle. [2] With simple subdivisions and combinations of the square and these last rectangles, the letters can be quickly and accurately proportioned. As can be seen in the "Construction Basics," they also form a related sequence of rectangles. [3, 4] Of course, the proportions of Roman capitals have been explained for a long time with reference to the square and the half square, and attempts have been made to proportion Roman capitals in relation to the golden section and golden rectangle. As far as I am aware, this is the first occasion since Roman times that a system of proportioning Roman capitals using both root-five and the golden rectangle has been attempted. Jay Hambidge explains the root-five rectangle as "the most distinctive shape which we derive from the architecture of the plant and the human figure...."[2] It is so-called because the relationship between the sides is as one to the square root of five, or 1:2.2360. The connection this rectangle has with growth patterns in plants or other natural organisms is fundamental, and the "vital" relationships expressed in such configurations may go some way to explaining the enduring quality of artifacts based on such proportions through the ages.

The root-five rectangle, either singly or in combination, is the key to many of the letter proportions. I had been vaguely aware that the *E* and *F* in the Trajan inscriptions were narrower than the half square usually ascribed to them, but was unaware of a specific rectangle, the root-five, which when in a vertical orientation gives a width slightly less than half square and could well account for this narrower proportion. Another characteristic is the high division on the *B*, resulting in a smaller upper bowl and a larger one at the base.[3] This contrasts with the quite low division in *P* and *R*, resulting in a generous bowl for these forms. As can be seen [here], these high and low divisions accord very well with the positioning of a square at opposite ends within the root-five rectangle.... [5] It is difficult to believe these characteristics are merely accidental.

The beauty of the system is that it not only provides key construction points, enabling rapid and precise proportioning of the letters, but also leaves the lettermaker free to interpret the precise details of the forms. It is essentially an underlying geometry, not one that rigidly dictates the finished form as in many Renaissance and later treatises.[4] It has made me aware of structural relationships between letters of which I previously had been unaware, and has greatly increased my confidence in handling these forms.

It seems unlikely to me that the proportioning of Roman capitals would have been left to chance and highly probable that some method of proportioning the letters would have been used, at least in the early stages of a letter-maker's training. Prof. E. A. Lowe's words seem particularly apposite here: "Calligraphy is distinguished by harmony of style. It is conscious of the methods by which it gets its results. Its forms are definite."[5] The Trajan inscription is a remarkable artifact and must have been the product of an equally remarkable lettermaking intelligence. It is not the product of a person working in isolation, but of a whole tradition of lettermaking reaching a peak in the early part of the 2nd century AD. It is possible that such sophisticated craftsmen would have been aware of, and made use of, such concepts as Hambidge's dynamic symmetry. It appears that the basic Roman letter proportions of square, half-square, and three-quarter width groups has been taken to a greater level of refinement, possible only to people in possession of such knowledge. We know that Roman architects possessed proportional dividers based on the golden section, though how widespread this kind of knowledge was among artists and craftsmen is, of course, difficult to gauge—but we do have the evidence of the artifacts.

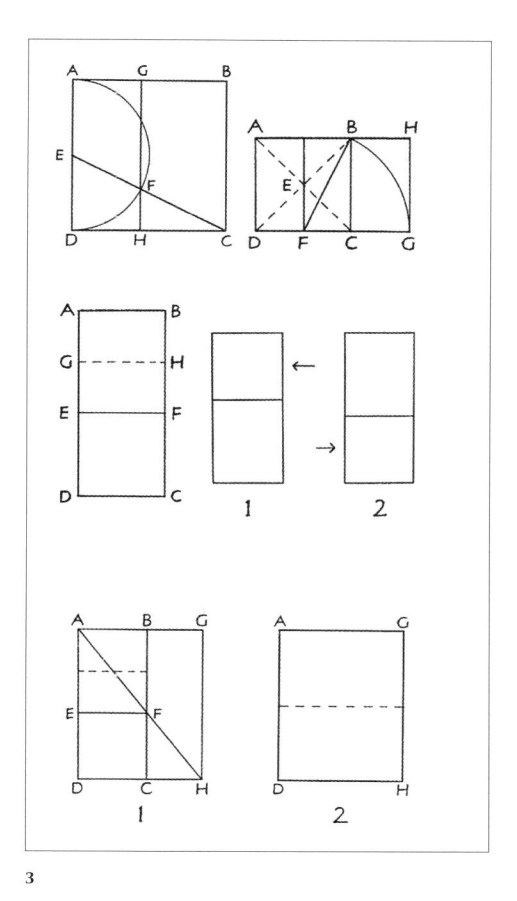

I am not advocating a form of "Trajan Orthodoxy." There are clearly other very good interpretations of Roman capitals, but certainly the Trajan letters represent, in terms of conventional letterforms, an achievement of the highest order—a fact recognized by most contemporary practitioners. A typeface closely modeled on its forms has been very successful in recent years, testifying to the continuing fascination of these letters.

Edited and excerpted from "The Trajan Secrets," published in The Edge *(November 2011).*

---

1 Edward M. Catich, *Letters Redrawn from the Trajan Inscription in Rome* (Davenport, Iowa: Catfish Press, 1961). Roman letterforms, Emil Hübner's *Exempla Scripturae Epigraphicae Latinae…* (Berlin, 1895). Some examples from Hübner's book are published in Edward Johnston, *Writing & Illuminating, & Lettering* (1906; repr. London: Adam & Charles Black, 1983).

2 Jay Hambidge, *The Elements of Dynamic Symmetry* (1926; repr. New York: Dover Publications, 1967), p. 17. Also see Matila Ghyka, *A Practical Handbook of Geometrical Composition and Design* (London: Alec Tiranti, 1952); and Matila Ghyka, *The Geometry of Art and Life* (New York: Sheed and Ward, 1946), p. 11, fig. 6, and pl. XLVI at the back.

3 This proportion of the *B* was commented on by Edward Johnston: "The extremely beautiful and finished B in the 'Trajan Alphabet' has the division a little higher, and a marked enlargement of the lower part." Johnston, *Writing & Illuminating, & Lettering* (London: John Hogg, 1906), p. 278.

4 Geometrical interpretations of Imperial Roman capitals flourished in the fifteenth and sixteenth centuries. See the bibliography for treatises by Feliciano, da Moylle, Pacioli, Dürer, Tory, and others. For geometrically constructed Trajan letters, see L. C. Evetts, *Roman Lettering: A Study of the Letters of the Inscription at the Base of the Trajan Column…* (London: Sir Isaac Pitman and Sons, Ltd., 1938). For brush-written Trajan letters see E. M. Catich, *Origin of the Serif: Brush Writing & Roman Letters* (Davenport, Iowa: Catfish Press, 1968), and Tom Kemp, *Formal Brush Writing* (Oxford: Twice Publishing, 1999).

5 Quotation from *Handwriting* by E. A. Lowe, written out by Irene Wellington (1951) and reproduced in Alfred J. Fairbank, *A Book of Scripts*, rev. ed. (Harmondsworth, Middlesex, U.K.: Penguin Books, 1960), pl. 61.

1 Chancery italic alphabet by Walter Kaech, written in chalk on a blackboard, 1950s.

2 Seal for Schulhaus-Einweihung Herrliberg by Kaech, 1967.

3 Rubbing of Early Christian inscription by Kaech. From *Bildzeichen der Katakomben* (1965).

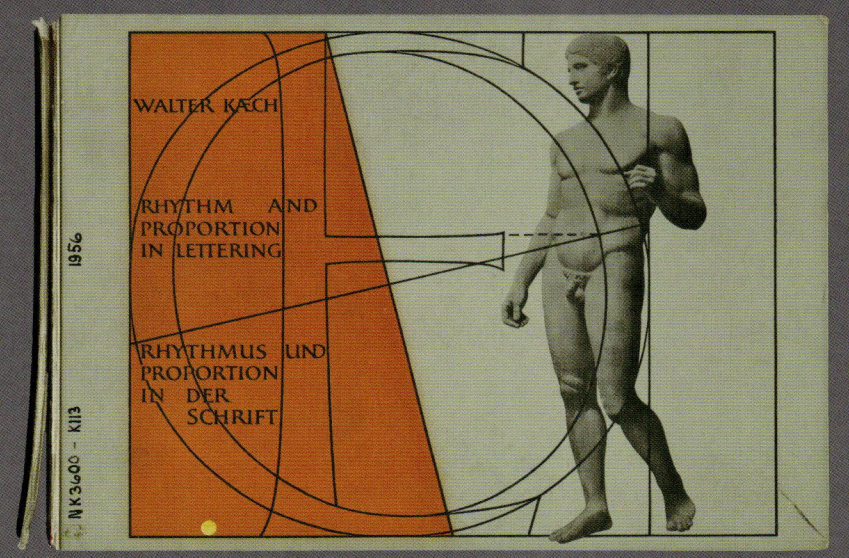

4 Cover of *Rhythm and Proportion in Lettering* (1956).

WALTER KAECH, CRAFTSMAN

JOST HOCHULI

WALTER KAECH WAS BORN IN Ottenbach, near Zürich, in 1901. He apprenticed as a lithographer before studying at the Kunstgewerblichen Abteilung der Gewerbeschule, in Zürich, with Ernst Keller, Rudolf von Larisch, Anna Simons, and Fritz Helmut Ehmcke. After graduating, Kaech became Ehmcke's assistant at the Kunstgewerbeschule in Munich during the year 1921–1922. He returned to Zürich, and from 1925 to 1929 was an instructor in design and woodcut at his old school. After 1929, he worked as a freelance graphic designer and, in 1935, he built his own house in Herrliberg, near Zürich. [2] Kaech returned to the Kunstgewerblichen Abteilung der Gewerbeschule in 1940, teaching writing and lettering there until 1967. [1] Among his students were Adrian Frutiger and I.[1] Kaech died in 1970.

Kaech was a craftsman, not a scientist. He spoke a little Italian, a few words of French, and not a single word of English. Unlike Father Catich, he received no education in Latin, since he never went to Gymnasium. What Kaech had, though, was an infallible sense for everything that had to do with craftsmanship. He knew immediately which tool created which forms, both two- and three-dimensional. His observations on the differences between the early *capitalis monumentalis* inscriptions of the 1st century and the 2nd century were remarkable. I've never read anything like them from anyone else.

Kaech wrote four books, all of which are currently out of print: *Schriften; geschriebene und gezeichnete Grundformen* (Olten, Switzerland: Otto Walter Verlag, 1949); *Rhythmus und Proportion in der Schrift* (Olten and Freiburg im Breisgau: Otto Walter Verlag, 1956); *Bildzeichen der Katakomben* (Olten and Freiburg im Breisgau: Otto Walter Verlag, 1965) and *Normalgrotesk (Blockschrift)* (Zürich: Verlag des Schweizerischen Maler- und Gipsermeister-Verbandes, 1964). [3] *Rhythm and Proportion in Lettering* was bilingual, English and German, and is considered his masterwork. [4, 7] Its influence spread to calligraphers, lettercarvers, and designers in England and the United States. In it he argued for the superiority of the Roman letter that had developed during the reigns of Augustus, Tiberius, Claudius, and Nero (27 BC–68 AD) over the form that emerged during the Flavian period (69–96 AD). He was especially critical of the letters of the inscription on Trajan's Column:

> A comparison of these earlier forms with those of the 2nd century, so far as aesthetic effect is concerned, is favorable to the form of the 1st century. The terminals in this original form are carried out logically on the baseline and headline as we can see in a proportionally and rhythmically settled way. The little terminal serifs in the rounded forms *C, G* and *S* are to be found at the same height as the serifs of the straight forms *E, F, L* and *T*. This means that the inner spaces of the letters are fully preserved and that the aspect of the line is one of monumental calm. The first oblique stroke in the *V* shows no serif, which is drawn inwards, but serves as a beginning like the beginnings of the analogous obliques in *A, M, N, X* and *Y*. A typical result of a script produced by the flat brush is that all straight lines become somewhat thicker toward the baseline.[2] [5]

5 Rubbing by Kaech of Roman inscription, 15–40 AD (Palazzo dei Diamanti, Ferrara). From *Rhythm and Proportion in Lettering* (1956).

6 Rubbing by Kaech of Roman inscription, c. 20 AD (Museo Archeologico Olivieriano, Pesaro). From *Rhythm and Proportion in Lettering* (1956).

7 Roman capitals by Kaech from *Rhythm and Proportion in Lettering* (p. 28).

Kaech favored "the immense value of the handwritten letter as against the designed form,"[3] railing against "The impossible practice of constructing lettering with the aid of geometry (with compass and ruling pen)... as if the laws of structure could give to dead matter the living beauty of lettering."[4] He believed that even the Trajan letters deviated from the written model. In his view they were so consistent in form and size that they must have been "obtained by drawing-like copying."[5] He supported his arguments with rubbings from 1st-century inscriptions in museums in Bologna, Ferrara, Padua, Pesaro, Rimini, and Verona. [6, 8]

8 Kaech making a rubbing in the courtyard of the Museo Civico Padua, February 1963.

1 Adrian Frutiger, while a student in Kaech's class, created the sans serif designs that would evolve into Univers. (See *Adrian Frutiger—Typefaces, The Complete Works*. Birkhäuser Verlag: Basel, Boston and Berlin, 2009.)

2 Walter Kaech, *Rhythmus und Proportion in der Schrift* (Olten and Freiburg im Breisgau: Otto Walter Verlag, 1956), pp. 36–37.

3 Ibid., p. 12.

4 Ibid., pp. 7–8. The preoccupation with written models was always important to Kaech; he believed that even sans serifs were not to be constructed with a ruler and compass, but rather should preserve as much of the written model as possible. This is a commonplace idea today, but it was new in the 1940s and 1950s.

5 Ibid., p. 37.

ON THE ORIGIN OF CAPITAL PROPORTIONS IN ROMAN TYPE

FRANK E. BLOKLAND

"ROMAN CAPITALS, AS NOW made by typefounders," wrote the American printer and printing historian Theodore Low De Vinne more than one hundred years ago, "are imitations of the lapidary letters used by the Romans."[1] The same sentiments were repeated recently by Robert Bringhurst, author of *The Elements of Typographic Style*: "Roman type consists of two quite different basic parts. The upper case, which does indeed come from Rome, is based on Roman Imperial inscriptions."[2]

There cannot be much doubt about what formed the template for capitals in roman type, but are they imitations of Roman Imperial inscriptions, as De Vinne and Bringhurst have suggested? A comparison of the Roman Imperial capitals, like the most famous ones on Trajan's Column, and the capitals Nicolas Jenson made for his archetypal roman type in 1470, used for instance in *Vitae illustrium virorum* (fig. 1), shows many differences of proportion and contrast. Many of Jenson's capitals are wider than their Imperial counterparts, and the relation found in the Roman inscriptions between half-square-based letters such as *B*, *E*, *F*, *L*, *P*, and *S*, and square-based letters, such as *H*, *N*, and *O*, is not preserved. (See "The Trajan Secrets," p. 34.) Also, the contrast is clearly lower in Jenson's type.

Yet, despite the differences, Jenson's archetypes have set the standard for type, and in the Western world we have been conditioned by them, mainly via Garamont's variants. In an article first published in the London *Times* in 1912, Bruce Rogers wrote that by "very general consent the types of the Italian Renaissance have been approved among modern printers as the most beautiful models upon which to base new attempts in letter design."[3] Not surprisingly, Rogers based his own Centaur type (see p. 19, fig. 32) on Jenson's Eusebius type, which had already provided the model for the types cut for William Morris and T.J. Cobden-Sanderson. In *The Alphabet*, Frederic W. Goudy tells us that "Jenson had an instinctive sense of that exact harmony in types, and he was so intent on legibility that he disregarded conformity to any standard…."[4]

The Roman Imperial capitals were not developed for typesetting, of course, but for making large inscriptions in stone. Their horizontal proportions were harmonized to one another and their contrast adjusted for lapidary use.[5] Combining the capitals with the roman lowercase letters forced Jenson to change their proportions accordingly. That these capitals were intended for relatively small point sizes (Jenson's type was around 16 digital pica points) encouraged a lowering of contrast and a thickening of the serifs. If one looks at the roman type of Jenson's contemporaries, such as Sweynheym and Pannartz and the Da Spira brothers, one sees comparable adaptations. Stanley Morison thought this was a natural development, declaring that "the necessities of architects and sculptors, though analogues, are not identical with those of punch-cutters and printers."[6]

How did Jenson and his contemporaries adapt the proportions of the capitals to the lowercase? Could their proportions have been distilled from Humanistic handwriting? According to Morison they did this by eye.[7] He further believed that the proportions of capitals in Renaissance type were derived from handwritten Carolingian models.[8] The enlarged widths of some of the capitals, such as *B*, *E*, *F*, *K*, *L*, *P*, and *S*, were explained by Morison as having been developed "in order to avoid a contrast between wide and narrow letters."[9] Edward M. Catich thought that the capitals in Latin book hands had no relation at all with the

1 Detail of roman capitals by Nicolaus Jenson from *Vitae Illustrium Virorum* by Plutarch (1478/1479), f. 2r.

lapidary capitals of the Romans.[10]

Browsing through the literature on the history of type design and typography, one comes across explanations for Jenson's letter proportions that mostly emphasize optical principles. Pierre-Simon Fournier's adage that "the eye should guide" is generally embraced and repeated (and possibly misunderstood).[11] Moreover, there would seem to be a special gift required for sophisticated type design, which is described by Allen Hutt as "some indefinable talent in the best punch-cutters and type designers who aimed and continue to aim at optical harmony."[12]

Patterns and the punchcutter's eye

The views of Goudy and Hutt place the Renaissance punchcutter mainly in the role of the type designer who relies on eye and instinct, but seem to ignore the fact that these all-around craftsmen invented, organized, and executed a complex and sophisticated manufacturing process that comprised, aside from design, the cutting of punches, the striking and justification of matrices, and the casting of type. The evidence suggests that strict systematization was most probably a prerequisite for controlling all of these aspects of font production and, hence, may have influenced the proportions of the capitals in both roman and italic type.

Could it be possible, then, that what is considered optically harmonic in type originated, at least partly, in the preconditions of Renaissance font production? And, if so, then why has this factor been completely overlooked in the literature? Is it a deliberate attempt to create an image of the type designer as someone gifted with instinctive qualities? How much of Jenson's "sense of exact harmony" was actually the result of standardization and systematization?

Perhaps it is a matter of conditioning, a case of what we see being influenced by what we know, as E. H. Gombrich suggests in *Art and Illusion*, discussing the psychology of the artist's perception.[13] Since the days of the first punchcutters, the emphasis has been on the role of the eye, taking for granted the technical restrictions. If one accepts Gombrich's argument, it becomes plausible that one can be conditioned to optically judge and reproduce established patterns without giving a second thought to their origin.

Horizontal patterns

The interval of stems and the relation between counters and the space between characters can be defined as the "rhythmic system" of type. Capitals and lowercase letters each have their own rhythmic system and hence their own spacing requirements. The stem interval of capitals is normally based on the distance between the stems of the *H*. Figure 2 shows "fence-posting" based on a repetition of the H and the related positioning of the *O*, of which the curves are treated as overshoots of the stems.

When the standard for the width of the capitals has been defined, the other capitals can be designed within a related rhythm. Figure 3 shows a fence of *H*'s of DTL Haarlemmer using a shift of half the letterform. The other capitals fit in this rhythm and the spacing of the capitals is a direct result of it; no optical corrections to the spacing have been made in the example. The required optical corrections were already made during the design process (initially by Jan van Krimpen and, later, in digital form, by the author of this article).

In roman type, capitals are forced into the rhythm of the dominant lowercase, as seen in figure 4. This implies that the rhyth-

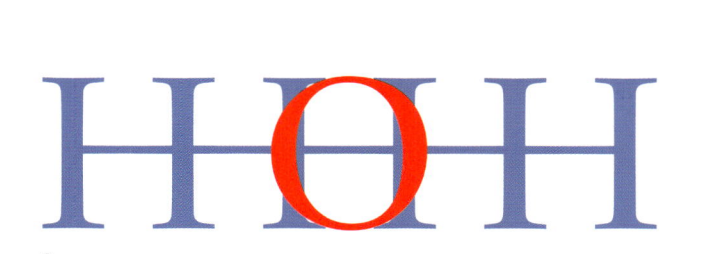

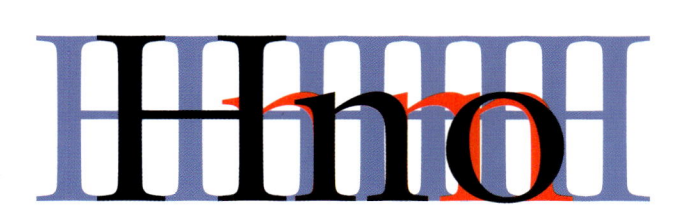

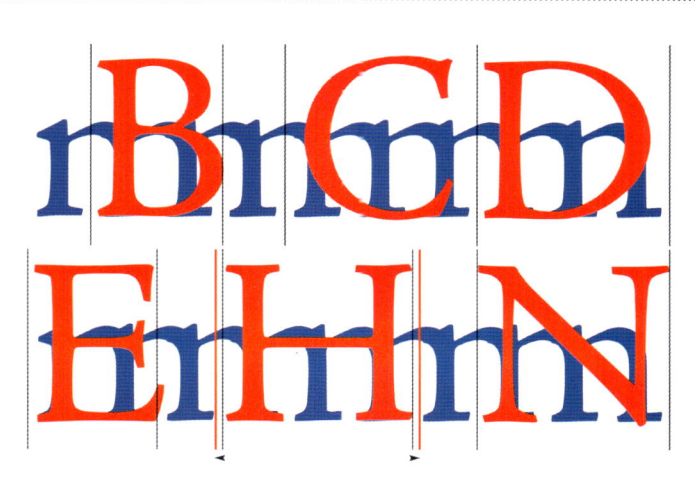

2

3

4

5

6

7

8

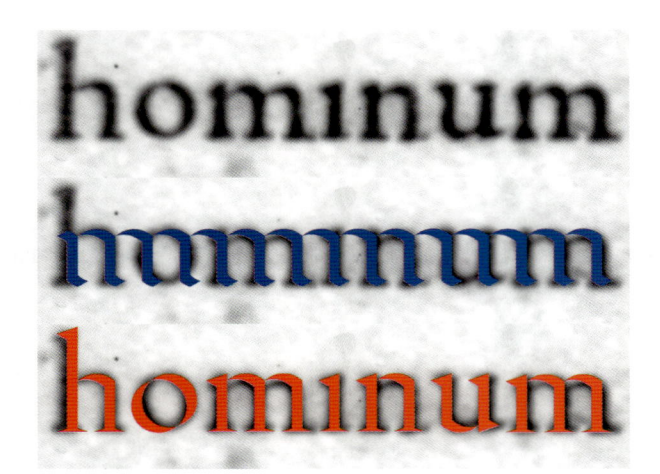

9

mic system of the capitals should in some way be synchronous with that of the lower case. The stem interval of Jenson's roman capital *H* is equal to twice the stem interval of the lower-case *n*, as shown in figure 5.

It is the traditional approach in type design and typography that the space between the counters is an optical repetition of the space within the counters. However, the problem in the Latin script is that, while this equilibrium concept works well for letters with enclosed counters, such as *n* and *o*, it works less well with "open" letters, like *a*, *c*, and *e*, or for letters that derive from the capitals and hence contain diagonals, such as *k*, *s*, and *v–z*. And, of course, compromises have to be made for combining lowercase letters with capitals.

The even distribution of white space is something that a calligrapher tries to achieve as much as possible; after all, writing offers a largely unlimited flexibility for making adaptive letter variants. In a typeset line, on the other hand, the division of spaces into equal parts in order to create rhythmic uniformity leads inevitably to problems. The written letters had not been developed to be placed within rectangles, as they are in type. For instance, the lowercase *a*, *c*, and *e* have partly open counters, which at some point becomes part of the letter's space. The question of where, exactly, the borderline between counter and space can be placed is relevant only to the typographer and not at all to the calligrapher.

The rhythm in Jenson's roman type shows a clear stem interval (see fig. 6) and curved parts are treated as overshoots of the stems. The spacing Jenson applied to his roman type also shows an equilibrium of white space. The length of the serifs helped Jenson to preserve the space between the letters—or, the other way around, worked as wedges that helped him to force the letters into the rhythmic system. Jan Tschichold briefly mentions the stem interval in his *Treasury of Alphabets and Lettering*: "The old lettering masters followed the rule that all the basic strokes of a word should be spaced at approximately equal distance. This rule is disregarded today; lower case letters are pushed together."[14]

Realizing that Jenson—leaving aside the question of whether or not he engraved the types himself—defined a standard for the production of roman type, it seems obvious that he needed a standardization of the letter shapes and proportions.[15] Jenson was not the first to make roman type, but he set the standard for its quality.[16] Figure 5 shows capitals of Adobe Jenson, a fairly faithful rendition by Robert Slimbach (although perhaps somewhat light to accommodate the taste of the 20th-century typographer), on an *n*-based fence. Like many other capitals, the *C*, *H*, and *N* fit within a doubled *n*, which equals the *m*. The *B* fits within one and a half *n*, as do the *E*, the *F*, and the *P*.

These proportions also imply that the positioning of the sidebearings is simplified, and therefore easier to adjust when casting with fixed mould-registers. Such standardization also makes it possible to limit the total number of character widths and, likewise, the number of widths of the copper bars used in the production of matrix making. It should be noted that the limitation of widths is *not* a prerequisite for justifying with fixed registers, and that it is possible to set the registers of the mould slightly wider for all capitals (indicated with the small arrows and the red lines in fig. 5).

The wonderful collection of the Plantin-Moretus Museum, in Antwerp, contains both raw strikes and justified matrices from Christophe Plantin's lifetime. There are justified matrices of type by the likes of Claude Garamont, Robert Granjon, and Hendrik van den Keere. The *Canon Flamande* and *Parangonne Flamande* of van den Keere, in figure 7, show a limited number of character widths. The justified matrices of Granjon's *Ascendonica Cursive* can be also placed in rows of equal widths, as in figure 8. The raw strikes of the *Ascendonica Cursive*, in figure 9, in possession of the museum show the same structure, and it looks as if the strikes were made in strings of copper that were pre-cut like chocolate bars. Strikes of characters that share widths could have been made in rows in an organized and standardized way. This, however, conflicts with the generally accepted theory that the punch was struck in "a lump of copper with one or two flat sides. Somewhere in this lump there floats a character. Justification in all directions was necessary."[17]

If Jenson used *n*-based proportions, then it is likely that Francesco Griffo followed the same scheme. The four examples of capitals of Monotype Bembo in figure 10 show the same *n*-based fence-posting. The *B* and *C* have an identical relationship to the *n* as in Jenson's type, though the *H* and *N* deviate somewhat from Jenson's relatively wide versions, which seems an attempt by Griffo to aesthetically improve the proportions of these capitals. One can imagine that when such a system was established, it was relatively easy to make improvements on it, which is what Griffo appears to have done. The capitals made by Garamont largely follow Griffo's scheme, and, as we know, the French master's œuvre influenced many subsequent punchcutters and type designers.

Standardization and unitization of widths

A closer look at Gutenberg's textura type reveals a limitation of character widths (fig. 11). The fitting of textura type is fairly simple because of its vertical stresses; the vertical strokes can be placed at equal distances, and hence the space between the strokes and the sidebearings is generally also equal.

Figure 12 shows that textura type can be fitted by placing the sidebearings exactly in between the stems. The division by vertical lines automatically leads to a simple unit arrangement: one unit for the *i*, two for

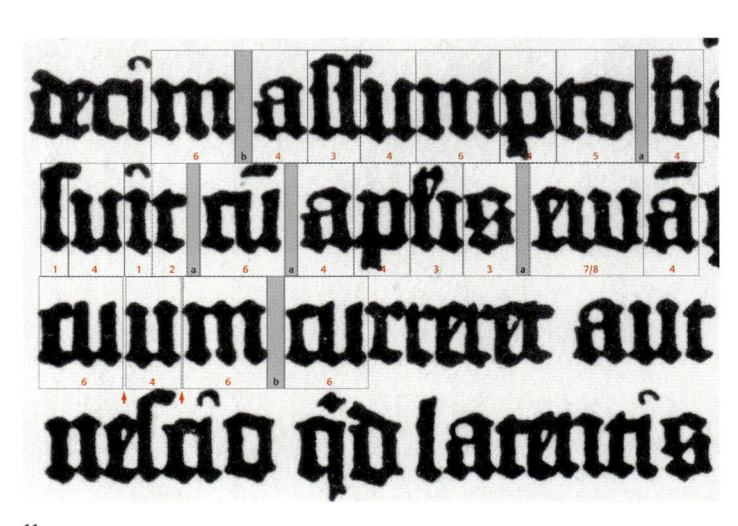

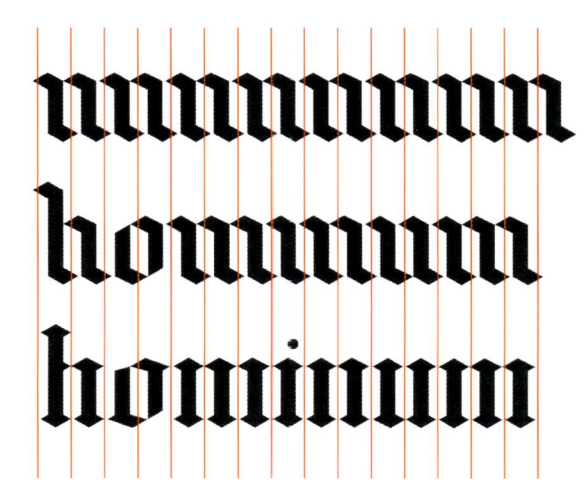

10

11

12

CAPITAL PROPORTIONS   43

the *n*, *o*, and *u*, and three for the *m*. In the bottom row, the stroke endings have been moved backwards because, otherwise, the difference between them and the arches becomes too small. This also helps to retain the position of the *o*, i.e., to keep it on two units like the *n*. Otherwise, the character width of the *o* would have to be reduced, thereby disrupting the rhythm of the vertical strokes. The units can be made smaller by further division, as in figure 13.

While the fitting of a textura type may not be complex, roman types have the complication of straight verticals that are combined with curved shapes. Yet the rhythmic systems for both textura and roman types are essentially identical, wherein the curved shapes can be considered as overshoots of the straight strokes. Defining the sidebearings for roman type can therefore be done in the same simple way as for textura type (fig. 14), implying that the same number of letters share widths in both textura and roman types.

Standardization makes the production of punches and matrices, the incorporation of spacing "intelligence," as well as the casting of type easier. It is likely that the production of roman type was standardized in a similar manner as that of textura, because there is a detectable and reproducible organic-morphological relationship between written textura ("quadrata") and the humanist minuscule that formed the basis for roman type. It also makes sense to reuse established, i.e., standardized, production methods for other types, if possible. Considering that the Da Spira brothers, Sweynheim and Pannartz, and Jenson worked in Germany, where they all cut gothic types before they went to Italy, makes it is even more plausible that elements from the textura type production were applied to roman type.

The unitization of Jenson's roman

Jenson's roman type seems to be positioned on a simple unit-arrangement system, comparable to the ones that can be distilled from Gutenberg's type and those of Fust and Schöffer. The question that inevitably comes up is how refined such a system could have been, considering the small sizes punchcutters had to execute.

Preliminary research into the unitization of Jenson's roman reveals that it can be fitted on a grid that uses eight units for

13

14

15

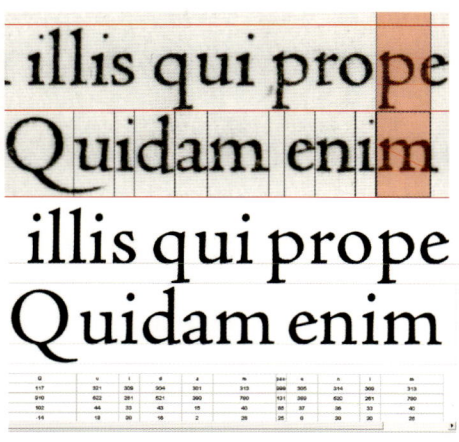

16

44

17

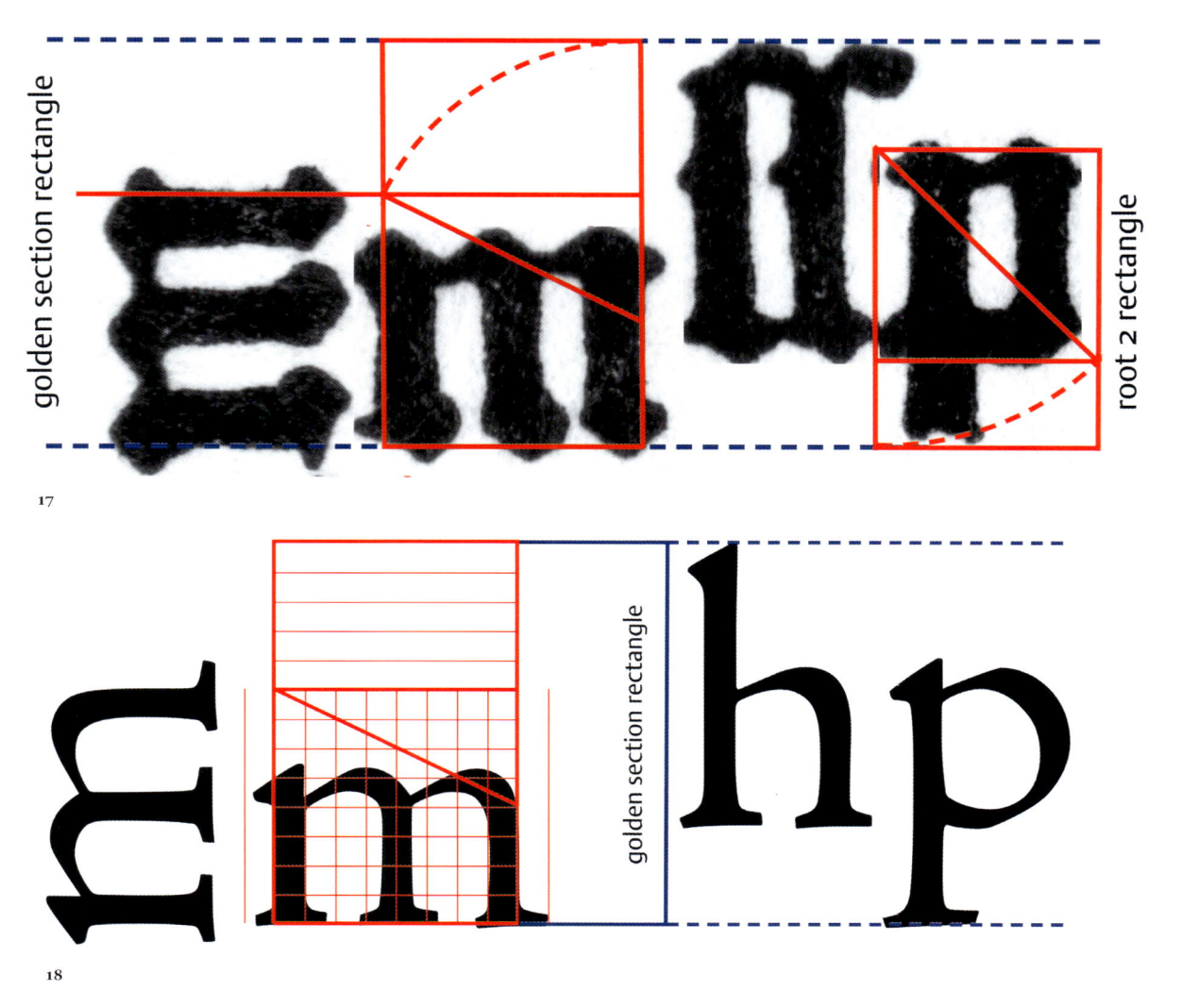

18

the *n* and fifteen units for the *M*. Figure 15 shows the results of this idea, using Adobe Jenson. The fitting of Adobe Jenson on eight units for the n resulted in a total of nine different widths, which are displayed here in vertical rows. The widths of the capitals fit into seven rows. Rows with (slightly) smaller widths can be configured as kerned versions in the adjacent rows, such as in the case of the capital *T*. It is an interesting challenge to try to reduce the number of widths even further.

One has to take into consideration that the original size of Jenson's type is quite small and that it inevitably resulted in some deviations along the path of triking-casting-printing. (Adobe Jenson is an interpretation, which may explain some deviations.). But the first test of the theory was encouraging when compared with enlarged prints of the 15th-century original (fig. 16). They seem to show the same kind of irregularities as can be seen in the original spacing, which cannot easily be explained optically, but can be explained by distilling the underlying unitization. The wordspace used here is two units. It must be said that this is really a very simple system.

Vertical patterns

If there was a standardization of horizontal widths in Renaissance type, was there also a related standardization in the vertical direction? The relationship between em-square and ascenders/descenders in Gutenberg's textura type from his 42-line Bible (1455) can be captured in a golden section rectangle and a root-2 rectangle (fig. 17).

Many Renaissance punchcutters, including Gutenberg, Griffo, and Granjon were trained as goldsmiths. The historian Richard A. Goldthwaite, who has exhaustively researched the byways of Renaissance Florence, tells us that building patrons looking for architectural ideas often turned to goldsmiths, who knew how to make drawings and possessed the requisite working knowledge of geometry.[18] The first printed edition of Euclid's *Elements* was published in 1482 by Erhard Ratdolt (1442–1528), a German printer working in Venice during the years 1476 to 1486.

Assuming that Jenson treated his roman type as a variant of textura type, then it is likely that his practice was not restricted to the horizontal patterns. Indeed, Jenson's roman type shows the same relation between the em-square and the length of the ascenders and descenders as Gutenberg's textura type (fig. 18). Interestingly, the vertical heights can be translated easily into the same units applied horizontally. The units are equal to the stem widths and also to the lengths of the serifs as fit into the grid. If one wished to change the relation between x-height, the length of ascenders and descenders, and the capital height, a serif, i.e., one unit, could be added to the rotated *m*, as in Guillaume Le Bé's *Double Canon Romain*, shown in figure 19.

As one would expect, the relation between em-square and the length of the ascenders and descenders in Gutenberg's and Jenson's types can also be found in the types of Griffo and Garamont. A closer look at Garamont's *Parangon Romain* (fig. 20—the digital revival Adobe Garamond by Robert Slimbach has been used here), shows

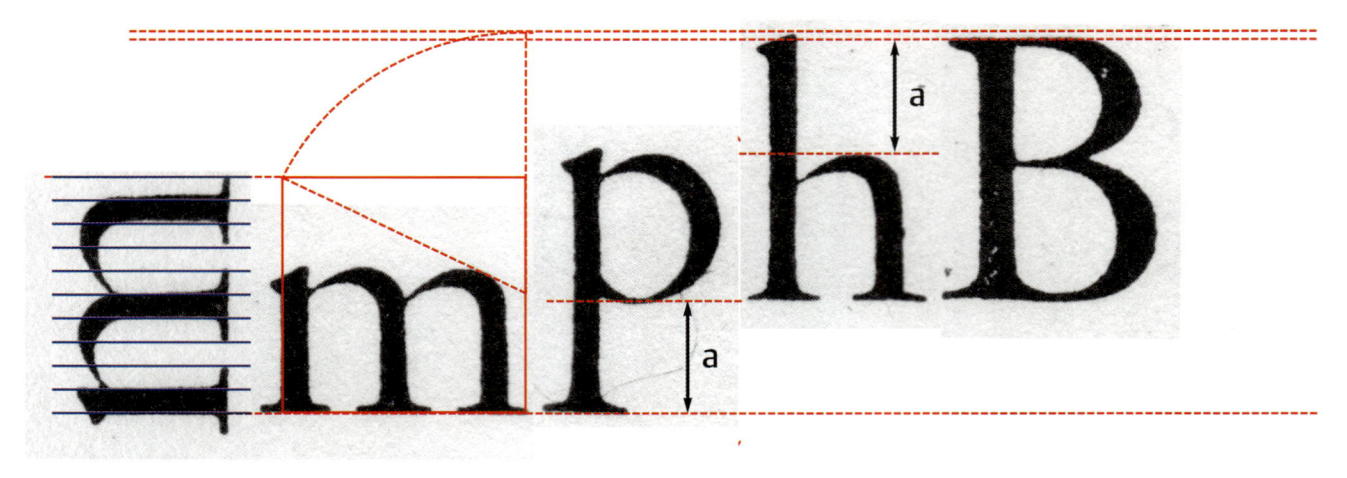

19

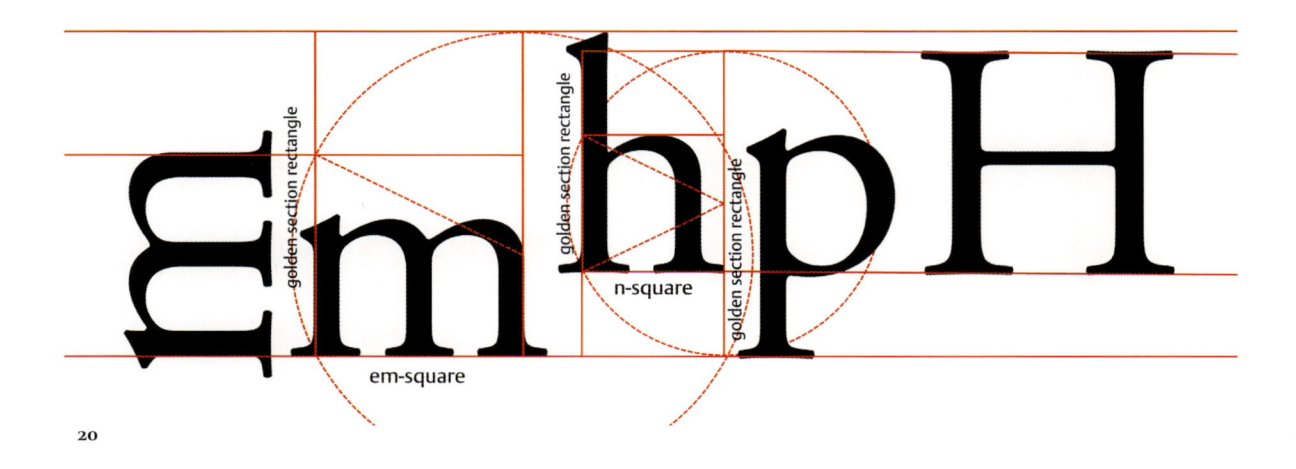

20

a related system for defining the height of the capitals.

This dynamic framework works in all directions; changing one of the proportions automatically changes all others, as well; all hierarchical relationships are covered by the system. For example, horizontal compression of the letters results in the shortening of ascenders and descenders, and a reduced height of the capitals in relation to the x-height.

Figure 21 shows the effect of compression on the relation between x-height and space remaining for the ascenders and ascenders. To get the same point size, the second image has to be enlarged, which results in a larger x-height and bolder image. This is precisely the relationship between textura and roman type. The next thing to investigate is whether the justified matrices of, say, van den Keere's *Parangon Romain* and *Parangonne Flamande* may also share widths.

Conclusion

There can be little doubt that the Roman Imperial capitals formed the basis for the design of the capitals that appear in 15th-century roman type. That the proportions and contrast of the typographic versions differ from their classical counterparts was the result of adaptations to the proportions of the lowercase letters. While the optical sensibilities and skill of the early punchcutters (who were truly "type designers" in a modern sense) played a key role in their work, it must also be acknowledged that they were involved with the invention, organization, and execution of a complex and sophisticated industrial process, which required *reproducible* systematization resulting in a standardization of letter proportions.

Later punchcutters could place a greater emphasis on the eye, because for them, optical judgment took for granted the underlying patterns, almost without consciousness—it was simply the framework in which things were done. In comparison to Renaissance punchcutters, present-day digital type designers have almost unlimited freedom to define the proportions and widths of characters. But this freedom should not be used to explain the proportions of typographic letterforms that, including the capitals, have been an intrinsic and salient characteristic of typography since the second half of the 15th century. Rather, the Renaissance patterns might be seen as highly useful when defining the parameters for newly designed digital typefaces. Our reading culture has been dominated by them for well over five centuries.

21

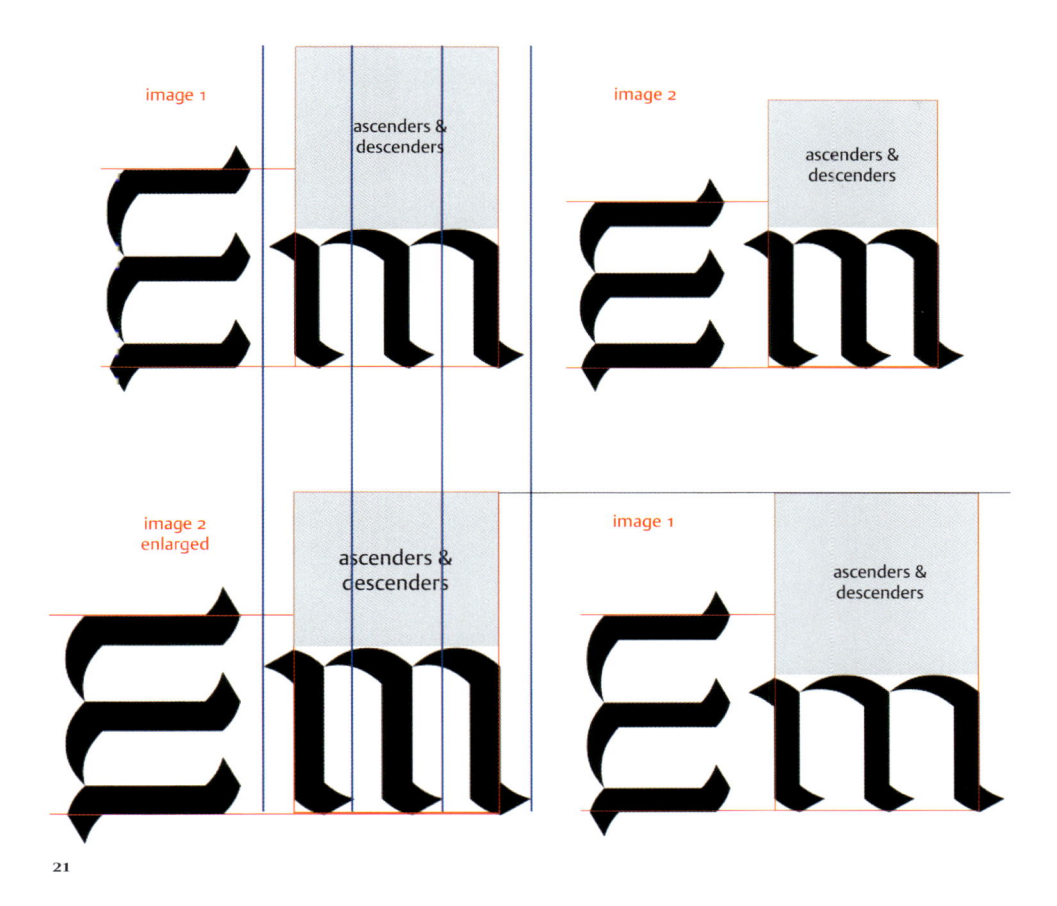

1 Theodore Low De Vinne, *The Practice of Typography* (New York: The Century Co., 1900), p. 186.
2 Robert Bringhurst, *The Elements of Typographic Style* (Vancouver, BC and Point Roberts, Washington: Hartley & Marks, 1992), p. 124.
3 Republished in Bruce Rogers, *Pi, A Hodge-Podge of Letters, Papers, Addresses, written during a period of 60 years* (Cleveland and New York: World Publishing, 1953), p. 17.
4 Frederic W. Goudy, *The Alphabet: Fifteen Interpretative Designs* (New York: Mitchell Kennerley, 1922), p. 30.
5 Morison writes, "The most conspicuous difference between the lettering derived from the old Roman *scriptura monumentalis* and the uppercase used by present-day printers is in the extension of several characters which, according to the classical letter-cutters and their disciples of the Renaissance, occupied half a square." Stanley Morison, *Fra Luca de Pacioli* (New York: The Grolier Club, 1933), p. 77.
6 ibid. p. 78
7 "Having learned and memorised the true proportions of Roman letter as taught in the manuals of Moille, Pacioli and others, the goldsmiths, punch-cutters and printers relied on their eyes and not upon their measuring tools." ibid. p. 78

8 "Although not always very literally, the bulk of the roman capitals used by 15th-century printers derive from titles employed in the books of that earlier Renaissance which Charlemagne had directed in the 8th century. Thus, Jenson's capitals are by no means immediately classical; they descend from Caroline models." Ibid p. 79
9 ibid. p. 80
10 "There seems to be no basis for this assumption. On the contrary it is disproved by the use of thin strokes in the bookhand which do not occur in the monumental letters," Edward M. Catich, *The Origin of the Serif* (Davenport, Iowa: Catfish Press, 1968), p. 113.
11 Harry Carter, *Fournier on Typefounding* (London: Soncino, 1930), p. 9.
12 Allen Hutt, *Fournier: The Compleat Typographer* (London: Muller, 1972), p. xii.
13 "The distinction between what we really see and what we infer through the intellect is as old as human thought on perception. Pliny had succinctly summed up the position in classical antiquity when he wrote that 'the mind is the real instrument of sight and observation, the eyes act as a sort of vessel receiving and transmitting the visible portion of the consciousness.'" E.H. Gombrich, *Art and Illusion: A Study in the Psychology of Pictorial Represen-

tation* (Oxford: Oxford University Press, 1987, 2nd edition), p. 12.
14 Jan Tschichold, *Treasury of Alphabets and Lettering* (New York: Reinhold Publishing Corporation, 1965), p. 34.
15 Stanley Morison and Kenneth Day, *The Typographic Book 1450–1935* (London: Ernest Benn, 1963), p. 28.
16 "The general calligraphic scheme of the letter does not differ from that of Da Spira. It is the technical excellence, such as might be expected from an engraver of Jenson's experience, that confers distinction upon his types." Ibid. p. 28.
17 Fred Smeijers, *Counterpunch* (London: Hyphen Press, 1996). p. 120.
18 Richard A. Goldthwaite, *The Building of Renaissance Florence: An Economic and Social History* (Baltimore: Johns Hopkins, 1980), p. 358.

ANNO HVMANATI DEI
MCCCCLXVIII
NONIS SEPTEMB

DIVO·VENETORVM·PRINCIPE·CHRISTOPHORO·MAVRO
CLARISS·Q·VIRIS
MARINO·MARIPETRO·PRAET·ET·DOMINICO·GEORGIO·PRAEF
S·P·Q·VERONENSIS
MACELLVM·HOC·VSVI·ORNAMENTO·Q·CIVITATIS·AERE·PVB·F

PESCHERIA

FELICE FELICIANO AND THE INSCRIPTIONS ON THE MACELLO OF VERONA

JAMES MOSLEY

THE INSCRIPTIONS THAT ARE SHOWN opposite (figs. 1, 2) are cut over the central doorway of the western side of a building in Verona that is known as the *Pescheria*, or fish market.[1] It was built during the long period of Venetian rule of the region of mainland Italy that is known as the Veneto. As the lower inscription notes, it was originally the public *macello*, or slaughterhouse of the city, which was also known as the *beccaria*. It is a single-story building, located in the Piazzetta della Pescheria, built of brick with a cement rendering that is now in poor repair. There are decorative battlements, or *merli*, at the skyline, done in the local style. In about 1860, its function as *macello* was transferred to another part of the city.[2]

A stone tablet bearing the word PESCHERIA was set in the wall of the present building, perhaps in about 1900, with large letters in the style known in Italy as "Liberty," or *art nouveau* (fig. 3). The eastern side of the building was largely demolished in 1882 by the violent flooding of the river Adige, which drove many floating mills on shore and did extensive damage to surrounding buildings, destroying the nearby Ponte Nuovo over the Adige. This side of the *Pescheria* was later rebuilt in a style that was intended to resemble the original form.[3]

The building was again damaged during the World War II. During repairs, while some of the stones surrounding the central doorway of the western façade appear to have been temporarily removed from the building, the opportunity was taken by Giovanni Mardersteig to have photographs made of the two inscriptions (figs. 1, 2). According to the Italian edition of Giovanni Mardersteig's reproduction of the alphabet of Felice Feliciano, the height of the letters in the top line of the inscriptions is 6.5 cm and in the bottom line it is 4.3 cm.[4] This is the text of the two inscriptions:

ANNO · HVMANATI · DEI
M · CCCC · LXVIII
NONIS · SEPTEMB

DIVO · VENETORVM · PRINCIPE · CHRISTOPHORO · MAVRO
CLARISSQ · VIRIS
MARINO · MARIPETRO · PRAET · ET · DOMINICO · GEORGIO · PRAE[F]
S · P · Q · VERONENSIS
MACELLVM · HOC · VSVI · ORNAMENTO · Q · CIVITATIS · AERE · PVB · F · F .[5]

1 (*opposite top*). Upper inscription on the façade of the Pescheria (ex Macello), Verona, 1468.

2 (*opposite center*). Lower inscription on the façade of the Pescheria (ex Macello), Verona, 1468.

3 (*opposite bottom*). Late 19th c. inscription on the façade of the Pescheria, Verona.

The importance of these inscriptions derives from their style and date, as well as their probable association with Felice Feliciano (born in Verona, in 1433), calligrapher, collector of the texts of early inscriptions, and a friend of the painter Andrea Mantegna.[6] Feliciano's manuscript alphabet in the Vatican Library,[7] written on vellum and colored to simulate the V-cut of an incised letter, was carefully redrawn and published in an edition with a commentary by Mardersteig, printed in 1960 at his Officina Bodoni. A facsimile edition, one of several made from manuscripts at the Vatican Library that were scanned there directly from the originals, was issued in 1985 by Belser Verlag, Zürich. The Feliciano manuscript is undated, but apparently it was made about 1460 or not long after. It is the earliest known example of the long

5 (*above*). Detail of the upper inscription on the façade of the Pescheria (ex Macello), Verona, 1468.

4 (*below*). Detail of the inscription on the façade of the Tempio Malatestiano in Rimini designed by Leon Battista Alberti, 1446–1468.

series of alphabets, many of them printed ones, that show a geometrical construction of classical Roman capitals based on the circle and the square, the forms prescribed by Vitruvius in the 2nd century AD as the basis of architecture.[8]

In addition to his claim that such letters were based on geometrical forms, Feliciano says that his are modeled on examples he had seen "in Rome and other places." One feature of Feliciano's letters, a redeeming one for those who find that a rigid "geometrical construction" can sometimes be a straitjacket on their design, is that in describing the making of letter *R*, for example, not only does he remark that "the most difficult part is the tail [leg], because it has no shape that the compass can make—you need to follow the guidance of your eye," but he adds a leaf showing a second *R*, saying that the leg needs to be made "more by practice than by rules, so you must draw it several times to make it come right."[9] (See p. 215, fig. 5.)

Perhaps this emphasis by Feliciano on the importance of personal taste is one reason why the graceful inscription on the *Pescheria* has such strong appeal. Whether or not he was directly involved in its making or its design, the details of the letters strikingly resemble those of his manuscript alphabet. Earlier exercises in making "antique letters" had often deviated from the exact forms of the Roman models that they were claimed to follow, and in the later examples that were more faithful to them, the constructed design tended to remain relatively static, as it is in several inscriptions of which the design or the direction is attributed to Leo Battista Alberti, first at Rimini (about 1450), on the façade of the Tempio Malatestiano, and later in the inscriptions on the Santo Sepolcro at San Pancrazio (1467), and on the façade of Santa

Maria Novella (1470), in Florence.[10] [4]

The "antique letters" incorporated as majuscules in the roman printing types based on the humanistic script that were made from about 1470, and which in due course replaced the earlier gothic forms, were one of the major formative influences on the letters of the "Latin script" that is used today. The inscriptions on the *Pescheria,* delicately cut on the variegated pink and white Veronese marble, are not easy to see today, let alone to photograph well. [5] They are located on a plain and utilitarian building that has suffered much physical damage. Writing in 1959, Mardersteig remarked that the lower inscription could not be seen because it was covered up by a sign, presumably one that gave the name of the shop.[11] [6]

Since these precariously surviving inscriptions constitute a document that relates to a critical step in the evolution of our present alphabet, their value can hardly be overestimated. Their safe custody, preservation, and a record of their form is important to those who are concerned with the history of letters, and that is one reason why the excellent images that were so providently made for Giovanni Mardersteig some sixty years ago have been republished here.[12]

6 Façade of the Pescheria with entrance to Punto Supermercato in 2010.

1. For help in writing this piece on the Pescheria's inscriptions I am much indebted to Dr. Pierpaolo Brugnoli for letting me see the study of the early history of this building that he has prepared for publication in *Atti dell'Accademia di Agricoltura Scienze e Lettere di Verona*. Much help has also been given by James Clough and Massimo Gonzato.
2. A topographical poem relating to Verona by Francesco Corna da Soncino, written in 1477, which refers to the *beccaria*, or slaughterhouse, with three big entrances that can be seen today, shows that the piazzetta was already known as the location of a fish market. Pierpaolo Brugnoli, *Le Strade di Verona* (Rome: Newton Compton, 1999), p. 434.
3. Details of the reconstruction of the building were provided, as Dr. Brugnoli notes, by Cecilia Trucchi, in her unpublished doctoral thesis for the Istituto di Architettura at the University of Venice on the works undertaken in Verona after the disastrous flood, "Verona nel secondo Ottocento. Problemi di recupero del patrimonio monumentale." The repairs to the Pescaria included the reconstruction of the eastern façade of the building and much work on the interior. Brugnoli, *Le Strade di Verona*, p. 435.
4. Giovanni Mardersteig, *Felice Feliciano, alphabetum romanum* (Verona: Officina Bodoni, 1960), p. 55.
5. "In the year of the manifestation of God as man 1468, 5 September. This slaughterhouse was built at public expense as an ornament and a utility for the city during the reign as Doge of Venice of Cristoforo Moro by the senate and people of Verona, Marino Maripetro and Domenico Giorgio being mayors." Cristoforo Moro (1390–1471) became Doge of Venice in 1462.
6. Among contemporary artists, Mantegna is outstanding for the quality of the Roman capitals that are used in his paintings. For a useful recent overview, see Stefano Zamponi, "Andrea Mantegna e la maiuscola antiquaria," in *Mantegna e Padova 1445–1460*, edited by D. Banzato, A. De Nicolò Salmazo, A. M. Spiazzi (Milan: Skira, 2006), pp. 73–79. On a celebrated occasion in 1464 recorded by Feliciano himself, he and Mantegna, accompanied by other friends, made an excursion on Lake Garda in search of inscriptions.
7. Vat. Lat. 6852.
8. A number of recent studies relating to the movement for the revival of the "antique letter" and Feliciano's place in it have been published by Stefano Zamponi, Florence. A recent contribution explores possible links with Feliciano in inscriptions at the Castello del Buonconsiglio at Trento, to whose proprietor, the Prince Bishop Johannes Hinderbach, Feliciano supplied several manuscripts: "*Epigrafi di tradizione antiquaria nel Castello del Buonconsiglio di Trento*," in *Studi di antiquaria ed epigrafia. Per Ada Rita Gunnella*, edited by C. Bianca, G. Capecchi, P. Desideri (Roma: Edizioni di storia e letteratura, 2009), pp. 73–85. It has recently been followed by the wide-ranging study "La capitale nel Quattrocento: verso la fissazione di un modello (Firenze, Padova, Roma)," in *Studium medievale. Revista de Cultura visual* 3 (2010): 63–77. His initial paper relating to the antique letter, "Le metamorfosi dell'antico: la tradizione antiquaria veneta," delivered at the conference *I luoghi dello scrivere da Francesco Petrarca agli albori dell'età moderna* (Arezzo, October 2003), is accessible online.
9. Criticism of the use of rigid geometrical forms for making letters was eloquently expressed by Giovan Francesco Cresci, who, in his writing manuals of 1560 and 1570, showed beautiful freely drawn capital letters based on Roman models, and who denounced the stultifying effect of the use of geometrical construction by his rival, the calligrapher Palatino. See James Mosley, "Giovan Francesco Cresci and the Baroque Letter in Rome," *Typography Papers* 6 (2005): 115–55. (See also Mosley, p. 59 in this volume.) It is worth noting that the "calligraphic" use of a broad brush, which determines the sequence of thick and thin strokes in the Roman capitals of the Imperial period and the angle of the stress of the curves, the thesis of a book by Edward M. Catich, *The Origin of the Serif* (1968), was originally advanced by W. R. Lethaby in the editor's preface that he contributed to Edward Johnston's *Writing & Illuminating, & Lettering* (1906).
10. Giovanni Mardersteig, "Leon Battista Alberti e la rinascita del carattere lapidario romano nel Quattrocento," *Italia medioevale e umanistica*, II (1959), pp. 285–307. English translation, "Leon Battista Alberti and the Revival of the Roman Inscriptional Letter in the Fifteenth Century," *Typography Papers* 6 (2005): 49–65. See also Christine M. Sperling, "Leon Battista Alberti's Inscriptions on the Holy Sepulchre in the Cappella Rucellai, San Pancrazio, Florence," *Journal of the Warburg and Courtauld Institutes*, 52 (1989): 221–28, pls. 42–47.
11. "Una seconda iscrizione, sull'architrave dello stesso portone, non è leggibile, perché ancora coperta da una grande segno commerciale." Mardersteig, "Leon Battista Alberti," 1959, p. 304 note. At a later date, certainly by 1990, the sign had been removed.
12. They are from originals kindly supplied by Martino Mardersteig, son of Giovanni Mardersteig, and are published by his courtesy. They were originally reproduced by the photogravure process in the *Alphabetum romanum* of Felice Feliciano that was printed at the Officina Bodoni, but, being sewn into the binding, they cannot easily be seen without maltreating the book.

THE TOMB OF NICCOLÒ FORTEGUERRI IN S. CECILIA IN TRASTEVERE

(c. 1474–1476)

BY PAUL SHAW
AND GARRETT BOGE

NICCOLÒ FORTEGUERRI, NEPHEW OF PIUS II, was a general in the papal armies before becoming a cardinal in 1460. He was born 7 October 1419 in Pistoia, in Tuscany, and died 23 December 1473, in Rome. His tomb is in S. Cecilia in Trastevere, Rome, the church that was his seat as a cardinal.

The Forteguerri tomb is considered to be the work of Tuscan sculptor Mino da Fiesole (1429–1484). It was Mino's first work in Rome upon his return to the city, in 1474, after a decade's absence. There is evidence that the work was rushed. Mino's Florentine assistants were not able to handle all of the work, so he turned for help to the Roman workshop of Andrea Bregno (1418/21–1503/6). Based on the style of lettering, the inscription was undoubtedly carved in Bregno's workshop. [1—other side of fold-out]

The lettering is in a style frequently called Sistine, after Pope Sixtus IV (reigned 1470–1484), but it is more accurately Bregnoesque, as it coincides more closely with the career of Bregno, the leading Roman sculptor of the time. It is an inscriptional interpretation of the distinctive calligraphic capitals associated with the Paduan scribe Bartolomeo Sanvito (1435–1511). [2, 3] Both men arrived in Rome in the early 1460s, a time when inscriptional lettering in the Eternal City was in flux: Medieval capitals were still in use, but the Florentine Sans was finally beginning to supplant them, and newer capitals, with serifs, were beginning to appear as well. Some of these seriffed letters had proportions and shading that mimicked, in varying degrees, Imperial Roman capitals. But they lacked the verve of Sanvito's written capitals. It is that extra dimension of liveliness—asymmetrical serifs, for example—that Bregno's workshop injected into the tomb inscriptions it turned out from 1465 until the early 1490s. [34]

Although the first instance of Bregnoesque lettering can be found on the tomb of Cardinal Ludovico d'Albret (d. 1465), the high point of the style came in the mid-1470s, with the inscriptions on the tombs—in presumed order of execution—of Cardinal Pietro Riario (d. 1474) in Santissimi Apostoli, Cardinal Alessandro Oliva (d. 1463) in Sant'Agostino, Cardinal Alain de Coëtivy (d. 1474) in Santa Prassede, and of Forteguerri, which is the best of them. The layout of the Forteguerri inscription is simple, with only one size of letter, its word- and letterspacing is superior to those of the others, and its letters are consistent, confident, and well-cut.

The Bregnoesque letter was subsequently imitated, in the 1480s and 1490s, by other sculptors and *scalpellini* (stonecarvers in a sculpture workshop). However, in the hands of these artists outside of the Bregno workshop, the letter underwent significant changes, becoming at times highly mannered. In the mid-1490s, it began to be supplanted by a more subdued, typographically influenced Roman capital, such as that seen in the inscription on the façade of the Cancelleria in Rome. [5]

For more on the Bregnoesque letter, see Starleen K. Meyer and Paul Shaw. "Towards a New Understanding of the Revival of Roman Capitals and the Achievement of Andrea Bregno," in *Andrea Bregno: Il senso della forma nella cultura artistica del Rinascimento*, edited by Claudio Crescentini and Claudio Strinati (Rome: Artout—Maschietto Editore, 2008), pp. 276–331.

2 Rubricated initial letter *M* by Bartolomeo Sanvito and Gaspare da Padova from *Scriptores Historiae Augustae* (Biblioteca Nazionale Centrale di Roma, Vitt. Em. 1004), 1477–1483.

3 Detail from *Epigrammata* by Martial (Biblioteca Raccolta Durazzo, Ms. A III 3, f. 17) written out by Bartolomeo Sanvito and rubricated by Gaspare da Padova, 1477–1483.

NICOLAO PISTORI
SANCTAE CAECILIA
SVPERATA FLAM
NISQVE HOSTIBVS
PIENTISSIMI FAC
INVICTI ITA DOMI
CONSTANTIS ANIM
·D·

1 Rubbing by Garrett Boge of the inscription on the tomb of Niccolò Forteguerri (d.1473) in S. Cecilia in Trastevere, Rome, 1997.

titling letters

initial letters

Ludovico d'Albret 63 mm

4 (*top*). Rubbing of selected letters from inscription on the tomb of Cardinal Ludovico d'Albret (d.1465) in S. Maria in Aracoeli, Rome.

5 (*middle*). Unretouched recreations by Nicholas Benson of large *M* from d'Albret inscription (see above) at same size using a broad-edged brush.

6 (*below*). Detail of façade inscription on the Palazzo Cancelleria, Rome, c.1495.

FORTEGUERRI TOMB 57

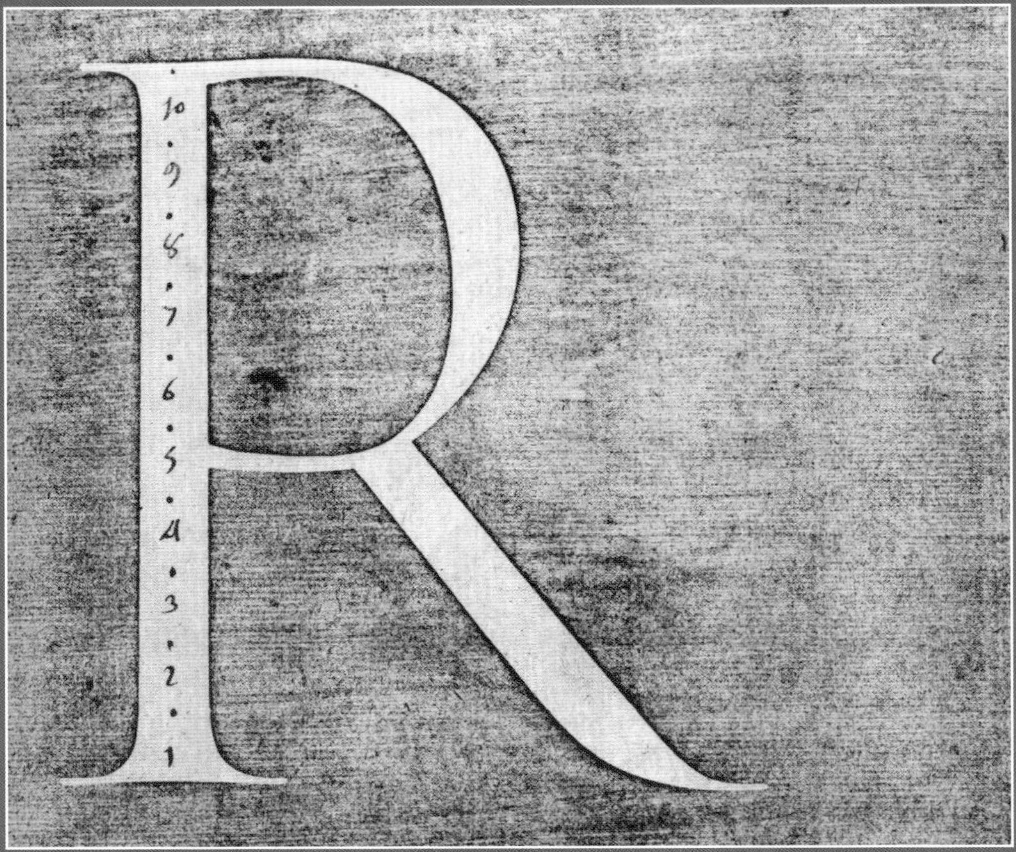

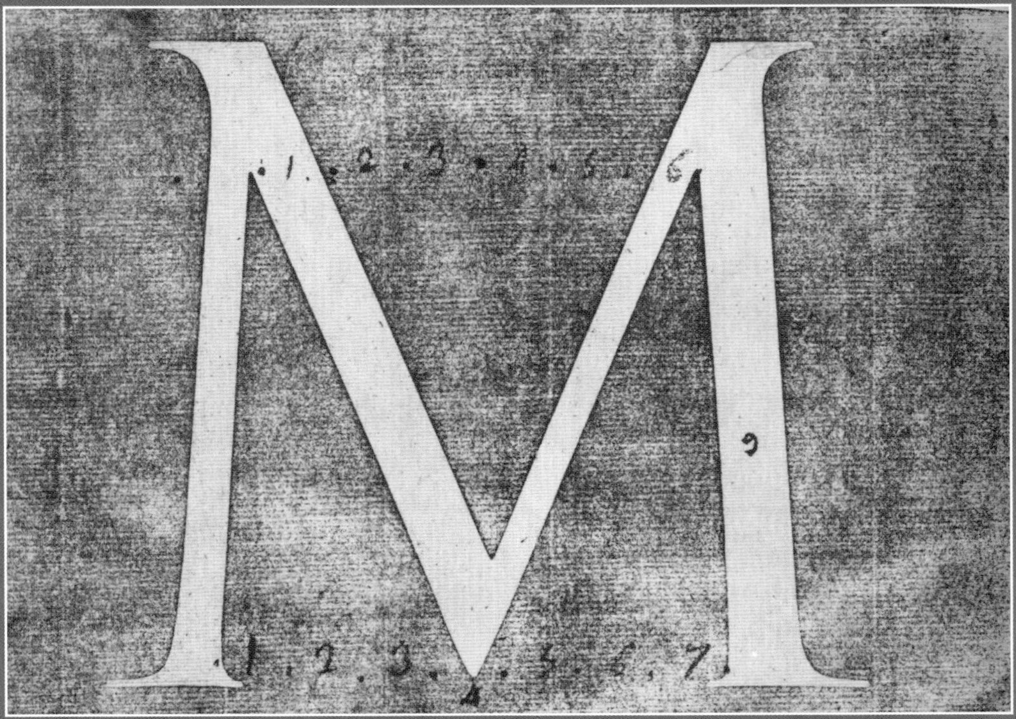

THE BAROQUE INSCRIPTIONAL LETTER IN ROME

JAMES MOSLEY

TO A VISITOR TO ROME with an interest in letterforms, the baroque buildings of the 16th and later centuries have an added attraction. Almost without exception, they are adorned with inscriptions, the high quality and consistency of whose lettering has led to the conclusion that in Papal Rome a uniform pattern of inscriptional capitals had been adopted, one to which architects and lettercarvers would remain faithful for more than two centuries. [10]

During the second half of the 16th century, the city of Rome began a process of renewal which restored its self-confidence after a half-century of disaster. The Church has been split by the doctrinal difference with the Protestants, which lost it the allegiance of much of Northern Europe. Ottoman Turkish power, established in Constantinople, the old capital of the Eastern Roman Empire, had continued the advance of Islam in Eastern Europe. And in 1527, the States of the Church had joined an elaborate alliance against the territorial claims of the Imperial Hapsburg family in Italy. This was fatally ill-advised. As a consequence the city of Rome was devastated for two years by armies of occupation that looted, burned, and killed. The calligrapher and printer Ludovico degli Arrighi was one of the many inhabitants who disappeared at this time.

Recovery, though never complete, was swift. At the great Council held at Trento, concluded in 1564, the Roman Church defined and reaffirmed its doctrine. Ottoman maritime power was destroyed for a generation by combined Catholic naval forces at the Battle of Lepanto, in 1571. Militant missionary movements, among whom the most prominent were the Jesuits, took the Gospel into the heart of the pagan and heretical faiths, and into the newly-discovered world from America to Japan. The leading French punchcutter, Robert Granjon, was recruited, against Protestant competition, to aid the missionary presses in Rome by making punches for types with which to print the scriptures in Arabic and other non-Latin scripts. Work on the rebuilding of the Basilica of St. Peter, which had started at the beginning of the century, was carried forward to completion. New churches and palaces were erected. The ancient Roman aqueducts were repaired and the fresh water that they brought to the city was triumphantly displayed by means of the many great fountains that still fill the air of Rome with the sound of their cascades. A great formal street plan was devised, aligned on viewpoints that were marked with the obelisks that had been brought to ancient Rome from Egypt. These pagan relics were re-erected and surmounted with a cross, as a symbol of the Christian domination of the world. The Rome we see today is still, to a large extent, the baroque city created during these years of renewal.

Credit for the model that was employed for the inscriptions applied to the new buildings appears to be due above all to one person, Giovanni Francesco Cresci. Milanese in origin, an official "writer" to the Vatican Library in Rome, Cresci was the creator, or at least the chief teacher, of a new style of calligraphy which replaced the older, more rigid chancery cursive. Its smooth, fluid curves and its swelling and diminishing line, created by means of a thin, flexible pen, would bring about a radical change in handwriting and ultimately in printing types, leading to the typographical innovations of Baskerville, the Didots, and Bodoni.

The writing books of Cresci promoted the new calligraphic style. The brilliant *Essemplare di più sorti lettere* (1560) and *Il perfetto scrittore* (1570) annihilated his competitors and gained many imitators. They both included alphabets of "ancient Roman capitals" for cutting in

1, 2 Capital *R* and *M* from *Il Perfetto Scrittore* (1570) by Giovanni Francesco Cresci. Cut in wood by Francesco Aureri da Crema. Cresci reproduced each capital letter twice in his book, once with a solid black background and once with a light gray one. The figures, written in the stem of the *R*, were added by a later owner and appear to be calculating the relationship of stem width to letter height. Cresci's capitals were the basis for the font Cresci (1997) by Garrett Boge.

stone, and an accompanying text which emphasized the superior value of freehand practice over rigid geometrical construction; and directed attention to specific existing models among the surviving inscriptions of antiquity, notably the inscription on Trajan's Column. [1, 2] Cresci's second alphabet of capitals is the model for the *Cresci* typeface in the The Baroque Set series. (See p. 69. fig. 1.)

In one of his last published works, Cresci gave a list of his pupils, among whom were several of the professional writing masters who would establish the new calligraphy in the practice of the next generation. One of these was Luca Horfei (or Orfei) of Fano. Horfei was the designer of the inscriptions which appear on many of the monuments that were erected to the order of the energetic and autocratic pope who gave the greatest impetus to the process of the renewal of the urban fabric: Felice Peretti of Fermo, who took the name of Sixtus V. Like Sixtus, Horfei came from the proudly independent region known as the Marche on the Adriatic Coast, an origin which may help to account for the favor of his patron. Among the examples of Horfei's work that he included in an illustrated book entitled *Varie inscrittioni* (fig. 3), is the circular inscription at the apex of the interior of the cupola of St. Peter's, nearly four hundred feet above the floor, which records its completion in 1590. They include the militantly Christian inscriptions for the bases of the pagan obelisks re-erected in the Piazza S. Pietro and the Piazza S. Giovanni in Laterano, and also the great inscription—to which Horfei added his own signature—on the fountain of the Acqua Felice. [5, 6] This was a project initiated under the reign of Pope Gregory XIII, for which Sixtus, his successor, shamelessly took the credit by naming it after himself. A manuscript (Vat. Lat. 5541) by Horfei survives in the Vatican Library with drawings for the construction of Roman capitals, and in 1590, he published a book of copperplate engravings showing the capitals, closely related to those of Cresci, that he employed in his inscriptions, the *Alfabeto delle maiuscole antiche romane*. The Pontif typeface is derived from this work, from Horfei's manuscript alphabet, and from other examples of his mature style. [4]

The new inscriptional style was modelled on the Roman letter of the early Imperial period, the 1st and 2nd centuries. Serifs are carefully delineated, sometimes with delicacy, depending on the character of the work in question, and sometimes robustly, perhaps following the model of the huge bronze letters which once filled the entablature of the façade to the Pantheon. The apexes to *M* and *N* are occasionally pointed, following the Trajan inscription (as in the inscriptions of the Vatican obelisk), but more usually they have the shoulder serifs that have become familiar in oldstyle roman type. *H* is narrow. *R* has a conspicuously large bowl, compared with the models that were followed during the early Renaissance, a feature which is found in many Roman inscriptions of the early Empire, and its leg is long, with an extended and flattened terminal. The new style has an identity that makes it unmistakeable, especially when seen outside the Papal States, in locations like the Biblioteca Ambrosiana, in Milan, the library founded by Cresci's patron Cardinal Federigo Borromeo. One of the most impressive examples in Rome itself is the inscription in huge mosaic letters, dark blue on gold, around the base of the cupola in St. Peter's, which is erected over the location of the crucifixion of Peter. [9] It employs the punning words from the Vulgate, "you are Peter and upon this rock I shall build my church":

TV ES PETRVS ET SVPER HANC PETRAM
AEDIFICABO ECCLESIAM MEAM ET
TIBI DABO CLAVES REGNI CAELORVM

3 (*top*). Plate 74 from *Varie inscrittioni del santiss. S. N. Sixto V Pont. Max.* (1589) by Luca Horfei (Newberry Library, Wing ZW 14.067).

4 (*above*). A resetting of the text above using Pontif (1997) by Garrett Boge.

60

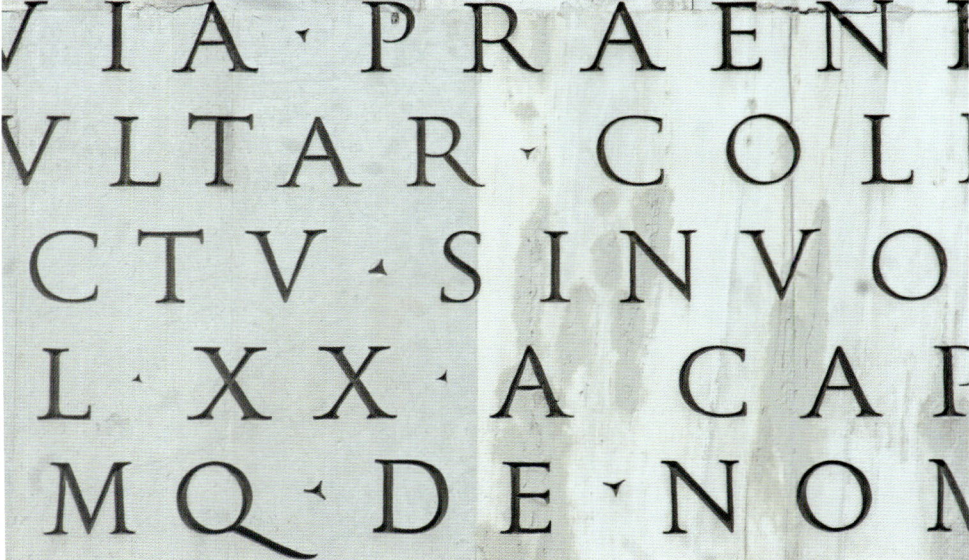

5 (*top*). The inscription on the attic of the Fontana dell'Acqua Felice, Rome, 1589. The acqueduct, whose source is the springs at Pantano Borghese, regathered the waters of the ancient Aqua Alexandrina. The fountain was designed by Domenico Fontana in 1587 and the inscription was designd by Luca Horfei (see plates 43–48 of *Varie inscrittioni*.)

6 (*top*). Detail of the inscription on the Acqua Felice, Rome, 1589. Notice the presence of *puncti* between the words.

In this inscription, for whose design the calligrapher Ventura (or Bonaventura) Sarafellini was paid in 1605, the robust proportions and well-drawn serifs of the letters ensure that their shape is maintained against the halation of the brilliant reflective background. This letter is the inspiration for the Pietra typeface, which exists in two styles: the capitals show the slightly condensed letters as they appear when viewed horizontally, whereas the small caps demonstrate the broader foreshortened forms that are seen by the viewer from the floor of the basilica one hundred and fifty feet below. One of the finest displays of the new inscriptional style is the inscription of the Acqua Paola, erected in 1612 to the designs of Giovanni Fontana and Flaminio Ponzio. Known in Rome as the *fontanone*, or "big fountain," it is the edifice on the hill of the Gianicolo which is clearly visible from the center of the city. Like that of the Acqua Felice, the structure of this fountain is based on the form of the Roman triumphal arch. Water flows abundantly through the three apertures and, like the arches which form its model, the fountain has a panel running the width of the entire structure for the placing of an inscription, which in this case records the bringing of water from the lake of Bracciano, some thirty miles away. [7, 8]

Roman buildings continued to bear inscriptions in the same style during the 18th, 19th, and even into the 20th centuries. A fine example is from the beautifully proportioned initials S P Q R on one of the plinths at the head of the staircase leading up to the Capitol. The fidelity with which the style was repeated often makes it difficult to assign a date. In the 18th century, as seen on the façade of the cathedral church of S. Giovanni in Laterano, for example, and in the architectural engravings of Piranesi, the letters sometimes become weighty and ample in proportion, not unlike the appearance of the more worldly Popes, but in general the continuity of design is remarkable. I have been present during the laying-out of inscriptions in the workshops of the Vatican City by means of carefully preserved brass stencils of some age, which have clearly been the means of repeating the "house style" from generation to generation.

In his writing book of 1570, Cresci had offered to make designs for printing types if a patron should present himself. However, the inscriptional capital letter of which he appears to be the progenitor—the "Sixtine letter" as Stanley Morison liked to call it—made only a brief entry into printing: it appears on the woodcut title page of the folio Vulgate Bible printed at the Vatican press under the authority of Sixtus V, in 1590, and in some fine decorative initials made for the press. It appears to have made little impact on contemporary types. Its appearance in the typefaces Cresci, Pontif, and Pietra can be said to be a realization, after four hundred years, of Cresci's intentions.

Postscript

My foregoing text, from 1996, needs some afterthoughts. For one thing, the term "Sixtine letter" that was used by Morison needs some comment. The Pope Sixtus that Morison had in mind was Felice Peretti, Sixtus V (reigned 1585–1590). But an earlier pope called Sixtus, who had similarly ambitious plans for rebuilding Rome, left some major buildings and many beautifully cut inscriptions that record his work, of which the forms might also deserve the name 'the Sixtine letter'. The name of Sixtus IV, Francesco della Rovere (reigned 1471–1484), is widely familiar from the so-called Sistine Chapel in the Vatican, and also the Ponte Sisto, the first new bridge to be built over the Tiber since antiquity. His aims are recorded in an inscription on the Capitol: XYSTUS QUARTUS PONT MAX URBIS RESTAURATOR (Sixtus the fourth, pope, who restored the city of Rome).

The work that is mentioned by Luca Horfei, showing his inscriptions, was called *Varie inscrittioni*, more fully *Varie inscrittioni del santiss. S. N. Sixto V Pont. Max. da Luca Horfei da Fano scrittore dissegnate*

7 (*upper left*). The inscription on the attic of the Fontana dell'Acqua Paola, Rome, 1612. The acqueduct regathered the waters of the ancient Aqua Traiana and also tapped water from Lago di Bracciano.

8 (*lower left*). Detail of the inscription on the Acqua Paola, Rome, 1612. The *puncti* are tri-pointed rather than triangular.

This essay, without the postscript, was originally published in 1996 by Legacy of Letters. It was commissioned to accompany the release of three new typefaces (Cresci, Pontif, and Pietra) designed by Garrett Boge for LetterPerfect.

Selected Bibliography

Anderson, Donald M. *A Renaissance Alphabet* [from *Il perfetto scrittore*, 1570], (Madison, Wisconsin: University of Wisconsin Press, 1971).

Cresci, Giovanni Francesco. *Essemplare di più sorti lettere*, 1560 (facsimile of edition of 1578). Edited with an introduction and translation by A.S. Osley. (London: Nattali & Maurice, 1968).

D'Onofrio, Cesare. *Le fontane di Roma*, 3rd ed. (Rome: Romana Società, 1986).

Fassina, Silvano. "Roman capitals: Five itineraries in Rome," *Calligrafia*, no. 7/8 (Rome: Stampa Alternativa, 1994). Text in Italian. Reprint in English by LetterPerfect, 1997.

Horfei (Orfei), Luca. *Alfabeto delle maiuscole antiche romane di Luca Orfei* [c.1590] (facsimile). Introduzione di Armando Petrucci. (Milano: Edizioni il Polifilo, 1986).

Marzoli, Carla. *Calligraphy 1535–1885: A collection of seventy two writing-books and specimens from the Italian, French, Low Countries and Spanish schools*, introduction by Stanley Morison (Milano: La Bibliofila, 1962).

Stanley Morison, *Early Italian Writing Books, Renaissance to Baroque*, edited by Nicolas Barker (Verona: Stamperia Valdonega, 1990).

Mosley, James. "Trajan Revived," *Alphabet*, no. 1 (London, 1964), pp. 17–48.

Osley, A.S. *Luminario: An introduction to the Italian writing books of the 16th and 17th centuries* (Nieuwkoop: Miland Publishers, 1972).

Petrucci, Armando. *Public Lettering: Script, Power and Culture* (Chicago: University of Chicago Press, 1993). Translation by Linda Lappin.

in pietra e dal medesimo fatte intagliare in rame per mostrare la lettera antica Romana in diverse grandezze & compartimenti, con alcune cancellaresche corsive variate et altre maniere di lettere necess. (Various inscriptions by Pope Sixtus V, drawn on the stone by Luca Horfei da Fano, who has had them engraved on copper in order to show the antique Roman letter in different sizes and constructions, with some chancery cursives and other kinds of writing.) Some examples of the plates are shown here. "(See fig. 3 and p. 15, fig. 23.) It is worth recalling that Domenico Fontana, the architect who was responsible for the moving and re-erecting of the Vatican obelisk, published not only his account of the operation, *Della trasportatione dell'obelisco vaticano* (1590), but added a list of other architectural achievements of Sixtus V and gave the texts of the inscriptions that accompanied them.

Lastly, it should be recalled that Horfei's inscriptional work is not an isolated achievement but the beginning of a tradition. The name of Ventura Sarafellini is mentioned above; another lettering artist who gained a reputation not long afterwards, but about which we know too little, was Fabrizio Badesio, who was responsible for admired inscriptions in Rome; and some later calligraphers like Leopardo Antonozzi published models for inscriptional capitals in their writing books. I offered a summary of this work in a later and more detailed essay: "Giovan Francesco Cresci and the baroque letter in Rome," *Typography Papers* 6 (2005), pp. 115–55.

7 (*upper left*). Detail of the inscription at the base of the cupola of St. Peter's designed by Ventura Sarafellini, c.1605. The letters were the model for the font Pietra (1997) by Garrett Boge.

8 (*lower left*). Inscription in the ceiling of S. Carlo alle Quattro Fontane, Rome, 1640. The church, designed by Francesco Borromini between 1638 and 1641, is considered to be one of the preeminent examples of Baroque architecture in Rome.

Some Principal Sites for Baroque Lettering in Rome

Base and platform at top of Column of Marcus Aurelius, 1589
Platform at top of Trajan's Column, 1589
Base of the obelisk in Piazza di S. Pietro (St. Peter's Square), 1586
Base of the obelisk in Piazza di S. Giovanni in Laterano, 1588
Base of the obelisk in Piazza del Popolo, 1587
Base of the obelisk at Piazza Navona, 1651
Façade of St. Peter's, 1612
Inscriptions on exterior of S. Giovanni in Laterano, 1586 and 1735
Inscriptions on exterior of S. Maria Maggiore, 1587 and 1611
Façade of S. Sebastiano fuori le Mura, 1622
Façade of S. Maria della Pace, 1667
Ceiling of S. Carlo alle Quattro Fontane, 1640
Attic of Fontana d'Acqua Felice, 1589
Attic of Fontana d'Acqua Paola, 1612
Attic of Fontana di Trevi, 1735
Arco di Sisto V at Termini, 1585
Inscription on the Teatro delle Acque at the Villa Aldobrandini (in Frascati), 1605

BAROQUE INSCRIPTIONAL LETTER IN ROME 63

THE BAROQUE SET

GARRETT BOGE

HOW COULD A DESIGNER of letters not be enamored with the Baroque inscriptions of Rome? They are literally engraved into the fabric of the city—on its obelisks and monuments, the flooring and apses of its churches, and on the pediments and friezes of its monumental buildings. (See pp. 61–63.)

In 1995, I went to Rome for the third time. I was no longer a tourist; I was in search of classical Roman lettering. This I found in abundance, thanks to numerous guidebooks, especially Silvano Fassina's superb *Cinque itinerari per le strade di Roma* ("Roman Capitals, Five Itineraries in Rome") (1995). Classical Roman capitals were not only to be found in the ancient Forum, but they seemed to be everywhere in the city— and even in the surrounding countryside as at the ruins of Ostia Antica. Once one begins looking long and hard at inscriptions, the variations of design—the result of period, material, and purpose—become apparent. Thus began my infatuation with Roman letters.

I was following the trail of artists and designers from the Renaissance and later who appreciated the grace and proportions of the Imperial Roman letter, as canonized in the inscription of Trajan's Column. Yet time, place, and circumstance necessitates adaptation, and this is what was done so brilliantly as part of Pope Sixtus V's rebranding of Rome in the late 16th century. (See p. 60, fig. 3.) Seeking to surmount the pagan foundation of the city with his triumphant Christian imprint, classical Roman lettering was appropriated and recanonized with the "Horfeian" letter, created by Luca Horfei, the Pope's scribe. A poignant example is the Augustan obelisk in Piazza del Popolo on which two inscriptions by Horfei flank two 1st-century inscriptions carved in his Christianized "Trajan" style. [4, 5]

Because this style, so prevalent in Baroque Rome, was documented by Horfei himself in *Alfabeto delle maiuscole antiche romane* (1587), it was a prime candidate for digitizing as a typeface. The name "Pontif," a corruption of the Pope's moniker, seemed a natural title since the letter was tied to papal renewal of the city. Giovan Francesco Cresci, Horfei's mentor demonstrated a somewhat more delicate Christianized "Trajan" in his alphabet in *Il perfetto scrittore* (1570). (See p. 59.) It became the model for the Cresci font. The Biblioteca Nazionale Centrale Vittorio Emanuele II, in Rome, and The Newberry Library, in Chicago, provided both sources for digitizing.

The Pietro typeface, the third one in The Baroque Set, is based on a later and more exhuberant source—the frieze of massive six-foot tall mosaic lettering high above the floor running around the inside of the dome of St. Peter's. (See p. 63, fig. 10) Upon first seeing it circling hundreds of feet over my head, I immediately knew it should be a typeface. Its forms are solid and authoritative, and like so many of the visual elements in that grand basilica, designed to inspire awe. The Fabbrica di San Pietro, which administers and maintains the basilica, provided photos for digitizing. However, I realized that the true proportions (photographed straight on) did not carry the power and authority of the squatter foreshortened effect seen from the floor. So a second set of capitals, conforming to video stills shot from the basilica's floor, was captured and encoded in the font's lowercase position, serving as a "small caps" variant (fig. 1, lines 3 and 4).

All three original sources had tapered vertical stems, like architectural columns slightly broader at the base as favored by both classical and Renaissance designers. The decision to preserve this subtle effect, despite the low-resolution displays available in the early 1990s, was the correct one, both for its trueness to the source and for the fonts' intended use as display type. Another, not so subtle feature of the Pietra source, its curious bulbous serifs, was also faithfully preserved. [2] This detail, though mannered, shows the bold confidence of early 17th-century inscriptions and flaunts the font's Baroque pedigree.

Although Adobe's Trajan typeface had not yet achieved the dominance it now has in the design, advertising, and packaging fields, I felt even then that variations on the classical Roman capital theme, reflecting the nuanced differences of the Baroque age, should be available. The relative obscurity of The Baroque Set has not diminished my view. Indeed, there seems to be a an even greater need today for its three fonts as potential choices for those seeking a fresh alternative to Carol Twombly's ubiquitous design.

BMQRT
BMQRT
BMQRT
BMQRT

1 Comparison of key letters of the typefaces in The Baroque Set: Cresci, Pontif, Pietra caps, Pietra small caps.

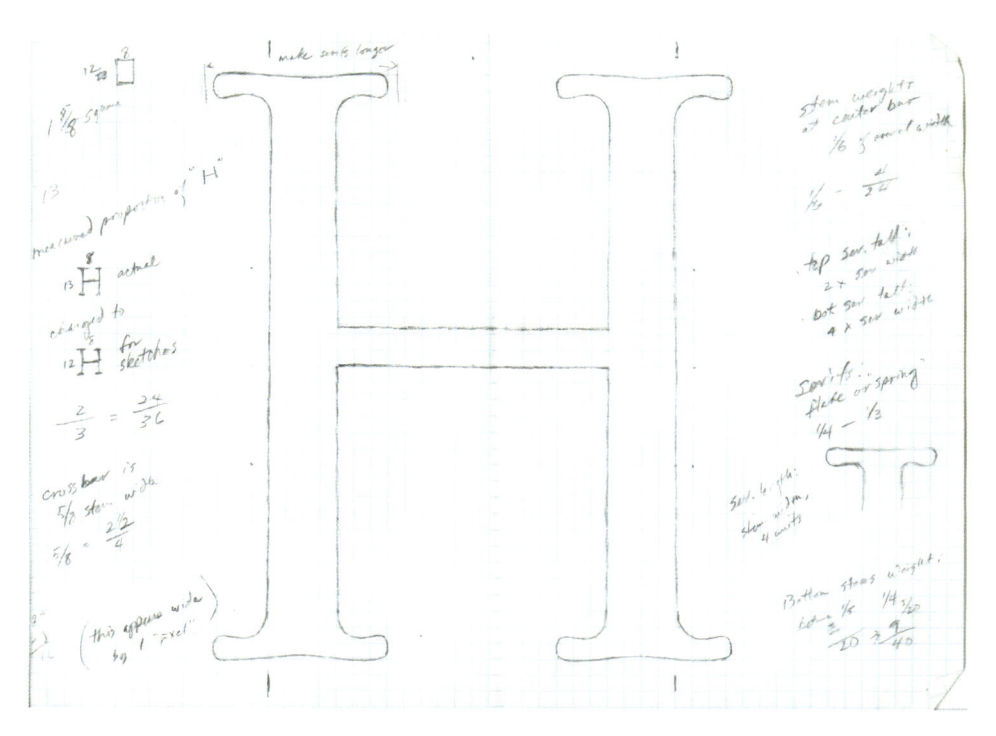

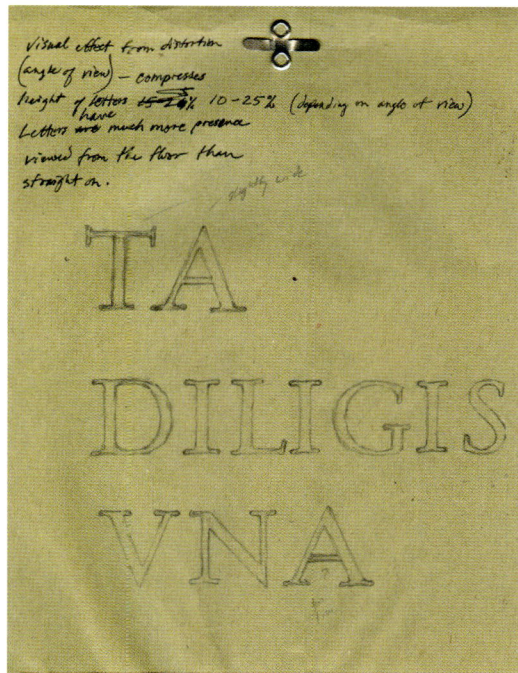

2, 3 Notes and sketches by Garrett Boge for Pietra, c. 1996.

4, 5 Left: one of the two Augustan inscriptions (1st century AD) on the obelisk in the Piazza del Popolo, Rome. Right: one of the two inscriptions by Luca Horfei on the same obelisk.

I FIND THE ROM
SO BEAUTIFUL T
INTELLECTUAL

Katharine Wolff

[THE TRAJAN INSCRIPTION] CAN BE REGARDED AS THE BEST BASIC FORM IN THE EVOLUTION OF OUR LETTERS. WE SHOULD STUDY AND ADMIRE THE GREAT BEAUTY OF THE INDIVIDUAL LETTERS, AND ALSO THE RHYTHM OF THEIR RELATIONSHIP.

Jan Tschichold

AN CAPS
HAT THEY DEFY
NALYSIS.

THE APPARENT SIMPLICITY OF THE ROMAN CAPITALS BELIE THEIR COMPLEXITY—THERE ARE FEW PLACES TO HIDE.

Jeremy Tankard

GOUDY'S INSCRIPTIONAL LETTERS

> "The curves in the Trajan capitals are not simple geometrical lines, but are carefully considered quantities which impart a character to the forms that no mechanical construction can possibly give. So far as we of today are concerned, the Trajan alphabet, in its spontaneity, is primal."

1 Detail of Frederic W. Goudy's hands as he draws the typeface Scripps College Oldstyle, 1941.

STEVE MATTESON

FREDERIC W. GOUDY WROTE THESE WORDs in 1925. It is this "primal" or "original" spirit that draws so many to study these ancient letters. And while Goudy undeniably imparted his own personality to his interpretations of historical letterforms, his epigraphic types seem to capture the very essence of the genre. He successfully modeled various styles of inscribed letters and infused their spirit into static type forms. [9, 10, 14, 15, 17] Classical inspiration came relatively late in Goudy's life. He spent his first thirty-odd years moving about the edge of America's frontier, before settling down in Chicago in 1889. His father had been a school superintendent and Goudy credits him for his unusually well-read youth. However, Goudy had little or no exposure to "art books" before his arrival in Chicago. It was not until 1910, during his first trip to Europe, that he saw Roman antiquities firsthand. That trip and one the following year, when he took rubbings of inscriptions, informed his lapidary sensibilities for the remainder of his life. [2]

Of Goudy's hundred or so typefaces, only four are modeled strictly on epigraphic letterforms: Forum (1911), Hadriano (1918), Record Title (1927) and Trajan Title (1930). The capitals in Goudy Oldstyle (1916), his best-known typeface, are clearly influenced by lapidary models as well. Each of these designs came about in a different manner, illustrating the various forms of inspiration that can lead to a new type design. Of each typeface, Goudy claimed that he did

2 Photograph by Goudy of unidentified Roman inscription taken during 1910 trip to Europe.

not "copy directly the exact makeup of each letter in a particular inscription," but instead captured the overall affect of the spirit imparted by the craftsmen who cut them. "Since, unfortunately I have no great knowledge of epigraphy," he wrote in *The Capitals from the Trajan Column at Rome* (1936), "nor opportunity to make accurate measurements of the actual letters, I rely mainly on an innate feeling for the forms of letters, on photographic reproductions, and a vivid recollection of the characters in place on the column where I studied them during a visit to Rome."

LETTERING

Goudy's lettering style was highly sought after during his years in Chicago—Marshall Field's, Gimbel's, and Kuppenheimer & Co. were just a few of his regular clients. [3] His own advertisement in the 1903 *Inland Printer* illustrates his characteristic, inked-in letterforms. [4]

After Goudy's visits to Europe, his approach to lettering changed. The advertisements for Peerless Automobiles show a significant shift in style to classically modeled capital letters. The refinement and proportions of the letters are distinctly Trajan-influenced, particularly the key letters *M* and *R*. [5]

3 (*top left*) Handlettered advertisement by Goudy for Marshall Field & Co., the Chicago department store. From The *Inland Printer* (vol. 30, no. 3, December 1902), p. 416

4 (*top right*) Handlettered advertisement by Goudy for his services as a graphic designer and lettering artist, 1903.

5 (*bottom*) Handlettered advertisement by Goudy for the Peerless Motor Car Company, 1910.

FORUM TITLE

Forum Title was designed in 1911 in a literal sprint of productivity surrounding the design of a book for the publisher Mitchell Kennerley (1878–1950). *The Door in the Wall*, a selection of H. G. Wells short stories, was the impetus for a new text typeface, Kennerley Oldstyle, that later brought Goudy worldwide acclaim. Goudy added a typeface with a lapidary quality for chapter headings, later naming it Forum Title. [7] Remarkably, drawings for both typefaces were completed within the same week.

Forum had its origins in the rubbings Goudy made the previous year in and around the Arch of Titus, in the Roman Forum. His first use of the rubbings were as inspiration for the lettering of the masthead of *The Forum*, a literary journal published by Kennerley from 1910 to 1916. [6] The lettering was further refined until 1911, when it became the Forum typeface. Goudy was quick to point out that while the typeface (caps, figures, and punctuation only) incorporated features of many inscriptions, it was not a replica of any one of them.

Forum Title is a lively design; the serifs and diagonal strokes reveal the brush-written letters underlying classical Roman inscriptions. Even Stanley Morison, often disdainful of Goudy's efforts, praised it. "It is a very handsome letter," he wrote in *On Typefaces* (1923), before delivering the predictable criticism, "completed, however, with a less satisfactory set of Arabic figures." Forum Title and Kennerley Oldstyle were extraordinary successes. [8] This was because of their beauty in execution and also because the time was ripe for new, original type designs based on classical ideals of proportion, balance, and harmony far from the wildly ornamental display types and attenuated Moderns characteristic of the 19th century.

HADRIANO

During his 1910 trip to Europe, Goudy made several rubbings of Roman inscriptions, most famously one in the Louvre. While his wife, Bertha, stood lookout for any guards, Goudy took rubbings from a 9' x 4' marble slab from the time of Hadrian: a large *E*, *P*, and *R*, and a smaller *I*, *A*, *N*, and *O*. [11] Eight years later he came across the rubbings and decided to design the missing letters in what he imagined "would be their harmonious form." The result was Hadriano, which embodies a distinctive style of lettering, even though its model was executed within three decades of the famous Trajan inscription. [10] (Hadrian was Trajan's successor and ruled from 117 to 138 AD.) The letters are heavier and less refined, and their widths are more regular than inscriptions in the Trajan vein. The typically narrow *E*, *F*, and *L* are more closely related to the width of *H* and *O* in Hadriano. The rubbing reveals an *A* with an exaggerated flourish at its apex and strong serifs on all letters, indicating that the broad brush, as per Father Edward M. Catich's theory, was clearly at work. These letters have more verve than many people associate with classical inscriptions. (This apex flourish can also be found in the calligraphy of 15th-century scribe Bartolomeo Sanvito—see p. 55.)

6 (*top*). Detail of masthead for *The Forum* (July 1910). Reproduced in *Typographica* No. 5 (Summer 1927).

7 (*bottom*). Detail from *The Door in the Wall* by H. G. Wells (New York: Mitchell Kennerley, 1911) showing the first use of Forum for chapter headings and Kennerley Oldstyle for the text. Goudy was responsible for the decorative initials in the book as well as its typography and design.

CHARACTERS APPEAR TO LOCK INTO ONE Another With A Closeness Common In Early Types But Not So Often Seen In Later-Day Creations. Serifs are strong and well defined and each letter is open and round. Although essentially a book letter, Kennerley Old Style has had more use as a face for publicity work. Regarded by many as one of the finest of Frederic W. Goudy's numerous type faces, Kennerley Old Style has enjoyed great popularity since it was first introduced. Although inspired by the Dutch types of $1234567890

8 (*top*). Detail from specimen of Kennerley Oldstyle.

9 (*left*). Goudy Title, a variant of Goudy Oldstyle designed by Morris Fuller Benton for American Type Founders, 1918. From *A Composite Showing of Goudy Types: A Pamphlet Supplementing the Specimen Book of 1923, Showing Important Additions to the Goudy Family* (1927).

THE GOUDY TITLE

SPECIALLY DESIGNED FOR THE AMERICAN TYPE FOUNDERS COMPANY BY FREDERIC W. GOUDY & CAST WITH MINIMUM AMOUNT OF SHOULDER AT THE BOTTOM OF THE LETTERS, PERMITTING LINES TO BE SPACED CLOSE TOGETHER

SPACE-SAVING TYPE

HADRIANO

HADRIANO IS UNIQUE IN THE ANNALS OF TYPE DESIGN. MR. GOUDY MADE A RUBBING FROM 3 LETTERS IN STONE, IN THE LOUVRE, PARIS. TO THESE 3 LETTERS HE ADDED THE BALANCE OF THE ALPHABET IN THE SPIRIT OF INSCRIPTIONS OF THE FIRST CENTURY A. D. · IT HAS NO PROTOTYPE ·

❖

A B C D E F G H I J K L M N
O P Q R S T U V W X Y Z &
QU 1 2 3 4 5 6 7 8 9 0 , - . ·

[24 PT.　　HADRIANO　　CAPS ONLY　　$6.75　　11A]

10 (*opposite*). Specimen showing of Hadriano. From *Typographica* No. 5 (Summer 1927).

11 (*above*). Rubbing by Goudy of Hadrian fragment in the Louvre, Paris. Made 12 August 1910.

12 (*below*). Constructed letter by Damiano da Moylle c.1480. From *The Architectural Record* (May 1928), p. 442.

RECORD TITLE

In 1927, Goudy was asked to create the title lettering for *Architectural Record*. He believed that monumental letters, commonly inscribed on buildings in the past, would make an appropriate typeface for an architectural magazine. He used a reprint of a treatise on classical letter design by Damianus Moyllus (Damiano da Moylle; now known as Damiano Moilli) from circa 1480 as a model for his alphabet. [12] (A facsimile edition of da Moylle's text, edited by Stanley Morison, was printed in 1927 following the discovery of a copy of da Moylle's *Alfabeto* the previous year.[1]) Goudy quickly found inadequate da Moylle's mathematical attempts to describe classical letters. "Beauty is too illusive [*sic*] to be snared by geometry," Goudy wrote. He noted that changes in their form had to be made "to fit them to modern eyes and uses; certain features had to be exaggerated or they would disappear in cutting, curves strengthened, stems and hairlines thickened or brought into greater harmony with each other."[2] As with other mathematically derived alphabets, such as those by Albrecht Dürer (1525) and Geoffroy Tory (1529), Goudy believed that the form of the letters, though accurate enough, lacked "feeling and the subtle, minute differentia that defy analysis that are inherent in the original."

In *The Elements of Lettering* he quoted Tory to indicate that even the theorists of geometrically constructed letters acknowledged the need for a "fudge factor":

> Now O you shall make this way in its square. Set in the square the diameter c. b. and bisect it in the point e., so that e. may form a middle point between the two points f. and g. which are to be your two centers; and from each let a circle be described touching two sides of the square; and where the circles cut one another, there with your hand you must shape the slender outline of the letter to a juster proportion.

Record Title is successful in its attempt to adhere to constructive formulae while retaining an organic spirit. "Harmony, grace, beauty and symmetry are secured by blending the fine strokes, stems and swells in their proper relations," Goudy wrote, "and not by merely combining the approximate geometric quantities." The flamboyant Q, typical of Goudy, is out of place; and the 2 and 3 are livelier than the other figures. Overall, it is a handsome alphabet that does honor to its inscriptional roots. [13, 14]

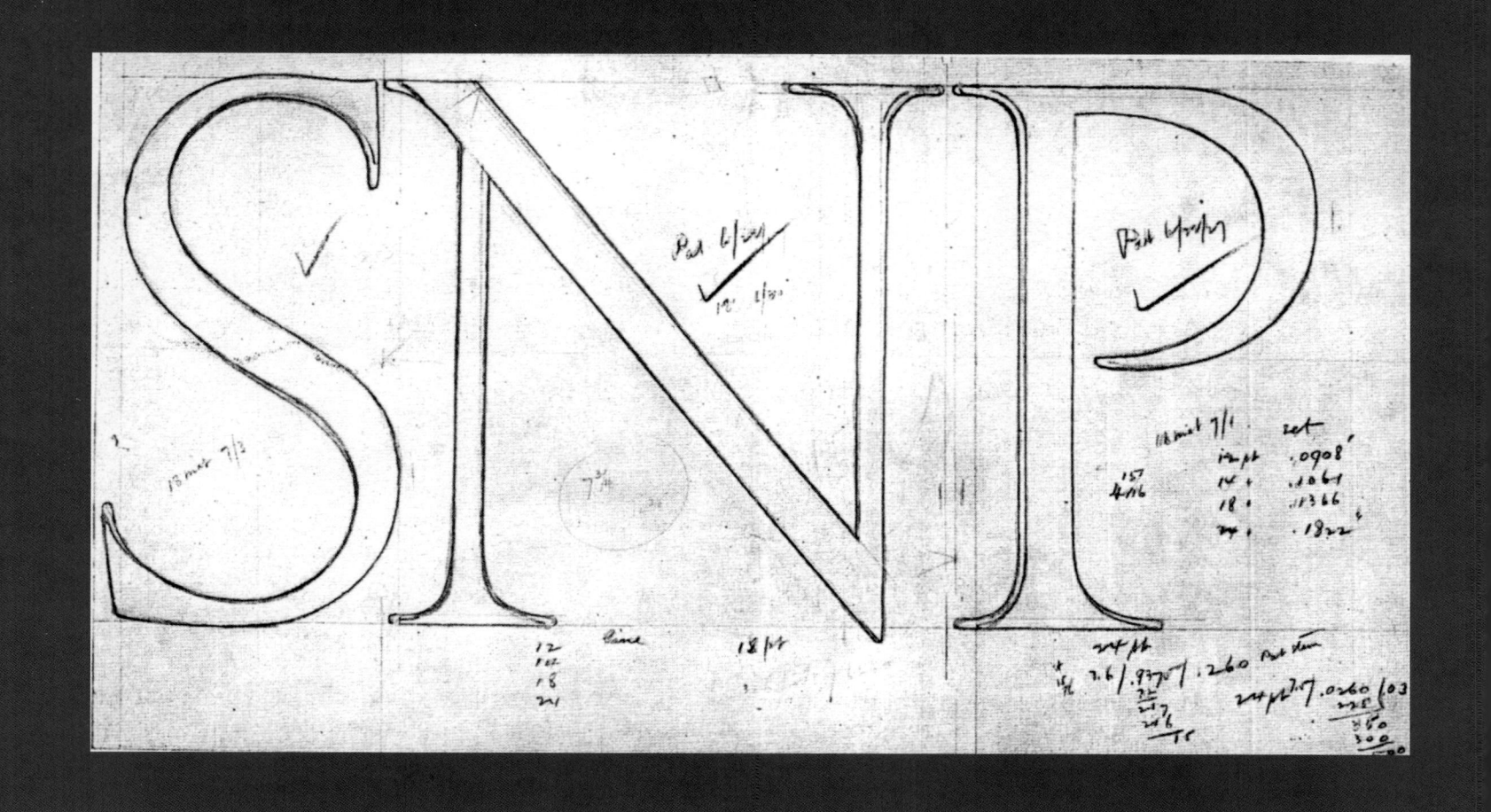

'RECORD TITLE,' A FONT OF MAJUS-
CULES OF CLASSIC FORM DESIGNED,
CUT AND CAST BY MR. GOUDY FOR
· THE ARCHITECTURAL RECORD ·
MCMXXVII

A B C D E F G H I J K L M N O P
Q R R S T U V W X Y Z &
: 1 2 3 4 5 6 7 8 9 0 ;

13 (*opposite, top*). Working drawing for Record Title typeface dated 22 June 1927. The letters (8") high were the basis for pantograph patterns. From *The Architectural Record* (May 1928).

14 (*opposite, bottom*). Showing of Record Title in *The Architectural Record* (May 1928).

15 (*below*). Showing of Trajan Title (1930). From *Typographica* No. 6 (1934). The *M* is unbalanced, reflecting Goudy's reliance on the inperfect cast of the Trajan Column in the Victoria & Albert Museum. Also note the design of *Q* and *U* intended to alleviate the need for a ligatured *QU* character.

TRAJAN TITLE

Trajan Title was the last (and arguably the best) of the purely epigraphic typefaces Goudy designed and it was among his favorites. In 1929, Goudy lettered the title page for the Limited Editions Club printing of *Rip Van Winkle* (1930). He based his forms entirely on the Trajan inscription in Rome. [15, 16] Satisfied with the result, he went on to draw the remaining alphabet when commissioned to create a list of 800 names of those who contributed to a community building project in Forest Hills, New York.

The letters are neither based on individual letters found in photos of the Trajan inscription, nor are they wholly fanciful renderings from Goudy's imagination. [17] Somehow, he conjured them from his memories of inscriptional lettering and managed to capture the spirit of the famous inscription as well as metal type would allow. Trajan Title is one of the typefaces whose drawings and matrices were lost in the fire that destroyed his studio in 1937.

THIS IS AN ORIGINAL FACE DE-
SIGNED WITHOUT FREAKY OR
FLAMBOYANT FEATURES.
ABCDEFGHIJKLMN
OPQRSTUVWXYZ
1234567890 & . , '

GOUDY TRAJAN TITLE

TRAJAN TITLE

CONTINENTAL
TYPEFOUNDERS
ASS'N, INC.

GOUDY TRAJAN TITLE, 48 PT.

2 THIRTY·SIX TRAJAN

GOUDY TRAJAN TITLE, 36 PT.

THIRTY PT·TRAJAN TITLE

GOUDY TRAJAN TITLE, 30 PT.

T·FLAVIVS VITALIT FECIT SIBI ET POSTERIS EIVS LIB·LIBERTA-

GOUDY TRAJAN TITLE, 24 PT.

L·TARQUITIO MARTIANO FILIO DVL- CISSIMO QUI VIXIT AN·VIIII·MENS·VI·

GOUDY TRAJAN TITLE, 18 PT.

TRAJAN TITLE IS A NEW ALPHABET OF CAPITALS
BASED ON THE LETTERS OF THE MONUMENTAL IN-
SCRIPTION AT THE BASE OF THE TRAJAN COLUMN

GOUDY TRAJAN TITLE, 14 PT.

ERECTED ABOUT 114 A.D., BUT THE DESIGN HAS NOT BEEN
SLAVISHLY COPIED. THE LETTERS ARE PRIMAL. STONE-CUT
FORMS ARE COMPOUND, BUILT UP A PART AT A TIME, & A

GOUDY TRAJAN TITLE, 12 PT.

ABDEGNRS

16 (*opposite*). Showing of Trajan Title (1930). From *Typographica* No. 6 (1934).

17 (*above*). Selected letters from the Trajan inscription drawn by Goudy. From *The Elements of Lettering* (New York: Mitchell Kennerley, 1922), p. 24.

18 (*below*). Showing of Forum Title (1910) combined with Goudy Oldstyle (1915). From *Typographica* No. 6 (1934).

```
AVRELIO
AVG · LIB
APHRODISIO
PROC · AVG
A · RATIONIBVS
S · P · Q · L
DEDIC · Q · VARINIO · Q · F
MAEC · LAEVIANO · AED
```

INSCRIPTION FROM BASE OF STATUE IN A ROMAN PALACE

TEXT TYPEFACES

If the Kennerley typeface won global recognition for Goudy, Goudy Oldstyle (1915) secured his posterity. This successful marriage of inscriptional capital letters with an Aldine-influenced minuscule formed the basis for most of Goudy's later typefaces. Goudy Oldstyle was so successful that ATF, under the direction of Morris Fuller Benton, extended the family. [9]

Although he was dissatisfied with American Type Founders' truncation of Goudy Oldstyle's descenders to fit their common line, Goudy felt confident that the overall design was solid and distinctive. In his *Elements of Lettering*, two very different inscriptional alphabets, Forum Title and Goudy Oldstyle, are used together harmoniously. [18]

B When examined carefully, several points of interest are to be found; first, the slight gradual increase in width of stem from top to bottom, the serifs merging gracefully into the stem outlines. Then note the serifs themselves as they flow by graceful movement into the body of the letter. The curve of the upper bowl at the top and the start of the lower bowl from the stem strongly indicates to my eye that the letter was *first* drawn or painted *on* the stone by a master writer who used a reed-pen or brush, which by its position in the hand would produce naturally just such a shape, a shape not indicated as the product of any cutting tool in the first instance, but a product easily gained by following the outlines of a written or painted original design.

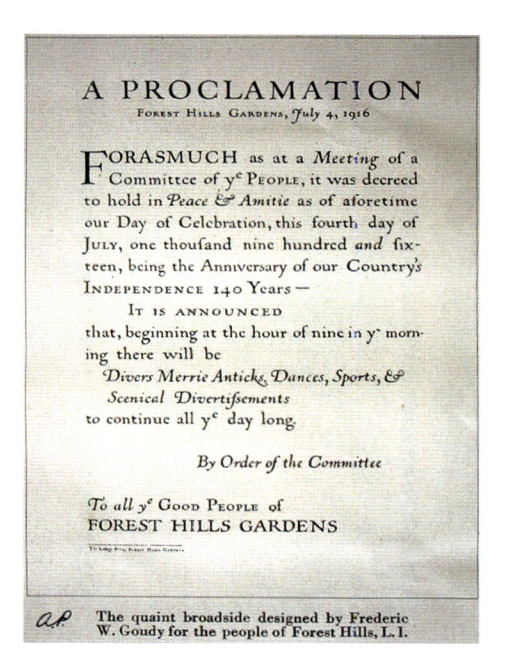

19 (*opposite*). Page from *The Capitals from the Trajan Column at Rome* (1936) showing Goudy's rendering of the Trajanic *R*. See "Father Catich and the Trajan Inscription," p. 25 for Goudy's rendering of the *B*.

20 (*above*). Broadside designed by Goudy for residents of Forest Hills Gardens, Queens, New York, 1916.

21 (*right*). Title page of *Why We Have Chosen Forest Hills Gardens for Our Home* (1915), a promotional booklet designed by Goudy and set in his Forum Title typeface.

Goudy and his wife Bertha were active in the new community of Forest Hills in the years 1913 to 1922. In addition to lettering for the community center already mentioned, they produced a promotional booklet called "Why We Have Chosen Forest Hills Gardens for Our Home" [20]. Forum Titling is featured prominently on the title page. Goudy also hand-lettered a whimsical Fourth of July flyer [19]. From these contributions to the neighborhood one can presume that Goudy's typographic talents were well known in the area. Thus, it is possible that his expertise was also employed in the creation of the World War I monument that stands in Flagpole Green between the two arms of Greenway Terrace. The inscription honors all of the local veterans who served in the war, including Goudy's son, Frederick [*sic*] T. Goudy. The inscriptional capitals are Goudy-esque in style with special ligatures (like *CT* and *ST*) for fitting difficult letter combinations.

BEYOND TYPE

In *The Alphabet, Elements of Lettering,* and *The Trajan Capitals,* Goudy drew and engraved several more variations of epigraphic letterforms with the intention of illustrating the proper spirit, power, and delicate balance of these influential exemplars. None was ever cast as type [16, 19]. These three publications, and the typefaces described, provide excellent examples for studying the most enduring principles of alphabet design.

Will Ransom, Goudy's former student and business partner in the Village Press, recalled Goudy's instructions for learning the Roman capitals: "Yes there are rules, and geometrical drawings by Dürer, and Tory and some of the Italians. Study them and copy them. You should know what has been done, and how, and why. But you will find that each one of those interpretations differs in details from all the others, which indicates that no particular form is the only correct one. Then lay them aside and forget them. They are foundation material only. Experiment with your own geometrical constructions if you must, but outgrow them, too. A human face, like a letter, has certain fixed elements arranged in relatively similar positions, but every portrait has its own peculiar characteristics."

1 *A Newly Discovered Treatise on Classic Letter Design, Printed at Parma by Damianus Moyllus circa 1480: Reproduced in Facsimile,* edited by Stanley Morison (Paris: At the Sign of the Pegasus, 1927).
2 George L. McKay, *A Half-Century of Type Design and Typography, 1895–1945, by Frederic W. Goudy,* 2 vols. (New York: The Typophiles, 1946).

FREDERIC W. GOUDY

/HITMOR
WILLIAM
TTSCHIEB
OUNG

22, 23 Details from *The Call to Overseas*, 1920, a monument to soldiers and sailors who fought in World War I, sculpted by Adolph Alexander Weinman. Located in Flagpole Green, Forest Hills, Queens, New York. Note the presence of Frederic T. Goudy, Goudy's son, in the honor roll.

Wood type Perpetua Titling. Reproduced at original size.

ERIC GILL'S CAPITAL LETTER

EWAN CLAYTON

BRITISH LETTERING ARTISTS have had a special relationship to classical Roman capitals for much of the last century and this has been particularly true for lettercarvers. At the root of this tradition, broadly characterized as a classical revival, lies the work of Eric Gill (1887–1940). By the mid-20th century, those who noticed the gradual demise of a British vernacular letter from the built environment regretted the dominance of "Trajan revived."[1] Yet if we look more carefully at the work of Gill and his legacy, we can see a complex story of influences and outcomes.

2 Drawing by Eric Gill for the gravestone of William Humble Ward, 2nd Earl of Dudley, 1933. This is an example of Gill's mature style, classical yet all his own. Ward was Lord Lieutenant of Ireland between 1902 and 1905, and the fourth Governor-General of Australia between 1908 and 1911. Patronizing and pompous, he was immortalized by James Joyce, who described his vice-regal cavalcade through Dublin in *Ulysses*.

3 (*above*). Roman capitals by Giovantonio Tagliente copied by Edward Johnston 8 November 1899 from *Alphabets* by Edward Strange (London: George Bell and Sons, 1895). (See also Tagliente's original letters on p. vi.)

4 (*below*). Inscription by Gill from *Writing & Illuminating, & Lettering* (1906) by Edward Johnston, plate XXIV.

In his *Autobiography*, Gill confesses that he was already "mad on letters" well before he went up to London, in April 1900, to be articled (the name for an apprentice in a profession rather than a trade) to the architectural practice of William Caroë.[2] As a young boy he had carefully copied the nameplates on the steam engines that shunted in the sidings below the family's house, in Brighton. Then, as a teenager, he was introduced to decorative lettering at the Chichester Art and Technical Institute.

Caroë required his articled clerks to carry out some form of extracurricular study. Rather than sign up for the customary art historical courses, Gill joined classes in monumental masonry and lettercarving at the Westminster Institute and also enrolled as a student at the London County Council Central School in Edward Johnston's classes on writing, illuminating, and lettering. Before joining Johnston's class, Gill had cut a number of inscriptions.[3]

It was through his classes in calligraphy that Gill made his first connection with classical Roman letters. At the time, Johnston's principal teaching hand was based on half-uncial letters, but he also taught a basic Roman capital that could be built up with pen or pointed brush. It is clear when comparing the surviving Johnston exemplar sheets with Gill's inscriptional work that Gill's idea of an essential Roman capital letter was formed here. Contrary to the common belief that Johnston's capitals were modeled on the letters on Trajan's Column, however, his handout of 9 November 1899 shows that his exemplar came from *Lo Presente* (1524), by the Venetian writing master Giovanni Antonio Tagliente.[4] [3] Subsequent sheets, dated November 1902 and December 1903, make it apparent that Tagliente's letters formed the basis for Johnston's teaching throughout the period that Gill studied with him.[5] It is from Johnston's rendering of Tagliente's capitals[6] that Gill acquired the beaked crossing on the apex of his *A* (see Johnston's sheets of 1902 and 1903), which characterized his letters until circa 1909, and the beaked serifs on his *N* and *M*, which he used all his life. From here also came the proportions of his letters: the wide *D*, the early large-bowled *P*, the narrow *X* and *Y*, and the elongated serifs that are a feature of his early carved forms. He gives full rein to these serifs in his later engraved and painted forms, a tendency that makes his engagement with sans serif letters in the late 1920s satisfyingly different.

Within three years Gill was showing promise in his understanding of the craft. He substituted as a teacher when Johnston traveled north to Scotland for his wedding, in late summer of 1903, and that same year he was elected to The Art Workers Guild as a letterer and signwriter. By then, drawn and painted lettering had become one of his specialties, as had inscriptions. In 1903, he designed a new fascia board for W. H. Smith, the stationery store, and this

ERIC GILL 87

5 (*top*). Eric Gill in front of the Trajan Column, 1906.

6 (*above*). Photograph by Gill of storefront in Rome, 1906.

work, which began with the store in Paris, gradually spread across stores throughout the United Kingdom. A year later, he was commissioned by Count Harry Kessler, the German private press owner, to draw title pages for an edition of classics in German to be published by Insel Verlag, of Leipzig. The series extended to eleven titles over a nine-year period. The lightweight letter Gill employed during these years is more at home in a drawn and painted medium than cut in stone, where extended serifs tend to disappear—even when colored with Gill's favored vermilion paint.

In title pages and inscriptions of this time, Gill's spacing (particularly the *IN* combination) feels uncomfortably close. He is still focused on the line; space can look after itself. Also noticeable in these early title pages and inscriptions is the steeply canted emphasis of *O*. It is the casualty of an over-enthusiastic reliance on the edged pen, which in Johnston's early Roman lettering is marginally steeper than in his later. We have here a phenomenon any teacher of lettering will recognize: idiosyncrasies in a teacher's exemplar become exaggerated in the student's work. Yet, this same year, 1903, sees the habit broken in the inscription that was eventually included in Edward Johnston's *Writing & Illuminating, & Lettering* of 1906. [4]

By 1906, Gill was ready for greater challenges. His business had grown to such an extent that he had taken on an assistant, 15-year-old Joseph Cribb. In the spring of that year he took his wife, Ethel, to Rome for a belated honeymoon. Gill's photograph album from the trip, now in the museum at Ditchling, in Sussex, shows him visiting Trajan's Column and photographing street signs and painted fascias. [5, 6] He spent his time "carefully looking at inscriptions ancient and modern…," as he later wrote, "from a lettercutter's and signwriter's point of view."[7] Many of the images are of classical letterforms more widely spaced than Gill had used heretofore—an approach he moves toward over the succeeding decades. One blurred photograph taken in the Basilica of S. Giovanni in Laterano shows the tomb of Cardinal Antonio Martino de Chaves of Portugal (1447), carved by Isaia of Pisa. The letters are Florentine sans serif in form. [7] James Mosley noted the similarity of an inscription by Gill from 1907, for the tomb of Irene Nichols in Ryde, on the Isle of Wight, to lettering such as this. (His main points of comparison are a round *G* and *E*, a high *M*, and an arched stem to the tail of *R*.[8]) He also points out an affinity between this inscription and a monument to the Marchese Spinetta Malaspina (second quarter of the 15th century) in the Victoria and Albert Museum, but originally from a vanished church in Verona. [8] The photograph from Rome is evidence of Gill's prior interest in these forms, but Mosley's essay contains an apt note of caution to any Gill scholar: "Gill was not historically minded, and his freedom from dependence on obvious models is not the least of the secrets of the appeal of his lettering at its best."[9] He was certainly capable, however, of absorbing influences.

Perhaps the most striking feature of the 1906 photograph album is that it shows classical letters from antiquity, the 16th century, and the 20th century as the public lettering of a civic society.

In 1906, Johnston's *Writing & Illuminating, & Lettering* was published. Gill helped Johnston with many of the practical aspects of putting the book together, and contributed to an appendix on lettercarving, which he had worked on since the late summer of 1904. His inscription (see fig. 4) was included as plate XXIV.

Gill had an intimate knowledge of Johnston's book and followed many of Johnston's recommendations in his own work, notably the advice on treatment of "the characteristic parts of a letter." These are the parts that distinguish one letter from another—Johnston gives the example of the leg of an *R*, the cross bar on *T*, the bottom stroke of *L*—and can properly be exaggerated. This, for Johnston, is a special form of decoration: "Rational exaggeration usually amounts to the drawing out or flourishing of tails or free stems, or branches—very often to the magnifying of a characteristic part."[10] We see this in much of Gill's early work.

It was Johnston who gave Gill his first lessons in wood engraving.[11] As Gill's inscriptional work took off and his use of assistants grew, it is in his engraving that we can find his more personal adventures in letterform. His 1908 Christmas card is crude, but progress is fast. Engraving is a halfway house between stonecarving, calligraphy, and painted lettering; it has the bite of the tool but greater momentum, leading to extensions and an exuberance of line when exuberance is sought. Just a

Edward Johnston (1872–1944) was a self-educated British calligrapher who began, in 1898, researching historical methods and practices of calligraphy and illumination in the British Museum. His mentors W. R. Lethaby, principal of the Central School, and Sydney Cockerell, former secretary to William Morris, ensured Johnston's studies were built upon the pioneering work of Morris himself. Johnston's main realization was that the edged pen, rather than a pointed nib, was the tool that had defined book hands down to the invention of printing. He made it his life's work to articulate the implications of this concept. His findings, edited by Heather Child, were published posthumously as *Formal Penmanship and Other Papers* (1971). Following his years at the Central School, Johnston moved with Lethaby to the Royal College of Art, in 1909, and taught there until the mid-1930s. Johnston was one of the architects of the 20th-century revival in calligraphy, along with Rudolf von Larisch (1856–1934), in Vienna, and Rudolf Koch (1876–1934), in Offenbach, Germany.

7 Detail of inscription on tomb of the Cardinal of Portugal, Maria de Chaves (d.1447) in S. Giovanni in Laterano, Rome sculpted by Isaia da Pisa. Note the *R* with curved leg in ROME.

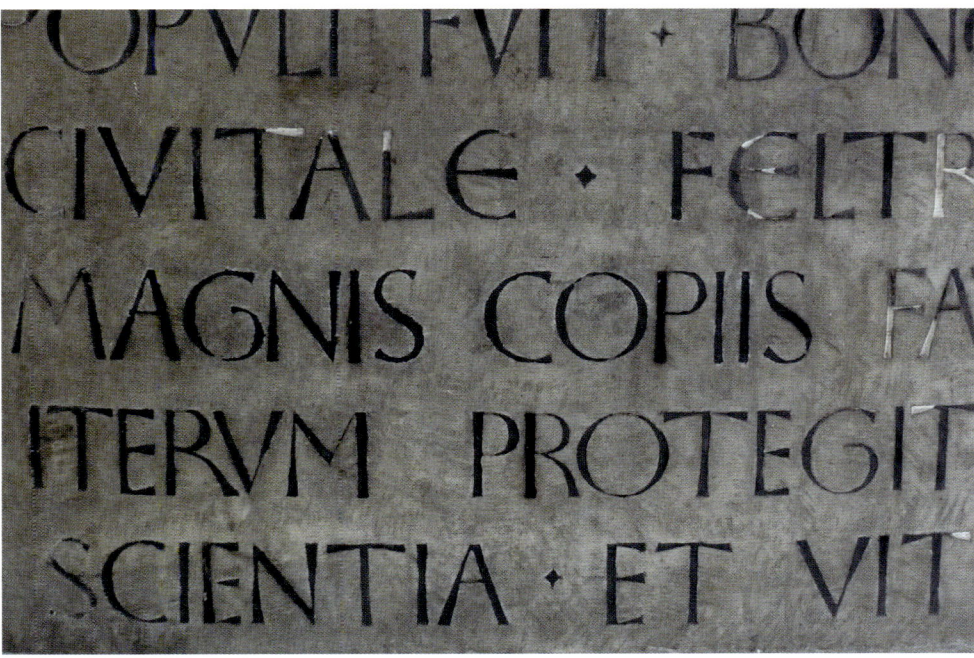

8 Detail of inscription at the base of the Monument to Marchese Spinetta Malaspina (c.1430–1435) attributed to Antonio da Firenze. Note the *M* in ITERVM and the *R* in PROTEGIT.

ERIC GILL 89

DIE ODYSSEE
NEU INS DEUTSCHE ÜBERTRAGEN VON RUDOLF ALEXANDER SCHRÖDER
DREIZEHNTER BIS VIERUNDZWANZIGSTER GESANG

9 Lettering by Gill for title page of *Die Odyssee* (Weimar: Cranach-Presse, 1910).

year after the rough-cut Christmas card, Gill's ex libris for Isabella Hildebrand is a confident display. [10] We see here for the first time the characteristic drooping *D* (a feature of his handwriting), extended serifs on *L* and *E*, and a sloping italic. By 1910, Gill had become sufficiently confident in his engraving technique to suggest the medium to Count Kessler for the title page to his Cranach Press Homer. (Compare fig. 9 to fig. 11.) He believed it would bring a livelier look. He designed the forms with the brush and then had them photographed onto the boxwood block. The cutting rendered the letters with sharper angles. With this in mind, Gill had chosen a different model to follow than Tagliente's capitals. The tapered stems of the arms of his *E*, the high center bars on *M*, and the thin slab serif on most terminals call to mind the versal letters of the Benedictional of St. Aethelwold (London, BL Add. MS 49598), a 10th-century manuscript that Johnston used for teaching pen-made Roman capitals.[12] Copies of the manuscript had become available through the plates and line blocks reproduced in *Writing & Illuminating, & Lettering*, as well as Johnston's class handouts.[13] From this experiment a new family of engraved forms developed. The letters had straight stems and thin slab serifs, forms we see on the Hammersmith Bakery bag he designed in 1915 (fig. 12) and ultimately implicated in Gill's personal typeface Joanna, used by the Hague and Gill Press in the 1930s. Forever after, even on Gill's forays into the more classical Roman capital, there can appear a slight turn-out to the serifs on the curved letters *C*, *G*, and *S* that comes from the pen-made versal form.

From 1913 onward, a new *U* shape (a unified curve rather than one that branches from a stem) makes an appearance in Gill's work, first in the wood engravings for Kessler and then fairly consistently in other engraved work, though not always. It remains interchangeable with the branched *U* in stone inscriptions until the end of his life. The *U* differs from the shape of the *U* in Caslon Old Face by having both sides as weighted stems rather than the left side only. A sample of Caslon had been reproduced in Johnston and Gill's *Manuscript and Inscriptional Letters* (MIL), a portfolio of instruction sheets issued in 1909. In the carved capital alphabet that Gill made for the portfolio, we see the introduction of an *E* with a shorter central arm, a Caslon feature. Caslon is infiltrating into the possibilities Gill can imagine for letterforms. The portfolio also sees a strengthened emphasis on the Trajan inscription; it includes Gill's own hand-drawn rendering of these letters and a statement that they can be considered "the root form of western lettering."[14] But the only additional trace of this renewed influence, over and above the forms Gill had already developed from Johnston's Tagliente-based model, is a smaller bowl to the *P* (which was long-lived) and a pointed top to the capital *A* (not long-lived). As Gill would write in his *Essay on Typography*, "while we may remember Trajan lovingly in the museum, we must forget all about him in the workshop" (p. 58). Gill is indeed casting his eye more widely and on Plate 16 of MIL, which shows his painted capitals, he comments, "The writing on the doorways in any of the Inns of Court is an admirable example of right method and good style." [13]

Caslon became a recurring influence on Gill's forms over the next few years. As the favored type for many British private presses, it also became the type that Gill's onetime neighbor Hilary (Douglas) Pepler began to employ at his newly acquired press, in Hammersmith, in 1915.

The brush writing of Plate 16 introduces a more weighty appearance to Gill's letters—similar to that of Caslon's type. This weightier letter is consolidated in the inscriptions for the Stations of the Cross of Westminster Cathedral (1914–18). Despite this consolidation in the forms of the letters, the Stations show surprising irregularities in the scale and placement of the inscriptions along the lower pediment across the fourteen tablets.

Plate 15 of MIL shows a raised alphabet, which, though based on the essential forms of Gill's Roman capitals, includes a pointed *A* and *N* as in the Trajan inscription. These letters have a more vernacular feel to them, and in certain earlier inscriptions Gill has allowed these letters to run together. [14] They are reminiscent of some of the tombstones of Sussex iron masters, themselves originally derived from techniques for carving in wood and casting in sand.

In 1907, Gill moved his family down to Ditchling, in Sussex. They were followed by the Johnstons, in 1912, and the Peplers, in

10 Ex libris designed by Gill for Isabella Hildebrand, 1907.

11 Lettering by Gill for title page of *Menschliche Komödie* by Honoré de Balzac (Insel Verlag, 1908).

ERIC GILL 91

12 Design by Gill for Hampshire House Bakery bag label, 1915.

ABCDEFGHIJK LMNOPQRSTU VWXYZ

13 Plate 16 (Roman Capitals—Example of Letters for Sign-Writing) from *Manuscript & Inscriptional Letters* by Edward Johnston and Eric Gill (London: John Hogg, 1909).

14 Plate 15 ("Raised" Letters—Capitals & Numerals) from *Manuscript & Inscriptional Letters* by Edward Johnston and Eric Gill (London: John Hogg, 1909). Carved by Gill in Hopton Wood stone.

ERIC GILL

1915. Pepler brought his Stanhope press with him, to try to earn his living from printing. In 1917, Gill began to supply him with initials for his books and pamphlets. A year later, he cut a series of initials in wood that are almost direct renderings of Caslon so that Pepler had some larger sizes of letters to use. He did narrow some of the letters (*D*, *G*, *L*, *M*, *T*, *X*, and *Z*), and kept his own more open form of *S* and the *U* weighted equally on both stems.[15] He also retained the dished serif at the apex of *A*, a shape we see in some of his engravings in the early 1920s. It is a feature he subsequently introduced into his type and the initials for the Golden Cockerel Press. The form saw its full flourishing across the alphabet in his headings for *The Four Gospels*, of 1931.

In 1915, Gill was offered the commission, jointly with Edward Johnston, to design a new block-letter typeface for the London Underground. He refused the work because of his prior commitment to finishing the Stations of the Cross. But in the early 1920s, a slim, sans-serif form makes its first appearance in his work—again, the innovation begins in his engravings. The 1922 bookplate for Thomas Lowinsky[16] has a Florentine feel to the letters: there is a high-waisted *R* with arched tail, an *M* with raised vertex that had appeared in his work from 1914 onward, and a palmate *Y*. [16] The same year also saw David Jones's first full year at Ditchling, and this bookplate was engraved by Gill to one of his designs. It is a seminal piece for both artists. The lettering is a departure for Gill, yet it also has something of the flavor of Jones's later lettering. It includes the introduction of a looped, double-bowled *E* that would become a feature of Jones's painted and engraved forms. The sans serif letterform is used again the following year in a bookplate for the bibliographer James Comly McCoy. From then on, a sans serif letter became a regular visitor to Gill's engravings, seen again in engravings from 1926 and 1927. It was during those years, when Gill had moved to the greater seclusion of Capel-y-ffin in the Black Mountains of Wales, that Gill used a block-letter sans serif for signs around the property, for a fascia board he painted for the bookseller Douglas Cleverdon,[17] and for notices developed for the Army and Navy Store in London. It was a time for experimentation. The engraved block for the chaliced ordination card for Gill's friend Desmond Chute

(1927) is particularly innovative. [15] The *O* is pointed, a shape Johnston had used in his calligraphy for some years, but in this case it appears in a capital alphabet and it affects the other letters, notably the *D*. These are narrow, lightweight versal-like letters. The pointed *O* makes an occasional appearance in Gill's carved lettering[18] and is subsequently featured in a long inscription within the creation initials in *The Four Gospels*.

An inscription of 1925 for a memorial to the painter John Singer Sargent[19] shows how strong Gill's inscriptional capitals became, growing in weight and confidence. [17] The flat-topped *A* gives strength to the form,[20] as does the unaccented weighting, a classical capital with a modern feel. However, the greater achievement in these years is probably the consolidation of Gill's lowercase romans rather than the capitals. It was this lowercase that drew him into type design—the preoccupying venture of the late

1920s. In his own imagination, and those of his assistants, the "house style" of capitals and lowercase romans had now settled down; there were no weak parts, few idiosyncrasies (barring the lowercase *r*), and no exaggeration of parts of forms. So, in 1925, when Stanley Morison, the type advisor to the Monotype Corporation, wanted to introduce a newly commissioned face into their existing program of type revivals, Gill was an obvious choice. [18] In 1927, having seen the drawings for Cleverdon's sans, Morison commissioned a further type, a sans serif, known today as Gill Sans. [19] These typefaces grew from the workshop practice of the previous decade and from his friendship with Johnston,[21] whose type for the London Underground had created the precedent for Gill Sans.

"The central problem in a type manufacturing system is communication between the parties," writes Richard Southall in

(2005). "The client has to make clear to the designer the requirements the new design is expected to fulfill. The designer has to convey to the producer the appearance the new types are to have. The producer, in consultation with the designer, has to ensure that the visual attributes of the character images the manufactured types give rise to will realize the appearance specifications the designer had in mind." In these circumstances, Gill's types took several years to evolve. Perpetua (Monotype Series 239), with the roman and italic together in one matrix case, was finalized only in March 1932. Gill, with his love of argument, lack of boundaries, and authoritarian approach to relationships, was not always best equipped to get the most from this negotiated design process. That Perpetua and Gill Sans have served the test of time is largely due to the modifications that Monotype's drawing office made during the design and manufacturing process.

Gill's third typeface, a design for Robert Gibbings's Golden Cockerel Press, originated in 1928 as a type made to work with the heavier line and black areas of wood engravings. [20] During Gill's time at Ditchling, the St. Dominic's Press had conducted experiments in bringing type and engraved block into visible association. In *A Child's Rosary Book* (1924), Pepler and Jones produced pages that worked as one unit of text and image, the type coming right up to the edge of the block. Now Gill had a chance to make a type of his own for that purpose. He had been working with Gibbings since 1924, and in Chaucer's *Troilus and Criseyde* (1927) Gill had cut loose with illustrations, titling, borders, and initials engraved for the purpose.[22] This was followed by *The Canterbury Tales*, issued in four parts from 1929 to 1931. Both Chaucer books are striking displays of lettering integrated with illustration in a classical typographic vein. The Golden Cockerel type, weightier than Gill's work heretofore, shows him reaching toward his belief that high contrast between thick and thin was not necessary in roman capitals; indeed, many historical Roman capitals lack such contrast.

The contract with Gibbings had originally required Gill to design type exclusively for his press. Gill circumvented this in typically agile fashion when working for Monotype by casting himself as a typographic advisor to the company, who would create concepts for others to carry out. There was a grain of truth to this: the Golden Cockerel type, cast by H. W. Caslon in 1929, was the first that Gill himself had overseen from first drawings to the final casting.

The year 1930 was critical for Gill. Two years earlier he had moved back from isolation at Capel to Pigotts, a farmhouse high on the Mendips in Buckinghamshire. He was once again in a maelstrom of activity—and definitely out of monastic seclusion. On the type design front he was continuing to be involved with designs for Perpetua; he had recently concluded a Perpetua Greek and began working on a new italic. He was still involved with the Golden Cockerel type, and had recently completed Gill Sans and Solus,

15 (*opposite*). Ordination card designed by Gill for Rev. Desmond Chute, 1927. Wood engraving.

16 (*this page*). Ex libris designed by David Jones for Thomas Martin Frances Esmond Lowinsky, 1922. Wood engraving by Gill.

ERIC GILL 95

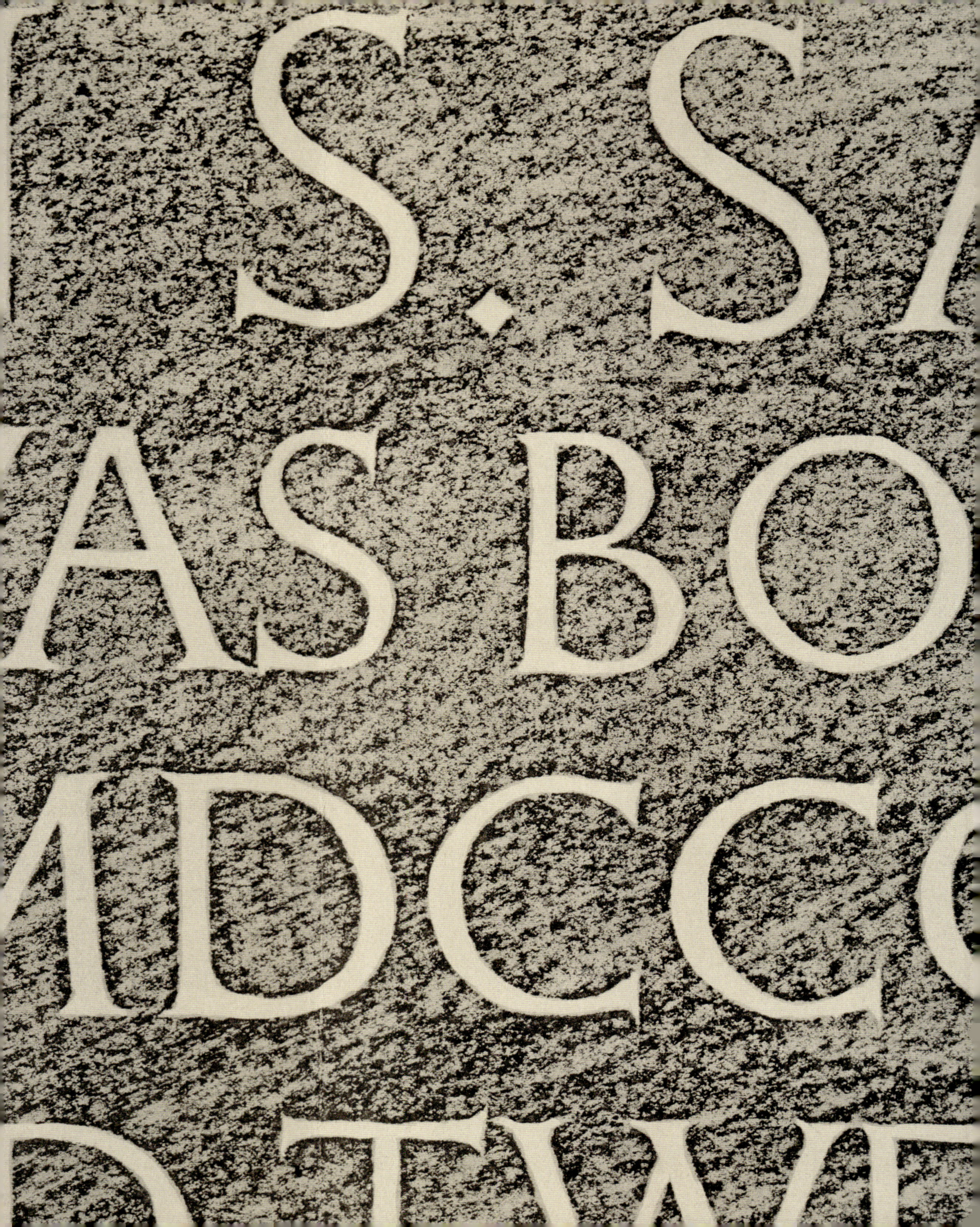
S · S
AS BO
DCC

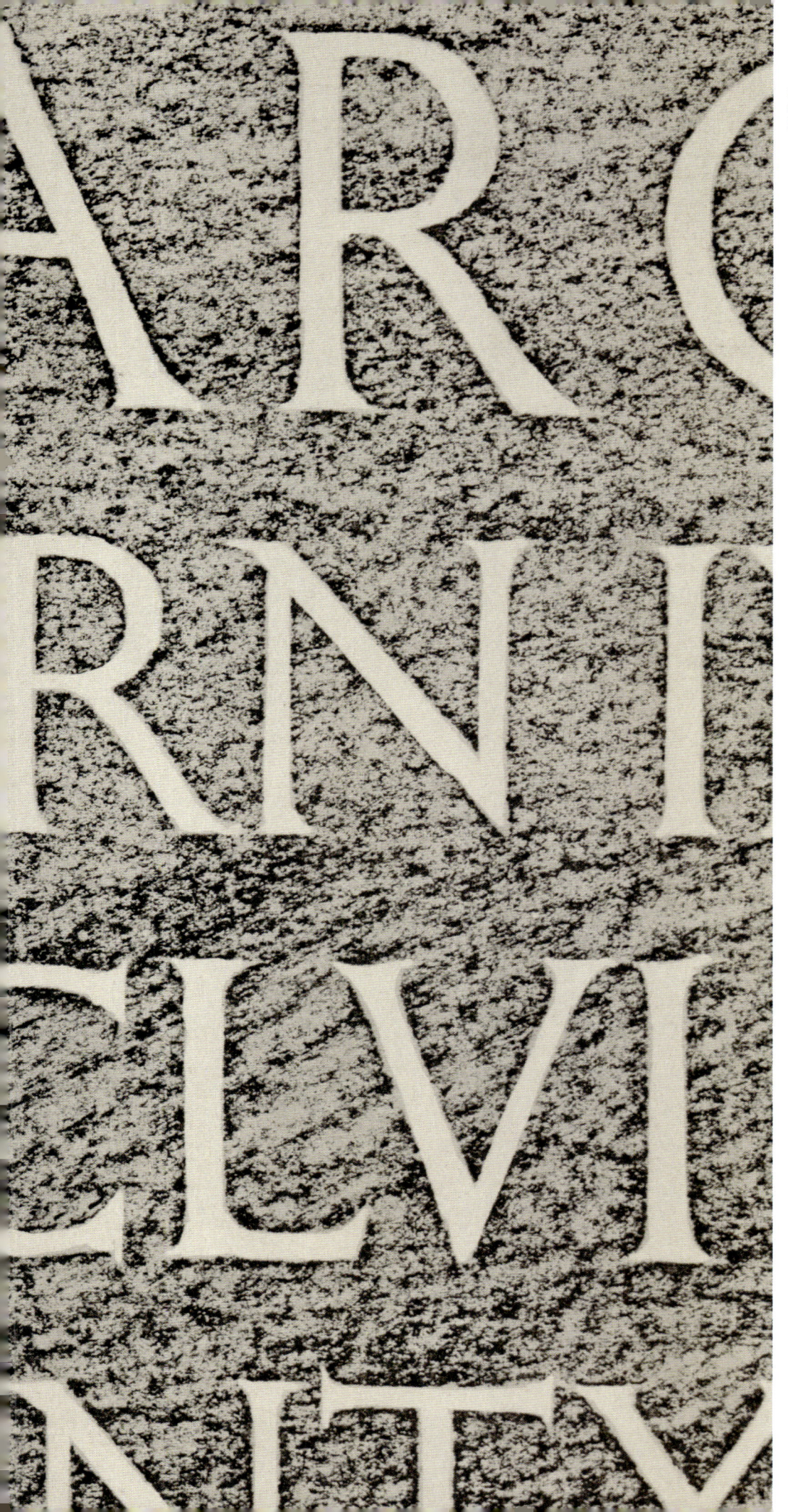

17 Detail of rubbing of inscription carved by Gill for memorial to John Singer Sargent, 1925. From *The Fleuron* No. 7 (1930).

ABCDEFG
HIJKLMN
OPQRSTU
VWXYZ

18 Perpetua Titling (Monotype Corporation, 1928).

ABCDEFGHIJKLMNO
PQRSTUVWXYZ

19 Gill Sans capitals (Monotype Corporation, 1928), early version with splayed *M*.

ABCDEFG
HIKLMN
OPRSTUV
WXYZJQ

20 Golden Cockerel Press Initials (Golden Cockerel Press, 1928).

ERIC GILL 99

MWHKT
CGDSEB

a subtle and light slab serif type that never achieved success. He was also finishing up Joanna, a new typeface destined for the commercial press that he subsequently set up at Pigotts with his future son-in-law, René Hague. It is the fourth of Gill's successful typeface designs. [21] Like Solus of the previous year, it has its roots in his wood-engraved work of the war years.

Robert Harling was the first to notice the family likeness among most of Gill's types. [22] The Golden Cockerel Type is Perpetua "expanded and rounded." Monotype Solus has such "obvious Perpetua parentage" in its smaller sizes that "most readers would probably be unaware of differences" (p. 52). Across these forms (and including Pilgrim, originally named Bunyan, of 1933–1934), "the differences are subtleties, and it was in the sensitive and judicious control of such subtleties that Gill showed his true skill as a maker of alphabets, for it is far easier to design an altogether novel *A* than to refine

the authority of the Trajan initial."

In his personal life Gill was entering more choppy waters in these years. One morning, in September 1930, he was found by his daughter Petra wandering lost in the workshop yard. Shockingly, Gill had lost all memory of where, and who, he was. A stroke was ruled out; the cause appeared to be psychological. Today we call such episodes a "fugue," a loss of identity brought on by some kind of personal trauma. Gill was hospitalized, and his condition perplexed his doctors and friends. For six weeks death seemed a possibility, and from that time onward he was never really physically well again. But it was then, from his hospital bed, that Gill began to dictate his first substantial book, *An Essay on Typography*, with its picture of two worlds split apart because each answered to fundamentally different motives. On the one hand there was the world of business, where avarice (read "desire") ruled, and on the other the

RRRR

21 (*above*). Showing of Joanna capitals (Monotype Corporation, 1931). Several letters have been "ganged up" to save space: *E* and *F*; *I*, *H*, and *K*. They are not ligatures. From *The Letter Forms and Type Designs of Eric Gill* by Robert Harling (London: Eva Svensson and the Westerham Press, 1976)

22 Comparison of *R* in Gill's typefaces. From left to right: Gill Sans, Golden Cockerel, Perpetua, and Golden Cockerel Initials.

JJXZYN

PR¶ÆŒ

world of the free craftsman, the home and family where "reason" reigned. In the essay Gill acknowledges their co-existence—he had, in David Jones's phrase, at last "made space for the warring factions"—but he was reaching toward something else. The essay has a slow-burning fuse, which detonates in an additional, final chapter in 1936, coincidentally a year in which he had a very brief recurrence of memory loss. The second edition of this essay ends paradoxically: "Lettering has had its day.... The only way to reform modern lettering is to abolish it."

When much of a lifetime's preoccupation has been with making letters, this is an extraordinary end point. The statement was not wholly negative, however; Gill was suggesting an alternative, shorthand, in which the correspondence between shape and sound is close. Gill subsequently experimented with carving a shorthand inscription in stone.

If we read this resolution to *An Essay on Typography* as a personal statement rather than as a prescription, it could be understood that, as in the structure of the argument of the book as a whole, Gill's subterranean self (he would have said his "soul") had made a diagnosis of his condition and was drawing him into better balance (his Dominican friends would have said a greater "grace"). Typically, Gill had sought to overcome historical complexities by simply abolishing them, but now he had become aware not only of a lack, but of something new. In short, movement must be added to strict form: the embodied, the gestural to the geometric; the response in the present moment to the eternal verities—in a lyrical partnership. Gill usually set up a move that was too radical to make—the abolition of the Roman alphabet. Yet even in the old forms, renewed movement crept in. A series of seemingly one-off experiments that peppered his final decade, often dismissed as random and eccentric, now appear to have a common theme. Apart from the late and commercially unsuccessful typefaces Aries and Bunyan/Pilgrim, which trod old ground, Gill's new ventures were types that involved a different relationship between form and movement. The letters in the *Four Gospels* stand on tiptoe, in tableaux like those the family used to enact with the guildsmen at Ditchling under Pepler's direction, and figures weave through them (figs. 23, 24). The weighty Jubilee (1933–1934) revisited the influence of the pen in letterforms. Gill Floriated, from 1936, picked up an experiment from 1930 resulting in a floriated capital typeface in which the lines of the letters stretch, arch, round out, and branch. [25] This is Gill's Roman capital alphabet literally coming alive with movement—a flame of organic growth—rather different in application to Johnston's notion of acceptable exaggeration. Gill also designed a Hebrew font and an Arabic font. As typographer, he was lured into a new kind of life. In wood engravings, for the first time, he began to engrave a written lowercase, a cursive writing, rather than carefully drawn forms. His inscriptions at last gained felt space, as in the tablet for Lady Ottoline Morrell, the large-scale carving for the League of Nations, in Geneva, and the tombstone for Gertrude Harris and her husband at Little Compton, Gloucestershire, where line and space operate as one. [26] Line no longer carves out or into space but sits in it. And finally, it was the apprentices from this post-1930 period who successfully carried forward Gill's vision for letter carving, while able to adapt and change in their own work. Although Gill's life was cut short by illness in November 1940, the last decade of his life saw him moving toward a new kind of balance between line and movement, a new space, a blending of reason and desire. Even though he was clouded by depression and increasing disillusion, "something" was voyaging on, the same something that, despite a flawed inheritance, had reached toward images of integration throughout his life. An integration he saw in the ground plan of the town of Chichester when compared with Brighton, in the community of Salies-de-Béarn in the foothills of the Pyrenees, and now in the mid-1930s, in Jerusalem "the Golden." His 1934 visit to the Holy City profoundly affected him, stirring him to a new commitment to his Blakean vision of heaven built in England's pleasant land.

23 & 24 Two chapter openings from *The Four Gospels* (Golden Cockerel Press, 1931) designed and engraved in wood by Gill.

25 Gill Floriated (Monotype Corporation, 1936).

26 (*below*) Inscription carved by Gill for tomb of Gertrude Harris at Little Compton, Gloucestershire, 1938.

1. See Nicolete Gray, *A History of Lettering* (Oxford: Phaidon, 1986), p. 202; James Mosley, "English Vernacular: A Study in Traditional Letter Forms," *Motif* 11 (winter 1963/64), pp. 3–55, also "English Vernacular" on James Mosley's blog http://typefoundry.blogspot.co.uk/2006/02/english-vernacular.html (accessed September 23, 2013).
2. Eric Gill, *Autobiography* (London: Jonathan Cape, 1940), p. 88.
3. See www.wilfrid.com/images/chichester/chi_cath_gill_hiscock.jpg
   A memorial in Chichester Cathedral for the organist Percy Hiscock (No. 2 in Evan Gill's inventory of his brother's inscriptions) shows Gill working with squat capitals with widely flaring stems, typical of the work of monumental masons of the day.
4. See Central Saint Martins MIS 22.2 at www.csm.arts.ac.uk/museum/object.php?objectid=1368
5. It appears that Gill studied with Johnston from sometime after April 1900 to 1903, when he acted as substitute teacher. By May 1902, they were sharing rooms in Lincoln's Inn Fields.
6. Johnston first saw Tagliente's capitals in E.F. Strange, *Alphabets* (1895), which he bought while living in Edinburgh and whose plates he copied as his first introduction to calligraphy. After he had moved to London, he consulted a copy of Tagliente's work in the British Museum. Johnston would make further use of Tagliente when he based his Cranach Press italic type on his forms.
7. Gill, *Autobiography*, p. 159, n. 1.
8. "Eric Gill's R: The Italian Connection" at http://typefoundry.blogspot.co.uk/2009_12_01_archive.html (accessed 23 September 2013).
9. Mosley's essay contains an annotation relevant to anyone making a study of Gill's letters: "Gill was not historically minded, and his freedom from dependence on obvious models is not the least of the secrets of the appeal of his lettering at its best."
10. Edward Johnston, *Writing & Illuminating, & Lettering*, 2nd ed. rev. (London: J. Hogg, 1908), p. 252.
11. 20/21 November 1906, recorded in both Gill's and Johnston's diaries.
12. The same manuscript served more recently as the model for the capitals in Carol Twombly's Charlemagne and Jovica Veljović's Silentium Pro.
13. Johnston, *Writing & Illuminating, & Lettering*, figs 80, 166. Gill also owned reproductions of this manuscript.
14. Class handouts produced by Johnston for a series of lectures at Leicester School of Art in 1907 also show him producing a hand-drawn alphabet of outline letters copied from Trajan's Column.
15. See, e.g., "Camouflage of Ships," a poster for the Groupil Gallery made in 1918 using Gill's letters for the gallery's name. www.iwm.org.uk/collections/item/object/8805 (accessed 18 January 2012).
16. "...who produced imaginative paintings and illustrations inspired by classical mythology but modern in feeling," Monica Bohm-Duchen, *Thomas Lowinsky* (London: Tate Gallery, 1990).
17. Gill, *Autobiography*, p. 229.
18. A striking example is the now-lost Resurrection Gravestone (1928) No. 180 in Judith Collins, *Eric Gill: The Sculpture* (London: Herbert Press, 1998).
19. A rubbing of the inscription was reproduced in Paul Beaujon [Beatrice Warde], "Eric Gill: Sculptor of Letters," *The Fleuron* 7 (1930).
20. The flat-topped *A* that became a feature in Gill's work from 1913 onward can be seen in an example from Emil Hübner, *Exempla Scripturæ Epigraphicæ Latinæ* (Berlin: G. Reimer, 1885), reproduced in Johnston's *Writing & Illuminating, & Lettering*. Sydney Cockerell claimed he was the first to introduce Hübner to Gill.
21. Its heyday had been the period up to 1917. Gill shared rooms with Johnston in Lincoln's Inn Fields from the spring of 1902 until Johnston's marriage the following year. From 1917, however, there was a slight distancing after Mrs. Johnston fell out with Gill and banned him from their house on Ditchling Common at Hallets. Eventually the Johnstons moved from Ditchling Common back to the village.
22. The working method that Gibbings and Gill evolved was for Gibbings to send Gill the proof pages on which Gill drew directly before transferring the design to a block, which Gill then freely engraved, keeping a freshness throughout the process.

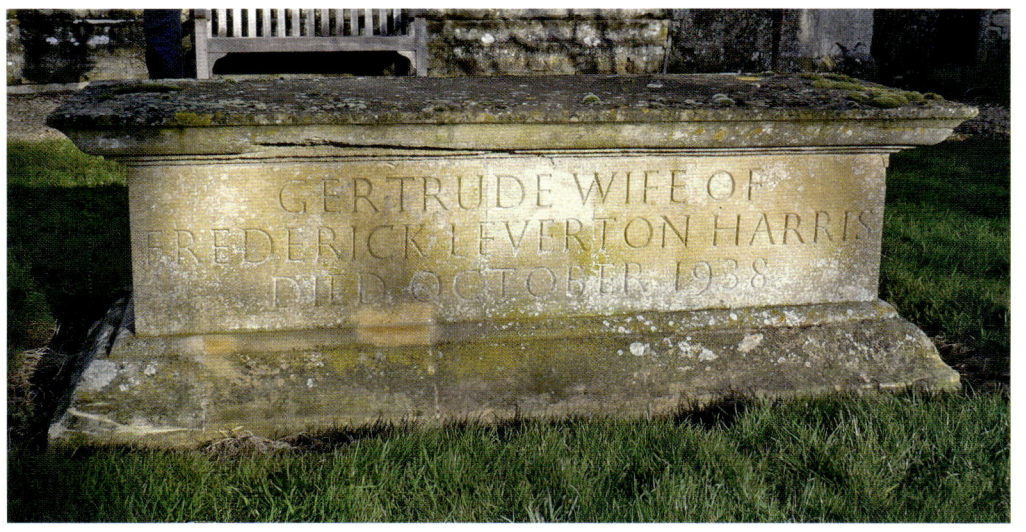

ERIC GILL 103

ABCDEFGHIJK
LMNOPQRSTU
VWXYZ

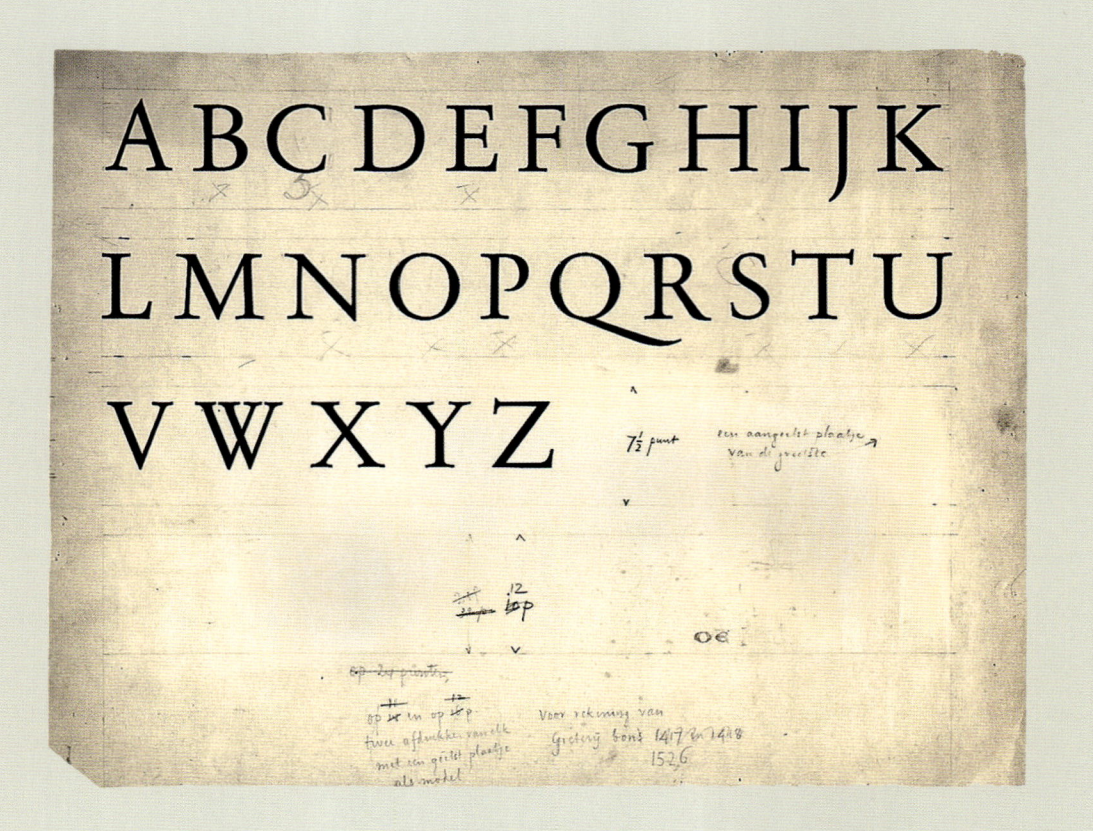

DR G. STUIVELING

EEN EEUW
NEDERLANDSE
LETTEREN

QUERIDO·AMSTERDAM

JAN VAN KRIMPEN AND ROMAN CAPITALS

MARTIN MAJOOR

One of the last texts Jan van Krimpen (1892–1958) published, *On Designing and Devising Type* (1957), can be seen as a definitive comment on his own work. "Of letters... it would be saying much too little to declare that I was interested in them: they have fascinated me from the very first time I saw a picture of a Roman inscription," he wrote in the introduction. Although there is a direct connection between van Krimpen's type designs, his book typography (notably the title pages), and his lettering (especially for dustjackets), it is useful to separate each of these activities.

Type design
By his own admission, Jan van Krimpen followed a path of "improving and perfecting," during which he chose to imitate and emulate rather than attempt to be original over and over again. "I prefer...the method of basing one's work on old patterns, even if, as a result, not more than two types may be produced by a man during his life." As a result of this approach, his typefaces are sometimes hard to tell apart. [3]

His sources, however, were not singular. For Lutetia (1925), his first type design, van Krimpen referred to the lowercase of types in Venetian incunabula, whereas the italic was based on the work of 16th-century Italian writing masters. For the capitals he looked toward Roman inscriptions as reproduced in Emil Hübner's *Exempla Scripturae Epigraphicae Latinae* (Berlin, 1885). The same path was followed for his successive type designs: Romaneé, 1928; Romulus, 1931; and Spectrum, 1952.

Van Krimpen was well aware of the influence of Roman inscriptions on type design. He discussed and argued about it with Stanley Morison, of whom he wrote, "Shall I be able ever to convince him that sculptured script, inscriptions and the like, derive from some form of calligraphy and that, therefore, neither calligraphy nor sculpturing nor engraving should be disregarded when we think of type? I almost doubt it" (*On Designing and Devising Type*, p. 15). The proportions within the capitals of van Krimpen's type designs were based unequivocally on those of Roman inscriptions, though he never followed their shapes too literally. This can be seen clearly in the capitals of Romanée—often considered van Krimpen's best typeface—in which the characters *B*, *E*, *F*, *L*, and *S* are wider than classical Roman inscriptions, and the characters *C*, *D*, and *G* are narrower. In van Krimpen's view, this "leveling out" was necessary to fit the capitals better with the lowercase. Be that as it may, van Krimpen made "a capital Q with an excessively long tail, *peccavi!*" [1]

Book typography
Before Jan van Krimpen started designing typefaces he was already active as a book typographer, focusing much effort on title pages. "The history of printing is in large measure the history of the title-page," wrote Stanley Morison in *First Principles of Typography* (a Dutch translation of which, made by Van Krimpen, was published in 1951). Van Krimpen followed Morison in his preference for title pages set solely in capitals: "As lower-case is a necessary evil, which we should do well to subordinate since we cannot suppress, it should be avoided when it is at its least rational and least attractive—in large sizes. . . . The main line of a title should be set in capitals; and, like all titling capitals, they should be spaced."

---

1 (*opposite, above*). Drawings for Romanée (Joh. Enschedé en Zonen, 1928) by Jan van Krimpen.

2 (*opposite, below*). Handlettered book jacket design by van Krimpen for *Een Euw Nederlandse Letteren* by Garmt Stuiveling (Amsterdam: Querido, 1941).

3 (*below*). Comparison of key letters in typefaces by van Krimpen. From top to bottom: Lutetia, Romanée, Romulus and Spectrum.

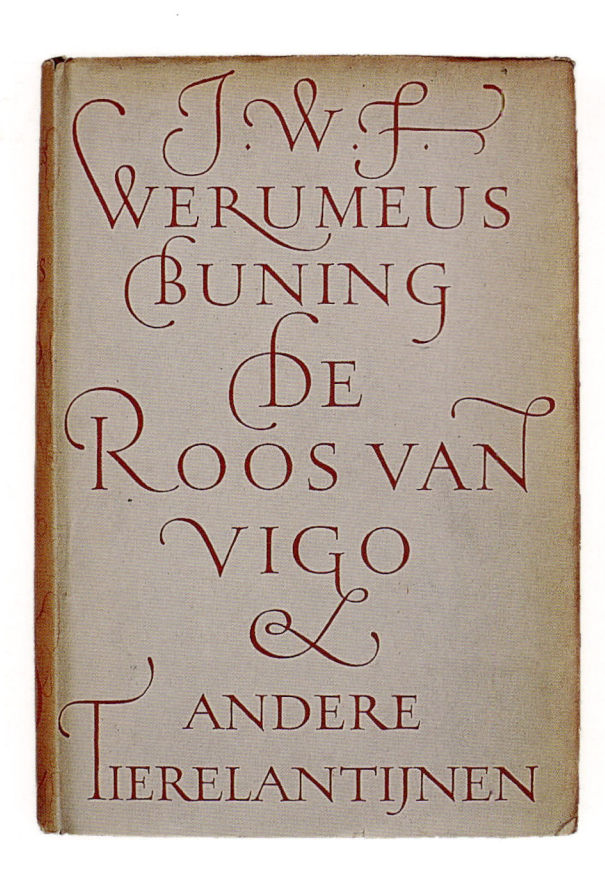

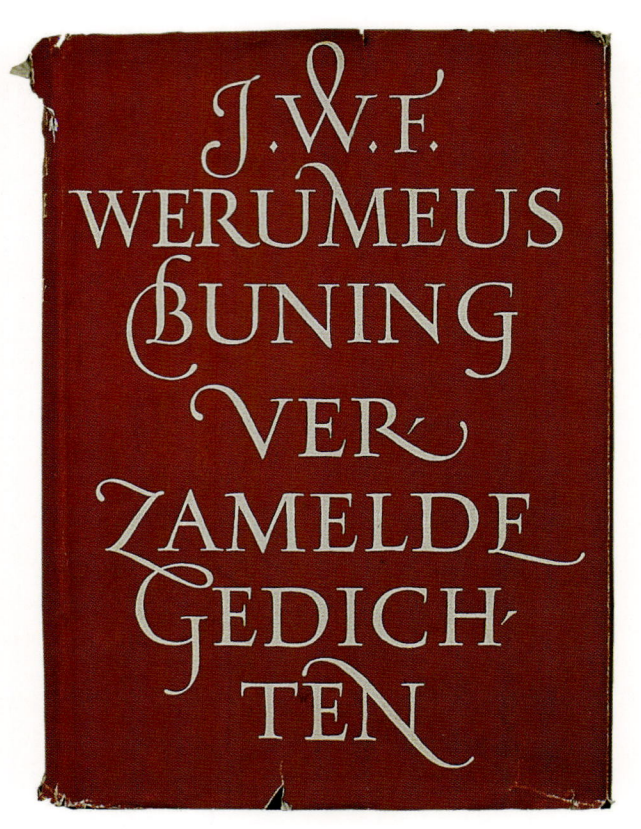

Van Krimpen regarded the title page as a monumental façade, using rather widely, but perfectly, spaced capitals and small capitals. He often replaced a needed comma with a specially designed punctuation mark that was based on the *punctus* mark, the triangular raised center dot, found in Roman inscriptions. In Holland, it became known as the "van Krimpen comma," one of the few new typographic signs of the 20th century. The symbol eventually was included in most of van Krimpen's typefaces.

Book jackets and other lettering
Although Van Krimpen made numerous dustjackets, his attitude toward them was one of ambivalence. "I think that [dustjackets] hardly belong to the book as such," he opined. "They are rather a signboard advertising the book itself and in very many instances indeed they have nothing to do with typography." Despite this bias, van Krimpen produced many beautiful ones, almost without exception using hand-drawn capitals. Where his type designs and title pages rarely show signs of exaggeration, his colored book jackets are often full of flourished capitals and swashes. [2, 4] These hand-lettered designs are closely related to inscriptional Roman capitals, especially the delicate serifs. Van Krimpen's roman capitals—often with Renaissance flourishes attached—also graced Dutch postage stamps from 1923 through the 1950s. His non-pictorial, low-value postage stamps from 1946 are considered among his most elegant designs. [5]

There are a few designs in which van Krimpen came very close to Roman inscriptional letters. In 1927, he designed a typeface called Dubbel Augustijn Open Kapitalen, a titling font of open capitals (fig. 7); and in 1956, he designed the lettering for the National Monument on the Dam in Amsterdam, cut in travertine stone (fig. 9). The latter was the closest he ever came to true Roman inscriptional style. It was the culmination of a lifelong fascination.

4 Handlettered book jacket designs by van Krimpen for two books by J.W.F. Werumeus Buning: *De Roos van Vigo en andere tierelantijnen* and *Verzamelde Gedichten* (Amsterdam: Querido, 1944 and 1948).

5 Series of stamp designs by van Krimpen for the Dutch postal service, 1946–1947. Below is the Red Cross 90th anniversary stamp, 1957. It was the last stamp design of nearly 500 done by van Krimpen.

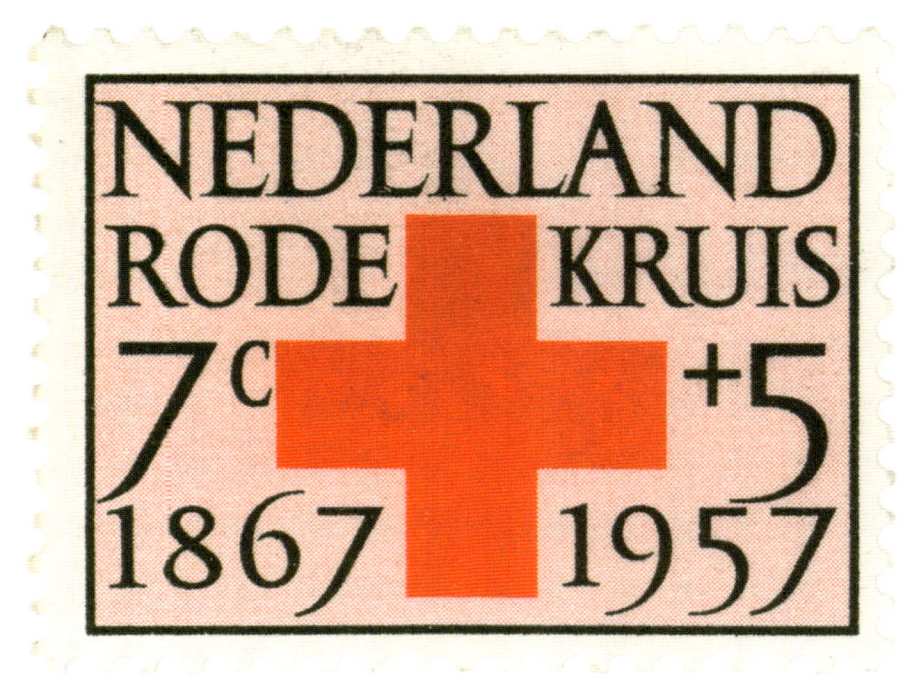

JAN VAN KRIMPEN 107

ABCDEFGHIJKLM NOPQRSTUVWXYZ

TER GELEGENHEID VAN DE INWIJDING VAN
HET GEBOUW AAN DE BAKENESSERGRACHT
SYMBOOL VAN DE HECHTE BAND MET HET
STAATSBEDRIJF DER PTT
SPREEKT DE DIRECTIE NAMENS GEHEEL
JOH·ENSCHEDÉ EN ZONEN
DE HOOP UIT DAT DE SAMENWERKING VAN
HET STAATSBEDRIJF EN DE VENNOOTSCHAP
NOG VELE JAREN BESTENDIGD ZAL BLIJVEN

HAARLEM I SEPTEMBER MDCCCLIIII

ABCDEFGHIJKLMNO PQRSTUVWXYZ

6 (*opposite, top*). Romulus capitals (Joh. Enschedé en Zonen, 1931) by van Krimpen.

7 (*opposite, middle*). Open Capitals (Joh. Enschedé en Zonen, 1929) by van Krimpen.

8 (*opposite, bottom*). Spectrum capitals (Joh. Enschedé en Zonen, 1952; Monotype Corporation, 1955).

Vol. 11
No. 1

FINE PRINT

THE REVIEW FOR THE ARTS OF THE BOOK

TENTH ANNIVERSARY ISSUE *January 1985*

January 1975–January 1985

Hermann Zapf '84

HERMANN ZAPF'S ROMAN CAPITALS: AN APPRECIATION

PAUL SHAW

THE RELEASE OF PALATINO IN 1950 WAS A SENSATION.[1] Although ubiquitous today (and therefore often unfairly reviled), Palatino represented a new direction in text types in the aftermath of World War II. It was not a revival, like many of the faces that dominated Stanley Morison's program at Monotype, nor was it historically based, like most of Frederic W. Goudy's types or W. A. Dwiggins's Caledonia. Palatino was different from previous German attempts at an oldstyle roman, though it, too, was a product of the *schriftkünstler* tradition. Despite being full of individuality, it lacked the eccentricity of Koch Antiqua; its lightness contrasted with the darkness of Weiss Antiqua; and its modeling differed sharply from the even tone of Schneidler Mediaeval. [3] Simply put, Palatino was the freshest old-style face since Perpetua.

Palatino's freshness can be directly attributed to its calligraphic roots, something that was rare in text faces at the time. It was calligraphically inflected but not overtly so. It was unlike Humanistic (William Dana Orcutt, 1904), Post Roman (Herbert Post, 1937), or even Zapf's own Novalis (an unreleased roman designed from 1946),[2] which explicitly showed their broad pen origins. [2] Palatino ushered in an era of modern "calligraphic" types—from Delphin (Georg Trump, 1951) to Leipzig (Albert Kapr, 1963)—that flourished in the 1950s and early 1960s. Its success turned the previously unknown Zapf into an international typographic star.

Palatino seemingly came out of nowhere in postwar Germany. Although Zapf had already designed two typefaces before it, the fraktur Gilgengart (1941) and Novalis, neither was released. Palatino was essentially his typographic debut. One reason for its quick success and its spread beyond Germany was its immediate availability as both a foundry type for display and as a Linotype face for text.[3] [4, 6] This came about through the close relationship that D. Stempel AG and Mergenthaler Setzmaschinen-Fabrik (later Linotype GmbH) had shared since 1900.[4] The Linotype connection was especially important because it made Palatino easier to be imported—with only minimal trouble caused by differences in type size—into both the United States and England via the sister companies Mergenthaler Linotype and English Linotype. Mergenthaler, especially, promoted the face in the United States, using it to set Willi Mengel's celebratory history of the company's founder, *Ottmar Mergenthaler and the Printing Revolution* (Mergenthaler Linotype Co., 1954). Palatino also benefited from Paul Standard's proselytizing on its behalf and Zapf's in general.

Palatino is not a classical roman typeface in the Renaissance manner of Centaur or Bembo. Its capitals have the variable letter widths and high stroke contrast associated with classical romans, but they have idiosyncratic features. In the Stempel foundry version, the *A* is slightly unbalanced and has a high crossbar; there are no spur serifs on *C*, *G*, and *S*; there are no serifs on the midstrokes of *E* and *F* (and *F*'s midstroke is visibly lower than *E*'s); the jaw of *G* is unusually low; *M* is abnormally wide; *Q* has a calligraphic tail that is joined to

---

1 (*opposite*). Cover of *Fine Print* (January 1985) designed and hand lettered by Hermann Zapf.

2 (*below*). Proof of pilot 10 pt size of Novalis (1946). From *Hermann Zapf and His Design Philosophy* (Chicago: Society of Typographic Arts, 1987), p. 21.

3 (*below*). Cover of type specimen for Koch Antiqua by Rudolf Koch (Gebr. Klingspor, n.d.).

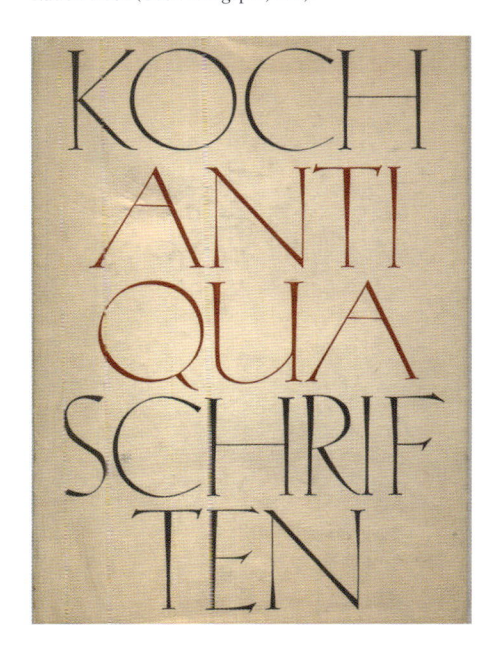

PALATINO

ABC
DEFGHI
JKLMNOP
QRSTUV
WXYZ
& Qu

This article is about the original metal versions of typefaces by Hermann Zapf, not about their subsequent film or digital incarnations. In the case of Palatino there are substantial differences among the various versions that have been issued—the most recent being Palatino Nova (2005)—and the discussion of proportion here is not applicable to them.

ABCDEFGHIJKLMNQPRSTU
ABCDEFGHIJKLMNQPRSTU
VWXYZ;ey th ng sp st ß Hamburg
VWXYZ;ey th ng sp st ß Hamburg
abcdefghijklmnopqrstuvwxyzw
abcdefghijklmnoqprstuvwxyzw

März 1948   *Hermann Zapf*

ABCDEFGHIJKLM
¶abcdefghijklmnopqrst
NOPQRSTUVWXYZ
uvwxyzchckfffififlftßtz
ÆŒQu & EFSpqsvwy*

4 (*opposite*). Enlarged photograph of 24 pt foundry Palatino printed on Arches Johannot paper.

5 (*above*). Proof of early version of Palatino, dated March 1948.

6 (*right*). Linotype version of Palatino. The letters in red were designed for the Anglo-American market. From *Eine Weitverzweigte Familie mit der sie Immer Zusammen-Arbeiten Sollten* (Frankfurt: D. Stempel and Linotype GmbH, c.1960), a type specimen devoted solely to Zapf's typefaces.

HERMANN ZAPF 113

MICHELANGELO

ABC
DEFGHI
JKLMNOP
QRSTUV
WXYZ
KQRS

7 (*opposite*). Enlarged photograph of 24 pt foundry Michelangelo printed on Arches Johannot paper. Note the alternate forms of *K*, *Q*, *R* and *S*.

8 (*below*). Two early sketches for Michelangelo dated 1947 (top) and 1949 (bottom) respectively. From *About More Alphabets* by Jerry Kelly (New York: The Typophiles and RIT Cary Graphic Arts Press, 2011), p. 32.

SISTINA

ABC
DEFGHI
JKLMNOP
QRSTUV
WXZ
& Q

9 (*opposite*). Enlarged photograph of 24 pt foundry Sistina printed on Arches Johannot lightweight paper. Note the alternate Q.

10 (*below*). Rubbings from Roman inscriptions by Zapf made 8 October 1950, and drawings of Aurelia (the original name for Sistina) dated November 1950. From *About Alphabets* by Hermann Zapf (New York: The Typophiles, 1960), p. 97.

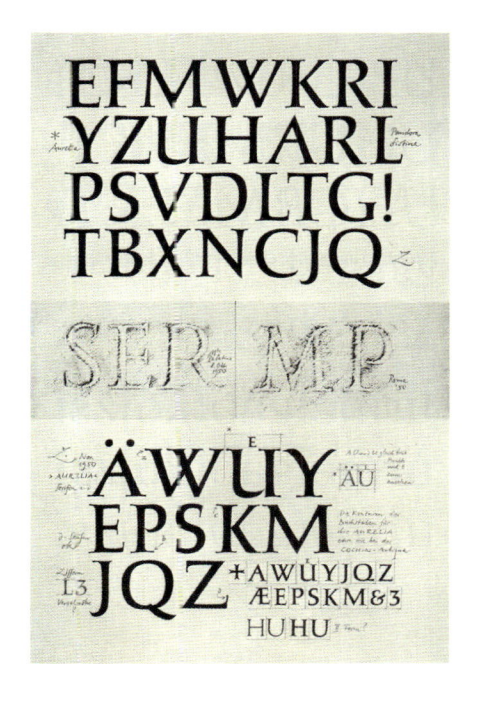

11 (*right, upper*). Comparison of stroke width to letter height ratios of typefaces by Hermann Zapf using the digital Palatino Nova family. From left to right: Michelangelo, Aldus, Palatino, Sistina, and Palatino Bold.

12 (*right, lower*). Comparison of Zapf's typefaces (using the digital Palatino Nova family) with Trajan. From left to right: Palatino nova Regular (Palatino), Trajan, Palatino nova Titling (Michelangelo), and Palatino nova Imperial (Sistina).

the bowl at 6 o'clock rather than the more familiar 5 o'clock position; *R* has an open bowl; *S* has an upward kink in its spine; *X* has partial serifs on its right-leaning diagonal and none on its left-leaning diagonal; and *Y* follows the Greek ypsilon in having curved arms without serifs. (At some point in the early 1950s, Stempel modified the foundry version made for sale in the United States and England. Serifs were added to the midstrokes of capitals *E* and *F*, and the *S* was given a more traditionally sloped spine.[5]) The Linotype version is a little more conventional, with *A* being more symmetrical and having a lowered crossbar, and the spine of *S* being more horizontal. Palatino's serifs are bracketed but not tapered; plus they are slightly cupped, making them simultaneously sturdy and graceful.[6] [6]

Any doubt that Palatino was intended by Zapf as a classical Roman typeface would have been erased with the release of Michelangelo that same year and Sistina the following year. Despite their differing names, both Zapf and Stempel conceived of these titling faces as members of the Palatino family. Michelangelo is lighter in weight than Palatino, but has much of its genetic makeup. [7] There are structural differences, however. The *A* is balanced, *B* has an open bowl, the midstrokes of *E* and *F* are optically aligned, *G* has an even lower jaw, *J* curves upward, *M* is even wider, the tail of *Q* is wavier, *R* has a higher waist, the spine of *S* slopes slightly downward, *U* has a leg, *Y* has a deeper crotch, and *Z* has a different distribution of weight with a thin diagonal and thick horizontals. (There are also alternate swash forms of *K*, *Q*, and *R*, and an alternate *S* with a curvier spine.) Despite the deviations from the classical ideal, the overall appearance of Michelangelo is one of great elegance.

Sistina is the polar opposite of Michelangelo in weight, yet has the same degree of sophistication. [9] Its design was one of the fruits of Zapf's visit to Italy in autumn 1950.[7] He made a rubbing of a Roman inscriptional fragment in the Foro Romano with the letters *SER* and *MP*. [10] Sistina has the high-waisted, off-balance *A* and the Greek *Y* of Palatino, but other details have been changed. There are serifs on the midstrokes of *E* and *F*, *Q* has a short tail sitting on the baseline, *R* has a closed counter, *S* has a sloping spine, *U* (like Michelangelo) has a leg, and *W* has crossing middle strokes. There is an alternative wider *T* and an alternative *Q* with a descending tail. The serifs are slightly bulbous at the ends, like ink pooling at the end of a pen stroke.

Given all of these variations, Palatino, Michelangelo, and Sistina would not constitute a type family by contemporary standards.[8] But the details did not seem to matter to Zapf, who saw their overall structure, their classical armature, as a unifying element. In his view, the key difference

13 (*opposite*). Detail of calligraphic broadside by Zapf with quotation by Douglas C. McMurtrie, c. 1959. Reproduced from *About Alphabets* (1960).

among them was their weight. In *About Alphabets* (1960) he wrote, "Since the Palatino family was intended mainly for display, it became essential for optical reasons to use a most careful gradation of scale in the weights of the several sizes. The ratio of capital height to thickness of the main stroke in the Michelangelo becomes 1:12, in the Aldus 1:11, in Palatino 1:9, in Sistina 1:7 and in Palatino Bold 1:5."[9] [11] Both Palatino Bold (released in 1951) and Linotype Aldus Buchschrift (released in 1954) were considered by Zapf and Stempel to be part of the larger Palatino family. Zapf created Aldus as a book-face companion to Palatino, which, despite its popularity over the past six decades as a book type, had been intended as a jobbing or advertising text face.[10] The ratios that Zapf was working with echo the Renaissance concern with establishing the true proportions of the classical Roman capital as embodied by the letters of the Trajan inscription. Scribes and artists theorized and argued over the proper proportion, with Ferdinando Ruano (1554) and Giovanni Francesco Cresci (1560) urging 1:8; Fra Luca Pacioli (1509), Francesco Torniello (1517), Albrecht Dürer (1525), Cesare Domenichi (1602), and Leopardo Antonozzi (1638) opting for 1:9; Felice Feliciano (c. 1460), Geoffroy Tory (1529), Cresci (1570), and Marc'Antonio Rossi (1598) arguing for 1:10; and Damiano da Moyle (c. 1483) and Sigismondo Fanti (1514) preferring 1:12.[11] Zapf, who was keenly aware of this tradition, sided with Pacioli et al. [12]

Zapf's reinterpretation of classical Roman capitals can be found in a series of calligraphic broadsides that he executed over the years. They tend to have the same format: an alphabet of capitals surrounded by one or more quotations about letters, type, or printing written out in italic. The earliest appears to be one that was reprinted in *About Alphabets*, bearing a quotation by Douglas C. McMurtrie, with capitals that have the lightness of Michelangelo.[12] [13; also see p. 146] Another from 1964, with slightly heavier capitals, has quotations from Thomas Carlyle, Emerich Kner, Albert Einstein, and Raymond Blattenberger. In both, the letters have some of the same personal quirks as the three typefaces cited above.[13] The crossbar on *A* is high, *G* has a low jaw, *M* is abnormally wide, and *Y* is in the Greek manner. But, notably, there are serifs on the midstrokes of *E* and *F* and the bowl of *R* is closed—and, with scale not an issue, the serifs are sharply bracketed. [13]

"The type of today and tomorrow will hardly be a faithful recutting of a 16th-century roman of the Renaissance, nor the original cutting of a classical face of Bodoni's time—but neither will it be a sans-serif of the 19th century," Zapf wrote in 1960.[14] The latter portion of his complaint was undoubtedly directed at Neue Haas Grotesk (Helvetica) and Univers, which he considered inappropriate for promoting modern furniture and products. In his view, his own Optima, released a year after them, was a truer type of its time. [14]

Optima, described by Zapf as a "serifless roman" to distinguish it from grotesques, was designed "to accompany the Palatino-Melior group" of typefaces.[15] Whereas grotesques attempted to be monoweight, Optima was built "on the principle of alternating weights of stroke," which Zapf claimed was an old principle in sans serif lettering, going back as far as ancient Greece, but rarely found in sans serif printing types. He applied a "constant axial direction" or stress throughout its curves in order to give the letters a consistent, logical structure. The distinctive flaring of the strokes and cupping of the terminals was done to counteract wear and tear at small sizes. But Zapf also added them because they were features of Roman inscriptional capitals,[16] and it is Optima's roots in classical letters that make it an essential part of any discussion of Zapf's Roman capitals.

However, Optima's origins lie not in ancient Rome but in Renaissance Florence. The idea for the typeface came to Zapf during the same 1950 trip to Italy that yielded the inspiration for Sistina. While visiting Santa Croce, in Florence, he sketched (on 1000-lira banknotes because he had run out of paper) several quattrocento floor tombs with "unserifed letters" whose "simple, vigorous forms" delighted him.[17] [17] These letters were part of a revival of Roman capitals in the first half of the 15th century in Florence, led by the artists Lorenzo Ghiberti, Donatello, and Luca della Robbia that took its cues from Romanesque letters. [18] While there are variations among the Florentine sans serif examples both in Florence and elsewhere—the style can be found as far afield as Rome and Venice—the most common style is marked by letters with strong thick/thin contrast and wedge-shaped strokes.[18] Zapf replaced those wedge shapes with tapering that

ABC DEFGHI JKLM NOPQ RSTUVW XYZ

We use the letters of our alphabet every day with the utmost ease and unconcern, taking them almost as much for granted as the air we breathe. We do not realize, that each of these letters is at our service today only as the result of a long & laboriously slow process of evolution in the age-old art of writing.

Douglas C. McMurtrie

OPTIMA

ABC
DEFGHI
JKLMNOP
QRSTUV
WXYZ
& N

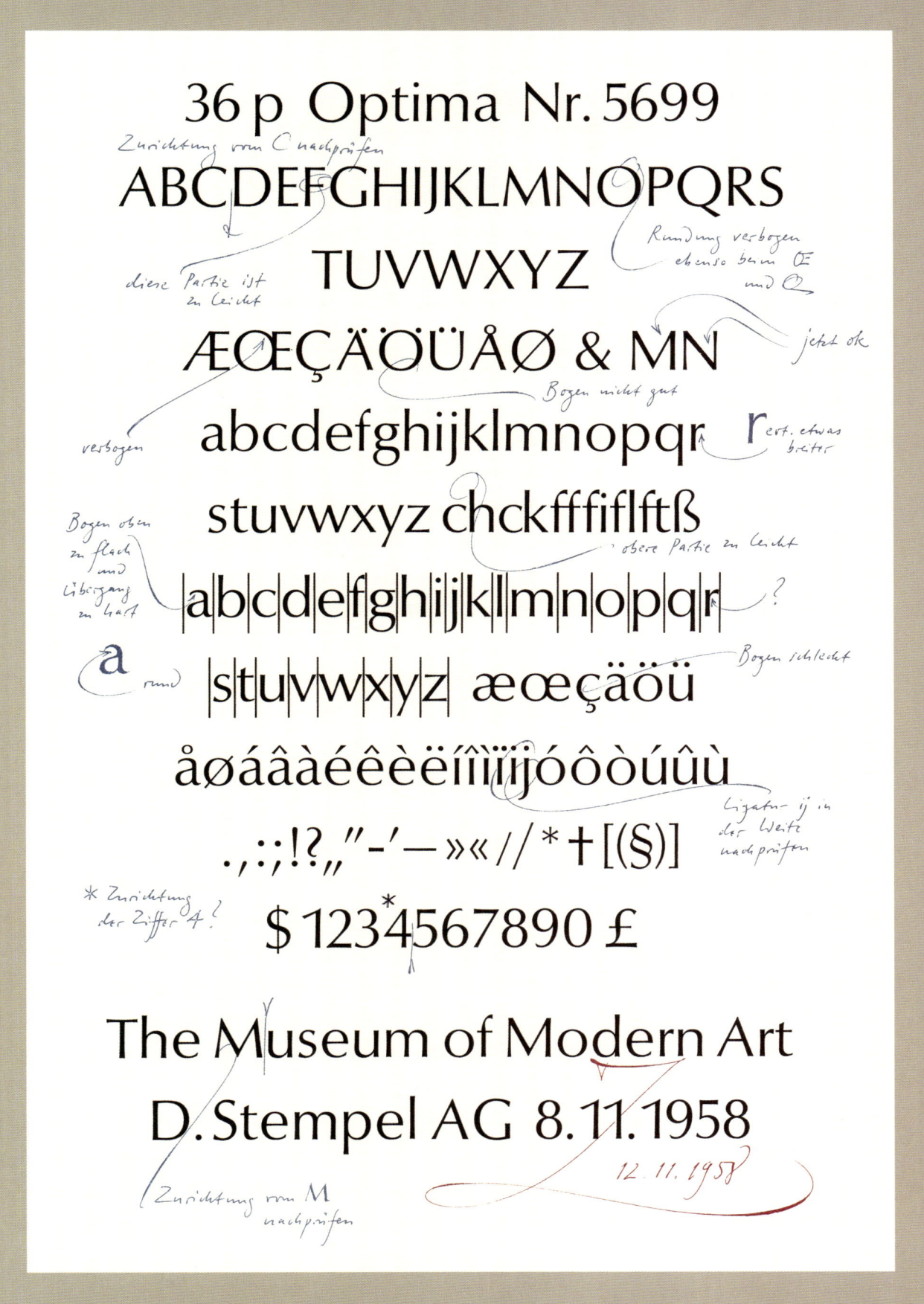

14 (*opposite*). Enlarged photograph of 24 pt foundry Optima printed on Arches Johannot paper. Note the alternate *N*. The alternate *M* is missing.

15 (*above*). Annotated proof of Optima dated 11 December 1958. Note the presence of the alternate forms of *M* and *N*.

MBRV
FIRENZE   B   ·   Buchstaben
S. CROCE   AB N D   aus der Inschrift
1950   A   N D   (Schrift läuft
           E S D   im Kreis, in der
                          Mitte befindet
Grabplatte   sich das
 in Santa Croce   Familienwappen)

BERTO · DILIONARDO · BERTI · ESVORVM · M · CCCC · XXX

16 (*above*). Sketches by Zapf in 1950 of letters from the floor tomb of Berto di Lionardo (d.1430) in S. Croce, Florence. From *The World of Alphabets* by Hermann Zapf, CD-ROM (Rochester, New York: Melbert B. Cary, Jr. Graphic Arts Collection and Wolfenbüttel, Germany: Herzog August Bibliothek, 2001).

17 (*below*). Sketches of letters on Quattrocento floor tombs in S. Croce, Florence made by Zapf 3 October 1950. He used a 1000 lire note because he had run out of paper. From *The World of Alphabets* by Hermann Zapf, CD-ROM (Rochester, New York: Melbert B. Cary, Jr. Graphic Arts Collection and Wolfenbüttel, Germany: Herzog August Bibliothek, 2001).

122

18 Detail of the *cantoria* by Luca della Robbia, 1437. The *cantoria*, now in the Museo dell'Opera di Santa Maria del Fiore, was originally installed in the Duomo in Florence.

calmed down the sprightliness of the letters and gave them a more classical aura. Furthermore, in adding a lowercase, seemingly spun out of thin air, he adjusted the proportions of the type to fit the Golden Section: the ratio of stroke thickness to height is 1:3 for the ascender/descender portions of the lowercase letters, 1:5 for the body of the lowercase letters, and 1:8 for the capitals; or an overall ratio of 3:5:8 that follows the Fibonacci Series.[19] Essentially, Zapf took letters that were quasi-classical and, other than their lack of serifs, made them fully classical. [15]

Although released in 1958, Optima was designed between 1952 and 1955.[20] Like Palatino, it was originally intended as an advertising face, but a 1954 meeting with Monroe Wheeler, director of exhibitions and publications for the Museum of Modern Art, New York, led Zapf to adjust it for text use instead. He saw Optima as an "eminently practical roman with a destined area of utility in books of art and photography, in technical or scientific publications, and in children's books and periodicals."[21] In his view it was a pleasantly legible and neutral design. He did his part to promote Optima as a book face, using it for many books and publications, most notably *About Alphabets* and *Hermann Zapf & His Design Philosophy* (1987), but Zapf did not foresee its popularity for cosmetic packaging and advertising.[22]

The use of Optima by the cosmetics and fashion inustries should come as no surprise, since the type exudes grace and elegance. Yet, with its lack of serifs, it is also modern, just as Zapf envisioned. In Optima, his masterpiece, classicism and modernity are harmoniously blended. The capitals have none of the peculiarities found in Palatino, Michelangelo, or Sistina. Despite their Renaissance Florentine origins, they are extremely close in structure to the letters of the Trajan inscription. The lone exception is the *R* with its leg joining the bowl at the stem.[23]

Today, Palatino and Optima are, at best, taken for granted and, at worst, unfairly looked down upon. Nevertheless, in the span of a decade—from 1948, the year that Palatino was designed, to 1958, the year that Optima made its debut—Hermann Zapf managed to reinvent the classical Roman capital for the 20th century, sidestepping the revivalism of Renaissance types that dominated the fine-printing movement, and challenging, with Optima, the neo-grotesques championed by the adherents of Swiss typographic modernism. It was a singular achievement that still resonates more than a half century later.

ABCDEFGH
IKLMNOPQRS
TUVWXYZ
1234567890
abcdefghijlmnopq
rsftuvwxyzßk
ÄEFHMPRÜ

19   Romann-Schrift by Joachim Romann (Gebr. Klingspor, 1943). From *Atlas zur Geschichte der Schrift* 7 (Darmstadt: Technische Universität Darmstadt, 2001), p. 93.

1. Palatino was designed in 1948 and originally named Medici. Hermann Zapf, *About Alphabets: Some Marginal Notes on Type Design* (New York: The Typophiles, 1960), p. 30. Jerry Kelly explains, "With Palatino the Stempel typefoundry wanted to offer printers a new, modern-looking generally useful Renaissance roman and italic front, which could be used to replace the older typefaces depleted during the war due to destruction or wear (lead was used mostly for ammunition, not type, between the late 1930s and 1945)." Kelly, *About More Alphabets: The Types of Hermann Zapf* (New York: The Typophiles, 2011), p. 27. While the first half of this claim is undoubtedly true, the second half—that Palatino was intended to replace depleted older typefaces—is debatable.

2. "I had started in 1948 another roman [besides Novalis], based on Renaissance models; this face, lacking the edged-pen emphasis of Novalis, was more suited to a broad field of utility printing, because it reflected modern feeling and its open counters seemed more adapted to offset and letterpress printing." Zapf, *About Alphabets*, p. 30. A sample of Novalis (dated 25 October 1948) is shown in ibid., p. 25. Although the design has a Germanic feel (e.g., *J* with a top stroke), the roots of Palatino can be detected in it. [2]

   Zapf has always credited the punchcutter August Rosenberger (1893–1980) with contributing to the success of the typefaces he designed while associated with Stempel. See ibid., p. 30. Rosenberger, who worked at Stempel from 1927 to 1962, cut all of the Zapf typefaces discussed here. Some have suggested that the increased romanization of Palatino during its development was the result of Rosenberger's influence, but Matthew Carter disagrees: "If Rosenberger had any effect (which I doubt) I would expect it to be in the opposite direction, towards the Gothic." He speculates that Walter Cunz, the managing director of Stempel with an eye toward the lucrative American market, may have had greater influence on the design. Private correspondence, 19 August 2013; see also note 6.

3. Zapf claims that Palatino was designed for the composing machine from the outset. Hermann Zapf, *Hermann Zapf & His Design Philosophy: Selected Articles and Lectures on Calligraphy and Contemporary Developments in Type Design, with Illustrations and Bibliographical Notes, and a Complete List of His Typefaces* (Chicago: Society of Typographic Arts, 1987), p. 22.

4. D. Stempel AG began making matrices for linotype casting machines in 1900. That same year, the company signed a contract with Mergenthaler Setzmaschinen-Fabrik to produce typefaces for linotype machines. See linotype.com/49-14023/history.html. Mergenthaler Setzmaschinen-Fabrik became Linotype GmbH after World War II.

5. The original 1948 drawing of Palatino is reproduced in Kelly, *About More Alphabets*, p. 27. [5] It shows an italic whose lowercase is very Germanic compared with the issued typeface. In contrast, the roman is fairly close to the final design. Jerry Kelly states that the basic difference between the two is that the serifs were strengthened to withstand high-speed printing.

6. To see the differences among these versions of Palatino, see *Hermann Zapf & His Design Philosophy*, p. 22, and, more important, the Stempel specimen *Eine weitverzweigte Familie mit der sie immer zusammenarbeiten sollten* (Frankfurt am Main: D. Stempel AG and Linotype GmbH, c. 1960). "The calligraphically stressed letters *E F S q p s v w* and *y* in the Palatino roman were given more traditional forms for the British and American markets—forms derived essentially from conversations with Franz C. Hess of Huxley House, New York, and with the American type designer W. A. Dwiggins, Hingham, Mass." *About Alphabets*, p. 36. The Stempel specimen refers to these alternate forms as pica letters. [6] Despite Zapf's comments about their origins, they predate his 1952 meetings with Hess and Dwiggins. They are already present in the 36-pt. pilot size of Palatino, shown in *August Rosenberger 1893–1980: A Tribute to One of the Great Masters of Punchcutting, an Art Now All but Extinct* (Rochester: Melbert B. Cary, Jr. Graphic Arts Collection, Rochester Institute of Technology, 1996), p. 29. Scott-Martin Kosofsky and Matthew Carter suggest that Stempel may have created alternate pica letters because the American market was the most viable in the aftermath of World War II. The European economies were devastated and did not begin to recover until 1951. "It was extremely difficult to begin again in Germany during the years following the war," writes Zapf. "The Stempel type foundry suffered relatively little damage in comparison to the heavily bombed Bauer foundry or the Klingspor foundry in Offenbach. Nonetheless, the working conditions in Stempel's punchcutting department and printing office were very poor. It was not easy to get machines repaired or even to purchase the simplest materials needed for producing type. The heating did not work, and food continued to be rationed in those years after the war." See *August Rosenberger*, pp. 7–8.

   It is odd that the illustration showing Palatino in Zapf's *About Alphabets* (p. 90) mistakenly includes the alternate pica letters twice, leaving out the original versions.

   Prior to its public release, handset Palatino was first used in 1949 for the original edition of *Feder und Stichel*, Zapf's calligraphic showcase. Linotype Palatino made its appearance in 1950 in *Feschrift zum 50-jährigen Bestehen des Gutenberg-Museums in Mainz*, Gutenberg-Jahrbuch 25, which celebrated the 50th year of the Gutenberg-Gesellschaft. (Most sources, including *About Alphabets*, say that *Feder und Stichel* was first published in 1950, but in *Hermann Zapf & His Design Philosophy*, p. 22, Zapf says 1949, as does Jerry Kelly in Martin Hutner and Kelly, *A Century for the Century: Fine Printed Books from 1900 to 1999* (Boston: David R. Godine, Publisher, 2004), p. xlvii.

7. Sistina was originally called Aurelia. The better-known typeface to emerge from Zapf's 1950 Italian sojourn was Optima. Zapf, *About Alphabets*, p. 33.

8. In 2005 Linotype Library issued the Palatino Nova family, which included not only a redesigned Palatino, but also a redesigned Michelangelo, Sistina, and Aldus. Michelangelo and Sistina were renamed Palatino Titling and Palatino Imperial, respectively, thus cementing the familial relationship.

9. Ibid., p. 34.

10. Zapf has attributed the idea for Aldus to Gotthard de Beauclair (1907–1992), a book designer who, in 1951, became the artistic director of D. Stempel AG. Ibid., p. 37. At Stempel, de Beauclair established the Trajanus-Presse as an in-house imprint.

11. For more on Renaissance concepts of ideal Roman proportions, see Donald M. Anderson, *The Art of Written Forms: The Theory and Practice of Calligraphy* (New York: Holt, Rinehart and Winston, 1969), pp. 125–33. For Domenichi and Rossi, specifically, see A. G. Osley, *Luminario: An Introduction to the Italian Writing Books of the Sixteenth and Seventeenth Centuries* (Nieuwkoop, The Netherlands: Miland Publishers, 1972), pp. 110, 143.

12. The broadside is undated. Zapf, *About Alphabets*, p. 111.

13. The broadside was designed for Container Corporation of America at the request of Albert Kner.

14. Zapf, *About Alphabets*, p. 39.

15. Ibid., pp. 40, 44.

16. Ibid., p. 44.

17. Ibid., pp. 40–41, and "Back to the Sources: Some Reflections on Calligraphic Types," in *Calligraphic Type Design in the Digital Age: An Exhibition in Honor of the Contributions of Hermann and Gudrun Zapf*, edited by John Prestianni (San Francisco: The Friends of Calligraphy and Corte Madera: Gingko Press, 2001), p. 38. Zapf referred to Optima during its design stage as Fiorentina or Firenze. He disliked the name Optima bestowed on the type by the marketing people at Stempel; he thought it was pretentious and said the type should have been called Neu Antiqua instead.

    There is also the question of whether Zapf was aware of Romann-Schrift (Klingspor, 1943), a design that strikingly seems to anticipate Optima. [19] He certainly was familiar in later years with its designer, Joachim Romann, since he recommended him to design a typeface for Hallmark Cards. For a showing of Romann-Schrift, see *Atlas zur Geschichte der Schrift 7: Das 20. Jahrhundert* by Walter Wilkes (Darmstadt: Technische Universität Darmstadt, 2001), p. 93.

18. The pioneering work on the Florentine sans serif is Nicolete Gray, "Sans Serif and Other Experimental Inscribed Lettering of the Early Renaissance," *Motif* 5 (Autumn 1960), pp. 66–76; it was reprinted with additional material by LetterPerfect in 1997.

19. "Back to the Sources," p. 38.

20. The importer for Stempel types in the United States was Amsterdam Continental. Their Optima brochure (c. 1967) states that the type was not available here until 1960.

21. Zapf, *About Alphabets*, p. 41. In shifting the emphasis of Optima from display use to text use Zapf abandoned the German common line so that the face could have long descenders.

22. In his various writings, Zapf is silent about when he designed the lowercase letters for Optima, the truly innovative aspect of the typeface. Was Optima strictly a titling face prior to the meeting with Wheeler?

23. Optima originally sported non-Trajanic alternative forms of *M* and *N* that were more typical of printing types. [15]

А

азъ боукн꙽

ба ве гі
да se зі

Ondeessendo
Antiqua agli

ЕЖ
ИС

Щю
Щю

Impresso in Vinegia nelle case
d'Aldo Romano, nel anno
MDXIIII del mese di
Agosto

Qui Я
Qui Я

ꞓ Q ⱦ

THE TRAJAN LETTER IN RUSSIA

MAXIM ZHUKOV

I FELL IN LOVE WITH THE TRAJAN letter early in my life. I was fifteen or younger when I noticed how beautiful and elegant the title of an American art book looked. Later, I learned that the typeface that caught my eye was Goudy Oldstyle, created by an American designer Frederic W. Goudy, and much later, that the book was among the winners of the prestigious *Fifty Books of the Year* competition held annually by the American Institute of Graphic Arts. I tried to copy those letterforms as closely as I was able to. I even ruined the jacket by tracing the caps and marking the baselines and the horizontal boundaries of the letters.

In the USSR, the late 1950s was a time of big change in politics, culture, education, art—in virtually all walks of life. That period is often referred to as "the thaw," as it followed the long decades of Stalin's chilling rule. The opening of Druzhba ("friendship"), a bookstore in downtown Moscow that offered books in foreign languages, was one of the notable events in the life of Moscow intelligentsia. Predictably, Druzhba carried books only in the languages of the socialist countries (German, Czech, Polish, Chinese, etc.), but even that felt exciting. It was, indeed, a breakthrough from cultural isolation.

Artists and designers used to stop by Druzhba quite often, because within a couple of days, many new arrivals would be all gone. The mid- and the late-1950s saw the appearance of some seminal books on type, typography, lettering, and calligraphy. Those were the subjects barely explored by the domestic experts, with one notable exception: the milestone monograph *Russkii grazhdanskii shrift, 1703–1958* ("Russian Civil Type, 1703–1958") by Abram Shitsgal, which was published in commemoration of the 250th anniversary of Peter the Great's typographic reform.

Two books of note briefly showed up at Druzhba in the late 1950s: Albert Kapr's *Deutsche Schriftkunst* (1955) and František Muzika's *Krásné písmo* (1958). [2] One common—and distinctive—feature of those books was the showing of the Trajan letters, which made their way even to the dustjackets. I think the last time Trajan letters were mentioned in a Russian-language book, before those German and Czech books reached Moscow, was in 1946, in Boris Kissin's *Graficheskoye oformlenie knigi* (1946).

1 (*opposite*). "The Birth of a Printing Type," wall chart by Vadim Lazurski (1973).

2 (*below*). Detail of spine lettering for *Krásné Písmo* by František Muzika (1958)

The respectful and careful showing in Muzika's and Kapr's books looked very convincing compared to Kissin's casual and inaccurate rendition. Kapr's featured a stunning 3-page fold-out picture of the inscription on the base of Trajan's Column. Somehow, those showings seemed to possess an authenticity that was missing in Soviet architectural lettering of the 1950s (which, by the way, looked and felt very similar to the American monumental inscriptions of the 1910s–1920s in the Beaux-Arts style). [3, 4] In fact, that lettering style had a lot more to do with the Renaissance treatises on letter construction—those by Dürer, Tory, Pacioli, Arrighi, et al.—than with the classical *capitalis monumentalis*.

The large-scale, credible showings of the Trajan letters in Muzika's and Kapr's books made a lasting

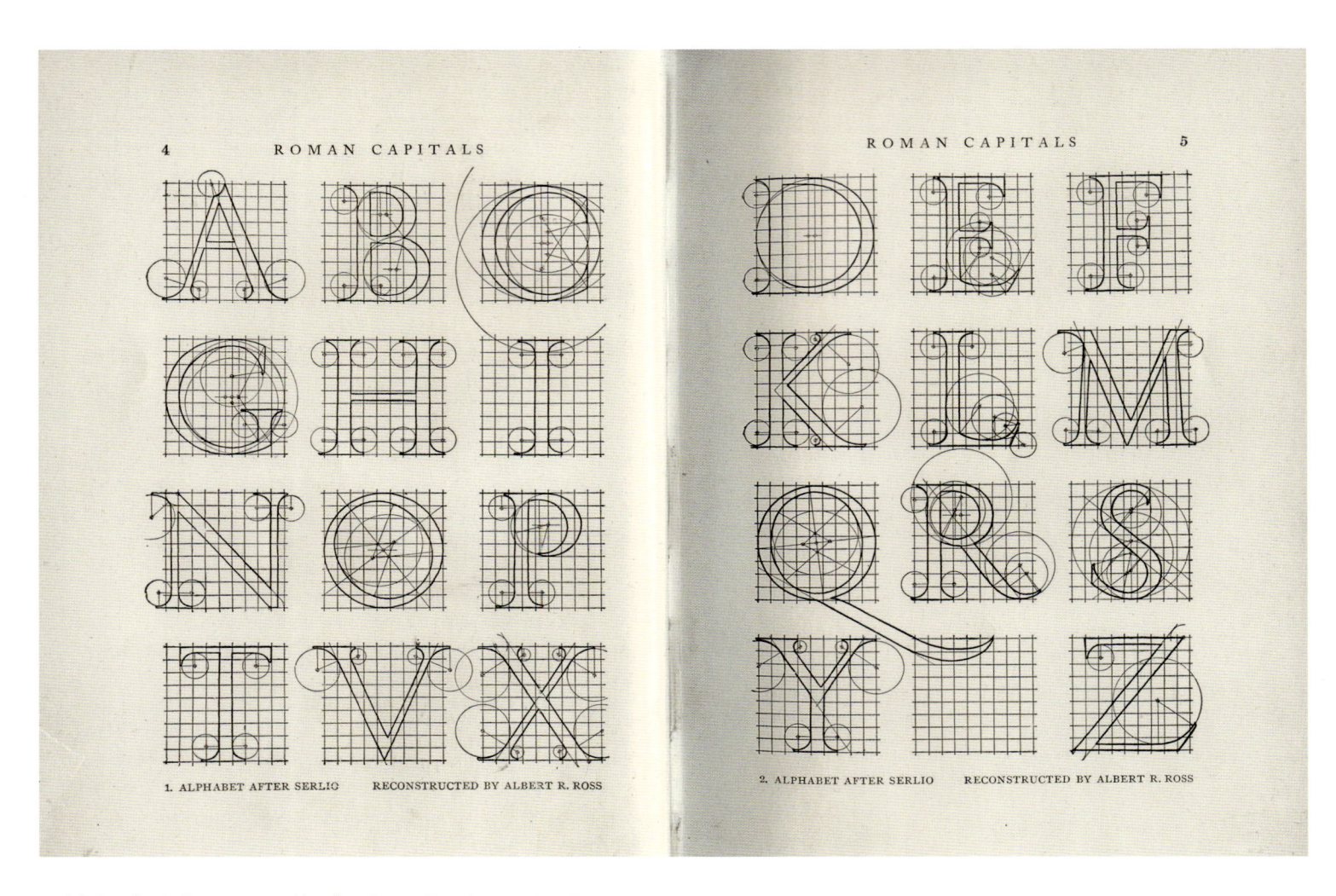

3 Alphabet after Serlio reconstructed by Albert R. Ross. From *Letters & Lettering* by Frank Chouteau Brown (Boston: Bates & Guild Company, 1902), pp. 4–5.

impression on the development of type design in the USSR. In 1958, Vadim Lazurski became the first Russian designer to create a Cyrillic adaptation of the Trajan inscriptional letter. [5, 7] Much later, in 1973, Lazurski acknowledged the influence of the Trajan letter on the development of his 1962 typeface when he referenced it in a wall chart titled *The Birth of a Printing Type*. [1]

The same powerful influence is clearly visible in the letterforms of a typeface Solomon Telingater was working on at the time, which was issued in 1959 under the name of Telingater Display. [6]

Around the same time—in 1958 or 1959—I came across a genuine trove of books and periodicals on type and typography. At the instigation of Telingater, I applied for a library card to the Rare Book Department of the Lenin Library, the national library of the USSR. It had the richest collection of typographic literature in the country, and three books in particular caught my attention: *Roman Lettering* by L.C. Evetts (1938); [9] *The Alphabet* by Frederic W. Goudy (1922), especially its chapter 4, "The Development of the Roman Capital" with its magnificent plates [8]; and last but not least, an intriguing monograph by Walter Kaech, *Rhythm and Proportion in Lettering* (1956).

I was so impressed by those resources that I actually translated most of Evetts's text into Russian, and copied all drawings using my own pencil, compass, and ruler, since cameras could not be used in the Rare Book Department at that time.

In 1960, I was admitted to the Moscow Printing Institute (MPI). For a couple of semesters, lettering was taught to us by the very same Vadim Lazurski. Predictably, exploring *capitalis monumentalis* was an important part of his course. I lent him my handmade translation of Evetts's *Roman Lettering*, and he happily used it in class. For almost the entire semester we assiduously worked on the Trajan letterforms, trying to build Cyrillic glyphs to match the Latin originals. [10]

When, twenty years later, I myself lectured at MPI, my students drew the letters

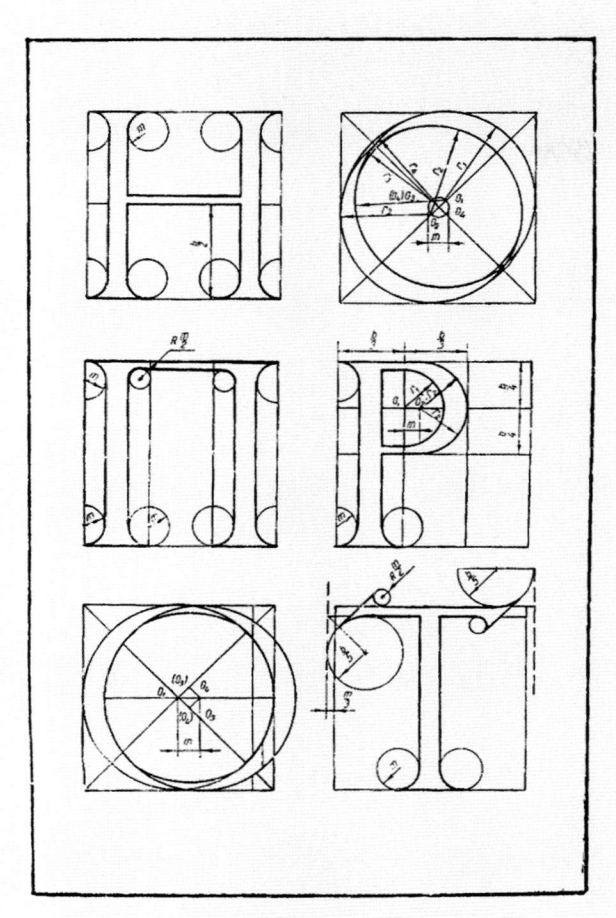

4 Typical Soviet architectural lettering of the 1950s. From *Nachertanie Shriftov: Posobie dlia arkhitektorov i inzhenerov* by Tikhon Kutsyn (Moscow: Gosudarstvennoe Izdatel'stvo Arkhitektury i Gradostroitel'stva, 1950), plate 10.

5 Cyrillic "adaptation" of the Trajan inscriptional letter by Vadim Lazurski, 1958.

АБВГДЕЁЖЗИЙКЛМНОП
РСТУФХЦЧШЩЪЫЬЭЮЯ

6 Telingater typeface by Solomon Telingater, 1959.

АБВГДЕЁЖЗИЙКЛМНОП
РСТУФХЦЧШЩЪЫЬЭЮЯ

7 Lazurski typeface by Vadim Lazurski, 1962.

THE TRAJAN LETTER IN RUSSIA 129

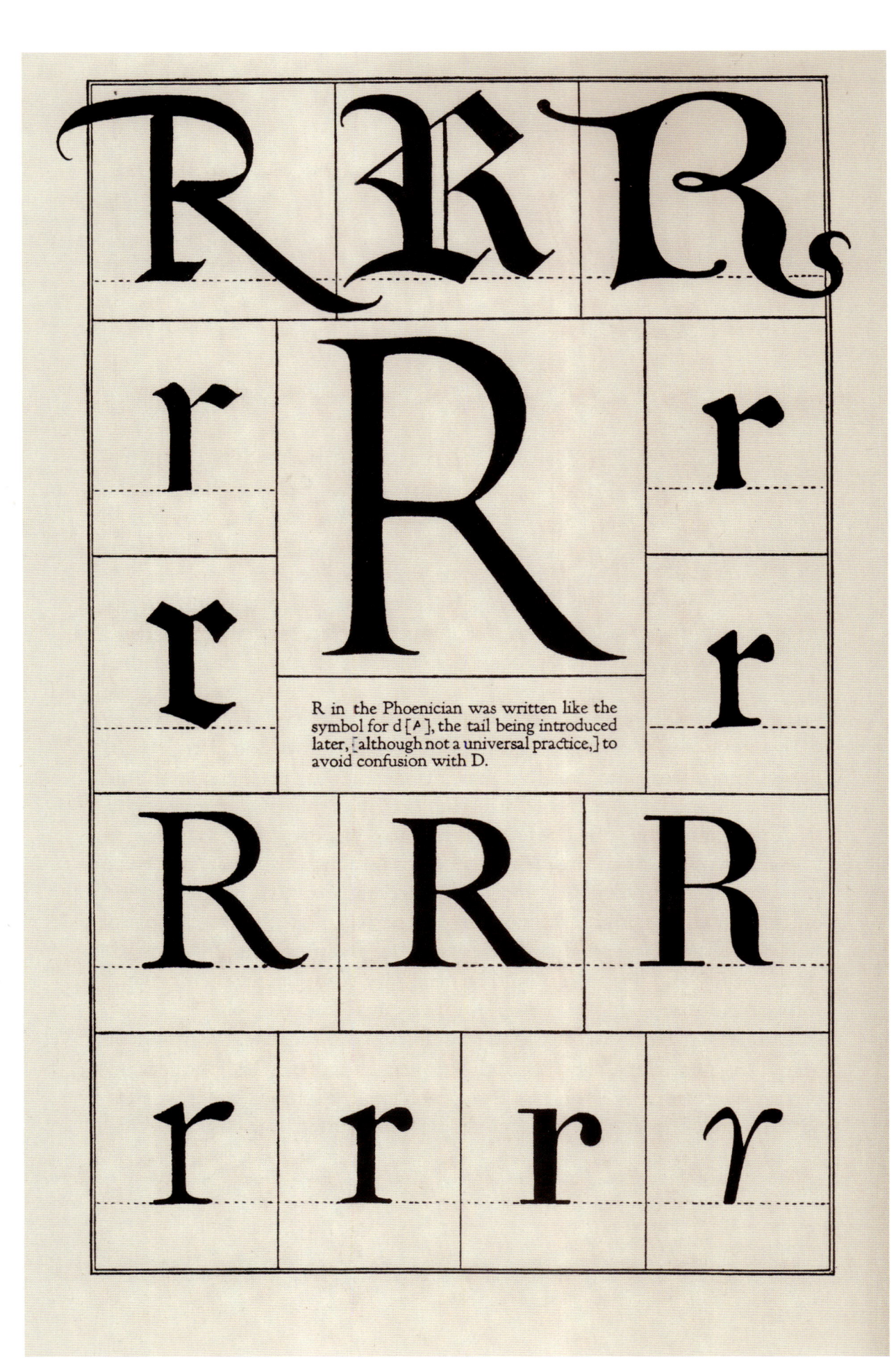

R in the Phoenician was written like the symbol for d [◁], the tail being introduced later, [although not a universal practice,] to avoid confusion with D.

from Trajan's Column for about three weeks. They also designed Cyrillic letters matching the original, in the original cap size, approximately 4½-inch high. From the jointly developed A–Z (А–Я) alphabetical glyph sets—each student drew several glyphs—a class list was composed in two versions, one Russian and one Latin (e.g., *Данила*/Danielis, *Дмитрий*/Demetrius, *Мария*/Maria, *Елизавета*/Elisabetha, etc.). Also, as a tribute to Lazurski, who was a guest speaker at my course, my students came up with an inscription on a scroll using the extra-large size of the same style (cap-height around 1 meter) saying, *Ave Vadimo*, paraphrasing the *Ave, Caesar, morituri te salutant*.

Our informational resources were still the same as in my own school years: Evetts' and Goudy's monographs, but they were complemented with a study that did not yet exist when I was Lazurski's student: Father Edward M. Catich's *The Origin of the Serif* (1968). That book not only shook up the world of lettering in the West, but it also had a lasting impact on my understanding of the Trajan letter.

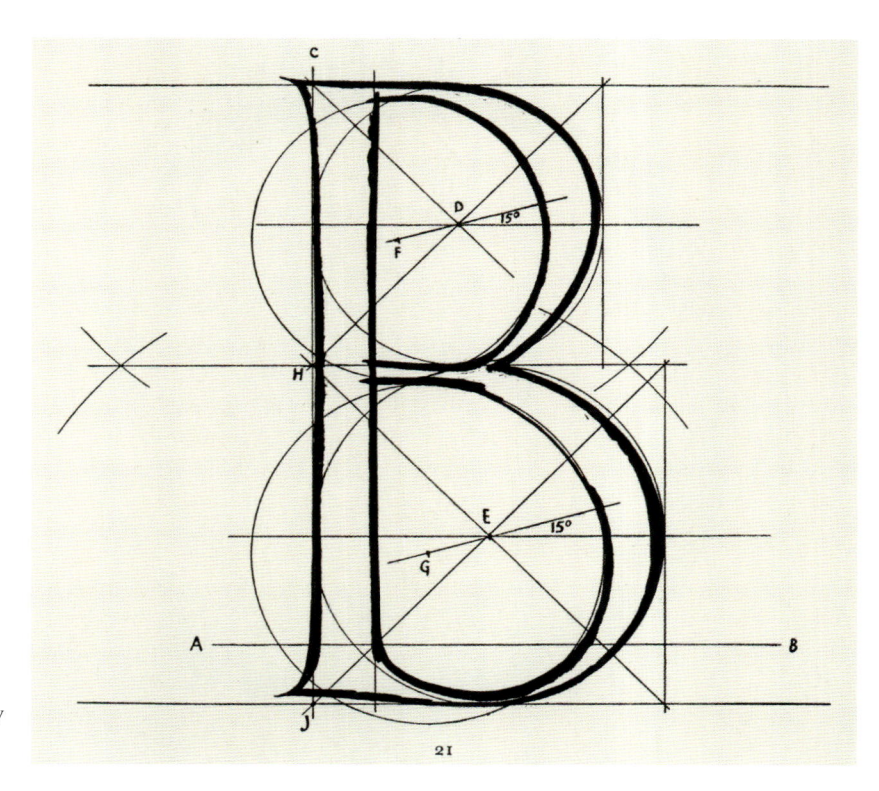

8 (*opposite*). Plate showing fifteen forms of the letter R from *The Alphabet* by Frederic W. Goudy (New York: Mitchell Kennerley, 1922). The large capital *R* is derived from the Trajan inscription.

9 (*right*). Constructed Trajanic B from *Roman Lettering* by L. C. Evetts (London: Isaac Pitman, 1938).

10 (*above*). *Bog* ("God") by Maxim Zhukov. Drawn with China ink on paper, 1963.

GILL'S LEGACY

EWAN CLAYTON

IN BRITAIN TODAY, THE THING FOR WHICH we can be most grateful to Gill (other than the things he created) was his establishment of a workshop tradition of lettercarving and monumental masonry. In the workplace, his particular blend of kindness, conviviality, and self-discipline found creative tinder. Many of the apprentices he taught went on to found their own workshops: Joseph Cribb (1892–1967), David Kindersley (1915–1995), John Skelton (1923–1999), and Ralph Beyer (1921–2008), as well as those, such as Reynolds Stone (1909–1979), whose brief two-week visits marked them for life.[1] In turn, most taught their own apprentices and today we are well into the fourth generation. In Britain, lettercarvng is flourishing as never before, and there is real diversity.

Although Gill's personal repertoire of forms contained a number of different approaches to letters, the prevalence of a classical Roman letter for public inscriptions and signage was encouraged by a number of institutional forces. In the early part of the 20th century, casts of Roman lettering[2] were distributed to art colleges across the country. Also, classical models were adopted for basic education in signpainting classes— a move that seems to have begun with Gill and Johnston. Some practitioners, such as the craftsmen of the Dorian workshop in London (particularly William Sharpington, who later worked from the City and Guilds of London Art School), achieved remarkable refinement in painting such letters with the pointed brush. The War Graves Commission, which continues to supply thousands of memorials for fallen servicemen and servicewomen, also set a standard. Memorials originally designed by Eric's brother Max Gill, with the assistance of Joseph Cribb, are in graveyards across the nation and in many countries overseas.

Within a decade or so of Gill's death, however, the times were changing. Joseph

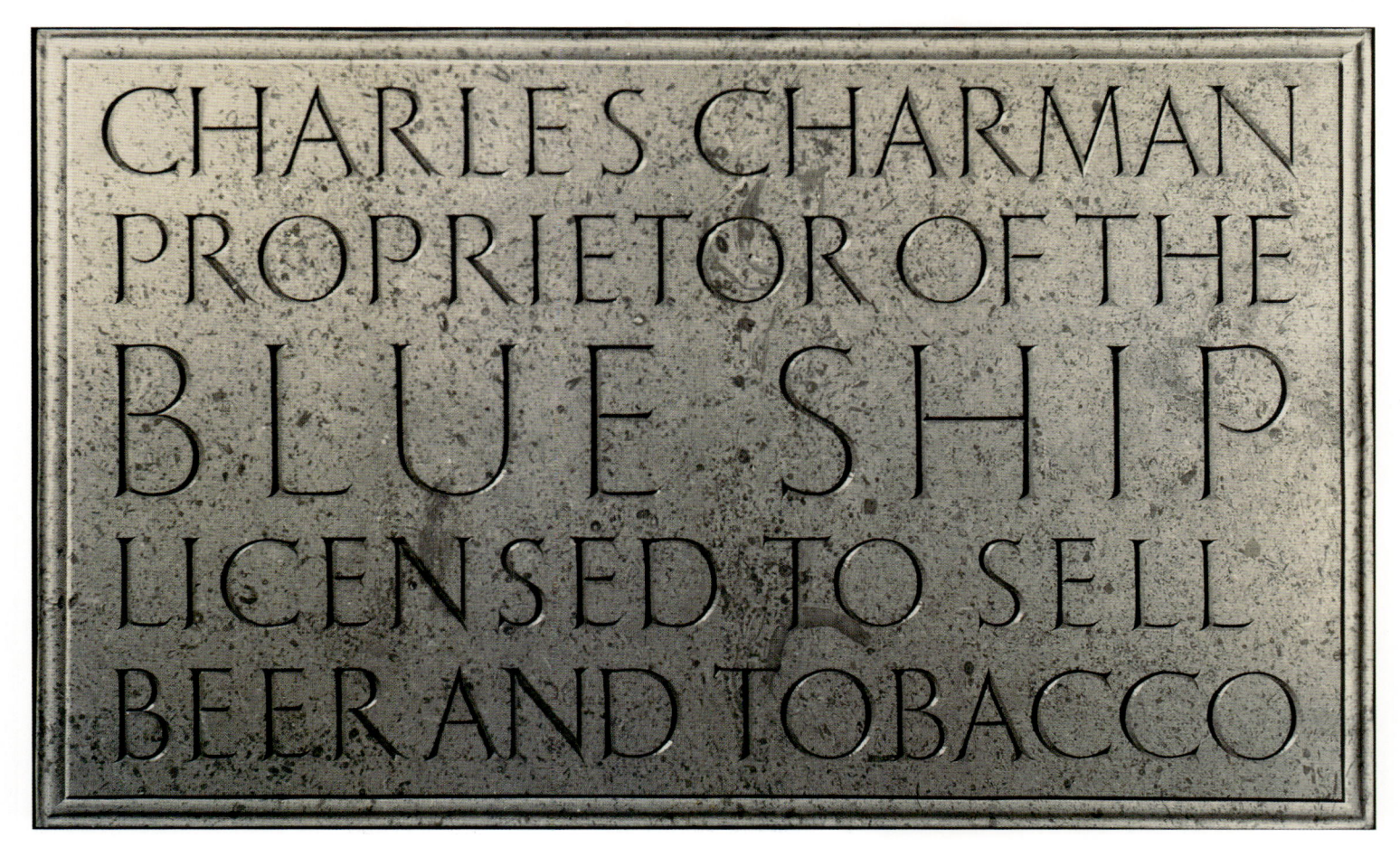

1 (*opposite page*). Inscription carved by David Kindersley, 1939.

2 (*below*). Arbora Decora (1956) by David Jones from *The Painted Inscriptions of David Jones* by Nicolete Gray (London: Gordon Fraser, 1981).

Cribb and his brother Laurie (1897–1979), Gill's longest-serving coworkers, continued carving at Ditchling until Joseph's death in 1967. He had introduced Michael Harvey (1931–2013) to lettercarving and saw John Skelton through his apprenticeship after Gill's early death. Joseph's Roman letters remained as Gill had taught him. Laurie Cribb went on to work for David Kindersley, who had established a workshop in Cambridge, in 1946. The workshop continues under the direction of his third wife, Lida Lopes Cardozo Kindersley Beck. Kindersley developed a finely finished and sturdy capital (narrower *H*, more upright *M*), and a subtle and beautiful italic which is shown to its best advantage on the fine-grained slate he favored. [1] Yet he was also an adventurous spirit; he cut letters in Rustic and was spurred by technical challenges or new materials (perspex, glass, lithography). In Joseph Cribb's book *Variations on the Theme of Twenty-Six Letters* (1969), the Gill tradition collided with pop art and psychedelia but was informed by a sense of history (runes), world culture (kufic forms), and the drawn line.

In the early 1960s, David Jones (1895–1974) and Ralph Beyer were principally responsible for breathing new life into the classical formulae. Some, no doubt, thought them wayward influences, but Jones, whose commitment to words made him a poet as well as a painter, discovered an abstract quality in lettering that enabled him to be true to both vocations. In his painted inscriptions from the late 1940s on, he strove to discover ways of working that kept him psychologically free, making a space for the accidental and slightly rough. Above all he wanted his inscriptions to have vitality. He drew on a rich vocabulary of letterforms, incorporating into his writing Latin, Welsh, and other modern European languages. [2] In a letter to Nicolete Gray, Jones remarked of habergeon (a jacket of chain mail) that, "you simply can't inscribe that word—so utterly of the North-European Middle Ages—in Roman capitals."[3] His informal arrangements of letters, his preference for the vernacular and the early Christian, counterbalanced Gill's more Roman Renaissance and Imperial influence. Jones's letters were primitive Romans, sloped at angles; *E* was wide, the serifs blunt, yet finely angled to collect the eye and turn it in specific directions. David Jones looked at a painted inscription as if it were a painting: every part must fit and the whole surface must be alive. Mostly private works made for friends,

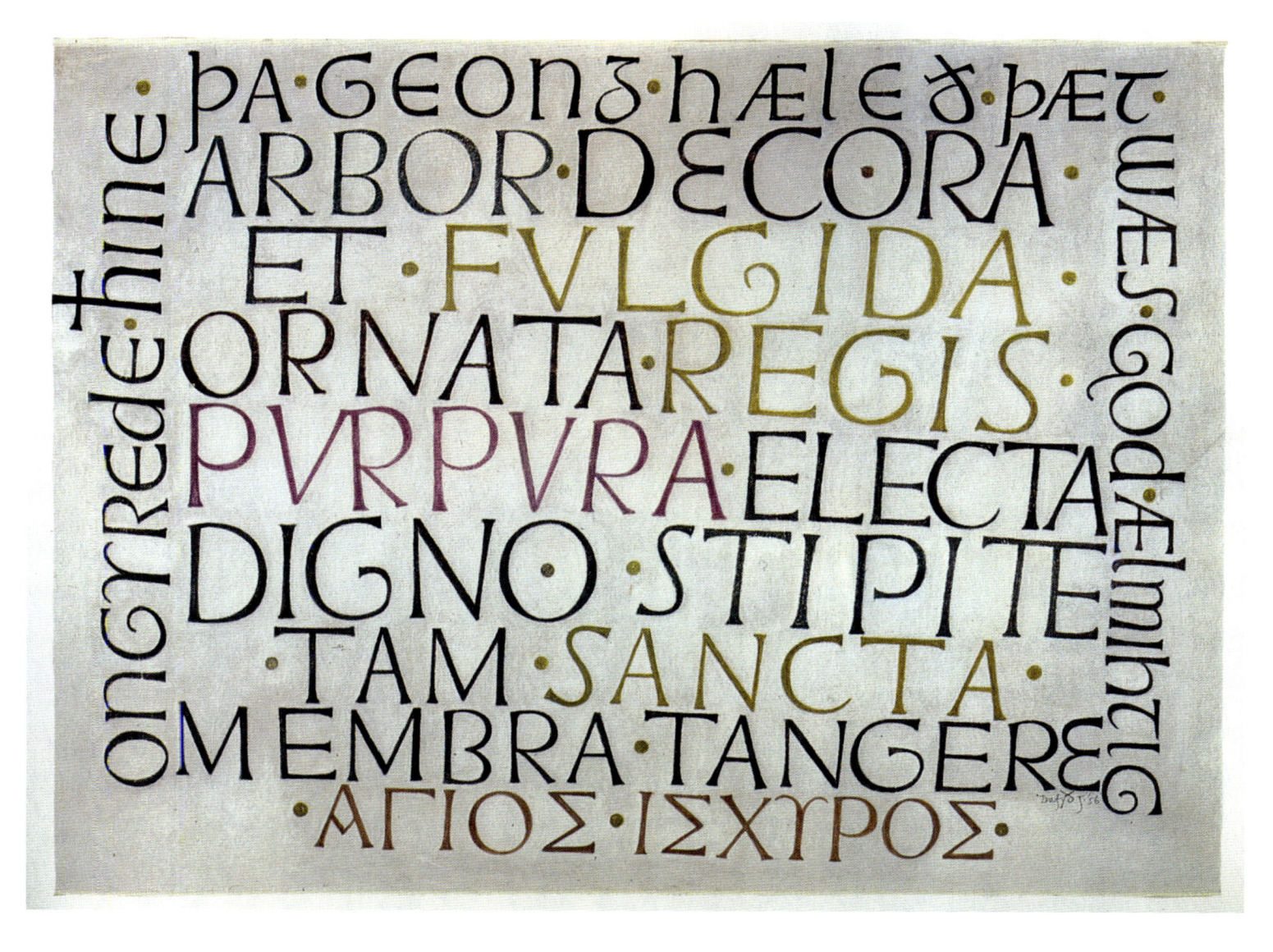

3 (*left*). Tomb of Joan Palmer (1918–1970) designed and carved by John Skelton.

4 (*above*). Inscription in St. Mary's churchyard, Haddington, East London. Carved in sandstone by Ralph Beyer, 1974.

5 (*below*). Churchill Memorial designed by John Skelton, 1965.

they continue to influence the current generation of letter carvers in Britain and on the Continent.

The German-born Ralph Beyer survived the war in Britain. He had been sent to England at age sixteen by his father, Oskar, who was a writer on primitive art, founder of Kunst Dienst (a German liturgical art movement), and an admirer of Rudolf Koch and his Offenbacher Werkstatt. Beyer, who had always resisted an overfinished letter, was confirmed in his own direction in lettercarving by seeing reproductions of Jones's work in a 1953 *Architectural Review* article by Nicolete Gray, as well as by his father's writings on the Christian inscriptions of the catacombs.[4] [4] Beyer went on to carve the immense Tablets of the Word[5] (eight tablets, each measuring 15' x 6') in Basil Spence's new Coventry Cathedral (1956–1961).

Beyer's slightly squared-off forms (perhaps just the design aesthetic of the times: Henry Moore, Barbara Hepworth) seemed to provide inspiration to Gill's nephew John Skelton. The Skelton workshop, at Streat in Sussex, was responsible for some of the more influential developments in lettercarving in the late sixties and seventies.

Skelton was both a sculptor and a lettercarver, which helped him to think more freely about shape [3, 5]. He stood at the center of an important network of influences that included the Belgian calligrapher Jef Boudens (1926–1990) and the French lettercarver Jean Claude Lamborot (b. 1921). John Skelton's house was full of work by Jones and Gill. Jack Trowbridge, one of Skelton's apprentices, who also worked as a silversmith, was given the freedom by John to develop his own distinctive silhouetted and chunkily serifed forms that became a Skelton trademark. It was the high weight-

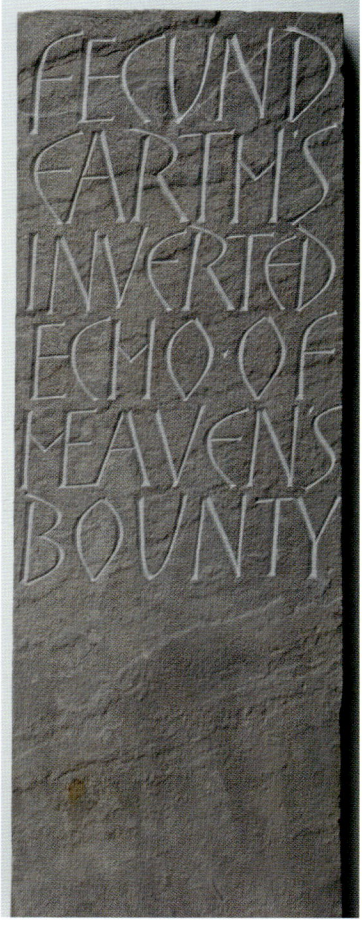

6, 7 (*right*). Two stones carved by Tom Perkins. Left: quotation from Hans Coper carved in Welsh slate, 1994. Right: Fecund Earth quotation from Brian Keeble carved in Herefordshire red stone, 2010.

8 Latin inscription carved by Richard Kindersley in limestone, 2009.

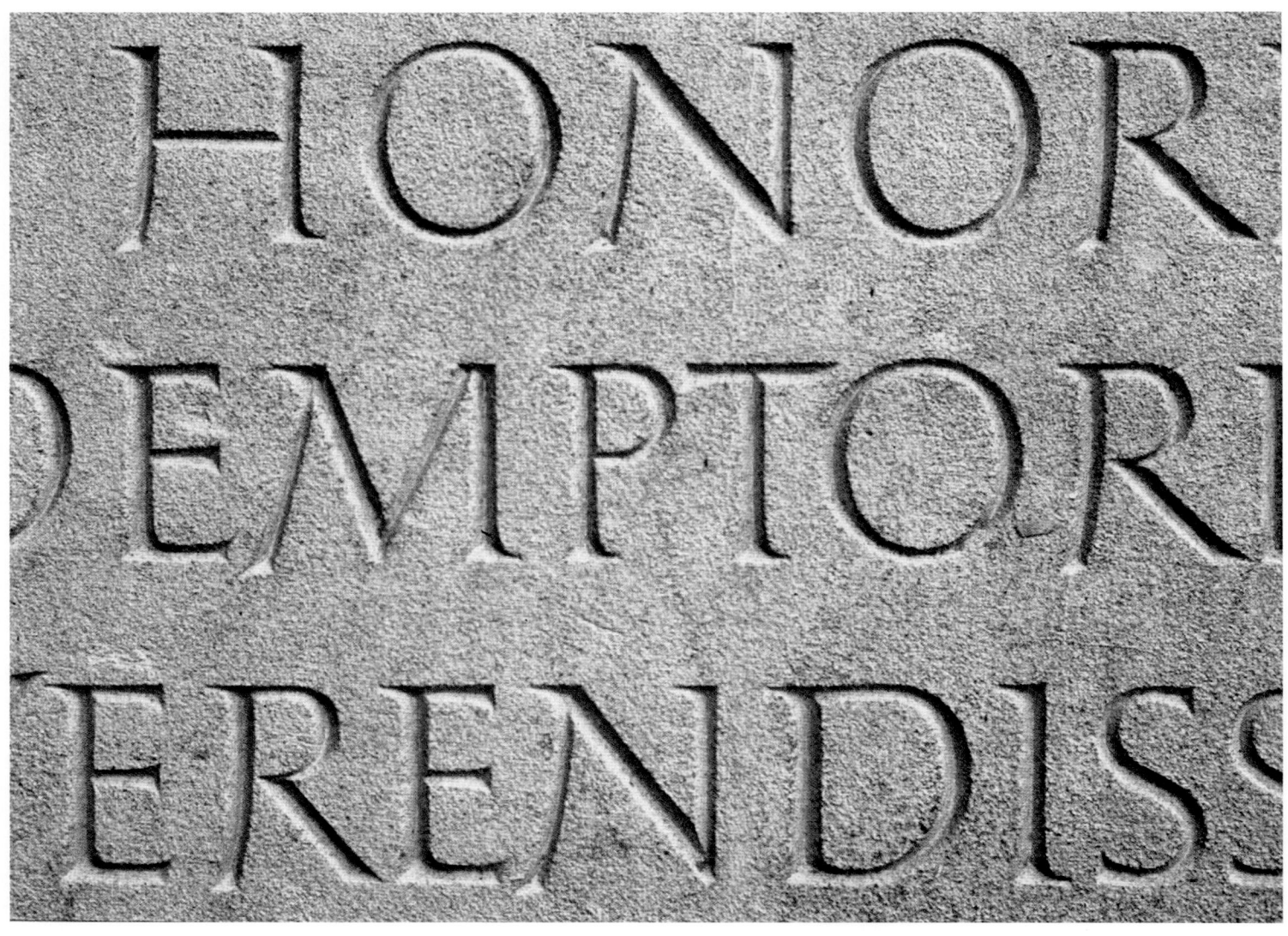

9 Detail of unidentified inscription carved by Michael Harvey, 1961. From *Adventures with Letters: A Memoir* by Michael Harvey (2012). The letters were influenced by the typeface Codex (C. E. Weber, 1955) designed by Georg Trump.

ing in these forms (on the *O* in particular) that would lead the young letter carver Tom Perkins (b. 1957) to develop the wide (and sometimes triple-weighted) *O*[6] that has become characteristic of his refined letter-carving. [6, 7] Perkins, who trained initially with Richard Kindersley (b. 1939), David's son, has also developed forms that take Gill's excursions with a pointed *O* as a basis for letter design.

Richard Kindersley too broke from a classical model when occasion demanded. [8] He has relished exploring an inscription's relationship to its setting in a more architectural way, sometimes stretching or compressing letters to achieve an overall composition carefully attuned to its environment. He has carved directly into brickwork and cast letters in concrete when required, and, true to Gill's philosophy, both materials and casting processes were allowed to affect the forms (often sans serif) and so they evolved.

Reynolds Stone focused principally on wood engraving; Gill had perspicaciously handed him an engraving tool as he left after his fortnight's stay at Piggots. (In 1939 Stone took up lettercarving.) Although his work came to span the medium, his contribution to engraved lettering was distinctive. Morison thought him the best after Gill. [10] He took the late Gill capital with its blunt serifed and open *C* and its more heavily weighted, and thus slightly more angular, leg to the *R* and added an influence taken from the engraved works of the 16th-century writing masters. In his work, the 20th-century capital had come full circle.[7]

Both David Kindersley and Reynolds Stone designed typefaces: the narrow and weighty Octavian by Kindersley (co-designed with Will Carter)[8] and Janet by Stone, based on his engraved forms. The most prolific and mainstream type designer of the Gill stable has been Michael Harvey. Having left Stone's workshop in 1961, he found work in dustjacket design, a trade whose fast turnaround stretched Harvey into exploring a wider repertoire of forms, one so diverse it is difficult to characterize. The forms were influenced by a burgeoning interest in the 1960s in vernacular letters, sparked by the writings of Nicolete Gray, Alan Bartram, and James Mosley. There was no longer an Imperial orthodoxy. Harvey's work in a more English vernacular tradition reached its apex in his commission for the inscriptions on the Sainsbury Wing of the National Gallery, London. [9] He drew direct inspiration from the great inscription—with its wide letters, chunkily serifed and high in stroke contrast—across the façade of St. Martin-in-the-Fields (1721–1726), which also flanks Trafalgar Square. (For more on Harvey, see p. 138.)

Gill's influence had begun to weaken in the 1960s with the rediscovery of the "English Letter," as Bartram dubbed it. In the 1980s, another tradition, that of contemporary German lettercarving as exemplified by Sepp Jakob of Freiburg im Breisgau, challenged his interpretation of letters. German attitudes toward stone in particular, shaped partly by the lack of machine technology immediately after World War II, meant that their volumes were more sculptural and surfaces textured. Letters were often raised rather than recessed. Upon seeing a copy of *Letters Slate Cut,* by David Kindersley, Jakob exploded, "*Nicht stein, nicht stein,*" pounding the table, "*ist Graphik!*" Yet Jakob had himself been taught by Alfred Riedel, a student of Rudolf Koch. Riedel used gothic forms, as well as both classical and monoline Romans, and had developed a fine uncial. His work and philosophy, especially as outlined in *Schrift + Symbol in Stein, Holz und Metall* (1995), heavily influenced the younger generation of English lettercarvers. Yet British lettercarving has kept its grounding in classical form, thanks to the continuing stream of public inscriptional lettering requiring functional legibility. Gill's letters are no longer dominant but, directly or indirectly, they remain a visible part of the English landscape.

1   A complete list of apprentices and coworkers can be found in David Peace, *Eric Gill: The Inscriptions* (London: Herbert Press, 1994), p. 173.
2   The Trajan inscription and the Wroxeter inscription from the Victoria & Albert Museum and British Museum, respectively, and Gill's inscriptions from *Manuscript and Inscriptional Letters.* See also James Mosley's comments in "Trajan Revived," *Alphabet* (1964): 17–36, esp. 29–33.
3   4 April 1961 in Nicolete Gray, *The Painted Inscriptions of David Jones* (London: Gordon Fraser, 1981), p. 106.
4   Oskar Beyer, *Frühchristliche Sinnbilder und Inschriften, Lebenszeugnisse der Katakombenzeit* (Kassel: Bärenreiter-Verlag 1954).
5   See http://en.wikipedia.org/wiki/File:Coventry_Cathedral.jpg
6   Tom Perkins's training in calligraphy at Reigate School of Art was also crucial to his understanding of the movement of weight around a letter; see his article "Calligraphy as a Basis for Letter Design," in *The Calligrapher's Handbook*, edited by Heather Child (London: A & C Black, 1985).
7   The capitals of Cresci (from *Il Perfetto Scrittore* [1570]), his contemporaries, and immediate successors (who believed in direct observation and rendering rather than geometry) followed a model closer to carvings from later in the reign of Hadrian (r. 117–38) and his immediate successor, Antonius Pius (r. 138–61), than from Trajan, who died in 117. The letters *M* and *H* are often the ones to watch.
8   Will Carter (1912–2001), founder of the Rampant Lions Press, designer of the Klang typeface and Dartmouth, a titling face for the college of that name. He learned letter cutting from David Kindersley and was a cousin of Reynolds Stone. In 1938, he spent some time in Germany in the studio of Paul Koch, son of the type designer Rudolf Koch.

10   Design by Reynolds Stone for specimen showing of his typeface Minerva (Linotype & Machinery, Ltd., 1954). Courtesy of Humphrey Stone.

STRAIGHT, NO CHASER
The Work of Michael Harvey

MICHAEL HARVEY WAS AN ENGLISH book jacket designer, lettercarver, type designer, and teacher. He was both part of the strong modern English lettering tradition begun by Eric Gill (1882–1940) and someone who stood in opposition to that tradition. Born in 1931 in Putney, Surrey, the son of the secretary of the Society of British Printing Ink Manufacturers, Harvey began his professional career at age sixteen, as a trainee engineering draftsman in a firm with the singularly unpretentious name Drawing & Tracing.

Dissatisfied with the rote nature of the work, Harvey sought a more creative outlet for his talents. In 1952, he discovered Eric Gill's *Autobiography* and found new inspiration for his drawing skills. He sought out Joseph Cribb (1892–1967), Gill's first assistant, to learn lettercarving. Following two summers of instruction from Cribb, in Ditchling, Sussex, Harvey joined Reynolds Stone (1909–1979), in 1955, as an assistant on large commissions. Although best known for his work as a wood engraver, Stone also cut letters in stone. Harvey's first job for him was prestigious: a three-panel inscription for the tomb of the Conservative Party politician Duff Cooper.

While working for Stone, Harvey enrolled in an evening class in lettering at the Epsom & Ewell School of Arts & Crafts. His first assignment was a book jacket design. It set him on the next phase of his career as a jacket designer for London publishers when, in 1961, he left Stone and became a full-time freelance designer, a status he maintained for the remainder of his life.

Harvey's lettering skills were honed by doing nearly 1,500 dustjackets over the course of nearly four decades. His clientele expanded to include publishers outside of London and Great Britain. In the late 1950s and early 1960s, Harvey zealously embraced letters outside of the Gill/Stone canon—sans serifs, slab serifs, pointed serifs, ligatures—along with new graphic tricks, such as reversing letters out of shapes, giving them rough textures or applying Zipatone patterns.

Over time these graphic tricks disappeared as Harvey became more confident about his lettering abilities, and the ability of letters to tell a story on their own. His jackets became simpler yet bolder. They were direct and without artifice or pretentiousness. In this he was influenced by a love of modern architecture and its purity of form. The perfect example of his mature style is the jacket for The Bodley Head edition of James Joyce's *Ulysses* (1975). [2]

During the 1960s, Harvey designed alphabets as a means of speeding up the design of some of his book jackets. He was thus well prepared when R. Hunter Middleton, of the Ludlow Typograph Company, commissioned him to design a typeface in 1966. The resultant design, a sloping "semi-serif" titling face with shading called Zephyr, harked back to a 1961 inscription he had carved under the influence of Georg Trump's Codex typeface. Both the inscription and Zephyr showed how much Harvey had moved beyond his hero Gill and his mentor Stone.

At the time, Zephyr was a one-off. Harvey did not become a serious type designer until the early 1980s, when Monotype Corporation agreed to take on the design that was eventually issued as Ellington (1990). The typeface was begun in the phototype era but not completed until the digital revolution had affected type design. Harvey was grateful for the change from drawing on paper to drawing on screen and lectured several times on the difference between designing type before and after the introduction of the Macintosh, PostScript, and programs such as Fontographer. "No longer did I need to make large character drawings," Harvey wrote in *Adventures with Letters*.

A sketch was enough as a background layer on which to draw outline bézier curves on

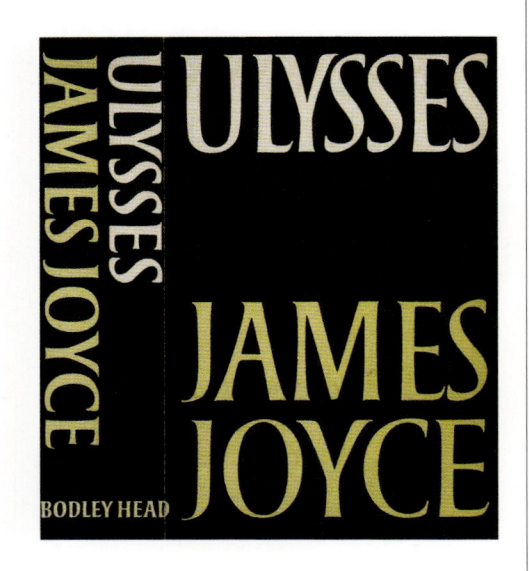

1 Book jacket for *Ulysses* by James Joyce (London: The Bodley Head, 1975). Designed and lettered by Michael Harvey.

2 (*left*). Detail of carved inscription on birdbath, 1996. The birdbath was a punning tribute to the alto saxophonist Charlie "Bird" Parker.

3 (*below*). Comparison of Ellington (Monotype Corporation, 1990) and Strayhorn (Monotype Corporation, 1992) typefaces.

ABEGMQRS
ABEGMQRS
abefghksty
abefghksty

WORKING WITH MICHAEL HARVEY was both an honor and a pleasure. It was after attending his letterforms course at the University of Reading that he asked me about working together as partners. I was flattered, but let it pass. Nine months later he asked me again, and then I knew he was serious—and thus Fine Fonts was born. We decided at the outset that we would create fonts from letterforms Michael had drawn for other purposes, such as book jackets and monuments. I was astounded when we went through his "back catalogue." Almost everywhere we looked there was gold, and thus the strapline to Fine Fonts—"Of Originality & Distinction"—suggested itself. Songlines and Balthasar are but two letterforms I had never seen before and they became two of our earliest fonts.

There was also innovation, primarily in the form of Mentor—the culmination of Michael's life in letters. Mentor incorporated those influences upon him that he held most dear. For both of us, the Mentor family—serif and sans serif—was a labor of love. After five years of forging the letterforms and the fonts on the anvil, thirty-two fonts emerged. Never was work so pleasurable as when Michael knew what he wanted, yet he was always was open to suggestion.

In Michael's studio archive* there is still much to discover and develop. Several typefaces, begun before his passing, are already in progress. Work will continue without "The Master" in the form of new very Fine Fonts.

—ANDY BENEDEK

* In addition to the material that remained in Michael's studio at the time of his death, many of his working drawings for typefaces, book jackets, and inscriptions, are now housed at the University of Reading Library, Special Collections Service, Papers of Michael Harvey (URL MS 5115).

4 Notes for Letterforms Unlimited workshop "Discover Yourself Drawing", 1989.

5 "Capital Letters" from *Creative Lettering: Drawing and Design* by Michael Harvey (London: The Bodley Head, 1985), p. 75.

Michael Harvey's Typefaces
(including unreleased designs)[1]

Methuen (1963)—photographic alphabet for book jacket titles; the basis for Braff
Grot R (1964)—listed by Macmillan but not in *Adventures with Letters*
Zephyr* (Ludlow Typograph, 1966; Fine Fonts, 2005)
Millbank (Tate Gallery, 1982)
Olympus (experiment, 1986)
Stamford (The Bodley Head, 1987)
Ellington (Monotype Corporation, 1990)
Strayhorn (Monotype Corporation, 1992)
Studz (Adobe, 1993)
Mezz (Adobe, 1994)
Andreas (Adobe, 1996)
Conga Brava (Adobe, 1996)
Childness (experiment, 1998)
Hotshot (experiment, 1998)
Zoot (experiment, 1998)
Jazzbo (experiment, 1999)
Moonglow (Adobe, 2000)
Aesop Script (Fine Fonts, 2000)
DTL *Unico* (Dutch Type Library, 2000)
Songlines (Fine Fonts, 2001)
Balthasar (Fine Fonts, 2002)
Braff (Fine Fonts, 2002)
Fine Gothic (Fine Fonts, 2006)
Tisdall Script (Fine Fonts, 2006)
Marceta (Fine Fonts, 2003)
Mentor and *Mentor Sans* (Fine Fonts, 2005)
Frieze (Fine Fonts, 2010)
Ruskin (Fine Fonts, 2012)
Victoriana (Fine Fonts, 2012)
Kaycee (Fine Fonts, in progress)
Scorpio (Fine Fonts, in progress)

*Michael redesigned and expanded Zephyr in 2008 for Fine Fonts, adding a lowercase to it.

screen with the mouse. And no more retouching; everything could be adusted through manipulating the curves. From then on, all of his typefaces were designed on the computer. Even so, they all had roots in letters made by hand. Harvey designed typefaces for Monotype, the Dutch Type Library, Adobe, and, in the final fifteen years of his life, for Fine Fonts, a partnership he shared with Andy Benedek.

Some of Harvey's type designs—notably Mezz, Braff, and Balthasar—came directly from lettering originally done for book jackets, but others came from custom lettering for such clients as The Bodley Head or The Tate Gallery (now Tate Britain) or from his inscriptional work. The length of the stultifying name of a trade publication, *Purchasing & Supply Management*, forced Harvey to devise a condensed letter for the masthead, which led to the design of Ellington. The design of Strayhorn (1996), Ellington's sans serif companion, can be traced to the 1986 inscription he designed for The Clore Gallery at the Tate. [3]

Through his client and friend John Ryder, of The Bodley Head, Harvey was enticed to write four books on lettermaking: *Lettering Design: Form & Skill in the Design & Use of Letters* (1975), *Creative Lettering: Drawing & Design* (1985), *Carving Letters in Stone & Wood* (1987), and *Calligraphy in the Graphic Arts* (1988). The latter three are especially notable for his use of drawings rather than photographs to illustrate techniques. "Drawing is the key," wrote Harvey. "Drawing frees the hand from the demands of the broad-edged pen, the sign-writer's brush. The pencil is neutral. Eye and mind are in control." [5] As much as he appreciated the labor-saving aspects of designing with a computer, he always retained his passion for drawing, the common link in his work as lettercarver, book jacket designer, and type designer.

Drawing and making were at the heart of Harvey's teaching. He taught lettering at Bournemouth & Poole College of Art and Design from 1961 to 1980, but got discouraged as educational "reform" in the late 1960s replaced craft with research. In contrast, his experience teaching "Letterforms" at the University of Reading, from 1993 to 2001, was more enjoyable. There he was encouraged to teach the students a range of crafts "including drawing, writing, carving, writing with brushes and pens, cutting letters in stone, wood, lino and rubber, [and] drawing letters with instruments and freehand." The Reading class was the culmination of ideas about teaching lettering that Harvey had honed while teaching workshops for calligraphy societies in the United States and Canada. [4]

One of Michael Harvey's most important and long-lived clients was the Scottish concrete poet Ian Hamilton Finlay (1925–2006), whose poems he lettered for print and inscribed in stone for more than thirty years. [6] Harvey served on the Royal Mint Advisory Committee for the Design of Coins and Medals from 1991 to 2004, and in 2001 he was awarded an MBE (Member of the Most Excellent Order of the British Empire).

Besides lettering and making things, Harvey was passionate about jazz, photography, and bicycling. He named a number of his typefaces after jazz musicians or compositions—though he was not always successful in this, as his attempts to name typefaces Jelly Roll and Jeru both foundered. At the end of his life he started a small publishing venture, 47 Editions, to showcase his photography.

Michael Harvey was that rare individual who seemed truly beloved by everyone, whether student or colleague—even by those who were not enamored of his style of lettering. This is all the more surprising given that he always spoke his mind about lettering and design. But he did so in a cheery manner that was disarming, and with a nonchalance that suggested he was more satisfied to voice his opinions than to convince others to share them. Most of his opinions were spoken and not written, but in *Adventures with Letters* he closed with a flurry of them, as if he wanted to make sure that before he died his views would not be forgotten.

Michael Harvey's work was never stilted nor contrived. His lettering—whether on paper, in stone, or on screen—was a reflection of the man himself: warm and full of life. It will be missed and so will he.
—P.S.

---

6 "Battle Flag for a Catamaran" (1995) by Ian Hamilton Finlay. Postcard designed and lettered by Harvey.

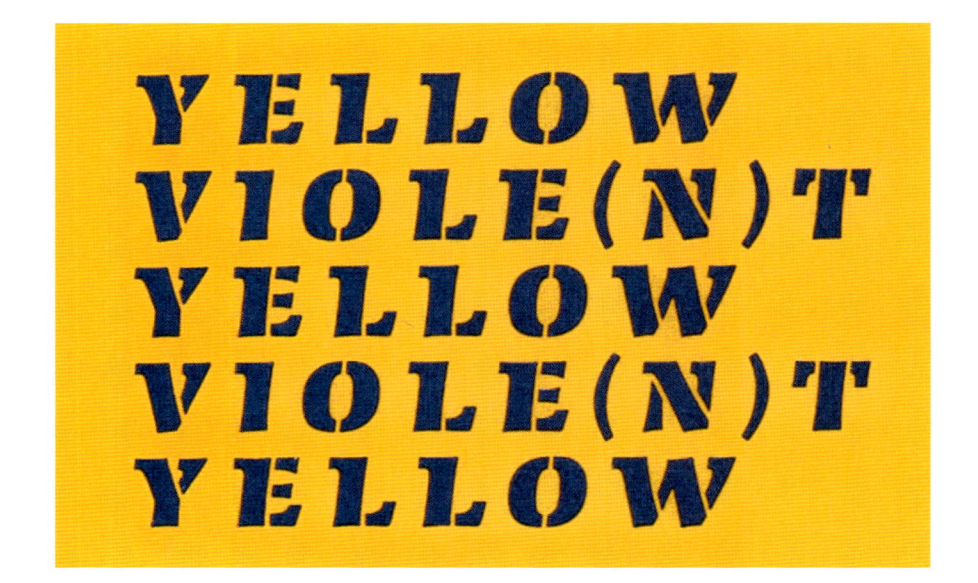

1 For completed typefaces, the dates signify the year the typeface was released, based on information provided by Andy Benedek of Fine Fonts or derived from *Adventures with Letters* by Michael Harvey (Bridport, UK: 47 Editions, 2012). Some of these dates contradict those given in sources by others, such as *An A-to-Z of Type Designers* by Neil Macmillan (New Haven, Conn.: Yale University Press, 2006).

ABCDEFGHIJKLM
abcdefghijklmnopqrst
NOPQRSTUVWXYZ
uvwxyz & 1234567890
abcdefghijklmnopqrstuvwxyz.

HB 1947

RICHARD KINDERSLEY [RK] How did John Howard Benson come to buy the John Stevens Shop? Why was he driven to re-create the Shop's lettercarving tradition?

JOHN BENSON [JEB] After studying art in New York, my father returned to Newport intending to be a sculptor and graphic artist. He secured a few commissions for stone sculptures and carried them out in the shop, which he first rented and eventually purchased from the Stevens family. He also was asked to make a gravestone for the wife of a prominent local clergyman. He knew, and to some extent had studied, the 18th-century colonial gravestones here in Newport, many of which had come from the Stevens Shop. Work was carried on there until the time he took it over, in 1927. The gravestone commission was a welcome addition to the job list because it was profitable. The letters he carved on it were drawn in outline in pencil, then traced down on the stone for carving. Their forms and the design of the stone were derived from the carving of John Stevens II. No brush was involved.

RK What role did Graham Carey play in the Shop?

JEB Graham Carey was a very intelligent and well-educated man from a wealthy family. He was a devout Catholic, as my father became, perhaps through his influence. He loaned my father some money to help buy the Shop, or perhaps to improve its facilities. My father and he were partners in the Shop, although, being well-to-do and not needing to work, Carey's casual lifestyle did not blend easily with Dad's work ethic. They did, however, have lots of fun together and the friendship lasted throughout JHB's life.[4]

RK That is a very clear image of how your father began, drawing with pencil and using local references. It would seem that the Benson capitals grew naturally from very practical needs, but as all the Bensons developed and brought in their particular style and growing erudition, the letters themselves became more sophisticated. Can you comment further on this evolution?

JEB As you suggest, the "Shop Roman" developed individually with the three Bensons who produced it. JHB's might seem to be the simplest, but is far from it [1, 5]. In inscriptions, his concern was mostly with pattern and overall design. The individual letters were strongly drawn but not at all fussy. His penlike brushwork was done quickly. In mass, the bold and relaxed geometry of the skeletons under his strokes produced patterns not unlike those of the inscriptions of 2nd-century AD Rome.

THE JOHN STEVENS SHOP 145

CDEF
IJK
OPQRS
WYZ

A ma könyvművésze feladatát nagy részben építészeti, főként pedig a szó tiszta értelmében grafikai feladatnak érzi.   Emerich Kner

Printing is an international art — it belongs to the people of all nations & is an effective instrument for world peace. For, if peace is the product of mutual understanding, then there is no work of man which is better designed to promote that understanding than the printing press.
Raymond Blattenberger

My letters were influenced by Hermann Zapf [see fig. 6] and W. A. Dwiggins, and the great Arnold Bank, who used to visit here in the summers. [7] Always looming over them all was my father's vital example. Nick learned mainly from me, heaven help him, but he has established a fine, personal style. I have tried to keep my nose out of his business since he started to run the Shop. He is the one to talk about his influences. We are less venturesome than JHB and you English, but we love the marriage of depth and surface tension in the v-cut letter and how it can enliven a surface sculpturally.

NICK BENSON [NB] My father did his best to make Roman capitals according to his father's examples, but he quickly realized that JHB brought all of his artistic talents to the task of lettering and carving. JEB realized that his talents were slanted toward technical proficiency. Not only was he inspired by the work of Zapf and Dwiggins, as he says, but he spent a lot of time looking at Emil Hübner's outline drawings of Roman inscriptions. (See p. 253.) He and his colleague John Hegnauer developed a Roman capital letter that was not at all like JHB's. [9, 10] At its best, it is a lean and beautifully stroked, broad-edge brush Roman, and the carving of these forms is as fine as any lettering cut in stone.

RK I think in our case, in the United Kingdom, there is a serious tendency to follow venturousness at the expense of having confidence in sound design. "The marriage of depth and surface tension in the v-cut letter and how it can enliven a surface sculpturally" is a beautiful articulation of our craft.

NB Early in the 1940s, Edward Catich demonstrated his broad-edge brush technique to my grandfather and his business partner, Graham Carey. He made a very strong case as to just how important this technique was in producing the Trajan inscription. Catich dedicated his life to the idea that the Trajan inscription is "the best Roman letter designed in the Western world, and the one which most nearly approaches an alphabetical ideal." He designed and carved Roman capital letters in strict adherence to this ideal. [4; see also p. 25]

RK Did Catich's demonstration of his broad-edge brush technique change JHB's practice or influence your father's work? I know that my father [David Kindersley] (fig. 11) resisted Catich's claim—it was almost an edict—that the brush was the overwhelming influence on the form of the Imperial Roman capitals. He believed that Catich never gave enough credit to the influence and effect of the chisel when carving over the painted letter.

NB JHB spent quite a bit of his young adult life looking at the work of the first three generations of Stevens family stone carvers. The Stevenses did not use brushes to lay out the letters they carved. Their letters evolved solely through use of the mallet and chisel. They may have used a roughly scratched layout to give some idea of placement, but the act of carving the forms developed the aesthetic of the lettering. Over fifty-odd years of evolution, this lowercase form was refined to a point of exceptional beauty. JHB saw and understood this. He also understood the merits of the brush technique that Catich espoused, but he chose to use this skill—along with what he had learned from Gill, Johnston, and

6 (*opposite*). Detail of alphabet broadside by Hermann Zapf, 1964. From *Hermann Zapf and His Design Philosophy* (Chicago: Society of Typographic Arts, 1987), pp. 172–173.

7 (*right*). Detail of Credo by John Rockefeller, Jr. (Rockefeller Center, New York City). Designed and lettered by Arnold Bank; carved and gilded by James Casey and John E. Benson, 1962.

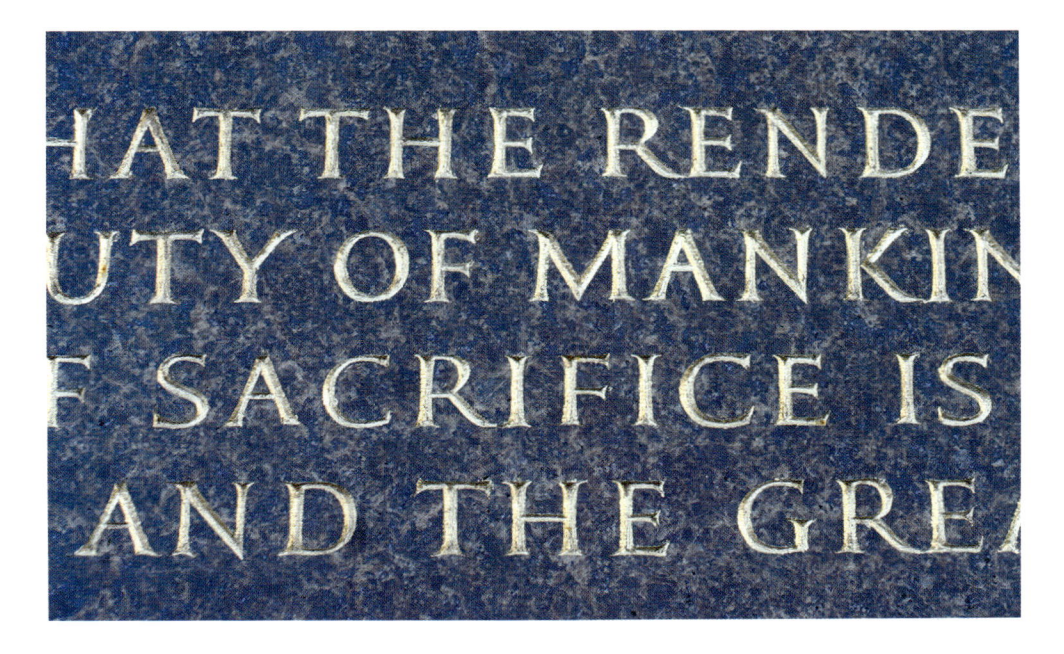

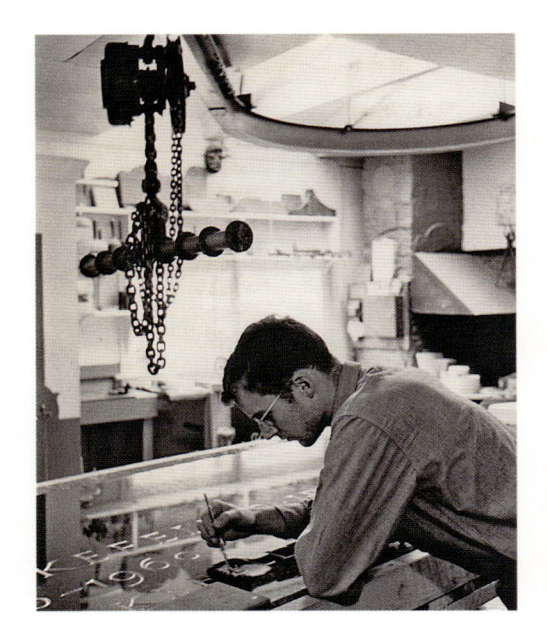

8 (*right*). John E. Benson painting letters, 1964.

9 (*below*). Alphabet stone for Philip Hofer carved by John E. Benson, 1964. Gold leaf on Monson slate. (Houghton TypS-2, Houghton Library, Harvard University.)

10 (*above*). Rubbing of alphabet stone carved by John Hegnauer for Erik Stocker, 2000.

11 (*right*). Memorial inscription for Stanley Morison carved by David Kindersley, 1976. Welsh slate. Commissioned by Brooke Crutchley, University Printer at Cambridge for the Stanley Morison Memorial Room, Cambridge University Library.

THE JOHN STEVENS SHOP 149

numerous other sources—as a jumping off point in developing a Roman capital letter that was entirely his own. [12]

RK   What are your views on how the Benson capitals compare with the original Trajan inscription or the English tradition of Eric Gill? [13]

JEB   In addition to his graphic and sculptural skills, JHB was a gifted mathematician. He was very interested in the theory of dynamic symmetry as put forward by Jay Hambidge.[5] Mathematics played an important role in his design work. Oddly enough, this did not affect his approach to letterforms, which was initially based on 18th-century models and later, in the 1930s, the study of classical Roman capitals and historic, continental pen forms. In the thirties, with his partner Carey, he wrote and drew all the illustrations for their book *The Elements of Lettering* (1940), a solid, practical treatise.[6] [14] JHB had found and carried with him a copy of Johnston's *Writing & Illuminating, & Lettering* (1906), which he wore out from daily use. From this, and his exposure to Johnston's and Gill's work, his lettering rapidly grew in sophistication and took on a more classical form. Carey was a patron of Gill, corresponded with him at length, and commissioned work from him. This association contributed greatly to my father's understanding of the craft. And yet, his Roman caps were highly personal, vigorously drawn and cut, and did not adhere to the Trajan standard. Lowercase letters were more related to the Johnstonian models, and his personal italic style grew out of those influences. Only later in life, when he became interested in the Renaissance writing masters, did this develop into more italianate forms, eventually leading to his edition of Arrighi's *Operina*. It is worth remembering that JHB had no formal training in lettering, and that any such work being done around him in New York was very commercial and largely free from English or Continental influence. Once established in the Shop, he taught himself.

RK   Can you say more about the book JHB and Carey wrote?

JEB   *The Elements of Lettering* owes a great debt to *Writing & Illuminating, & Lettering*. Graham Carey wrote the text, with JHB editing and collaborating on the technical parts. It was printed in 1940 and again in 1950, after the Italian influence came into Dad's italic. Some of the pen-lettered plates, to our eyes today, seem more than a bit crude, but they served their purpose well. Many were redrawn for the 1950 edition. The marginal illustrations, some first done as wood engravings, are splendid, and show Dad's characteristic gift for design.

RK   Your mention of JHB's interest in dynamic symmetry through people like Hambidge is tantalizing, since from the Renaissance onward so many letterers have tried to discover the mathematical paradigms underlying classical capitals.

JEB   My father did not use Hambidge's system to draw letters, but to help him place lines of words on the stones. The words were formed spontaneously with little concern for typographic convention. He sometimes did sketches with no lettering at all, just the shape of the lettered surface covered with lines and formulas.

RK   JHB had the foresight to explore lettering through the brush. I believe that the geometry of the wrist, elbow, and shoulder brings its own mathematics to the production of pen and brush letters, giving them a unity and rhythm that the mathematical method of discovery has attempted to uncover. I am reminded of William Blake's drawing of Newton bending down with paper and dividers, his reductionist take on the scientific method. My library is littered with books showing attempts at finding mathematical paradigms. All of the results are unappetizing. What, in your view, makes the Benson capitals unique?

NB   So many people refer to "The Roman" as some sort of definitive ideal; perhaps this is with the Trajan inscription in mind, thanks to Johnston, Catich, and others. The form has a broad range of styles. It reached the refined quality we see in the Trajan between the birth of the Roman Empire and the end of the 3rd century. [15, 18] There are many other inscriptions equally as beautiful as the Trajan, and there were obvious stylistic choices made by those who produced them that help to differentiate them. Roman capital lettering, V-cut into stone, is directly influenced by both the painted layout and the way in which the letters are carved. The brushwork may be a bit more important than the carving, but the carving is vastly more important than many people understand.

RK   I very much agree with all you have said. In my view. there are about five great seminal inscriptions surviving in Rome. I photographed a letter *D* on the Via Appia in Rome that says it all: the gestural quality of the brush and the refinement of the chisel. [16] It sits abandoned by the side of the road, a testament to a beauty which transcends the mere utilitarian letter *D*.

NB   That is a gorgeous *D*! I assume you have seen the tablet on the tomb to the freed children of Sextus Pompeius Justus on the Appian Way. In my opinion it is the finest Roman inscription that exists. [18] I am traveling to Rome this October to examine it in the flesh, along with a number of other inscriptions.

RK   In your work, how does the type of stone and the scale of lettering affect the design of the letters?

JEB   JHB's approach to inscriptions on structures was governed largely by practical considerations, architectural aesthetics, and issues of material, visibility, and legibility. It is still our approach. Coming of age as a designer in the sixties, my experience with architects was complicated. Most of them wanted no lettering on their buildings at all. Furthermore, they seemed unconcerned with geology, other than to select stone of agreeable—or bland—and noninvasive coloring. I was always being told to make the letters smaller. I took to making my first submission of design ideas much larger than needed so we could compromise to a size more near the ideal. On architectural projects, we usually came in late on the job and were required to cut whatever material they gave us.

RK   In England, too, modernism—derived from the Bauhaus conceit that the building should articulate its purpose by its function—led architects to view lettering as a distracting embellishment. Luckily, the *fatwa* has lost potency in recent years, and

12 Latin inscription carved by JHB in Monson black slate.

13 (*left*). Rubbing of a stone cut by Eric Gill. From *The Elements of Lettering* by John Howard Benson and Arthur Graham Carey (Newport: John Stevens Shop, 1940), Plate XXIII.

14 (*right*). "Built-Up Letters" by JHB. From *The Elements of Lettering* by John Howard Benson and Arthur Graham Carey (Newport: John Stevens Shop, 1940), Plate XVIII, p. 68.

THE JOHN STEVENS SHOP 151

15 (*above*). Tomb of Flavia Irene, wife of Titus Claudius Secundus (CIL. VI. 1859) on the Via Appia, Rome, 1st c. AD.

16 (*left*). Fragment of tomb on the Via Appia, Rome.

17 (*below*). Copy of Appian Way *D* carved by Richard Kindersley as a teaching aid.

now we can work occasionally as part of a team with architects, and indeed, show them that lettering on buildings can be strikingly beautiful and effective. Of course, the great irony is that on the 1923 Bauhaus building there is a splendid piece of vertical architectural lettering.

JEB Roger that! I had a book about the Bauhaus in college. Read the covers off it.

RK Do either of you have a repertoire of digitized alphabets that you apply to various jobs, or do you always begin with a new design for each commission?

JEB To support a shop with five or six employees, I took on more of the graphics requirements for buildings and made a few custom alphabet designs. This actually started with photographic styles, but with the computer it grew much easier. Prior to this, we had to do all our sketches by hand. [18, 19]. Many in a long list of benefactors, rendered in two or three design variants, begged for an easier methodology. With the computer and its typographic capabilities, I began, in the late '80s, to make digital alphabets for assistance in laying out larger and more complex commissions. Although we have done several such jobs this way, the alphabets tend to be so specifically designed for one job and its physical attributes that they are less broadly applicable than one might think. Nick does, however, use some of them for certain initial design sketches.

NB I design all of the lettering by hand for gravestone work. I have designed a few in-house typefaces to use for my sketches. Unfortunately, I find that many of the clients I work with these days want the option to amend my designs. This may well be in response to the limited desktop design work they do on their own computers, and the idea that we can make immediate changes with the click of a button, but I have found that I simply cannot make hand-drawn sketches pay. These "sketch faces" are really just placeholders for the lettering that I work up with a brush at full scale. [20]

RK Nick, you must find that extremely difficult and frustrating, having put your professional judgment into something and then have your client want to "fiddle" with it on their computer.

NB Such is the curse of desktop editing, I suppose. I take most of it with a grain of salt. The architectural typefaces are typically one of a kind. I design with the material, architecture, scale, and subject in mind. [20, 23] Each of the faces I have designed looks heavy, typographically, but keep in mind that at least 10% of the weight of these forms is lost once they are carved in stone.

RK The digital lettering you both do, I assume you save them as a font. Can you say a little more about the process? Do you draw on paper and scan into a program like Adobe Illustrator? Or do you work directly onscreen, bringing up in the background one of your previous designs, which might need tweaking for a current client?

JEB No more ridiculous system of drawing has ever been devised than the one(s) governing digital design. Anyone who claims to be able to draw letters solely on the screen and/or without extensive, hand-drawn trials in graphic media can cheerfully lay claim to the dismal aesthetic of most digital type design. The practitioners who produce the best stuff—Rich Lipton, Sumner Stone, Carol Twombly, Matthew Carter, Jovica Veljović, et al.—all cut their teeth with pen or brush or steel or stone. Computer drawing of individual letters and

18 Detail of the tomb of the children of Sextus Pompeius Justus on the Via Appia, Rome, 2nd century AD. (CIL VI 24520)

THE JOHN STEVENS SHOP 153

19 (*below*). The Four Freedoms monument, Roosevelt Island, New York City. Carved in Mount Airy granite by Nicholas Benson and Paul Russo, 2012.

20 (*opposite, above*). Martin Luther King Memorial font (2010) designed by Nicholas Benson.

21 (*opposite, below*). Stone of Hope, the Martin Luther King Memorial, Washington, DC. Carved in Atlantic green granite by Nicholas Benson, 2010.

> IN THE FUTURE DAYS WHICH WE SEEK TO MAKE SECURE, WE LOOK FORWARD TO A WORLD FOUNDED UPON FOUR ESSENTIAL HUMAN FREEDOMS. THE FIRST IS FREEDOM OF SPEECH AND EXPRESSION – EVERYWHERE IN THE WORLD. THE SECOND IS FREEDOM OF EVERY PERSON TO WORSHIP GOD IN HIS OWN WAY – EVERYWHERE IN THE WORLD. THE THIRD IS FREEDOM FROM WANT... EVERYWHERE IN THE WORLD. THE FOURTH IS FREEDOM FROM FEAR... ANYWHERE IN THE WORLD. THAT IS NO VISION OF A DISTANT MILLENNIUM. IT IS A DEFINITE BASIS FOR A KIND OF WORLD ATTAINABLE IN OUR OWN TIME AND GENERATION.
>
> — FRANKLIN D. ROOSEVELT
> JANUARY 6, 1941

ABCDE
FGHIJK
LMNOP
QRSTU
VWXYZ

MARTIN LUTHER KING, JR. NATIONAL MEMORIAL SITE SPECIFIC LETTER DESIGN 3.75" CHARACTER
THE JOHN STEVENS SHOP

INJUSTICE ANYWHERE IS A THREAT TO JUSTICE EVERYWHERE. WE ARE
CAUGHT IN AN INESCAPABLE NETWORK OF MUTUALITY, TIED IN
A SINGLE GARMENT OF DESTINY. WHATEVER AFFECTS
ONE DIRECTLY, AFFECTS ALL INDIRECTLY.

ALABAMA, 1963

shoehorning them into digital fonts is the rule of the day and it is a very thin one at that.

I always started with hand-drawn body copy as near final scale as my hand would allow. [23] The letters were extracted from scans of such examples and digitized in Fontographer or Illustrator. Many proofs, many full-size trials of text. For small-scale fonts, when the Laserwriter only had 300 dpi output, I used to scan pages of handwriting and make bitmap fonts from them before resorting to the Bezier drawing tool for the final version. The bigger stuff was often drawn with a chisel-edged marker.

RK I notice that the Shop often uses a humanist sans serif letter, as for example in the Martin Luther King Memorial. [21] How did this letter evolve?

JEB The Martin Luther King alphabet, a sans serif letter somewhere between the Greco-Roman stone graffiti models and such modern work as Hans Meier's Syntax or Carol Twombly's Lithos, was drawn to meet very specific needs. The originals were from brush-drawn, full-size studies by Nick. [20] The American black community was the client for this job, and had no desire for a traditional Latin, continental, or Anglo-Saxon letterform. Furthermore, just when the MLK job was maturing, a strong and intelligent criticism of tribal African and "Black" poster-style letterforms appeared in the press. We had first considered this avenue, but the criticism linked it to slavery. In that precise time frame, it was thus made unacceptable. The stone selected by the architect was a strongly colored granite with a coarse crystalline structure and a honed finish. In the matrix of the stone, the junctions of the large crystals formed tiny fracture lines, which, if cut across with a driven chisel in a near-polished face, tended to produce chips. Coupled with the large letter counts involved and the fussiness of all that laying out and tracing down, we decided to use computer-cut sandblast stencils and very lightly blast the layouts into the stone, to form a clean line across these fractures up to which a sharp-edged v-section could be cut.

RK This is an interesting description of how the lettering arrived from the need to express an impartial archetypal letterform rather than an Anglo-Saxon letter with all its baggage. I thought it looked most elegant, whatever its derivation, and that it worked well with the granite while being humanist. It carries power because of its interaction with a hard material. Your initial, very light sandblasting is a process that people use from time to time in England. Has this particular letterform for the King Memorial led to architects being interested in using it? I notice that on the FDR inscription you cut directly in from the drawing. Photographs show the work being cut by hand. Was that the case for all the lettering, or did you use a small air tool? I detect a strong Roman influence in the Martin Luther King inscriptions.

JEB Well, why not? Nick and I both love the early, Greco-Roman, sans serif capitals. Many were carved directly into bronze or copper plates. In stone they have the dynamism of graffiti, with the glorious Greek skeletons overlaid by the barbaric aspirations of early Rome. The digital letter I sandblasted for the longer quotes on the FDR job was taken quite shamelessly from these models. [22] Nick's MLK font is more subtly drawn and gracefully spaced. They were taken from brush letters he drew at full scale. Other uses of these alphabets do occur, but not in any major works without redrawing. [19]

NB The sans serif form I chose for the MLK Memorial also had much to do with its architectural style. It is certainly considered contemporary design, with nods to the classical world. The Martin Luther King Memorial Foundation liked the idea of the lettering having some contemporary overtones.

RK I think this works particularly well, because the inscription looks fresh and contemporary, yet has an underlying humanist quality shining through from classicism. The humanist element is of course very apposite to the memorial and its message.

Could you say a little more about how you came to design the letterform? You mentioned the architectural style having an input, yet there also seems to be much more emerging from the tradition of the Stevens Shop into the letters.

NB The funny thing about all of the typefaces I have designed for large architectural jobs is that I have a hard time getting away from the capital, skeletal form we have developed over the past seventy years. [23] Much of what makes the letters work well on the MLK Memorial is the skeletal form. When one sees the inscriptions from a distance, they read well because of it. In turn, as one gets closer and sees the attention to the details and the finish of the letters, they work well on that front, too, I think.

RK What is your process of drawing up capital letters? Do you begin with the brush and work the letters over with a pencil drawing? Does computer software have any input into the design process?

JEB Once JHB got a brush in his hands, known from the work of Gill and others, his letters took on a strong and characteristic style. He held the brush like a pen in thumb and forefinger, with the hand resting lightly and moving on the stone. Full-size cartoons were done in watercolor on paper and pounced down through lively perforations. My method was to use a chisel-edged carpenter's pencil for a rough layout on brown paper and then paint over it with white poster paint. Toward the end of my time in the Shop, I took to doing this pencil layout with no guidelines and only casual reference to my sketch. After the broad-edged, rough pencil layout, I brushed down directly over it, and on the same paper an adjusted, white poster paint layout. Over this I would do a tracing paper overlay, correcting the form and spacing where needed, and then trace this down on measured lines on the stone. [27, 28] The final layout was done over this with the same white poster color. This rather laborious technique I learned from Jim Casey, a good carver and sign painter. He worked briefly with my father when he returned, heavily decorated, from World War II, and then joined the Shop again after my father died from his lifelong heart condition in 1956.

RK Do you believe that classical Roman letters have a place in the 21st century? If so, what are they good for and why?

JEB Carol Twombly's Adobe Trajan has proven the viability of the Trajan letterform in a graphic context, at least in this country. It can be seen everywhere. Efforts to use it in carved work are less successful and tend to reveal the spindly quality of the design at small sizes and the compromises Carol had to make for it to function as a digital typeface. Even in the original, to the extent that we can reconstruct it today, it is a very lightweight letter for a carved form. The bold version Adobe produced was a valiant effort but, to me, a failure. [See "Democratizing the Empire," p. 181, and "Trajan Revived Redux," p. 185.] Far more workable carved forms exist, both in Claudian examples and in other, unexploited originals, like the glorious inscription on the tomb of the children of Sextus Pompeius Justus on the Via Appia. [18] In general, the Roman majuscule, used in every modern serifed typeface, remains the standard of legibility today. Classic forms of this model are as good as any.

NB   The Roman majuscule will most likely remain the standard for legibility until we find another form of communication. I also agree with my father that typographic interpretations all tend to fall flat when carved in stone. So many of the variants of the Imperial Roman capital that were carved throughout the Empire—in Europe, Turkey, and Africa—are worthy of inspection and contemporary interpretation for future inscriptions.

RK   The take-up of Carol Twombly's Trajan has been phenomenal. It is used in the United Kingdom in many areas of advertising and in particular for film posters. You are right about the thinness, but of course she took the Trajan model, which has lost at least 1.5 mm of surface due to weathering and the ill-founded attempt by the Italian authorities in the 19th century to clean it through acid etching. You can see the residue of the letter in Carol's design. The serifs are oddly stunted and misshapen, whereas the Sextus Pompeius Justus inscription is much clearer, particularly the serifs. It was, of course, only dug up in the 19th century. It had been buried and therefore protected. But what Trajan has shown is the enduring quality of those original letters.

JEB   Trajan is a huge and deserved success. [See "Democratizing the Empire," p. 181.] The Trajan inscription, now horribly degraded, was captured—in the early '50s, I think—by Catich. A full-size copy of his excellent

22 (*above*). Room Three, Franklin Delano Roosevelt Memorial, Washington, DC. Carved by JEB, 1997.

23 (*right*). National World War II Memorial alphabet (2003) designed by Nicholas Benson.

THE JOHN STEVENS SHOP   157

rubbing was at Adobe when they did the design. Oddly enough, I had a similar rubbing, though nowhere near as precise, in the Shop for awhile. Someone wanted to sell it to me. I declined but did take a few same-size xeroxes of it. It sure is a pretty letter, though more like a fashion model than a dancer. [See "Census of Trajan Inscription Reproductions," p. 238 .]

RK John, when you took over the Shop, how did the work change? Was there a different attitude toward producing letters? Did the client base change?

JEB When I entered the Shop, in 1961, it had been in a slow period following the death of my father, its artistic and spiritual leader. My mother had kept the place going doing solid work of good quality. John Hegnauer came to work with me in 1964, and Jim Casey stayed on through the early seventies. My lettering and design work developed and, through one of my father's old connections, at the age of twenty-five I was given the job of inscribing the gravesite memorial to John F. Kennedy. It was a complicated undertaking but it served to establish both me and the Shop in the architectural lettering business, where we have stayed, together with our traditional gravestone work, for sixty years. We gained a reputation for the design and carving of refined and classically elegant inscriptions. [25] In no sense was I the equal of my father in artistic talent, but I had good hands, excellent eyesight, and my Quaker mother's devotion to duty. We had a wonderful time at the Shop. [8]

After I turned over the management of the Shop to Nick, in 1993, following several years in which he worked with me, I conducted my own carving business from a studio I built on the shop premises. That lasted for seven years and during that time I worked on the FDR Memorial in Washington, D.C. [22] I also did a suite of hand-carved and digitally designed, sandblasted inscriptions at the new Joseph Moakley Federal Courthouse in Boston. In the year 2000, I retired from the trade to pursue sculpture in what has become a relaxed and low-pressure lifestyle.

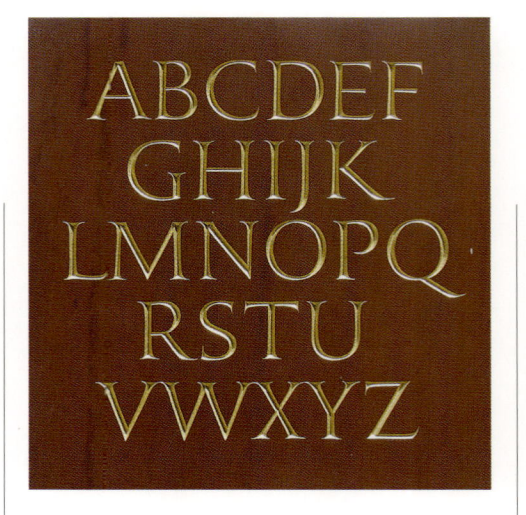

RK It must have been intimidating to take over the Shop from your father, though the loyalty of Jim Casey must have helped. I notice you say you have handed the management to your younger son, Nick. The word "management" sounds a little curious, yet it may well be very precise because it would suggest that you are still, in spite of your sculpture, drawn back to lettering. Is this the case?

JEB I meant that Nick took over the responsibilities that he had not already assumed: fiscal management, client contact, labor relations—the whole enchilada, as we say.

No more lettering for this old body. Hands degraded from too much abuse on building sites and windsurfers.

RK Sometimes, when I struggle out of bed, I share your thoughts about too much time on building sites, and climbing scaffolding. Well before the modern-day regimes of health and safety, I remember as a young man scrambling up and down scaffolding like a monkey. We even had our own scaffolding spanner to make adjustments. If we did that on a modern site, we would find ourselves on the outside pavement in nanoseconds!

Nick, do you feel obliged to make changes in the Shop's working practice or in the nature of its designs since you have taken over?

NB I did not take any overt action to put my own spin on the Shop process or product when I took over in 1993. [26] It has been difficult to stop and make a deeply critical assessment of the stylistic direction I intend to take while trying simply to keep the place going. The John Stevens Shop has an awfully long history, even by continental standards. The Stevenses' work and my family's efforts offer so very much to look at and consider. I have come to realize that my grandfather was not at all interested in painting and carving letters to a highly polished typographic standard. He saw bodies of text as an interwoven fabric of singular design. See his design for the Latin phrase "QUONDOQUE LICEBIT." [12] These letters were not perfectly painted or maniacally carved, but the rhythm of the strokes, the continuity of forms, and the overall unity of the text are undeniable. This work, and others like it, enthralls me. It seems to me that this quality is at its best when produced by people who have been carving for at least a decade. They don't think over-critically about the process. They move quickly, effectively, and without pretention. If there is any personal imprint I would wish to make during my tenure at the John Stevens Shop, it would be to produce work along these lines. [24]

RK Most eloquently put.

NB Thank you, Richard.

RK I think the Bensons and the John Stevens Shop are a genuine ornament and inspiration in the history of American lettering and design, in particular to hang in through the last century and early current century to the craft of carving, not as a fossilized relic from the past, but with foresight to have reinvented the art and craft.

JEB This is far too much about much too little. It is, after all, a simple little craft shop that has contrived, by accident and stubborn application, to survive through three centuries. [33]

24 (*opposite*). Alphabet stone carved by Nicholas Benson, n.d. Gold leaf on red Vermont slate.

25 (*above*). Alphabet stone carved for Robert Boyajian by JEB, 1974. Gold leaf on Monson slate.

26 (*left*). Nicholas Benson adjusting painted layout of inscription, 1996.

27 (*below*). Rough sketch by JEB of inscription for the Melbert B. Cary, Jr. Graphic Arts Collection at Rochester Institute of Technology. Dated 22 September 1970.

28 (*bottom*). Plaque for the Melbert B. Cary, Jr. Graphic Arts Collection carved by JEB, 1970. Gold leaf on wood.

29 (*opposite, above*). John E. Benson and Nicholas Benson in The John Stevens Shop, 2013. On the wall in the background at right is a portrait of John Howard Benson, painted by the English artist Thomas Derrick and commissioned by Graham Carey.

30 (*opposite, below*). Richard Kindersley in his workshop in London.

1. For a fuller history of the John Stevens Shop, see Esther Fisher Benson, "The History of the John Stevens Shop," in *Bulletin of the Newport Historical Society*, no. 112 (October 1963); Fisher Benson, "John Howard Benson and The John Stevens Shop," in *Newport History: Bulletin of the Newport Historical Society* 62, pt. 1, no. 213 (Winter 1989).
2. John Howard Benson, *The First Writing Book: An English Translation & Facsimile Text of Arrighi's Operina, the First Manual of the Chancery Hand*, Studies in the History of Calligraphy, 2 (New Haven: Yale University Press, 1954).
3. For more about John Howard Benson, see Philip Hofer, "The Work of John Howard Benson," in *The New Colophon* (New York: Duschnes Crawford, Inc., 1950), pp. 208–22, and Hofer, *John Howard Benson & His Work, 1901–1956* (New York: The Typophiles, 1957).
4. John Benson relates: "See the photograph of my father and Graham Carey with, between them, the American calligrapher James Hayes. The occasion, around 1952, was one of their twice-yearly parties at which they all wore paper stone carver's hats adorned with heraldic emblems signifying the skills they practiced in the imaginary John Stevens University. John Howard, who seldom took himself too seriously, was a wryly amusing and fun-loving man."
5. Hambidge wrote several books based on his theory of dynamic symmetry. The most influential have been *Dynamic Symmetry in Composition* (Cambridge, Mass.: The author, 1923) and *The Elements of Dynamic Symmetry* (New York: Brentano's, 1926). The latter is available as a Dover Publications paperback.
6. John Howard Benson and Arthur Graham Carey, *Elements of Lettering*. (Newport, R.I.: John Stevens Shop, 1940). A second, revised edition was published in 1950 by McGraw-Hill Co.

THE JOHN STEVENS SHOP 161

THERE ARE SOME PEOPLE W
GOOD CAPITAL R, NO MAT
ARE TRAINED. JUST AS 'PERS
HANDWRITING, CHARACTER

Eric Gill

THE ROMAN CAPITALS INFLUENCED THE EARLIEST TYPE DESIGNS AND CONTINUE TO INFLUENCE MUCH OF TYPE DESIGN TODAY. WITHOUT ROMAN CAPITALS, WE WOULD NOT HAVE LOWER CASE AND WITHOUT CAPS AND LOWER CASE THIS EMAIL WOULD BE BLANK.
Jim Parkinson

HO CAN NEVER DRAW A
ER HOW LONG THEY
ONALITY' IS EXPRESSED IN
IS REVEALED IN LETTERING.

THE ROMAN CAPITALS SET A MODEL OF LETTER SKELETON THAT WE CAN'T REALLY NOT THINK ABOUT. WE CAN REACT TO IT, AND POSSIBLY ADJUST PROPORTIONS, BUT CANNOT ESCAPE IT ENTIRELY. THE ROMAN CAPS SET A MEASURE OF HOW TO WORK WITH THE WIDTHS OF CAPITALS—EVEN IN A CONTEMPORARY SANS.

Peter Bil'ak

BEARDSLEY'S
CAFÉ RESTAURANT

SECOND ANNIVERSARY CELEBRATION
27 JUNE 1977 NORTHAMPTON MASSACHUSETTS

PENUMBRA
THE OFFSPRING OF TRAJAN AND FUTURA

LANCE HIDY

WHEN MY TYPEFACE PENUMBRA was published by Adobe Systems, in 1994, I wrote in the accompanying specimen book that Futura and Trajan [2] had influenced the design. In fact, my early attempts at poster lettering, in the late 1970s, were suggestive of those two letterforms. Be that as it may, the Trajan-Futura explanation of Penumbra's origin obscures the real story: the designs were inspired as much by images as they were by letters. Making and using letters and images had until then been two separate arenas in my career; in poster design, which would become a dominant medium in my work, I found the opportunity to integrate them. In the best posters, the image and the letterforms are "equivalents," to use Alfred Stieglitz's term for his first experiments in abstraction. Just as Stieglitz's cloud photographs were equivalents to his feelings of the moment, I wanted my letterforms to become the equivalents of my pictorial style. This was the quest that would lead me to Penumbra.

By the late 1970s, I had achieved some mastery of book typography, though I found that bookish typefaces were ill-suited to my posters. They were too complicated and stylized to be equivalents to the flat, hard-edged, photography-based style I was developing. The geometric simplicity of Futura was tempting, but I felt it was too industrial to accompany the organic contours in my poster art. I considered humanist sans serif faces such as Gill and Syntax, but they had aesthetic connotations that did not feel right, either. Typefaces are stamped with the personality of their creators, and colored by their times and places of origin. Using pre-existing types in my posters felt like wearing hand-me-down clothes. If I were to follow the example of poster artists I admired—Toulouse-Lautrec, Höhlwein, Cassandre, and Shahn—I would have to tailor the letterforms specifically for my poster art.[1] [1]

1 (*opposite*). Beardsley's Café Restaurant poster designed and silkscreened by Lance Hidy, 1978. The lettering was inspired by the Trajan inscription.

2 (*below*). Relationship of Penumbra to Trajan and Futura.

AEGHJKMQRS
+ AEGHJKMQRS
= AEGHJKMQRS

Of the thirty-three posters I produced between 1977 and 1987, fifteen of them featured capital letters that were forerunners of Penumbra. [3, 4, 8–11] To understand the equivalence I sought for the letters, I should explain the thinking behind the artwork. [5–7]

My poster images were composed of flat, hard-edged colors such as one finds in Egyptian wall painting, Greek ceramics, textiles, Japanese prints, and comic books. Bridging many subjects, centuries, and civilizations, the style I had cultivated was simultaneously old, at least in the flatness of the colors, and modern in my use of the camera to capture the fleeting gestures and subtle contours of my subjects. For example, after shooting 180 photographs of a woman and her collie, the chosen one was transformed into simple, flat shapes, minus the distracting details. The distilled essence of the photographic form and idea was retained without artistic additions. My style, if it can be called that, is the result of trying to have no style—only a pure, pictorial idea, simplified as far as I could take it.

NICARAGUA
MARYLAND
CHILDREN
BOSTON
CHILDREN'S
GRADUATE

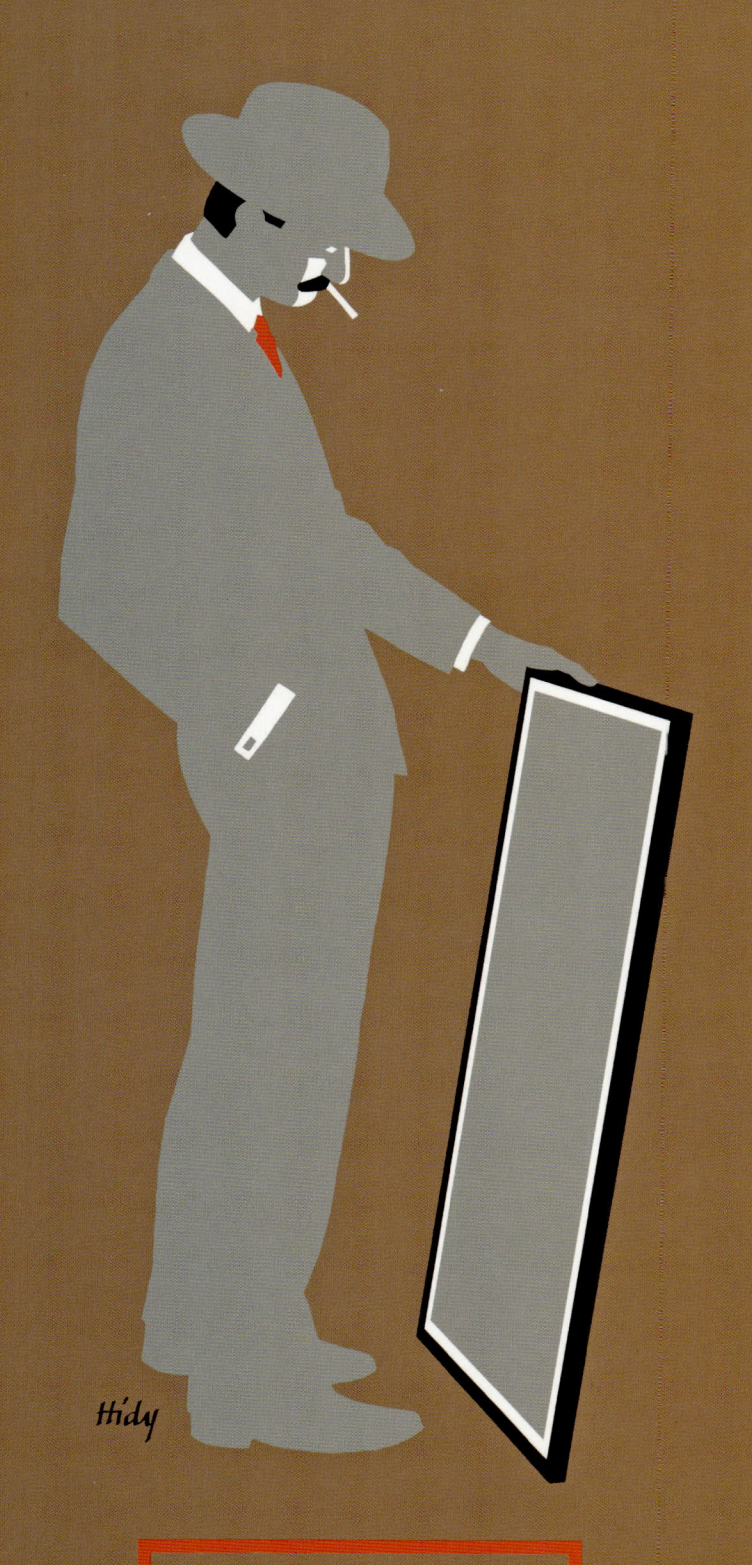

3 (*left*). Dow and Frosini Framing & Posters poster designed and silkscreened by Hidy, 1979. The lettering was traced from Futura.

4 (*above*). Samples of Hidy's poster lettering, 1977–1978, showing variations in weight, serif, and formality.

5, 6, 7 (*clockwise from upper left*). These three images show the sequence of steps that Hidy went through in the design of his mature posters: original photograph, outline drawing, and final design. Poster designed by Hidy for Davis-Kidd Bookseller, 2000; silk-screened by Robert Preston.

DAVIS-KIDD BOOKSELLERS
NASHVILLE · MEMPHIS · JACKSON

PENUMBRA 167

8 (*above*). Godine for Children poster designed by Hidy for David Godine, Publisher, 1982; silkscreened by Rob Day.

9 (*below*). Poster lettering by Hidy, 1985.

BLACK OAK BOOKS

1491 SHATTUCK AVENUE ▲ BERKELEY ▲ CA 94709

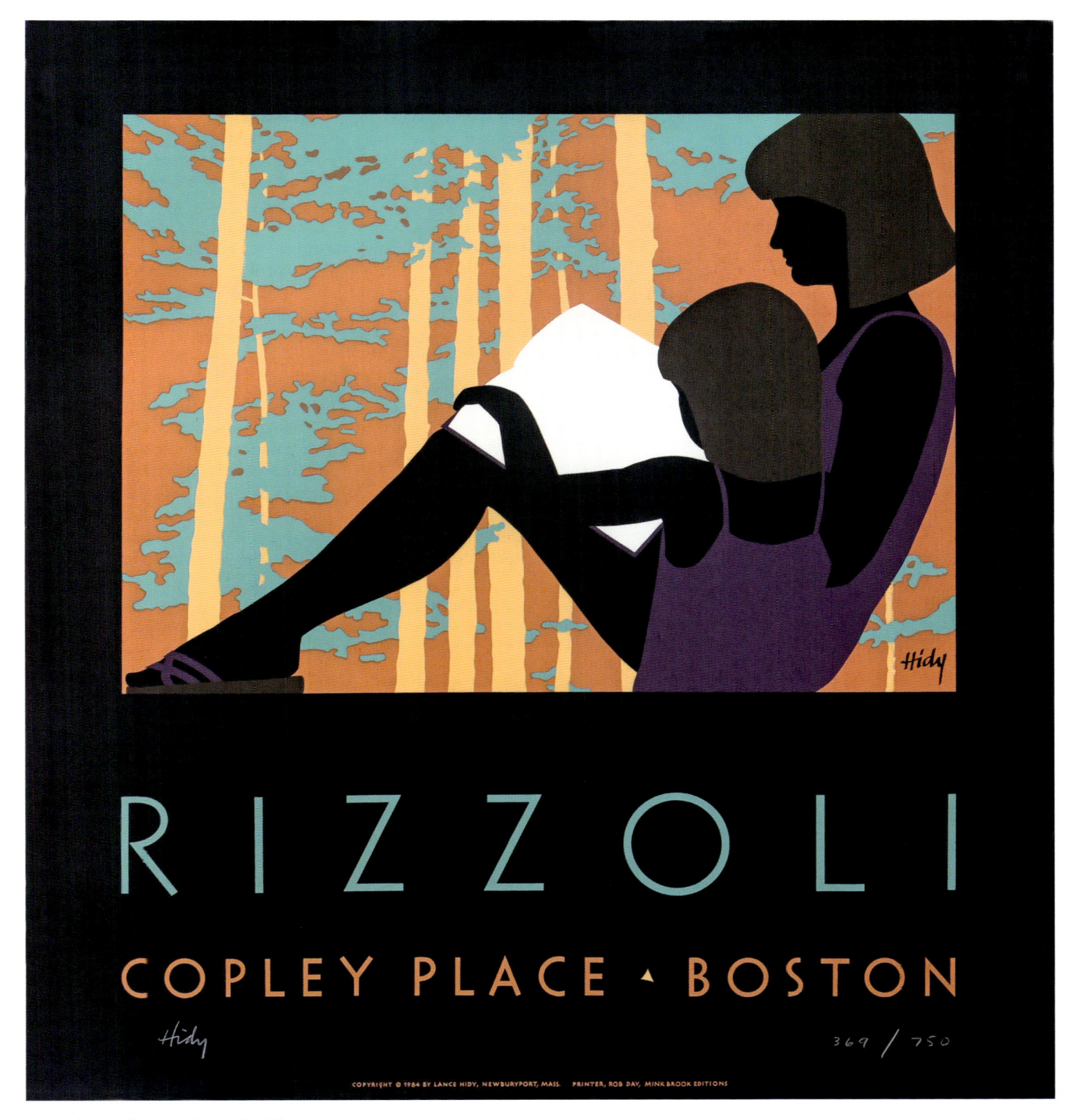

10 Rizzoli Booksellers poster designed by Hidy, 1984; silkscreened by Rob Day. The lettering for this poster and the "Godine for Children" poster (opposite), designed to blend in with the illustrations as "equivalents," were both precursors to Penumbra.

WHITE MOUNTAINS FESTIVAL '80 · BRETTON WOODS, N.H.

Terra, June 15, 1992, Lance Hidy

11 (*opposite*). White Mountains Festival poster designed and silkscreened by Hidy, 1980. The first proto-Penumbra lettering, it was written with a Speedball B-series nib, with the round corners squared off with a technical pen. The silkscreen mask was cut with a knife at actual size (⅜" high).

12 (*above*). Gino Lee (left) and Lance Hidy (right) in 1994.

13 (*above*). Early proof (June 15, 1992) of Penumbra with interpolations. The four masters are marked in red and the interpolations are in black.

What letterform, then, would be the equivalent? It, too, would need to be distilled down to an essence, but still strong enough to be readable amidst the large areas of color. And I wanted it to have a living, organic quality like the contoured shapes drawn from my photographs—neither too mechanical nor industrial.

The first crude ancestor of Penumbra appeared as a single line of capitals in a lily-pad poster design of 1980. [11] Lettered with a round-nib Speedball B-series pen, the stroke endings were squared off with a fine-tipped technical pen. The small bowls of the *D*, *B*, and *R*, the sharp points on the angled joins, and the monoweight strokes would all survive, more or less, in the typeface I would make fourteen years later. The sloped sides of the *U* appeared in some of the posters but eventually were replaced with verticals. Over the next seven years I experimented with this basic idea, varying the weight, sometimes adding serifs or swelled stroke endings—all of which would be built into the typeface design, though my occasional experiments with irregular letter shapes and strokes would be left behind. [4, 9]

Sumner Stone, then director of type development at Adobe, was the first person to suggest making a typeface from my poster lettering. Ironically, by seating me on Adobe's Type Advisory Board and giving me access to the latest technology, Sumner unwittingly played a role in bringing my lettering career to an end.

As a consultant, I had access to the growing Adobe Type Library, including beta versions of the new line of Adobe Originals. While experimenting with the beta version of Trajan, my poster-lettering experience taught me that it was too thin to be very useful, at least for my kind of work, which was certainly not atypical of the way Trajan might be used by others. When I suggested making a bold version, the idea was dismissed at first as sacrilege. But after sleeping on it, the Adobe team reconsidered and decided to take my advice. (See p. 181.)

After Sumner left Adobe, at the end of 1989, his idea of making a typeface from my poster lettering continued to circulate among the Adobe Originals team. Robert Slimbach and Fred Brady were skeptical about the idea until I pointed out that there was a shortage of classically inspired display fonts that had mono-weight strokes, or at least minimally tapering ones. Other than Albertus, Open Capitals, Sistina, and Weiss Initials, what was there? [2] Agreeing that Penumbra could help fill this void, they gave me a contract in 1992.

Adding Penumbra to the Multiple Master library created some excitement because, unlike the previous efforts that involved only the axes of weight and width, it was to be the first one with a style axis for serif. While other recent typefaces—Lucida, Scala, Rotis, and Sumner's own Stone family—included both a sans serif and a serif version of the same typeface, Penumbra was

PENUMBRA 171

VERBSGOHUMANTLD
VERBSGOHUMANTLD
VERBSGOHUMANTLD
VERBSGOHUMANTLD

14 (*above*). The first formal ink drawings of Penumbra, drawn on mylar (13/16″ high). In red are the final Penumbra letters for comparison.

15 (*right*). Screen shot of the Multiple Master Font Utility. Weight and serif values were chosen with the sliders. After clicking the create button, this instance would have "355 WT 800 SR" added to its name. As new instances accumulated in the font menu, it was easy to be confused by all of the numbers.

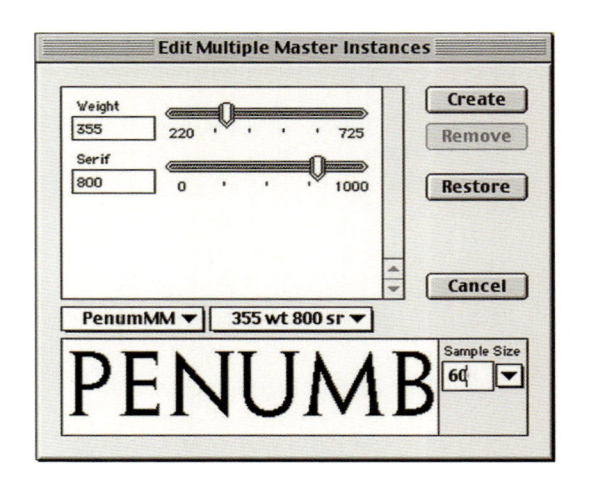

designed to offer intermediate versions of serif.[3] In all, I created four masters for Penumbra: sans serif light, sans serif bold, serif light, and serif bold.

My first step toward creating Penumbra MM was to hire Gino Lee (1962–2011), a brilliant Harvard student with a talent both for letterpress typography and for computer technology.[4] It was he who did most of the digitization, while I did the art direction. At the Adobe team's suggestion, I produced ink drawings of medium-weight letters .8125 inches high—one set of sans, and another of serif. [10] The light and bold masters were to be extrapolated from these. Gino and I also kept samples of my old poster lettering on hand as a reference. Together, he and I converted the drawings to vectors, working in collaboration with the Adobe group that included Slimbach, Carol Twombly, Brady, and Jocelyn Bergen.

Penumbra MM had two variables: 506 increments of weight from light to bold, and 1,001 increments from sans serif to full serif. [15] Two sliders in the Multiple Master utility allowed the user to potentially create more than a half-million variations of Penumbra—506,506, to be exact. Each user-created instance was given a cumbersome name with the numbers of the weight and serif coordinates. Trying to sort through them in the font menu could be perplexing. In retrospect, limiting the increments to ten or twenty per axis would have been sufficient for even the most demanding typographer.

Unfortunately, Multiple Master technology proved too good to be true, at least as a consumer product (Adobe and others still use it as an essential font development tool). The complex coding caused so many output failures that some printers refused to accept jobs containing MM fonts.

Therefore, none of us was surprised when the Multiple Masters were made obsolete by the new OpenType formats, which often add new sizes and weights to previously released designs. And so Penumbra was converted to a family of sixteen fonts: four serif variations, each with four weights.

[16] While this limited palette seems not to have hurt the popularity of Penumbra too much, the limited weight options can be frustrating to typographers. In particular, I miss the middle weight, halfway between the light and the bold. Fortunately there is a work-around in Adobe Illustrator. After setting the type in two weights, intermediate weights can be created using the blend tool. Serif variations can be interpolated with this method too.

An interesting postscript to the Penumbra story emerged from Sumner Stone's research into the origins of Roman capitals. I still remember his excitement when he first showed me pre-Trajan, Penumbra-like inscriptions with monoline strokes and serifs. These important letterforms had escaped my notice, including one example rather close to my home: the funerary relief of the Publius Gessius family (30–20 BC) in Boston's Museum of Fine Arts. [17, 18] I must have seen it several times, so it is possible that its carved letters entered my unconscious mind.

THE PENUMBRA FAMILY

16 (*left*). OpenType version of Penumbra with sixteen variations replacing the original Multiple Master version.

SERIF

AEGHJKMQRS
AEGHJKMQRS
AEGHJKMQRS
AEGHJKMQRS

HALF SERIF

AEGHJKMQRS
AEGHJKMQRS
AEGHJKMQRS
AEGHJKMQRS

FLARE SERIF

AEGHJKMQRS
AEGHJKMQRS
AEGHJKMQRS
AEGHJKMQRS

SANS SERIF

AEGHJKMQRS
AEGHJKMQRS
AEGHJKMQRS
AEGHJKMQRS

17 (*top*). Recreation of the Publius Gessius inscription using Penumbra Serif Light.

18 (*above*). Part of the inscription on the funerary relief of the Publius Gessius family (Museum of Fine Arts, Boston).

---

1 Henri de Toulouse-Lautrec (1864–1901), Ludwig Hohlwein (1874–1949), A. M. Cassandre (1901–1968), and Ben Shahn (1898–1969)
2 Albertus (Monotype Corporation, 1936–1940) by Berthold Wolpe; Open Capitals (Joh. Enschedé en Zonen, 1928) by Jan van Krimpen; Sistina (Stempel AG, 1951) by Hermann Zapf; and Weiss Initials (Bauersche Giesserei, 1931) by E. R. Weiss. The Weiss Initials comprised Series I (Weiss Kapitale), Series II (Weiss Lapidar and Weiss Lapidar Mager), and Series III (Weiss Kapitale Mager) initials. Series II bears a resemblance to Penumbra.
3 Lucida Serif (1985) and Lucida Sans (1985) by Charles Bigelow and Kris Holmes; Scala (1988; FontShop, 1990) and Scala Sans (FontShop, 1993) by Martin Majoor; Rotis (Agfa, 1989) by Otl Aicher (consisting of a serif, semi-serif, semi-sans and sans); ITC Stone (International Typeface Corporation, 1987). There is also Ellington (Monotype, 1990) and Strayhorn (Monotype, 1995), a matching pair of serif and sans serif types designed by Michael Harvey that belongs to this period.
4 Gino Lee also digitized the initial version of Zapfino.

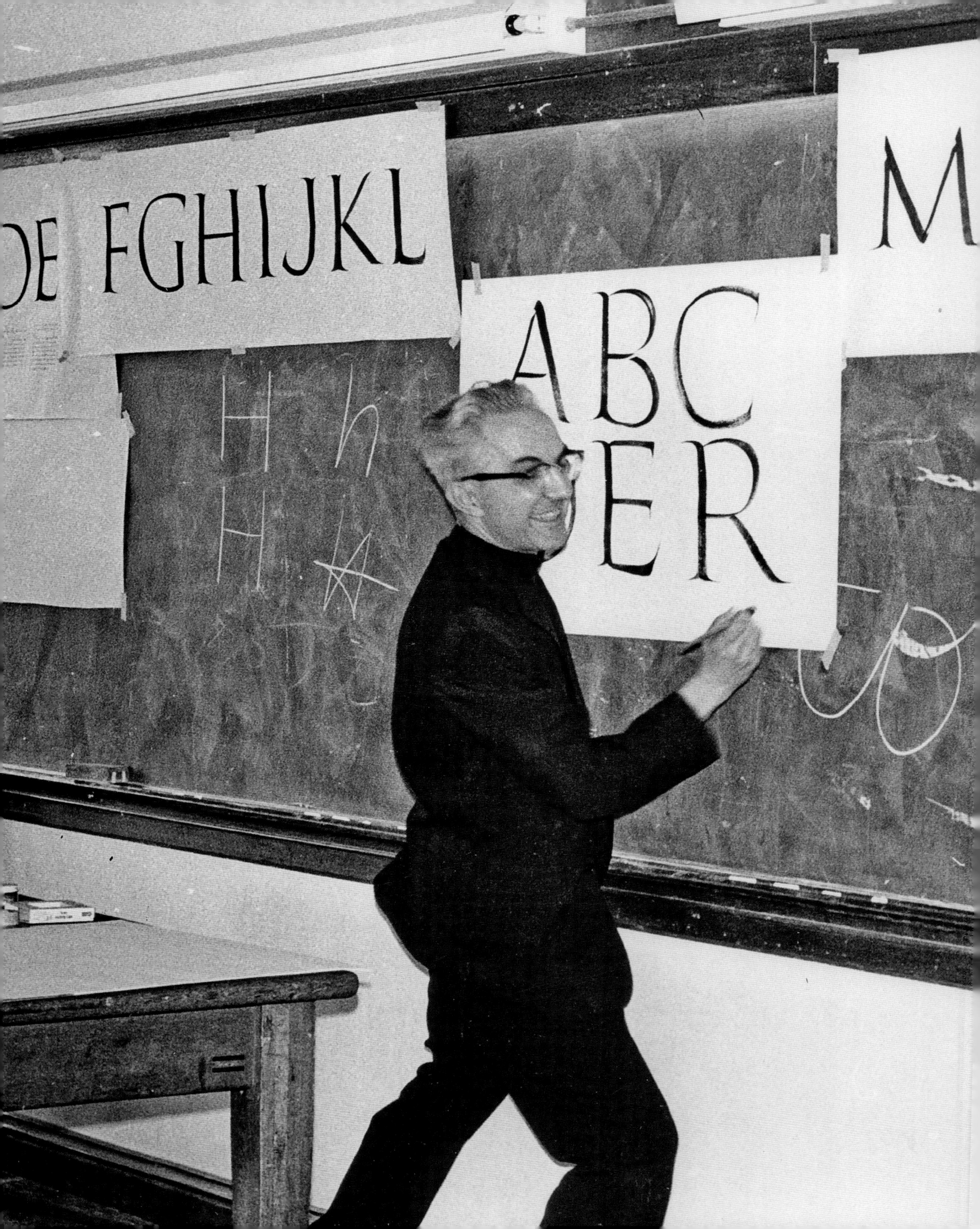

DE FGHIJKL
M
ABC
ER

FATHER CATICH AT REED COLLEGE

GREGORY MACNAUGHTON

EDWARD CATICH (1906–1979) WAS born in Montana, orphaned at eleven years old, and sent to Illinois, where he was apprenticed to a sign painter. He paid his way through college painting signs and working as a professional musician, eventually becoming a Catholic priest. He later became an accomplished artist, creating liturgical work that, among other things, depicted Christ as a black man in contemporary clothes (for which he received a *monitum*, an official warning from the Vatican). But Catich is remembered primarily as a world-renowned expert in classical Roman letterforms, who rocked the paleographical establishment with groundbreaking theories about their making. These were elucidated in two major works, *Letters Redrawn from the Trajan Inscription in Rome* (1961) and *The Origin of the Serif: Brush Writing & Roman Letters* (1968). In these two volumes, Catich claimed that the flat brush he knew so well as a commercial signwriter was directly responsible for the serifs on Roman lapidary inscriptions from the 1st century. This theory was a direct challenge to the conventional wisdom of the time.

For Lloyd J. Reynolds (1902–1978), "conventional wisdom" was an oxymoron. He was born into poverty in Minnesota, moved west as a child, and grew up to be a professor of art and literature. He earned his undergraduate degree in the Department of Forestry at Oregon State University, but he was also an autodidact, a talented engraver, actor, and puppeteer. He is widely remembered as one of the most influential calligraphers in America. Like his heroes John Ruskin and William Morris, Reynolds railed against the materialism of consumer culture and famously refused to cooperate when summoned before the House Un-American Activities Committee, in 1954. He spoke of the practice of calligraphy as a spiritual path and encouraged his students to see with their third eye. Both Reynolds and Catich founded the art departments at the colleges where they taught: Reynolds at Reed College in Portland, Oregon, and Catich at St. Ambrose College (now St. Ambrose University) in Davenport, Iowa. For twenty years the two men engaged in a lively and spirited correspondence, which culminated in the design of a series of lapidary inscriptions for the Reed College campus.

1 (*opposite*). Father Catich demonstrating writing Trajanic capitals with a flexible broad-edged brush at Reed College, 1964.

2 (*below*). Father Catich carving letters at Reed College, 1964.

Their correspondence was initiated by Reynolds in January 1956. [3] "Dear Father Catich," he wrote. "I have just received a notice of your coming talk on the 'The Origin of the Serif.' Would I were at least within hitch-hiking distance of Chicago!... I am destroyed with suspense." Reynolds then requested a one-sentence précis of Catich's theory and closed the letter with, "I have heard good things of you—and now I admire your audacity!" Their correspondence grew over the next two years, leading Reynolds to ask Catich to contribute an inscribed Roman alphabet for a calligraphy exhibition he was curating at the Portland Art Museum. Through a series of lectures, Reynolds personally raised the funds for the museum

March 26 1956

Dear Mr. Reynolds:
Thank you very much for the
writing that you sent. You astonish me when
these were done for a class demonstration.
I'd tackle that especially in that size in
I get around the problem of demonstrating
the blackboard in letters about 15" tall
chalk on its side. I hold the chalk between
ginger, first giving it a few strokes so
evenly. This saves all the bother of having
paint, paper, brushes or reeds. At first
difficult to handle the chalk holding it
with a little practice it comes quickly
naturally. It also has the advantage that
being vertical, no one has to leave his
is being written. One can also use the
of chalk but I find that it is not as cl
blackboard chalk, ~~narrow~~ One can conve
chalk into any length he wishes whereas
so easily with the inch squares of chalk
is 1" x 1" x 3". You recall this. It is so
lecturere's chalk and comes in colors.

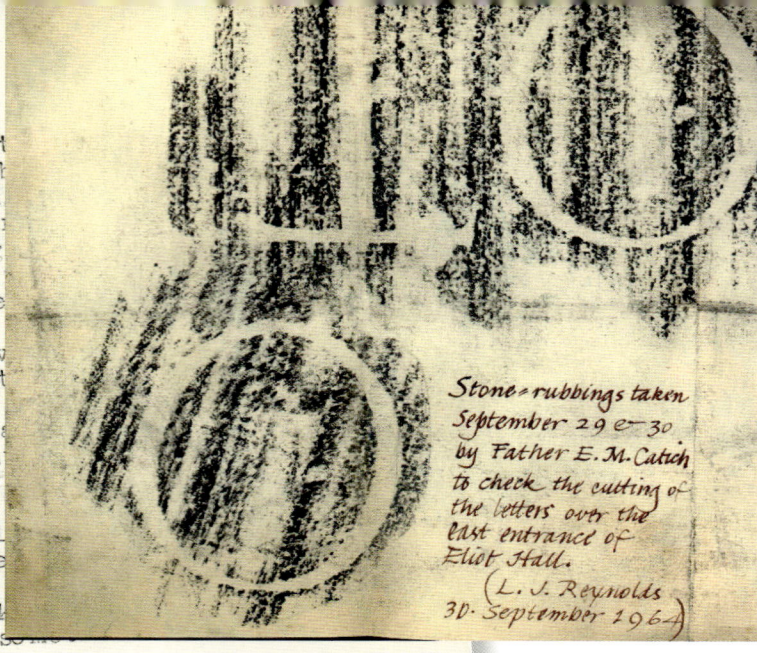

Stone-rubbings taken
September 29 & 30
by Father E.M. Catich
to check the cutting of
the letters over the
east entrance of
Eliot Hall.
(L. J. Reynolds
30. September 1964)

I did not intend to wait so long in writing. Your inquiry
originally caught me at a very bad time. The day I got your
original inquiry I had a bad fire in the studio, got burnt
(all bandages off now) and everything was in a mess. Fortunately
nothing important by way of research material was lost. This
happened the day before the Chicago lecture. I had to lecture
and demonstrate with bandages on the hands. It was embarrasing
for I could not do as well as I am able. It was well received
though and I tried to quit after an hour of lecture-demonstrating
but had to go on for 50 mins. more answering questions and such.
Much interest even though I was rather disjunctive in the present-
ation. I only had an outline of what to say and, with a subject
like that which has been very close to me since my days in Rome
from 35 through 39, an outline was all I needed to get going.

For demonstration
^I use a sable brights brush, the kind used by oil painters.
The hair is not too long and gives a crisp stroke. It is shorter
than the ordinary showcard-writer's flat brush. After long experimenting I settled on this and it answers all the questions.
I cannot go into detail why but, the brush is not held like
the usual lettering brush, near the ferule. Instead the brush,
which is twelve inches long, is held between thumb and forefinger
at the tip twelve inches away from the hairend. It is not easy
to write at first in this fashion but with some experience it
can be done expertly. There is no support for the hand such
as mahl stick or hand bridge, nor does one use the left hand as
a support. Really it looks impossible but it can be done.
It is a three-directional movement, the usual two directions
on the surface plus the thrid direction ~~from~~ rotating the brush
between thumb and forefinger.

I have made many rubbings of the Trajan inscription in Rome
and have been immersed in these letters for yrs. Many things
puzzled me at first and what I do now are answers to many of these
vexing problems. An understanding of the place of brush and reed
writing in Roman lettering supplies the internal dynamics and
makes up the whole theory of the fine Imperial inscriptions.
The brush writing I do is an outcome of this experience.

I have mailed a tube containing some letters made in 1940
which shows some of the dynamics of brush to chiseling. I
have included a set of the writing and lettering charts we
use in our classes. I enclosed three cut reeds, in case you
are not familiar with these. All our students cut their own
reeds. I use watch springs. Jewellers usually throw these away
and we get ours from one in town here. A lighted match will soften
the spring in the middle allowing one to bend it into shape.
Good reeds can be had from the florist. He uses these to sustain
potted plants. The green dye can be washed off. You will find
them superior to Coit pens, the sharpness of the edge commends
itself.

to acquire Catich's inscribed alphabet stones that are now a part of the museum's collection. (Although the agreement stated that these stones would be on permanent public display, they never have been.) One of the Catich stones explicitly demonstrates the brushstrokes used in creating the letters for the inscription. (See p. 25.) Reynolds wrote at the time, "there is no doubting the extreme importance of his [Catich's] thesis and of these controversial stones; so the Portland Art Museum is fortunate to have them." Then, in 1963, an opportunity presented itself for Reynolds to invite Catich to Reed, not just to visit but to leave his mark on the campus in perpetuity. Portland's fire marshall had recently determined that the design of Eliot Hall (c. 1912), one of two original buildings on the Reed College campus, lacked adequate egress and constituted a fire hazard. The proposed remodeling would create a new entrance to the building and the new entrance would need an inscription bearing the building's name. [6, 7] For Reynolds, there was no question of who should cut these letters; the job had to go to the nation's foremost authority on classical Roman lapidary inscriptions, his friend Father Edward Catich.

In a letter dated December 1, 1963, Catich confirmed his visit to Reed and negotiated the final price, $75 plus railroad coach fare. "No meals," he wrote. "I'll be eating with you, I hope.... The letters will be the best Trajan Imperial." [5]

Catich was coming from his home in Davenport and planned to visit Reed on his way to Los Angeles, where he expected to begin working on inscriptions for the new Los Angeles County Museum of Art. The museum was being designed as a complex of concrete, fountains, and reflecting pools in the midst of the desert, and despite the futuristic leanings of William L. Pereira, the building's architect, his firm had retained Catich as their consultant for the lettering on the building. However, in March 1964, Catich wrote to Reynolds to say that the work on the museum had been delayed and that he needed to find some interim work.

3 (opposite, left). Detail of letter from Father Catich to Lloyd J. Reynolds (26 March 1956). See the third paragraph where Father Catich discusses his brush technique and the fourth paragraph where he mentions his rubbings of the Trajan inscription.

4 (opposite, right). Detail of a rubbing made by Father Catich to test the progress of his cutting of the new lettering for Eliot Hall (29 and 30 September 1964). The notation was written out by Reynolds in his distinctive italic hand.

5 (left). Detail of second page of letter from Reynolds to Father Catich (1963) describing his plan for the inscriptions he wants to have carved for the Reed College buildings.

6 (top). The original carved lettering for the front entrance of Eliot Hall, 1912.

7 (above). The new carved lettering by Father Catich for the side entrance of Eliot Hall, 1964. This is the only Catich inscription at Reed College that was painted instead of gilded; and the only one carved directly into a building.

8, 9, 10 (*clockwise from upper right*). Rubbings of details of the inscriptions carved by Father Catich for Abingdon, Quincy and Eastport dormitories.

11 (*right*). Carved and gilded inscription by Father Catich for Kerr dormitory.

"I want to pick up some stone lettering jobs.... I'm willing to do any small signs gilded with either gold or palladium at rock bottom prices. Do you need any signs at the College?"

In the margins of Catich's letter, next to this proposal, Reynolds wrote, "v[ery]. reasonable."

Reynolds wasted no time in organizing a work order for Catich and, in June 1964, he wrote to him with a proposal for forty-five slate plaques identifying the names of buildings all over the Reed campus. [5] Reynolds expressed his concern that some of the proposed inscription sites were problematic because the recessed areas above the doors had already been inscribed. It was an ambitious project that was never completed, on account of misunderstandings regarding fundraising. One donor reduced his gift from $1,000 to $440, but this was sufficient for work to begin on signs for Abington, Chemistry, Doyle, Eastport, Kerr, Ladd, the Library, Music, Quincy, Westport, and Winch—all of which were scheduled to be cut in the summer of 1964. Of the original forty-five plaques planned, only these eleven were ordered and completed. [8–11]

The fact that these were the first plaques Reynolds ordered is especially interesting, because they included the dormitory inscriptions that were the very ones he had highlighted as being problematic. When the dormitories were built in 1912, the lintels above the doorways had been left bare, and for many years the dormitories were known simply as A through H. In 1935, however, they were named in honor of important individuals in Reed's history and the lintels were inscribed with the names they bear today—Ladd, Abington, Doyle, Westport, Eastport, Kerr, Quincy, and Winch—although in a style that might be described as Gothic Uncial. [6] This was likely a decision based on the architecture of the buildings themselves, a Tudor Gothic style inspired by the buildings of Oxford. But the lettering lacked a paleographical pedigree, and Reynolds apparently made the decision that, if he could afford only eleven plaques, the first thing to do was to cover these abominations with Catich's Trajan Imperial letters.

Reynolds sent Catich detailed measurements for the slate plaques, which were cut to size and inscribed in Davenport.[1] Each plaque is rectangular, approximately twenty-four inches long and eighteen inches high, with the exception of those for Eastport and Westport, which are shaped like shields. Reynolds sent rubbings of the shields to Catich so that their shapes could be accurately reproduced and slates cut to fit inside the existing forms. However, the shields were not large enough to accommodate the names as single words; the letters would have to be no more than an inch high. To solve this problem, Catich split each name into two rows of four letters, inscribing the words *East* and *West* above the word *Port*. [10] The V-cut trenches of the letters were gilded in gold leaf. The Eliot Hall inscription, cut into the original limestone of the east entrance of the building, was not gilded but painted a light blue instead.[2] (Of the original 1935 inscriptions on the Reed campus, *Eliot Hall*, above the south or frontal entrance, is the only one that is visible today.) [4, 7]

The timing of Catich's manufacture of these slate inscriptions coincided with his work on *The Origin of the Serif*. In the same 1964 letter in which Catich asked Reynolds whether the college needed any signs, he wrote, "The mss for the Serif book is out among the experts who are asked to chew it to pieces... I'm counting the enemies gleefully. Hewitt, Gill, Ogg, Goudy, Ency. Britannica, Edw. Maurde Thompson, Kapr, Chappell, et al. West, Brown, Egbert. I am naming them in the book. Someone has to stick the neck out."[3]

Catich believed that most of his contemporaries were mistaken about the methods of making Roman lapidary inscriptions, as well as the actual form of the Roman majuscule letters. Reynolds had long admired Catich's willingness to upset convention: "I suspect that you enjoy being a hornet—although gadfly would probably please you more. I prefer it." He was no stranger to making enemies himself. He delighted in promoting Catich and his controversial theories to the Portland printing and academic establishment. Reynolds was instrumental in introducing Catich and his ideas to the West Coast, first by securing commissions for the Portland Art Museum and then by inviting Catich to inscribe letters on the buildings of Reed College. He wrote to Catich, "Europe and the effete East may raise eyebrows at you, but out here a wheat-bender and sign-writer from Helena is just one of the boys and probably the one authority who would be listened to." At Reed, Reynolds provided Catich with an opportunity to publicly demonstrate the role of the flat brush in the creation of Roman majuscule inscriptions, four years before *The Origin of the Serif* was published, in what was likely one of the first such demonstrations west of Davenport, Iowa. [1, 2] Since Reed College was, at that time, the epicenter of a West Coast letter-arts revival, Catich's visit and the beautiful letters he left behind have become part of Reed's calligraphic legacy. And through Reynolds's students, such as Charles Bigelow and Sumner Stone, they continue to have a far-reaching impact on contemporary typography and letter arts.[4]

---

1   Catich was assisted in cutting the dormitory plaques by Frank Kickel and Lloyd Alterra.
2   Catich wasted no time getting started on the Reed College commission. In one of Reynolds's "scribble books" is a note dated 29 September 1964: "Catich arrived 9:30—R.R. [railroad] Wrote out Eliot Hall & started cutting before noon."
3   The enemies Catich was counting were Graily Hewitt, Eric Gill, Oscar Ogg, Frederic W. Goudy, *Encyclopedia Britannica* [i.e., Stanley Morison], Edward Maunde Thompson, Albert Kapr, Warren Chappell, Aubry West, Frank Chouteau Brown, and James C. Egbert.
4   Sumner Stone was present when Catich inscribed the letters on Eliot Hall, in September of 1964. The moment was one of the inspirations behind the formation of Adobe Trajan.

21   22   23

DEMOCRATIZING THE EMPIRE: THE BIRTH OF ADOBE TRAJAN

SCOTT-MARTIN KOSOFSKY

IN HIS BOOK *ANCIENT LAW* (1861), the British historian Henry Sumner Maine wrote that the laws of the Roman Empire marked the "triumph of ideas" over the "empire of primitive notions," drawing a sharp distinction between government by social contract and rule by presumed status. A society based on contract, he said, is a secure one that produces innovation by the free and open dissemination of knowledge. And so, periodically, when the world becomes too tangled, too Byzantine, we find ourselves turning back to Ancient Rome to look for curatives, for the basics. It happens even in typography.

The neoclassical urge to get back to Rome found a perfect typographic moment in the late-1980s, as a new technology held the promise of cleaning up the chaos of the preceding thirty years of constant change. The technology was PostScript, the page description language developed by Adobe Systems. The founders of Adobe understood that type was the prime element of pages and so they hired Sumner Stone to be their Typographic Director in 1984. Stone was a graduate of Reed College, where he had come under the powerful influence of the calligrapher Lloyd Reynolds, a humanist with a deep sense of the classical, and a force in the italic handwriting movement. It was there that, twenty years earlier, at the invitation of Reynolds, Father Edward M. Catich, had cut inscriptions for the old dormitory block and the administrative building, in the process "educating" a group of students that included not only Stone, but also Charles Bigelow and Michael McPherson. (See "Catich at Reed College," p. 175.)

Reynolds' influence went beyond inscriptions. His calligraphy and that of his students appeared everywhere on campus, from posters to cabinet drawers. Years later, after Reynolds had retired and had been replaced by Robert Palladino (a Catich student), it was still true. Steve Jobs, during his brief time on campus, noticed this and was inspired to take a calligraphy class with Palladino, an experience that proved to be a turning point in his life—and in that of all of us who use personal computers today.

The Bézier drawing tools developed at Adobe for its Illustrator application were a far cry from brushes, chisels, and pens used by Catich and Reynolds, yet they appeared to have the suppleness necessary to capture exceedingly fine letterforms, especially as they could be manipulated directly over scanned images of drawn or photographed letters. Stone was determined to find out if they could really work with a subtlety sufficient to reproduce classic forms. While much of Adobe was occupied with converting existing type libraries to its Type 1 font format, Stone embarked on a program called Adobe Originals, types that he, along with Robert Slimbach, Carol Twombly, and others created from scratch. The Originals program was overseen by Adobe's Type Advisory Board, which included Stone, Roger Black, Max Caflisch, Alvin Eisenman, Stephen Harvard, Lance Hidy, Erik Spiekermann, and Jack Stauffacher. [6]

Slimbach's first major project was Adobe Garamond, issued in 1989 to considerable acclaim, establishing Adobe as a typographic force. Twombly (fig. 3), a graduate of the Rhode Island School of Design who had become a student in Charles Bigelow's computer typography program at Stanford University, was assigned to work on three titling faces—

1 (*opposite, upper*). Detail of rubbing of the Trajan inscription by Father Catich, 1966.

2 (*opposite, lower*). Selected *E*s traced by Father Catich from his rubbings of the Trajan inscription (in black) with outlines of Adobe Trajan *E* (in turquoise) overlaid for comparison. The numbering indicates that these are the first three *E*s in the second line of the inscription.

3 (*inset*). Carol Twombly, 1989.

4 (top). Early proof of Adobe Trajan (c.1988) with unresolved characters such as *Y* and *7*.

5 (above). Early test of interpolation of Adobe Trajan characters (c.1988) to establish weights of the family.

6 Members of the Adobe Type Advisory Board, c.1988: from top to bottom and left to right, Roger Black, Chris Pullman, Lance Hidy, Jack Stauffacher, Sumner Stone, and Alvin Eisenman.

all caps, no lowercase—based on pre-Gutenberg designs, to be released the same year: Lithos, inspired by Greek sans serif capitals; Charlemagne, based on lettering in the 10th-century Benedictional of St. Aethelwold of Winchester, a latecomer in the Carolingian program to revive classical letterforms; and Trajan, based directly on the inscription on Trajan's Column. [7] For the Trajan type project, an undertaking that everyone regarded as a kind of holy grail, Twombly was given access to a scanned set of Father Catich's drawings, as well as life-size photocopies of a rubbing of the Trajan inscription that had been made available to the company by lettercarver Christopher Stinehour. [1, 2]

Making digital replicas of old letters is an academic exercise; making a useful typeface based upon them requires innumerable acts of interpretation. In the case of the Trajan inscription, there are the variables, such as multiple examples of the same letter; then there are the letters *J*, *U*, and *W* that did not exist in the early Latin alphabet, or the *H*, which, by chance, does not appear in the Trajan text, and finally there are the Greek letters *K*, *Y*, and *Z*, which only occasionally occur in Roman inscriptions. Whereas *J* is a variant of *I*, and *W* is a double *V*, the *U* is a vexing form for achieving harmony amongst the Imperial forms (for Eric Gill's difficulties with it, see p. 90). How wide should it be? Will both stems curve, or will the right be straight? Lastly, there are Arabic figures and punctuation to be invented. The figures were especially troublesome for Twombly and she reported that, in seeking the right balance, she consulted numerous type specimens, but eventually came up with her own glyph-to-glyph reference scheme to achieve a harmony of forms (e.g., using *C* and *E* as references for *3* and *5*; and then *S* and *3* as the basis for *8*). She had already used a similar method for the missing alphabetic letters (e.g., deriving *K* from *R*, and *Y* from a mix of *A*, *I*, and *M*). [4]

Design is, after all, a practical matter and overreliance on historical documents can take its toll on modern type design. To turn the Trajan letters—or any carved forms—into type, one must adapt very large three-dimensional letters that were V-cut into stone. Moreover, one must consider how weather, age, and occasional cleanings have contributed to the Trajan letters' overall thinning as seen today, especially with respect to the serifs. Literal-mindedness in this particular case could have led to a very anemic typeface and, indeed, the regular weight of Adobe Trajan, tends to be a little light.

The Type Advisory Board commented on the design as it progressed. Lance Hidy, who made his reputation as a poster designer, suggested that there be a bold version, to make the design useful for a variety of circumstances. Some of his colleagues were aghast at the suggestion, as if making a bold would be a sacrilege, but Hidy's sense of professional practicality prevailed and his advice turned out to be prescient, as the bold became the weight of choice for many uses. It could have been argued, too, that there were heavier letters in other inscriptions from the Imperial period.

For Twombly, adjusting the weight of the letters meant working with the new interpolation tools, though not without a considerable amount of manual adjustment. [5] Her early performances were amazingly good considering that the tools she was using were being invented as she worked. The appearance in the same year of these two unquestioned classics, Claude Garamont's types and the letters of the Trajan inscription, in fresh new versions available on people's desktop computers, made 1989 an *annus mirabilis* in the history of type and graphic design. The issues of optical size and weight would be addressed later on by Adobe's Multiple Master project, which, though a failure in the marketplace, continues to be used as a development tool. Years later, it played a role in the redesigned

ABCDEFGHIJKL
MNOPQRSTUVWXYZ&
1234567890

ABCDEFGHIJKL
MNOPQRSTUVWXYZ&
1234567890

ABCDEFGHIJKL
MNOPQRSTUVWXYZ&
1234567890

Trajan family and its new companion, Trajan Sans. (See "Trajan Revived Redux," p. 185; and also "Penumbra," p. 172, and "Waters Titling," p. 229.)

Unlike Lithos, which was a great success from the start, Trajan was slower to catch on. It seemed to require a cultural shift to take off, a public realization that we were, once again, at a neoclassical moment and that it might as well be embraced. The shift came and Trajan more than took off—it rocketed! Suddenly, in the mid-1990s, the Trajan letters were appearing everywhere, nowhere more so than on movie posters, and soon it could be found on the most quotidian things—even pet food manufacturers found themselves mingling amongst the *senatus populusque romanus*. Once again, the Empire had struck back triumphantly.

The author thanks David Lemon and Lance Hidy for their help with this article.

7 From top to bottom: Trajan, Lithos, and Charlemagne (Adobe, 1989). All designed by Carol Twombly and released as a set.

...FANC...
...NSI...
...GNITV VI...
...DE TYR...
...TIONE...
...M PVBLI...
...M TR...

TRAJAN REVIVED REDUX

TRAJAN PRO 3
Robert Slimbach and Carol Twombly
Adobe, 2011

TRAJAN SANS PRO
Robert Slimbach
Adobe, 2011

STEVENS TITLING
John Stevens and Ryuichi Tateno
Linotype, 2011

CANTO
Richard Lipton
Font Bureau, 2011

POPVLVS
Sumner Stone
Stone Type Foundry, 2011

ROMA
Thomas Lincoln
Canada Type, 2011

BY PAUL SHAW

HALF A CENTURY AGO, James Mosley, in "Trajan Revived," his seminal article in the first and only issue of *The Alphabet*, traced the deification of the letters found on the base of Trajan's Column from their first resurrection in the Renaissance to their adoption, c. 1963, as a model for painted signs by the British Ministry of Works. Twenty-five years later, the Trajanic letters reached a new apotheosis with the release of Adobe Trajan. The typeface met with unexpected success, proving that the classical Roman capital is still relevant in a digital world, and that letterforms originally carved in stone two millennia ago have as much meaning as letters glowing on screens as they do as ink on paper. Another quarter century on, these letters continue to exert a fascination. Evidence for this is the remarkable release—within a single year, 2011—of five major suites of typefaces that reference it to varying degrees: Trajan Pro 3 and the ancillary Trajan Sans Pro by Robert Slimbach; Stevens Titling by John Stevens and Ryuichi Tateno; Canto by Richard Lipton; Popvlvs by Sumner Stone; and Roma by Thomas Lincoln.

TRAJAN PRO 3

Trajan Pro 3 is an extension of Twombly's original Trajan font by her former colleague Robert Slimbach, who updated it for OpenType and the Web. Twombly's Trajan was a highly faithful interpretation of the stone-cut letters. Twombly invented the missing letters, Arabic figures, punctuation, and other symbols, and added a bold weight. Some criticized the bold as not authentic, yet it is very close in heft and style to the flat-cut letters (originally filled in with metal) found on the fragment of the Arch of Claudius (51 AD), now on display at the Capitoline Museums in Rome, or the Arch of Constantine (315 AD). [1, 2]

Trajan Pro 3 has six weights, ranging from Extra Light to Black, with the new Semibold matching the old Bold. Although the publicity for the new design touts the versatility these additional weights provide, their desirability is a matter of debate. The Extra Light weight looks emaciated, while the Black feels chubby. The latter is a caricature, the antithesis of the elegance the Trajan letter has represented for so long.[1] The problem is inherent in the Trajanic letters themselves, as the distinctive pointed apices of *A*, *M*, and *N* cannot be maintained at heavier weights without serious distortion to counters and the angles of the diagonal strokes. [5] There is no acceptable solution short of changing those forms, as the book jacket designer Muriel Nasser did in her brush-lettered Roman capitals. [3, 6]

1 (*opposite*). Detail of the main inscription on the Arch of Constantine, 315 AD. These Imperial capitals are bolder than those of the Trajan inscription because they were originally filled with bronze. The dark spots mark the holes for the prongs of the missing metal letters.

2 (*above*). Fragment of the Arch of Claudius, 51 AD.

3 (*right*). Detail of lettering by Muriel Nasser from book jacket for *Beyond Equality: Labor and the Radical Republicans, 1862–1872* by David Montgomery (New York: Alfred A. Knopf, Inc., 1967).

4 Inscription from Aquileia, 1st century AD. Note the Greek Y.

5 Sample letters from Trajan Pro 3 showing the range of weights in the family. From left to right: Extra Light, Regular, and Black.

6 Jacket design and lettering by Muriel Nasser for *White Lotus* by John Hersey (New York: Alfred A. Knopf, Inc., 1965).

The extension of Trajan Pro 3 to include Greek and Cyrillic characters is more understandable and defensible. After all, the Greek alphabet underpins the other two, providing many of their basic forms; and the Cyrillic alphabet has been heavily Westernized since the reforms of Peter the Great in the early 18th century. The Greek and Cyrillic characters will be the most important legacy of Trajan Pro 3. An additional benefit of the former is the presence of *ypsilon*, the Greek Y with curved arms, which Renaissance scribes such as Bartolomeo Sanvito loved to insert into manuscripts and which Hermann Zapf revived in Palatino. [4] It is a character that can be substituted with impunity for the more familiar seriffed Y in Trajan. However, there is no tall Greek Y nor tall *I*, *L*, or *T*—all letters found in Roman inscriptions. On the plus side, Slimbach resisted the urge to create a slew of ligatures, nested letters, and swash capitals as have befouled several recent typefaces in the classical mode.[2] The only additions to the Roman character set are two extra ampersands and double-*N* and double-*T* ligatures. Although neither ligature is found in classical Roman inscriptions, the latter is always something modern typographers desire.

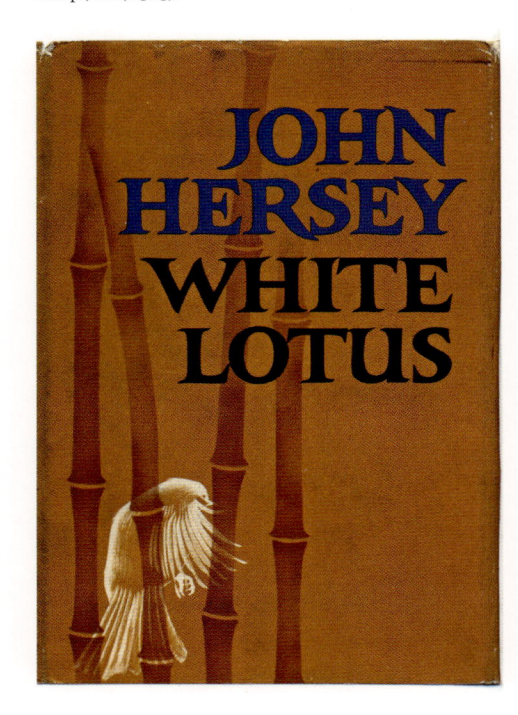

186

ABCDEFGHIJKL
MNOPQQRSTUV
WXYYZ&&&NNTT
12334567890

7 Basic character set of Trajan Sans Pro with alternates and ligatures. The second Y is from the Greek character set.

TRAJAN SANS PRO

The real news associated with Trajan Pro 3 is the accompanying Trajan Sans Pro. [7] The notion of a sans serif based on the classical proportions of the Trajan inscription letters has intrigued designers for several decades. The idea is not far-fetched. Sans serifs, contrary to the beliefs of Bauhauslers, are not modern letters but ancient ones. The Greeks and the Romans carved sans serif letters centuries before Jesus's birth. The capitals of Futura (1927), the quintessential geometric sans serif, follow the variable proportions of Imperial Roman capitals but are monolineal. Lance Hidy's Penumbra (1994), originally a Multiple Master font whose axes were weight and serif style, included a monoweight sans that reflected Trajanic proportions and forms (note the splayed M) while remaining resolutely contemporary. The same is true of Sumner Stone's Basalt (1998) and Magma (2004). Hermann Zapf's Optima (1958), based on Florentine Renaissance inscriptions that were, in turn, inspired by Roman inscriptions, managed the feat of maintaining a thick/thin contrast in a sans serif. However, none of these designs is directly descended from the letters of the Trajan inscription. This is where Trajan Sans Pro is unique. [8]

A precedent for Trajan Sans Pro are the so-called Ideal Letters that Father Catich included in his portfolio *Reed, Pen, & Brush Alphabets for Writing and Lettering* (1972). But these letters, based on the proportions of the Trajanic capitals, and existing only in a skeletal weight, never became the basis for a typeface—and, they are resolutely monoline. In contrast, Trajan Sans Pro retains the subtle stroke modulation of Trajan, something that may seem easy to do but is actually quite challenging. The removal of serifs changes the balance of the letters as well as the spacing. Slimbach has successfully captured the elusive vitality of the Trajan letters while avoiding any similarity to Optima or Basalt.

Other than the absence of serifs, Trajan Sans Pro is the same as Trajan Pro 3. That is, it has the same glyph set and the same six weights. But this time the Extra Light and Black weights are more successful. Stripping the letters of serifs has changed the proportions of these extreme weights—for instance, Trajan Sans Pro Black is not as squat as Trajan Pro 3 Black—and that makes a world of difference. Trajan Sans Pro is proof of the adage that sans serif typefaces tend to be more conducive to a wide range of weights than serif ones.

EMR
EMR
EMR
EMR
EMR

8 Top to bottom: Trajan Pro 3, Trajan Sans Pro, Roma, and Optima nova. For a more direct comparison the heights of the fonts have been equalized.

TRAJAN REVIVED REDUX 187

STEVENS TITLING PRO

John Stevens is, in the opinion of many, including me, the preeminent Western calligrapher in the world today. (See "Artist of the Written Word," p. 202.) He is equally at home working with a pen as a brush, whether pointed or broad-edge, and he can wield a ruling pen with aplomb, too. He is extremely versatile, able to create vibrantly expressive scripts as easily as a formal chancery cursive. Trained initially as a signwriter, Stevens's specialty has been the Imperial Roman capital in the Catich manner (i.e., written with a flexible, broad-edged brush). [9, 10] In this, he has shown an amazing ability to give these ancient letters new life, both through wringing subtle variations on the classical theme, and simply by imbuing his strokes with an ineffable energy. Thus, a typeface by Stevens based on his deep knowledge of Imperial Roman capitals is an exciting event. [11–14]

Yet, Stevens Titling falls short of my lofty expectations. It is his first typeface and the lack of experience shows. The digitization was done by Ryuichi Tateno, the Japanese calligrapher and type designer responsible for Pirouette (notable for its overlapping swash capitals). Stevens Titling consists of a suite of four fonts, each of which is progressively "brushier": from the solid Sable Brush through the slightly looser Badger Brush and Boar Brush to the very streaky Wolf Brush. [11] This is a novel concept—or would be if Richard Lipton had not thought of something similar at nearly the same time with Canto—but not a wholly workable one. The problem is one of scale. The sheer beauty of the letters is lost at ordinary display print sizes. The striated brushstrokes clog up and the weight of the letters becomes attenuated. It is only at large sizes—such as 120 pt and up—that Stevens Titling, especially the Wolf Brush font, comes into its own. The bigger the letter, the more one can appreciate the nuances of the diverse brushstrokes.

Stevens Titling is aptly named. It is a capitals-only font set, but several letters are rendered in two or more ways. [13, 14] Some are structurally different, with changes in serifs or the addition of swashes; some are texturally different, with fluctuating degrees of brushiness. The alternates are not identical from font to font within the Stevens Titling suite, though there is more similarity among the Badger Brush, Boar Brush, and Wolf Brush fonts than there is with the Sable Brush font. Because it is solid, the last has the fewest alternates—though it makes up for this deficiency by having the only set of small capitals. The two swash *T*s, which appear in all four of the fonts, are intended for use at the beginning and ending of words. There are no ligatures (other than diphthongs), nested letters, or tall letters. But Stevens Titling does include a collection of Aldine leaves, which have their origins in Roman inscriptions. [13, 14]

Stevens Titling, even in the basic Sable Brush font, is jauntier than Trajan (or Trajan Pro 3) and, at large sizes, an excellent alternative to it.

9 (*above, left*). Brush written Imperial Roman alphabet by John Stevens, 1995.

10 (*above, right*). "Thank You" by Alice Walker. Calligraphic painting by John Stevens, 2007. Watercolor and raised gilding.

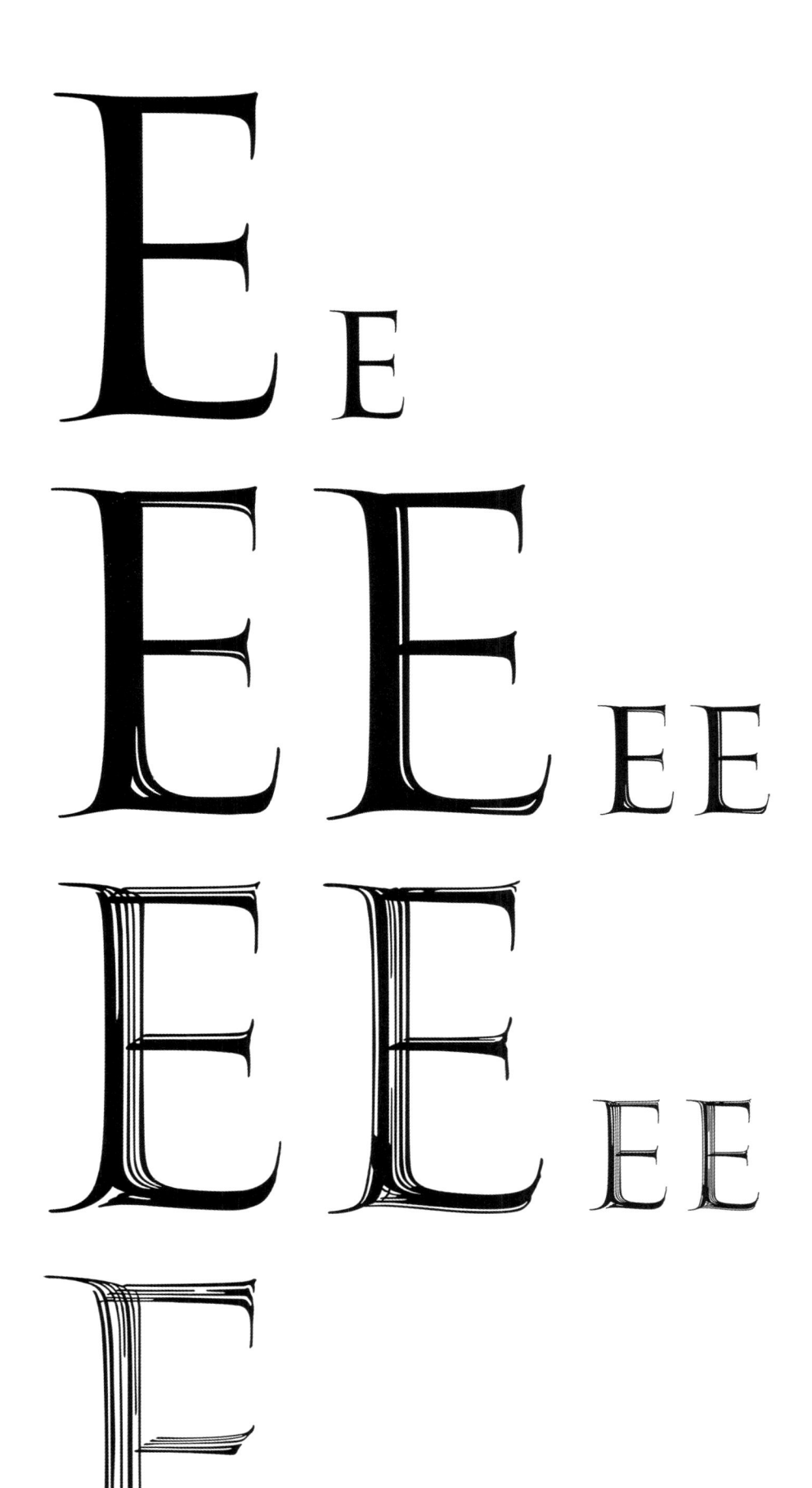

12 (*above*). Some of the alternate characters available in the Stevens Titling family. The specific alternates vary from font to font, but they can be mixed.

11 (*left*). Comparison of the different members of the Stevens Titling family at two sizes. From top to bottom: Sable Brush, Badger Brush, Boar Brush, and Wolf Brush.

TRAJAN REVIVED REDUX 189

AAABBCCCDDEEFF
GGHHIIJKKKLL
MMMMNNNNOOOPP
QQRRRRRSSTTTT
UUVVVVVWWWWW
XXXXXYYYYYZZZ
1234567890&
{[(.,;:!?/-*)]}

13 Stevens Titling Badger Brush by John Stevens (Linotype, 2011). Basic character set with alternates.

14 Stevens Titling Wolf Brush by John Stevens (Linotype, 2011). Basic character set with alternates.

AAAAAAAAA
BBCDDEEFFGG
HIJJKKKLLMMM
NNNNOPPQQRRR
SSTTUVVVV
WWWWWXXXX
YYYYYZZ&

abcdefghijklmnopqr
stuvwxyz

Th Th ct ff ffi ffl fj ft fi fl ß s tt t

ABCDEFGHIJKLMNOPQRSTUV
WXYZ&1234567890
1234567890 {[(.,;:!?/-·*)]}

CANTO

Before focusing his energies on type design, Richard Lipton had proven himself to be an outstanding calligrapher, able to wield a broad-edged brush in the Catich manner with a deft touch. [16] His intimate familiarity with Imperial Roman capitals was evident in the distinctive bifurcated serifs that characterize the underrated Arrus (1991), the first font he designed at Bitstream. [18] The cupping of the serifs is decorative at large sizes but melts away at small sizes, allowing Arrus to function equally well in both circumstances. This is important since, unlike most typefaces sparked by Imperial Roman capitals, it has a lowercase and thus is suitable for text usage. Similarly, Canto, Lipton's latest riff on the Trajan letters, also has a lowercase, making it more than a titling face. [15]

Canto is another suite of fonts, in this case the variations are called Roman, Pen, Brush, and Brush Open. The sequence moves from the typographic to the calligraphic, becoming looser along the way—or perhaps in the opposite direction, as Font Bureau proclaims, from the expressive, preparatory brush through the informal pen to the formal roman. The direction does not really matter as much as the notion, shared with Stevens Titling, of building a type family on different degrees of formality.

Canto Roman is typographic. Its serifs are crisp and fully formed, its strokes are cleanly joined, and its weight takes into consideration the small sizes in which most type is set. Small caps and oldstyle figures are included. Its very large number of swash characters—up to nine for the *A* alone—indicates that Lipton sees it doing duty as a display font as well as a text font. But he has not gone hog wild with alternates.[3] There are no lowercase swash letters and no all-capitals ligatures. The only ligatures beyond the usual lowercase *f*-ligatures are *Th*, *tt*, and quaint *ct* and *st*. One thing lacking in Canto Roman as a text face is a companion italic, which Arrus has.

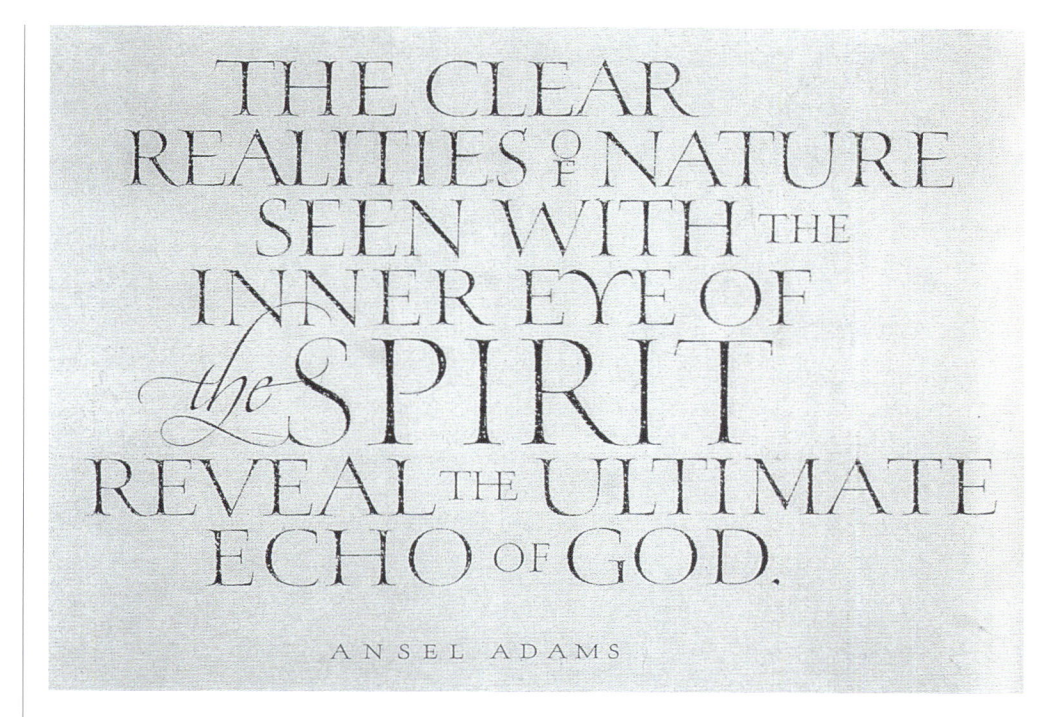

Canto Pen and Canto Brush are both calligraphic in nature. [17] They have sharper serifs and more voluptuous fillets than Canto Roman, along with fuller curves and a hint of waisting on the stems. This is the Catich effect. The lowercase stems have serifs that reflect the movement of broad-edged tools. The brush font is more gestural than the pen one, with overlapping and streaked strokes that reveal each letter's ductus. The streaking is not as pronounced as in the Badger Brush, Boar Brush, or Wolf Brush fonts of Stevens Titling. In the Canto Brush Open font it is stronger, so that it remains visible at small sizes.

Lipton's restraint extends beyond the character set to the composition of the Canto family. The four regular members each have bold companions and nothing more.

16 (*above*). Calligraphic broadside by Richard Lipton, 1980s. Stick ink and gold on paper.

17 (*far left*). Comparison of members of the Canto family: from left to right, Canto Roman, Canto Pen, Canto Brush (with alternates).

18 (*left*). Comparison of selected letters from Arrus (top) and Canto Roman (bottom).

15 (*opposite*). Canto Roman by Richard Lipton (Font Bureau, 2011). Full Latin character set of with alternates, swash capitals and ligatures.

TRAJAN REVIVED REDUX 193

19 Popvlvs by Sumner Stone (Stone Type Foundry, 2011).

POPVLVS

Sumner Stone, former director of typography at Adobe, has a distinguished calligraphic pedigree, having studied with Lloyd Reynolds at Reed College—where he watched Father Catich carve Trajan-inspired capitals into slate for the names of the older buildings on the campus (See "Catich at Reed College," p. 175)—and then worked for Hallmark Cards. At Adobe, he was responsible for instigating the original Trajan typeface, so it is fitting that he should try his hand at a typeface in the Roman Imperial capital tradition himself. The result is Popvlvs (its spelling in Roman lapidary style), one of a trio of typefaces reflecting the Western lettering heritage. [19] The other two are the calligraphic Davanti and the typographic Sator. [20] Together they embody, respectively, the aesthetic of the broad-brush, the broad-edged pen, and the graver. In this, Stone has, independently, come up with a concept similar to the one that underlies Lipton's Canto.

Popvlvs looks at first glance like Trajan, but close inspection reveals the many substantive ways in which it differs. Stone has created a synthesis of the Imperial Roman capital based on the Trajan inscription, the children of Sextus Pompeius Justus inscription along the Via Appia, and other inscriptions that he photographed during trips to Rome between 1996 and 1998. Unlike Trajan, his *M* and *N* have seriffed apices (though not *A*), as in the Sextus Pompeius Justus inscription; his *Q* has a shorter tail and his *Y* is narrower. Other differences are more subtle: sharper and more abrupt bracketing of serifs and changes in the distribution of weights (see the lower leg of *E*, the curve of *G*, the bowl of *R*, and the bottom serif on *S* for instance).

What sets Popvlvs apart from Trajan Pro 3 and Stevens Titling is Stone's attempt to concoct a lowercase complement to the Imperial Roman capitals. [19] It is a formidable task and, ultimately, one that is not satisfactory. The question is, why undertake it? [21]

In inventing a lowercase for Popvlvs, Stone was confronted with two choices for his models: the brush-written Roman Imperial capitals and the French Renaissance types of Garamont and Granjon. He chose a combination of the two. Most letters are clearly offshoots of the capitals, which is not surprising since that is how they evolved. Thus, the round letters (*b*, *c*, *d*, *o*, *p*, *q*, and *s*), vertical letters (*i* and *l*) and diagonal letters (*k*, *v*, *w*, *x*, *y*, and *z*) are irreproachable. The arched group of letters (*h*, *m*, *n*, *u*, and perhaps *r*) is also satisfactory. The remaining lowercase letters, which deviate the most from the form of the capitals, have been based on French Renaissance typefaces. The major problem with Popvlvs occurs within this group (specifically *a*, *e*, and *g*).

The Imperial Roman capitals have proportions that, as Stone himself has pointed out, are carefully balanced and thus not subject to tinkering without repercussions. The *a*, *e*, and *g* are all double-story letters, which is where the difficulty lies. Their vertical space reflects Renaissance aesthetics. Thus, the eye of the *e* is small, the bowl of *a* slopes downward, and the *g* has a small bowl and an elongated loop. These letters lack the equilibrium of the capitals. Though counterintuitive, a better model for the lowercase might have been the types of Richard Austin rather than those of Claude Garamont. They have fuller curves and a more even balance of counters and negative space that seems to fit with the quiet authority

ABCDEFGHIJKLMNO
PQRSTUVWXYZ
abcdefghijklmnopqrstu
vwxyz&fffiflßffiffl
1234567890

20 Sator by Sumner Stone (Stone Type Foundry, 2011).

of the Roman Imperial capitals. Stone's lowercase for Popvlvs is lively, especially the g with its sharply bent link (a Stone trademark) and the sharply sheared top of *t*. These letters lack the calm and self-effacing quality found in the Trajan capitals.

Lipton's Arrus has a lowercase with fuller, rounder letters that manages to blend harmoniously with its capitals. One subtle aspect to them is the deeper crotch where arches and bowls join the stems. This is something Stone also did in Sator, which is a more cohesive typeface than Popvlvs. [20] Then again, it is a design built on centuries of tradition as well as Stone's deep knowledge of pen-made letterforms. In the end, the problem with Popvlvs is not the quality of the lowercase but its ability to work seamlessly with the capitals. In some words, the two work together like longtime musical partners, but in others they feel awkward and the lowercase often seems to overpower the capitals. Although the lowercase is a work in progress, Popvlvs is a noble experiment and Stone deserves to be commended for his effort.

il jt
vwyxkz
ocqdbp
nhmu rf
aegs

IHTLFE
VWX
AZ YKNM
OQCG S
DPRB JU

21 Grouping by form of Popvlvs lowercase and capital letters.

TRAJAN REVIVED REDUX 195

ABCDEFGHIJKLM
NOPQRSTUVWXYZ&
abcdefghijklmno
pqrstuvwxyz
fffifjftffi
1234567890

ARCH
ARCH
ARCH
ARCH
ARCH
ARCH

ABCDEFGHIJKLMNOP
QRSTUVWXYZ&
1234567890
ABCDEFGHIJKLMNOP
QRSTUVWXYZ&
1234567890

22 (*opposite, top*). Roma Solid by Thomas Lincoln (Canada Type, 2011).

23 (*opposite, bottom left*). The members of the Roma family. From top to bottom: Roman Solid, Roman Outline, Roma Shaded, Roma Inscribed, Roma Inline, and Roma Fill.

24 (*opposite, bottom right*). Roma Shaded and Roma Inline by Thomas Lincoln (Canada Type, 2011).

25 (*right*). Carved and painted Trajanic *R* by Thomas Lincoln, n.d. Marble.

ROMA

Full disclosure: Although I had not met him at the time, Tom Lincoln contacted me for advice on Roma when it was in its infancy, and I consulted on the work as it developed, between 2009 and 2011. But the design is entirely his.

Thomas Lincoln, the designer of Roma, is not as well known as Slimbach, Lipton, or Stevens, yet he has solid credentials as a lettering artist and designer. In the 1960s, he studied with the legendary calligraphers Lloyd Reynolds—mentor to type designers Sumner Stone and Charles Bigelow—at the Museum Art School in Portland, Oregon, and Arnold Bank at Reed College.[4] Through his studies with Reynolds, Lincoln came in contact with Father Catich's theories about the Trajan inscription, though he never studied with the signwriter-turned-priest. [25] He subsequently moved to New York City, where he worked with Herb Lubalin, who gave him a different perspective on letters. In 1965, his typeface Lincoln Gothic, a forerunner to Roma, was a winner in the first typeface competition organized by the Visual Graphics Corporation (VGC), makers of the Typositor, a photosetting device for headlines. For the past several decades, Lincoln has worked as a graphic designer in his native Oregon.

Roma began life as Trajan Sans—before Adobe appropriated the name. Lincoln's idea was to use the Trajan letters as the armature or grounding for a contemporary sans serif. The difficulties Lincoln went through in trying to translate the subtleties of the Trajan capitals to sans serif form reinforce the exceptional quality of Slimbach's Trajan Sans. This is not to say that Roma is inferior, only that it is different. It is not a direct derivative of the Trajan letters, but a freer interpretation. Lincoln has eschewed a brush-driven modulation of the strokes in favor of a more rigorously epigraphic/typographic approach. [22] Yet, there is still a faint thick/thin contrast to them that prevents them from being too static. In spirit, Roma is closer to Schneidler Initials than to Carol Twombly's Trajan.

What truly separates Roma from Trajan Sans is the presence of a lowercase. It was also one of the most difficult aspects of the typeface's development. From the moment he began drawing the lowercase, Lincoln was acutely aware of Optima, worried that his design was encroaching too much on Zapf's. But how could it not? Zapf had hit the sweet spot when he designed Optima's lowercase, a set of original letters that, unlike the capitals, owed nothing to historical models but all to the theoretical concepts of classical balance, proportion, and harmony. Classicism provides designers with a narrow space in which to work. The best carve out their own territory by exploiting small yet significant differences within its strict parameters. Anything worthwhile that Lincoln did with Roma would inevitably be close, though not identical, to Optima.

Ultimately, what keeps Roma from being too close to Optima is its Trajan DNA. The curves of round letters are flatter, the proportions of key letters such as *R* are those of Imperial Rome rather than Renaissance Florence, and there is no waisting of strokes. Lincoln has successfully navigated the tricky balancing act of designing a typeface that is both personal and classical.

Cementing its credentials as a classical design, Roma has small capitals and old-style figures, though it is a display face rather than a text one. Lincoln has eschewed ligatures, alternates, swash characters, and other distractions. There are four weights (Light, Regular, Semibold, and Bold) and six additional, dimensional variations (Fill, Inline, Inscribed, Outline, Solid, Shaded). [23, 24] The latter group bring Roma into the world of Cecil B. DeMille and may prevent some people—influenced by the traditional prejudice against display faces, especially dimensional ones, as somehow being not properly typographic—from seeing it as a serious design in the same league as Trajan, Stevens Titling, and Canto. But such designs make perfect sense for letters whose origins are three-dimensional inscriptions.

Not all six of the dimensional variations of Roma are meant to be used independently. Roma Fill combines with Roma Inscribed, Roma Inline pairs with Roma Shaded, and Solid mates with Roma Outline for situations where designers want multi-colored type. Only Roma Inscribed, Roma Shaded, and Roma Outline should be used on their own. (Roma Solid is simply Roma Regular, the redundancy due to the need to pair the outer and inner dimensional fonts for greater ease of use.) Roma's dimensional variants exist only in a single weight and none has a lowercase. They are strictly titling fonts.

The number of dimensional *classical* typefaces has always been small. Although Alessandro Butti and Aldo Novarese's Augustea Open (Nebiolo, 1951) is sold by Letraset, and Monotype Imaging offers John Peters's Castellar (1957), Columna (Bauer, 1953) by Max Caflisch is only found in a solid version from URW++, and Jan van Krimpen's Open Roman Capitals (Enschedé, 1929) is not available in digital form. These are all metal faces; there are no new digital designs of comparable note. Thus, there is a niche to be filled by Roma Open, Roma Shaded, and Roma Inscribed.

QUO CAPITALIS MONUMENTALIS?

The overuse and misuse of Trajan has blinded us to its merits, in the same manner that we have become inured to the good qualities of Helvetica, Times New Roman, and Palatino. Trajan Pro 3, with its iffy extra weights, is not likely to change anyone's hostile opinion about the original, though it may provide a teachable moment to show that typefaces have optimal proportions and weights. For those disposed to like Trajan, but who still feel that it is time to try something else, Stevens Titling and Canto will suffice, depending on the situation. Stevens Titling is more vivacious than Trajan, a quality greatly prized today, though one that goes against the historical roles that Trajan often fulfills. Canto, on the other hand, is versatile and thus might find more favor—and triumph where Arrus never has. It can even be used at a wider range of sizes than Trajan or the other fonts mentioned here.

Of course, there are still other alternatives to Trajan, older typefaces that have never managed to gain widespread popularity despite their virtues. This is because they all have shortcomings. Shángò (2007), Jason Castle's digital re-creation of Schneidler Initials, is, at heart, a beautiful design that has gone underappreciated. [26] But the original has several annoying characters, notably the *A* with an abnormally low crossbar and the odd, lowercase-style *Y*. Hermann Zapf's Michelangelo (Stempel, 1951, but now subsumed under Palatino nova as Palatino Titling) has been largely forgotten in the digital era. It is elegant, though some of its proportions are idiosyncratic (e.g., *A*, *M*, *R*, and *U*). Nero (Berthold, 1982) by Friedrich Poppl is a graceful contemporary interpretation of Imperial Roman capitals that includes several ligatures (even THE) and nested letters that anticipate revivals like Shángò. [26] Unfortunately, depending on one's position toward "handcrafted" typefaces, the letters all have a roughened edge. Senatus (Berthold, 2003) by Werner Schneider, Poppl's protegé, is similar but without the abraded

26 Alternates and ligatures from Shango Classic Regular by Jason Castle (Castletype, 2007). Shango is derived from Schneidler Text by F. H. E. Schneidler (Bauer, 1936).

edge and the extra characters. However, it *is* a personal interpretation of the Imperial Roman capitals, and it is fairly light. (See "The Origins of Senatus," p. 209.) In contrast, Matthew Carter's Mantinia (Carter & Cone, 1993) may be too heavy for some tastes. It is actually a Renaissance interpretation of Imperial Roman capitals. (See "Mantinia," p. 213] Garrett Boge's trio of Cresci, Pontif, and Pietra (all LetterPerfect, 1997) are Baroque versions of Imperial Roman capitals. Each is lovely in its own way, yet stiffer than Trajan. Finally, there are Arrus, already mentioned, and Waters Titling (Adobe, 1997; OpenType version 2001) (See "Waters Titling," p. 225.) The latter, by calligrapher Julian Waters, is a contemporary vision of classical capitals complete with alternates, tall capitals, and numerous ligatures; there are also condensed and semicondensed versions, of which none of the other fonts under discussion can boast. But Waters Titling lacks the tautness of Trajan, has letters that diverge significantly from the Imperial Roman model (notably *A* with a serif at the apex, *M* with nearly straight sides, and *R* with an open bowl) and has elongated serifs.

In the end, there is no effective substitute for Trajan, only alternatives that are excellent in their own right and must be accepted on their own terms.

That being said, Trajan Sans Pro opens new possibilities for those who want something else besides Trajan. It holds out the promise of being both classical and modernist at the same time—not such a strange combination when one realizes there is a shared love of simplicity. The question is whether modernists can stomach its slightly curved stems, flared stroke endings, and clear-cut stroke contrast. In this regard, the more severe Roma may be preferred. Or designers can resurrect the overlooked Penumbra (1994)—Lance Hidy's Multiple Master typeface (now offered as separate fonts) that encompasses a sans, flare, half-serif, and serif options—if they want more control over the degree of sans serifness to their letters. (See "Penumbra," p. 155.)

The flurry of typefaces released in 2011/2012 that were inspired by Imperial Roman capitals in general, and the Trajan inscription in particular, was a rare occurrence. That they generated so little publicity is a shame. Whether or not one finds them flawed, they are typefaces worthy of our notice. They are the work of supremely skilled and smart designers who understand the Imperial Roman capitals through their hands as well as their minds. Their differing interpretations of the same source material are fascinating. Together, Trajan Sans Pro, Stevens Titling, Popvlvs, Canto, and Roma are proof that the past, rather than being stultifying, can hold the seeds of new ideas.

---

1 Discussions of the beauty of Imperial Roman capitals, and especially of the Trajan letters, often have centered on the proper proportion of stroke thickness to letter height. Theorists have advocated several ratios: 1:8 was preferred by Ludovico Vicentino degli Arrighi (1523), Juan de Yciar (1548), and Giovanni Francesco Cresci (1560); 1:9 was the choice of Fra Luca Pacioli (1509) and Francesco Torniello (1517); 1:10 was favored by Felice Feliciano (c. 1463), Albrecht Dürer (1525), Geoffroy Tory (1529), and Giovanni Francesco Cresci (1570); and 1:12 was promoted by Damiano da Moylle (c. 1480) and Sigismondo Fanti (1514). See *The Art of Written Forms: The Theory and Practice of Calligraphy* by Donald M. Anderson (Holt, Rinehart and Winston, 1969), pp. 125–33. Hermann Zapf, in designing his Palatino family, used ratios of 1:5 (Palatino Bold), 1:7 (Sistina), 1:9 (Palatino), 1:11 (Aldus), and 1:12 (Michelangelo). Trajan Pro 3 Regular has a ratio of 1:8, with stem widths of the other members of the family being one-third (Extra Light), two-thirds (Light), four-thirds (Semibold), twice (Bold), and just under three times (Black) that of the Regular.

2 Some examples of typefaces inspired by classical Roman capitals that, in my view, have gone overboard with the addition of characters that go against the classical spirit are Shángò (2007), Castle Type's revival of F. H. E. Schneidler's Schneidler Initials (1936), Canada Type's 2011 update of Walter Tiemann's Orpheus (1928) and Euphorion, and PF Monumenta Pro (2009) from Parachute. Patrick Griffin, the designer of Orpheus Pro, is clearly aware of the madness behind the extra characters. On Canada Type's website, he sheepishly admits:

"The Orpheus Pro fonts started out as a straightforward revival of Tiemann's Orpheus and Euphorion. It was as simple as a work brief can be. But did we ever get carried away, and what should have been finished in a few weeks ended up consuming the best part of a year, countless jugs of coffee, and the merciless scrutiny of too many pairs of eyeballs. The great roman caps just screamed for plenty of extensions, alternates, swashes, ligatures, fusions from different times, and of course, small caps. The roman lowercase wanted additional alternates and even a few ligatures. The italic needed to get the same treatment for its lowercase that Tiemann envisioned for the uppercase. So the lowercase went overboard [with] plenty [of] alternates and swashes and ligatures. Even the italic uppercase was augmented by maybe too many extra letters. Orpheus Pro has been a real ride."

3 Lipton has resisted the contemporary urge to turn a classical typeface into a Victorian free-for-all, full of swash letters, ligatures, nested letters, alternates, decorative doodads, as has happened with the typefaces listed in note 2.

4 Although Arnold Bank (1908–1986) is not as well-remembered as Lloyd Reynolds (1902–1979), he was the more influential figure in the 1950s and 1960s. He was art director in *Time* magazine's promotion department from 1941 to 1947. In 1951, Reynolds invited Bank to teach at the Museum Art School, in Portland, and at Reed College, resulting in the publication of Bank's only "book," a set of loose cards composed of photographs of Bank's chalkboard demonstrations (He taught additional summer sessions at Reed College in the 1960s.) From 1954 to 1957, he lectured at the Royal College of Art, in London, on a Fulbright grant. His lectures were bravura performances in which he astonished the English audience by being able not only to write from memory a wide range of historical calligraphic hands, including the obscure Beneventan and several varieties of bastarda, but he did so using both hands. New York designers tell of seeing a similar feat at the Type Directors Club in the 1960s. For the last twenty-five years of his life, Bank taught calligraphy and typography at Carnegie Tech, now Carnegie-Mellon University.

TRAJAN PRO 3 CYRILLIC

MAXIM ZHUKOV

DISCLOSURE: *Maxim Zhukov consulted on the development of the Cyrillic parts of both Trajan Pro 3 and Trajan Sans Pro. He prepared historical and stylistic research, tested prototypes, gave feedback on specific letterforms, and provided sample art and copy for specimens.*

MANY CYRILLIC VERSIONS OF TYPEFACES based on historical models are not, strictly speaking, *revivals*. There is not much to revive: Cyrillic typefaces that could be classified as oldstyle (e.g., Venetian oldstyle or French oldstyle) did not exist in 15th- and 16th-century Russia, or in any other lands where Cyrillic was used. However, credible and convincing oldstyle typefaces can be developed by extrapolating the visual features of the Latin originals and applying them to the letters of the Cyrillic alphabet.

What makes the "cyrillization" of designs originally created for the Latin script easier is the presence of so many letters in both alphabets that share similar forms, even if those glyphs relate to different characters. For example, in English and Russian glyph sets, the uppercase *A, B, C, E, H, K, M, O, P, T*, and *X* are all letters derived from the Greek script, the common ancestor of both the Latin and the Cyrillic alphabets, and thus are virtually the same. The balance of the Russian capital glyph set—*Б, Г, Д, Ё, Ж, И, Й, Л, П, У, Ф, Ц, Ч, Ш, Щ, Ъ, Ы, Ь, Э, Ю*, and *Я*—remain to be designed to "match" the look and feel of the original (Latin) version. But that is where the difficulty lies.

Predictably, there is a lot more to a Cyrillic font complement than the Russian glyph set. Most digital Cyrillics support the processing of text in dozens of languages. The most common language set covered by Unicode code page Windows 1251 (Cyrillic Standard) includes six Slavic languages—Belarusian, Bulgarian, Macedonian, Russian (modern and pre-1918), Serbian, and Ukrainian—and twenty-one non-Slavic languages—Abaza, Adyghe, Aghul, Avar, Chechen, Dargwa, Ingush, Kabardian, Kabardin--Circassian, Karachay-Balkar, Karakalpak, Kumyk, Lak, Lezgian, Mordvin-Erzya, Mordvin-Moksha, Nogai, Rutul, Tabasaran, Tat, and Tsakhur. And then there is a Cyrillic Asian code page (ParaType 154) covering forty languages, both Slavic and non-Slavic.

This is where the design job becomes really challenging, even if the typeface under construction, like Trajan Pro 3, is all majuscule, with no lowercase glyphs. Not only is the Cyrillic version expected to be consistent with the design of the Latin, but it also has to conform to the design conventions endemic to Cyrillic.

As with Latin-based typefaces, there are letterforms in Cyrillic that work better in the "modern" (neoclassical) idiom than in the oldstyle one (for example, the wavy, tilde-like terminals in the *З, Ц, Щ,* and *Э*). To ensure the design integrity of a Cyrillic typeface, it is standard practice to coordinate the construction of certain glyphs that are visually related (for example, *С, О,* and *Э*; or *Г, Е, Ё* and *Т*; or *Н, П, Ц, Ш,* and *Щ*; or *Б, В, Р, Ч, Ь, Ы, Ъ,* and *Я*). In a multilingual typeface, those design groups correlate logically, extending across the boundaries of either glyph set, so the treatment of the Cyrillic *С* is coordinated with the Latin *D, G,* and *Q*; the *Г* with the *F* and the *L*; the *Б* and the *Я* with the *R*; and so on.

One convincing manifestation of the interdependence of glyph shapes is the belonging of certain letters to more than one group of correlates. The *Б*, for one, is subject to coordination with *В, Р, Ч, Ь, Ы, Ъ, Я,* and *R*, but its construction is also related to *Г, Е, Ё, Т, Ц, Щ, F,* and *L*. The lineup of those rows of glyphs that share certain visual features is not rigid: it is design-dependent. For example, the *Ж* may be harmonized with *К, Я,* and *R* (as in most Cyrillic faces issued after 1750), or it may be treated as a singular form, visually unrelated to its sister glyphs (as it looked in the typefaces before Peter the Great's typographic reform).

Some design features of Trajan Pro 3 called for a judicious revision of the common, habitual correlations in Cyrillic glyph construction. [1] The pointed apices and vertices of the original *A, M, N, V, W,* and the spiky *Z* called for the use of the isosceles

АБВГДЕЖЗИЙКЛ
МНОПРСТУУФФФ
ХЦЧШЩЪЫЬ
ЭЮЯТТ
АБВГДЕЖЗИІКЛМН
ОПРСТУУФФФХ
ЦЧШЩЪЫЬЭЮЯТТ

1 Trajan Pro 3 Cyrillic by Robert Slimbach (Adobe, 2011).

TRAJAN PRO 3 GREEK

GERRY LEONIDAS

DISCLOSURE: *Gerry Leonidas has been an unpaid advisor to Adobe on nearly all of its Greek types since Minion Pro. For Trajan Pro 3, he gave general feedback on the approach taken once the design was done, and specific feedback on how to deal with accents (whether to include them, and in which characters).*

TRAJAN PRO 3 GREEK IS A SIMPLE all-caps extension to an existing Latin display typeface. [1] It is done well, but it is a typical adaptation. That is, the same inscriptional style has been applied to an Eastern script that has no equivalent lapidary tradition, ignoring its own separate manuscript display style. The extension is somewhat necessary to insure the wider use of the parent Trajan typeface, but it is predictable and unsurprising. It might have been more interesting if Adobe had explored equivalent historical sources in the Greek tradition instead of taking the "safe" route. As it is, Trajan Pro 3 Greek works well for graphic designers who tend to value uniformity of texture over typographic identity, rather than those who look for display typefaces that offer some research-informed individuality. There is no doubt that it is competent and efficient—but it will not raise any eyebrows.

ΑΒΓΔΕΖΗΘΙΚΛΜ
ΝΞΟΠΡΣΤΥΦΦΦΧ
ΨΩΝΝΤΤ
ΛΜΝΞΟΠΡΣΤΥΦΦΦ
ΧΨΩΝΝΤΤ

1 Trajan Pro 3 Greek by Robert Slimbach (Adobe, 2011).

---

2 Sans serif Cyrillic alphabet by Vadim Lazursky, 1965.

Д and Л (delta- and lambda-like), and the unusual, zigzag ("inverted-N") form of the И. Preference was given, unhesitatingly, to the straight-limb, kappa-like construction of the К, the matching Ж and Я, and the stiff, v-like, not sagging, form of the У. Simple, austere, geometric forms, reminiscent of classical Greek inscriptions, were invariably preferred to a more elaborate, fanciful pattern of a latter-day printing type. No fancy finials, bulbous or lachrymal—usually found in Cyrillic type design—were allowed. The hanging terminals of the Д, Ц, and Щ were reduced almost to naught.

NOTE: In 1958, Vadim Lazurski became the first Russian designer to create a Cyrillic "adaptation" of the Trajan inscriptional letter. (See p. 129, fig. 5.) He subsequently created a sans serif interpretation of the Trajanic letter in 1965 (see fig. 2) and, in 1978, sketched a multi-weight Cyrillic alphabet in the Roman Imperial capital vein. In all of this he anticipated both of the main innovations of Trajan Pro 3 Cyrillic.

ARTIST OF THE WRITTEN WORD

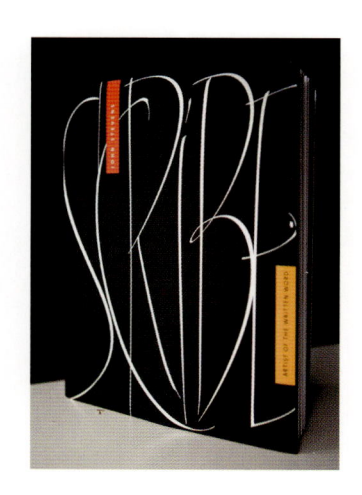

I FIRST MET JOHN STEVENS IN 1981, when he was just beginning to explore calligraphy after completing his training as a signwriter. Even then he was extremely accomplished, so much so that his entries to the first "Calligraphy in the Graphic Arts" competition that I organized for the Society of Scribes, Ltd., were rejected by the judges—led by Milton Glaser—on the mistaken assumption that they must have been drawn. (The next year I changed the name of the competition to Calligraphy *and Lettering* in the Graphic Arts.) Since that time Stevens has continued to hone his skills to the point where it is not hyperbole to call him the premier calligrapher working in the Western tradition today. His versatility sets him apart from his contemporaries—whether established luminaries, such as Hermann Zapf, or rising stars such as Luca Barcellona. Stevens is adept at the use of broad-edged pens, broad and pointed brushes, and ruling pens: he can execute any of the major Western calligraphic hands, from Imperial Roman capitals to fraktur to chancery cursive, and he is equally skilled at expressive work. [2–7] He is as comfortable doing traditional scribal work as creating commercial work for reproduction; his portfolio ranges effortlessly from certificates and awards to book jackets, advertising and logos. (Among his many clients are Yale University, Macy's, Newsweek, Robert Mondavi Wines, Victoria's Secret, and Lucasfilm.) An additional aspect of Stevens's work that stands out is his impeccable sense of design, something lacking in many otherwise accomplished contemporary calligraphers.

Scribe: Artist of the Written Word (Greensboro, North Carolina: Letter Arts Book Club for John Neal Books, 2013) has been five years in the making. [1] Given that it is the first book by or about Stevens, it is a landmark work. It is also a frustrating one, for *Scribe* is several books in one: an extensive portfolio; a long meditation on the place of the scribe in the 21st century; an abbreviated instructional manual; and a short history of modern calligraphy. Stevens's ambitious attempt to weave these various elements together is only partially successful, something that becomes evident to those who stop to read the text rather than merely flip through the book to savor the beautiful work.

As a portfolio or showcase of Stevens's work, *Scribe* is stunning, a feast for the eyes for anyone who loves letterforms. Choose an adjective and the odds are it describes at least one piece in the book: elegant, delicate, decorative, spare, direct, controlled, rough, expressive, wild, powerful, funky, sensuous, aggressive, and more. The work is continually exciting and amazing (How did he do that? is a question I kept asking myself). In fact, one criticism of *Scribe* is that there is so much work at such a high level that it is easy for a reader—especially one who has never tried writing with a broad-edged pen or a brush—to become jaded and to forget that this is not type but rather the product of a supremely skilled hand.

Although done in the 1980s, the most astonishing work in *Scribe* is arguably the series of complex multitext pieces shown on pages 156–61, including two calendars for Headliners/Identicolor and a greeting card for United Airlines. [8] There is less elaborate work that is also thrilling, however.

All images are from *Scribe: Artist of the Written Word* by John Stevens.

1 (*opposite, top*). Cover of *Scribe: Artist of the Written Word*.

2 (*opposite, bottom*). Letterhead illustration.

3 (*right*). Single-stroke, brush-written block letter used as a step toward learning Imperial Roman capitals.

A warm-up transition, single stroke block letter (with some calligraphic touches). This practice will ease our way into Roman. John Stevens

4 (*above*). Brush-written fraktur capitals with italic minuscule, 2009.

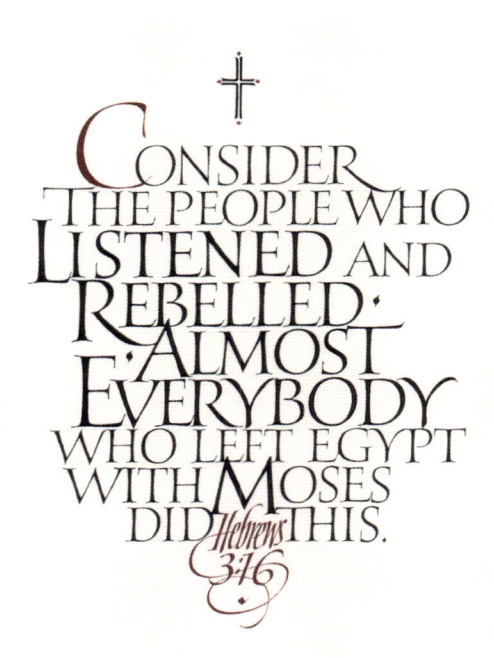

5 (*left*). Hebrews 3:16 (1985). Pen-written Roman capitals. Stick ink on handmade paper.

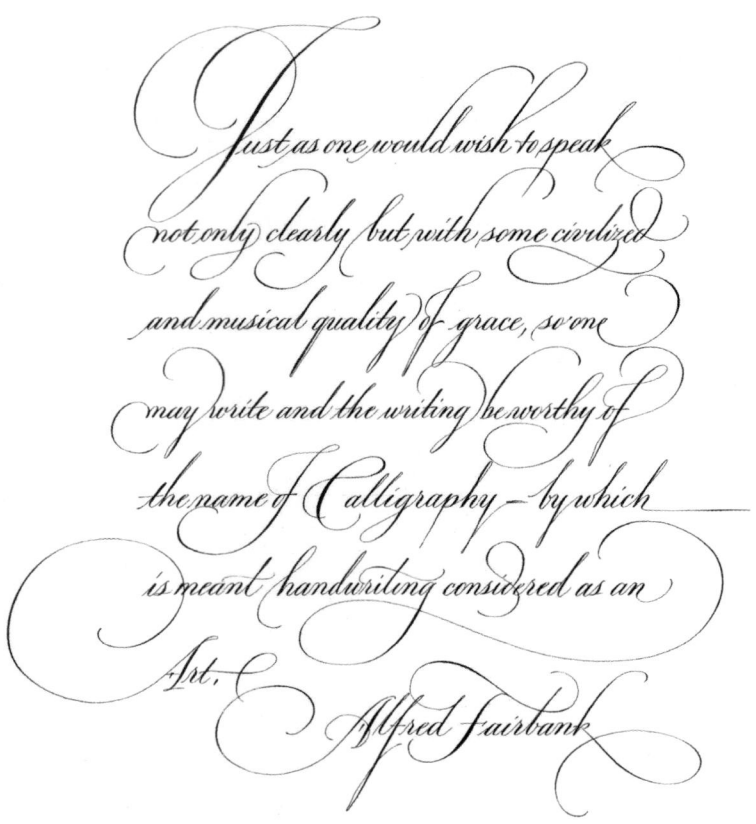

6 "Even the Gods" (2002). Written with a ½" flat brush.

7 (*above*). Quotation by Alfred Fairbank, 1990. Stick ink on handmade paper.

8 (*right*). Poster for Headliners Identicolor, 1987. Written in a wide variety of scripts (including several variants of Imperial Roman capitals) with a mix of brushes and pens.

Picking somewhat at random (I could easily pick seven other works), I would nominate the book title *Water Shaper*, the quotation from Cratylus (p. 77), the word "breath" (p. 73), the selection from Hebrews 3:16, the "Letterhead" pictorial composition (p. 142), the birth announcement for Quentin Keoni Teta, and the Alfred Fairbank quotation on writing. [2, 5, 7, 9]

Enough gushing over Stevens's work. What about his text? Stevens seems to have tried to tackle every major issue that has arisen in the world of calligraphy since its second modern revival in the 1970s, as well as others that have been present since the first modern revival during the Arts & Crafts era: bias toward the broad-edged pen at the expense of the brush and other tools; calligraphy vs. lettering (or writing letters vs. drawing letters); original calligraphy vs. calligraphy for reproduction (or direct writing vs. retouched letters); calligraphy vs. type; formal scripts vs. expressive lettering; calligraphy as a transparent vehicle vs. calligraphy as an interpretive vehicle; and—the big one today—calligraphy as a craft vs. calligraphy as art. That is a lot of ground to cover. Unfortunately, Stevens engages these issues in a peripatetic manner rather than through sustained argument.

Scribe opens with a ringing declaration: "Artist of the written word means we focus on letters as image rather than being servants of the text." Embedded in this short sentence is the calligraphy as craft vs. calligraphy as art debate. But the introduction that follows does not immediately take up the argument. Instead, Stevens flits about. At first, he rightly complains about the limitations of the word *calligraphy* and the biased perceptions it engenders in non-calligraphers, though he fails to take up the problems inherent in it—it is a compound of the Greek words "kallos" and "graphia," meaning "*beautiful* writing"—or to explain how its meaning has morphed (degenerated?) over the past century. He then goes on to argue against choosing sides in the many dichotomies prevalent in the calligraphic world. Finally he addresses the notion of calligraphy as art, only to declare, "I don't feel it is our job to decide what is art." His answer is to trust in quality, a concept that he circles back to several times yet never attempts to define. The dichotomy of form vs. content that opened the introduction is addressed four pages in, followed quickly by thoughts on the importance of line in calligraphy, the lack of visual awareness among calligraphers, a diatribe against short attention spans, and finally a meditation on why he and others are so deeply intrigued by letters. It is a heady mix of ideas.

This summary of the introduction is emblematic of *Scribe* as a whole. The points that Stevens makes are good ones, even important ones, but they are not always made in a systematic manner, nor in the most forceful or resonant way. For instance:

> If we think of ourselves as servants of the text, we seek to become transparent and to convey the meaning of the words without imposing our own interpretation on them. It is my belief that this transparency is an impossible idea or, at best, naïve. . . . I have found letterforms to be a

NINETEEN HUNDRED EIGHTY SEVEN
1987
January February March April May June July August September October November December
Январь бевраль март апрель май июнь июль август сентябрь октябрь ноябрь декабрь весна лето осень
MCMLXXXVIII
MONDAY 2
MONDAY'S CHILD IS FAIR OF FACE
3 TUESDAY
TUESDAY'S CHILD IS FULL OF GRACE
WEDNESDAY 4
WEDNESDAY'S CHILD IS FULL OF WOE
5 THURSDAY
THURSDAY'S CHILD HAS FAR TO GO
FRIDAY 6
FRIDAY'S CHILD IS LOVING AND GIVING
7 SATURDAY
SATURDAY'S CHILD WORKS HARD FOR A LIVING
SUNDAY 1
THE CHILD THAT IS BORN ON THE SABBATH DAY IS BONNY, BLYTH, GOOD AND GAY
1 9 8 7
CALENDER
WINTER SPRING SUMMER FALL
THE WINTER SOLSTICE
THE VERNAL EQUINOX
THE AUTUMN EQUINOX
THE SUMMER SOLSTICE
1987
SUMMER
WINTER
MARTIN LUTHER KING
New Years Day
St. Valentine's Day
St. Patricks
PASSOVER
Easter
Mothers Day
Memorial
Fathers Day
Fouth of July
YOM KIPPUR
Labor Day
VETERANS
Halloween
ELECTION
Thanksgiving
Christmas
CHANUKAH
THE SEASONS OF THE CHINESE CALENDER
The spring begins
the rain water
the excited insect
the vernal equinox
the clear and bright
the grain rains
The summer begins
the grain fills
the grain in ear
the summer solstice
the slight heat
the great heat
The autumn begins
the limit of heat
the white Dew
the autumn equinox
the cold Dew
the hoar frost Descends
THE WINTER BEGINS · THE LITTLE SNOW · THE HEAVY SNOW · THE WINTER SOLSTICE · THE LITTLE COLD · THE SEVERE COLD.
THOTH PHAOPHI ATHYR CHOIAK TYBI MECHIR PHAMENOTH PHARMUTHI PACHONS
PAYNI EPIPHI MESORE INUNDATION CULTIVATION HARVEST EGYPTIAN 1500 B.C.
Janeiro Fevereiro Março April Mai Junho Julho Agosto Setembro Outubro Novembro Dezembro
HEADLINERS
Identicolor
A B C D E F G H I J K L M N O P Q R S T U V W X Y Z
JS
John Stevens © 1986

9 Book jacket lettering for *Water Shaper* by Laura Williams McCaffrey (New York: Clarion Books, 2006).

potent force in representing content and that they can be content themselves, since they are made of lines, shapes, spaces, and other graphic elements. You simply cannot mark a surface and have it be devoid of any content created by the maker. [p. 18]

Qualifiers and other forms of equivocation—"My guess," "My thought," "I believe," "I think," and so on—mar his sentences and hinder his arguments.

Furthermore, Stevens often seems to be involved in a dialogue with unnamed allies and opponents. Many of his views either spring from or run counter to ideas voiced by others over the past century, but those others—Arthur Baker, Hans Joachim Burgert, Father Edward M. Catich, Ray DaBoll, Alfred Fairbank, Nicolete Gray, Edward Johnston, Brody Neuenschwander, Friedrich Neugebauer, and more—are never quoted and rarely cited. Stevens does mention and quote from thinkers outside of the calligraphy world, such as Milton Glaser, Paul Klee, and the Buddhist teacher Pema Chödrön. And he does explicitly acknowledge those in the calligraphy world—John Howard Benson, Father Catich, Karl-Erik Försberg, Hermann Zapf, and others—who have had a major influence on his work. For those outside of the hermetic calligraphy world—or even those inside it but without familiarity of the debates that have been animating it since the 1970s—many of the arguments Stevens is making will not be fully understood. This is a shame because Stevens, by dint of his skill and versatility, is in a prime position to make outsiders, those in the worlds of art and design, sit up and take notice of what is possible under the term *calligraphy* today.

In *Scribe*, Stevens aims to have it all—an attitude with which I am wholly sympathetic. He believes that lettermaking—let's drop the problematic term *calligraphy*, as he suggests—can be a craft, an art, *and* an integral aspect of design. There is no need to choose among these possibilities. They can all exist, as indeed they do in his work. Furthermore, letters can be made with any tool that reveals the personality of its maker. Stevens's tools of choice are the broad-edged pen, the broad and pointed brush, and the ruling pen, but he is willing to embrace the chisel and mallet, the spray can, or the marker.

As indicated at the beginning of this review, *Scribe* is more than a portfolio and an artist's statement. It also includes much information about making letters, although, to the likely disappointment of many, it assiduously avoids being a how-to book. There are only two exemplars (a brush-written minuscule alphabet on p. 57 and brush-written sans serif capitals on p. 60) and a few exercises (pp. 87, 89). This is deliberate. At the end, in a section titled "Teaching Ideals," Stevens explains that he prefers to teach "themes" rather than specific hands or lettering styles. His basic concepts (outlined on pp. 256–57, but many are detailed earlier) are: Form and Animation; Capitals, Minuscules, and Cursive; Form, Rhythm and Movement; Form, Proportion and Weight; Gesture and Modularity; Two Lines Interacting; Working with Dissimilar Ideas; Diverge/Converge; Edging or Hybrid Form; Losing the Grid; Visual/Verbal Relationships; and Automatic Drawing.

Stevens is not interested in providing detailed explanations about making specific letters, preferring instead to discuss the concepts behind lettermaking in general.

And it is here that *Scribe* is both at its best and at its most frustrating. For instance, his chapter on brush sensibilities ("plastic lines, subtle swells and nuances"), with its notion that such attributes can be carried over to pen-made letters, and its discussion of hybrid (or nonclassical) forms, is revelatory. Yet, other than general comments in some captions (for example, "Brush-written on rough paper using Chinese pointed brush and watercolor"), there is little specific information on the effects possible with different kinds of brushes. Nor are there any "process" illustrations to assist the reader in visualizing techniques such as "cornering, squashing, lifting, or wrong-weighting" (except for a portion of a tiny one at the bottom of p. 73), or understanding what Stevens means when he writes, "The outline of the form is not an exact copy of the basic stroke. It is usually balanced but not symmetrical." Essentially, Stevens expects the reader to follow the path he trod in arriving at his present skill level: "You must look, see, and study in order to know." There are no shortcuts.

There is much more in *Scribe* that warrants discussion, but suffice it to say that the book is essential reading for all calligraphers, and could be equally of interest to anyone seriously interested in type. Stevens shows us what the human hand is capable of, the extraordinary forms it can conjure without any mechanical or digital assistance. *Vive la plume et vive il pinceau!*
—P.S.

...N WISSEN...
...UND KRIEG...
...MPHIEREN...
...WERDEN...
DASS SICH D...
...ER DER ERD...
...IGEN WERDE...
...ZU ZERSTÖR...
SONDERN...
...ZU BAUEN...

THE ORIGINS OF SENATUS

**WERNER SCHNEIDER
WITH DAN REYNOLDS**

Notes from a conversation with Dan Reynolds. In my work as a type designer, classical forms occupy a high priority. Their high design quality and functionality serve as timeless models. Their expressiveness fascinates me as well, with their inherent dynamism and immediacy. The development of the Roman capitals occurred over a period of many centuries, and it was only in Augustus's time that the process reached its final heights. It is lucky for us to still be able to witness these letters and to understand how the Roman lettering artists recognized the broad-edged writing instrument as the ideal tool for the expression of their artistic imagination. Even after 2,000 years, these letters are held in high regard by the typographic world. Because of their timeless, formal qualities, they show no signs of aging. Aesthetic quality, proportional beauty, and high functionality should remain the benchmark for all letter design. Roman capitals exemplify this like no other.

The example on the base of Trajan's Column—made a century after the time of Augustus—is the epitome of high aesthetics and it serves as a role model to this day. The Trajan inscription outshines everything else created by letter artists before or since. The secrets behind its success lie primarily in the capable hands of a gifted artist, no matter which tool he used: a reed, a brush, or a chisel. Also, I am convinced, contrary to Father Catich's claim, that the written design of the Imperial capitals and their sculptural implementation were performed by the same person. The homogeneity of the work suggests this.

I think of my collaboration with the late Günter Gerhard Lange (1921–2008), artistic director of Berthold, as a godsend for my work as a lettering artist. He was regarded internationally as the epitome of visual connoisseurship and valuable criticism. His lectures, known for their bawdy language, were legendary. They earned him the nickname, "Gutenberg's Machine Gun." His recommendations from previous projects, Schneider-Antiqua for example, proved to be very constructive for me and formed the basis of trust between us.

Before my work on Senatus, my admiration had focused primarily on the almost perfectly executed inscription on the base of Trajan's Column. The impetus for designing another Roman inscriptional typeface came from Lange. He called me one day, in 1989, to say, "Schneider, we are going to make a classical serif type with the name Inskriptur and I want classical capitals straight out of your hand. Got it?!" He was determined and concise in his language, mentioning "orientation on the Arch of Titus model." [8] I responded, "How about an orientation on the Trajan inscription?" He replied, "No! Carol Twombly at Adobe has already done an excellent typeface based on that! It's good! We don't need another Trajan!"

At first I had considered creating a lowercase for the typeface as well, but I recognized GGL's preference for a purely capital typeface with a classical feeling and accepted his vision. Senatus keeps the spirit of the classical Roman capital alive. It is not a copy of an ancient Roman inscription, but it is infused with its qualities. During the Senatus project, Lange and I discussed corrections over the telephone. Unfortunately, he had already stopped marking up typeface correction sheets by hand at this point, which was really too bad. [3] The change to the width of Senatus' *R*, for instance, came as a request from GGL. The form of the *R* found on the Arch of Titus is much wider than the more typographic shape in Senatus. Also, the weight of Senatus' letterforms is deliberately lighter in comparison with the Arch of Titus inscription.

1 Louis Pasteur broadside by Werner Schneider, 1988. Built-up lettering with a broad-edged pen. Printed in white on dark blue paper.

This was done in order to help obtain an ample progression of weights via interpolation, but the final version of the typeface was released only in a single weight. [5, 6]

About fifteen years went by before Senatus was released in 2004. [2] There were many interruptions along the way, including delays caused by H. Berthold AG's business difficulties during the early 1990s.[1] By the time Senatus was to be finished, I mailed my 1:1 production drawings to Dieter Hofrichter (the designer of Carat, the typeface you are reading now), in Munich, who was a close colleague of Harvey Hunt and GGL in Berthold Types Ltd., the new company.

I went to Rome for study purposes in 2003, quite late in the Senatus development process. During the trip I took a few photos and made sketches of the inscriptions on the Arch of Titus, which proved to be particularly valuable. The inscription on the Arch begins with the words "SENATUS POPULUS," which later gave the typeface its final name. [7, 8] "This is exactly what I wanted to call the typeface in the first place," Lange later remarked to me.

Many of my classical calligraphic works, especially those made with the Hiero note pen [a pointed-nib pen], show a certain affinity with Senatus' formal language. [1] For me, it was the most important tool in the process of finding the right form for the typeface. The diagonal forms that taper to a point in the letters are especially indicative of that. This flexible writing instrument provides a more sensitive result than what can be achieved with a wide bamboo pen or a broad-nib metal pen.

Without a doubt the idealized Roman alphabet is still the best means of learning about visual form today. All elementary design laws are present in its letters, including the theory of proportion, optical phenomena and their dimensional ratio, contrast values, rhythmic values, light and dark, movement, ductus, etc. For each letter artist struggling to achieve high-quality forms, an intensive examination of this model is an essential duty.

---

1 In 1993, H. Berthold AG became insolvent. It was reformed as H. Berthold Systeme GmbH in 1993, a company that was dissolved in 1995. Prior to dissolution, the company licensed its typefaces to a company in Chicago, which, in 1997, took on the name of Berthold Types Ltd. It is now called Berthold Direct Inc. Lange retired from Berthold AG in 1990, but then returned to work with Berthold Types Ltd. in 2000, where he remained until his death in 2008.

ABCDE
FGHIJKL
MNOPQR
STUVW
XYZ

2 (*above*). Senatus by Werner Schneider (H. Berthold AG, 2004)

3 (*right*). Detail of annotated proof (22 February 1985) of Schneider Antiqua BQ (H. Berthold AG, 1987). The notes are by G.G. Lange, Berthold's longtime artistic director.

4 (*below*). Comparison of Schneider Antiqua (top) and Senatus (bottom).

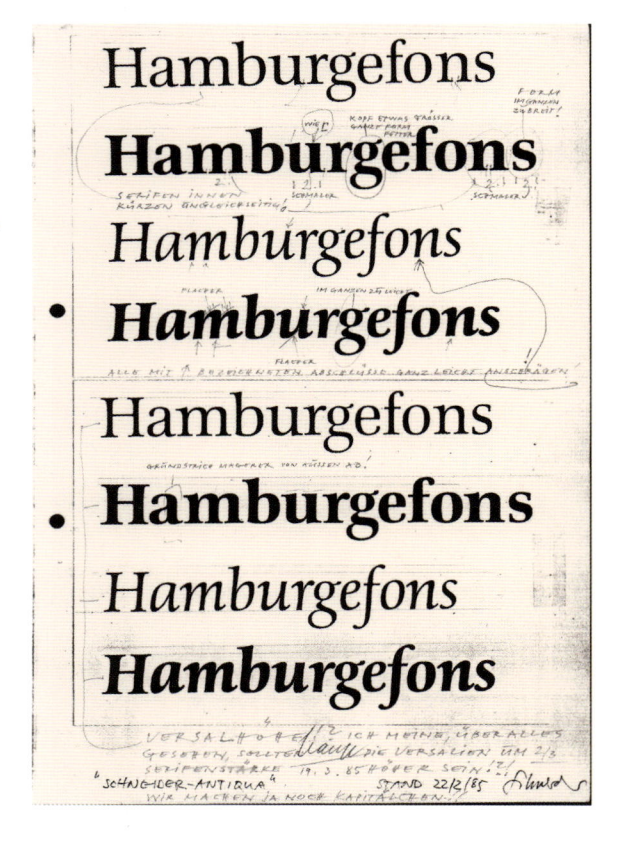

AEGMQRW
AEGMQRW

ABCM 12
ABCM 12
ABCM 12
ABCM 12

QRSTU
VWXYZ
E1267

5 (*above*). Tests of weights for Inscriptur, an early name for Senatus (undated but probably 2001 or 2002).

6 (*above, right*). Paste-up of drawings of proposed Senatus Bold (8 August 2001).

7 (*below*). Recreation of the Arch of Titus inscription using Senatus.

8 (*bottom*). Inscription on the attic of the Arch of Titus, 79 AD.

SENATVS
POPVLVSQVE·ROMANVS
DIVO·TITO·DIVI·VESPASIANI·F
VESPASIANO·AVGVSTO

SENATUS 211

TMLBZI
VIEPCOURN
DATISŒRFXLHK
THQUINGAZWUP
UNCÆKLER
HEYXJ&N
TZQYGR
NK VA

Lettres de deux Points de Cicero, Romaines,
Italiques & Grecques.

Numero Premier.

ABCDEF
GHIJKL
MNOPQ
RSTVUX
YZÆŒ

Numero Troisiéme.

ABCDEF
GHIJKL
MNOPQ
RSTVUX
YZÆŒ

Numero Second.

ABCDEF
GHIJKL
MNOPQ
RSTVUX
YZÆŒ

Numero Quatriéme.

ΑΒΓΔΕΖ
ΗΘΙΚΛΜ
ΝΞΟΠΡΣ
ΤΥΦΧΨΩ

ABCDEF
GHIJKL
MNOPQ
RSTUVX
YZÆŒ

NUMERO
PREMIER
CAPITALS

MANTINIA

MATTHEW CARTER

MY FIRST ATTEMPT AT DRAWING classically inspired Roman capitals was done in the late 1970s, an alphabet with several alternative forms and a few two-letter ligatures (some of them now looking awkward and best forgotten). [1] These never got beyond inch-high drawings taped to a mounting board, but I kept them with the idea that they might come in handy one day.

When Cherie Cone and I started Carter & Cone Type Inc., in January 1992, the first job I did was to digitize the regular weight of ITC Galliard Roman and Italic. Our digitization included expert sets that restored to the face the small caps, old-style figures, and other ancillary sorts that had been part of the original photocomp version released by Mergenthaler in 1978. At the same time the idea of adding a titling face to the Galliard family came up. The inspiration for Galliard had been the roman and italic types of the French punchcutter Robert Granjon (1513–1590). In deciding to not simply make a Galliard Titling, but to design a complementary face, I think I was also influenced by a set of capitals cut by Granjon on two-line pica that are immediately recognizable as his workmanship, but do not conform exactly to any of the capitals of his roman types. Granjon's titling caps (known as "La Plaisante" to Christopher Plantin, who owned matrices for them) are well printed in the *Épreuves générales des caractères . . .* of the typefounder Claude Lamesle (Paris, 1742) as Numero Premier, the first of four "Lettres de deux Points de Cicero . . ." shown on the same page (the *J, U, Æ,* and *Œ* are additions by a less skilled hand). [2] I liked the weight and proportions of La Plaisante very much. I scanned Lamesle's specimen and digitized the letters, with the intention of building a fully fledged titling face that shared with Galliard's romans and italics the presiding influence of Granjon. [3]

There the matter rested until the spring of 1992, when I wandered into the Royal Academy in order to get out of the rain and, serendipitously, saw in London an exhibition of the Italian Renaissance artist Andrea Mantegna (c. 1431–1506). I was gobsmacked by the exhibition, especially by the beautiful lettering in many of Mantegna's paintings and engravings. [4] I sketched several letters on the back of an airline ticket.

Back home I read references to Mantegna's classically inspired lettering in Nicolete Gray's *A History of Lettering* (1986) and the account in James Wardrop's *The Script of Humanism* (1963) of a congenial inscription-collecting expedition in 1464, on Lake Garda, by Mantegna and friends that included Felice Feliciano.[1] Feliciano's report on the excursion survives (they found twenty-two inscriptions), as does his alphabet of capitals, a manuscript in the Vatican Library that is the earliest known example of the desire to record the incised letters of classical Rome, and a forerunner of other Renaissance treatises that gave mathematical rules for reconstructing Roman letters. [5, and p. 12]

Mantegna, in keeping with the revival of interest in the remains of classical antiquity on the part of artists and humanist scholars of his time, is known to have studied Roman inscriptions. (He is thought to have been the only Renaissance artist who knew Latin.) The humanist craze for epigraphy seems to have been centered in Padua, where Mantegna grew up. His lettering is obviously derived from Imperial Rome, but not from its purest form as typified by the Trajan inscription. His letterforms are the interpretations of an artist rather than copies of an antiquary: they have unorthodox characteristics, such as the double serifs on the apexes of *A, M,* and *N,* three letters that, perhaps not coincidentally, are prominent in his name, both

---

1 (*opposite, top*). Titling alphabet drawn by Matthew Carter in the late 1970s as part of an exploration of alternates and ligatures.

2 (*opposite, bottom left*). "La Plaisante" titling caps by Robert Granjon, reproduced as Numero Premier in *Épreuves generals des caractères . . .* by Claude Lamesle (Paris, 1742).

3 (*opposite, bottom right*). The Numero Premier Capitals as digitized by Carter with new characters for *J, U,* and the dipthongs *Æ* and *Œ*.

4 Entombment engraving by Mantegna, 1465/1470.

in Italian and in its Latin form, *Mantinia*, by which he also signed himself. [4]

In my enthusiasm for the Mantegna exhibition, my titling face became more idiosyncratic—and acquired its name. I adopted the un-Trajanesque and un-Granjonian *A*, *M*, and *N*. My first set of classical capitals, drawn some fifteen years earlier, reasserted themselves as a continuing fascination with ligatures and other eccentricities that are more epigraphic than typographic in origin.

Two more influences were stirred into the mix. When I moved to Boston, and then Cambridge, in the 1980s, I found two wonderful examples of lettering: the inscriptions on the façade of the Boston Public Library and gravestones from the late 17th and early 18th centuries in local burial grounds. The library's main building was designed by Charles Follen McKim, of the partnership McKim, Mead & White, and opened in 1895. Its exterior was very obviously influenced by Henri Labrouste's Bibliothèque Sainte-Geneviève, in Paris, including the panels beneath the windows on which are inscribed the names of the great minds whose works are contained within. Which of the architects, Labrouste or McKim, designed the better elevation is open to discussion, but in the lettering of the inscriptions, McKim is clearly the winner. Labrouste's capitals look like printers' letters of the mid-19th century, and when a name is too long to fit in the width of the stone panel the capitals are condensed, as in typographic practice. [6] McKim's capitals, by contrast, are splendidly epigraphic; overly long names are made to fit by combining letters in ingenious double or triple ligatures or by nesting them. [7] I tried to research the source of McKim's lettering, but without success until I found, by chance, a book called *Letters & Lettering*, by Frank Chouteau Brown, first published in Boston in 1902. This interesting treatise was aimed chiefly at architects at a time when drawing letters was part of their training. (Brown was later the editor of *Architectural Review*.) Plate 7 is a photograph of an alphabet cut in stone, captioned "Model for incised Roman capitals. McKim, Mead & White." [8] On the following page, Brown says it was used for the Boston Public Library. The alphabet is immediately recognizable as Felice Feliciano's (the curious *G*-like character that Felice appended to his alphabet is the best clue),[2] but a close comparison with a facsimile of Felice's manuscript reveals some puzzling differences: for example, the *S* in the stone is even more ungainly than the one in Felice's drawing. I could not imagine how McKim knew Felice's alphabet; it seemed too unlikely that he had encountered the original in the Vatican Library, and the only facsimiles I knew were of much later dates: 1960 by Giovanni Mardersteig; and 1985, a superb reproduction by Belser Verlag. (See "Felice Feliciano and the Inscriptions on the Macello of Verona," p. 49) However, in Mardersteig's description of his edition, I found a mention of "R. Schöne, 'Felicis Feliciani Veronensis opusculum ineditum,' in *Ephemeris Epigraphica*, 1" (Berlin, 1872). The Classics Library at Yale yielded up a copy of this obscure work, which does indeed contain a reproduction of Feliciano's alphabet as *Tab. II.*, but one that does it less than justice. [9] This single-page copy was clearly the source of McKim's model stone, and the less-than-faithful rendering of Feliciano's Roman capitals the fault, therefore, of Schöne's engraver, not McKim's stonecutter. In practice, the lettering of the names on the Boston Public Library departed considerably from Felice and the model stone, for the good functional reason that the letters are cut very deeply into the granite and have lost the thick-thin contrast and the fine detailing of Felice's manuscript. The resulting gain in legibility of these sturdy capitals when read from below on the street is another way in which McKim improved on Labrouste.

I cannot claim that my fascination with the sources of the lettering on the Boston Public Library contributed directly to my typeface design; it was no more than an enjoyable red herring. In the end, it was the way the letters were used rather than their forms or history that most intrigued me, in particular when combined into space-saving ligatures. The same could be said of the gravestones that I photographed in Boston, Cambridge, and Watertown. Early New

5 Two forms of R from Felice Feliciano's *Alphabetum Romanum* (Vat. Lat. 6852), c. 1460. Two other letters from the manuscript are reproduced on p. 12.

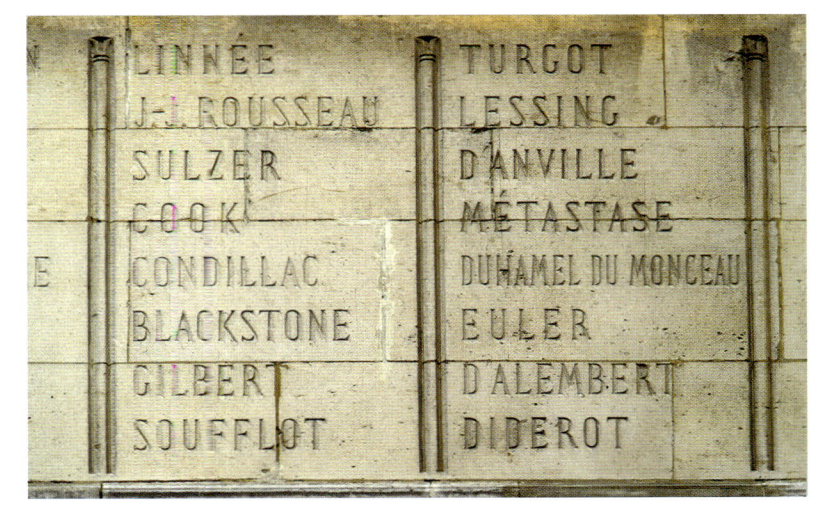

6 Detail of inscriptions on the Bibliothèque Sainte-Geneviève in Paris (Henri Labrouste, 1850).

7 Detail of inscriptions on the façade of the Boston Public Library (Charles Follen McKim, 1895).

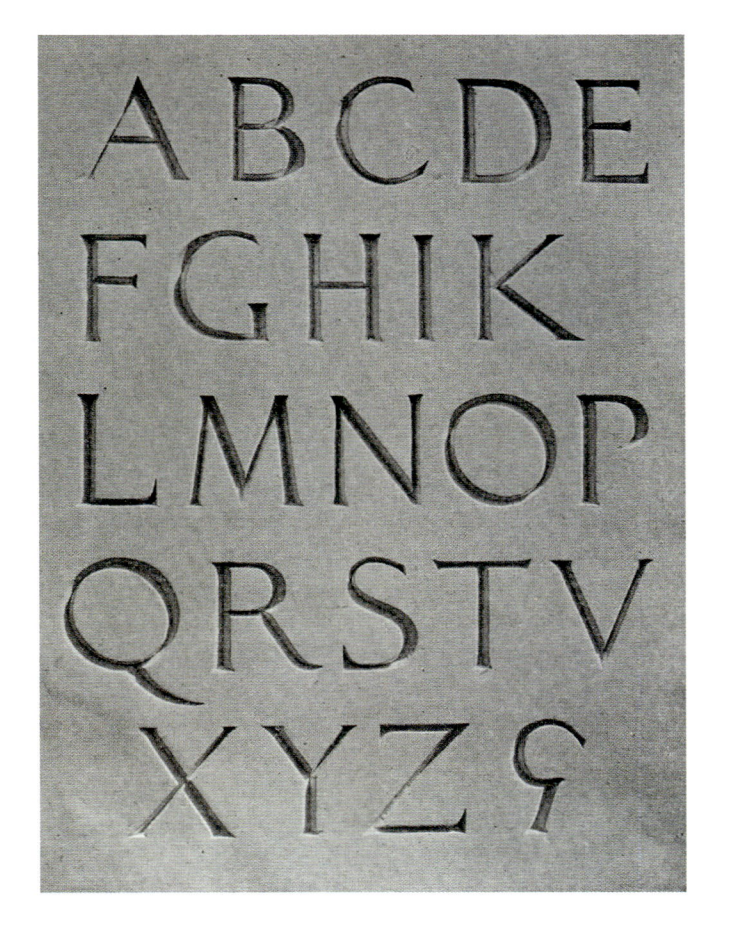

8 "Model for incised Roman capitals. McKim, Mead and White" from *Letters & Lettering* by Frank Chouteau Brown (Boston: Bates & Guild, 1902), p. 13.

MANTINIA 215

9 Feliciano's *Alphabet* (Tab. II) from *Ephemeria Epigraphica* by Rudolf Schöne (Berlin, 1872).

10, 11 (*opposite*). Details of two colonial gravestones showing unusual ligatures.

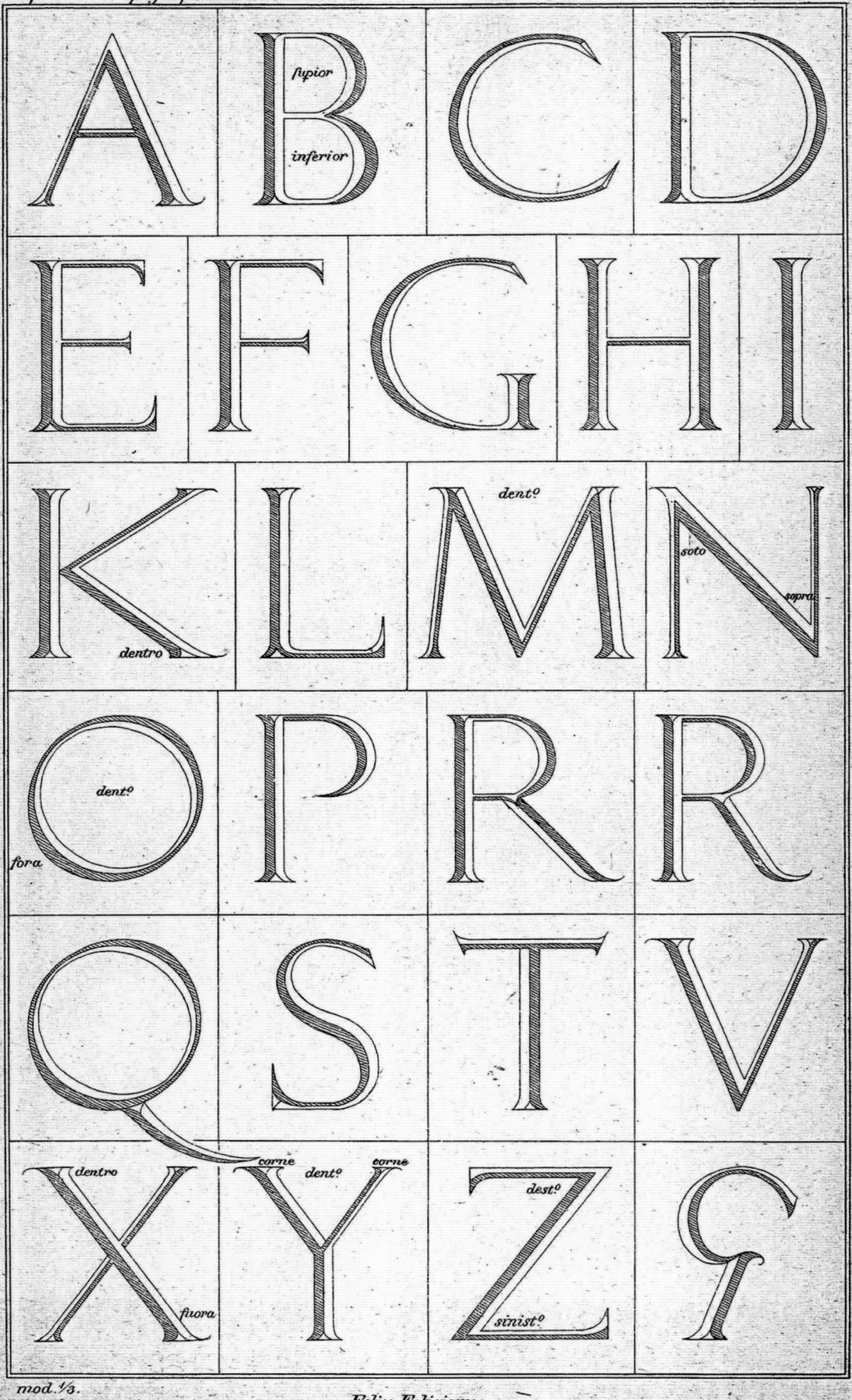

MANTINIA 217

MANTINIA · MCMXCIII

CAPS AABBCCDDEEFFGGHH
AND IIJJKKLLMMNNOOPQQ
SUPERIOR RRSSTTUUVV
CAPS WWXXYY&&ZZÆÆŒŒ

FIGURES 1234567890

SMALL CAPS ACEHIORSTUWYZ

LIGATURES HVCTHEUPLA
TTCTUTWTYMEMPMDMBE

ALERNATIVES T&YRRQQ
TALL CAPITALS ITLY
INTERPOINTS ♠ ♠ ▼

England gravestones have been studied for their symbolic decorations, but their lettering has had less attention. I found the letterforms fascinating and elusive in the sense that the styles have no obvious precedents, least of all in contemporary printing types. Ligatures are common. [10, 11] In Renaissance inscriptions, the use of complex ligatures appears to be decorative, playful even. (See p. 11, fig. 16.) This is not likely to be the case with Puritan gravestones in America, where more pragmatic reasons for merging letters must have applied: saving the stonecarver's time and labor, and sometimes reducing the length of words to fit the stone.

Capital ligatures are much less common in type than in stone, of any period. They do exist, however. ITC Avant Garde Gothic, with its plentiful and vigorous overlapping forms, is one encouraging example—notwithstanding Herb Lubalin's oft-cited remorse at seeing them badly used. Having decided to include ligatures in Mantinia I found them unexpectedly hard to design. Cobbling together any two capitals seldom works—they can be very stubborn about their freestanding independence—something I should have learnt from my attempts in the 1970s. I drew and rejected many more than I adopted, and I managed to concoct very few that did not have Roman or Renaissance precedents, *TW* being one with a claim to originality.

As a completed typeface, Mantinia (released in 1993) is really a medley of influences and its eventual relation to Galliard is, frankly, tenuous. [12] I liked the idea of giving it an unconventional character set (this was in the days of the PostScript Type 1 format). Inscriptional models suggested many of the characters. In addition to the ligatures were tall capitals, an alphabet of superior small capitals, and three interpoints. The numerals, for which Rome gave no models and the Renaissance very few, were largely improvised, except for the *8*, which was contributed by Carlo Crivelli, a contemporary of Mantegna, in the date "1486" on his painting of the *Annunciation* (National Gallery, London).

---

12 (*opposite*). Mantinia by Matthew Carter (Carter & Cone Type Inc., 1993). This is the full alphabetic/numeric character set.

1 Anyone interested in reenacting the outing should read Gillian Riley's suggestions in her *Renaissance Recipes* (1993) for meals that might have been enjoyed at lakeside inns: stuffed trout with lemon, and pumpkin tortelloni— both highly recommended. We do not know what wine was served on that happy occasion, but modern-day followers in the footsteps of Mantegna and company could do worse than to drink Mantinia, a dry white wine from Greece, one variety of which, bottled by Tselepos, has its label set (Jonathan Hoefler tells me) in Mantinia.

2 I knew this non-letter [a Tironian *et*] all too well. When Giovanni Mardersteig was preparing his *Felice Feliciano Veronese Alphabetum Romanum*, printed in 1960, he asked me to cut a punch that would sort with his Dante type. I did so, but not very successfully. Dr. Mardersteig was very fond of Feliciano, who was from Verona, Mardersteig's adoptive home. The stone that Brown illustrated cannot be traced. Brown's photograph was also reproduced by Michael Harvey in his very informative contribution to *Inscriptions at the Old Public Library of San Francisco*, edited by Jack W. Stauffacher (San Francisco: The Book Club of California, 2003). I would guess that Monotype's Felix Titling of 1934 was also derived from *Tab. II.* of *Ephemeris Epigraphica* at one remove from the original.

ROME

ROME

VICENZA VERONA

BOLOGNA

PADUA

VENICE

ARRIGHI

LA OPERINA

NUMERO·TRE

CODEX

REQUIEM
A TRUE RENAISSANCE LETTER

JONATHAN HOEFLER

REQUIEM CELEBRATES THE FERTILE world of Renaissance humanism. The idea for it began in 1990, with a request from Fred Woodward, then art director at *Rolling Stone*, to develop a typeface from the Roman capitals in *Il modo de temperare le penne* (1524/1525), the second writing manual by Ludovico Vicentino degli Arrighi (c. 1490–c. 1527), a calligrapher at the Apostolic Chancery in Rome. [5] But before I could start developing a prototype, he had already discovered Adobe's then-new Trajan and begun using it for the magazine's purposes. However, a few years later, I was able to revive the project when Giovanni Russo, the art director at *Travel & Leisure*, inquired about a custom typeface.

What intrigued me about Arrighi's Roman capitals was that they were approached from the perspective of a practitioner, not a theoretician. In the half century prior to the publication of *Il modo* there had been a growing trend among prominent Renaissance minds to dissect capital letters scientifically. Among the contemporary treatises on this subject were: *De divina proportione* (1509) by Fra Luca de Pacioli, the inventor of double-entry bookkeeping; *Of the Just Shaping of Letters* (1525), a section of a longer work on applied geometry by the celebrated artist Albrecht Dürer (see p. 15, fig. 21); and *Champ fleury* (1529) by the Parisian polymath Geoffroy Tory. Arrighi's letters, one of the most elegant renderings of the classical alphabet, were freed from the shackles of geometry. Instead, they are simply shown floating in a solid field of black.

Arrighi's capitals became the basis for Requiem's Display Roman and Small Caps. But missing from most of the Renaissance writing manuals—including *La operina* (1522), his first book, and *Il Modo*—is a viable roman lowercase, which *Travel & Leisure* needed. The upright lowercase was more the province of typefounding than calligraphy, so the few writing masters who attempted a lowercase did so with hesitation. Arrighi's few lowercase characters seemed too calligraphic and contrived to me. I spent some time experimenting with the lowercase in Giovanni Francesco Cresci's *Il perfetto scrittore* (1570) but found them a little too bitter to go with Arrighi's saucy caps. [3] There is a staid, "constructed" quality to Cresci's lettering that is at odds with Arrighi's spirit. I also tried to build a lowercase from the sparkling letters in "La paraphrasi," a 16th-century manuscript by Ferdinando Ruano in the British Library. I thought that they bridged the gap between the calligraphic and the typographic very smartly, but in the end, little of Ruano's lettering made it into the Requiem lowercase, which is an invention, a caprice.

However, studying Ruano's letters did help me diagnose one of the font's early problems. Most printing types designed in upper- and lowercase presume that the primary function of capital letters is to serve as initials, and that the bulk of what is read will be printed in lowercase. The widths of these lowercase letters differ greatly, so their composition produces a sort of modulated effect. On the other hand, most of the capitals hew to a narrow range of widths. The obvious outliers are *I*, *M*, and *W*. But in alphabets that have no lowercase, this modulation must be effected through the capitals themselves. Thus, classical letters such as those found on the base of Trajan's Column exhibit widely different character widths: *E* and *S* are nearly half the width of *N* and *R* for instance. This allows the inscription (SENATVS POPVLVSQVE ROMANVM...) to achieve a varying rhythm that is comfortable for reading.

The difficulty in outfitting a font of capitals with a lowercase is that caps of dramatically

1 (*opposite*). Decorative cartouches from Requiem. The top line shows how the cartouches are assembled using cameo letters and separate handles.

2 (*below*). Page from *Libro da scrivere* by Giovanni Battista Palatino (Rome, 1561), f. 10r. (The Newberry Library, Chicago, Vault Wing ZW 535 .P174.)

different widths are not comfortable with a similar lowercase. For instance, a lowercase *n* designed to accommodate a narrow capital *S* will be dwarfed by a wide capital *H*. Most of the various Trajan-with-a-lowercase fonts suffer this problem as a fundamental design defect. (See "Trajan Revived Redux," pp. 194–195.) The problem is exacerbated by a small x-height, which is characteristic of Renaissance letters such as those of Arrighi or Cresci.

Ruano cleverly sidestepped the problem by combining his capitals with a lowercase of unusually large x-height. Thus, a sufficiently large lowercase *n* is at home with both a narrow *S* and a wide *H*. I borrowed Ruano's strategy for Requiem, additionally lengthening the font's ascenders and descenders to help camouflage the large x-height—and giving the font the grace that Arrighi's capitals deserve.

Unfortunately, a large body is exactly what one does not want in a chancery italic. So, when the order came from *Travel & Leisure* for an italic to go with the roman, reconciling the two required a bit of chicanery. For the italic I turned again for inspiration to Arrighi, whose full-blooded *cancellaresca corsiva* is his chief claim to fame.

By the time Requiem was commercially released, in 1999, I had added optical size masters for small sizes (Text) and very large sizes (Fine); italic ligatures; ornaments; and two sets of alphabets contained within decorative "cartouches" whose endpieces are inspired by the work of Giovanbattista Palatino (c. 1515–c. 1575) and Vespasiano Amphi-areo (c. 1501–c. 1563), two other Renaissance writing masters. [2] A single set of elegant Renaissance revival Roman capitals had become a full-fledged contemporary digital font. [4] *Viva Arrighi!*

3 (*below*). Minuscules by Giovanni Francesco Cresci from *Il Perfetto Scrittore* (1570). Cut in wood by Francesco Aureri da Crema.

4 (*opposite, above*). Capitals, small capitals and figures from Requiem by Jonathan Hoefler (Hoefler Type Foundry, 1992).

5 (*opposite, below*). Roman capitals by Arrighi from *Il Modo de temperare* (Venice, 1523–1525). Cut in wood by Eustachio Celebrino. (The Newberry Library, Wing ZW 535 .L961)

ABCDEFGHIJKK
LMNNOPQQRR
STTUVWXYYZ&
ABCDEFGHIJKKLMNNO
PQQRSTTUVWXYYZ&
1123456789o

JJKQR

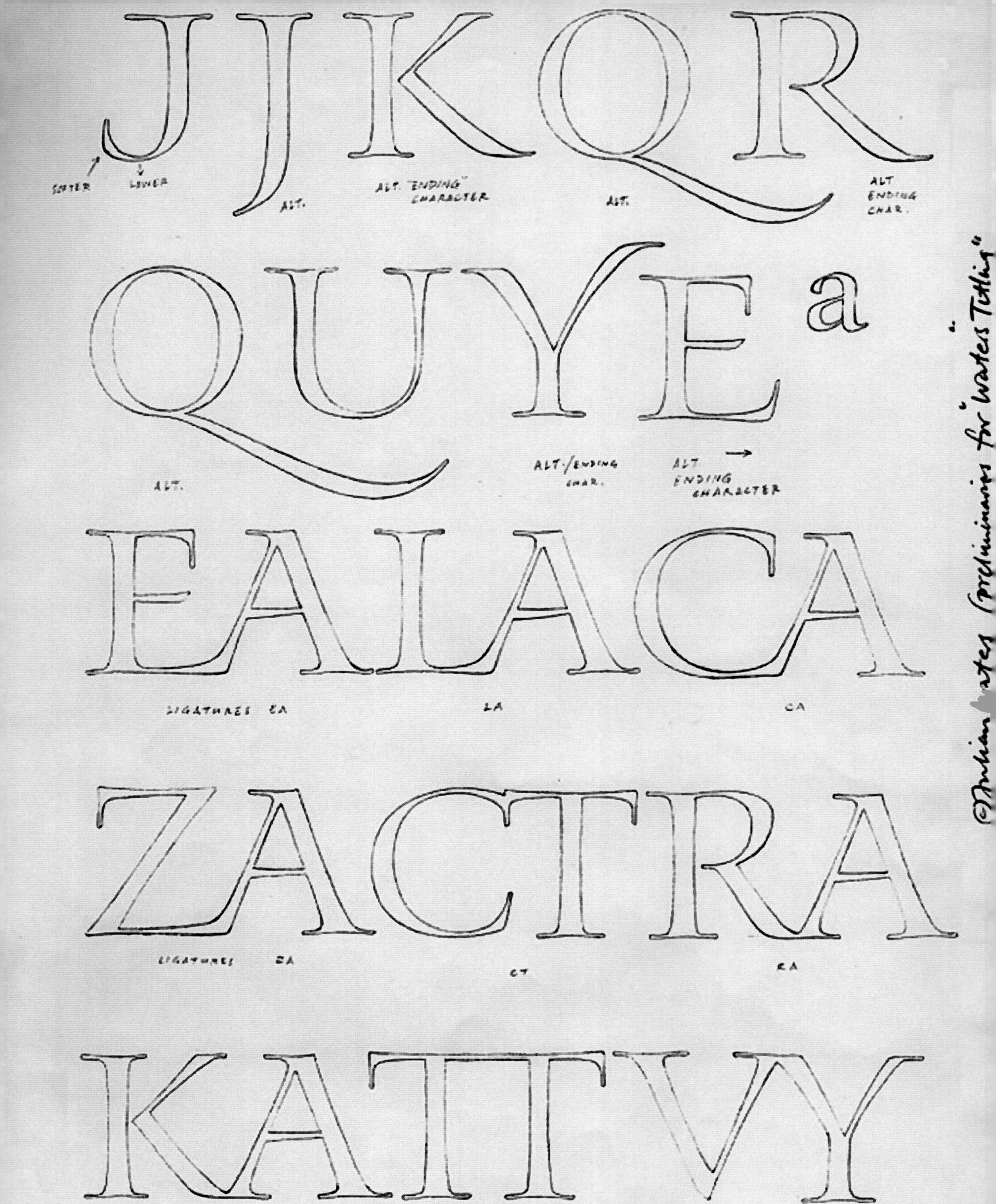

SERIF | V LOWER | ALT. | ALT. "ENDING" CHARACTER | ALT. | ALT ENDING CHAR.

QUYE ª

ALT. | ALT./ENDING CHAR. | ALT ENDING CHARACTER

EALACA

LIGATURES EA | LA | CA

ZACTRA

LIGATURES ZA | CT | RA

KATTVY

LIGATURES KA | TT

©Dorian Mattar (preliminaries for "Waters Tuthig")

WATERS TITLING

JULIAN WATERS

I AM A CALLIGRAPHER AND LETTER-ING designer. I began my career in the mid-1970s, learning initially from my mother, Sheila Waters, a renowned calligrapher trained in the Edward Johnston tradition in England, and then from the legendary Hermann Zapf, with whom I first studied in 1979. The English tradition gave me a strong foundation, but the work of Zapf and other Europeans inspired me to become a lettering designer. Zapf's aesthetics in letter design can be seen in much of my work and that of many letterers of my generation. By the time that I had established my lettering practice in Washington, D.C., in the mid-1980s, I was developing a variety of styles to cope with a wide range of commissioned lettering and design work. Among them were several variations of drawn and pen-made capitals designed for book jackets, posters, and calendars (including a notable series for the Audubon Society). [2–4] Sumner Stone, then typographic director at Adobe Systems, saw some of this work in the late 1980s and invited me to develop a typeface based on my formal lettering. The result was Waters Titling, released by Adobe in 1991.

My font work for Adobe started with a pen-made, semi-formal turned serif (and semi-seriffed) cap and lowercase alphabet I had made for the 21st edition of *The Speedball Textbook* (1985). [5] I called it Aura and started developing it into a font. I scanned and redrew the letters in Adobe Illustrator with bezier curves and then imported them into FontStudio, where I refined their shapes, established sidebearings, and so forth. This was a very different way of drawing compared to working with my familiar pen and ink. At the time, one of the new developments at Adobe was the "blend" tool in Illustrator and I made several early tests of it. In one, I drew the letter *B* in four different weights and then blended (interpolated) between them to create in-between shapes. [6] This was the same principle at the core of Adobe's Multiple Master (MM) typefaces that were then in development.

As the typeface developed, Adobe changed their minds about it, urging me to focus on a larger project, a Multiple Master titling typeface. I based the new design on a more formal, fully seriffed alphabet that I had used in different iterations for a number of my lettering projects. This became Waters Titling MM. Adobe's goal was for me to produce a contemporary alternative to their own Trajan typeface.

Although Adobe Trajan had just begun to become popular in the mid-1990s, it was a limited design of only two weights. Adobe envisioned my Waters Titling MM as a more versatile counterpart, having an almost infinite range of weights and widths that would make it useful for everything from movie titling to book jackets to logos. While Trajan has pointed tops to the *A, M,* and *N*, Waters Titling has flat-seriffed tops on those letters. [8] In this it follows other Roman inscriptions, such as the memorial to the children of the freedman Sextus Pompeius on the Appian Way. [7] I also gave Waters Titling a contemporary, personal aesthetic with dramatic thick-thin contrast, crisp details, and extended thin serifs, resulting in a distinctive font family unlike anything on the market.

Sumner left Adobe in 1989, and as I developed the typeface family further I worked with Fred Brady, his successor. Robert Slimbach, Adobe's in-house type designer (and an excellent calligrapher in his own right), gave me much needed technical help and feedback; I returned the favor by providing feedback on his Poetica typeface. Waters Titling was planned as a 2-axis MM family with wide variation in both width and weight.

1 (*opposite*). Annotated drawing (c.1996) of ligatures and alternate characters for Waters Titling.

2 (*above*). Book jacket for *Goines Posters* by David Lance Goines (Boston: Alphabet Press, 1985). Design and lettering by Julian Waters.

3 (*right*). "Generations" poster by Waters for the Smithsonian's International Gallery, 1987.

4 (*opposite*). Cover of the Audubon Nature Calendar 1991 (Audubon Society) with lettering by Waters.

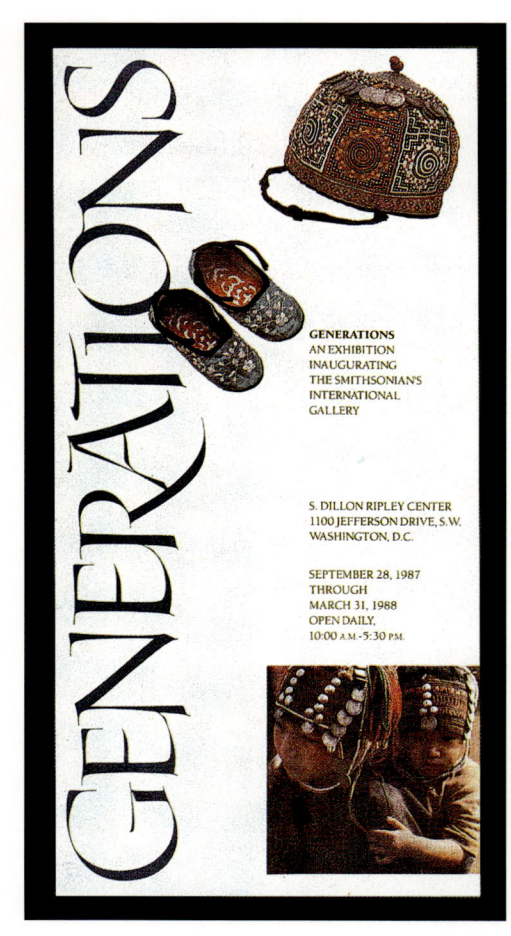

AUDUBON

NATURE CALENDAR 1991

5 (*far left*). Alphabet by Waters for *The Speedball Textbook*, 22nd edition (1991).

6 (*left*). Interpolated weight and width test for Waters Titling MM (n.d.).

7 (*below*). Detail of the inscription on the tomb of the children of Sextus Pompeius Justus (2nd century AD) on the Via Appia, Rome. Also see p. 153.

AEMRS
AEMRS

8 Comparison of Trajan (above) and Waters Titling (below).

Using FontStudio, I digitized a medium weight set of letters, based on a style I had used for several projects. From there I developed four "outer" weights and widths: a light condensed, a light extended, a bold condensed, and a bold extended. What I had done earlier as an interpolation experiment with the B was now expanded into full character sets in the extreme weights, all designed to blend together and be capable of seamlessly creating all the weights in between. In order for the Multiple Master interpolation to work properly, each of the extreme weights of any given shape had to be drawn with the same number of bezier points, placed very carefully in relation to those of the other weights. This was quite challenging. Making outline curves on the computer is not the same as drawing with your hand what you imagine in your mind. Moreover, the Multiple Master designer must think of all the weights at once while drawing any single shape. It is very easy to lose sight of one's original vision.

As I expanded the design, each weight included regular capitals and tall caps, weighted to visually match initial capitals set slightly larger than regular caps. I also designed many ligatures for each weight. [1] These ligatures help the flow and spacing of particular letter combinations that leave visual holes (*LA* or *CT*) or create "hot spots" (*OO*) when spaced too closely. Some ligatures were intended to allow adjoining serifs of two letters to fit closely together in normal settings without clashing (*TT*). And, of course, all of the ligatures would be useful for logo design. In my calligraphy I often make such connections between letters on the fly, as needed, to help the cohesiveness of a lettering design, so their inclusion in the type family felt natural to me. [2] I avoided self-conscious and overly decorative combinations, but included some surprises, such as ks and rs, where the *K* or *R* leg flows directly into the bottom of the *S*. Along with the ligatures, I designed some italic "tag words"—such as *for*, *of*, *from*, and *the*—for each weight. These were often found in 19th-century decorative typefaces but are an unusual feature for a classical titling typeface. I also included many alternate characters in every weight, including extended and swash versions of *K* and *R*, suitable to end a line or to place somewhere in a layout needing some breathing room. There is also a round, "uncial" *E*. Swapping this for the normal *E* will give a very different feel to a text, softer or somewhat more medieval, depending on the weight.

When Adobe abandoned the consumer version of its Multiple Master technology in 2003, Waters Titling was reissued in OpenType format with twelve distinct weights and widths, retaining all the ligatures, alternates, tall caps, and italic tag words. [9]

ABCDEEE
FGHIJJKKK
LMNOPQQRRR
STTTUVVWWXYYYZ
CACCCECOCTDCDGDO
EAESEYEEEEOKSLA
NNOOOOCOGRSST
THTTTYZA
ABCDEFGHIJKL
MNOPQRSTU
VWXYZ
1234567890
&&

Wisdom

LISTEN TO
& ADVICE
& ACCEPT
INSTRUCTION
THAT YOU
MAY GAIN
WISDOM
FOR THE
FUTURE

9 (*opposite*). Waters Titling by Julian Waters (Adobe, 1997) showing alternates, ligatures, and tall capitals.

10 (*above*). "Wisdom" (Proverbs 19:20). Calligraphy by Julian Waters. The capitals have been built up using a broad-edged pen and then retouched.

TYPEFACES WITH CLASSICAL ROMAN INFLUENCES: 1900 TO THE PRESENT

Presented here is an alphabetical list of typefaces whose capitals have variable or classical proportions that are derived from Roman inscriptional capitals either directly or indirectly via Renaissance and Baroque models. Several reference the Trajan inscription explicitly by the presence of *M* and *N* with pointed apexes. These are noted, as are those that have the Greek or palmate form of *Y*. The focus is entirely on the capitals, not on the lowercase. As it is, many of the typefaces are titling faces, which means that they lack a lowercase. A number of them attempt to simulate letters carved in stone with shading or inline effects, while others are open rather than solid. A few sans serifs are included because they either allude to inscriptional sans serifs, such as those in ancient Rome or quattrocento Florence, or are derived from seriffed types in a classical vein. The letters F, C, P, and D signify foundry casting, metal machine composition, photocomposition, and digital, respectively. The typefaces marked in red are mentioned in the articles in *The Eternal Letter*. N.B.: the dates are those of the year when the typeface was released. —P.S.

Albertus (Berthold Wolpe, Monotype 1938) C
Aeterna [Jost Medieval] (Heinrich Jost, Ludwig & Mayer 1927) P—Trajanic *M* and *N*; seriffed alternates
Arrus (Richard Lipton, Bitstream 1991) D—brush-influenced bifurcated serifs
Augustea (Alessandro Butti and Aldo Novarese, Nebiolo 1951) P—titling face; also Augustea Open and Nova Augustea (with lowercase)

Baker Signet (Arthur Baker, Visual Graphics Corporation 1965) P
Basalt (Sumner Stone, Stone Type Foundry 1998) D—a warm sans serif inspired by Republican Roman Capitals; several characters available in wide and narrow versions.
Bembo (Monotype 1929) C
Brudi Medieval (Walter Brudi, Berthold 1953–1954) F—Trajanic *M* and *N*

Canto (Richard Lipton, Font Bureau 2011) D—Trajanic *M* and *N*; Greek *Y*; roman, pen, brush and brush open variants
Capitolium (Gerard Unger 1998) D—inspired by Giovanni Francesco Cresci's minuscule alphabet in *Il Perfetto Scrittore* (1570)
Carolus (Karl-Erik Forsberg, Berling 1954) F—titling face; calligraphic; not Trajanic in width but squarish
Castellar (John Peters, Monotype 1957) C—titling face; shaded
Centaur (Bruce Rogers, Metropolitan Museum of Art 1914; Monotype 1929) F, C
Columna (Max Caflisch, Benteli AG private typeface; Bauer 1955) F—titling face; open; Trajanic *M* and *N* (and seriffed alternates); *R* with short leg and long leg
Cristal (Rémy Peignot, Deberny & Peignot 1955) F—titling face; inline decoration
Cresci (Garrett Boge, LetterPerfect 1996) D—titling face; inspired by Giovanni Francesco Cresci's capitals in *Il Perfetto Scrittore* (1570)
Cycles (Sumner Stone, Stone Type Foundry 1993–1997) D—a family of 8 optically sized faces ranging in size from 7 pt to 48 pt

Dante (Giovanni Mardersteig, Officina Bodoni 1957; Monotype 1959) F, C—also Dante Titling
Dartmouth Titling (Will Carter, 1964) F—titling face; designed for Dartmouth College
Davanti (Sumner Stone, Stone Type Foundry 2010) D—part of a trio with Popvlvs and Sator
Delphian (R. Hunter Middleton, Ludlow 1928) C—titling face; inline decoration
Delphin I (Georg Trump, Weber 1951) F
Delphin II (Georg Trump, Weber 1955) F
Diotima (Gudrun Zapf-von Hesse, Stempel 1954) F; Trajanic *M* and *N*

Elizabeth (Elizabeth Friedlander, Bauer 1937) F—narrow but with Trajanic *M* and *N*
Ericus (Karl-Erik Forsberg, Berling 1964) F—titling face; Trajanic *M* and *N*

Felix (staff, Monotype 1934) C—titling face based on constructed capitals by Felice Feliciano (1460)
Forum Title (Frederic W. Goudy, Village Letter Foundery 1911; Lanston Monotype 1924) F, C—titling face
Galba (Claude Mediavilla, Mecanorma 1987) P—titling face
Garda Titling I, II, and III (Mario Feliciano, Feliciano Type Foundry, 1998 and 2001) D—titling face; inspired by capitals of Giovanni Francesco Cresci; serif, short serif, and sans variants
Goudy Oldstyle (Frederic W. Goudy, American Type Founders 1915–1916) F
Goudy Trajan (Jason Castle, Castle Systems 2001) D—titling face; revival of Trajan Title
Goudytype (Frederic W. Goudy, American Type Founders 1916) F

Hadriano (Frederic W. Goudy, Village Type Foundery 1918; Lanston Monotype 1929) F, C—titling face; inspired by Hadrian inscriptional fragment in the Louvre
Hadriano Stonecut (Sol Hess, Lanston Monotype c. 1932) C—titling face; shaded
History (Peter Bil'ak, Typotheque 2009) D—the underlying structure (seen most clearly in layers 2 and 3) is classical.

Le Beaune Classic (Damien Gautier, 2002) D

Magma (Sumner Stone, Stone Type Foundry 2004–2009) D—a humanist sans serif; family includes Titling Thin

Mantinia (Matthew Carter, Carter & Cone 1993) D—titling face; inspired by engraved lettering of Andrea Mantegna

Marcus (Robbie de Villiers, Wilton Foundry 2013) D—based on lettering by Julian Waters

Meridien (Adrian Frutiger, Deberny & Peignot 1957) F

Michelangelo (Hermann Zapf, Stempel 1950) F—titling face; companion to Palatino

PF Monumenta Pro (Panos Vassiliou, Parachute 2009) D—titling face; with swash capitals and ligatures; Shaded and Metallica variants

Mramor Pro (Frantisek Storm, Storm Typefoundry 1994; 2013) D

Nero (Friedrich Poppl, Berthold 1982) P—titling face; with some swash capitals; rough-edged.

Open Roman Capitals (Jan van Krimpen, Enschedé 1929) F—titling face; open; companion to Romulus

Optima (Hermann Zapf, Stempel 1958) F

Optima nova Titling (Hermann Zapf and Akira Kobayashi, Linotype 2008) D—titling face; with tall capitals and ligatures

Orpheus (Walter Tiemann, Klingspor 1928) F—Trajanic M and N

Orpheus Pro (Patrick Griffin and Kevin Allan King, Canada Type 2011) D—redesign and extension of Orpheus; "The great roman caps just screamed for plenty of extensions, alternates, swashes, ligatures, fusions from different times, and of course small caps."

Palatino (Hermann Zapf, Stempel 1950) F—Greek Y

Palatino nova Imperial (Hermann Zapf and Akira Kobayashi, Linotype 2005) D—titling face; redesign of Sistina

Palatino nova Titling (Hermann Zapf and Akira Kobayashi, Linotype 2005) D—titling face; redesign of Michelangelo

Phidias (Hermann Zapf, Stempel 1950) F—titling face; Greek companion to Michelangelo

Penumbra MM (Lance Hidy, Adobe 1994) D—titling face; Multiple Master originally with axes for weight and serif length: now available as Sans, Fine Serif, Half Serif, Serif

Perpetua (Eric Gill, Monotype 1925–1930) C—also Perpetua Titling

Pietra (Garrett Boge, LetterPerfect 1996) D—titling face; inspired by the lettering of Ventura Sarafellini at the base of the cupola of St. Peter's in Rome (1605)

Poetica (Robert Slimbach, Adobe 1992) D—small caps

Pontif (Garrett Boge, LetterPerfect 1996) D—titling face; inspired by lettering of Luca Horfei da Fano that was part of the urban restoration of Rome by Pope Sixtus V (1587–1590)

Popvlvs (Sumner Stone, Stone Typefoundry 2012) D—part of a trio with Davanti and Sator

Requiem (Jonathan Hoefler, Hoefler Type Foundry 1999) D—capitals inspired by those of Ludovico degli Arrighi da Vincenza in *Il Modo Temperare le Penne* (1523)

Roma (Tom Lincoln, Canada Type 2011) D—titling face; Inline, Fill, Solid, Shaded, Inscribed, and Open variants

FS Rome (Jason Smith, Fontsmith 1996–2000) D—titling face; based on the cast of the Trajan inscription in the Victoria & Albert Museum

Romulus (Jan van Krimpen, Enschedé 1931; Monotype 1936) F, C

Sator (Sumner Stone, Stone Type Foundry 1995) D—part of a trio with Davanti and Popvlus

Schneider Antiqua (Werner Schneider, Berthold, 1987) D

Schneidler Initials (F. H. E. Schneidler, Bauer 1937) F—titling face; Trajanic M and N

Senatus (Werner Schneider, Berthold 2003) D—titling typeface

Serlio (staff, Linotype 1990) D—titling face; based on lettering associated with architectural theorist Sebastiano Serlio (1475–c. 1554)

SFPL Roman (Sumner Stone, Stone Type Foundry 1999) D

Shángò (Jason Castle, Castle Systems 2007) D—titling face; revival of Schneidler Initials; classic, sans, chiseled, and gothic variants as well as swash capitals and ligatures

Sistina (Hermann Zapf, Stempel 1951) F—titling face; companion to Palatino and Michelangelo

Spectrum (Jan van Krimpen, Enschedé 1952; Monotype 1955) F, C

Stevens Titling (John Stevens and Ryuichi Tateno, Linotype 2011) D—titling typeface

ITC Stone (Sumner Stone, International Typeface Corporation 1987; 2005) D—available as Serif, Sans and Informal. ITC Stone Sans updated in 2009 as ITC Stone II.

Trajan Title (Frederic W. Goudy, 1930) F—titling typeface

Trajan (Carol Twombly, Adobe, 1989) D—titling face originally packaged with Lithos and Charlemagne; based on lettering of Trajan Column inscription (AD 114)

Trajan Pro 3 (Carol Twombly and Robert Slimbach, Adobe 2012) D—titling face; weight and linguistic extension of Trajan

Trajan Sans (Robert Slimbach, Adobe 2012) D—titling face; derived from Trajan

Trajanus (Warren Chappell, Stempel 1940) F—Trajanic M and N

Trump Mediaeval (Georg Trump, Weber 1954) F

Trump Gravur (Georg Trump, Weber 1961) F—titling typeface; companion to Trump Mediaeval

Tuff (Sumner Stone, Stone Type Foundry 2009) D—a softer version of Magma

Unknown (Freeman Craw, Headliners c. 1964) P—titling face; name unknown; used by Craw for various design projects

ITC Veljovic (Jovica Veljovic, International Typeface Corporation 1984) P

Vendôme (Francois Ganeau, Olive 1952) F

Waters Titling MM (Julian Waters, Adobe 1997) D—titling face; Multiple Master with weight and width axes; also has tall capitals, ligatures, and swash capitals; Greek Y

Weiss Antiqua (E. R. Weiss, Bauer 1926) F—Trajanic M and N

Weiss Initials [Kapitale Kräftig, Kapitale Mager, Lapidar Mager, and Lapidar Kräftig] (E. R. Weiss, Bauer 1931) F—titling typefaces; mix of classical (Trajanic M and N) and medieval (curled G, uncial E) letters

The census below is based on a search of movie sources and images on the Internet. It is not scientific or exhasutive, but it offers a reasonably accurate picture of Hollywood's embrace of the Trajan typeface over the past twenty-three years. Here, year by year, is the number of movies whose posters featured Trajan in their title.

1991: 1	1999: 26	2007: 42
1992: 4	2000: 11	2008: 33
1993: 3	2001: 22	2009: 28
1994: 11	2002: 28	2010: 31
1995: 16	2003: 19	2011: 11
1996: 16	2004: 19	2012: 18
1997: 14	2005: 36	2013: 14
1998: 18	2006: 38	2014: 20

TRAJAN AT THE MOVIES

YVES PETERS

NO OTHER TYPEFACE IS SO INTIMATELY connected with the film industry as Trajan. Within five years of its release it was ardently embraced by Hollywood. Now, it seems to be a *de rigeur* feature of nearly every movie poster, shouldering aside all other typefaces. How did this happen?

Trajan was part of the inaugural release of the Adobe Originals in 1989. The first film poster* ever designed with Trajan, as far as I have been able to discover, was *At Play in the Fields of the Lord* (1991). The next year, four movies employed Trajan, among them the blockbusters *The Bodyguard* and *Scent of a Woman*. The latter achieved three important Oscar nominations and an Academy Award for Al Pacino, in addition to three Golden Globes. In 1993, the count was down to three: *Indecent Proposal, The Joy Luck Club,* and *The Pelican Brief.* But from 1994 onwards the number of films featuring Trajan on their posters started to increase dramatically. The many awards for *Scent of a Woman,* in combination with the box office performance of *The Body Guard* and *Indecent Proposal,* must have made the film studio executives sit up and take notice of the typeface. Film studios are hesitant to take risks and seem to be on the lookout for the *last* success story. Whenever something seems to work, they want to be the first to replicate its success by copying its elements, whether it be a screenplay idea or something as mundane as the typeface on a publicity poster.

Over the course of twenty years, from 1991 until 2011, I found over 450 films that featured Trajan on their posters. Marked out on a graph, the use of Trajan shows a rise until 2008 after which there is a leveling off. Two exceptional spurts in use can be correlated to specific occurrences. The first was the conversion of Trajan in 1999 to the OpenType format, which led to an expansion of its character set. The second was tied to the bundling of Trajan with Adobe's Creative Suite 2, in 2005. (A more modest rise in usage can be correlated to its inclusion in Adobe's Creative Suite 3, two years later.) It is well known that a typeface available for free with software or hardware will be used more heavily than fonts that must be purchased independently. In this respect, Trajan benefited from the same sort of default laziness that has led Helvetica, Times Roman, Palatino, Arial, and even Comic Sans to become widespread.

While many film genres have their own recognizable type styles—big red sans serifs for comedies, squarish grotesques for action movies, delicate didones for romantic comedies—the usage of Trajan defies categorization. Initially, its stately and classic character made it the go-to choice for epics, historic movies, inspirational dramas, and sweeping love stories; but the typeface also appeared on posters for movies with subjects ranging from war to romance, suspense, action, adventure, science fiction, and more. However, over the course of the two decades studied there was a noticeable shift towards the "lower end" of the spectrum with Trajan being used for dystopian futures, murder stories, horror flicks, and slasher films such as the remakes of *Day of The Dead, A Nightmare on Elm Street, Friday The Thirteenth*, and *The Hills Have Eyes,* or the torture porn of *The Human Centipede* films.

Recent films using Trajan that appear to be more upmarket are actually movies made to go straight-to-video or for television. This movement is consistent with the life-cycle of overused typefaces. Through its initial success and subsequent persistent use in the marketing collateral for films, Trajan somehow became the Arial of the film poster. Many designers turned their backs on it, leaving it to become the property of the "common users." Instead of being consciously selected for its formal qualities and emotional/cultural connotations, it now ends up being used simply because it has become the default "movie poster font." It is omnipresent in the credits, tag lines and localized versions of film posters. Other designers use its cultural cachet to polish the sheen of run-of-the-mill productions.

Although my survey stopped in 2011, there is no sign that Hollywood has grown tired of Trajan. Informally I have counted eighteen uses of it in 2012, fourteen in 2013, and twenty in 2014—nearly all of them downmarket and only one with an historical excuse (*Pompeii*). Trajan may have become an instance of the undead, a vampire typeface that cannot be slain, giving a whole new meaning to the notion of a "timeless typeface."

*My survey was only concerned with the original posters for movies in which Trajan is the principal typeface, used for the movie's title, but not for its tagline or credits. One measure of Trajan's hold on Hollywood is in the number of movies that use Trajan for taglines, in newspaper and magazine advertisements and, astonishingly often, for titles in second releases and re-releases intended for the DVD market. The best example of the latter is *Titanic* (1998) whose original poster featured a condensed, riveted grotesque typeface for the title, but whose post-Oscar nomination posters used Trajan instead.

LEARNING FROM CHAIRS

BY CYRUS HIGHSMITH

with special guest
Father Catich

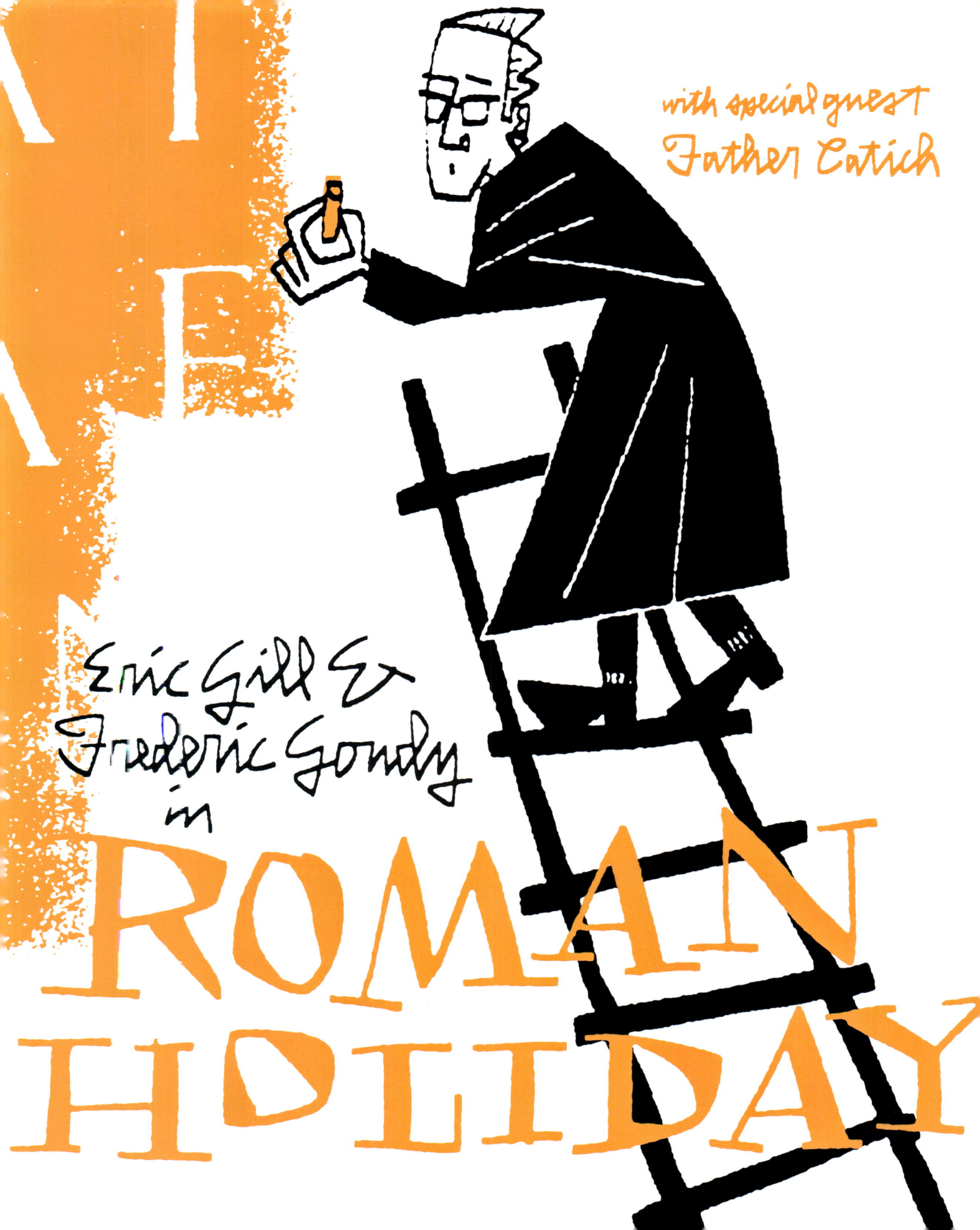

Eric Gill & Frederic Goudy in

ROMAN HOLIDAY

CENSUS OF TRAJAN INSCRIPTION REPRODUCTIONS

This census of reproductions of the inscription on Trajan's Column is a continuation and expansion of a census of rubbings begun in 2007 by Ryan L. Roth, then the program director of the Rare Book School at the University of Virginia. It excludes photographs. —P.S.

Casts

The oldest known reproduction of Trajan's Column was a bronze cast carried out circa 1806 at the direction of Napoleon and erected in the Place Vendôme, in Paris. It was surmounted by a statue of the emperor, whose appearance was changed in 1831 and again in 1862. The column was destroyed in 1871.[1]

The most famous copy of Trajan's Column is in the Cast Courts (formerly the Architectural Courts) of the Victoria & Albert Museum, in London. In 1864, pieces of relief were cast in sections from metal moulds in the Louvre that had been cast under the direction of Napoleon III. The gallery at the V&A is not high enough to accommodate the column in one piece, so it is displayed in two sections. The cast of the base, which includes the inscription, was made in 1872 as an afterthought, according to Diane Bilbey of the museum's Sculpture Department.

The V&A cast of the inscription became the basis for early 20th-century study of the Roman Imperial capitals. Plaster casts of it were made and distributed to British art schools.[2] The V&A cast became Father Edward M. Catich's *bête noire*. He complained about it in his writings and conspired against it in his correspondence. In 1961, he wrote to calligrapher Lloyd J. Reynolds, "With a few good sets of rubbings in this country we can thumb our noses all around at the V&A Museum. Wouldn't it be something if we could get a really good plaster cast from the Rome original???" He hoped that the V&A would get a better cast once they "learned how bad" theirs was.[3]

The Muzeul Național de Istorie a României (National Museum of Romanian History), in Bucharest, has a plaster cast of the entire Trajan Column, fully displayed in one piece, which Catich considered to be "far, far better than the one at the V&A Museum in London."[4] The cast was supposedly made about 1923 by Ivan Meštrović (1883–1962), a sculptor Catich visited several times in Zagreb between 1936 and 1938.[5]

Both Catich and Reynolds, in their 1961–62 correspondence, mention seeing a plaster cast of the Trajan inscription, complete with the winged female figures at either side, "under the pavement" at Trajan's Forum. I take this description to mean that the cast was in the storage areas under the Via dei Fori Imperiali, the road built between 1924 and 1932 under Mussolini's direction, that divides the Roman Forum from Trajan's Forum. Catich had his eye on it: "the cast probably is better than the stone in the Forum since the cast was made before the acid-scrubbing incident [1897]." He asked the Roman archaeological authorities if he could purchase it, but was told it was the property of the government.[6] The current location of the cast is unknown.

There is no mention of a cast of the Trajan inscription at the Museo della Civiltà Romana (Museum of Roman Civilization) on the EUR website, though the museum does have a cast of the spiral reliefs from the column. Catich said that the museum did not have a cast when he visited it in 1961..

The Archäologisches Institut und Archäologische Sammlung, Universität Zürich (Archaeological Collection of the University of Zürich) has several plaster casts of the reliefs of Trajan's Column, donated by the Gesellschaft Zürich in 1897, but none of the base with the inscription.

From the moment Catich saw the plaster cast of the Trajan inscription in Rome he was determined to have a similar one made for himself. He finally achieved his goal in 1964. "With the help of Italian workmen," he wrote, "we made sectional negatives of the inscription using *argiller Creta*, a tenacious and firm siena-colored molding clay. We next assembled these negative sections and made a plaster positive of the complete inscription." The negative was not made in plaster because Catich was afraid of defacing it, since plaster could "by its tenacity, break out parts of the letters."[7]

Catich used the plaster cast to make a polyester cast. He chose polyester for its toughness, light weight, and dimensional stability. He painted the cast "a light, warm, bone gray to simulate the color of the Greek marble in which the Trajan inscription is cut" and the letters "a toned burnt siena similar in value and color to *minium* (basic carbonate of lead) commonly used by the ancients for overpainting their inscriptions."[8] In 1966, Catich sold the polyester cast to R. R. Donnelley & Sons, the large Chicago printing firm, for $750 and destroyed the plaster cast. The polyester cast now hangs in Donnelley's corporate headquarters.[9]

Squeezes

A squeeze is formed by pressing soft, wet, moldable paper, pulp, latex, or plaster into a low relief inscription. When the material is dry and removed, it becomes a multidimensional mirror-image representation of the original inscription. Although squeezes were a common method of recording inscriptions by archaeologists and epigraphers, there is little information on any made from the Trajan inscription. Catich told Reynolds that he made squeezes of it before 1956, as well as in 1962 and 1966.[10] The pre-1956 squeezes were lost in a studio fire, and the whereabouts of Catich's other squeezes are unknown. None is recorded as part of The Catich Collection, the digitized collection at St. Ambrose University.

Rubbings

Rubbings are the most common method of recording inscriptions. An undated note by Catich mentions rubbings by the great German epigrapher Emil Hübner, but their existence has not been confirmed. The earliest rubbings that have been located are both by Ernst F. Detterer (1888–1947), the custodian of the John M. Wing Collection on the History of Printing at the Newberry Library, Chicago, from 1931 until 1947. They were made circa 1921–22, when he was a teacher at the School of the Art Institute of Chicago. They were made with cobbler's wax (a substance that Belgian lettercarver Kristoffel Boudens used in 1995, when he was in Rome investigating inscriptions) on kraft paper. Although Detterer had been his mentor, Catich was dismissive of his efforts:

> I saw Detterer's rubbing… which he and Phipps made of the Roman inscription. They were having a study session at the Newberry with Jim Hayes, [Robert Hunter] Middleton, et al., working from this rubbing. It was pathetic and I admired it for them. I did not have the heart to tell them how really bad their rubbing was. I had parked my car just around the corner from the Newberry on this occasion and had my fine rubbing with me. I decided against showing them the real thing for it would have been a real blow to Ernst Detterer whom I admired very much and who was a good friend. They have never seen the real thing by way of rubbings.[11]

Ernst Detterer Rubbings

University of Kentucky, King Library Press (Margaret I. King Library)
Kraft paper using cobbler's wax. Mounted on cloth and varnished.
c.44 x 109 in.
Donated to the Press by Robert Hunter Middleton in 1968.
c.1921

Newberry Library
(Case Wing Detterer Rubbing 1922)
Shoe polish on craft paper mounted on linen and varnished.
1922

Father E.M. Catich Rubbings

Catich made many rubbings of the Trajan inscription over the years—as well as inscriptions in the Museo Archeologico Nazionale di Napoli (National Archeological Museum in Naples), the Vatican epigraphic collections, and the Rome catacombs. There is documentation that he made rubbings in 1935–39, 1949, 1950, 1951, 1952, 1961 (5 sets), 1962, 1966 (3 sets), 1969, and 1970. He made five sets in 1961 and three in 1966. How many he made in the other years is unknown. Catich said that his two best rubbings (as of 1961) were destroyed in a studio fire in 1956 and that, in 1962, three sets of rubbings he had been working on were ruined by wind and rain.[12] In the 1960s, he began to make rubbings with an eye to selling them to individuals or institutions. His price in 1961 was $75 for a set (two rubbings, each of three lines of the Trajan inscription); by 1969, the price was $100.[13]

Catich's rubbings took time, especially if they were to be accurate. He told Reynolds that each one took three to four hours "and for this I had to have at least 2 assisting workmen."[14] His rubbings were not done with shoe wax or rubbing crayons but with *graffito polverato* (powdered graphite), the substance that photoengravers used for electrotyping. The paper he used was *carta senza collo* (unsized paper), obtained from the Gregorian University printshop, where it was used for interleaving. Catich stretched the paper tightly over the surface of the inscription using strips of surgical tape. The powdered graphite was firmly rubbed over the paper using a cotton-padded, soft chamois skin stretched over a 2.5-inch-diameter tin can lid.[15]

The information on the extant Catich rubbings comes from the various owners, which accounts for the variable detail. They are listed in chronological order.

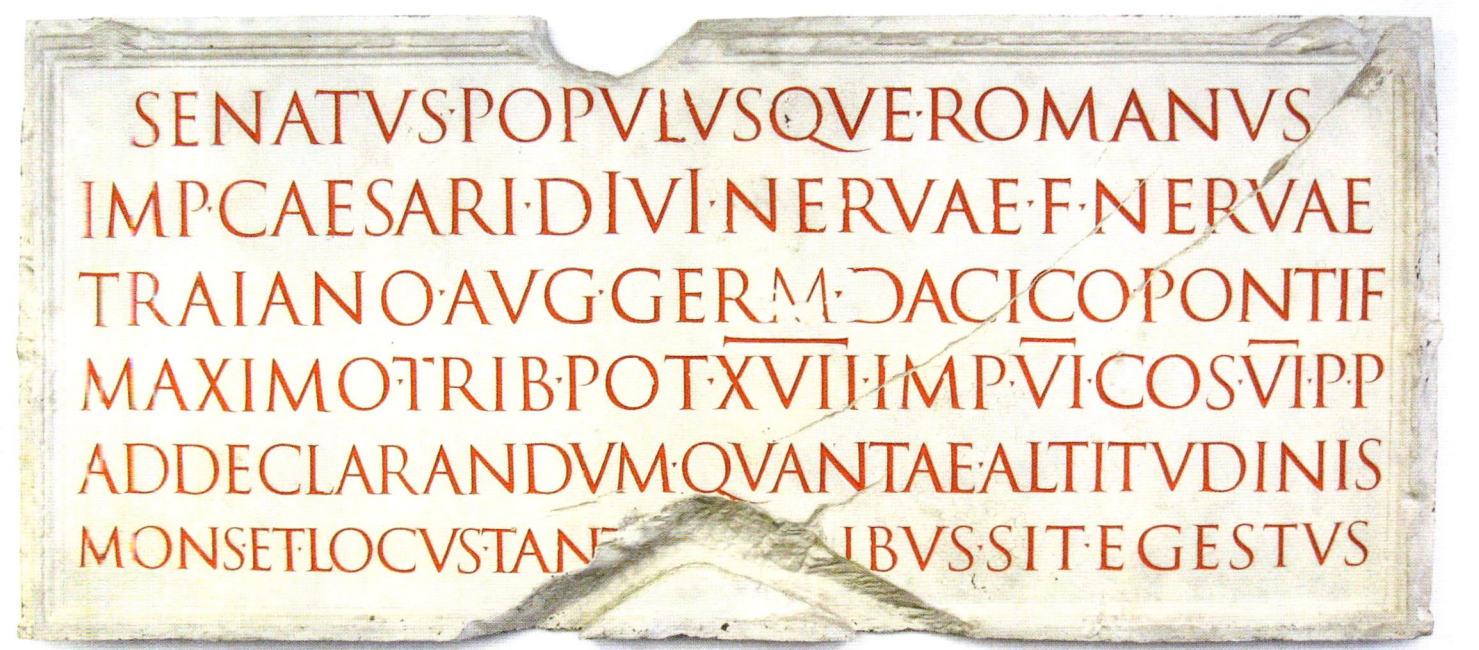

Polyester cast of the Trajan inscription by Father Edward Catich, 1964. R. R. Donnelley & Co.

University of California at Los Angeles
(exact location unknown)
Inscribed: "Inscriptio nuncupata Traiana / E. Catich, June 16, 1950"
16 June 1950
[Rubbing not confirmed by UCLA librarians. However, a photocopy is owned by Christopher Stinehour. It was used by Carol Twombly in the design of Adobe Trajan typeface. A photocopy of the photocopy later hung in the San Jose offices of Adobe Systems.]

Hermann Zapf
Two sheets joined together; currently framed and glassed.
Powdered graphite
Inscribed: "Romae, in basis columnae cochlidis Traiani in foro eius. Haec fecit E. Catich, 14 Julii, 1950."
Acquired from Rick Cusick.
14 July 1950

University of Chicago (R.R. Donnelley & Sons Company Archive, 1844–2005)
Series XX: Artifacts, Artwork and Memorabilia; Subseries 4 (Paintings, Drawings and Art Prints)
Powdered graphite
1951
[rubbing not confirmed by University of Chicago librarians]

Newberry Library (Case Wing oversize ZW 14 .C297)
Two individual sheets
Powdered graphite
62 x 281 cm
Inscribed: "Romae, in basis columnae cochlidis Traiani in foro eius. Haec fecit E. Catich, 7 Junii 1966."
7 June 1966

Carnegie Mellon University
(Arnold Bank Collection)
Three sheets, two 10 ft and one 5 ft in length
Thick tissue paper (Japanese Masa?) tacked onto plain backing paper
Inscribed: "Romae, in basis columnae cochlidis Traiani in foro eius. Haec fecit E. Catich, 7º Junii '66."
7 June 1966

Harvard University, Department of Printing and Graphic Arts, Houghton Library (Edward M. Catich Papers [MS Typ 537]; acc. no. *66M-82)
Two individual sheets
Purchased from Catich 10 November 1966.
1966

Society of Printers (in the Society of Printers archives now at the Boston Public Library, formerly in the Mugar Memorial Library, Boston University)
Commissioned by Harold Chevalier, President of the Society of Printers in 1969.
1969

Newberry Library
(John M. Wing Collection; no further details)
Partial rubbing
February 1970

Sheila Waters
Two sheets of three lines, each c. 2 ft x 9.5 ft
Powdered graphite
Lower sheet inscribed: "Inscriptio nuncupata / 'Traiana' in basi / Columnae cochlidis / Traiani in foro eius / Rome. Feb. 14 1970 E Catich"
Gift from Paul Herrera in 1979.
14 February 1970
Digital facsimile at Rare Book School, University of Virginia

Rick Cusick
Powdered graphite on rag paper
Inscribed: "Inscriptio nuncupata / Traiana in basi / Columnae cochlidis / Traiana in foro eius. / Rome Feb.14.1970 E.Catich"
Acquired from John Schmits c.1980 who inherited it from Catich.
14 February 1970

Paul Herrera
Two individual sheets, three lines each.
Powdered graphite
Inscribed: "Inscriptio nuncupata / Traiana in basi / Columnae cochlidis / Traiana in foro eius. / Rome Feb. 14. 1970 E. Catich."
14 February 1970

Suzanne Moore
Two individual sheets, three lines each.
Powdered graphite
Inscribed: "Inscriptio nuncupata / 'TRAIANA' in basi / Columnae cochlidis / Traiani in foro eius. / E. Catich. Feb. 21, 1970"
21 February 1970
"My rubbing is an original Catich in its tube with the verification. I must admit it gets little use—a collector traded it for a fine binding by my husband Don Glaister some time ago." The rubbing came in a tube covered in marbled paper designed by Catich and with both a top label ("TRAJAN / RUBBING / INSCRIPTION") and side label ("TRAJAN / INSCRIPTION / rubbing made in Rome / Feb. 1970—E.M. Catich"). The rubbing was originally owned by James Thielman of Terre Haute, Indiana. On the back of an envelope sent to Thielman, Catich wrote, "Nine sets of rubbings were made." Presumably this refers to his February 1970 trip to Rome, all of which are documented here.

Rochester Institute of Technology, Cary Library (CSC 048)
Powdered graphite
112 x 149 cm (44 x 110 in)
Inscribed: "Inscriptio nuncupata / 'TRAIANA' in basi / columnae cochlidis / Traiani, in foro eius / E. Catich, Feb. 21, 1970"
Commissioned by the Melbert B. Cary, Jr. Graphic Arts Collection in 1969.
21 February 1970

Smith College
Two individual sheets of three lines each
Inscribed: "Inscriptio nuncupata / 'TRAIANA' in basi / columnae cochlidis / Traiani in foro eius. / Feb. 22, 1970, E. Catich."
Acquired by Elliott Offner, who helped defray Catich's trip to Rome.
22 February 1970

San Francisco Public Library
Inscribed: "Inscriptio nuncupata / 'Traiana' in basi / Columnae cochlidis / Traiani in foro eius. / Feb. 22, 1970, E. Catich"
Gift of Don Moy.
22 February 1970

University of Wisconsin
Two sheets, 2 ft x 12 ft each
Commissioned by Donald M. Anderson and purchased by University of Wisconsin Department of Art for $250; currently in possession of Phil Hamilton.
February 1970

Newberry Library (James Hayes Papers)
Fragmentary rubbings cut down from larger rubbings
September [unknown year]

St. Ambrose University
Two sheets. No other details available.

Gunnlaugur SE Briem
Rubbing of the R.R. Donnelley & Sons Company cast of the Trajan inscription made while it was on display in New York City in

the 1980s. Made with a graphite stick on a single sheet of Japanese paper.

Garrett Boge
Rubbing of the R. R. Donnelley & Sons cast of the Trajan inscription.
In addition to complete rubbings of the Trajan inscription by Father Catich there are also individual letters. These accompanied 130 numbered copies (out of 230) of *The Trajan Inscription: An Essay* by Father Edward M. Catich (Boston: Society of Printers, 1973). The letters were cut from a 1969 rubbing by Catich. At least two of the remaining unnumbered copies have rubbings that were added by Catich after publication.

Paul Herrera
"OA"
Inscribed: "The letters opposite are from the third line of the Trajan Inscription in Rome. I made this rubbing in 1936. E. Catich. Nov. 27, 1973 / TRAIANO.AVG". The letters "OA" are underlined.

Iowa State University (Parks Library)
"LA"
1936
Inscribed: "These letters are from the 5th line of the Trajan Inscription in Rome. I made this rubbing in 1936. E. Catich Nov 27th, 1973." Below this is written "ADDECLARANDVM" with the "LA" marked with a red square.

Christopher Stinehour
"CL"
1936
Inscribed: "The letters opposite are from the fifth line of the Trajan Inscription in Rome. I made this rubbing in 1936. E Catich Nov. 27.1973." Below this is written "ADDECLARANDVM" with the "CL" marked with a red square.

Several other individuals have made rubbings of the Trajan inscription in the 20th century.

Lloyd J. Reynolds Rubbings
Reed College (Eric V. Hauser Library)
Three fragmentary rubbings: GE, N, and SA.
Wax crayon on yellow tracing paper
Spring 1960
Lloyd J. Reynolds said that he made a complete rubbing of the inscription on a single sheet of "architect's tracing paper" using "a heavy (lumber) wax crayon" in January 1960, but its whereabouts are not known.[16] These three fragmentary rubbings were made on the same trip to Rome. Reynolds apparently did not follow Catich's advice to use powdered graphite on newsprint.[17]

Mark van Stone Rubbing
Two pieces of rice paper: one for lines 1–5 and one for line 6
Wax crayons
Rubbing made collaboratively by van Stone and nine other participants in his lettering tour of Rome. Four of the participants have been identified: Amanda Adams, Bonnie Ebbs, Cheryl Jacobsen, and Lisa Niccolini.
1991
Twelve blueprints of the rubbing were made for sale; one is owned by Cheryl Jacobsen.

Masahiko Kimura Rubbing
Graphite stick on a single sheet of drawing paper
Rubbing made by Kimura and Yukari Haruta on their honeymoon.
10 May 1999
Recounted and reproduced in *Trajan Inscription* (Tokyo: Vignette Books; Robundo Publishers, 2002).

"While in Rome on commission, I erected the scaffolding anew in fron[t] [of] the Trajan Inscription in order to get some hpotos [sic] of me at work for the brochure to be put out by Donnelley & Sons of Chicago who now own the polyester cast cast [sic] which I made or the[m]. While the scaffolding was up I made several sets of rubbings[.] If you know of anyone who might be interested in a set of the rubbings at 75.00 let me know."[18]

"I made several additional rubbings in Rome this summer. I worked in the epigraphic museums in Athens, Naples and the Vatican this summer doing research. Do you know of anyone who might be interested in a set of these rubbings? I have three sets on hand. They are $75.00 per set. I have also written to three others abt. These so that it is a case of 'first come[,] first served.'"[19]

---

1. John Hungerford Pollen, *A Description of the Trajan Column* (London: George E. Eyre and William Spottiswoode, 1874), p. 94.
2. David Diringer, *Staples Alphabet Exhibition: The Alphabet throughout the Ages and in All Lands* (London: Staples Press, 1953).
3. Catich to Reynolds, 18 September 1961 and 4 November 1961 (unless otherwise noted, all correspondence between Catich and Reynolds cited herein is from the Lloyd J. Reynolds Papers, Reed College).
4. Catich to Donald M. Anderson, 31 December 1970 (unless otherwise noted, all correspondence between Catich and Anderson cited herein is from the Donald M. Anderson Archives Papers, Newberry Library).
5. Catich to Reynolds, 4 November 1961.
6. Catich to Reynolds, 4 November 1961 and 14 April 1962.
7. Catich to Reynolds, 4 November 1961; *The Trajan Inscription in Chicago* (Chicago: Lakeside Press, R. R. Donnelley & Sons, [c. 1968]).
8. Ibid.
9. Catich to Reynolds, 19 May 1964.
10. Catich to Reynolds, 14 April 1962 and 8 April 1966.
11. Catich to Reynolds, 29 January 1961.
12. Catich to Reynolds, 26 March 1956, 8 April 1956, 8 January 1961, 18 September 1961, 30 September 1961, 30 August 1966, 8 October 1966, and 13 September 1969.
13. Catich to Reynolds, 18 September 1961 and 13 September 1969.
14. Catich to Reynolds, 30 September 191.
15. Catich to Reynolds, 3 March 1960, and see note accompanying some of Catich's post-1966 rubbings. The technique was the result of experimentation between 1935 and 1949.
16. Reynolds to Catich, 21 October 1960.
17. Catich to Reynolds, 3 March 1960.
18. Catich to Reynolds, 8 October 1966.
19. Catich to Reynolds, 13 September 1969; Catich to Donald M. Anderson, 31 December 1970.

SELECTED COLLECTIONS OF ROMAN INSCRIPTIONS

Indicates collections of major importance.

UNITED STATES

ANN ARBOR
*The Dennison & De Criscio Collections, Kelsey Museum of Archeology
University of Michigan,
434 South State Street,
Ann Arbor, Michigan 48109-1390
Tel (734) 764-9304

UNITED KINGDOM

ENGLAND

BATH
The Roman Baths
Abbey Church Yard,
Bath BA1 1LZ
Tel +44 (0)1225 477785

CARLISLE
Tullie House Museum & Art Gallery
Castle Street, Carlisle,
Cumbria CA3 8TP
Tel +44 (0)1228 618718

CHESTER
Grosvenor Museum
27 Grosvenor Street,
Chester CH1 2DD
Tel +44 (0)1224 972197

LINCOLN
The Collection / Art and Archaeology in Lincolnshire
Danes Terrace, Lincoln LN2 1LP
Tel +44 (0)1522 782040

LONDON
*British Museum
Great Russell Street,
London WC1B 3DG
Tel +44 (0)20 7323 8299

SHREWSBURY
Shrewsbury Museum & Art Gallery
The Square, Shrewsbury,
Shropshire SY1 1LH
Tel +44 (0)1743 258885

SCOTLAND

GLASGOW
The Hunterian
University of Glasgow,
University Avenue,
Glasgow G12 8QQ
Tel +44 (0)141 330 4221

WALES

NEWPORT
*The National Roman Legion Museum
High Street, Caerleon NP18 1AE
Tel +44 (0)029 2057 3550

EUROPE

BELGIUM

ARLON
Le Musée Archéologique d'Arlon
rue des Martyrs 13, 6700 Arlon
Tel +32(0)63 212 849

BULGARIA

PLOVDIV
Archeological Museum of Plovdiv
Saedinenie Square 1,
Plovdiv 4000
Tel +359(0)32 633 106

FRANCE

ARLES
*Museum of Ancient Arles (Musée départemental Arles Antique)
rue du Cirque Romain,
13635 Arles
Tel +33 04 13 31 51 03

AUTUN
Musée Rolin
5 rue des Bancs, 71400 Autun
no telephone number available

BORDEAUX
Musée d'Aquitaine
20 cours Pasteur, 33000 Bordeaux
Tel +33 05 56 01 51 00

LYON
*Gallo-Roman Museum of Lyon (Musée Gallo-Romain de Fourvière Lyon)
6 Rue de l'Antiquaille, 69005 Lyon
Tel +33 (0)4 72 38 49 30

NARBONNE
Musée Archéologique de Narbonne
Place de l'Hôtel de Ville, Ancien Palais des Archevêques, 11100 Narbonne
Tel +33 (0)4 68 90 30 54

*Musée Lapidaire
Eglise Notre-Dame,
de Lamourguie
Place Lamourguié,
11100 Narbonne
Tel +33 (0)4 68 90 30 65

NÎMES
*Musée Archéologique
13 Boulevard Amiral Courbet,
30000 Nîmes
Tel +33 (0)4 66 76 74 80

PARIS
*Musée du Louvre
Greek, Etruscan, and Roman Antiquities
75058 Paris
Tel +33 (0)1 40 20 53 17

Musée du Cluny (Musee National du Moyen Âge)
6 place Paul Painlevé, 75005 Paris
Tel +33 (0)1 53 73 78 00

REIMS
Musée Historique Saint-Remi
53 rue Simon, 51100 Reims
Tel +33 (0)3 26 85 23 36 / (0)3 26 35 36 90

ROUEN
Musée départemental des Antiquités
198 rue Beauvoisine, 76000 Rouen
Tel +33 (0)2 35 98 55 10

SAINTES
Musée Archéologique
Esplanade André Malraux,
17100 Saintes
Tel +33 (0)5 46 74 20 97

STRASBOURG
Archeological Museum (Palais Rohan)
Palais Rohan , 2, Place du Château, 67000 Strasbourg
Tel +33 (0)3 88 52 50 00

TOULOUSE
*Musée Saint-Raymond
1 Ter place Saint-Sernin,
31000 Toulouse
Tel +33 (0)5 61 22 31 44

GERMANY

AUGSBURG
*Kunstsammlungen und Museen Augsburg
Römisches Museum
Dominikanergasse 15, 86150 Augsburg
Tel +49 (0) 821 324 ext. 41 31

BERLIN
*Pergamonmuseum der Staatlichen Museen zu Berlin
Antikensammlung, Am Kupfergraben, 10117 Berlin

COLOGNE [KÖLN]
*Römische-Germanisches Museum
Roncalliplatz 4, 50667 Köln

MAINZ
Römische-Germanisches Zentralmuseum
Ernst-Ludwig-Platz 2 D,
55116 Mainz
Tel +49 (0)613191240

*Landesmuseum Mainz
Grosse Bleiche 49-51, 55116 Mainz
Tel +49 (0)613128570

MUNICH [MÜNCHEN]
Glyptothek und Antikensammlung
Staatliche Antikensammlungen
Königsplatz, 80333 München
Tel +49 (0)89 59988830

REGENSBURG
***Historisches Museum**
Dachauplatz 2–4, 93047
Regensburg
Tel +49 (0)941 507 2448

TRIER
Rheinisches Landesmuseum Trier
Weimarer Allee 1, 54290 Trier
Tel + 49 (0)651/9774-0

GREECE
ATHENS
National Archaeological Museum
44 Patission Street, Athens 10682
Tel +30 213214 4800

EPIDAURUS
Archeological Museum of Epidaurus
21052 Iero Asklipiou, Argolis
Tel +30 27530 22009

HUNGARY
BUDAPEST
Aquincumi Múzeum
Szentendrei út 135, 1031 Budapest
Tel +36 1 250-1650

ITALY
AGRIGENTO
Museo Archeologico Regionale di Agrigento
Contrada San Nicola 12, Agrigento
Tel +39 (0)922 401565

AQUILEIA
***Museo Archeologico Nazionale di Aquileia**
Via Roma 1, 33051 Aquileia (UD)
Tel +39 (0)431 91035

Museo Nazionale Paleocristiano di Aquileia
Piazza Pirano 1, Loc. Monastero, 33051 Aquileia (UD)
Tel +39 (0)431-91035 91131

ASSISI
Museo Civico e Foro Romano
via Portica 2, Assisi (PG)
Tel +39 (0)75813053

BENEVENTO
***Museo del Sannio di Benevento**
Piazza Santa Sofia, 82100 Benevento
Tel +39 (0)824 2 1818
Fax +39 (0)824 32 6238

BOLOGNA
Museo Civico Archeologico
Via dell'Archiginnasio 2, 40124 Bologna
Tel +39 (0)51 2757211

BRESCIA
***Museo del Monastero di Santa Giulia**
Via Musei 81/b, 25121 Brescia

BRINDISI
Museo Archeologico Provinciale F. Ribezzo
Piazza Duomo 7, 72100 Brindisi
Tel +39 (0)831 565501/508

FERRARA
***Museo Lapidario**
Via Camposabbionario, Ferrara
Tel +39 (0)532 24 49 49

FLORENCE [FIRENZE]
Museo Archeologico Nazionale
Via della Pergola 65, 50121 Firenze
Tel +39 (0)55 23575

***HERCULANEUM [ERCOLANO]**
Ufficio Scavi di Ercolano, Corso Resina, 80056 Ercolano (NA)
Tel +39 081 7324311

MILAN [MILANO]
Civico Museo Archeologico di Milano
Corso Magenta 15, 20123 Milano
Tel +39 (0)2 88445208

NAPLES [NAPOLI]
***Museo Archeologico Nazionale di Napoli**
Piazza Museo Nazionale, 19, 80135 Napoli
Tel +39 (0)81 4422149

OSTIA ANTICA
***Museo Archeologico Ostiense**
Viale dei Romagnoli 717, Località Ostia Antica
Tel +39 (0)6 56358099

PADUA [PADOVA]
***Museo Archeologico di Padova**
Piazza Eremitani 8, 35121 Padova
Tel +39 (0)498204579
Fax +39 (0)498204566

PALERMO
Museo Archeologico Regionale
Piazza Olivella 24, Palermo, Sicily
Tel +39 (0)91 611 6805

PALESTRINA
Museo Archeologico di Palestrina
Piazza della Barberini-Cortina, Palestrina
Tel +39 (0)69538100

PARMA
***Museo Archeologico Nazionale di Parma**
Piazza della Pilotta 5, Palazzo della Pilotta, 43121 Parma
Tel +39 (0)521 233718

PERUGIA
Museo Archeologico Nazionale dell'Umbria
Piazza Giordano Bruno 10, 06121 Perugia
Tel +39 (0)75 572 7141

PESARO
Museo Archeologico Oliveriano
Via Mazza 97, 61121 Pesaro
Tel +39(0)721 33344

*POMPEII
Pompei Scavi, via Villa dei Misteri 2, Pompeii
Tel +39 081/5365154

RAVENNA
***Museo Nazionale di Ravenna**
Via San Vitale 17, Ravenna
Tel +39 (0)544 215618

RIMINI
***Lapidario Romano**
1 via Gaetano Tonini, Museo della Città, 47900 Rimini
Tel +39 (0)541 2 1482

ROME [ROMA]
***Il Museo Epigrafico Museo Nazionale Romano**
Terme di Diocleziano, Viale Enrico De Nicola 79, Rome

Palazzo Massimo alle Terme
Largo di Villa Peretti 1, Rome
Tel +39 (0)6 399 67 700

***Musei Capitolini**
Palazzo Nuovo, piazza del Campidoglio 1, 00186 Rome
Tel +39 (0)60608

***Foro Romano**
Via della Salaria Vecchia 5/6, Rome
Entrances from largo Romolo e Remo,
via Sacra (piazza del Colosseo),
via Foro Romano
& via di San Teodoro
Tel +39 (0)6 3996 7700

Sant'Agnese Fuori le Mura
Via Nomentana 349, 00162 Rome
+39 (0)6 8620 7644

S. Sebastiano Fuori le Mura
Via Appia Antica 136, 00179 Rome
+39 (0)6 785 0350
www.catacombe.org

***Appian Way (Via Appia)**
this ancient Roman road is lined with inscriptions and monuments

SYRACUSE [SIRACUSA]
Museo Archeologico Regionale Paolo Orsi
Viale Teocrito 66, 96100 Siracusa, Sicily
Tel +39 (0)931 489511

TARANTO
Museo Nazionale Archeologico di Taranto
Via Cavour, 10, 74100 Taranto, Sicily
Tel +39 (0)994 53 21 12

TRIESTE
Museo di Storia ed Arte ed Orto Lapidario
Piazza della Cattedrale 1, 34121 Trieste
Tel +39 (0)40 310500 / 040 308686

URBINO
***Museo Archeologico Lapidario**
Palazzo Ducale
Piazzale Duca Federico 13, 61029 Urbino
Tel +39 (0)722/2760

VATICAN CITY
***Vatican Museums Musei Vaticani**
Viale Vaticano, 00165 Rome
Tel: +39 (0)6 69884676 or 0039 06 69883145
Includes the Lateran Profane Museum, Pio Christian Museum, and Lapidary Gallery

VELLETRI
Museo Civico Archeologico Oreste Nardini
Palazzo Comunale, Via Goffredo Mameli 4-6, 00049 Velletri (RM)
Tel +39 (0)6 96158268
Fax +39 (0)6 96158239

VENICE [VENEZIA] AND TORCELLO
***Museo Archeologico Nazionale**
San Marco 52, 30124 Venezia
Tel +39 (0)41 296 7663

Museo Archeologico di Torcello
Palazzo del Archivio, Piazza Torcello 30012 Torcello VE
Tel +39 (0)41/730 761

VERONA
***Museo Lapidario Maffeiano**
Piazza Bra 28, 37122 Verona
Tel +39 (0)45 590087
Founded 1745 by Scipione Maffei; oldest public lapidary museum in the world

---

LUXEMBOURG
LUXEMBOURG
Musée national d'histoire et d'art Luxembourg
Marché-aux-Poissons,
L-2345 Luxembourg
Tel +352 47 93 30 1

PORTUGAL

LISBON
Museu Nacional de Arqueologia
Praça do Império 1400,
206 Lisbon
Tel (351) 213620000

ROMANIA

CONSTANTA
Muzeul de Istorie Nationala si Arheologie
Piata Ovidiu 12, Constanta
Tel +40 (0) 241 618 763

SPAIN

ÁLAVA
Bibat Museo de Arqueología de Álava
Calle Cuchillería, 54, 01001
Vitoria-Gasteiz (Araba-Álava)
Tel +34 945-203700

BARCELONA
Museu d'Història de la Ciutat
Plaça del Rei, Barcelona
Tel +34 932 562 100

MÉRIDA
***Museo Nacional de Arte Romano**
Calle José Ramón Mélida, 2,
06800 Mérida (Badajoz)
Tel +34 924-311690/
+34 924-311912

SEVILLE
Museo Arqueológico de Sevilla
Plaza de América, s/n, Pabellón de Bellas Artes, 41013 Seville
Tel +34 954786474

TARRAGONA
Museu Nacional Arqueològic de Tarragona
Plaça del Rei, 5, 43003 Tarragona
Tel +34 977 23 62 09

ÚBEDA
Museo Arqueológico de Úbeda
Calle Cervantes 6, (Casa Mudéjar),
23400 Úbeda (Jaén)
Tel +34 953779432

SWITZERLAND

AVENCHES
Musée Romains Avenches
Av. Jomini 16, ch 1580 Avenches
Tel +41 (0)26 557 33 15

BASEL
Antikenmuseum Basel und Sammlung Ludwig
St. Alban-Graben 5, CH-4010 Basel
Tel +41 (0)61 201 12 12

MIDDLE EAST

LEBANON
HELIOPOLIS [NOW BAALBEK]
ruins with inscriptions

SYRIA
BOSRA
Omar Mosque built with stones containing Roman inscriptions

DAMASCUS
National Museum of Damascus
Shoukry Al-Qouwatly, Damascus

HAMA
***Apamea**
Ruins of a Roman theatre
Due to the Syrian civil war there is no reliable contact information available.

TURKEY
ANTIOCH (ANTAKYA)
Antakya Archaeological Museum; Hatay Archaeological Museum (Hatay Arkeoloji Müzesi)
Cumhuriyet Mah. Gündüz Caddesi No. 1, Antakya/Hatay
Tel +90 326 214 6168

GEYRE BELDESI, KARACASU
***Aphrodisias Archaeological Site**
Geyre Beldesi, Karacasu
Tel +90 (0)256 448 8003

ISTANBUL
Istanbul Archaeological Museums (Arkeoloji Müzeleri)
Alemdar Cad. Osman Hamdi, Bey Yokuşu Sk, 34122, Gülhane/Fatih, Istanbul
Tel +90 (0)212 520 7740

IZMIR
Izmir Archeology Museum / Izmir Arkeoloji Müzesi
Halit Rıfat Paşa Caddesi 4.
Konak, Izmir
Tel +90 0232 489 0796

SELÇUK
***Ephesus Museum (Efes Müzesi)**
Ataturk Mah. Uğur Mumcu Sevgi Yolu, Selçuk (Izmir)
Tel +90 (0)232 892 6010

SIDE
Side Museum
Selimiyeköyü, Side
Tel +90 242 753 10 06

NORTH AFRICA

LIBYA
KHOMS (FORMERLY LEPTIS MAGNA)
***Leptis Magna Archeological Museum**

TUNISIA
CARTHAGE [CARTAGO, NEAR TUNIS]
Carthage National Museum
Colline de Byrsa, BP 33
2016 Cartago
Tel +216 1/34 10 77
(++216) 71 733 866

DOUGGA
Archeological site near Tunis has inscriptions; but most of them are in the Bardo Museum.

SOUSSE
Sousse Archeology Museum
Khalef al Fata Tower, Kasbah, Sousse

TUNIS
***The National Bardo Museum**
Rue Mongi Slim 2000, Tunis
Tel +216 71 513 650

Museo Lapidario Maffeiano, Verona. Founded 1745 by Scipione Maffei, it is the oldest public lapidary museum in the world.

FURTHER READING ON ROMAN CAPITALS

*Indicates treatises on constructing Roman Capitals

GENERAL HISTORIES AND SURVEYS OF WRITING AND LETTERING

Anderson, Donald M. *The Art of Written Forms: The Theory and Practice of Calligraphy.* New York: Holt, Rinehart and Winston, 1969.

Baines, Phil and Catherine Dixon. *Signs: Lettering in the environment.* London: Laurence King, 2003.

Bartram, Alan. *Lettering in Architecture.* London: Lund Humphries, 1975.

———. *Tombstone Lettering in the British Isles.* London: Lund Humphries, 1978.

———. *Fascia Lettering in the British Isles.* London: Lund Humphries, 1978.

———. *Street Name Lettering in the British Isles.* London: Lund Humphries, 1978.

———. *The English Lettering Tradition from 1700 to the Present Day.* London: Lund Humphries, 1986.

Capelli, Adriano. *Lexicon abbreviaturarum: Dizionario di abbreviature latine ed italiane usate nelle carte e codici specialmente del medio-evo…* 3rd ed. Milano: Casa Editrice Libraria Ulrico Hoepli, 1929.

Degering, Hermann. *Die Schrift. Atlas der Schriftformen des Abendlandes vom Altertum bis zum Ausgang des 18. Jahrhundert.* 4th ed. Tübingen: Verlag Ernst Wasmuth, 1964.

Diringer, David. *The Alphabet: A Key to the History of Mankind.* 3rd ed. rev. with the collaboration of Reinhold Regensburger. 2 vols. London: Hutchinson, 1968.

Gray, Milner, and Ronald Armstrong. *Lettering for Architects and Designers.* London: Batsford, 1962.

Gray, Nicolete. *Lettering on Buildings.* London: The Architectural Press, 1960.

———. *A History of Lettering: Creative Experiment and Letter Identity.* Oxford: Phaidon Press Ltd., 1986.

Gürtler, André. *Die Entwicklung der lateinischen Schrift = L'évolution de l'écriture latine (The development of the Roman alphabet).* St. Gallen: A.G. Zollikofer, 1969. *Typographische Monatsblätter* no. 11.

Kinneir, Jock. *Words and Buildings: The Art and Practice of Public Lettering.* London: Architectural Press, 1980.

Knight, Stan. *Historical Scripts from Classical Times to the Renaissance.* 2nd rev. and expanded ed. New Castle, Del.: Oak Knoll Press, 1998.

Mediavilla, Claude. *Histoire de la calligraphie française.* Paris: Albin Michel, 2006.

Morison, Stanley. *Politics and Script: Aspects of Authority and Freedom in the Development of Graeco-Latin Script from the Sixth Century B.C. to the Twentieth Century A.D.* The Lyell Lectures, 1957. Edited by Nicolas Barker. Oxford: Clarendon Press, 1972.

Mosley, James. "English Vernacular." *Motif* 11 (Winter 1963–64): 3–55.

———. "Trajan Revived." In *Alphabet 1964: International Annual of Letterforms*, vol.1, pp. 17–48. London: James Moran Ltd. for The Kynoch Press, 1964.

Nash, John R. "In Defence of the Roman Letter." in *EJF Journal* 7 (Autumn 2002): 11–31.

Petrucci, Armando. *La Scrittura: Ideologia e rappresentazione.* Torino: Piccola Biblioteca Einaudi, 1986.

———. *Public Lettering: Script, Power, and Culture.* Translated by Linda Lappin. Chicago and London: University of Chicago Press, 1993.

Sutton, James, and Alan Bartram. *An Atlas of Typeforms.* London: Lund Humphries, 1968.

MODERN LETTERING MANUALS AND TREATISES

Benson, John, and Graham Carey. *The Elements of Lettering.* Newport, R.I.: The John Stevens Shop, 1940.

Brown, Frank Chouteau. *Letters and Lettering: A Treatise with 200 Examples.* Boston: Bates & Guild Co., 1902.

Catich, Edward M. *Reed, Pen, & Brush Alphabets for Writing and Lettering.* Davenport, Iowa: Catfish Press, 1972.

*Goines, David Lance. *A Constructed Roman Alphabet: A Geometric Analysis of the Greek and Roman Capitals and of the Arabic.* Boston: David R. Godine, 1982.

Harvey, Michael. *Lettering Design.* London: The Bodley Head, 1975.

———. *Creative Lettering, Drawing and Design.* London: The Bodley Head, 1985.

Johnston, Edward. *Writing & Illuminating, & Lettering.* London: John Hogg, 1906). With "Inscriptions in Stone" by A.E.R. Gill, app. B, chap. XVII, pp. 389–406.

———. *Manuscript & Inscription Letters for Schools & Classes & for the Use of Craftsmen.* 2nd impression, rev. London: John Hogg, 1911. With 5 plates by A.E.R. Gill.

Kaech, Walter. *Rhythmus und Proportion in der Schrift* (Rhythm and proportion in lettering). Translated by Elizabeth Friedländer. Olten, Switzerland: Walter Verlag, 1956.

Kemp, Tom. *Formal Brush Writing.* Oxford: Twice Publishing, 1999.

Koch, Rudolf. *Schreibbüchlein: Eine Anleitung zum Schreiben.* Kassel-Wilhelmshöhe, Germany: Bärenreiter-Verlag, 1930. With woodcuts by Fritz Kredel.

*Muess, Johannes. *Das römische Alphabet: Entwicklung, Form und Konstruktion.* (The Roman alphabet: development, form, and construction). Munich: Callwey, 1989.

Ohlsen, Walter. *Monumentalschrift · Monument · Mass: Proportionerung des Inschriftalphabets und des Sockels der Trajanssäule in Rom* (translation). Hamburg: Friedrich Wittig Verlag, 1981.

LETTERCARVING

Grasby, Richard. *Lettering and Carving.* Dorchester, England: Sacketts, 1988.

———. *Lettercutting in Stone: A Workbook.* Oswestry, England: Anthony Nelson, Ltd., 1989

Harvey, Michael. *Carving Letters in Stone & Wood.* London: The Bodley Head, 1987.

Jakob, Sepp, and Donatus M. Leicher. *Schrift + Symbol in Stein, Holz und Metall.* Munich: Callwey Verlag, 1977.

Kindersley, David, and Lida Lopes Cardozo. *Letters Slate Cut: Workshop Practice and the Making of Letters.* New York: Taplinger Publishing / A Pentalic Book, 1981.

Kindersley, Lida Lopes Cardozo. *The Annotated Capital: On the Thinking Behind the Capital Letter of the Cardozo Kindersley

Workshop. Cambridge: Cardozo Kindersley, 2009.

Perkins, Tom. *The Art of Letter Carving in Stone*. Ramsbury, Marlborough, Wiltshire: The Crowood Press, 2007.

ANCIENT ROME

Adobe. *Lithos*. Mountain View, Cal.: Adobe Systems Inc., 1989.

———. *Trajan*. Mountain View, Cal.: Adobe Systems Inc., 1989.

Avrigemma, Salvatore. *Rimini: guida ai più notevoli monumenti romani e al Museo archeologico*. Bologna: L. Cappelli, 1934.

Borger, Hugo, and Helga Schmidt-Glassner. *Das Römisch-Germanische Museum Köln*. Munich: Callwey Verlag, 1977.

Burdy, Jean, and André Pelletier. *Guide du Lyon gallo-romain*. Lyon: ELHA, 1997.

Camodeca, Giuseppe, Heikki Solin, Fara Nasti, Aniello Parma, Mika Kajeva, et al., eds. *Le Iscrizioni Latine del Museo Nazionale di Napoli*. Vol. 1, *Roma e Latium*. Naples: Loffredo Editore Napoli S.p.A., 2000.

Catich, Edward M. *Letters Redrawn from the Trajan Inscription in Rome*. Davenport, Iowa: Catfish Press, 1961.

———. *The Origin of the Serif: Brush Writing & Roman Letters*. Davenport, Iowa: Catfish Press, 1968.

———. *The Trajan Inscription: An Essay*. Boston: Society of Printers, 1973.

Christol, Michel, and Jean Charmasson. *Inscriptions antiques de la cité de Nîmes*. Cahiers des musées et monuments de Nîmes, 11; Travaux du Centre de recherches d'épigraphie et d'histoire de l'Empire romain, Université de Paris I, Panthéon-Sorbonne 1. Nîmes: Musée archéologique de Nîmes, 1992.

Corpus Inscriptionum Latinarum (CIL). Berlin: 1862–1955.

Degrassi, Attilio. *Inscriptiones Latinae Liberae rei Pvblicae: Imagine*. Berlin: Walter de Guyter & Co., 1965.

Dobson, Brian, and Valerie A. Maxfield. *Inscriptions of Roman Britain*. London: London Association of Classical Teachers, 1995.

Espérandieu, Émile-Jules. *La Maison carrée: Notice du monument et guide sommaire des collections*. Nîmes: Imprimerie générale, 1923.

Evetts, L. C. *Roman Lettering: A Study of the Letters of the Inscription at the Base of the Trajan Column…* London: Sir Isaac Pitman and Sons, Ltd., 1938.

Friggeri, Rosanna. *Terme di Diocleziano: La Collezione Epigrafica*. Milan: Electa, 2012.

Gondi, F. Grossi. *I Trattato di Epigrafia Cristiana Latina e Greca del Mondo Romano Occidentale*. Rome: Università Gregoriana, 1920.

Gordon, Arthur E. *An Illustrated Introduction to Latin Epigraphy*. Berkeley, Los Angeles, and London: University of California Press, 1983.

———. and Joyce Gordon. *An Album of Dated Latin Inscriptions*. 3 vols. Berkeley and Los Angeles: University of California Press, 1958.

Goudy, Frederic W. *The Capitals from the Trajan Column at Rome*. New York: Oxford University Press, 1936.

Grasby, Richard. "Latin Inscriptions: Studies in Measurements and Making." *The Papers of the British School at Rome* 70 (2002): 151–76.

———. *The Making of Roman Inscriptions*. Studies 7 to 11. Oxford: The Centre for the Study of Ancient Documents, 2009.

Henzen, Wilhelm, et al., eds. *Ephemeris Epigraphica: Corporis Inscriptionum Latinarum, Supplementum*. Rome: Institutum; Berlin: Georgium Reimerum, 1872–1913.

Hübner, Emil. *Exempla scripturae epigraphcae latinae a Caesaris dictatoris morte ad aetatum Iustiniani*. Berlin: G. Reimerum, 1885.

Keppie, Lawrence. *Understanding Roman Inscriptions*. Baltimore: Johns Hopkins University Press, 1991.

Kimura, Masahiko. *Trajan Inscription*. Tokyo: Vignette Books; Robundo Publishers, 2002.

Lettich, Giovanni. *Itinerari Epigraphici Aquileiesi: Guida alle epigraphi esposte nel Museo Archeologico Nazionale di Aquileia*. Trieste: Editreg SRL, 2003.

Limentani, Ida Calabi, and Attilio Degrassi. *Epigrafia Latina*. Milan and Varese: Istituto Editoriale Cisalpino, 1968.

Manzella, Ivan Di Stefano. *Mestiere di epigrafista*. Rome: Edizioni Quasar, 1987.

———. *Index Inscriptionum Musei Vaticani. 1. Ambulacrum Iulianum sive "Galleria Lapidaria". Inscriptiones Sanctae Sedis I*. Rome: Ex Officina Libraria Pontificia, 1995.

Martines, Giangiacomo, ed. *Colonna Traiana: Corpus dei disegni 1981–2001*. Rome: Edizioni Quasar di Severino Tognon, 2001.

May, Alan. "Roman Bronze Inscriptional Lettering: A Note on Methods of Production." *Typography Papers* 1 (1996): 123–29.

Modonesi, Denise. *Museo Maffeiano: iscrizioni e relievi sacri latini*. Rome: "L'Erma" di Bretschneider, 1995.

Nazari, Oreste. *L'iscrizione della colonna Traiana*. Turin: C. Clausen, 1908.

Ohlsen, Walter. *Monumentalschrift, Monument, Mass: Proportionierung des Inschriftalphabets und des Sockels der Trajanssäule in Rome*. Hamburg: Wittig, 1981.

Perkins, Tom. "Trajan Secrets." *The Edge* (January 1997).

Petersen, Lauren Hackworth. "The Baker, His Tomb, His Wife, and Her Breadbasket: The Monument of Eurysaces in Rome," *Art Bulletin* 85, no. 2 (June 2003): 230–57.

Rossi, Giovanni Battista de. *Inscriptiones Christianae urbis Romae septimo saeculo antiquores*. Rome: Officina libreria pontificia, 1888.

Shaw, Paul. "A Recent Discovery in Trajan's Forum: Some Implications for Understanding Bronze Inscriptional Letters." *Typography Papers* 5 (2003): 23–32.

Susini, G. C. *Il lapicida romano: Introduzione all'epigrafia latina*. Edizione anastatica. Rome: "L'Erma" di Bretschneider, 1968.

———. *Epigrafia romana*. Rome: Jouvence, 1982.

Susini, Giancarlo. *The Roman Stonecutter: An Introduction to Latin Epigraphy*. Oxford: Blackwell, 1973.

———. *Epigraphica Dilapidata: Scritti Scelti di Giancarlo Susini. Epigrafica e Antichità 15*. Faenza: Fratelli Lega Editore, 1997. Includes "Il lapicida romano. Introduzione all'epigrafia latina," "Concetto e tecnica del tempo nelle iscrizioni romane," and "Per una classificazione delle iscrizioni itinerarie."

Travagli, Anna Maria Visser. *Il Lapidario del Museo civico di Ferrara: la nuova sistemazione a Santa Libera: notizie sulla raccolta*. Florence: Centro Di, 1983.

Tuck, Stephen. *Latin Inscriptions in the Kelsey Museum: The Dennison and De Criscio Collections*. Ann Arbor: University of Michigan Press, 2005.

Wallace, Rex E. *An Introduction to Wall Inscriptions from Pompeii and Herculanum*. Wauconda, Ill.: Bolchazy-Carducci Publishers, 2003.

Wright, David H. *The Vatican Vergil: A Masterpiece of Late Antique Art*. Berkeley: University of California Press, 1993.

———. *The Roman Vergil and the Origins of Medieval Book Design*. London: The British Library, 2001).

CAROLINGIAN ERA AND THE MIDDLE AGES

Adobe. *Charlemagne*. Mountain View, Cal.: Adobe Systems Inc., 1989).

Gray, Nicolete. "The Paleography of Latin Inscriptions in the Eighth, Ninth, and Tenth Centuries." *Papers of the British School in Rome*, n.s., 3, vol. 16 (1948), 38–167.

Rossi, Giovanni Battista de. "Le inscription du tombeau d'Hadrien I composée et gravée en France par l'ordre de Charlemagne." *Mélanges d'archéologies et d'histoire de lécole Françaises de Rome* 8 (1888): 478–501.

Wallach, Luitpold. "The Epitaph of Alcuin: A Model of Carolingian Epigraphy." In *Alcuin and Charlemagne: Studies in Carolingian History and Literature*, pp. 178–97. Ithaca,: Cornell University Press, 1959. First published in *Speculum* 30 (1955): 367–73.

———. "The Epitaph of Hadrian Composed for Charlemagne by Alcuin." In *Alcuin and Charlemagne: Studies in Carolingian History and Literature*, pp. 178–97. Ithaca: Cornell University Press, 1959. First published in *American Journal of Philology* 72 (1951): 128–44.

THE RENAISSANCE AND THE BAROQUE

Alexander, Jonathan J.G. "Initials in Renaissance Illuminated Manuscripts: The Problem of the So-called 'litera Mantiniana.'" In Johanne Autenrieth, ed., *Renaissance- und Humanistenhandschriften / Schriften des Historischen Kollegs: Kolloquien 13*. Munich: Oldenbourg, 1988.

Amphiareo, Frate Vespasiano. *Opera*. Venice: Gabriele Giolito de Ferrari, 1554.

Antonozzi, Leopardo. *De caratteri*. Rome: 1638.

Arnoldi, Francesco Negri. "Il Monumento sepolcrale del Card. Niccolò Forteguerri in Santa Cecilia a Roma e il suo Cenotafo nella Cattedrale di Pistoia." In *Egemonia Fiorentina ed Autonomie Locali nella Toscana Nord-Occidentale del Primo Rinascimento Vita, Arte, Cultura*. Pistoia: Centro di Studi, 1978, 211–221.

Campana, Augusto. "Le Iscrizioni di Sisto IV." In Gaetano Miarelli Mariani et al., *Ponte Sisto (1475–1975; 1877–1977): Ricerche e proposte*. Rome: Palazzo Braschi, 1977.

Carter, Matthew. "Theories of Letterform Construction, Part I," *Printing History: The Journal of the American Printing History Association* 26/27 [vol. 13, no. 2] (1991–92): 3–16.

Casamassima, Emanuele. "Lettere Antiche: Note per la Storia della Riforma Grafica Umanistica," *Gutenberg Jahrbuch* (1964): 13–26.

———, ed. *Luminario. Facsimile dell'esemplare Palatino della Biblioteca Nazionale Centrale di Firenze*. Florence: Leo Olschki, 1966.

Chambers, David, Jane Martineau, and Rodolfo Signorini. "Mantegna and the Men of Letters." In Jane Martineau, ed., *Andrea Mantegna*. Milan: Olivetti / Electa, 1992), 8–30.

Covi, Dario A. "Lettering in Fifteenth Century Florentine Painting," *The Art Bulletin* 45, no. 1 (March 1963), 1–17.

———. *Lettering in the Inscriptions of 15th Century Florentine Paintings*. Hanover, NH. Extract from *Renaissance News* 7 (1954).

Cresci, Giovanni Francesco. *Essemplare di piu sorti lettere*. Edited, introduction, and translated by A. S. Osley. London: Nattali & Maurice, 1968.

———. *Renaissance alphabet; Il perfetto scrittore, parte seconda [by] Giovan Francesco Cresci*. With an introduction by Donald M. Anderson. Madison: University of Wisconsin Press, 1971.

De la Mare, Albinia. "Bartolomeo Sanvito da Padova, copista e minatore." In *La Miniatura a Padova dal Medioevo al Settecento*. Edited by Giordana Canova Mariani, with Giovanna Baldissin Molli and Federica Toniolo. Modena: Franco Cosimo Panini Editore, 1999, 495–505.

———, and Laura Nuvoloni. *Bartolomeo Sanvito: The Life & Work of a Renaissance Scribe*. Edited by Anthony Hobson and Christopher De Hamel. Paris: Association internationale de bibliophilie, 2009.

*Dürer, Albrecht. *Of the Just Shaping of Letters: From the Applied Geometry of Albrecht Dürer, Book III*. Translated by R. T. Nichol. New York: Grolier Club, 1917.

*———. *Vnderweysung der Messung, mit dem Zirckel vn[d] Richtscheyt, in Linien Ebnen vnnd gantzen Corporen*. Nuremberg: 1525.

*Fanti, Sigismondo. *Theorica et practica… de modo scribendi fabricandique omnes litterarum species*. Venice: Giovanni Rosso, 1514.

Feld, Maury. "Constructed Letters and Illuminated Texts: Regiomontanus, Leon Battista Alberti, and the Origins of Roman Type." *Harvard Library Bulletin* 28, no. 4 (1980): 357–79.

*Feliciano, Felice. *Alphabetum Romanum Vat. Lat. 6852 aus der Bibliotheca Apostolica Vaticana*. 2 vols. (commentary and facsimile). Zurich: Belser Verlag, 1985.

Gallerani, Paola Isabella. "La T di Mantegna: Dai modelli epigrafici a un'iscrizione nascosta nella pala di San Zeno" in *Quaderni di Palazzo Te* 9 (2000): 9–21.

Gehl, Paul F. "The Newberry Alphabet with a Note on Provenance." *Typography Papers* 6 (2005): 5–18.

Gombrich, Ernst H. "From the Revival of Letters to the Reform of the Arts: Niccolò Niccoli and Filippo Brunelleschi." In *Essays in the History of Art presented to Rudolf Wittkower*. Edited by Douglas Fraser, Howard Hibbard, and Milton J. Lewine. London: Phaidon Press, 1967, pp. 71–82.

*Gray, Nicolete. "The Newberry Alphabet and the Revival of the Roman Capital in Fifteenth-Century Italy." *Typography Papers* 6 (2005): 19–48.

———. "Sans Serif and Other Experimental Inscribed Lettering of the Early Renaissance." *Motif* (1960): 67–76; reprint, with corrections and additional commentary, edited by Paul Shaw. Seattle and New York: LetterPerfect, 1997.

Guerrini, Paola. "L'Epigrafia Sistina come Momento della 'Restauratio Urbis'" in *Un Pontificato ed Una Città Sisto IV (1471–1484): Atti del convegno Roma, 3–7 Dicembre 1984*. Istituto Storico Italiano per Il Medio Evo / Studi Storici Fasc. 154–162. eds. Massimo Miglio, Francesca Niutta, Diego Quaglioni, Concetta Ranieri. Roma: Nella Sede dell'Istituto Palazzo Borromini, 1986), 453–468.

———, Silvia Maddalo, Francesca Niutta, and Daniela Porro. "Iscrizioni Romane Sistine." In *Un Pontificato ed una città: Sisto IV (1471–1484): Atti del convegno Roma, 3–7 Dicembre 1984*. Istituto Storico Italiano per Il Medio Evo / Studi Storici Fasc. 154–62. Edited by Massimo Miglio, Francesca Niutta, Diego Quaglioni, and Concetta Ranieri. Rome: Nella Sede dell'Istituto Palazzo Borromini, 1986, pp. 469–79.

Hartt, Frederick, Gino Corti, and Clarence

Kennedy. *The Chapel of the Cardinal of Portugal 1434–1459 at San Miniato in Florence.* Philadelphia: University of Pennsylvania Press, 1964.

Huelsen, Christian, ed. *Il libro di Giuliano da Sangallo: Codice Vaticano Barberino Latino 4424.* Codices e Vaticanis Selecti 11. Leipzig: Otto Harrassowitz, 1910.

Kajanto, Iiro. *Classical and Christian: Studies in the Latin Epigraphs of Medieval and Renaissance Rome.* Helsinki: 1980.

Kajanto, Iiro. *Papal Epigraphy in Renaissance Rome.* Tammisaari, Finland: Suomalaisen Tiedeakatemian Toimnituksia Annales Academiæ Scientiarum Fennicæ, 1982. With chapters on paleography by Ulla Nyberg.

Kühlenthal, Michael. "Andrea Bregno in Rom." *Römisches Jahrbuch der Bibliotheca Hertziana* 32 (1997/1998): 179–272.

Maddalo, Silvia. "'andrea scarpellino' antiquario: La studio dell'Antica nella bottega di Andrea Bregno." In *Roma, centro ideale della cultura dell'Antico nei secoli XV e XVI: Da Martino V al Sacco di Roma 1417–1527.* Edited by Silvia Danesi Squarzina. Milan: Electa, 1989, 229–36.

———. "Il Monumento Funebre tra Persistenze Medioevali e Recupero dell'Antico." In *Un Pontificato ed una città: Sisto IV (1471–1484): Atti del convegno Roma, 3–7 Dicembre 1984.* Istituto Storico Italiano per Il Medio Evo / Studi Storici Fasc. 154–62. Edited by Massimo Miglio, Francesca Niutta, Diego Quaglioni, and Concetta Ranieri. Rome: Nella Sede dell'Istituto Palazzo Borromini, 1986, 429–52.

Marcon, Suzy. "La silloge dell'Anomino Marucelliano: Un episodio di calligrafica epigrafica." *Studi di Storia dell'Università e della Cultura* (Sec. XV–XX) Quaderni per la Storia dell'Università di Padova 24 (1991): 31–56.

*Mardersteig, Giovanni, ed. *Alphabetum Romanum. Felice Feliciano Veronese.* Verona: Editiones Officianae Bodoni, 1960.

*Mardersteig, Giovanni. "Francesco Torniello e il suo alfabeto romano." In *Tra Latino Volgare per Carlo Dionisotti*, vol. 2, 521–44. Padua: Editore Antenore, 1974.

———. "Leon Battista Alberti e ola Rinascita del Carattere Lapidario Romano nel Quattrocento." *Italia medioevale e umanistica* 2 (1959): 285–307. Reprinted in *Scritti di Giovanni Mardersteig sulla storia dei caratteri e della tipografia*, edited by Alberto Vigevani. Milan: Edizioni il Polifilo, 1988, 33–56. Translated into English by James Mosley as "Leon Battista Alberti and the Revival of the Roman Inscriptional Letter in the Fifteenth Century," *Typography Papers* 6 (2005): 49–65.

Meiss, Millard. *Andrea Mantegna as Illuminator: An Episode in Renaissance Art, Humanism and Diplomacy.* New York: Columbia University Press, 1957.

———. "Toward a More Comprehensive Renaissance Paleography." *The Art Bulletin* 42 (1960): 97–112.

Meyer, Starleen K., and Paul Shaw. "Towards a New Understanding of the Revival of Roman Capitals and the Achievement of Andrea Bregno." In *Andrea Bregno: Il senso della forma nella cultura artistica del Rinascimento.* Edited by Claudio Crescentini and Claudio Strinati. Rome: Artout—Maschietto Editore, 2008, 276–331.

Mitchell, Charles. "Felice Feliciano Antiquarius." *Proceedings of the British Academy* 47 (1961): 197–222.

Moschetti, Andrea. "Le iscrizioni lapidarie romane negli affreschi del Mantegna agli Eremitani." *Atti del Reale Istituto Veneto di scienze, lettere, ed arti* 99 (1929–30): 227–39.

*Moille, Damiano. *A Newly Discovered Treatise on Classic Letter Design.* Introduction by Stanley Morison. Paris: At the Sign of the Pegasus, 1927.

*Morison, Stanley. *Fra Luca de Pacioli of Borgo San Sepolcro.* New York: The Grolier Club, 1933.

Mosley, James. "Giovan Francesco Cresci and the Baroque Letter in Rome." *Typography Papers* 6 (2005): 115–55.

Niutta, Francesca. "Temi e Personaggi nell'Epigrafia Sistina." In *Un Pontificato ed una città: Sisto IV (1471–1484): Atti del convegno Roma, 3–7 Dicembre 1984.* Istituto Storico Italiano per Il Medio Evo / Studi Storici Fasc. 154–62. Edited by Massimo Miglio, Francesca Niutta, Diego Quaglioni, Concetta Ranieri. Rome: Nella Sede dell'Istituto Palazzo Borromini, 1986, 381–408.

*Pacioli, Fra Luca de. *Divina proportione: opera a tutti glingegni perspicaci e curiosi necessaria oue ciascun studioso di philosophia: prospettiua pictura sculptura: architectura: musica: e altre mathematice: suavissima: sottile: e admirabile doctrina consequira: e delecterassi: co[n] varie questione de secretissima scientia / [frater Lucas Patiolus Burgensis Minoritanus et sacrae theologie professor];* M. Antonio Capella eruditiss[imo] recensente. Venice: A. Paganius Paganinus characteribus elegantissimis accuratissime imprimebat, 1509.

Palatino, Giovanbattista. *Libro nuouo d'imparare a scriuere tutte sorte lettere antiche et moderne di tutte nationi: con nuoue regole misure et esempi, co vn breue & vtile trattato de le cifere.* Rome: Appresso Campo di Fiore, 1540.

Pasini, Pier Giorgio. *Il Tempio Malatestiano: Splendore cortese e classicissimo umanistico.* Milan: Skira Editore, 2000. Introduction by Antonio Paolucci, documents edited by Oreste Delucca.

*Petrucci, Armando. *Alfabeto delle maiuscole romane.* Milan: Il Polifilo, 1986. [Luca Horfei Alfabeto delle maiuscole romane c. 1589.]

Pines, Doralynn Schlossman. "The Tomb Slabs of Santa Croce: A New Sepoltuario." PhD diss., Columbia University, 1985.

Porro, Daniela. "La Restituzione della Capitale Epigrafica nella Scrittura MonumentaleL Epitafi ed Iscrizioni Celebrative." In *Un Pontificato ed una città: Sisto IV (1471–1484): Atti del convegno Roma, 3–7 Dicembre 1984.* Istituto Storico Italiano per Il Medio Evo / Studi Storici Fasc. 154–62. Edited by Massimo Miglio, Francesca Niutta, Diego Quaglioni, and Concetta Ranieri. Rome: Nella Sede dell'Istituto Palazzo Borromini, 1986, 409–27.

Ricci, Corrado. *Il Tempio Malatestiano.* Rimini: Bruno Ghigi Editore, 1974. With appendix by Pier Giorgio Pasini "Cinquant'anni di studi sul Tempio Malatestiano." Originally published 1924.

*Rossi, Attilio, ed. *Omaggio all'Alfabeto: Felice Feliciano, Luca Pacioli, Giovannino de' Grassi, Giuseppe Maria Mitelli.* Milano: Luigi Maestri Tipografo, 1990.

Sabelli, Rita, Laura Giovannini, and Carlo Biliotti. *Le tombe terragne della Basilica di Santa Croce.* Firenze: Edizioni Città di Vita, 2001.

Saxl, F. "The Classical Inscription in Renaissance Art and Politics." *Journal of the Warburg and Courtauld Institutes* 4 (1941): 19–46.

———. "Jacopo Bellini and Mantegna as Antiquarians." In *Lectures.* London: The Warburg Institute, University of London, 1957, 151–60.

Schöne, Richard. "Felicis Feliciani Veronensis Opusculum ineditum." *Ephemeris*

Epigraphica 1 (1872): 255–69.

Shaw, Paul. "Bartolomeo Sanvito, Part I." *Letter Arts Review* 18, no. 2 (2003): 40–49.

———. "Bartolomeo Sanvito, Part II." *Letter Arts Review* 19, no. 2 (2004): 14–23.

Sperling, Christine Margit. "Artistic Lettering and the Progress of the Antique Revival in the Quattrocento." 2 vols. PhD diss., Brown University, 1985.

*———. "Leon Battista Alberti's Inscriptions on the Holy Sepulchre in the Cappella Rucellai, San Pancrazio, Florence." *Journal of the Warburg and Courtauld Institutes* 52 (1989): 221–28, illus. 42–47.

Stiff, Paul. "Brunelleschi's Epitaph and the Design of Public Letters in Fifteenth-Century Florence." *Typography Papers* 6 (2005): 66–114.

*Torniello da Novara, Francesco. *Opera del modo de fare le littere maiuscole antique*. Milan: Gotardo da Ponte, 1517.

*Tory, Geoffroy. *Champ flevry. Au quel est contenu Lart & Science de la deue & vraye Proportio[n] des Lettres Attiques, quo[n] dit autrement Lettres Antiques, & vulgairement Lettres Romaines proportionnees selon le Corps & Visage humain.* Paris: A Pot Casse, 1529.

*Tory, Geoffroy. *Champ fleury*. Translated into English and annotated by George B. Ives. New York: Grolier Club, 1927.

Tschichold, Jan. *Das Alphabet des Damianus Moyllus, Parma un 1483*. Basel: Bucherer, Kurrus & Co., 1971.

Tucci, Pier Luigi. *Laurentius Manlius: La riscoperta dell'antica Roma; La nuova Roma di Sisto IV*. Rome: Edizioni Quasar, 2001.

Tura, Adolfo. *Fra Giocondo et les textes français de géométrie pratique*. Hautes Études médiévales et modernes. Paris: Librairie Droz, 2008.

Turchini, Angelo. *Il Tempio Malatestiano, Sigismondo Pandolfo Malatesta e Leon Battista Alberti*. Cesena: Società Editrice "Il Ponte Vecchio," 2000.

*Verini, Giovanni Battista. *Luminario; or, The Third Chapter of the Liber Elementorum Litterarum on the Construction of Roman Capitals.* Translated by A.F. Johnson with an introduction by Stanley Morison. Cambridge, Mass.: Harvard College Library, 1947.

SEVENTEENTH TO NINETEENTH CENTURIES

Morison, Stanley. *Latin Script Since the Renaissance*. Cambridge: University Press, 1938.

Mosley, James. "The Nymph and the Grot: The Revival of the Sans Serif Letter." *Typographica* 12 (1965): 2–19.

Ponot, René. *Louis Perrin & L'enigme Des Augustaux*. Paris: Editions des Cendres, 1998.

TWENTIETH AND TWENTY-FIRST CENTURIES

Aicher, Otl. *Typographie*. Berlin: Ernst & Sohn; Lüdenscheid: Edition Druckhaus Maack, 1988.

Benson, Esther Fisher. *The History of the John Stevens Shop*. Newport, RI: The John Stevens Shop, 1963.

Bernard, Laure. *Lettres de Pierre: Jean-Claude Lamborot graveur lapidaire.* Alain Piccoud Edition, 2004. n.p.

Burke, Chris. *Paul Renner: The Art of Typography*. London: Hyphen Press, 1998.

Cady, Lanore. *Houses & Letters: A Heritage in Architecture & Calligraphy*. Freeport, Me.: Bond Wheelwright Co., 1977.

Dreyfus, John. *The Work of Jan van Krimpen: A Record in Honour of His Sixtieth Birthday.* London: Sylvan Press, 1952.

Fleuss, Gerald. *Tom Perkins Lettercarver, Calligraphic Enterprises*. Ditchling, England: 1998.

Garman, James C., and John Dorato. *The Stone Carver's Business: Three Centuries of Craft Tradition at the John Stevens Shop*. Newport, R.I.: Salve Regina University Gallery, 2006.

Graphos et al. *Stèle à Jean-Claude Lamborot*. With contributions by Eric Valat, Roger Gorrindo, Jacques Le Roux, Pierre Bourgain, Jean-François Cochard, Rodolphe Giuglardo, and Pierre-François Besson. Marseilles: Arqa, 2006.

Harling, Robert. *The Letter Forms and Type Designs of Eric Gill*. Rev. and expanded ed. [Westerham], England: Eva Svensson, 1976.

Hochuli, Jost. *Schriften, in Holz geschnitten*. St. Gallen, Switzerland: Verlagsgemeinschaft St. Gallen, 1980.

Monotype Corporation. *Monotype Recorder* 41, no. 3 (1958). Commemorating an exhibition of lettering and type designs by Eric Gill held at Monotype House, London, October 1958.

Monotype Corporation. "Eric Gill: The Continuing Tradition. "*Monotype Recorder*, n.s., no. 8 (1990).

Shaw, Paul. *Werner Schneider Schriftkunst: A Catalogue of Recent Works.* City, Va.: Privately published by Michael Clark Design, 1999.

Sierman, Koosje, Sjoerd van Faassen, and Sjaak Hubregtse. *Adieu Aesthetica & Mooie Pagina's: J. van Krimpen en het 'schoone boek', Letterontwerper & boekverzorger, 1892–1958*. The Hague: Museum van het Boek, Amsterdam: Uitgeverij de Buitenkant and Haarlem: Museum Enschedé, 1995.

Skelton, Christopher, comp. *Engravings of Eric Gill.* Wellingborough, Northamptonshire, England: Christopher Skelton, 1983.

Society of Typographic Arts. *Hermann Zapf and His Design Philosophy: Selected Articles and Lectures on Calligraphy and Contemporary Developments in Type Design, with Illustrations and Bibliographical Notes, and a Complete List of His Typefaces.* Chicago: Society of Typographic Arts, 1987.

Stone, Reynolds, and Kenneth Clark. *Reynolds Stone Engravings*. London: John Murray, 1977.

Zapf, Hermann. *About Alphabets: Some Marginal Notes on Type Design*. New York: The Typophiles, 1960. [Typophiles Chap Book No. 37: *A Tribute to Paul a Bennett, Publisher and Onlie Begetter of the Typophile Chap Books*.]

116

NEVR
S   1 3/8 – 1 1/2" high; 1/8" leading

most interpoints are triangles, except left/right last line & end of line 7 & after ET line 6
ET line 4

Duomo (S. Lorenzo) / Perugia   117

1451 tomb (left side of back entrance)

Florentine sans, crowded; minimal leading; justified except final 2 lines; no margins

HEC · BREVIS · ILLVSTRI · BALIONA · ABORIGINE ·
CRETVM · ANDREAM · EGIT · VRNA · GRAEMVN
ERANDA · IOANNEM · INGENTI VRTVE · VRM · QI · INIV
RE · SACRORVM · DOCTOR · POTIFICVM · ET · EGIS ·
SVRGENTIBVS · AVGOR · LAVRENT · ECLESIE · PER
YSINVS · PRESVL · ET · INGENS · ANTISTES · VIX
IT · NVNC · ALTA · INPACE · QVIESCENS ·· (short)
·· M · CCCC · LI ·· (centered)

MMVMNACLISE ᴀ ◦ (heavy)

GTRVPXCNDO

HNDHVBNVQ·   end of line

not accurate for thick/thin; only for proportion & structure

Duomo (S. Lorenzo) / Perugia

RECORDING INSCRIPTIONS: METHODS AND TIPS

This is a summary of the different methods for recording inscriptions. It applies to all inscriptions, whether from ancient Greece and Rome, Renaissance Italy, Colonial America, or any other time and place. Although focused on stone, it can apply equally to inscriptions in metal and wood.

1 (*opposite, above*). Transcribed text of inscription on Renaissance tomb (1451) in S. Lorenzo, Ferugia, with notes and drawings of letters. Sketchbook by Paul Shaw, 2002.

2 (*opposite, below*). Detail of S from 1st-century inscription (no. 168) in Musées d'Archéologie, Nîmes showing the movement of the brush in writing the letter prior to carving. Note the extremely long serifs.

3 (*below, left*). Photograph of detail of inscription on the Pyramid of Cestius, Rome, c. 12 BC showing barrel distortion of letters.

4 (*below, right*). Detail of inscription on the façade of the House of Lorenzo Manilio, Rome, 1457/1475 showing the effect of pollution, weathering and shadows on letters.

Notes

Epigrapher Arthur E. Gordon emphasizes the importance of taking good on-site notes about inscriptions no matter what technique is used for recording them.[1] These include a transcription of the text with ligatures, abbreviations, nesting characters, interpoints, line breaks, and indents indicated; comments on distinctive features of individual letters; and measurements of letter height, line spacing, and line length.[2] Make sure that stray marks, scratches, cracks, dirt, and so forth are not mistaken for parts of letters. Ivan Di Stefano Manzella, author of *Mestiere di epigrafista* (1987), recommends the use of a .5mm mechanical pencil with a grade B lead hardness and graph paper with a metric scale. [1]

Photography

Photography is probably the most common method of recording inscriptions today. Photographs have many advantages and disadvantages. They allow recording of inscriptions that are in precarious condition or inaccessible locations. Zoom or telephoto lenses make it possible to study inscriptions that are high up on buildings, monuments, columns, arches, and other structures, while macrophotographs can reveal details of inscriptions that are often invisible to the naked eye. [2]

Among the disadvantages of photography is the distortion of letters resulting from perspective (e.g. shooting from below or from the side) and barrel distortion. Sun and shadows also present problems. Sun can bleach out an inscription while shadows can obscure letters. The vagaries of light can also make it difficult to tell whether letters in a photograph are inscribed or in relief. Painted inscriptions are easier to photograph but the accuracy of the paint vis-à-vis the carved letter needs to be taken into account.[3] Inscriptions should be photographed head-on with raking light, which brings out the edges of the carving. Ideally, a chromatic scale and a ruler should be included in photographs to help with subsequent identification of color and, most important, scale.[4] [3, 4]

5 Collection of *A*s from inscriptions on the Orkney Islands. The enlarged *A* in the lower right corner has landmarks (key points) marked out indicating where the shape changes abruptly. This information is a valuable part of the geometric morphometric study of inscriptions. Comparison created by George Thomson.

6 Detail of inscription on the façade of S. Anastasia in Verona, c. 1471, showing the influence of the deteriorated, pink-veined stone on the deciphering of letterforms.

7 (*opposite*). Drawing of Claudian inscription fragment (CIL VI 920) from Emil Hübner's *Exempla Scripturae Epigraphicae Latinae* (1885), plate no. 86.

Digital Photography

Digital photography has advantages over traditional photography. Not only is it more affordable, but it is also faster and more precise. And many of the problems inherent in traditional photography can be mitigated or overcome entirely. "Digital images can be enhanced, distortion due to perspective can be corrected and, with appropriate equipment, acceptable images can be recorded in poor light conditions, even in almost complete darkness," asserts George Thomson, author of *Inscribed in Remembrance: Gravemarker Lettering: Form, Function and Recording* (2009) and *Lettering on Gravemarkers: A Guide to Recording and Analysis* (2011). Thomson argues that digital images can be subjected to more sophisticated analysis than analog photographs. "One such procedure is geometric morphometrics or shape analysis," he explains. "The procedure can reveal much about letterforms, one particularly valuable outcome can be the grouping of related forms and the construction of classifications."[5] [5]

Drawings

Drawing is the oldest and simplest method of recording an inscription. It was the approach used by the artists and antiquarians of the Renaissance such as Jacopo Bellini, Ciriaco d'Ancona, and Giovanni Marcanova; the great 19th-century epigrapher Emil Hübner; and authors of modern lettering manuals such as Frank Chouteau Brown. As Ivan Di Stefano Manzella remarks, it is immediate and it is personal.[6] It is a useful mnemonic technique, but it is not the most reliable one for those interested in the forms of letters as opposed to their content. Its accuracy depends entirely on the skill of the draftsman. Arthur E. Gordon found those of Hübner and other early epigraphers to be untrustworthy.[7] One problem with drawing inscriptional letters is that people often unconsciously sketch what they know, not what they see. [7]

Tracings

Di Stefano Manzella views tracing as a rapid, low-cost, durable, relatively faithful, and easily copiable method of recording inscriptions. The technique involves drawing the outline of the letters with a marker on acetate or mylar held in place on the surface with tape. It is not recommended for curved, rough, or porous surfaces.[8]

Rubbings

Rubbings are a time-honored method for studying inscriptions, used by both epigraphers and amateurs. They are two-dimensional representations of inscriptions. Rubbings record letters in their exact size, form, and proportion, without any of the distortion endemic to photography or the subjective interpretation found in drawing.

Di Stefano Manzella considers rubbings to be superior to photographs when the letters are worn or lightly cut, or where the stone itself is covered with lichen, stains, or other discolorations.[9] They can give a more accurate representation of the edges of letters and they often pick up subtle details of letters—such as hairlines or thin serifs—that are not visible to the naked eye. Moreover, they can tune out the "noise" of variegated surfaces, such as the veining of the red marble typical of Verona. [6]

Rubbings do have a few limitations and drawbacks, however. The letters are in reverse, white on a dark background, which subtly affects how they are perceived. They also appear heavier than they are to the naked eye or in photographs since they record v-cut incisions at their widest point. The quality of rubbings depends on the method used, the nature of the stone, and the neatness of the lettercarving. Slate, limestone, marble, and granite are smoother surfaces than travertine or tufa. But weathered (sugared) marble is a problem. Rubbings of inscriptions that have been exposed to the elements are much cruder than those made from tombs in churches or other interior inscriptions.

There are three basic materials for making a rubbing: wax, carbon paper, and powdered graphite.

WAX METHOD

In this method a crayon, rubbing stick, or

rubbing disk is laid flat on the surface of the stone and, with light pressure, rubbed over the letters. In the Victorian era, cobbler's wax, or "heel ball," was used for rubbings; today, specially formulated rubbing sticks (White Winds) and disks (Oldstone) are available.[10] [10] Japanese masa papers have traditionally been used for rubbings, but other papers can work if they are light and durable. Both White Winds and Gravestone Rubbing Supplies sell special rubbing paper.[11]

The quality of wax rubbings depends on the hardness of the crayon, the surface of the stone, and the direction of the rubbing motion. Wax crayons work best on smooth surfaces, such as tombstones inside churches, and are less effective for inscriptions that have weathered. (See p. 38 for a rubbing made with cobbler's wax; pp. 178 for wax rubbings of slate outdoors and p. 57 for a wax rubbing of marble indoors.) Type designer Garrett Boge discovered that the best results were achieved by rubbing in two opposing directions, ideally with black in the first direction and then, more lightly, with gold or another metallic in the second one. This method picks up more of a letter's edge than rubbing with a single color in one direction. (See pp. 52–54 for an example of Boge's multiple color wax method.)

CARBON PAPER METHOD

The use of carbon paper to make a rubbing is considered a low-impact technique, and in general it is used more often by genealogists than by epigraphers. Cover the inscription with paper. Then rub a kitchen sponge wrapped in half a sheet of carbon paper (black is preferable to blue) over it. An alternative to carbon paper is Carboff, a special wax-coated engravers paper.

POWDERED GRAPHITE METHOD

Father Catich was critical of the wax crayon method for making rubbings, finding it unsuitable for bringing out subtle details of letters from rough surfaced stones. His preferred technique, the one used by professional epigraphers today, involved powdered graphite. (See pp. 26–27 for a graphite rubbing on weathered marble.) He applied the powdered graphite to an unsized paper with a cotton-padded chamois skin stretched over the lid of a small tin can. Another method is pouncing, the technique signpainters use to lay out a design. A small bag made of cheesecloth or a finely woven handkerchief is filled with powdered graphite and then rubbed softly across paper.[12]

Rubbings made with powdered graphite are not as sharp as those made with wax crayons. They are also subject to smudging unless the surface is fixed.

Squeezes

"Squeezes" are paper casts of the face of an inscription. They have long been used by epigraphers because of their accuracy. Because they are three-dimensional, Gordon and Di Stefano Manzella consider them superior to rubbings. Squeezes can show small details of incisions.[13] Along with accuracy, Di Stefano Manzella cites simplicity, rapidity, lightness, portability, and low cost as advantages of squeezes. The drawbacks, he says, are that they cannot be used for lightly incised inscriptions or with rough surfaces (especially travertine). Also they can be affected by temperature and humidity, and are limited by the available dimensions of paper. Once made, they need to be carefully stored to avoid becoming flattened. [8, 9]

To make a squeeze, the surface needs to be carefully cleaned with a brush. Then an absorbent, unsized paper (Di Stefano Manzella recommends blotter or filter paper) is spread over the inscription, wetted with a spray bottle, and worked into the incisions using sculptors' palette knives. Once dry, the paper is carefully peeled off. The result is a copy of the inscription in relief and in reverse. Gordon says that it is important to photograph a squeeze in order to turn it from a relief into an incision and to reverse the print to make the inscription right-reading.[14]

Gordon says that latex squeezes are possible, but warns that they could damage the stone.[15] Di Stefano Manzella suggests the use of aluminum foil as a simple, fast substitute for a proper paper squeeze, but notes that such copies are delicate and hard to conserve.[16]

Casts

In the 19th century, casts were a common means of studying the past: sculpture, monuments, buildings, and, in some cases, inscriptions. Like squeezes, casts also provide a very accurate means of recording an inscription; casts are more durable. They are also expensive, time-consuming, and difficult to make. The biggest hurdle to making one today is obtaining permission. Although casts could be made of bronze or lead, the preferred material in the past was gesso (made from *argilla cruda*) or plaster. But today, casts can be made from such modern materials as silicone, sculpting resins, *creta plastica* (sold under the brand name Plastibò), or *plastilina bianca* (white plasticine). The latter two, which use forms of highly malleable plastic modeling clay, are fast but not very durable.[17] (See p. 239.)

Di Stefano Manzella describes how to use plasticine to make an impression of an inscription:

> In order to avoid getting an incomplete or inaccurate reproduction, one must use the palm of one's hands to model a piece of plasticine into a ball (without any cracks) that will suffice for one or two letters roughly two centimeters high. Once the ball is ready, set it atop the letters and press it into the furrows using the thumbs. If the plasticine becomes too thin during this process, add more so that the resulting cast is thick enough to be peeled off without becoming deformed. To prevent it from sticking to the inscription (which can happen even with smooth marble if the temperature is warm enough), sprinkle or spread talcum powder across the letters [to act as a release agent].[18]

Not all methods for viewing and assessing inscriptions are of equal value, as indicated above. Often it is best to combine methods. Sumner Stone sets forth the hierarchy of methods in this order of usefulness:

1. the actual inscription
2. a cast of the actual inscription
3. a rubbing or squeeze of the actual inscription
4. a photograph of a rubbing of the inscription
5. a photograph of the inscription; or, if the inscription is in poor condition (e.g. badly discolored), a photograph of a squeeze of the inscription
6. a drawing of an inscription

Ideally, it is best to have multiple representations of an inscription, for example a photograph and a squeeze, or a drawing and a rubbing. It should be noted that Thomson cautions against the use of a number of the techniques described above. "It used to be common and perfectly acceptable practice to scrub and clean gravestones or apply anything to the stone which would enhance the lettering and make it easier to read or photograph," he writes. "This includes soap, detergents, talc, shaving foam and a range of acid or alkaline liquids. The other commonly used method, of course, is to make rubbings. The dangers of utilizing almost any contact method to record an inscription are now recognized, even from such an apparently innocent product as the tape used to hold the paper on the stone for rubbings. The general consensus is to avoid using any of these procedures, with the possible exception of making impressions using aluminum foil. Even this method, however, is not recommended unless the substrate is sound, which is often not the case with old inscriptions." Although Thomson notes that the use of non-contact methods presents no danger to artifacts, they have the disadvantages already outlined above.[19]

Basic Materials And Tools
This list excludes the materials needed for making squeezes and casts, as well as the items associated with professional photography. For them, see the more extensive list in Di Stefano Manzella, Mestiere di epigrafista, *pp. 20–21. —P.S.*

Pencil
Paper or notebook/sketchbook
Loupe or magnifying glass
Tape measure or ruler
Cleaning brush
Flashlight
Rubbing stick or disk
Powdered graphite
Cheesecloth
Masking tape
Carrying tube
Camera
Zoom lens, wide angle lens, and macro lens
Lens filters
Tripod
Remote shutter release cable
Compact flash card reader
Camera battery

8 Squeeze of 43 BC Pansa inscription (CIL VI 37077). From *Album of Dated Latin Inscriptions*, Part I by Arthur E. Gordon and Joyce S. Gordon (No. 5a).

9 Photograph of Pansa inscription (CIL 6.37077), 43 BC. From *Album of Dated Latin Inscriptions*, Part I by Arthur E. Gordon and Joyce S. Gordon (No. 5b).

10 (*left*). Detail of rubbing of the Trajan inscription by Ernst Detterer, 1922. (The Newberry Library, Case Wing Detterer Rubbing, 1922).

11 (*right*). Lettercarver Richard Grasby measuring the letters of the Trajan inscription, June 1995.

1. Arthur E. Gordon, *Illustrated Introduction to Latin Epigraphy* (Berkeley: University of California Press, 1983), p. 39. See also Ivan Di Stefano Manzella, *Mestiere di epigrafista: Guida alla schedatura del materiale epigrafico lapideo* (Rome: Edizioni Quasar, 1987), pp. 20–21.
2. Here are some suggestions for measuring inscriptions:
   a. the height of capital letters should be based on vertical strokes not on diagonals or curves; *E* and *H* are the best letters to use.
   b. the height of minuscules (small letters) should include x-height (body), ascender height, and descender depth.
   c. to determine the left margin of a text, use the stem of a letter, not a serif or other extremity as a guide.
   d. to determine the right margin of a text, follow the advice for the left margin; but ragged line lengths make it necessary to indicate minimum and maximum margins (or even right margins of every line).
   e. for centered lines, it is necessary to measure both the left and right margins, which may be different since centering is often not mathematically accurate.
   f. to determine the top margin of a text, measure to the top of a letter like *E* or *T*, which has a horizontal stroke at the top.
   g. to determine the bottom margin of a text, measure from the baseline of the last line.
   h. measuring leading (line spacing) is useful, especially when there is a clear break between portions of a text. Measure from the baseline of the upper line to the top of a letter at the line below.
3. It is important to remember that letters are often painted inaccurately. Paint frequently extends beyond the incision, whereas delicate serifs and tendrils are left unpainted.
4. Di Stefano Manzella, *Mestiere di epigrafista*, pp. 22–23; Gordon, *Illustrated Introduction*, p. 32. Di Stefano Manzella's discussion of photography is extensive but pre-digital.
5. Thomson: "Morphometrics is a branch of analytical research which uses measured differences in the size and shape of organisms or objects. Simpler 'traditional' procedures or 'size morphometrics' involve measurement of heights, widths and other linear measurements. They can also include areas and the measurement of angles. Shape analysis or 'geometric morphometrics' is based on landmarks which define the shape of a physical entity. Shape is the geometric definition of an object, not the sum of a series of linear measurements of it.
   "Its most important attribute is that it is independent of displacement, rotation and scale. The value of geometric morphometrics as an analytical tool could be used to demonstrate the changes in inscriptional style over time and to determine whether evolution was gradual or took place in a series of sudden changes." See also George Thomson, *Inscribed in Remembrance: Gravemarker Lettering: Form, Function and Recording* (Dublin: Wordwell, 2009), and idem, *Lettering on Gravemarkers: A Guide to Recording and Analysis* (Waterbeck, Scotland: George Thomson, 2011).
6. Di Stefano Manzella, *Mestiere di epigrafista*, p. 29.
7. Gordon, *Illustrated Introduction*, p. 32. Similarly, Thomson, in "Beyond the Record" (2012, unpublished, p. 1) has this to say: "often these illustrations [by epigraphers] misrepresent the true nature of the lettering, and demonstrate a somewhat inferior understanding of letterform. While they give a reasonable impression of the inscription, they are useless if we want to gain a full understanding of the inscriptional forms."
8. Di Stefano Manzella, *Mestiere di epigrafista*, p. 31, in which he describes tracings as *calchi su carta lucida* or *calchi su carta velina*.
9. Ibid., p. 30.
10. Ernst Detterer made rubbings of the Trajan inscription in 1922 using cobblers wax. Since the early 1990s, Belgian lettercarver Kristoffel Boudens has used a block of shoe polish (brand unknown) to make rubbings of his own work as well as inscriptions in Rome. Sticks of black cobblers wax are available today from the Edinburgh Bagpipe Company Limited (they are used by bagpipers to waterproof pipers hemp). In the 1950s, Swiss designer Walter Kaech used American Art Clay Company (AMACO) wax crayons for rubbings of Roman inscriptions he made in Ferrara, Pesaro, and elsewhere in Italy. AMACO stopped making wax crayons in the 1970s. In a pinch, I once used Crayola crayons, with the paper peeled away, to rub the inscription on a Revolutionary War cannon.
11. In the early 1960s, American calligrapher Lloyd Reynolds used architects' yellow tracing paper to make rubbings. Type designer Garrett Boge prefers 70 lb and 80 lb text weight Mohawk Letterpress for making full-scale, art rubbings. For research purposes, I tend to use inexpensive 16 lb layout bond (usually 11x14 Borden & Riley pads) for rubbings of individual letters or words. One advantage of small sheets of paper is that they do not require carrying tubes as larger rubbing sheets do.
12. In the 1960s Catich purchased his powdered graphite from shops in Rome that catered to photoengravers, who used the substance in electrotyping. Today, there are a number of online sources for powdered graphite.
13. Di Stefano Manzella, *Mestiere di epigrafista*, p. 30; Gordon, *Illustrated Introduction*, pp. 30–31.
14. Gordon, *Illustrated Introduction*, p. 31.
15. Ibid., p. 32.
16. Di Stefano Manzella, *Mestiere di epigrafista*, p. 31.
17. Ibid., pp. 29–30.
18. Ibid., p. 30.
19. The Association for Gravestone Studies has a summary of good rubbing practices—for example, "Test paper and color before working on stone to be certain that no color bleeds through," and "Don't use detergents, soaps, vinegar, bleach, or any cleaning solutions on the stone, no matter how mild!"—available online at www.gravestonestudies.org/faq.htm. Also see historicgraves.com/blog/how/low-impact-headstone-rubbings

Acknowledgments

THE TYPOGRAPHIC 20TH CENTURY ended much as it began, with a rush of revivals of classical letterforms. The wildly popular Adobe Trajan (1989) was just the beginning. In 2011, a flurry of Trajan-inspired typefaces appeared, requiring a review for *Codex: The Journal of Letterforms* that soon sparked into a broader, deeper investigation of the roots of the classical Roman capital and its smoldering influence over two thousand years. As I gathered material I came to realize that *Codex*, despite its excellence, was no longer the proper vehicle for the subject, which needed more space. Thus was born the idea of *The Eternal Letter* as a book, and the transformation of *Codex: The Journal of Letterforms* into Codex Studies in Letterforms.

From the outset, John Boardley, the founder of *Codex*, encouraged the idea of a varied investigation of the classical Roman capital. He was equally supportive of the suggestion that the topic become a book, the first of what is intended to be a series of volumes exploring aspects of letterforms. I am deeply grateful for his generosity in allowing his journal to evolve into something on a grander scale that will have greater permanence.

Linda Florio has been more than just the designer of *Codex* and of *The Eternal Letter*. She has been an invaluable sounding board throughout the tortuous path that the topic of the classical Roman capital has followed as it went from journal to book. Her visual arrangement of the contents of *Codex* elevated it to the first rank of art history and graphic design monographs. With *The Eternal Letter*, she has injected style, color, and vibrancy into what might otherwise be a sleepy academic subject.

The Eternal Letter would not exist as a book were it not for Scott-Martin Kosofsky, a Codex board member, who conceived and oversaw the transition of the journal into book form, and who brought MIT Press on board as our publisher. He has gone beyond the call of duty in overseeing the production and editorial aspects of the book, as well as contributing an article. Sumner Stone, Alta Price, Mary Gladue, and Allen Tan all made significant contributions in the early stages of planning.

Roger Conover, Executive Editor of The MIT Press, deserves thanks for having the vision of transforming the contents of *Codex* 4 into a book and suggesting the title of *The Eternal Letter*.

I want to thank Steve Dyer for doing the final proofreading of a complicated text on short notice, and to Erik Spiekermann whose typographic eye is unfailing. The sponsorship of Monotype Corporation, Adobe Systems, Mark Simonson Studio, and Courier Corporation, has enabled *The Eternal Letter* to be a book of quality in both content and appearance.

Without authors there are no books. *The Eternal Letter* would not exist without Andy Benedek, John E. Benson, Nicholas W. Benson, Garrett Boge, Matthew Carter, Ewan Clayton, Lance Hidy, Jost Hochuli, Jonathan Hoefler, Richard Kindersley, Scott-Martin Kosofsky, Gerry Leonidas, Martin Majoor, Steve Matteson, Gregory MacNaughton, James Mosley, Tom Perkins, Dan Reynolds, Ryan L. Roth, Werner Schneider, Julian Waters, and Maxim Zhukov. I am grateful to all of them for their contributions and for being so patient during the long gestation of *The Eternal Letter*. I want to thank Peter Bil'ak, Jim Parkinson, Jeremy Tankard, and Katharine Wolff for their insightful remarks about classical Roman capitals, which appear on the section dividers.

Without images, a book such as this would not only be visually dull, but it would be nigh impossible to properly explain the subtleties of a subject like the classical Roman capital. Thus, I owe a deep debt of gratitude to the following individuals for providing photographs, fonts and reproduction rights: Erich Alb, Archives d'Académie d'Architecture (Paris), Michael Babcock of interrobang letterpress, Phil Baines, James Birchfield, Larry Brady, Priscilla Brüsilauer of the Stiftsbibliothek St. Gallen, Jason Castle of Castle Type, Emanuela Brignone Cattaneo, Caroline Duroselle-Melish of the Houghton Library at Harvard University, Paul Gehl of The Newberry Library, David Lance Goines, Richard Grasby, Patrick Griffin, Phil Hamilton, Clint Harvey, Michael Harvey, Jake Hegnauer, John Hegnauer, Paul Herrera, Otmar Hoefer of Linotype, Dieter Hofrichter of Hoftypes, Amelia J. Hugill-Fontanel of the Cary Graphic Arts Collection at Rochester Institute of Technology, Mark Jamra, Masahiko Kimura, Lida Lopes Cardozo Kindersley, Gloria Kondrup of the Archetype Press at Art Center College of Design, David Lemon of Adobe/TypeKit, Thomas Lincoln, Richard Lipton, Mathieu Lommen of the Special Collections at the University of Amsterdam, Heather Lovewell of the St. Ambrose University Library, Martino Mardersteig, Suzanne Moore, John Neal, John Neilson, Harry Parker of Font Bureau, Michael Russem of Kat Ran Press, Jane Siegel at the Rare Book & Manuscript Library of Columbia University, Helen Skelton, Robert Slimbach, Jason Smith of FontSmith, Paul Soady, Donna Steele of The Ditchling Museum, John Stevens, Christopher Stinehour, Humphrey Stone, Joanna Storey, Jakob Straub, George Thomson, Carol Twombly, Mark van Stone, the Victoria & Albert Museum, Gay Walker of Reed College, Sheila Waters, and Stefano Della Zana of Scrinium.

Finally, in the course of the peregrinations that *The Eternal Letter* underwent, there is much material that ended up on the cutting room floor. Even though their contributions did not make it into the volume, I want to give a hearty thanks to the following individuals for being kind enough to send them in the first place and gracious enough to accept their absence: Ron Arnholm, Wim Crouwel, Michael Doret, Nikola Djurek, Ken Garland, Tim Girvin, Milton Glaser, Carol Goldenberg, Christopher Haanes, Michael Harvey, Jonathan Hoefler, Incisive Letterwork (Brenda Berman and Annet Stirling), Mark Jamra, Lida Lopes Cardozo Kindersley, Richard Kindersley, Willi Kunz, Rod McDonald, John Nash, David Quay, Paula Scher, Werner Schneider, Nick Shinn, Nick Sloan, Rick Valicenti, Massimo Vignelli, and Wolfgang Weingart.

Credits

vii Courtesy of the Rare Book and Manuscript Library, Columbia University.
xii Photograph by Paul Shaw, 2007.
2 Photograph by Paul Shaw, 2007.
3 Photograph by Matteo Della Corte, 1916. Courtesy of the Soprintendenza alle Antichità di Napoli e Caserta, via James Mosley.
4 Photograph by Francis Frith. ©Victoria & Albert Museum, London.
5 Photograph by Richard Kindersley, 1997.
6 Photograph by Paul Shaw, 2010.
7 (*left*) Photograph by Paul Shaw, 2013.
7 (*right*) Photograph courtesy of the Stiftsbibliothek St. Gallen.
8 Courtesy of Prof. Joanna Story.
9 (*left*) Photograph courtesy of Bibliothèque Municipale, Abbeville.
9 (*right*) Photograph courtesy of the Stiftsbibliothek St. Gallen.
10 (*left*) Photograph by Paul Shaw, 2007.
10 (*right*) Courtesy of Beinecke Library, Yale University.
11 (*top*) Photograph courtesy of Opera del S. Maria del Fiore, Florence.
11 (*second*) Photograph by Paul Shaw, 2008.
11 (*third*) Photograph by Paul Shaw, 2013.
11 (*fourth*) Photograph by Paul Shaw, 2014.
12 (*top*) Reproduction courtesy of Arch. Emanuela Brignone Cattaneo.*
12 (*bottom*) Photograph courtesy of Scrinium exclusive world distributor Codicum Facsimiles Bibliothecae Apostolicae Vaticanae, www.scrinium.org.
15 (*top*) Courtesy of the Rare Book and Manuscript Library, Columbia University.
15 (*middle*) Courtesy of the Rare Book and Manuscript Library, Columbia University.
15 (*bottom*) Courtesy of The Newberry Library, Chicago.
16 (*top left*) Romain du Roi
16 (*top right*) Courtesy of the Rare Book and Manuscript Library, Columbia University.
16 (*middle*) Courtesy of the Rare Book and Manuscript Library, Columbia University.
16 (*bottom*) Courtesy of the Rare Book and Manuscript Library, Columbia University.
19 (*top*) © Victoria & Albert Museum.
19 (*bottom*) Courtesy of Dan Rhatigan and Monotype.
20 (*top*) Photograph by Paul Shaw, 2009.
20 (*bottom*) Photograph by Paul Shaw, 2008.
21 (*right*) Courtesy of Herb Lubalin Study Center of Design and Typography, Cooper Union.
24 Courtesy of St. Ambrose University.†
25 Image courtesy of St. Ambrose University.†
26 (*top*) Courtesy of The Newberry Library, Chicago (Case Wing ZW 14.C251, Catich Rubbing 1966).
27 Image courtesy of St. Ambrose University.†
29 Image courtesy of St. Ambrose University.†
33 Images courtesy of St. Ambrose University.†
38 (*top*) Image courtesy of Jost Hochuli.
39 Photograph by Peter Stahl. Courtesy of Jost Hochuli.
48 (*top and middle*) Photographs courtesy of Martino Mardersteig.
48 (*bottom*) Photograph by Paul Shaw, 2010.
50 (*top*) Photograph by Clint Harvey, 2012.
50 (*bottom*) Photograph by Paul Shaw, 2010.
51 Photograph by Paul Shaw, 2010.
52–54 Reproduction courtesy of Garrett Boge. The rubbing is now part of the Garrett A. Boge Papers, The Newberry Library, Chicago.
55 Courtesy of the Biblioteca Nazionale Centrale di Roma.
56 Reproduction courtesy of Arch. Emanuela Brignone Cattaneo.
57 (*top*) Rubbing by Paul Shaw, 2002.
57 (*middle*) Courtesy of Nicholas Benson.
57 (*bottom*) Photograph by Paul Shaw, 2007.
61 (*top*) Photograph by Paul Shaw, 2008.
61 (*bottom*) Photograph by Paul Shaw, 2007.
62 (*top*) Photograph by Paul Shaw, 2005.
62 (*bottom*) Photograph by Paul Shaw, 2005.
63 (*top*) Photograph by Garrett Boge, 1997.
63 (*bottom*) Photograph by Paul Shaw, 2010.
65 (*bottom*) Courtesy of The Newberry Library, Chicago (The Garrett A. Boge Papers, Box 12, Folder 161).
70 Courtesy of the Cary Graphic Arts Collection at The Wallace Center, Rochester Institute of Technology.
73 (*bottom*) Courtesy of the Rare Book and Manuscript Library, Columbia University.
75 Courtesy of the Library of Congress.
84–85 Wood type Perpetua Title printed especially for *The Eternal Letter* by Gloria Kondrup, Archetype Press (Art Center College of Design, Pasadena, California).
86 Image courtesy of the Central Lettering Record, Central Saint Martins College (London).
87 (*top*) Courtesy of Paul Soady.
89 (*top*) Photograph by Paul Shaw, 2007.
89 (*bottom*) Photograph by James Mosley used with kind permission of the Victoria & Albert Museum, London.
90 Courtesy of the Rare Book and Manuscript Library, Columbia University.
91 (*top*) With permission of the Trustees of the Ditchling Museum.
94 Photograph by Ewan Clayton.
96–97 Courtesy of the Rare Book and Manuscript Library, Columbia University.
104 (*top*) Courtesy of the Jan van Krimpen Archive, Special Collections, University of Amsterdam.
104 (*bottom*) From the collection of Martin Majoor.
106 From the collection of Martin Majoor.
107 Courtesy of Michael Russem, Kat Ran Press.
109 Photograph by Martin Majoor.
112 Letterpress proof provided by Michael Babcock of Interrobang Letterpress.
113 (*top*) Courtesy of Matthew Carter.
114 Letterpress proof provided by Michael Babcock of Interrobang Letterpress.
116 Letterpress proof provided by Michael Babcock of Interrobang Letterpress.
120 Letterpress proof provided by Michael Babcock of Interrobang Letterpress.
122 Courtesy of Otmar Hoefer and Linotype.
123 Photograph by Paul Shaw, 2005.
132 Courtesy of Lida Lopes Cardozo Kindersley.
134 (*top right*) Photograph by John Neilson.
135 (*top*) Photographs by Tom Perkins.
135 (*bottom*) Photograph by Richard Kindersley.
137 Courtesy of Humphrey Stone.
138 (*top*) Photograph by Dennis Letbetter.
143 (*top*) Photograph by John E. Benson.
143 (*bottom*) Photograph by William K. Covell.
144 Image courtesy of St. Ambrose University.†
145 Image courtesy of Nicholas Benson.
147 Photograph by Paul Shaw, 2006.
148 Photograph by Henry Curtis.
149 (*top*) Photograph of rubbing courtesy of Jake Heganauer.
149 (*bottom*) Courtesy of Lida Lopes Cardozo Kindersley.
151 (*top*) Image courtesy of Nicholas Benson.
152 (*top and lower right*) Photographs by Paul Shaw, 2005.
153 Photograph by Paul Shaw, 2005.
154 Photograph by Nicholas Benson.
155 (*bottom*) Photograph by Nicholas Benson.
160 (*top*) Photograph by Alexander Nesbitt.
160 (*middle and bottom*) Courtesy of the Cary Graphic Arts Collection at The Wallace Center, Rochester Institute of Technology.
161 (*top*) Photograph by Christine Dunn.
161 (*bottom*) Photograph by Peter Kindersley, 2013.
171 (*left*) Photograph by Greg Nikas.
174 Courtesy of Special Collections, Eric. V. Hauser Memorial Library, Reed College.
175 Courtesy of Special Collections, Eric. V. Hauser Memorial Library, Reed College.
176 Courtesy of Special Collections, Eric. V. Hauser Memorial Library, Reed College.
177 (*left*) Courtesy of Special Collections, Eric. V. Hauser Memorial Library, Reed College.
177 (*right*) Photographs by Paul Shaw, 2011.
178 Rubbings by Paul Shaw, 2011.
178 Photograph by Paul Shaw, 2011.
180 (*top*) Courtesy of The Newberry Library, Chicago (Case Wing ZW 14.C251, Catich Rubbing 1966).
181 Courtesy of Adobe Systems, Inc.
182 (*top* and *middle*) Courtesy of Adobe Systems, Inc.
182 (*bottom*) Photograph by Sumner Stone.
184 Photograph by Paul Shaw, 2010.
185 Photograph by Paul Shaw, 2007.
186 (*top*) Photograph by Paul Shaw, 2010.
188 Images courtesy of John Stevens and John Neal Bookseller.
193 Image courtesy of Richard Lipton.
197 Image courtesy of Thomas Lincoln.
198 Font courtesy of Jason Castle of Castletype.
202–206 All images courtesy of John Stevens and John Neal Bookseller.
210 (*middle*) Image courtesy of Werner Schneider.
210 (*top left and right*) Images courtesy of Werner Schneider.
211 (*bottom*) Photograph by Paul Shaw, 2010.
214 Image courtesy of the National Gallery of Art (Washington, DC).
215 (*top*) Photograph courtesy of Scrinium, exclusive world distributor Codicum Facsimiles Bibliothecae Apostolicae Vaticanae, www.scrinium.org.
215 (*lower left*) Photograph by Paul Shaw, 2010.
217 Photographs by Matthew Carter.
221 Image courtesy of The Newberry Library, Chicago.
222 Courtesy of the Rare Book and Manuscript Library, Columbia University.
223 Image courtesy of The Newberry Library, Chicago.
224 Image courtesy of Julian Waters.
228 Photograph by Paul Shaw, 2005.
239 Photograph courtesy of Paul Herrera.
250 (*bottom*) Photograph by Paul Shaw, 2005.
251 Photographs by Paul Shaw, 2007.
252 (*left*) Image courtesy of George Thomson.
252 (*right*) Photograph by Paul Shaw, 2010.
255 (*right*) Photograph courtesy of Margaret Sasanow and the Centre for the Study of Ancient Documents, Oxford.
255 (*left*) Courtesy of The Newberry Library, Chicago (Case Wing Detterer 1922).
257 Courtesy of The Newberry Library, Chicago.

* *Tutti diretti di riproduzione riservati.*
† *Images provided by St. Ambrose University, Davenport, Iowa, are for educational purposes only, and may not be reproduced or distributed in any format without prior written permission of St. Ambrose University, 518 West Locust Street, Davenport, Iowa 52803.*

Contributors

John E. Benson, a sculptor and lettercarver, is the former owner of the John Stevens Shop, in Newport, Rhode Island, where he began working for his father, John Howard Benson, at the age of fifteen. His lettercarving work includes John F. Kennedy Memorial in Arlington National Cemetery, the Civil Rights Memorial in Montgomery, Alabama, the Franklin Delano Roosevelt Memorial and the date stones of the Vietnam Veterans Memorial, in Washington, DC, and many American museums.

Nicholas W. Benson began working at the John Stevens Shop at the age of fifteen under his father, John E. Benson, and is now its owner and creative director. He also studied at the Kunstgewerbeschule in Basel. His work includes the World War II Memorial and the Martin Luther King Memorial, in Washington, D.C. He was awarded a National Endowment for the Arts National Heritage Fellowship in 2007 and named a MacArthur Foundation Fellow in 2010.

Frank E. Blokland, founder of the Dutch Type Library (DTL), is a type designer. He is also a Senior Lecturer in type design at the Koninklijke Academie van Beeldende Kunsten (KABK), in The Hague, and Professor and Research Fellow at the Plantin Institute of Typography, in Antwerp. Currently, he is finishing a PhD dissertation at Leiden University on the standardization and systematization of roman and italic type since its Renaissance origins.

Garrett Boge is a type designer with a deep interest in letterforms from Ancient Rome to the Baroque era. He is noted for his meticulous, multicolored rubbings of inscriptions. His archive was acquired in 2013 by the Newberry Library, Chicago.

Matthew Carter, principal of Carter & Cone Type Inc., is a type designer with over fifty years' experience of typographic technologies ranging from hand-cut punches to screen fonts. He was named a MacArthur Foundation Fellow in 2010.

Ewan Clayton is a calligrapher and Professor of Design at the University of Sunderland, in England, where he co-directs the International Research Centre for Calligraphy. He lives near the village of Ditchling, Sussex, where three generations of his family have worked as members of a guild of craftsmen formed in 1921 by Eric Gill and the printer Hilary Pepler. He is the author of *The Golden Thread* (2013).

Linda Florio, designer of this book, is the principal of the New York studio Florio Design, whose clients include some of the major cultural institutions in the city. She specializes in editorial and content-driven print and digital media, focused on the visual arts. For nine years she was a senior designer at The Metropolitan Museum of Art.

Lance Hidy is an illustrator, graphic designer, and graphic design educator. He is best-known for his photography-based illustrations for posters and United States postage stamps, and for his design of a series of books of Ansel Adams's photographs. He studied calligraphy with Lloyd Reynolds.

Cyrus Highsmith is a senior type designer at Font Bureau and an instructor at the Rhode Island School of Design. He is the author of *Inside Paragraphs* (2012).

Jost Hochuli studied with Walter Kaech in Zürich. Since 1959, he has run his own commercial graphics and book design firm in St. Gallen. He has taught lettering, writing, and typography at design schools in Zürich and St. Gallen. Jost is the author of *Detail in Typography* (2008) and *Designing Books: Practice and Theory* (1996).

Jonathan Hoefler, principal of Hoefler & Co., is a type designer and writer on things typographic. Hoefler has designed original typefaces for *Rolling Stone* magazine, *Harper's Bazaar*, *The New York Times Magazine*, *Sports Illustrated*, and *Esquire* and several institutional clients, including the Solomon R. Guggenheim Museum.

Richard Kindersley, lettercarver and sculptor, began his career at the workshop of his father, David Kindersley. His work can be seen at many of Britain's most notable institutions, including Westminster Abbey, St. Paul's Cathedral, London Bridge, Tower Bridge, the universities of Exeter, Oxford, Cambridge, and elsewhere around the world.

Scott-Martin Kosofsky develops, produces, edits, designs, composes, writes, and makes types for books at The Philidor Company. He specializes in projects with complex, multi-script typographic requirements (he is an expert in biblical and liturgical Hebrew) and in image-driven books that touch upon issues of social and political policy. He is the author of *The Book of Customs,* which won a National Jewish Book Award in 2005.

Gerry Leonidas is Associate Professor in Typography at the University of Reading, in England, where he directs the MA program in type design. His specialty is Greek typography and typeface design, a subject on which he speaks and consults frequently.

Martin Majoor is a Dutch type designer, book typographer, and critic, perhaps best known for his typefaces Scala and Scala Sans. He designed *Adieu Aesthetics & Beautiful Pages!* (1995), a book on the life and work of Jan van Krimpen, whom he considers one of his main sources of inspiration in type design and book typography.

Steve Matteson is the Creative Director for Type at Monotype Corporation. He designed the fonts for Xbox and Xbox 360, the Segoe fonts for Windows Vista, as well as the Droid fonts for the Android operating system. Steve has been fascinated by Fred and Bertha Goudy for over twenty-five years, speaking and writing about their life and work. He has also designed digital versions of many of Fred's typefaces.

Gregory MacNaughton is the Education Outreach and Calligraphy Initiative Coordinator of the Douglas F. Cooley Memorial Art Gallery at Reed College in Portland, Oregon.

James Mosley is a Professor in the Department of Typography and Graphic Communication at the University of Reading, and a Senior Research Fellow of the Institute of English Studies in the University of London. He was Librarian of the St Bride Library, London, from 1958 until 2000. His highly-regarded blog, "Typefoundry," is based on "documents for the history of type and letterforms."

Tom Perkins is a lettercarver in Cambridge, England. He is the author of *The Art of Letter Carving in Stone* (2007).

Yves Peters is a graphic designer and rock drummer in Ghent, Belgium. He edits "The FontFeed" and writes about type for other websites and publications.

Dan Reynolds is an American type designer and educator living in Berlin. He is cofounder of the Offenbach Typostammtisch and was formerly a member of the marketing and font development team at Linotype. He currently teaches type design at the Hochschule Darmstadt.

Ryan L. Roth is a bibliographer. He has been a faculty member of the California Rare Book School at UCLA and program director of the Rare Book School at the University of Virginia.

Werner Schneider, one of the world's most highly regarded calligraphers, has been a professor at the Fachhochschule in Wiesbaden since 1971, and was the creator of five notable typefaces for Berthold AG and Linotype. His works have have been featured in exhibitions around the world.

Paul Shaw is the Editor in Chief of Codex. He teaches calligraphy and typography at Parsons School of Design and the history of graphic design at the School of Visual Arts. He is the author of *Helvetica and the New York City Subway System* (MIT Press, 2011).

Julian Waters is a calligrapher and lettering designer living near Washington, DC. His clients include many publishers, agencies, and design firms. He has designed typefaces for Adobe, corporations, memorials, and public spaces, including Thomas Jefferson's Monticello. He studied calligraphy with Sheila Waters and Hermann Zapf, and now teaches calligraphy workshops worldwide.

Maxim Zhukov specializes in multilingual typography and cross-cultural design. For many years he served as a Typographic Coördinator to the United Nations. He researches, lectures and writes on typography and type design; and often consults on Cyrillic type design for many individual designers and type foundries.